EXCLUSION FROM PUBLIC SPACE

Hardly known twenty years ago, exclusion from public space has today become a standard tool of state intervention. Every year, tens of thousands of homeless, drug addicts, teenagers, protesters and others are banned from parts of public space. The rise of exclusion measures is characteristic of two broader developments that have profoundly transformed public space in recent years: the 'privatisation of public space' and its increased control in the 'security society'. Despite the fundamental problems it raises, exclusion from public space has hardly received any attention from legal scholars. This book addresses this gap and comprehensively explores the implications that this new form of intervention has for the constitutional essentials of liberal democracy: the rule of law, fundamental rights and democracy. To do so, it analyses legal developments in three liberal democracies that have been at the forefront of promoting exclusion measures: the United Kingdom, the United States and Switzerland.

DANIEL MOECKLI is Assistant Professor of Public International Law and Constitutional Law at the University of Zurich and Fellow of the University of Nottingham Human Rights Law Centre. He is the author of *Human Rights and Non-discrimination in the 'War on Terror'* (Oxford University Press, 2008), for which he was awarded the Paul Guggenheim Prize, and co-editor of *International Human Rights Law* (Oxford University Press, 2014). Before joining the University of Zurich, Daniel was a Lecturer at the University of Nottingham and worked for the International Bar Association, Amnesty International and the Supreme Court of the Canton of Berne.

CAMBRIDGE STUDIES IN INTERNATIONAL AND COMPARATIVE LAW: 129

Established in 1946, this series produces high-quality, reflective and innovative scholarship in the field of public international law. It publishes works on international law that are of a theoretical, historical, cross-disciplinary or doctrinal nature. The series also welcomes books providing insights into private international law, comparative law and transnational studies which inform international legal thought and practice more generally.

The series seeks to publish views from diverse legal traditions and perspectives, as well as of any geographical origin. In this respect, it invites studies offering regional perspectives on core *problématiques* of international law, and in the same vein, it appreciates contrasts and debates between diverging approaches. Accordingly, books offering new or less orthodox perspectives are very much welcome. Works of a generalist character are greatly valued, and the series is also open to studies on specific areas, institutions or problems. Translations of the most outstanding works published in other languages are also considered.

After 70 years, *Cambridge Studies in International and Comparative Law* remains the standard-setter for international legal scholarship and will continue to define the discipline as it evolves in the years to come.

A list of books in the series can be found at the end of this volume

EXCLUSION FROM PUBLIC SPACE

A Comparative Constitutional Analysis

DANIEL MOECKLI
University of Zurich

CAMBRIDGE
UNIVERSITY PRESS

CAMBRIDGE
UNIVERSITY PRESS

University Printing House, Cambridge CB2 8BS, United Kingdom

Cambridge University Press is part of the University of Cambridge.

It furthers the University's mission by disseminating knowledge in the pursuit of education, learning and research at the highest international levels of excellence.

www.cambridge.org
Information on this title: www.cambridge.org/9781107154650

First published 2016

A catalogue record for this publication is available from the British Library.

Library of Congress Cataloging-in-Publication data
Moeckli, Daniel, author.
Exclusion from public space : a comparative constitutional analysis / Daniel Moeckli.
New York : Cambridge University Press, 2016.
LCCN 2016015464 | ISBN 9781107154650
LCSH: Assembly, Right of. | Public spaces – Law and legislation. | Civil rights. | Comparative law.
LCC K3256 .M64 2016 | DDC 342.08/54–dc23
LC record available at https://lccn.loc.gov/2016015464

ISBN 978-1-107-15465-0 Hardback

SUMMARY CONTENTS

CONTENTS

ACKNOWLEDGEMENTS

This book is a revised and updated version of my habilitation thesis submitted to the Faculty of Law of the University of Zurich in 2013. I would like to thank Professor Helen Keller and Professor Regina Kiener for acting as referees for the habilitation and for sharing their insightful comments with me. To Professor Helen Keller, as well as to Professor Thomas Gächter, I am also grateful for encouraging me to move to Zurich in order to embark on the habilitation project in the first place.

The colleagues at the University of Zurich who supported me in manifold ways are too numerous to name. Special thanks go to Dr Tilmann Altwicker, PD Dr Markus Schott, Dr Stefan Schürer, Professor Sarah Summers and Dr Andrea Töndury who were very generous in sharing their time and offering encouragement. Patrik Dudar, Raffael Fasel, Raphael Keller and Lea Raible provided excellent research and editorial assistance.

Parts of the book were written during a stay as a Visiting Fellow at the European University Institute, Italy, in autumn 2010. Everyone I met at the Institute made me feel extremely welcome. I am especially indebted to Professor Martin Scheinin for sponsoring my stay in Florence. Furthermore, I thank Dr Peter Ramsay from the LSE for his advice.

Four anonymous reviewers for Cambridge University Press provided thoughtful comments that helped me improve the manuscript. At the Press, I thank Elizabeth Spicer, who has been a very patient editor, and Chloé Harris, who ensured an efficient production process.

Last, and most importantly, I thank my family and friends. I am especially grateful to Irene Schumacher who, rather than just to endure my ramblings about public space, engaged me in intriguing discussions on the subject and supported me throughout my work. I would like to apologise to her and to our son Louis for having spent so much time on this book instead of with them.

Legal developments have been taken account of, to the best of my knowledge, up to September 2015. All websites were last accessed on 1 October 2015.

ABBREVIATIONS

A.2d	Atlantic Reporter, Second Series
AC	Law Reports, Appeal Cases
ACHR	American Convention on Human Rights
ADHR	American Declaration of the Rights and Duties of Man
All ER	All England Reports
Art.	Article
Arts	Articles
AS	Amtliche Sammlung des Bundesrechts (official collection of federal legislation)
AS	Amtliche Sammlung der Stadt Zürich (collection of the laws of the City of Zurich)
ASBO	Anti-social behaviour order
AuG	Bundesgesetz über die Ausländerinnen und Ausländer (Federal Act on Foreign Nationals)
BBl	Bundesblatt der Schweizerischen Eidgenossenschaft (collection of federal materials of the Swiss Confederation)
BehiG	Bundesgesetz über die Beseitigung von Benachteiligungen von Menschen mit Behinderungen (Federal Act on the Elimination of Discrimination against People with Disabilities)
BGE	Entscheidungen des Schweizerischen Bundesgerichts (decisions of the Swiss Federal Supreme Court)
bGS	Bereinigte systematische Gesetzessammlung des Kantons Appenzell Ausserrhoden (collection of the laws of the Canton of Appenzell Ausserrhoden)
BGS	Bereinigte Gesetzessammlung des Kantons Solothurn (collection of the laws of the Canton of Solothurn)
BGS	Bereinigte Gesetzessammlung des Kantons Zug (collection of the laws of the Canton of Zug)
BGST	Bundesgesetz über die Sicherheitsorgane der Transportunternehmen im öffentlichen Verkehr (Federal Act on the Security Units of Public Transport Companies)
BID	Business Improvement District

BR	Bündner Rechtsbuch (collection of the laws of the Canton of Grisons)
BSG	Bernische Systematische Gesetzessammlung (collection of the laws of the Canton of Berne)
BV	Bundesverfassung der Schweizerischen Eidgenossenschaft (Federal Constitution of the Swiss Confederation)
BVR	Bernische Verwaltungsrechtsprechung (Collection of administrative law decisions of the Canton of Berne)
BWIS	Bundesgesetz über Massnahmen zur Wahrung der inneren Sicherheit (Federal Act on Measures for the Protection of Internal Security)
CA	Court of Appeal
Cal. Rptr. 3d	California Reporter, Third Series
CBO	Criminal Behaviour Order
CCTV	Closed Circuit Television
Ch.	Law Reports, Chancery Division
Ch.	Chapter
Chs	Chapters
Cm	Command papers
col.	column
CRC	Convention on the Rights of the Child
CRPD	Convention on the Rights of Persons with Disabilities
D.C.	District Court
D.C.	District of Columbia
E.	Erwägung (consideration)
EC	European Community
ECHR	European Convention for the Protection of Human Rights and Fundamental Freedoms
EG	Estates Gazette
ETS	European Treaty Series
EU	European Union
EWCA Civ	Court of Appeal of England and Wales, Civil Division
EWCA Crim	Court of Appeal of England and Wales, Criminal Division
EWHC	High Court of England and Wales
F.2d	Federal Reporter, Second Series
F.3d	Federal Reporter, Third Series
F.Supp.	Federal Supplement
GA	UN General Assembly
GDB	Gesetzesdatenbank des Kantons Obwalden (collection of the laws of the Canton of Obwalden)
GS	Gesetzessammlung des Kantons Glarus (collection of the laws of the Canton of Glarus)

HRLR	Human Rights Law Reports – UK cases
ICCPR	International Covenant on Civil and Political Rights
ICERD	International Convention on the Elimination of All Forms of Racial Discrimination
ICESCR	International Covenant on Economic, Social and Cultural Rights
ICJ Statute	Statute of the International Court of Justice
ICRMW	International Convention on the Protection of the Rights of All Migrant Workers and Members of Their Families
IPNA	Injunction to Prevent Nuisance and Annoyance
Ir CLR	Irish Common Law Reports
IRLR	Industrial Relations Law Reports
JStG	Bundesgesetz über das Jugendstrafrecht (Juvenile Criminal Code)
KB	Law Reports, King's Bench
LAPD	Los Angeles Police Department
LGR	Local Government Reports
LS	Loseblattsammlung (systematische Gesetzessammlung des Kantons Zürich) (collection of the laws of the Canton of Zurich)
Mass.	Massachusetts Reports
MG	Bundesgesetz über die Armee und die Militärverwaltung (Military Act)
MStG	Militärstrafgesetz (Military Criminal Code)
N.E.2d	North Eastern Reporter, Second Series
N.W.2d	North Western Reporter, Second Series
NYPD	New York City Police Department
OAS	Organization of American States
OJ	Official Journal of the European Communities
PSPO	Public Spaces Protection Order
P.2d	Pacific Reporter, Second Series
QB	Law Reports, Queen's Bench Division
RB	Rechtsbuch Kanton Thurgau (collection of the laws of the Canton of Thurgau)
RB	Urner Rechtsbuch (collection of the laws of the Canton of Uri)
RSG	Recueil systématique de la législation genevoise (collection of the laws of the Canton of Geneva)
RSN	Recueil systématique de la législation neuchâteloise (collection of the laws of the Canton of Neuchâtel)
SAR	Systematische Sammlung des Aargauischen Rechts (collection of the laws of the Canton of Aargau)
S.E.	South Eastern Reporter
S.E.2d	South Eastern Reporter, Second Series
SG	Systematische Gesetzessammlung des Kantons Basel-Stadt (collection of the laws of the Canton of Basel-Stadt)

SGF	Systematische Gesetzessammlung des Kantons Freiburg (collection of the laws of the Canton of Fribourg)
SGS	Systematische Gesetzessammlung des Kantons Basel-Landschaft (collection of the laws of the Canton of Basel-Landschaft)
sGS	Systematische Gesetzessammlung des Kantons St. Gallen (collection of the laws of the Canton of St. Gallen)
SHPO	Sexual harm prevention order
SHR	Schaffhauser Rechtsbuch (collection of the laws of the Canton of Schaffhausen)
So.2d	Southern Reporter, Second Series
SOCPA	Serious Organised Crime and Police Act
SR	Systematische Sammlung des Bundesrechts (systematic collection of federal legislation)
SRL	Systematische Rechtssammlung des Kantons Luzern (collection of the laws of the Canton of Lucerne)
SRSZ	Systematische Gesetzessammlung des Kantons Schwyz (collection of the laws of the Canton of Schwyz)
StGB	Schweizerisches Strafgesetzbuch (Swiss Criminal Code)
StPO	Schweizerische Strafprozessordnung (Swiss Criminal Procedure Code)
TFEU	Treaty on the Functioning of the European Union
TPIM	Terrorism Prevention and Investigation Measure
UDHR	Universal Declaration of Human Rights
UK	United Kingdom
UKHL	UK House of Lords
UN	United Nations
UN Charter	Charter of the United Nations
UNESCO	United Nations Educational, Scientific and Cultural Organization
UN-HABITAT	United Nations Human Settlements Programme
UNTS	United Nations Treaty Series
US	United States
U.S.	United States Supreme Court Reports
U.S.C.	Code of Laws of the United States of America
VPB	Verwaltungspraxis der Bundesbehörden (decisions and opinions of the federal administrative authorities)
WEF	World Economic Forum
WLR	Weekly Law Reports
WTO	World Trade Organization
ZGB	Schweizerisches Zivilgesetzbuch (Swiss Civil Code)
ZR	Blätter für Zürcherische Rechtsprechung

1

Introduction

Christopher Lamb was seventeen years old when, in 2004, a youth court imposed an anti-social behaviour order (ASBO) under the Crime and Disorder Act 1998 on him for 'using disorderly behaviour or threatening abusive or insulting words likely to cause harassment, alarm or distress'.[1] The ASBO prohibited him from going into the town centre of Whitley Bay, a town with a population of about 40,000 in North East England, as well as from entering the metro system or any bus shelters in the region for two years.[2] Lamb repeatedly breached the ASBO by entering the prohibited area, although, as a court pointed out, none of these breaches involved anti-social behaviour or, indeed, impacted on the public in any way.[3] However, since any breach of an ASBO amounted to an offence punishable with up to five years imprisonment,[4] a judge sentenced Lamb to twenty-two months in a young offender institution.[5] This sentence was later reduced to six months.[6]

Patricia Johnson, a grandmother of several children, was arrested on suspicion of a marijuana trafficking offence in Over-the-Rhine, a neighbourhood near the city centre of Cincinnati, Ohio.[7] The arresting police officer served her with an exclusion notice that prohibited her from entering Over-the-Rhine for three months. The legal basis for this prohibition was an ordinance of the City of Cincinnati of 1996 that established 'drug exclusion zones' in areas with 'a higher incidence of drug-related activity'.[8] The city council had designated Over-the-Rhine as a 'drug exclusion zone'. Anyone arrested within such a zone for one of several enumerated offences was subject to exclusion for up to three months from

[1] *R.* v. *Lamb (Christopher)*, [2005] EWCA Crim 3000, para. 2. [2] Ibid.
[3] Ibid., para. 18. [4] Crime and Disorder Act 1998, s. 1(10) (repealed).
[5] *R.* v. *Lamb (Christopher)*, [2005] EWCA Crim 3000, para. 10. [6] Ibid., para. 20.
[7] *Johnson* v. *City of Cincinnati*, 310 F.3d 484, 488–9 (6th Cir. 2002).
[8] See Cincinnati Municipal Code, § 755-5 (repealed). For a description of the background and exact contents of the ordinance, see *State* v. *Burnett*, 755 N.E.2d 857, 858–9 (Ohio 2001).

the 'public streets, sidewalks, and other public ways' in all 'drug-exclusion zones'.[9] Violation of an exclusion order was subject to prosecution for criminal trespass. Johnson helped care for the five children of her daughter who lived in Over-the-Rhine, regularly taking two of them to school. She was found within the exclusion zone during the exclusion period and charged with criminal trespass. She was never indicted of the marijuana trafficking offence that had given rise to the exclusion order.[10]

Mario Gsell is a journalist who in 2001 wanted to observe, and report on, the World Economic Forum (WEF), which is held annually in the Swiss ski resort of Davos.[11] As every year, the police established checkpoints on all access routes (roads and railroad) to Davos where they carried out personal and vehicle searches.[12] Although there was no explicit legal basis for doing so, the policy of the police was, and apparently still is,[13] to deny access to Davos to all potential protesters and to turn back anyone who is not clearly identified as not posing a security risk as well as anyone whose identity cannot be reliably confirmed, except if they are known to the respective police officers.[14] The bus Gsell was travelling on was stopped by the police shortly before Davos. Despite presenting his press card and informing the police about his planned activities in Davos, Gsell, as all other passengers, was ordered to turn back.[15]

1.1 Exclusion from public space and its challenges to liberal democracy

These are just three of many examples that demonstrate that various states have started to prevent certain categories of people from gaining access to places that are normally publicly accessible. While the power of the police to temporarily remove people from a specific public place to defuse a dangerous situation has existed for some time,[16] in the last few years numerous liberal democracies have introduced laws that authorise the police and other authorities to exclude people from *large parts* of public space for *extended periods of time*. Among the new legal tools put

9 Cincinnati Municipal Code, § 755-5 (repealed).

10 *Johnson* v. *City of Cincinnati*, 310 F.3d 484, 488–9 (6th Cir. 2002).

11 BGE 130 I 369, 370–1 (2004). See also *Gsell c. Suisse*, no. 12675/05, 8 October 2009 (only available in French).

12 BGE 130 I 369, 370–1 (2004). See also BGE 128 I 167, 168 (2002).

13 Amtsblatt des Kantons Graubünden 2013/2, 10 January 2013, pp. 14–18.

14 BGE 130 I 369, 384–5 (2004). 15 Ibid., 371. 16 See Section 3.1.

at the disposal of state authorities are exclusion orders, dispersal orders, control orders, curfews and the establishment of zones where particular activities, such as demonstrating, are prohibited. In some instances, as in that of Gsell, law enforcement authorities have also banned individuals from public places without there being any explicit legal basis for doing so. The targets of these new exclusion measures include teenagers, drug addicts, protesters, homeless people, alcoholics as well as (potential) sex offenders, street gang members and football hooligans. As will be argued below, this rise of exclusion measures is characteristic of two broader developments that have fundamentally transformed public space in recent years: the 'privatisation of public space' and its increased regulation and control due to the rise of the 'security society'.[17]

Granting the state the power to exclude people from public space poses a number of challenges to the basic values and principles on which liberal democracies are founded. Exclusion measures are typically based – if they have an explicit legal basis at all – on legal norms that are very vaguely and broadly drafted, raising concerns with regard to the rule of law; they interfere with a range of guarantees of liberty and equality; and they prevent ever-larger sections of the population from being visible, and participating, in public life and are thus problematic from the perspective of democracy. Yet despite these fundamental constitutional problems, and the emergence of case law addressing some of them, exclusion from public space has not attracted much interest from constitutional lawyers. Most scholars who have tackled the issue of exclusion from public space so far have done so from the perspective of (critical) geography,[18] sociology,[19] criminology[20] or, to a limited extent, property/land law[21] or 'administrative law'[22] (understood in the sense of the continental European tradition).[23] This book aims to address this gap by comprehensively exploring the implications that powers of exclusion from

[17] See Section 2.5.

[18] Belina, *Raum, Überwachung, Kontrolle* (2006); Mitchell, *The Right to the City* (2003).

[19] Litscher/Grossrieder/Mösch-Payot/Schmutz, *Wegweisung aus öffentlichen Stadträumen* (2011); Beckett/Herbert, *Banished* (2010); Gasser, *Kriminalpolitik oder City-Pflege?* (2004).

[20] Von Hirsch/Shearing, 'Exclusion from Public Space' (2000).

[21] Gray/Gray, 'Civil Rights, Civil Wrongs and Quasi-Public Space' (1999); Ellickson, 'Controlling Chronic Misconduct in City Spaces' (1996).

[22] Finger, *Die offenen Szenen der Städte* (2006).

[23] On the different understandings of 'administrative law' in the common law and the continental European traditions, see Bell, 'Comparative Administrative Law' (2006), 1261.

public space have for the foundational elements of any liberal democratic constitution: the rule of law, fundamental rights and democracy. To do so, it analyses relevant laws, their application and the emerging jurisprudence of three liberal democracies that have been at the forefront of developing exclusion measures: the United Kingdom, the United States and Switzerland.

1.2 Methodology

In order to explore the issues set out above, a comparative constitutional analysis will be undertaken: the book examines the constitutional law implications of exclusion from public space, comparing the situations in the United Kingdom, the United States and Switzerland. This section explains the reasons for choosing this methodological approach.

1.2.1 A constitutional analysis

As explained above, the issue of exclusion from public space has so far mainly been examined from the perspectives of geography, sociology and criminology. These existing inquiries are predominantly *descriptive and explanatory*: their primary focus is on a description of various exclusion measures and an analysis of the reasons for their adoption and of their (geographical, sociological or criminological) implications. Although nearly all of the respective authors are evidently critical of exclusion from public space, they rarely explicitly state the basis for their criticism: at most, they *imply* that exclusion measures represent bad policy or that they are morally objectionable.[24] In contrast, I aim to explore exclusion from public space from a *normative* perspective. More precisely, I consider measures excluding people from public space in the light of the most relevant fundamental values and principles on which liberal democracies are founded, assessing them for their compatibility with these values and principles. In order to identify the latter, the constitutions of the three liberal democratic states referred to above will be examined, with a view to identifying common underlying 'constitutional values and principles'[25] or, in John Rawls' terms, 'constitutional essentials'.[26]

24 E.g. Beckett/Herbert, *Banished* (2010); Gasser, *Kriminalpolitik oder City-Pflege?* (2004).

25 For a definition of these terms, which are often used interchangeably, see Jacobsohn, 'Constitutional Values and Principles' (2012).

26 Rawls, *Political Liberalism* (1993), pp. 227–30. See Michelman, 'Rawls on Constitutionalism and Constitutional Law' (2002).

Measures excluding people from public space normally fall within the competence of municipal or local authorities, and the relevant legal powers are often provided by state (in the United States), cantonal (in Switzerland) or even municipal, rather than national, legislation. Since these laws, and their application, may differ considerably, the few legal analyses of exclusion from public space that do exist have focused, by and large, on particular local contexts and specific land law or administrative law aspects.[27] As a consequence, only very little attention has been paid to the 'broader issues' raised by exclusion from public space, that is, its implications in terms of constitutional law. This lack of attention is surprising, considering that the regulation of the use of public space is an issue that is at the heart of constitutional law as it has important implications for key constitutional values such as the rule of law, fundamental rights and democracy. This book seeks to address these so far largely unexplored constitutional law implications of exclusion from public space.

1.2.2 A comparative analysis

Vicki Jackson distinguishes several broad classes of methodological approach in comparative constitutional law ('classificatory', 'historical', 'normative' or 'universalist', 'functionalist' or 'consequentialist' and 'contextualist'), which, as she concedes, may overlap with each other and within which, in turn, different techniques may be used.[28] According to her classification, the present study would probably be characterised as primarily 'functionalist',[29] since, as will be explained in this section, the main objectives of the comparison are to facilitate a comprehensive analysis of various ways of excluding people from public space and to assess these for their compatibility with the fundamental values and principles that are common to liberal democratic states. In view of the last point, namely its aim of identifying common principles, Jackson

[27] E.g. Finger, *Die offenen Szenen der Städte* (2006); Ellickson, 'Controlling Chronic Misconduct in City Spaces' (1996).

[28] Jackson, 'Comparative Constitutional Law' (2012), 55–67.

[29] Ibid., 62–6. On functionalism in comparative law in general, see Michaels, 'The Functional Method of Comparative Law' (2006); Zweigert/Kötz, *Einführung in die Rechtsvergleichung* (1996), pp. 31–47. On functionalism in comparative constitutional law, see Tushnet, 'The Possibilities of Comparative Constitutional Law' (1999), 1238–69. For critiques of the functionalist approach to comparative constitutional law, see Teitel, 'Comparative Constitutional Law in a Global Age' (2003); Frankenberg, 'Critical Comparisons' (1985), 434–40.

might also assign this study to the category of comparative analyses she describes as 'universalist'.[30] At the same time, however, the inquiry also aspires to be 'contextualist': it is guided by the belief that legal norms and their application, especially in the field of public law,[31] should not be considered without paying due attention to their particular institutional and national contexts.[32] I therefore make an attempt to present the various principles and norms at issue before their respective historical and political backgrounds. I hope that, by contributing to an understanding of how the issue of exclusion from public space is addressed in other legal systems, the book will also help readers get a better grasp of the particularity of their own respective legal system and the context within which it operates.

The first objective of the comparative analysis is to explore various ways of approaching the issue of exclusion from public space. A number of states currently face the same social problem, namely that the presence of particular groups of people in (certain parts of) public space is seen as undesirable or even as a threat to society. As a reaction to this common social problem, they have created new laws or added new provisions to existing laws. Comparison across a number of states makes it possible, first of all, to gauge the extent to which the adoption of measures excluding people from public space represents a general trend in liberal democratic states. This in itself constitutes a worthwhile objective. More importantly, however, comparison allows for a more comprehensive analysis, and thus also a more reliable assessment, of the different ways of dealing with the social problem referred to above. How do the new legal regulations try to address the problem? How are they implemented? What are their consequences?

The second objective of the comparison is to identify fundamental values and principles relevant in the context of exclusion from public space that are common to liberal democratic states and to assess exclusion measures for their conformity with them. Which types of exclusion measures, if any, are compatible with the 'constitutional essentials' of liberal democracy and which ones are not? In order to answer these questions, the jurisprudence of UK, US and Swiss courts (as well as of international courts and adjudicatory bodies) dealing with these issues

30 Jackson, 'Comparative Constitutional Law' (2012), 60–2.

31 See Tushnet, 'Comparative Constitutional Law' (2006), 1253–7; Bell, 'Comparative Administrative Law' (2006), 1260; Starck, 'Rechtsvergleichung im öffentlichen Recht' (1997); Strebel, 'Vergleichung und vergleichende Methode im öffentlichen Recht' (1964).

32 Jackson, 'Comparative Constitutional Law' (2012), 66–7.

will be subject to a comprehensive and thorough analysis. A comparative approach makes it possible to move beyond specific local contexts and, by considering exclusion from public space from the perspective of the fundamental values of liberal democracy, to gain a better understanding of their wider implications. It should therefore also be clear that this book does not – and cannot – aim to explore each and every legal issue that is related to exclusion from public space.

A comparative approach is all the more pertinent given that there is a strong interplay between the constitutional values and principles of different liberal democratic states. As the following chapters try to demonstrate, the 'constitutional essentials' of such states have not developed in isolation but, on the contrary, have profoundly influenced each other. And they continue to do so: courts (both constitutional courts and lower courts) and legal scholars regularly refer to the law and case law of foreign jurisdictions (as well as international law and the jurisprudence of international courts) when applying and interpreting constitutional principles such as the rule of law, fundamental rights and democracy. It may thus be revealing to compare how the issue of the relationship between these constitutional principles and access to public space is conceptualised and tackled in various liberal democracies.

This observation holds especially true with respect to the fundamental rights conformity of exclusion measures. Today, the study of fundamental rights is linked to the study of international law and comparative constitutional law to such an extent that a scholarly work that deals with fundamental rights is arguably incomplete if it fails to take into account international human rights jurisprudence and, at the very least, key developments in other jurisdictions.

International human rights law is of great relevance to an inquiry such as the present one in that numerous states, including those considered here, have ratified at least the key human rights treaties and are thus obliged to comply with the guarantees contained therein.[33] Furthermore, both the creation and application of *domestic* guarantees of fundamental rights are frequently influenced by the jurisprudence concerning the respective guarantees at the international level.[34] How rights guarantees

[33] See Section 5.1.

[34] On how, for instance, the ECHR and the European Court of Human Rights have shaped domestic law in European states, see e.g. Spielmann, 'Jurisprudence of the European Court of Human Rights and the Constitutional Systems of Europe' (2012); Keller and Stone Sweet (eds), *A Europe of Rights* (2008); Blackburn and Polakiewicz (eds), *Fundamental Rights in Europe* (2001).

are articulated and interpreted in domestic constitutional law can today no longer be properly understood if one does not have a grasp of the degree to which national institutions might be responding to the supervision of international institutions such as the European Court of Human Rights or the UN Human Rights Committee. On the other hand, comparative constitutional law is important for an understanding of international human rights norms, as international institutions often consider the relevant jurisprudence of national courts when interpreting these.[35] As Mark Tushnet has concluded, today 'in some aspects the study of comparative constitutional law is continuous with the study of international human rights law'.[36]

As far as the domestic level is concerned, there is increasing assimilation of various constitutional systems in the field of fundamental rights. This development towards convergence is prodded in part by the emergence of international human rights law: the lists of fundamental rights in national constitutions have become more and more reflective of international human rights instruments and thereby also more and more reflective of one another.[37] At least in respect of fundamental rights protection, the claim that there is now what David Law has called 'generic constitutional law' seems therefore justified.[38] Law and Mila Versteeg analysed 729 constitutions adopted by 188 different states from 1946 to 2006 and found, first, that a significant number of rights-related provisions appear in virtually all constitutions and can therefore be described as 'generic'.[39] The guarantees of freedom of expression, freedom of religion and equality, for example, were contained in 97 per cent of all constitutions in force as of 2006.[40] Second, Law and Versteeg demonstrate that the number of 'generic rights' has been increasing over time.[41] The trend towards transnational convergence, it has been argued, is however not limited to the *codification*

[35] Accordingly, the European Commission for Democracy through Law of the Council of Europe (Venice Commission) regularly publishes the *Bulletin on Constitutional Case-Law*, containing summaries of the most significant decisions taken by constitutional courts in Europe: Council of Europe, Venice Commission, *Bulletin on Constitutional Case-Law* (Strasbourg) (1993). For the European Court of Human Rights, see McCrudden, 'A Common Law of Human Rights?' (2000), 522.

[36] Tushnet, 'Comparative Constitutional Law' (2006), 1233.

[37] See Thürer, 'Kosmopolitische Verfassungsentwicklungen' (2005), 38.

[38] Law, 'Generic Constitutional Law' (2005).

[39] Law/Versteeg, 'The Evolution and Ideology of Global Constitutionalism' (2011), 1187–94, 1199–200. See also Law/Versteeg, 'The Declining Influence of the United States Constitution' (2012), 770–9.

[40] Law/Versteeg, 'The Evolution and Ideology of Global Constitutionalism' (2011), 1200.

[41] Ibid., 1200–2.

of fundamental rights, but it also applies to the application and interpretation of these norms. As part of what is described by some as a 'global' or 'transnational judicial dialogue'[42] and by others as a 'constitutional engagement in a transnational era',[43] constitutional court judges around the world not only meet each other and exchange ideas more and more regularly but also refer to each other's decisions to an unprecedented degree. As a result, one of the leading texts on comparative constitutional law concludes that in the area of fundamental rights there is now 'widespread overlap – if not underlying universalism – at the core'.[44] This development towards convergence is particularly far advanced in Europe where, as an ambitious work tries to show, a *ius publicum europaeum* is emerging: a common European public law, consisting of both a common constitutional law and a common system of scholarship.[45]

There are good reasons to be sceptical about far-reaching claims that constitutional law all over the world is converging and that there is now 'a global community of courts',[46] which is engaged in an 'active and ongoing dialogue'.[47] Yet this is not the place to assess the different positions in this debate.[48] For present purposes it suffices to note that even authors who are sceptical about the alleged trend towards convergence acknowledge that, in the distinct area of human and fundamental rights, there is now indeed broad and substantial consensus among national constitutions and constitutional courts. Ruti Teitel, for instance, who is generally very critical of convergence claims,[49] argues that in

[42] E.g. Slaughter, *A New World Order* (2004), pp. 65–103, 268; Slaughter, 'A Global Community of Courts' (2003). See also Kirby, 'Transnational Judicial Dialogue, Internationalisation of Law and Australian Judges' (2008).

[43] Jackson, *Constitutional Engagement in a Transnational Era* (2010).

[44] Dorsen/Rosenfeld/Sajó/Baer, *Comparative Constitutionalism* (2010), p. 3.

[45] Von Bogdandy/Cruz Villalón/Huber (eds), *Handbuch Ius Publicum Europaeum, Bd. 1* (2007); von Bogdandy/Cruz Villalón/Huber (eds), *Handbuch Ius Publicum Europaeum, Bd. 2* (2008); von Bogdandy/Cassese/Huber (eds), *Handbuch Ius Publicum Europaeum, Bd. 3* (2010); von Bogdandy/Cassese/Huber (eds), *Handbuch Ius Publicum Europaeum, Bd. 4* (2011). For an English summary presenting some of the results of this research project, see von Bogdandy, 'The Past and Promise of Doctrinal Constructivism – A Strategy for Responding to the Challenges Facing Constitutional Scholarship in Europe' (2009). Peter Häberle claimed already in 1991 that there was a *gemeineuropäisches Verfassungsrecht* ('common European constitutional law'): Häberle, 'Gemeineuropäisches Verfassungsrecht' (1991).

[46] Slaughter, 'A Global Community of Courts' (2003).

[47] Slaughter, *A New World Order* (2004), p. 66.

[48] For a critical analysis of the idea of a 'global judicial dialogue', see e.g. Law/Chang, 'The Limits of Global Judicial Dialogue' (2011).

[49] See Teitel, 'Comparative Constitutional Law in a Global Age' (2003).

respect of what she calls 'transnational human rights law' there is now such a degree of agreement that one may speak of a limited universal 'law of humanity', which she describes as 'the logical peak of the comparativist project'.[50] Given that we may be witnessing the emergence of a 'common law of human rights'[51] or a 'global model of constitutional rights',[52] it is indeed in this particular field of constitutional (and international) law that adoption of a comparative approach promises to be especially fruitful.

In the following chapters on the rule of law (Chapter 4), liberty (Chapter 5), equality (Chapter 6) and democracy (Chapter 7), the first section of each chapter will explain how the three domestic constitutional systems (as well as the international legal system) have influenced each other with regard to these 'constitutional essentials' and draw out commonalities and differences. The main body of each of these chapters then compares the situations in the three states with specific regard to the issue of exclusion from public space.

1.2.3 Choice of states

The states selected for this comparative analysis of the constitutional law implications of exclusion from public space are the United Kingdom, the United States and Switzerland. It would be dishonest to claim that this choice is due to nothing else than scientific logic. As Günter Frankenberg has pointed out, it is inevitable that the selection of jurisdictions for any comparative study will hinge upon a range of contingent factors, including the author's biographic background, his or her academic interests and practical restraints (such as language).[53] Nevertheless, there are several objective reasons that justify a focus on these three countries for present purposes.

In older scholarly works it was sometimes claimed that comparisons will only make sense if they are made between countries that belong to what has variously been described as the same 'legal family',[54]

[50] Teitel, *Humanity's Law* (2011), p. 190. See also Teitel, 'Humanity Law: A New Interpretive Lens on the International Sphere' (2008), 695–702; Teitel, 'Comparative Constitutional Law in a Global Age' (2003), 2593.

[51] McCrudden, 'A Common Law of Human Rights?' (2000).

[52] Möller, *The Global Model of Constitutional Rights* (2012).

[53] Frankenberg, 'Critical Comparisons' (1985), 433–4.

[54] David/Jauffret-Spinosi, *Les grands systèmes de droit contemporains* (2003), pp. 15–23. For an English translation, see David/Brierley, *Major Legal Systems in the World Today* (1985), pp. 17–31. Despite the title of his work, David uses the term 'legal family'.

Rechtskreis[55] or 'legal tradition'.[56][57] It is of course true that comparisons between legal systems that are fundamentally different will rarely yield very useful results. However, the distinction between the Romano-Germanic, common law, Muslim law and further legal families, *Rechtskreise* or legal traditions has been mainly developed with a view to the private-law context and is of limited utility with regard to public-law systems. What is more important for comparative studies in the field of public law – and, since 'constitutions lie at the intersection of law and high politics',[58] especially constitutional law – is that the states to be compared are part of the same 'ideological community', for example that they share a liberal political ideology.[59] In any event, it is difficult to define criteria for choosing appropriate comparators that would be generally applicable: the selection of countries must always depend on the particular objective of the inquiry to be undertaken.[60] As will be briefly indicated in this section and then further elaborated in the following chapters, both with regard to their fundamental constitutional values and the particular issue to be explored in this study (namely, exclusion from public space), the selected states have exerted a considerable influence on each other and thus share important commonalities.

As far as fundamental constitutional values or 'constitutional essentials' are concerned, it should, first of all, be observed that exclusion from public space only poses a challenge for those states that would define themselves as liberal democracies, that is, states that are governed by a form of majority rule that includes the protection of the rights and liberties of the individual and subjects the exercise of decision-making power to the rule of law.[61] In states that are not based on the values of democracy, fundamental rights and the rule of law, granting the government the power to exclude people from public space will not normally pose problems with regard to constitutional law. The United Kingdom,

55 Zweigert/Kötz, *Einführung in die Rechtsvergleichung* (1996), pp. 62–73.

56 E.g. Glenn, *Legal Traditions of the World* (2014).

57 For an overview of works making this claim, see Constantinesco, *Rechtsvergleichung* (1972), pp. 49–50, 122–8. See also Bernhardt, 'Eigenheiten und Ziele der Rechtsvergleichung im öffentlichen Recht' (1964), 437–8.

58 Tushnet, 'Comparative Constitutional Law' (2006), 1228.

59 Barak, *Proportionality: Constitutional Rights and their Limitations* (2012), pp. 66–7; Bell, 'Comparative Administrative Law' (2006), 1265.

60 Zweigert/Kötz, *Einführung in die Rechtsvergleichung* (1996), p. 40; Constantinesco, *Rechtsvergleichung* (1972), p. 51.

61 Ball/Dagger, *Political Ideologies and the Democratic Ideal* (2011), p. 39; Beetham, 'Liberal Democracy and the Limits of Democratization' (1993), 55–7.

the United States and Switzerland are all liberal democracies and thus belong to the same 'ideological community'.

Indeed, historically, their constitutional systems, far from developing in isolation, have influenced each other. In a process described by Alfred Kölz as *atlantischer Kreislauf moderner Staatsideen* ('Atlantic cycle of modern conceptions of the state'),[62] the theories of European Enlightenment thinkers (foremost among them the Englishman John Locke and the French Baron de Montesquieu) as well as the models of parliamentarism and liberty as they had developed in the United Kingdom had a profound influence on the US founding fathers, manifesting itself most clearly in the Bill of Rights, the Federalist Papers and the Declaration of Independence drafted by them. Switzerland's political system of the time also had some, although rather limited, impact on the shaping of the US constitutional system.[63] The US constitutional documents, institutions and ideas, in turn, served as models for the protagonists of the French Revolution of 1789, which shaped constitutional developments throughout Europe.[64] Through the 'medium'[65] of the French Revolution the ideas and institutions developed in the United States also made their way to Switzerland.[66] In addition, leading political thinkers in Switzerland at the time, in particular Benjamin Constant, were directly influenced by the English parliamentary system.[67] Later on, the architects of the Swiss constitution of 1848 took inspiration from the bicameral parliament and the federal state model established by the US constitution.[68] Some of the direct democratic instruments developed in Switzerland, in turn, were adopted by individual US states.[69]

62 Kölz, *Neuere schweizerische Verfassungsgeschichte* (2004), pp. 919–20, 935; Kölz, *Der Weg der Schweiz zum modernen Bundesstaat* (1998), pp. 80–4, 228–9.

63 Hutson, *The Sister Republics* (1992), pp. 27–34; Widmer, 'Der Einfluss der Schweiz auf die amerikanische Verfassung von 1787' (1988).

64 Lester, 'The Overseas Trade in the American Bill of Rights' (1988), 537.

65 Kölz, *Der Weg der Schweiz zum modernen Bundesstaat* (1998), p. 6.

66 Ibid., pp. 5–6, 37–84; Kölz, *Neuere schweizerische Verfassungsgeschichte* (1992), pp. 98–123.

67 Kölz, *Der Weg der Schweiz zum modernen Bundesstaat* (1998), p. 20.

68 Auer/Malinverni/Hottelier, *Droit constitutionnel suisse* (2013), Vol. I, pp. 318–20; Haller, *The Swiss Constitution in a Comparative Context* (2009), p. 10; Kölz, *Neuere schweizerische Verfassungsgeschichte* (1992), pp. 562–7; Hutson, *The Sister Republics* (1992), pp. 47–57.

69 Kölz, *Neuere schweizerische Verfassungsgeschichte* (2004), pp. 919–20; Andreas Gross, 'Direkte Demokratie in Gliedstaaten der USA', *Neue Zürcher Zeitung*, 14 August 1999, p. 83; Hutson, *The Sister Republics* (1992), pp. 75–83; Cronin, *Direct Democracy* (1989), pp. 48–9, 164.

This historical background explains why the political systems of the three states share important characteristics. This observation might not come as a surprise as far as the relationship between the United Kingdom and the United States is concerned. However, also the Swiss constitutional tradition and system, which in general have been very open to influences from abroad,[70] are in many respects closer to those of the United Kingdom and the United States than – as one would perhaps expect – those of Germany or other continental European states. As Dietrich Schindler has pointed out, the authoritarian notions that characterised the constitutional systems of Switzerland's neighbouring states for a long time are rather alien to the Swiss political tradition with its emphasis on popular sovereignty and liberty.[71] Similarly, in terms of methodology, the pragmatic approach prevalent in Anglo-American constitutional doctrine is arguably closer to the Swiss tradition than the often abstract and theoretical approach of continental European constitutional scholarship.[72]

Not least due to the status of the United States as the politically and economically most powerful state in the world, the US legal system has exerted, and continues to exert, great influence worldwide, including in the United Kingdom and Switzerland.[73] This also holds true with regard to constitutional law and, especially, issues relating to fundamental rights.[74] Not only have numerous states of the world, as explained above, 'constitutional guarantees of fundamental human rights and freedoms derived from seventeenth-century England, the eighteenth-century enlightenment and the American and French Revolutions',[75] but their courts also regularly consider the jurisprudence of the US Supreme Court concerning the interpretation of the Bill of Rights. When fundamental rights are at stake, the relevant landmark judgments of the Supreme Court are studied with nearly as much attention in London, Lausanne and Strasbourg as they are in the United States.[76] To refer to only one example, albeit one that is of particular relevance in the present context, the change in understanding in Switzerland of the function of public

[70] Schindler, 'Die Staatslehre in der Schweiz' (1976), 260. [71] Ibid., 263. [72] Ibid.

[73] For the United Kingdom, see e.g. Loveland, 'The Constitutionalisation of Political Libels in English Common Law' (1998). For Switzerland, see Kiener/Lanz, 'Amerikanisierung des schweizerischen Rechts' (2000); Wiegand, 'The Reception of American Law in Europe' (1991); Wiegand, 'Die Rezeption amerikanischen Rechts' (1988).

[74] On the worldwide influence of the US constitution in general, see Billias (ed.), *American Constitutionalism Abroad* (1990).

[75] Lester, 'The Overseas Trade in the American Bill of Rights' (1988), 537. [76] See ibid.

streets as not being limited to a traffic function but also including a communicative function was influenced by the US Supreme Court's 'public forum' doctrine.[77] A similar development towards recognition of the 'public forum' function of streets and squares can be observed in the United Kingdom.[78]

Conversely, while the US Supreme Court used to refer to legal developments in foreign countries (especially those 'in the Anglo-Saxon tradition') quite regularly until about the 1950s,[79] it was reluctant to do so in the second half of the last century. However, the relevance of foreign constitutional law in the United States may now be gaining momentum again, as in recent years the Supreme Court has repeatedly referred to developments in other jurisdictions. In *Lawrence* v. *Texas*, concerning a ban on same-sex sexual activity, for example, it considered in detail the legal situation in the United Kingdom and other states as well as the case law of the European Court of Human Rights on the right to respect for private life.[80] Similarly, in *Roper* v. *Simmons*, the Supreme Court referred extensively to the position of foreign states, and in particular the United Kingdom, on the juvenile death penalty, explaining that '[t]he United Kingdom's experience bears particular relevance here in light of the historic ties between our countries and in light of the Eighth Amendment's own origins', the Eighth Amendment having been modelled on a parallel provision in the English Declaration of Rights of 1689.[81] It concluded more generally that '[i]t does not lessen our fidelity to the Constitution or our pride in its origins to acknowledge that the express affirmation of certain fundamental rights by other nations and peoples simply underscores the centrality of those same rights within our own heritage of freedom'.[82] In an earlier case Justice Breyer had also cited Switzerland's system of cantonal implementation of federal legislation in support of his conclusion that the US federal government may give directions to state officials.[83]

77 Saxer, *Die Grundrechte und die Benutzung öffentlicher Strassen* (1988), p. 124.

78 Feldman, *Civil Liberties and Human Rights in England and Wales* (2002), p. 1015.

79 McCrudden, 'A Common Law of Human Rights?' (2000), 508–9; Kadish, 'Methodology and Criteria in Due Process Adjudication' (1957), 328, 333.

80 *Lawrence* v. *Texas*, 539 U.S. 558, 568, 572–3, 576–7 (2003).

81 *Roper* v. *Simmons*, 543 U.S. 551, 575–8 (2005).

82 Ibid., 578. See also *Atkins* v. *Virginia*, 536 U.S. 304, 317 (2002) (taking account of the overwhelming international consensus against imposing the death penalty on mentally retarded persons).

83 *Printz* v. *United States*, 521 U.S. 898, 976 (1997) (Breyer, J., dissenting).

The commonalities among the three jurisdictions under consideration have been, and continue to be, reinforced by the influence of international law described in the previous section. This holds especially true with regard to commonalities between the United Kingdom and Switzerland. As signatory states of the European Convention on Human Rights (ECHR),[84] their domestic systems of fundamental rights protection have been shaped to a very considerable degree by this convention and the jurisprudence of the Strasbourg institutions.[85] It has rightly been argued that in these two states 'the ECHR constitutes a kind of surrogate, or shadow, Constitution'.[86]

Turning to the issue of exclusion from public space, the United Kingdom, the United States and Switzerland are among those liberal democracies that have been at the forefront of developing exclusion measures. Chapter 3 gives a comprehensive overview of the various types of exclusion measures adopted by these three states, so it is sufficient here to briefly highlight some of the most important and influential of them. The United Kingdom has been a pioneer in the creation of far-reaching legislation directed against anti-social behaviour, which includes governmental powers to exclude people from public space.[87] The British approach to anti-social behaviour has now begun to influence policy developments elsewhere.[88] The United Kingdom has also been instrumental in the development of exclusion measures directed against football-related violence.[89] The United States has some of the strictest exclusion measures against particular categories of (suspected) criminal offenders, such as sexual offenders, drug offenders and street gang members.[90] It is also the country in the Western world where juvenile curfews are probably most widespread.[91] In Switzerland, the cantonal police acts give the police remarkably broad powers to remove and keep away from public places for extended periods of time anyone who is suspected of threatening or disturbing public safety and order.[92] Finally,

[84] European Convention for the Protection of Human Rights and Fundamental Freedoms (ECHR) (adopted 4 November 1950, entered into force 3 September 1953) 213 UNTS 222.

[85] Besson, 'The Reception Process in Ireland and the United Kingdom' (2008); Thurnherr, 'The Reception Process in Austria and Switzerland' (2008).

[86] Keller/Stone Sweet, 'Assessing the Impact of the ECHR on National Legal Systems' (2008), 686.

[87] See Section 3.3.2.

[88] See e.g. for the Netherlands, Huisman/Koemans, 'Administrative Measures in Crime Control' (2008).

[89] See Section 3.3.1. [90] See ibid. [91] See Section 3.3.2. [92] See ibid.

the three states have been among the first to resort to exclusion measures in order to control protest activities, for example by deploying 'kettling' practices.[93]

Importantly, not only with regard to their 'constitutional essentials', but also with regard to exclusion from public space, the three states have influenced each other. Underlying all strategies of spatial exclusion directed against anti-social behaviour is arguably the *broken windows* thesis, which was developed and first implemented in the United States. *Broken windows* is now one of the leading criminal justice theories and has shaped policing strategies across the Western world, including in the United Kingdom and Switzerland.[94] One area where adoption of exclusion measures was directly influenced by the policy of another state is that of football-related violence. The United Kingdom was the first state to introduce football banning orders, which may include a requirement not to be in certain places at certain times, in 1986.[95] As a reaction to the violence at Euro 2000, football banning orders were then made applicable to even those who have not been convicted of a relevant offence.[96] In 2006, Switzerland followed the British model in preparation of Euro 2008 by adopting similar exclusion powers directed against violence related to sports events.[97] Introduction of these exclusion powers was justified with, among other things, the alleged success of football banning orders in the United Kingdom.[98]

To sum up, the constitutional systems of the United Kingdom, the United States and Switzerland are based on common values and principles, in particular – as will be demonstrated in more detail in the following chapters – with regard to the rule of law, fundamental rights and democracy. Furthermore, they belong to the liberal democratic states with the most far-reaching exclusion measures. At the same time, as will also become clear in the following chapters, there are some significant differences among the three states, both in terms of their 'constitutional essentials' and their approach to dealing with social problems such as crime, anti-social behaviour and (potentially) violent protest. For

[93] See Section 3.3.3. [94] See Section 2.5.2.

[95] Public Order Act 1986, ss 30–37 (repealed with saving by Football Spectators Act 1989).

[96] Football Spectators Act 1989 (as amended by the Football Disorder Act 2000), s. 14B in conjunction with s. 14G.

[97] Botschaft zur Änderung des Bundesgesetzes über Massnahmen zur Wahrung der inneren Sicherheit (Massnahmen gegen Gewaltpropaganda und gegen Gewalt anlässlich von Sportveranstaltungen) vom 17. August 2005, BBl 2005, 5613, pp. 5617, 5623, 5639.

[98] Ibid., p. 5624.

example, it is often maintained that the United States is a paradigmatic case of an exclusive society, whereas European societies are generally said to be much more inclusive.[99] As a further aspect, as even a cursory look at the sources referred to in this book demonstrates, there is a greater reliance on case law (rather than academic writing) in the common-law countries of the United Kingdom and the United States as compared to Switzerland. This combination of fundamental commonalities and significant differences in specific respects promises to yield interesting and fruitful comparative insights.

1.3 Scope of research

The different laws that form the legal basis for the exclusion measures to be explored are described in Chapter 3; Annex I reproduces the text of the most important legal norms authorising exclusion from public space. In the cases of the United States and Switzerland with their federal systems, most exclusion measures are based on state legislation (in the United States) or cantonal legislation (in Switzerland) as well as municipal laws. With regard to the most important exclusion measures, such as the blanket exclusion powers contained in Swiss cantonal police acts, the book provides a comprehensive overview. However, space does not allow coverage of all exclusion measures adopted in each and every state, canton and municipality. Therefore, I concentrate, on the one hand, on those exclusion measures that are applicable in the larger states (in particular California, Texas and New York), cantons (in particular Zurich and Berne) and cities (in particular New York City and Zurich) and, on the other hand, on those that have resulted in case law that is of particular relevance for the present inquiry. In the United Kingdom, exclusion measures are based on national legislation. The focus of the analysis is on the legal situation in England and Wales.

In terms of jurisprudence, the book concentrates on the analysis of the case law of the highest courts of the three states at issue (that is, the House of Lords and, since 1 October 2009, the Supreme Court of the United Kingdom, the US Supreme Court and the Federal Supreme Court of Switzerland) and the European Court of Human Rights. However, since a number of questions that are crucial for the present context have not (yet) been addressed by these courts, I also consider numerous decisions

99 Young, *The Exclusive Society* (1999).

of various courts of lower instance that have already had occasion to deal with these questions.

Having set out what this book aims to achieve and what issues it will explore, it may be helpful to specify what it does *not* intend to cover.

The book focuses on measures designed to exclude people from *public space* as defined in Section 2.1.1. It is this category of exclusion measures that raises the most pronounced and complex issues from the perspective of the fundamental constitutional values referred to above. In contrast, governmental powers to exclude individuals from certain parts of *private space* (as they exist in all three states at issue in the context of, for example, domestic violence)[100] will not be addressed. Nor does this study cover exclusion from so-called *semi-public space*, that is, property that is owned by private parties and that is, legally, subject to a private-law regime of use but is, in fact, publicly accessible, such as shopping malls, entertainment centres, sports stadiums and so on.[101] Nevertheless, since the increasing importance of semi-public space is also transforming traditional notions of 'proper' public space, it is necessary to briefly explain the concept and regulation of semi-public space.[102]

I concentrate on those measures that either completely ban access to certain parts of public space or prevent their use for *non-commercial* purposes (such as simply sitting on a public sidewalk or protesting). Again, this choice is due to the fact that these are the measures that are most relevant from the perspective set out above. Measures that 'merely' prevent people from using parts of public space for *commercial* purposes, for example to solicit prostitution or to set up sales stalls, will thus not be dealt with. It must be acknowledged that sometimes it may be difficult to distinguish between commercial and non-commercial use of public space. A good illustration of this difficulty is the substantial body of case law that various courts have elaborated in their attempts to establish a distinction between commercial and non-commercial speech.[103]

[100] For the United Kingdom, see Family Act 1996, ss 30–63; Children Act 1989, ss 38, 38A, 44, 44A. For an overview of the situation in the US states, see American Bar Association Commission on Domestic Violence, 'Domestic Violence Civil Protection Orders (CPOs) by State', June 2009, available at www.americanbar.org/content/dam/aba/migrated/domviol/pdfs/dv_cpo_chart.authcheckdam.pdf. For an overview of the situation in the Swiss cantons, see Schwander, *Häusliche Gewalt* (2006).

[101] See Section 2.1.3. [102] See Sections 2.1.3 and 2.5.1.

[103] For the United States and the United Kingdom, see e.g. Barendt, *Freedom of Speech* (2005), pp. 392–416. For Switzerland, see e.g. Müller/Schefer, *Grundrechte in der Schweiz* (2008), pp. 364–74. For the European Court of Human Rights, see e.g. Hertig Randall, 'Commercial Speech under the European Convention on Human Rights' (2006).

A broad definition of commercial use of public space is adopted here: any forms of use that are at least partly motivated by commercial considerations will not be addressed. Thus, for example, although the Swiss Federal Supreme Court has held that begging is not a 'private economic activity' in the sense of Article 27 of the Federal Constitution (the guarantee of economic freedom),[104] in most instances financial considerations form at least part of the reason why someone begs,[105] and therefore exclusion measures directed against begging will not be covered.

Finally, I do not address measures that prevent people from accessing parts of public space *in foreign states* by banning them from travelling abroad, as is the case, for example, with certain exclusion measures directed against football-related violence.[106] These kinds of exclusion measures raise specific issues with regard to the crossing of national borders, a thorough exploration of which would go beyond the scope of the present inquiry.[107]

1.4 Language and terminology

For the passages dealing with the situation in Switzerland, the text of laws, decisions, academic commentary, materials and so on has been translated into English where it appears in the main body of the text. Where not otherwise indicated, the translations are my own. The most important legal terms and key passages are, in addition, also reproduced in their original languages. In the case of key legal concepts, reference is made to the German and French versions (but not to the less common Italian or Rhaeto-Romanic versions). Where a text only appears in the footnotes, no translation is provided. English translations of the Federal Constitution and the most important federal acts and ordinances are available on the website of the Swiss federal authorities.[108]

The meaning of the most important terms and concepts used (such as 'public space', 'rule of law', 'democracy' etc.) will be explained at the beginning of the respective chapters. However, since there is a great deal

[104] BGE 134 I 214, 216 (2008). [105] See Moeckli, 'Bettelverbote' (2010), 545–8.

[106] For the United Kingdom, see Football Spectators Act 1989 (as amended by the Football Disorder Act 2000), ss 14(4)(b), 14E(3), 19. For Switzerland, see Bundesgesetz über Massnahmen zur Wahrung der inneren Sicherheit vom 21. März 1997 (SR 120) (Federal Act on Measures for the Protection of Internal Security) (BWIS), Art. 24c.

[107] See e.g. *Gough v. Chief Constable of Derbyshire*, [2002] EWCA Civ 351 (concerning the question of whether football banning orders that prevent the attendance of matches abroad are compatible with EU law).

[108] www.admin.ch/bundesrecht/00566/index.html?lang=en.

of terminological inconsistency in this area and there are repeated references to some of these terms from the very beginning, a clarification on the use of the terms 'fundamental rights' (*Grundrechte/droits fondamentaux*), 'human rights' (*Menschenrechte/droits humains* or *droits de l'homme*), 'constitutional rights' (*verfassungsmässige Rechte/droits consitutionnels*), 'individual rights' (*Individualrechte/droits individuels*) and 'freedoms' or '(civil) liberties' (*Freiheitsrechte/libertés*) is already due at this stage. 'Fundamental rights' is used in this study as a generic term to describe all basic entitlements held by an individual (or a group of individuals) towards the state, be they guaranteed by a constitution or international law. 'Human rights' are the rights that everyone is entitled to, simply by virtue of being human. In the United States and Switzerland, the term is used almost exclusively when reference is made to fundamental rights that are guaranteed by *international* law, but not in the context of the respective *domestic* systems of rights protection. In contrast, in the United Kingdom, where the guarantees of the ECHR have been incorporated into domestic law by way of the Human Rights Act,[109] the term 'human rights' is also regularly used in the domestic context.[110] I use the term 'human rights', first, to describe rights guaranteed by international law and, second, in the sections dealing with the situation in the United Kingdom when it seems more appropriate to use the common British terminology. 'Constitutional rights' are entitlements that have their legal basis in the (written) constitution of a state. 'Individual rights' are rights that are held by individuals, in contradistinction to 'group rights', which are rights held by groups of persons. 'Freedoms' or '(civil) liberties' are those fundamental rights that protect the individual's integrity – his or her freedom to do or not do certain things – with regard to particular spheres of life and that, accordingly, impose primarily negative obligations on the state.

Another term I use from the beginning and thus needs to be clarified at the outset is that of the 'police'. In the English language, including in legal terminology, the term 'police' is used to refer to an organisational unit or institution (typically of the state) in charge of maintaining order and preventing and detecting crime.[111] In contrast, in Swiss legal terminology

[109] See Section 4.1.2.

[110] E.g. Amos, *Human Rights Law* (2006). The respective sections of constitutional law textbooks are often entitled 'human rights'. E.g. Barnett, *Constitutional and Administrative Law* (2013), p. 397; Bradley/Ewing, *Constitutional and Administrative Law* (2011), p. 397.

[111] Emsley, *The English Police* (1991), p. 1.

(although not in everyday language), 'police' refers to a function rather than an institution.[112] To facilitate comparison among the three legal systems, I use the term in the first-mentioned, institutional, sense.

Throughout the book, the English style of citing legal materials is used. References to Swiss legislation and to decisions of Swiss courts in the footnotes are kept in the original (German or French) language. In the case of judgments of the Swiss Federal Supreme Court, as a chronological aid for non-Swiss readers, the year of the judgment is added in brackets to the original citation.

1.5 Structure of the book

The book starts, in Chapter 2, by providing a general definition of 'public space' that can be used for present purposes and by distinguishing public space from related concepts. It then briefly explains how, historically, the concept of public space has developed and why the availability of public space is important in, and for, a liberal democracy. Next, the chapter considers how access to, and use of, public space is regulated in the United Kingdom, the United States and Switzerland. Public space has undergone a fundamental transformation in recent years. The final section of the chapter singles out two particularly important aspects of this transformation, the 'privatisation of public space' and its increased control in the 'security society', and explores their implications for the present context.

Chapter 3 first retraces the history of exclusion from public space, explaining, in particular, how banishment declined and how (and why) new forms of exclusion from public space emerged. The bulk of the chapter (together with Annex I) provides an overview of the new exclusion measures adopted in the last few years in the United Kingdom, the United States and Switzerland. It shows that these measures are intended to address three types of social problems: criminal behaviour, anti-social behaviour and political protest. It then provides (together with Annex II) a typology of the different ways in which people are excluded from public space in the three states at issue. To my knowledge, no such overview and typology have yet been produced – not even for one of the three jurisdictions alone.

112 Mohler, *Grundzüge des Polizeirechts in der Schweiz* (2012), pp. 17, 35; Häfelin/Müller/Uhlmann, *Allgemeines Verwaltungsrecht* (2010), p. 558; Sauer, *Das Recht der Vollzugspolizeien von Bund und Kantonen* (2007), p. 51; Reinhard, *Allgemeines Polizeirecht* (1993), pp. 1–31.

Chapter 4 opens with a summary of the meaning of the rule of law in the three jurisdictions. The idea is not to offer a thorough comparative analysis but merely to show that there are a number of common elements underlying, and requirements following from, these conceptions of the rule of law. In the remainder of the chapter, existing exclusion measures are assessed for their conformity with these basic rule-of-law requirements. Are exclusion measures that are based upon general breach-of-the-peace powers (or, in Switzerland, the *polizeiliche Generalklausel*) compatible with these requirements? Are norms that authorise exclusion of those who pose a danger to 'public safety and order' or those who 'cause harassment or distress to others' sufficiently precise? How much discretion can be delegated to law enforcement authorities? Do exclusion measures circumvent existing procedural safeguards or undermine the right to an effective remedy?

Chapter 5 addresses the relationship between exclusion from public space and liberty. It first explains how fundamental rights are protected in the three states at issue and under international law. It then explores which guarantees of liberty may be engaged by exclusion measures. For example, do dispersal orders for anti-social behaviour amount to an interference with the freedom of movement? Next, the requirements for the limitation of these legally guaranteed freedoms are explained and exclusion measures are tested for their compliance with these requirements. Does the exclusion of people from public space who may cause feelings of insecurity in others serve a legitimate aim? Is it a proportionate means of achieving this aim to ban such people from going to the city centre for three months? These and similar questions are addressed with regard to the three categories of exclusion measures (measures designed to address criminal behaviour, anti-social behaviour and political protest). Throughout the chapter, specific examples from all three jurisdictions are used to illustrate the issues, with the respective exclusion measures being assessed for their compliance with the different fundamental rights requirements. The case law on exclusion measures that already exists is subject to a critical analysis.

Chapter 6, which addresses the relationship between exclusion from public space and equality, follows a similar structure. First, the chapter explains how the right to equality and non-discrimination is protected in the three jurisdictions and what obligations it entails. Then, the conformity of exclusion measures with these requirements is examined. To what extent do the three categories of exclusion measures involve differences in treatment among different social groups, be it due to distinctions made by the law, be it due to unequal enforcement (or disproportionate impacts) of neutral laws? On what criteria are the differences in treatment entailed by these measures based? Is there a justification for such differences in treatment (or outcome)? As in the previous chapter, specific examples of exclusion from public space and already existing case law are used to explore these questions.

Chapter 7 first briefly sets out the concepts of democracy that underlie the constitutional systems of the three states at issue, with a particular emphasis on two common elements: the notion that democracy necessarily implies the protection of fundamental rights and the idea of deliberative democracy. The chapter then explores the extent to which exclusion measures can be said to enjoy democratic legitimacy because they represent the will of the political community. Finally, the chapter provides an analysis of the consequences of exclusion from public space for the liberal and deliberative elements of democracy. Does exclusion from public space harm democracy by depriving people, especially marginalised groups, of an effective forum for the exercise of their political and civil rights? What are the consequences for the 'psychological conditions' of democracy if ever-larger sections of the population are banned from simply being present in public space for ever-longer periods of time?

Drawing together some of the main arguments made in previous chapters, Chapter 8 first highlights that the adoption of exclusion measures plays a central role in the current transformation of public space, through which its character as the space of liberty, equality, tolerance and democracy is undermined. It then shows how, as a reaction to this transformation, calls for a 'right to public space' have emerged in recent years. The main part of the chapter explores whether there is a need to legally guarantee such a right. Does a 'right to public space', be it understood as a right of *access* to public space or a right to the *existence* of public space, already exist in the law of the United Kingdom, the United States and/or Switzerland? If not, would it be helpful to create an explicit constitutional guarantee (or a guarantee in international human rights law) of such a right? Or is there, rather, a need for a new approach by courts and other law-applying authorities to cases involving access to public space within the existing legal framework?

The final chapter, Chapter 9, first briefly summarises the main findings. It then concludes the book with a short outlook to the future, asking whether maintaining public space should not primarily be a civic responsibility rather than a task that could be delegated to the police or, more generally, the state.

2

Public space and its transformation

The sort of exclusion measures that build the focus of this book are, in the case of most measures, exclusively and, in the case of the others, primarily applicable in what is commonly referred to as 'public space' (*öffentlicher Raum/espace public*). In any event, it is when they are used to ban people from this type of space that these measures raise the most pronounced issues with regard to the 'constitutional essentials' of liberal democratic states. Public space is, however, not a concept that has a clearly defined meaning, neither in law nor in any other academic discipline. Given the objective of this study set out in Chapter 1, it would go far beyond its scope to try to elaborate a legal definition – or even a legal theory – of public space. The purpose of this chapter is much more modest.

First, it tries to extract from existing definitions of public space those elements of this concept that are most relevant for the present context (Section 2.1). It then gives brief overviews of the historical development of the concept of public space (Section 2.2) and of its importance for liberal democracy (Section 2.3). Section 2.4 is devoted to an explanation of the legal regimes regulating access to, and use of, public space in the United Kingdom, the United States and Switzerland. The final section examines the fundamental transformation that public space has undergone in recent years and explores its implications, focusing on two aspects that are particularly relevant for present purposes (Section 2.5).

2.1 The definition of 'public space' and related concepts

This section explores how the term 'public space' should be understood in the present context and distinguishes it from a number of related concepts, including 'public place', 'semi-public space', 'public forum' and 'public sphere'.

2.1.1 *'Public space'*

The term 'public space' (as well as the related German term *öffentlicher Grund*) can be, and has been, defined in numerous various ways. As this book is concerned with legal measures excluding people from public space, its focus is on the *legal* definition of public space, as opposed to definitions used in, for example, geography, urban design, sociology, cultural studies, media studies, psychology or philosophy. Nevertheless, the legal understanding of public space is inevitably shaped by meanings attributed to the term in other subject areas. Already the terms 'space' and 'public' as such are open to diverse interpretations and, accordingly, the same holds true for 'public space'.

2.1.1.1 'Space'

'Space' (*Raum/espace*) is often presented as a natural given, a physical object in itself or a characteristic of physical nature.[1] However, as Pierre Bourdieu has pointed out, space as physical space can only be thought of on the basis of an abstraction, which ignores everything that is linked to space as being populated and appropriated.[2] Such an abstract concept of space is not helpful for a social science such as law. In the social sciences, space is neither just a physical object nor a mere idea. Instead, the nature of space is inextricably linked to social practice: space is always used as a means to achieve a certain objective.[3] Therefore, it is pointless to try to conceive of space as an ontological entity independent of its use: ' "What space is" is revealed only in the use of space.'[4] In Henri Lefebvre's words, '(social) space is a (social) product'.[5] This means that the law cannot abstractly define space but, as a social practice, itself contributes to the production of space.

2.1.1.2 'Public'

As Jürgen Habermas and others have pointed out, the adjective 'public' (*öffentlich/public*) as well as the corresponding noun 'publicness' or 'public sphere' (*Öffentlichkeit/publicité* or *espace public*) have multiple, and often conflicting, meanings.[6] For, just as in the case of 'space', the

[1] Läpple, 'Gesellschaftszentriertes Raumkonzept' (1991), 36.
[2] Bourdieu, 'Physischer, sozialer und angeeigneter physischer Raum' (1991), 28.
[3] Belina, *Raum, Überwachung, Kontrolle* (2006), pp. 26–35.
[4] Smith, 'Degeneracy in Theory and Practice' (1981), 115.
[5] Lefebvre, *The Production of Space* (2008), p. 26.
[6] Habermas, *Strukturwandel der Öffentlichkeit* (1990), pp. 54–8. See also Geuss, *Public Goods, Private Goods* (2001); Kohler, 'Was ist Öffentlichkeit?' (1999).

distinction between 'public' and 'private', on which these concepts rely, is a social, historical product.[7]

In its most common usage, the term 'public' refers to something that is open to everybody, as in 'public event' or 'public square'. This common understanding is reflected in the law. *Black's Law Dictionary*, for example, defines 'public' as '[o]pen or available for all to use, share, or enjoy'.[8] While Swiss and German law dictionaries do not normally contain definitions of the corresponding German adjective *öffentlich*,[9] one law dictionary defines the noun *Öffentlichkeit* as 'a group of people that is indeterminate in terms of number and identity (general public) and the accessibility of processes to this group'.[10]

However, 'public' has also other meanings. For example, the term 'public building' does not necessarily refer to the accessibility of the building but may simply mean that it is owned by the state. 'Public' changes its meaning again when it is used in an expression such as 'public interest', referring to the general welfare or common good,[11] or 'public law', meaning the body of law that deals with the relations between the state and private individuals and the structure and organisation of the state itself.[12] Furthermore, there are a range of quite specific meanings of 'public' that have to do with publicity (*Publizität/publicité*) and 'the public' (*das Publikum/le public*): 'public statement',[13] 'public opinion' or 'public trial', for example.[14] Therefore, the exact meaning of the term 'public' can only be determined by considering the context, the 'discursive field',[15] in which it is used. For our purposes this means that 'public' cannot be defined on its own, separately from the expression

[7] See e.g. Geuss, *Public Goods, Private Goods* (2001).

[8] Garner (ed.), *Black's Law Dictionary* (2009), p. 1348.

[9] See e.g. Metzger, *Schweizerisches juristisches Wörterbuch* (2005); Weber (ed.), *Creifelds Rechtswörterbuch* (2007).

[10] Köbler, *Juristisches Wörterbuch* (2007), p. 298 ('Öffentlichkeit ist der nach Zahl und Individualität unbestimmte Personenkreis (Allgemeinheit) sowie die Zugänglichkeit von Vorgängen für diesen').

[11] Garner (ed.), *Black's Law Dictionary* (2009), p. 1350. See Section 5.3.1.

[12] Garner (ed.), *Black's Law Dictionary* (2009), pp. 1350–1; Metzger, *Schweizerisches juristisches Wörterbuch* (2005), p. 461.

[13] Article 261bis of the Swiss Criminal Code, for example, makes it a criminal offence to 'publicly incite' (*öffentlich aufrufen/inciter publiquement*) racial hatred, which the Federal Supreme Court understands to refer to any statement that is not made in a private setting, defined as a setting characterised by relations of a personal nature or special trust: BGE 130 IV 111, 119 (2004).

[14] See Habermas, *Strukturwandel der Öffentlichkeit* (1990), p. 55.

[15] Kohler, 'Was ist Öffentlichkeit?' (1999), 199 ('diskursives Feld').

'public space' and without having regard to how that expression is used in different contexts.

2.1.1.3 'Public space'

Given these diverging and often conflicting meanings of the terms 'space' and 'public', it comes as no surprise that 'public space' (*öffentlicher Raum/espace public*) is not a legal term of art, that is, a term with a precise and fixed legal meaning. The same is true for the related German term *öffentlicher Grund* ('public ground').[16] I am not aware of any law dictionaries that would contain a definition of 'public space' or *öffentlicher Grund.* Rather, depending on the context, the term 'public space' may refer to different things. For example, it is sometimes used as a synonym for public property (that is, property owned by the state);[17] or it may include, as in the context of the surveillance of public places, all locations that are accessible to the public;[18] or, even more extensively, it may refer, as in US privacy law, to 'anywhere that is visible from a publicly accessible vantage point, such as parts of a house or garden that are visible from the street';[19] or it may describe, as in feminist legal studies, everything that traditionally has been treated as being outside the domestic, familial sphere;[20] or it may be used, in its broadest meaning, to refer to all relations between people that are governed by the principles of public interaction.[21] To complicate things further, 'public space' is sometimes used in a descriptive sense to refer to a factual situation and sometimes, as in the last example, in a normative sense to refer to a normative ideal or claim.[22]

As the two concepts logically depend on – and exclude – each other, a good starting point for defining 'public space' is by distinguishing it from 'private space'. A space is normally understood to be private if access to it can be determined by the owner at will.[23] Chief Justice Lord Camden held already in 1765 in the landmark case of *Entick* v. *Carrington* that '[o]ur law holds the property of every man so sacred, that no man can set his foot upon his neighbour's close without his

[16] See also Moser, *Der öffentliche Grund und seine Benützung* (2011), p. 141.
[17] See Glasze, 'Privatisierung öffentlicher Räume' (2001), 161–2.
[18] BGE 136 I 87, 111–19 (2009).
[19] Paton-Simpson, 'Privacy and the Resonable Paranoid' (2000), 322.
[20] Nash, 'From Lavender to Purple' (2005); MacKinnon, 'Disputing Male Sovereignty' (2000), 152–75.
[21] Mastronardi, *Verfassungslehre* (2007), p. 20. [22] Ibid., pp. 3, 18–20.
[23] Blackstone, *Commentaries on the Laws of England* (1967), Vol. II, p. 2; Cohen, 'Dialogue on Private Property' (1954), 370–1.

leave'.[24] At least traditionally, this has been understood to mean that persons in possession of land have a virtually unchallengeable discretion to determine who may enter or remain on their land.[25] In the United Kingdom and the United States, this notion finds its expression in the legal concept of trespass;[26] in Switzerland in that of the *Hausrecht/droit au domicile.*[27] By only being accessible to a limited number of people, private spaces offer their owners a space of retreat.

Accordingly, the most common legal understandings of 'public space' concentrate on the opposite concept of *general accessibility*. It is this issue that, as explained above, is already at the heart of most attempts to legally define the term 'public'.

Similarly, definitions of the concept of 'public place', which is closely related to (but more concrete than) that of 'public space',[28] also centre on the question of general accessibility. For example, the *Oxford Dictionary of Law* defines 'public place' as 'a place to which the public has access'.[29] The corresponding French term *lieu public* refers, according to the *Vocabulaire juridique*, to 'a place open to the public, a place where everyone is admitted without distinction'.[30]

This understanding is reflected in numerous definitions of the term 'public place' as contained in relevant laws regulating the use of public space, discussed in more detail in the following chapters. For example, in the United Kingdom, the Public Order Act 1986 defines 'public place', in the context of processions and assemblies, as 'any highway [. . .] and any place to which at the material time the public or any section of the public has access, on payment or otherwise, as of right or by virtue of express or implied permission'.[31] Exactly the same definition can be found in Section 35(10) of the Anti-social Behaviour, Crime and Policing Act

[24] *Entick* v. *Carrington* (1765) 19 Howell's State Trials 1029 (Lord Camden, CJ). See also *Wood* v. *Leadbitter* (1845) 13 M. & W. 838, 153 E.R. 351.

[25] Gray/Gray, *Land Law* (2011), p. 536.

[26] See ibid., pp. 508–35; Goldstein, *Real Property* (1984), pp. 8–24.

[27] See Schweizerisches Strafgesetzbuch vom 21. Dezember 1937 (StGB) (SR 311.0) (Swiss Criminal Code), Art. 186; BGE 90 IV 74, 76 (1964) ('Art. 186 StGB schützt das Hausrecht, nämlich die Befugnis, über einen bestimmten Raum ungestört zu herrschen und in ihm den eigenen Willen frei zu betätigen.'); Schweizerisches Zivilgesetzbuch vom 10. Dezember 1907 (ZGB) (SR 210) (Swiss Civil Code), Arts 641, 926. See also Bundesverfassung der Schweizerischen Eidgenossenschaft vom 18. April 1999 (SR 101) (BV) (Federal Constitution of the Swiss Confederation), Art. 13(1); ZGB, Art. 28.

[28] See Section 2.1.2.

[29] Law and Martin (eds), *Oxford Dictionary of Law* (2009), p. 440.

[30] Cornu (ed.), *Vocabulaire juridique* (2007), p. 498 ('Lieu ouvert au public; lieu où tout le monde est admis indistinctement').

[31] Public Order Act, s. 16.

2014, relating to the dispersal of persons from public places. In the United States, legal definitions of 'public place' similarly focus on the question of accessibility. For example, the Chicago Municipal Code defines 'public place', for purposes of prohibitions of loitering, as 'the public way and any other location open to the public, whether publicly or privately owned'.[32] According to the Dallas Code of Ordinances, a 'public place', in the context of juvenile curfews, is to be understood very broadly as including 'any place to which the public or a substantial group of the public has access and includes, but is not limited to, streets, highways, and the common area of schools, hospitals, apartment houses, office buildings, transport facilities, and shops'.[33] A similarly broad definition can be found in the New York City Administrative Code, which bans the consumption of alcohol in any public place, defined as '[a] place to which the public or a substantial group of persons has access including, but not limited to, any highway, street, road, sidewalk, parking area, shopping area, place of amusement, playground, park or beach located within the city'.[34]

In Switzerland, relevant laws do not normally employ the terms *öffentlicher Ort/lieu public* (public place) or *öffentlicher Raum/espace public* (public space) at all. Instead, they often simply refer to *'ein Ort/un lieu'* ('a place/location'), even when what is clearly meant primarily is a *public* place.[35] Some legal norms regulating political protest in public places or imposing juvenile curfews refer to *'öffentlicher Grund'* ('public ground');[36] others more specifically to *'öffentliche Strassen und Plätze'* ('public streets and squares'),[37] without however providing a definition of these terms. Government guidelines or similar documents, however, do sometimes provide definitions. For example, the guidelines for the improvement of safety in public and semi-public space of the City of

[32] Chicago Municipal Code, §§ 8-4-015(d)(5), 8-4-017(c)(2).

[33] Dallas, Texas Code of Ordinances, s. 31–33(a)(9).

[34] New York City Administrative Code, § 10–125(a)(2).

[35] E.g. Polizeigesetz (PolG) des Kantons Zürich vom 23. April 2007 (LS 550.1), § 33; Polizeigesetz des Kantons Bern vom 8. Juni 1997 (BSG 551.1), Art. 29; Loi sur la police du Canton de Genève du 26 Octobre 1957 (LPol, RSG F 1 05), Art. 22A (adopted on 19 February 2009).

[36] E.g. Verordnung der Stadt Zürich über die Benutzung des öffentlichen Grundes (Benutzungsordnung) vom 23. November 2011 (AS 551.210); Reglement der Stadt Bern über Kundgebungen auf öffentlichem Grund vom 20. Oktober 2005 (Kundgebungsreglement; KgR; SSSB 143.1); Gemeindepolizeireglement der Gemeinde Urtenen-Schönbühl vom 15. Mai 2006, Art. 6.

[37] E.g. Gemeindepolizeireglement der Gemeinde Interlaken vom 5. Dezember 2006 (552.11), Art. 9.

Zurich define 'public spaces' as 'streets, paths, squares, public buildings and other spaces, which are open for the free use of the public'.[38]

It follows from these meanings attributed to the terms 'public place' and 'public spaces' in existing legal regulations, including in norms that are central to the subject of the present inquiry, that the issue of accessibility is at the heart of the notion of 'public space'. A very general definition of 'public space' may be framed as follows: *Public space is that space which is accessible to, and can be used by, an indeterminate number of people (the public).*

Thus, whether a given place is part of 'public space' or not depends on its accessibility rather than ownership: 'public space' is not equivalent to 'public property'. Of course, ownership is an important indication of the accessibility of a place. After all, it is, as a general rule, in the discretion of the owner to determine who is given access to his or her property. As the US Supreme Court has put it, 'the right to exclude others' is 'one of the most essential sticks in the bundle of rights that are commonly characterized as property'.[39] Some authors have even argued that property is *exclusively* about control over access and should be defined as 'a power-relation constituted by legally sanctioned control over access to the benefits of excludable resources'[40] or 'a relationship among human beings such that the so-called owner can exclude others from certain activities or permit others to engage in those activities and in either case secure the assistance of the law in carrying out his decision'.[41] Private owners will normally exclude the public from accessing their property, whereas publicly owned property will normally be accessible to the public.

However, this is only the general rule and there are exceptions: ownership may be a convenient starting point, but it is not the determinative factor. In all three jurisdictions at issue it is well established in case law, as well as legal doctrine, that the public accessibility of a given place depends not on who the owner is but on what purpose it is meant to serve. The Swiss Federal Supreme Court has held that, irrespective of who the owner is, streets and squares are to be considered public if they are

38 Stadt Zürich, Mehr Sicherheit im öffentlichen und halböffentlichen Raum: Checklisten für das Planen, Projektieren, Bauen und Unterhalten, December 2003, p. 6 ('Öffentliche Räume sind Strassen, Wege, Plätze, öffentliche Gebäude und andere Räume, die der Allgemeinheit zur freien Benützung offen stehen.').

39 *Kaiser Aetna* v. *United States*, 444 U.S. 164, 176 (1979).

40 Gray, 'Property in Thin Air' (1991), 295.

41 Cohen, 'Dialogue on Private Property' (1954), 373.

designed to be open for the use of the public.[42] Swiss legal doctrine uses the term *öffentliche Sachen im Gemeingebrauch/domaine public* ('public goods in common use') to describe this category of goods, which, apart from streets, also includes, for example, squares, bridges, parks, public train stations, lakes and rivers.[43] In the United Kingdom, the public enjoys certain rights of access to land, most notably a right to use the highway and a right of passage over navigable waters, irrespective of ownership.[44] English common law defines the term 'highway' as 'a way over which there exists a public right of passage, that is to say a right for all Her Majesty's subjects at all seasons of the year freely and at their will to pass and repass without let or hindrance'.[45] The House of Lords has explicitly stated that such public accessibility does not depend on ownership: 'The nature of the public's right of use of the highway cannot depend upon whether the owner of the subsoil is a private landowner or a public authority.'[46] Thus, highways include not only all public streets, including adjoining pavements, and footpaths but may also include private streets.[47] The US Supreme Court, finally, made it clear very early on that streets and parks are crucial for the exercise of fundamental rights and must thus be accessible to the general public, irrespective of who their owner is. In its much-quoted judgment in *Hague* v. *CIO* of 1939, it famously made the following observation:

> Wherever the title of streets and parks may rest, they have immemorially been held in trust for the use of the public and, time out of mind, have been used for purposes of assembly, communicating thoughts between citizens, and discussing public questions. Such use of the streets and public places has, from ancient times, been a part of the privileges, immunities, rights, and liberties of citizens.[48]

That ownership is of no relevance is, moreover, implicit in the legal definitions of 'public place' referred to above and is even made explicit in

[42] BGE 94 I 569, 574–5 (1968). See also BGE 127 I 164, 178 (2001); BGE 104 IV 105, 108 (1978).

[43] Tschannen/Zimmerli/Müller, *Allgemeines Verwaltungsrecht* (2014), p. 469; Moser, *Der öffentliche Grund und seine Benützung* (2011), pp. 34–6; Hottelier, 'La réglementation du domaine public à Genève' (2002), 124–6; Jaag, 'Gemeingebrauch und Sondernutzung öffentlicher Sachen' (1992), 147; Moor, *Droit administratif III* (1992), pp. 253–4, 259–63, 269–70; Grisel, *Traité de droit administratif* (1984), pp. 526–7.

[44] Gray/Gray, *Land Law* (2011), pp. 546–9.

[45] *Halsbury's Laws of England* (1988–2008), Vol. 21, para. 1.

[46] *DPP* v. *Jones (Margaret)* [1999] 2 AC 240, 257 (Lord Irvine). See also ibid., 268 (Lord Hope).

[47] Ibid., 268 (Lord Hope).

[48] *Hague* v. *CIO*, 307 U.S. 496, 515 (1939).

the case of the Chicago Municipal Code, which defines 'public place' as 'the public way and any other location open to the public, whether publicly or privately owned'.[49]

There may be different reasons why a given place is characterised as publicly accessible. Public accessibility may follow from an act dedicating that place to a particular public use. In the United Kingdom and the United States, both public authorities and private landowners can dedicate a place in this manner.[50] In Switzerland, in contrast, dedication (*Widmung/affectation*) is always a sovereign act of a public authority. If the relevant piece of land is owned by a private party, the public authority will therefore first need to acquire the power of disposition over it if the owner refuses to agree to the dedication.[51] In addition, in all three jurisdictions public accessibility of a place may also follow from the fact that it has been used by the public for a long time or since times immemorial,[52] or from its particular nature, as, for example, with rivers, lakes and seashores.[53]

In summary, on the one hand, privately owned places also, such as certain streets, may be publicly accessible and thus form part of public

[49] Chicago Municipal Code, §§ 8-4-015(d)(5), 8-4-017(c)(2).

[50] For the United Kingdom, see *DPP* v. *Jones*, [1999] 2 AC 240, 256 (Lord Irvine). For the United States, see Goldstein, *Real Property* (1984), pp. 704–5; *Scott* v. *Cannon*, 959 S.W.2d 712, 718 (Tex. App., 1998).

[51] Moser, *Der öffentliche Grund und seine Benützung* (2011), pp. 37–42; Häfelin/Müller/Uhlmann, *Allgemeines Verwaltungsrecht* (2010), pp. 536–7; Moor, *Droit administratif III* (1992), pp. 272–3; Grisel, *Traité de droit administratif* (1984), pp. 529–30. For a comprehensive German treatise of the concept of *Widmung*, see Axer, *Die Widmung als Schlüsselbegriff des Rechts der öffentlichen Sachen* (1994).

[52] For Switzerland, see BGE 94 I 569, 574–5 (1968); BGE 74 I 41, 48–9 (1948); Moser, *Der öffentliche Grund und seine Benützung* (2011), pp. 42–4; Häfelin/Müller/Uhlmann, *Allgemeines Verwaltungsrecht* (2010), p. 537; Moor, *Droit administratif III* (1992), pp. 264–6, 272; Meier-Hayoz, *Berner Kommentar zum schweizerischen Privatrecht* (1965), p. 182. For the United Kingdom, see Highways Act 1980, s. 31(1) ('[w]here a way over any land [. . .] has been actually enjoyed by the public as of right and without interruption for a full period of 20 years'). For a good overview, see *R.* v. *Oxfordshire CC Ex p. Sunningwell Parish Council* [2000] 1 AC 335, 346–56 (Lord Hoffmann). For the United States, see *Gion* v. *City of Santa Cruz*, 2 Cal. 3d 29, 465 P.2d 50 (1970) (widespread public use of a beach during long periods is sufficient evidence of dedication to the public).

[53] For Switzerland, see Häfelin/Müller/Uhlmann, *Allgemeines Verwaltungsrecht* (2010), p. 536; Jaag, 'Gemeingebrauch und Sondernutzung öffentlicher Sachen' (1992), 147; Moor, *Droit administratif III* (1992), pp. 253–4. For the United Kingdom, see Gray/Gray, *Land Law* (2011), pp. 548–9; Feldman, 'Property and Public Protest' (2000), 34. For the United States, see e.g. *Matthews* v. *Bay Head Imp. Ass'n*, 471 A.2d 355 (N.J., 1984); Rose, 'The Comedy of the Commons' (1986).

space in its most common legal sense. On the other hand, not all property owned by the state is designed to be used by the public. A building housing a government ministry or a military base, for example, is typically not accessible to the public and thus does not form part of public space.

A narrow definition of 'public space' (or *öffentlicher Grund*) would only cover those locations that are accessible to the public for any purposes and activities, at any time and free of charge.[54] In contrast, there are a number of (legal) definitions, including some of those referred to above, that are wider and also include places that are only accessible to certain categories of people, for specific purposes, at specified times or on payment, such as schools, universities, hospitals, town halls, theatres or transport facilities.[55] I will focus on 'public space' in the first, narrow sense. What is of primary interest for present purposes is exclusion from exactly those places where access is normally *not* dependent on further conditions such as compliance with particular rules of conduct and that are accessible at any time and free of charge.

Furthermore, exclusion measures in the sense just referred to are used almost exclusively with regard to *urban* public spaces, most commonly in inner-city areas. Exclusion from public space consisting of natural resources such as lakes, rivers or seashores is of hardly any practical relevance. Therefore, the focus of the book will be on urban areas. This is, moreover, where the overwhelming majority of the population of the three states at issue live.[56] Urban spaces that are publicly accessible without further conditions include not only streets (including the pavement), footpaths, squares and parks but also, for example, certain parts of train stations.[57]

To sum up, this book uses the term 'public space' to refer to *space which is accessible to, and can be used by, the public (that is, everyone) without conditions, at any time and free of charge, in particular public*

[54] See Moser, *Der öffentliche Grund und seine Benützung* (2011), pp. 193–4.

[55] E.g. Public Order Act 1986, s. 16; Dallas, Texas Code of Ordinances, s. 31–33(a)(9).

[56] In the United Kingdom, 83 per cent of the total population live in cities and suburbs. In the United States, the percentage is 82 per cent, in Switzerland 74 per cent: Central Intelligence Agency, *The World Factbook*, 2015, available at www.cia.gov/library/publications/the-world-factbook/geos/us.html.

[57] On publicly accessible parts of train stations in Switzerland, see BGE 138 I 274, 284–5 (2012); Urteil des Bundesverwaltungsgerichts A-7454/2009 vom 29. März 2011, E. 8. 4–8.6; Moser, *Der öffentliche Grund und seine Benützung* (2011), pp. 172–93; Mathis, 'Die Ausübung politischer Rechte auf Bahnhofsarealen' (2011); Wyssmann, *Nutzungskonflikte im öffentlichen Raum* (2009).

streets (including the pavement), footpaths, squares, parks and publicly accessible parts of train stations.

This definition of public space is a descriptive one. According to the understanding underlying this definition, public space, as any type of space, is a social product: what makes a given space public is the fact that people cannot be, and are not, denied access to it. This means, conversely, that if people can be, and in fact are, excluded from a given place, this place ceases to be a truly public space. Thus, as norms regulating the use of public space and enforcement of these norms may change, so may the public nature of that space.

2.1.2 *'Public place'*

A 'place' is something concrete and particular, something that can be experienced. Accordingly, a 'place' is generally understood to be a concretisation of 'space'.[58] Although, as explained above, 'space' is not merely an idea but a social product, it is more general and abstract than 'place': it is an overarching category.[59] For example, a particular shopping centre is a place, whereas shopping centres as such represent a type of space ('semi-public space').[60] Therefore, I use the term 'public place' (*öffentlicher Ort/lieu public*) to refer to a specific part of 'public space', such as a particular town square.

2.1.3 *'Semi-public space'*

Certain places that are owned by private parties and that are, legally, subject to a private-law regime of use but that are, in fact, publicly accessible, such as shopping centres, entertainment centres, sports stadiums, parts of train stations that are privately owned and so on are often described as 'semi-public' or 'quasi-public space'[61] (*halböffentlicher* or *semi-öffentlicher Raum*).[62] The key difference between such semi-public space and 'proper' public space is that in the case of the former it is in the

58 Wehrheim, *Die überwachte Stadt* (2012), p. 130.

59 Läpple, 'Gesellschaftszentriertes Raumkonzept' (1991), 37, 46.

60 See Section 2.1.3.

61 E.g. Gray/Gray, 'Civil Rights, Civil Wrongs and Quasi-Public Space' (1999).

62 E.g. Gutachten des Bundesamtes für Justiz vom 3. Februar 2011, Zutrittskontrollen in Stadien: Durchsuchungen im Intimbereich, VPB 2012 Nr. 2, p. 21; Bericht des Bundesrates zu den privaten Sicherheits- und Militärfirmen vom 2. Dezember 2005, BBl 2006, 623, p. 648 ('*Halböffentliche Räume* sind Räumlichkeiten, die sich zwar privat zuordnen lassen, im Rahmen ihrer Zweckbestimmung nach aber öffentlich zugänglich sind') (original emphasis); Siehr, *Das Recht am öffentlichen Raum* (2016), p. 1.

discretion of the private owner to deny access to certain persons, regulate the use of the property and enforce these regulations. Semi-public space may be in fact open to the public, but, since it is subject to a private-law regime, members of the public do not have a legal claim to be granted access to it or to use it in a manner contrary to the wishes of the owner.[63] Whether and, if so, to what extent there are limits to the owner's discretion is contentious, and the case law on this question is in a state of flux.[64] The focus of this book is on exclusion measures that apply in 'proper' public space rather than semi-public space, and so a detailed examination of the issue is beyond its scope. Nevertheless, since the increasing importance of semi-public space is also transforming traditional notions of 'proper' public space, Section 2.5 will briefly return to the regulation of semi-public space.

2.1.4 'Public forum'

'Public forum' is a term of art in US constitutional law that refers to 'a public place where people traditionally gather to express ideas and exchange views'.[65] A public forum is thus one, particularly important, part of public space as defined above. The concept of the public forum has been developed by the US Supreme Court in its First Amendment case law, described in more detail in Section 2.4.3, which distinguishes different categories of fora.

2.1.5 'Public sphere'

A final distinction that needs to be drawn is that between public space and the 'public sphere' (*Öffentlichkeit/publicité* or *espace public*).[66] The concept of the 'public sphere' is most commonly associated with the work of Jürgen Habermas, who originally elaborated it in his 1962 book *Strukturwandel der Öffentlichkeit* (*The Structural Transformation of*

63 In contrast, Ursula Wyssmann uses a different definition: she argues that what distinguishes semi-public space from public space is that it does not serve a public purpose. Wyssmann, *Nutzungskonflikte im öffentlichen Raum* (2009), p. 43.

64 See Section 2.5.

65 Garner (ed.), *Black's Law Dictionary* (2009), p. 1349. See also Kalven, 'The Concept of the Public Forum' (1965).

66 On the problems of translating '*Öffentlichkeit*' as 'the public sphere', see Kleinstüber, 'Habermas and the Public Sphere' (2001).

the Public Sphere)[67] and developed it in his later work.[68] Habermas defined the public sphere – more precisely, the bourgeois model of the public sphere – as 'the sphere of private people come together as a public'.[69] It is a sphere that is situated between the private sphere and the sphere of the state.[70]

In contrast to the physical and, normally, descriptive notion of 'public space', Habermas's public sphere is distinctly aspatial and abstract – it is a purely *discursive* 'space'.[71] Furthermore, it is not only a historical phenomenon but also (and in his later work almost exclusively) a normative ideal of political action – an ideal that in his view has never been fully realised in practice.[72] Nancy Fraser, who has usefully described Habermas's public sphere as 'the space in which citizens deliberate about their common affairs, hence, an institutionalized arena of discursive interaction',[73] has highlighted this normative, idealistic character of the concept.[74] (It should be noted that writers such as Hannah Arendt[75] and Iris Marion Young,[76] who have elaborated a similar normative ideal, have chosen to describe it as 'public space', thus emphasising more its local, particular and contextual dimensions.)[77] Just as with public space, accessibility is at the heart of the notion of the public sphere. As Habermas has pointed out, a 'public sphere' from which certain groups are excluded would not only be incomplete but would not be a 'public sphere' at all.[78]

[67] Habermas, *Strukturwandel der Öffentlichkeit* (1990); Habermas, *The Structural Transformation of the Public Sphere* (1992).

[68] See in particular Habermas, *Theorie des kommunikativen Handelns* (1981). See also Calhoun (ed.), *Habermas and the Public Sphere* (1993).

[69] Habermas, *Strukturwandel der Öffentlichkeit* (1990), p. 86 ('die Sphäre der zum Publikum versammelten Privatleute').

[70] Habermas, *Strukturwandel der Öffentlichkeit* (1990), pp. 89–90.

[71] See Siehr, *Das Recht am öffentlichen Raum* (2016), p. 164 ('Bei Habermas ist die Öffentlichkeit hingegen "ortlos". ').

[72] Habermas, *Strukturwandel der Öffentlichkeit* (1990), p. 34.

[73] Fraser, 'Rethinking the Public Sphere' (1990), 57.

[74] Ibid. See also Howell, 'Public Space and the Public Sphere' (1993), 308–13.

[75] E.g. Arendt, *The Human Condition* (1998), pp. 199, 227; Arendt, *On Revolution* (1963), p. 253. Arendt sometimes also uses the term 'public realm': Arendt, *The Human Condition* (1998), pp. 22–78.

[76] Young, *Justice and the Politics of Difference* (1990), p. 119.

[77] See Howell, 'Public Space and the Public Sphere' (1993); Benhabib, *Situating the Self* (1992), pp. 89–114.

[78] Habermas, *Strukturwandel der Öffentlichkeit* (1990), p. 156 ('Die bürgerliche Öffentlichkeit steht und fällt mit dem Prinzip des allgemeinen Zugangs. Eine Öffentlichkeit, von der angebbare Gruppen eo ipso ausgeschlossen wären, ist nicht etwa nur unvollständig, sie ist vielmehr gar keine Öffentlichkeit.').

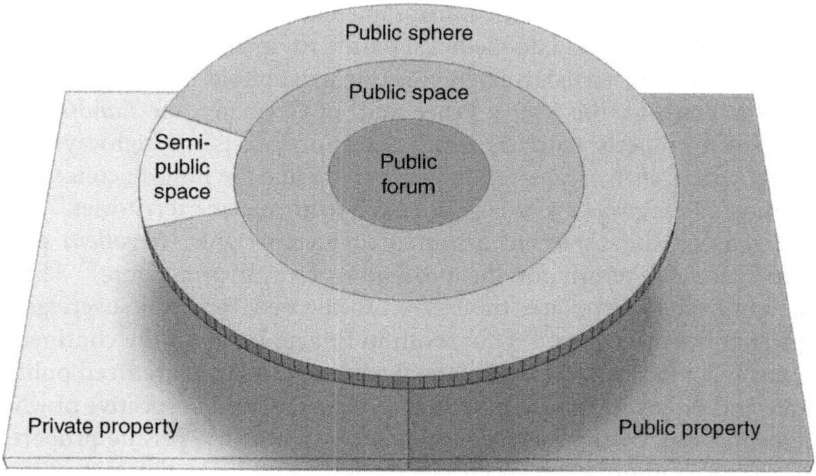

Figure 1 Public sphere, public space, public forum and semi-public space

It follows from the above that 'public space' as understood here is one part of the broader concept of the 'public sphere': it represents the *material* part of the public sphere where citizens can *physically* 'come together as a public'. Quite often, however, the term 'public space' is used, rather unhelpfully and confusingly, as a synonym for 'public sphere'.

2.2 Historical background

Public space as defined above is a relatively new concept. It is true that the categories of 'private' and 'public' have their origins in ancient Greece,[79] and the Greek agora and the Roman forum are often described as early forms of public space.[80] They were open and accessible places where people – or at least certain categories of people (women, slaves and foreigners were excluded from any political activities) – conducted public affairs.[81] However, a proper distinction between private and public space did not emerge until much later. There was no clear separation between the private and the public sphere during the medieval period.[82]

[79] Habermas, *Strukturwandel der Öffentlichkeit* (1990), p. 56.

[80] Mumford, *The City in History* (1961), pp. 148–57, 221–7. [81] Ibid.

[82] See e.g. Brunner, *Land und Herrschaft* (1970), pp. 242–8, 333–40; Hanson, *From Kingdom to Commonwealth* (1970).

Both in England and on the European continent the concept of public space developed in the late medieval period as an aspect of royal sovereignty. Monarchs started to extend measures to uphold what was referred to as, in England, the King's Peace and, in Germany, the *Landfrieden* from royal property (such as royal estates or forests) to highways and further spaces such as squares and parks.[83] While the English concept of the King's Peace was eventually delinked from specific territories,[84] the monarchs on the continent assumed sovereign rights (*Regalien*) over these spaces in return for the provision of royal protection.[85] These sovereign rights were later transferred to the new forms of sovereignty replacing the monarchs.[86] Thus, both in England and on the continent, gradually a physical domain emerged where the state guaranteed public peace and order. Authority over that domain existed irrespective of who the owner was: by the seventeenth/eighteenth century, private property and public authority had been clearly separated.[87] At the same time, natural rights theories were elaborated, providing the basis for the idea of a separate private realm that is free from the power of the state.[88] In the nineteenth century, the public/private distinction then became one of the central tenets of political and legal thought.[89] Most of the previously existing common spaces (described as 'commons' in English and as *Allmende* in German), which had been shared by the members of a particular (local) community but had not been open to everyone, disappeared.[90] All space became either public or private.

[83] Weber, 'The King's Peace: A Comparative Study' (1989).

[84] Feldman, 'The King's Peace, the Royal Prerogative and Public Order' (1988), 103–8.

[85] Saxer, *Die Grundrechte und die Benutzung öffentlicher Strassen* (1988), p. 46; Thieme, *Die Funktion der Regalien im Mittelalter* (1968), pp. 5–23.

[86] Thieme, *Die Funktion der Regalien im Mittelalter* (1968), pp. 27–31.

[87] Stern, 'Die Öffentliche Sache' (1964), 186.

[88] Horwitz, 'The History of the Public/Private Distinction' (1982), 1423.

[89] Ibid., 1424; Bullinger, *Öffentliches Recht und Privatrecht* (1968), pp. 37–74.

[90] On the transfer of resources from the commons to purely private ownership through enclosure in England, mainly between 1700 and 1840, see e.g. Neeson, *Commoners* (1993). On the same development in Germany, and for a comparison with developments in England, see Zückert, *Allmende und Allmendaufhebung* (2003). On the process of dissolution of the *Allmende* in Switzerland from the sixteenth to the nineteenth century, see Carlen, *Recht, Geschichte und Symbol* (2002), pp. 41–2; Mattmüller, 'Allmend – Version vom 17. Mai 2001', *Historisches Lexikon der Schweiz*; von Miaskowski, *Die schweizerische Allmend in ihrer geschichtlichen Entwickelung* (1879), pp. 16–86. While in Switzerland a number of *Allmende* have survived to this day, they are largely limited to mountainous areas where intense use is impossible. Carlen, *Recht, Geschichte und Symbol* (2002), p. 42; von Miaskowski, *Die schweizerische Allmend in ihrer geschichtlichen Entwickelung* (1879), pp. 1, 84–6.

2.3 The importance of public space

The notion of public space, as well as the distinction between 'public' and 'private' on which it rests, is thus closely linked to the emergence of the modern state and the rise of liberal thought in Europe. A state based on liberal and democratic principles depends on the availability of public space as defined above and a clear separation between public and private space. While the following chapters will further elaborate on this, the basic reasons for this importance of public space are already briefly set out here. They follow from the nature of public space as described above and, put in such general terms, will be fairly uncontroversial. The fundamental importance of public space to liberal democracy is due to the fact that, drawing on the work of Christoph Gusy and others,[91] public space can be conceptualised as the space of liberty, the space of equality, the space of tolerance and the space of democracy.

2.3.1 Space of liberty

Liberty depends on the availability of public space. Hannah Arendt described the connection between public space and liberty succinctly: 'Without a politically guaranteed public realm, freedom lacks the worldly space to make its appearance.'[92] Of course, also private space offers a degree of freedom, but of a freedom that is very different from that offered by public space. The liberty provided by private space is essentially individual: it is the freedom to be left alone and to do what one likes at home. Public space, in contrast, provides not only the possibility to move from one private space to another but also ensures access to common facilities and social goods. It is primarily through public space that the freedom to take part in social life can be realised. Thus, public space is the space of *common* liberty.[93] Certain liberties, such as the freedom of expression and the freedom of assembly, can only be meaningfully exercised in public space. Many other liberties, such as the freedom of association, the freedom of religion and economic freedoms, are at the very least heavily dependent on the availability of public space as

[91] Gusy, 'Der öffentliche Raum' (2009); Gusy, 'Polizei und private Sicherheitsdienste im öffentlichen Raum' (2001), 350–51. See also Hottelier, 'La réglementation du domaine public à Genève' (2002), 124; von Hirsch/Shearing, 'Exclusion from Public Space' (2000); Moor, *Droit administratif III* (1992), pp. 290–4.

[92] Arendt, *Between Past and Future* (1961), p. 149.

[93] Kohler/Thürer, 'Der Liberale und der öffentliche Raum' (2005), 133.

a forum of communication and exchange. Finally, it is in the nature of public space that it does not have a single predetermined function but that it is, as a general rule, open to be used for any purpose chosen by its users.[94] As such, public space is the space where people are free to define themselves in relation to others and as a community. In sum, liberty depends on the availability of both private and public space and, as the two concepts logically depend on each other, on a clear separation between the two. In the words of Harry Kalven, 'the generosity and empathy with which [public places] are made available is an index of freedom'.[95]

2.3.2 *Space of equality*

In private space, it is in the discretion of the owner to decide whom to grant access and what kind of behaviour to allow. In making these choices, the owner can be selective, even arbitrary: he or she is not required to treat everyone in the same manner. In contrast, public space is defined by the very fact that it is equally accessible to everyone. Everyone has the same rights to use public space and everyone is subject to the same set of rules.[96] Importantly, as a general rule, use of public space is free for everyone.[97] Whereas private space and the liberty that follows from it are very unequally distributed, the liberty linked to public space can, at least in principle, be exercised equally by everyone, regardless of how rich or poor they are.

2.3.3 *Space of tolerance*

Private space with its focus on individual liberty is the space of non-toleration. The owner can ask her guests to leave, or not invite them in the first place, if she does not like what they say or how they behave (for example, when they are drunk or noisy) or how they look or how they smell. In public space, in contrast, a wide range of behaviours and appearances must be tolerated. This is the flipside to the liberty and equality that are attached to public space. If I claim certain freedoms in

94 Hottelier, 'La réglementation du domaine public à Genève' (2002), 124.

95 Kalven, 'The Concept of the Public Forum' (1965), 12.

96 Gusy, 'Der öffentliche Raum' (2009), 218; Gusy, 'Polizei und private Sicherheitsdienste im öffentlichen Raum' (2001), 350.

97 Häfelin/Müller/Uhlmann, *Allgemeines Verwaltungsrecht* (2010), pp. 542–3; Moor, *Droit administratif III* (1992), pp. 293–4.

public space, I cannot deny others these same freedoms as this would run counter to the equality requirement implicit in the concept of public space.[98] Only in my private space can I claim a wider scope of liberty than that available to others. Thus, in public space I have to expect to be confronted with conceptions of liberty that might differ from my own and I have to tolerate that others exercise their liberties, even if it is in a controversial, confrontational or asocial manner.[99] As long as that conduct only causes moral outrage but does not violate any legally protected interests (such as the sexual integrity of others), I have to put up with it. In fact, not only do I have to tolerate others exercising their liberties, but I also have to be prepared to be confronted with the manifestations of political, social or economic problems that I might prefer to avoid, such as homelessness or drug addiction.[100] To put all of this the other way round, public space is the space where people have the right to present and express themselves in their otherness and to be accepted and respected in their otherness.

2.3.4 *Space of democracy*

Whereas private space is the space where people can retreat to attend to their personal affairs, public space as a central dimension of the public sphere is the space where different conceptions of the common good can find their expression and be debated, where political opinions can be formed. Public space is thus of central importance to theories of democracy, such as that developed by Hannah Arendt. Maurizio Passerin d'Entrèves has summarised Arendt's conception of democratic politics as follows:

> For politics to occur it is not enough to have a collection of private individuals voting separately and anonymously according to their private opinions. Rather, these individuals must be able to see and talk to one another in public, to meet in a public space so that their differences as well as their commonalities can emerge and become the subject of democratic debate.[101]

The availability of public space is crucial for the exercise of the rights that are at the heart of any democratic system, be it political rights in the narrow sense, such as the right to collect signatures, be it civil rights

[98] Gusy, 'Der öffentliche Raum' (2009), 218. [99] Ibid.

[100] Gusy, 'Polizei und private Sicherheitsdienste im öffentlichen Raum' (2001), 351.

[101] D'Entrèves, 'Hannah Arendt and the Idea of Citizenship' (1992), 152.

without which an effective political participation would be impossible, such as the freedoms of expression and assembly. 'In an open democratic society', it has been rightly observed, 'the streets, the parks, and other public places are an important facility for public discussion and political process.'[102] Indeed, public space is required so that a political community – a *demos* – can form and define itself in the first place. It is for this reason that one of the earliest forms of public space, the Greek agora, today stands as a symbol of the origins of the democratic tradition.[103]

2.3.5 *The importance of (physical) public space in the information age*

It is often argued that, due to the massive technological developments in recent decades, physical public space has diminished – and will continue to diminish – in importance. In the information age, publicity can be created, more than ever before, through non-physical sites of the public sphere: newspapers, the radio, TV, mobile phones, the Internet, computer networks and so on. People no longer require access to a common physical space to participate in public debate but can do so through means such as online discussion groups, Internet chat rooms, TV and radio talk shows. Thus, the argument goes, the public sphere has been 'virtualised': '[t]he media today *is* the public sphere',[104] and the real struggle is no longer about physical public space but about 'building a new public sphere in cyberspace'.[105]

Although it is undoubtedly true that new means of transmitting, presenting and sharing information have profoundly reshaped the public sphere, physical public space remains of crucial importance for at least three reasons.

The first reason follows from the nature of public space as the *space of liberty*. An increasingly large part of the virtual dimension of the public sphere is controlled by private actors. In Western states, nearly all newspapers, almost all of the Internet and numerous TV and radio stations are in, often very few, private hands.[106] As compared to public space, these privately controlled fora offer less liberty. The same statement that may

[102] Kalven, 'The Concept of the Public Forum' (1965), 11–12.
[103] Kohler/Thürer, 'Der Liberale und der öffentliche Raum' (2005), 133.
[104] Carpignano/Andersen/Aronowitz/Difazio, 'Chatter in the Age of Electronic Reproduction' (1990).
[105] Schuler and Day (eds), *Shaping the Network Society* (2004), p. 227.
[106] See Boyd-Barrett, 'U.S. Global Cyberspace' (2004). For the United States in particular, see Bagdikian, *The New Media Monopoly* (2004).

be made in the form of a placard held up on a public town square may never find its way into the media or attract any attention on the Internet because it appears unacceptable or uninteresting to those controlling the virtual space.

The second reason for the continued importance of physical public space follows from its nature as the *space of equality*. The obvious point that can be made in this regard is that most of the media are privately owned and operated for profit, so that not all social groups have the same opportunities of making use of their broad reach. But beyond this, there are also inequalities in gaining access to the virtual dimension of the public sphere in the first place: not everyone has physical access to technology or the resources and skills needed to effectively participate as a 'digital citizen'.[107] As a consequence of this 'digital divide'[108] (*digitale Kluft/Spaltung*),[109] the appropriation of physical public places may remain for marginal groups the only means of making themselves noticed as a part of society. In an exclusively virtual public sphere, some groups, such as homeless people, would simply be invisible.[110]

Finally, the third reason for the continued importance of public space follows from its nature as the *space of democracy*. Empirical evidence suggests that, despite the emergence of the virtual space, the appropriation of physical locations, for example through occupations and demonstrations, remains a central component of democratic politics. Since most people have to pass through (certain parts of) public space on a regular basis but do not have to visit the virtual public sphere (and certainly not specific parts of it, such as particular websites), it is possible to reach a much more diverse public in physical locations. For some political causes, the physical sites of demonstrations in their support have been of such crucial importance that they have become symbolised by them (for

107 In Switzerland, for example, more than half of the people with only basic education do not have access to the Internet. 'Fernsehen löst Zeitungen als Leitmedium ab', *Neue Zürcher Zeitung*, 27 April 2010. Only 28 per cent of persons with a basic education use the Internet, as compared to 80 per cent of persons with a higher education. Bundesamt für Berufsbildung und Technologie, *Digitale Spaltung in der Schweiz* (2004), p. 19. In the United States, 81 per cent of the total population, but only 54 per cent of people with disabilities, have access to the Internet. Fox, 'Americans Living with Disability and Their Technology Profile' (2011), available at http://pewinternet.org/Reports/2011/Disability.aspx. See generally Report of the UN Special Rapporteur on the promotion and protection of the right to freedom of opinion and expression, 10 August 2011, UN Doc. A/66/290.

108 Servon, *Bridging the Digital Divide* (2002); Compaine (ed.), *The Digital Divide* (2001).

109 Bundesamt für Berufsbildung und Technologie, *Digitale Spaltung in der Schweiz* (2004).

110 Mitchell, 'The End of Public Space?' (1995), 123.

example, Tiananmen Square, Seattle, Genoa, Tahrir Square or Maidan). As Linda Hershkovitz has observed, '[t]he power of oppositional movements rests on their ability to appropriate "the space of the other" and transform it in ways which articulate their own political vision'.[111] In fact, it can be argued that exactly because political debates are increasingly mediated, the occupation of physical locations has become even more important. The media, after all, heavily rely on the reproduction of symbols, as was illustrated, for example, by the Tiananmen Square, the Tahrir Square and the Occupy Wall Street protests.[112]

2.4 Regulation of the use of public space

The account above could leave the impression that public space is, or should be, a completely unregulated space where anything is permitted. This is, of course, not the case. Public space never has been, and probably never can be, completely unregulated. In every public place certain social norms and conventions apply, and most people will readily comply with them. Pretty much any legal system of the world has a set of legal regulations to back up these social norms and conventions. In fact, since everyone has the same rights to use public space, the risk that competing interests will collide is greater than in the case of private space. Thus, there is a need for regulation to preserve the nature of public space as a truly communal space.

In Switzerland and the United Kingdom, regulation of the use of public space has focused on the efficient coordination of different forms of use by giving priority to the free circulation of traffic over other forms of use characterised as more intense or unreasonable. Originally at least, fundamental rights considerations did not enter the equation. In contrast, the US Supreme Court acknowledged very early on that regulation of the use of public space is a fundamental rights – and in particular a freedom of speech – issue. Accordingly, it has developed the

[111] Hershkovitz, 'Tiananmen Square and the Politics of Place' (1993).

[112] Parkinson, *Democracy and Public Space* (2012), pp. 64–6; A. El Difraoui, 'Die Rolle der neuen Medien im Arabischen Frühling', Bundeszentrale für politische Bildung, 3 November 2011, available at www.bpb.de/internationales/afrika/arabischer-fruehling/52420/die-rolle-der-neuen-medien?p=all; Milz, *Die Bedeutung Sozialer Netzwerke in der arabischen Welt: Länderbericht der Konrad-Adenauer-Stiftung e.V.* (July 2011), available at www.kas.de/rpg/de/publications/23306/ (both with particular regard to the Tahrir Square protests); Calhoun, 'Tiananmen, Television and the Public Sphere: Internationalization of Culture and the Beijing Spring of 1989' (1989) (with particular regard to the Tiananmen Square protests).

applicable principles as part of its First Amendment case law, focusing on the communicative purpose of a given place – that is, its function as a 'public forum'. This notion of the public forum, which emphasises the importance of the availability of public places for the exercise of fundamental rights, has in recent years also become increasingly influential in both Switzerland[113] and the United Kingdom.[114]

2.4.1 *Switzerland*

As explained in Section 2.1.1.3, because of the public purpose they serve, Swiss legal doctrine describes streets, squares, parks and so on as *öffentliche Sachen im Gemeingebrauch/domaine public* ('public goods in common use'). According to the dualistic conception prevalent in Switzerland, both private and public law apply to this category of goods. Whereas private law determines, in particular, the content and transfer of the property rights over such goods, their use is regulated by public law.[115] The relationship between the state and the person using a street, square or park is thus always subject to public law.[116] Although *öffentliche Sachen im Gemeingebrauch* are usually owned by some public entity, they may also be the property of private actors, with the public entity having a private-law or public-law right to regulate their use.[117]

According to Article 664 of the Swiss Civil Code, public goods, including *öffentliche Sachen im Gemeingebrauch*, are under the authority of the cantons. The cantons have a comprehensive legislative competence in this regard, which includes determination of the purpose and permissible use of such public places.[118] With specific regard to streets and squares, the authority of the cantons also follows from the Swiss Federal Constitution.[119] It is common for cantons to make a distinction between

[113] Saxer, *Die Grundrechte und die Benutzung öffentlicher Strassen* (1988), p. 124.

[114] Feldman, *Civil Liberties and Human Rights in England and Wales* (2002), p. 1015.

[115] Häfelin/Müller/Uhlmann, *Allgemeines Verwaltungsrecht* (2010), pp. 539–40; Moor, *Droit administratif III* (1992), pp. 253–7; Grisel, *Traité de droit administratif* (1984), p. 534.

[116] Urteil des Bundesgerichts 6B_116/2011 vom 18. Juli 2011, E. 3.3; Häfelin/Müller/Uhlmann, *Allgemeines Verwaltungsrecht* (2010), p. 540.

[117] Häfelin/Müller/Uhlmann, *Allgemeines Verwaltungsrecht* (2010), p. 540; Moor, *Droit administratif III* (1992), pp. 270–2.

[118] Tschannen/Zimmerli/Müller, *Allgemeines Verwaltungsrecht* (2014), pp. 489–90; Häfelin/Müller/Uhlmann, *Allgemeines Verwaltungsrecht* (2010), p. 537; Meier-Hayoz, *Berner Kommentar zum schweizerischen Privatrecht* (1965), pp. 157–9.

[119] BV, Arts 3, 43 and (*e contrario*) 82.

major roads connecting different regions, falling within the competence of the cantonal authorities, and smaller, more local roads, falling within the competence of the municipalities.[120] In most cantons, the cantonal authorities have adopted legislation concerning the basic purpose, classification, construction and maintenance of streets and squares, whereas the regulation of specific, intense forms of use (such as markets, demonstrations, public events, street prostitution, etc.) is left to the municipalities.[121] Accordingly, many municipalities have introduced norms regulating the use of public ground, often including special regulations for different forms of use.[122]

It is thus up to the cantons (and municipalities) to regulate the use of public ground and to distinguish between different forms of use. Depending on the type and intensity of use, at least two broad categories are commonly distinguished: *Gemeingebrauch/usage commun* ('common use') and *gesteigerter Gemeingebrauch/usage accru* ('extended common use'). Some cantons know a third category, *Sondernutzung/usage privative* or *particulier* ('special use'), to describe a particularly intense use.[123] What category a specific form of use falls into cannot be answered in the abstract but depends on the context, in particular the purpose of the public good in question (which, in turn, depends on its dedication)[124] as well as the local and temporal circumstances.[125] As a consequence, the same activity that would qualify as *Gemeingebrauch* if exercised in a public park or on a weekend might qualify as *gesteigerter Gemeingebrauch* if exercised on a major road or on a weekday.[126]

[120] For the Canton of Berne, see Strassengesetz vom 4. Juni 2008 (BSG 732.11), Arts 7–8; Moser, *Der öffentliche Grund und seine Benützung* (2011), pp. 61–3, 127–8. For the Canton of Zurich, see Strassengesetz vom 27. September 1981 (StrG, LS 722.1), § 5.

[121] Saxer, *Die Grundrechte und die Benutzung öffentlicher Strassen* (1988), p. 52; Meier-Hayoz, *Berner Kommentar zum schweizerischen Privatrecht* (1965), p. 155. See e.g. for the Canton of Berne, Strassengesetz vom 4. Juni 2008 (BSG 732.11), especially Art. 68.

[122] For the City of Zurich, see Verordnung über die Benutzung des öffentlichen Grundes (Benutzungsordnung) vom 23. November 2011 (AS 551.210); Prostitutionsgewerbeverordnung vom 7. März 2012 (AS 551.140); Veranstaltungsrichtlinien mit Gebührenordnung vom 16. Mai 2007 (AS 551.280). For the City of Berne, see the overview in Moser, *Der öffentliche Grund und seine Benützung* (2011), pp. 352–67.

[123] For overviews, see Tschannen/Zimmerli/Müller, *Allgemeines Verwaltungsrecht* (2014), pp. 482–8; Häfelin/Müller/Uhlmann, *Allgemeines Verwaltungsrecht* (2010), pp. 541–53; Moor, *Droit administratif III* (1992), pp. 282–309; Grisel, *Traité de droit administratif* (1984), pp. 543–65.

[124] See Section 2.1.1.3. [125] BGE 135 I 302, 307 (2009).

[126] Moser, *Der öffentliche Grund und seine Benützung* (2011), pp. 209–11.

Gemeingebrauch is that use that conforms to the purpose of the relevant part of public ground and does not significantly impede the simultaneous use by others.[127] This includes, for example, driving on a street; walking, standing, waiting, meeting with others and various forms of communication on a street, pavement or square; strolling, relaxing or playing ball games in a park; and distribution of political leaflets and collection of signatures for popular initiatives by individuals in pedestrian zones.[128] A form of use that qualifies as *Gemeingebrauch* cannot be subject to a permission requirement and must normally be free of charge.[129] As a general rule, only police interests can justify restrictions of *Gemeingebrauch.*[130]

In contrast, *gesteigerter Gemeingebrauch* and *Sondernutzung* describe forms of use that are more intense than that for which the public good in question was originally intended for (for example, setting up a market stall in the middle of a traffic road, holding a circus on a public square, driving in a pedestrian zone) or that significantly impede the simultaneous use by others (for example, holding an assembly or demonstration on a public street, setting up a street theatre or open-air cinema on a public square, parking a car on a public street for an extended period of time).[131] To coordinate these more intense forms of use, public authorities can establish preventive control systems in the form of permission requirements.[132] However, as the Federal Supreme Court started to

[127] Tschannen/Zimmerli/Müller, *Allgemeines Verwaltungsrecht* (2014), p. 483; Moser, *Der öffentliche Grund und seine Benützung* (2011), pp. 209–16; Häfelin/Müller/Uhlmann, *Allgemeines Verwaltungsrecht* (2010), pp. 541–2; Moor, *Droit administratif III* (1992), pp. 282–4; Grisel, *Traité de droit administratif* (1984), pp. 544–6.

[128] For an overview with references to the case law and further literature, see Moser, *Der öffentliche Grund und seine Benützung* (2011), pp. 231–3. For the distribution of leaflets, see BGE 96 I 586, 589–93 (1970). For the collection of signatures, see BGE 135 I 302, 309 (2009).

[129] Moser, *Der öffentliche Grund und seine Benützung* (2011), pp. 216–30; Häfelin/Müller/Uhlmann, *Allgemeines Verwaltungsrecht* (2010), pp. 542–3; Moor, *Droit administratif III* (1992), pp. 290–4.

[130] Moser, *Der öffentliche Grund und seine Benützung* (2011), p. 217; Moor, *Droit administratif III* (1992), p. 291.

[131] Tschannen/Zimmerli/Müller, *Allgemeines Verwaltungsrecht* (2014), pp. 484–5, 487–8; Moser, *Der öffentliche Grund und seine Benützung* (2011), pp. 241–51, 269–73; Häfelin/Müller/Uhlmann, *Allgemeines Verwaltungsrecht* (2010), pp. 545–6, 552; Moor, *Droit administratif III* (1992), pp. 286–8.

[132] Tschannen/Zimmerli/Müller, *Allgemeines Verwaltungsrecht* (2014), pp. 485–7; Moser, *Der öffentliche Grund und seine Benützung* (2011), pp. 251–61, 273–80; Häfelin/Müller/Uhlmann, *Allgemeines Verwaltungsrecht* (2010), pp. 547–8; Malinverni, 'L'exercice des libertés idéales sur le domaine public' (2004), 25–30; Moor, *Droit administratif III* (1992), pp. 301–2; Grisel, *Traité de droit administratif* (1984), pp. 554–62.

recognise in about the mid-1970s, there is a *bedingter Anspruch/droit conditionnel* ('conditional right')[133] to be granted permission for 'extended common use' if such use is essential for the exercise of one's fundamental rights on public ground.[134] The denial of such permission therefore amounts to an interference with the respective fundamental right.[135] A denial can be justified by other than just police interests, including, for example, the public's interest in using the public place in question and the interest of third persons in exercising their rights there.[136] It is because these other interests must be taken account of (and may prevail), and because it only relates to already existing public facilities, that the right to be granted permission for extended common use is described as 'conditional'.[137]

2.4.2 United Kingdom

In the United Kingdom, all land, including publicly accessible places, is subject to the private law of land ownership. Even if streets, squares or parks are owned, as they normally are, by a public body, private property law applies. As a consequence, according to the traditional view, public authorities were allowed to invoke the 'fundamental right [. . .] to object to trespass'[138] in the same way as private landowners and restrict any use of the ground that was not reasonable – that is, any use that went beyond the purpose for which the dedication was made (in other words, any use that went beyond what would be described as *Gemeingebrauch* in Swiss legal terminology). Having said that, it is recognised today that 'reasonable use' must be understood broadly: as the House of Lords has put it, 'the public highway is a public place, on which all manner of reasonable

133 The term *bedingter Anspruch* was first used in this context by Moser, 'Besprechung von BGE 100 Ia 392' (1975), 270. The Federal Supreme Court used it for the first time in BGE 105 Ia 91, 95 (1979).

134 E.g. BGE 135 I 302, 308 (2009); BGE 132 I 256, 259–60 (2006); BGE 105 Ia 91, 95 (1979). See Moser, *Der öffentliche Grund und seine Benützung* (2011), pp. 426, 528–31; Moor, *Droit administratif III* (1992), pp. 297–301.

135 Moser, *Der öffentliche Grund und seine Benützung* (2011), pp. 538–43; Häfelin/Müller/Uhlmann, *Allgemeines Verwaltungsrecht* (2010), p. 550.

136 BGE 132 I 256, 259–60 (2006); BGE 107 Ia 292, 294 (1981). See Moser, *Der öffentliche Grund und seine Benützung* (2011), pp. 529–30, 532–8; Moor, *Droit administratif III* (1992), pp. 304–7.

137 BGE 138 I 274, 282 (2012). For a critique of the concept of a *bedingter Anspruch* ('conditional right'), see Section 8.3.1.

138 *Newbury District Council* v. *Russell* (1997) 95 LGR 705 (Rattee, J.).

activities may go on'.[139] This has been held to include, for example, a peaceful and non-obstructive demonstration on part of a highway.[140]

In addition to the private-law power of trespass, common law and statute law provide for a number of further restrictions on behaviour in public places. In particular, the common-law concept of public nuisance and the offence of wilful obstruction of the public highway according to Section 137(1) of the Highways Act 1980 prohibit behaviour that impedes others in their use of the respective public places.[141] Furthermore, under the Public Order Act 1986, police and local authorities may impose conditions on public processions and assemblies or prohibit processions altogether.[142] As opposed to Switzerland and the United States, where norms on the use of public places are typically found at the municipal level, there is thus national legislation on these matters, even though enforcement rests with local authorities. Sections 1–5 of the Public Order Act 1986 also criminalise certain types of behaviour in public places, such as using threatening, abusive or insulting words or behaviour, or disorderly behaviour, likely to cause harassment, alarm or distress.[143] Finally, the police may rely on their common-law power to prevent a breach of the peace,[144] which gives them wide discretion to control behaviour in public space.[145]

The traditional position described above has changed and it is now widely recognised that public bodies, even when they act as private landowners, do not have complete discretion in controlling use of their property. Rather, as has been confirmed by the courts, since public bodies hold property for public purposes, they are limited by the normal public-law principles. Thus, they have to act within their powers, for proper purposes and rationally when regulating the use of public space.[146] For example, a local council was held to have acted beyond its powers when it imposed on the organising committee of a community festival on a public recreation ground a condition that no political organisation would be allowed to attend the festival.[147] Similarly, the House of Lords decided that another local authority had acted unlawfully when it refused to allow a rugby club to use its training facilities because it did not prevent its members from playing in South

[139] *DPP* v. *Jones* [1999] 2 AC 240, 254 (Lord Irvine). [140] *DPP* v. *Jones* [1999] 2 AC 240.
[141] See ibid., 253 (Lord Irvine). [142] Public Order Act 1986, ss 12–14. [143] Ibid., s. 5.
[144] *R* v. *Howell* [1982] QB 416. See Section 3.2.3.
[145] Birtles, 'The Common Law Power of the Police to Control Public Meetings' (1973).
[146] See Feldman, 'Political Rights' (2009), 441.
[147] *R* v. *London Borough of Barnet, ex p Johnson* (1990) 89 LGR 581 (CA).

Africa.[148] Since the introduction of the Human Rights Act 1998, public authorities also have to make sure that any restrictions of the use of public places complies with the rights guaranteed by the ECHR, in particular the rights to freedom of expression and freedom of assembly. For example, in deciding whether a certain form of behaviour amounts to an unreasonable obstruction of the public highway contrary to Section 137(1) of the Highways Act 1980, an important consideration must be whether the person in question is exercising his or her Convention rights.[149] This has led David Feldman to argue that 'a new type of property, namely public authorities' property, which [is] subject to some different rules from other types of property by reason of the juridical nature of its owners' has emerged,[150] producing 'a hybrid system of property law which is part public, part private'.[151]

2.4.3 United States

Publicly accessible places such as streets, squares and parks may be owned by some public body, typically a municipal corporation, or the private owner of abutting land, subject to the easement acquired by the public.[152] As in the United Kingdom, the original rule was that public authorities as the property owners have the same powers to regulate these spaces as a private landowner would. That position was well reflected in an 1895 decision by the Massachusetts Supreme Judicial Court,[153] later confirmed by the US Supreme Court.[154] Upholding an ordinance that established a permit requirement for making a speech on Boston Common, the court held that '[f]or the Legislature absolutely or conditionally to forbid public speaking in a highway or public park is no more an infringement of the rights of a member of the public than for the owner of a private house to forbid it in his house'.[155] Accordingly, public authorities were free to limit the public use to certain purposes.[156] The Supreme Court changed its approach in 1939 when it held in *Hague* v. *CIO*, referred to above, that streets, squares and parks must be accessible to the public for purposes of assembly, communication and

148 *Wheeler* v. *Leicester City Council*, [1985] AC 1054.
149 *Westminster City Council* v. *Haw*, [2002] EWHC 2073 (QB).
150 Feldman, 'Property and Public Protest' (2000), 44. 151 Ibid., 50.
152 64 *Corpus Juris Secundum: Municipal Corporations*, §§ 1845–6.
153 *Commonwealth* v. *Davis*, 162 Mass. 510 (1895).
154 *Davis* v. *Massachusetts*, 167 U.S. 43 (1897).
155 *Commonwealth* v. *Davis*, 162 Mass. 510, 511 (1895). 156 Ibid.

discussion.[157] In the same decision, however, the court also made it clear that

> [t]he privilege of a citizen of the United States to use the streets and parks for communication of views on national questions may be regulated in the interest of all; it is not absolute, but relative, and must be exercised in subordination to the general comfort and convenience, and in consonance with peace and good order.[158]

Authority to regulate the use of public places such as streets and parks rests with the states as part of their police powers to protect the safety, health, morals and general welfare of the public.[159] States may delegate the power to regulate in these areas, completely or partially, to municipalities or counties, and most states have done so.[160] Accordingly, many municipalities, including virtually all larger cities, have passed ordinances on activities in public space such as demonstrating, picketing, street prostitution, begging, sleeping and so on.[161]

What forms of use states or municipalities may prohibit, or otherwise regulate, depends on the purpose of the property in question. Recognising that a public authority 'has power to preserve the property under its control for the use to which it is lawfully dedicated',[162] the Supreme Court has developed a sophisticated 'public forum doctrine'[163] to determine 'when the Government's interest in limiting the use of its property to its intended purpose outweighs the interest of those wishing to use the property for other purposes'.[164] According to this doctrine, there are three types of fora.[165] The first category, 'traditional public fora', includes places which by long tradition or by government fiat have been devoted to assembly and debate. With regard to this type of fora, which includes streets, sidewalks, squares and parks, limitations can only be imposed when it is shown that the regulation is necessary to serve a compelling state interest and is narrowly drawn to achieve that

[157] *Hague* v. *CIO*, 307 U.S. 496, 515 (1939). [158] Ibid., 515–16.

[159] See e.g. *National League of Cities* v. *Usery*, 426 U.S. 833, 851 (1976); *Lochner* v. *New York*, 198 U.S. 45, 53 (1905).

[160] See 64 *Corpus Juris Secundum: Municipal Corporations*, §§ 1852–5.

[161] See Section 3.3. [162] *Adderley* v. *Florida*, 385 U.S. 39, 87 (1966).

[163] See Kalven, 'The Concept of the Public Forum' (1965). For a helpful and critical overview of the relevant Supreme Court case law, see Tribe, *American Constitutional Law* (1988), pp. 986–97.

[164] *Cornelius* v. *NAACP Legal Defense and Educational Fund, Inc.*, 473 U.S. 788, 800 (1985).

[165] The categorisation was established in *Perry Education Assn.* v. *Perry Local Educators' Assn.*, 460 U.S. 37 (1983).

interest.[166] The second category, 'designated public fora', consists of non-traditional public fora which the state has intentionally opened for use by the public as a place for expressive activity, for example university facilities[167] or theatres.[168] Also with regard to this category of public space, any limitations must serve a compelling state interest. However, unlike with traditional public fora, the state is not required to indefinitely retain open access to these places.[169] Finally, the third category, 'non-public fora', includes all other state-owned property, such as military bases,[170] prison grounds[171] and, controversially, airport terminals.[172] States are granted much greater latitude in regulating these non-public fora. Restrictions can be imposed as long as they are reasonable, and access may be denied entirely or granted selectively.[173]

2.5 The transformation of public space

Especially in Western states, but also in other parts of the world, public space has undergone a fundamental transformation in recent years, which is increasingly undermining its nature as the space of liberty, equality, tolerance and democracy. The backdrop to this transformation is the increased mobility of capital and labour and the consequential heightened competition between cities – at the global and regional levels – in attracting investment and taxpayers and thus in marketing themselves as residential (and tourist) destinations.[174] Today, the prevailing notion among certain social classes is 'that one should choose where to live like one shops for a pair of socks – the idea that moving to a city is a question of deciding the kind of package of city services one wants to buy with city taxes'.[175] Whereas originally this competition between cities mainly turned on economic factors, in recent years socio-cultural factors,

166 *Cornelius* v. *NAACP Legal Defense and Educational Fund, Inc.*, 473 U.S. 788, 800 (1985); *Perry Education Assn.* v. *Perry Local Educators' Assn.*, 460 U.S. 37, 45 (1983).

167 *Widmar* v. *Vincent*, 454 U.S. 263 (1981).

168 *Southeastern Promotions, Ltd.* v. *Conrad*, 420 U.S. 546 (1975).

169 *International Soc. for Krishna Consciousness, Inc.* v. *Lee*, 505 U.S. 672, 678 (1992); *Perry Education Assn.* v. *Perry Local Educators' Assn.*, 460 U.S. 37, 45–6 (1983).

170 *Greer* v. *Spock*, 424 U.S. 828 (1976).

171 *Adderley* v. *Florida*, 385 U.S. 39 (1966).

172 *International Soc. for Krishna Consciousness, Inc.* v. *Lee*, 505 U.S. 672, 680–83 (1992). But see the concurring opinion by Kennedy, J., joined by three other members of the court, arguing that airport terminals are public fora. Ibid., 693–703.

173 Ibid., 683; *Perry Education Assn.* v. *Perry Local Educators' Assn.*, 460 U.S. 37, 46 (1983).

174 See e.g. Wehrheim, *Die überwachte Stadt* (2012), pp. 32–6; Harvey, 'The Right to the City' (2008); Smith, 'New Globalism, New Urbanism' (2002).

175 Frug, 'The Emergence of Private Cities in America' (1999), 583–4.

including shopping facilities, entertainment, cleanliness and safety, have become evermore important.[176] The regeneration of urban spaces and the capacity to present their city centres as clean and safe places to visit, shop and do business is today vital to the fortunes of cities: 'Place has become a product, to be branded and sold.'[177] What matters above all is the *image* or *feeling* a city conveys with regard to these factors.[178] As the strategy for the external affairs of the City of Zurich makes explicit, international competition between cities 'always also takes place on a symbolic level'.[179]

The transformation of public space resulting from this rise of the 'entrepreneurial'[180] or 'neoliberal city'[181] consists of a number of processes, the most important of which can be described under the broad headings of 'privatisation of public space' and 'increased control of public space'.

2.5.1 Privatisation of public space

'Privatisation of public space' is an often-heard term that is used to refer to several developments, not all of which actually involve privatisation in the narrow sense of transfer of ownership of a previously state-owned place to a private actor.[182] Such changes in ownership are in fact quite rare, although there have been a few instances in recent years, such as the taking over of (previously public) parts of train stations and airport terminals by private companies or the sale of a part of the downtown area of Salt Lake City by the municipality to the Church of Jesus Christ of Latter-Day Saints.[183] A broader understanding of 'privatisation of public space' refers to the social process whereby towns and cities are increasingly fragmented into separate private enclaves (residential segregation)

176 Healey, 'On Creating the "City" as a Collective Resource' (2002); Institut für Landes- und Stadtentwicklungsforschung des Landes Nordrhein-Westfalen (ed.), *Im Mittelpunkt der Städte* (2001).

177 Crawford, 'From the Shopping Mall to the Street Corner' (2011), 485.

178 Mitchell, *The Right to the City* (2003), p. 166.

179 Stadt Zürich, *Eine Strategie für die Aussenbeziehungen der Stadt Zürich*, 30 September 2009, p. 5 ('Der internationale Standortwettbewerb findet immer auch auf einer symbolischen Ebene statt.').

180 Hall and Hubbard (eds), *The Entrepreneurial City* (1998).

181 Hackworth, *The Neoliberal City* (2006).

182 See Siehr, *Das Recht am öffentlichen Raum* (2016), p. 1; Kohn, *Brave New Neighborhoods* (2004), pp. 4–7; Glasze, 'Privatisierung öffentlicher Räume' (2001).

183 See Kersten/Meinel, 'Grundrechte in privatisierten öffentlichen Räumen' (2007); Kohn, *Brave New Neighborhoods* (2004), pp. 4, 93–5.

and people spend less and less time in commonly shared spaces. This process is particularly advanced in the United States,[184] but it has also started to shape life in Europe.[185] As pointed out by Gerald Frug, it is today quite normal for the average US citizen never to enter public space during a typical day:

> He wakes up in the morning in his private homeowner association, gets in his own private car and drives at 60-miles-an-hour to the office park, stops at the shopping mall on the way home for groceries or, perhaps, a movie and meal, and then enters the gates (manned by a security guard) that surround the subdivision in which his home is located.[186]

This average person would also be likely, one might add, not to leave his holiday resort during his vacations and to visit an entertainment park on the weekend. While a broad range of factors contribute to the 'privatisation of public space' in this sense, including suburbanisation and the growth of private (and often gated) communities,[187] this section will focus on two factors that are particularly relevant for the present context: the proliferation of semi-public space and, as a reaction to it, attempts to improve public places by making them seem more like semi-public space. Both can be understood as attempts to produce 'public space' without its negative sides.

As explained above, the term 'semi-public space' refers to places that, even though publicly accessible, are owned by private parties and that are, legally, subject to a private-law regime of use. An increasingly large part of space is now semi-public in this sense: people spend more and more time in places such as privately owned sections of train or underground train stations, airport terminals, entertainment parks, sports complexes and plazas (that is, small, privately owned squares in front of, or sometimes within, large buildings). But the paradigmatic example of the proliferation of semi-public space is the rise of the shopping centre (or shopping mall). The first fully enclosed shopping centres were built in the United States in the 1950s;[188] by 2010, there were 107,773 shopping centres in the United States.[189] In Europe, the development of shopping

184 E.g. Kohn, *Brave New Neighborhoods* (2004); Frug, 'The Emergence of Private Cities in America' (1999); Wallin, 'The Stranger on the Green' (1998).
185 Glasze, 'Privatisierung öffentlicher Räume?' (2001).
186 Frug, 'The Emergence of Private Cities in America' (1999), 583.
187 Low, *Behind the Gates* (2003); Blakely/Snyder, *Fortress America* (1999).
188 Cohen, 'From Town Center to Shopping Center' (1996).
189 US Census Bureau, Statistical Abstract of the United States, 2012, Table 1061, available at www.census.gov/prod/2011pubs/12statab/domtrade.pdf.

centres started later, but they have now also become very widespread and popular. In the United Kingdom, there are 1,300 shopping centres, the largest number in any country outside North America;[190] 945,000 square meters of shopping centre space opened in the year 2008 alone, the highest figure since records began.[191] Switzerland is one of the countries with the highest density of shopping centres in Europe, with 30 square meters of shopping centre surface per hundred people in 2009,[192] a number that is set to grow further.[193] Selling and buying goods is just one of the functions performed by these shopping complexes. Often incorporating cafés, restaurants, entertainments, exhibitions, banks, a post office, a police station or the local library, they have become important social and cultural meeting places.[194]

The rise of semi-public spaces raises complex legal challenges. As privately owned places, they would normally be subject to private-law regulation, yet at the same time, in practice, they fulfil the same functions as public space. The largest US shopping centre, the Mall of America in Bloomington, Minnesota, describes itself as 'a city within a city', made up of 'town squares' and 'city streets'.[195] The US Supreme Court acknowledged the public functions of semi-public space as early as in 1968 in *Amalgamated Food Employees Union Local 590* v. *Logan Valley Plaza, Inc.*, a case involving picketing on the grounds of a large shopping mall:

> Here the roadways provided for vehicular movement within the mall and the sidewalks leading from building to building are the functional equivalents of the streets and sidewalks of a normal municipal business district. The shopping center premises are open to the public to the same extent as the commercial center of a normal town. So far as can be determined, the main distinction in practice between use by the public of the Logan Valley Mall and of any other business district, were the decisions of the state courts to stand, would be that those members of the general public who sought to use the mall premises in a manner contrary to the wishes of the respondents could be prevented from so doing.[196]

190 'The Shopping Centre Industry' (1999).

191 The Retail Bulletin, 'Record amount of new shopping centre space opens in the UK', 10 November 2008, available at www.theretailbulletin.com/news/record_amount_of_new_shopping_centre_space_opens_in_the_uk_10-11-08/.

192 RegioPlan Consulting GmbH, 'Shopping Center Listen Europa – Ausgabe 2/2009'.

193 S. Batthyany, 'Shoppingcenter Schweiz: Die Schweiz wird zur Shopping Mall – und niemanden stört es', *NZZ am Sonntag*, 5 October 2008.

194 Crawford, 'The World in a Shopping Mall' (1992).

195 See Coffin, 'The United Mall of America' (2000), 635.

196 *Amalgamated Food Employees Union Local 590* v. *Logan Valley Plaza, Inc.*, 391 U.S. 308, 319 (1968).

Similarly, the Supreme Court of North Dakota observed in 1991:

> In essence, they [shopping malls] are the functional equivalent of the city streets, squares and parks of earlier days. Indeed, in many instances, the shopping mall has displaced the shops along main street. With its controlled environment, it is an appealing place for the public to converse and socialize as well as to browse and shop in and about the stores there.[197]

Yet despite these acknowledgements, the jurisprudence of the Supreme Court and other US courts is inconsistent and conflicting.[198] In its earlier case law, including *Amalgamated Food Employees Union*,[199] the Supreme Court held that privately owned space may need to be considered public for First Amendment purposes.[200] However, it came to a different conclusion in *Lloyd Corp.* v. *Tanner*, decided in 1972.[201] In *Hudgens* v. *National Labor Relations Board*, decided in 1976, it finally overruled *Amalgamated Food Employees Union*.[202] Nevertheless, it has since suggested that this does not prevent states from granting broader liberties than those provided by the federal constitution to allow individuals to exercise free speech rights in shopping centres that are regularly held open to the public, subject to reasonable regulations.[203] Furthermore, some state and federal courts have held that exclusion from semi-public spaces should be subject to a reasonableness requirement, that is, that people may not be excluded for arbitrary or discriminatory reasons.[204]

In the United Kingdom, in contrast, the Court of Appeal has held that the owner of a private shopping centre, as part of his trespass powers, has an unchallengeable discretion to deny permission to enter the centre.[205] The case concerned a group of youths who were banned from entering a shopping centre for life, even though no rational ground of eviction had been substantiated. Despite the fact that the shopping centre made up the

[197] *City of Jamestown* v. *Beneda*, 477 N.W.2d 830, 837–8 (N.D., 1991).

[198] For a critical analysis, see Alexander, 'Attention, Shoppers' (1999).

[199] *Amalgamated Food Employees Union Local 590* v. *Logan Valley Plaza, Inc.*, 391 U.S. 308, 319–25 (1968).

[200] See also already *Marsh* v. *Alabama*, 326 U.S. 501 (1946).

[201] *Lloyd Corp.* v. *Tanner*, 407 U.S. 551 (1972).

[202] *Hudgens* v. *National Labor Relations Board*, 424 U.S. 507 (1976).

[203] *Pruneyard Shopping Center* v. *Robins*, 447 U.S. 74 (1980).

[204] *Streetwatch* v. *National R.R. Passenger Corp.*, 875 F.Supp. 1055 (S.D.N.Y., 1995); *Bock* v. *Westminster Mall Co.*, 819 P.2d 55 (Colo., 1991); *Matthews* v. *Bay Head Imp. Ass'n*, 471 A.2d 355, 366 (N.J., 1984); *Uston* v. *Resorts International Hotel, Inc*, 445 A.2d 370, 375 (N.J., 1982).

[205] *CIN Properties Ltd* v. *Rawlins*, [1995] 39 EG 148 (CA). See Gray/Gray, 'Civil Rights, Civil Wrongs and Quasi-Public Space' (1999).

larger part of the town centre and constituted the town's primary location of employment, the court effectively held that the shopping centre owner, just like any private property owner, did not need to show reasonable grounds for excluding members of the public. A challenge against the decision of the Court of Appeal before the European Commission of Human Rights was unsuccessful.[206]

The European Court of Human Rights came to a similar conclusion in *Appleby* v. *United Kingdom*.[207] The applicants were stopped from setting up a stand and distributing leaflets in the town centre of Washington (Tyne and Wear), consisting of a shopping centre, car parks and walkways, which were owned by a private company. The court reviewed the US case law referred to above and concluded that '[i]t cannot be said that there is as yet any emerging consensus that could assist the Court in its examination in this case'.[208] It went on to observe: 'While it is true that demographic, social, economic and technological developments are changing the ways in which people move around and come into contact with each other, the Court is not persuaded that this requires the automatic creation of rights of entry to private property, or even, necessarily, to all publicly owned property (government offices and ministries, for instance).'[209] Since in the present case the applicants had other means available to communicate their views to others, there was no violation of Article 10 of the ECHR, the right to freedom of expression.[210]

While these are just a few of many cases dealing with semi-public space,[211] they show how courts have struggled to come to terms with the special nature of semi-public space and to fit it within existing legal categories and doctrines. The general approach of courts still seems to be to treat shopping centres and other semi-public spaces in the same manner as any other private property. However, especially in the United States, there is increased recognition that the owners of such properties should not have complete discretion but should be subject to at least some of the limitations that apply in respect of public space. The appropriate way forward may be the 'sliding scale' test suggested by the Supreme Court of New Jersey, according to which 'the more

[206] *Anderson and nine others* v. *The United Kingdom*, no. 33689/96, admissibility decision of 27 October 1997.

[207] *Appleby and others* v. *The United Kingdom*, no. 44306/98, 6 May 2003, ECHR 2003-VI, 185.

[208] Ibid., para. 46. [209] Ibid., para. 47. [210] Ibid., paras 48–50.

[211] For a comprehensive overview, see Gray/Gray, 'Civil Rights, Civil Wrongs and Quasi-Public Space' (1999).

private property is devoted to public use, the more it must accommodate the rights which inhere in individual members of the general public who use that property'.[212]

As semi-public space is not the focus of this study, it is beyond its scope to explore these complex questions in more detail.[213] What is important to note for the present context is that the proliferation of semi-public space has also profoundly reshaped the notion of public space.

As the statement of the Supreme Court of North Dakota referred to above illustrates, semi-public space, '[w]ith its controlled environment', has a great appeal for the public: 'it is an appealing place for the public to converse and socialize'.[214] Shopping malls, entertainment parks and plazas convey a sense of publicness that public places seem no longer to be able to convey: the sense of a space that, while still appearing to be public, is clean, attractive and safe, a space where the user does not have to expect to be confronted with deviating or undesirable behaviour.[215] At the same time, the fact that people spend more and more time in semi-public space and less and less in public streets, squares and parks has made the latter even less attractive and safe. In response to this problem, many cities, often prompted by pressure from businesses located in the city centres, have tried to 'upgrade' inner-city spaces by making them appear more like semi-public space.

One example of this development is the rise of Business Improvement Districts (BIDs). A BID is a public/private partnership designed to improve a defined business or shopping area, normally in the inner city.[216] Businesses in a BID pay an additional tax or fee to fund services such as security patrols, street cleaning and garbage collection in addition to those provided by the municipality.[217] BIDs are created through legislation and the municipalities are involved in their administration.[218] As opposed to private or semi-public space, the ground on which BIDs are based is not private. The streets and squares are managed in a public/private partnership but remain state property.

212 *State* v. *Schmid*, 423 A.2d 615, 629 (N.J., 1980).

213 For the United Kingdom and the United States, see the comparative overview in Gray/Gray, 'Civil Rights, Civil Wrongs and Quasi-Public Space' (1999). For Switzerland, see Gamma, *Möglichkeiten und Grenzen der Privatisierung polizeilicher Gefahrenabwehr* (2000), pp. 88–9; Kälin/Lienhard/Wyttenbach, *Auslagerung von sicherheitspolizeilichen Aufgaben auf private Sicherheitsunternehmen* (2007), pp. 35–6.

214 *City of Jamestown* v. *Beneda*, 477 N.W.2d 830, 838 (N.D., 1991).

215 See Crawford, 'From the Shopping Mall to the Street Corner' (2011), 494–501.

216 Mallett, 'Managing the Post-Industrial City' (1994).

217 Briffault, 'A Government for Our Time?' (1999), 368–9.

218 Ibid., 379, 409.

BIDs first emerged in Canada and the United States in the 1970s and have become very widespread there since the 1990s – in New York City alone there are now over 130 BIDs, covering nearly every shopping area of the city.[219] In the whole of the United States, there are more than 1,500 BIDs.[220] BIDs have also become increasingly popular in Europe. In the United Kingdom, the Local Government Act 2003 provides for the possibility of establishing BIDs,[221] and by 2008 already fifty-nine BIDs had been established in England.[222] Although there generally seems to be more scepticism towards private involvement in Switzerland, similar public/private partnership models are emerging there too.[223] The BID model has also been applied to public parks, as with the Bryant Park Corporation in New York City.[224]

So, on the one hand, privately owned space is taking over an ever-larger share of the functions of public space: we spend more and more of our daily lives in shopping malls instead of city centres. On the other hand, as semi-public space with its controlled, safe and clean environment has become the new ideal, public space is adapting to this new ideal. Space that was previously public is now run in public/private partnerships designed to ensure a high standard of cleanliness and safety or, as with airport terminals and private parts of train stations, is completely privatised.

In short, the distinction between public and private space starts to blur. It has become difficult for the average citizen to tell whether he or she is in a public or a private space.[225]

With the hybridisation of public and private space, not only the functions of these previously separate forms of space start to overlap, but also the legal regimes governing them. As the examples referred to above demonstrate, courts struggle to categorise certain privately owned spaces. In some cases, they have treated them legally as public places. Conversely, as public space is being adapted to the ideal of controlled, semi-public space, it starts to be regulated in the same way private space is regulated.

219 Carmona/de Magalhães/Hammond, *Public Space* (2008), p. 161. 220 Ibid.

221 Local Government Act 2003, Part 4.

222 Cook, 'Policing, Partnerships, and Profits' (2010). See also Carmona/de Magalhães/Hammond, *Public Space* (2008), p. 180.

223 For the example of the Markthalle Basel, see Cavigelli, 'Kooperationen zwischen öffentlicher Hand und Privaten in der Stadtentwicklung' (2007).

224 See the website of the Bryant Park Corporation, at www.bryantpark.org.

225 Wehrheim, *Die überwachte Stadt* (2012), p. 116.

As will be shown in Chapter 3, in recent years a spate of laws has been passed in all three jurisdictions under consideration that prohibit behaviour in public space that, previously, would normally only have been banned by private property owners, such as loitering, spitting, drinking alcohol or even just sitting or lying down on the ground. Often these new regulations are almost direct copies of those applicable, and tested out, in semi-public space. Drinking alcohol outside of restaurants and sitting or lying down on the floor, for instance, are among the typical behaviours prohibited by shopping mall owners.[226]

The pressure to adjust urban public places to the ideal of the shopping centre is apparent, for example, in an ordinance of the City of Reno, Nevada, which prohibits sitting or lying down on public sidewalks in the downtown area. The preamble to the relevant provision justifies the prohibition by explaining that the primary purposes of the sidewalks were those of 'enabling pedestrians to safely and efficiently move about from place to place, facilitating deliveries of goods and services, and providing convenient access to entertainment, goods and services'.[227] It goes on to state that '[t]he public welfare is promoted by an economically healthy downtown area which attracts people to shop, recreate, work and be entertained',[228] but that 'people sitting or lying on the sidewalks deter many members of the public from frequenting the downtown area'.[229]

A further example of the assimilation of public space to the ideal of semi-public space is the prohibition of a number of anti-social behaviours in the City of Berne in Switzerland. Sitting and lying down on the ground, playing loud music, begging and several other forms of behaviour were first prohibited by the Swiss Federal Railway company in its code of conduct applicable in that part of the Berne train station that is owned by itself (the part leading to and surrounding the platforms).[230] (Although, since the Swiss Federal Railway company is state-owned, this is not semi-public space in the strict sense, it is still ground that is not owned or controlled by the local public authorities.) The City of Berne then felt compelled to introduce a virtually identical set of prohibitions in its part of the station and the entrances to it to ensure a consistent

226 Glasze, 'Privatisierung öffentlicher Räume?' (2001); Wakefield, 'Situational Crime Prevention in Mass Private Property' (2000), 130, 133–6.

227 Reno, Nevada, Municipal Code, s. 8.12.015(a)(1).

228 Ibid., s. 8.12.015(a)(5).

229 Ibid., s. 8.12.015(a)(6).

230 SBB Rail City Bern, Bahnhofordnung, reprinted in Wyssmann, *Nutzungskonflikte im öffentlichen Raum* (2009), p. 163.

standard throughout the station.[231] This, in turn, led to suggestions to extend at least part of this ban (namely, the prohibition of begging) to the whole of the city centre.[232]

Not only behavioural standards are transposed from the legal regimes governing privately owned space to those governing public space, but also enforcement powers. As explained above, the ultimate power for the regulation of a given space, namely the power to deny others access to it, used to be a typical private-law power. In fact, it was thought of as the very essence of private property. Public authorities, it became recognised over the years, could only avail themselves of this power under a number of important limitations: certain places, such as streets, squares or parks, should, as a rule, be accessible to everyone. As the numerous examples described in Chapter 3 demonstrate, this rule has now been undermined. The power of exclusion has made its way from privately owned space to public space.

Finally, also the way in which regulations are enforced may be transposed from semi-public space to public space. Private security companies, first set up to police 'mass private property' such as shopping malls, train stations or football grounds, now provide security in small municipalities,[233] protect critical infrastructure such as embassies[234] and patrol the public streets in BIDs.[235]

2.5.2 Increased control of public space in the security society

The transformation of modern society into a 'risk society' (*Risikogesellschaft*)[236] has fundamentally reshaped criminal justice systems. Crime has become just one of many risks that are taken for granted and that need to be predicted, anticipated and managed.[237] Rather than

231 Reglement betreffend die Benützung des städtischen Teils des Bahnhofs Bern vom 1. Juni 2008 (Bahnhofreglement, BHR; SSSB 732.21), Art. 2. See Wyssmann, *Nutzungskonflikte im öffentlichen Raum* (2009), p. 99.

232 See Protokoll der Stadtratssitzung vom 12. Juni 2008, pp. 1118–23 (Motion Fraktion SVP/JSVP: Schluss mit der Bettelei – der Gemeinderat muss endlich handeln!).

233 Gamma, *Möglichkeiten und Grenzen der Privatisierung polizeilicher Gefahrenabwehr* (2000), pp. 183–4.

234 BWIS, Arts 22(2) and (4).

235 Cook, 'Policing, Partnerships, and Profits' (2010); Barr, 'More Like Disneyland' (1997), 404–12.

236 Beck, *Risikogesellschaft* (1986); Beck, *Risk Society* (1996). See also Giddens, *Modernity and Self-Identity* (1991); Giddens, *The Consequences of Modernity* (1990).

237 Garland, *The Culture of Control* (2001), especially Chapters 5 and 7; Ericson/Haggerty, *Policing the Risk Society* (1997); Feeley/Simon, 'Actuarial Justice' (1994).

as social deviance and harm that can be attributed to responsible individuals who need to be held to account for their actions and punished, crime is now regarded as a 'normal social commonplace aspect of modern society'.[238] Thus, everyone has become a potential criminal and thus needs to be controlled.[239] The primary concern of contemporary criminal justice policies is the *prevention* of crime rather than the prosecution, punishment and rehabilitation of offenders.[240] This shift from a reactive to a preventive paradigm has given rise to the claim that we now live in what has been described as a 'control society'[241] (*Kontrollgesellschaft*)[242] or, in more recent years, a 'security society'[243] (*Sicherheitsgesellschaft*).[244]

The preventive logic entails new modes of classification and control that permeate all aspects of society. As crime is seen as inevitable and everyone has become a potential criminal, the focus of criminal justice policies in the 'security society' is reduced from concrete acts or individuals (or concepts such as guilt and responsibility) to groups of people: segments of the population that are categorised and controlled according to their levels of dangerousness.[245] Risk assessment through actuarial profiling,[246] registration of certain types of offenders[247] and civil preventive measures[248] are some of the tools that are central to this new approach.

In a further step of abstraction,[249] numerous preventive strategies have become completely depersonalised. In the 'security society', crime prevention is increasingly about the control of 'situations' and space rather than people.[250] A broad range of contemporary criminal justice practices

238 Garland, *The Culture of Control* (2001), p. 128.

239 Singelnstein, 'Jeder ist verdächtig' (2007).

240 Zedner, *Security* (2009), pp. 68–9, 73–4.

241 Garland, *The Culture of Control* (2001); Deleuze, 'Postscript on the Societies of Control' (1992).

242 Lindenberg/Schmidt-Semisch, 'Sanktionsverzicht statt Herrschaftsverlust' (1995).

243 Zedner, *Security* (2009), p. 68.

244 Singelnstein/Stolle, *Die Sicherheitsgesellschaft* (2012); Albrecht, *Der Weg in die Sicherheitsgesellschaft* (2010); Legnaro, 'Konturen der Sicherheitsgesellschaft' (1997).

245 Singelnstein/Stolle, *Die Sicherheitsgesellschaft* (2012), pp. 66–7, 87–9; Feeley/Simon, 'Actuarial Justice' (1994). See also already Cohen, *Visions of Social Control* (1985).

246 Feeley/Simon, 'Actuarial Justice' (1994).

247 E.g. 'Making Outcasts out of Outlaws' (2004).

248 Ashworth/Zedner, 'Defending the Criminal Law' (2008); Shute, 'New Civil Preventative Orders' (2004).

249 For an analysis of the different steps of abstraction, see Belina, *Raum, Überwachung, Kontrolle* (2006), pp. 103–33.

250 Lindenberg/Schmidt-Semisch, 'Komplementäre Konkurrenz in der Sicherheitsgesellschaft' (2000), 311–12; Legnaro, 'Konturen der Sicherheitsgesellschaft' (1997), 274–7.

that are designed to prevent crime through the increased control and restructuring of public space are evidence of this trend: various surveillance measures (such as CCTV, random controls or stops-and-searches, increased police presence on the streets or use of park attendants),[251] situational crime prevention techniques (such as target hardening, access control, deflection of offenders, entry/exit screening or improved street lighting)[252] and community safety initiatives (such as community policing and neighbourhood watches).[253] As part of this focus on space, certain places or local areas, for example 'red light' districts, underground stations, ethnic-minority areas and *banlieues*, are constructed as 'dangerous' or 'criminal' spaces, as 'no-go areas'. Others, such as government districts or shopping areas, are designed as high-security zones.[254] Accordingly, different strategies and means of control are applied in different spaces. An example of this are the 'security risk areas' designated in the City of Amsterdam, where, unlike elsewhere in Amsterdam, the police may subject anyone to a preventive search for weapons.[255] Often the primary purpose of such locally differentiated strategies is to displace certain activities from one place to the other.[256] *Why* people do certain things is now of less interest than *where* they do them.[257]

Strategies of spatial control have been boosted, and their scope has been widened, by the hugely influential *broken windows* thesis of James Q. Wilson and George L. Kelling, which constructs a link between space and criminality that makes intuitive sense. The thesis, first set out in an article in the *Atlantic Monthly* in 1982[258] and later developed into

[251] Lyon, *Surveillance Studies: An Overview* (2007).

[252] Singelnstein/Stolle, *Die Sicherheitsgesellschaft* (2012), p. 86; Killias/Kuhn/Aebi, *Grundriss der Kriminologie* (2011), pp. 271–86; Clarke, 'Situational Crime Prevention' (1995); Clarke, 'Situational Crime Prevention: Its Theoretical Basis and Practical Scope' (1983).

[253] For the United Kingdom, see Crawford, *The Local Governance of Crime* (1997). For Switzerland, see Gamma, *Möglichkeiten und Grenzen der Privatisierung polizeilicher Gefahrenabwehr* (2000), pp. 191–4.

[254] Belina, *Raum, Überwachung, Kontrolle* (2006), pp. 122–32; Legnaro, 'Die Stadt, der Müll und das Fremde' (1998), 273–4; Crawford, *The Local Governance of Crime* (1997), pp. 85, 275–85.

[255] The European Court of Human Rights held that an application directed against the respective designation order was manifestly ill-founded and thus declared it inadmissible. *Colon* v. *Netherlands* (dec.), no. 49458/06, 15 May 2012.

[256] Barr/Pease, 'Crime Placement, Displacement, and Deflection' (1990).

[257] Belina, *Raum, Überwachung, Kontrolle* (2006), p. 123; Lindenberg/Schmidt-Semisch, 'Sanktionsverzicht statt Herrschaftsverlust' (1995), 10.

[258] Wilson/Kelling, 'Broken Windows' (1982).

a book,[259] uses the image of broken windows to argue that tolerating even minor disorder and incivilities eventually leads to crime.[260] If a window in a building is broken and not repaired promptly, the argument goes, all the other windows will soon be broken too. Broken windows send a signal that no one cares about the neighbourhood – that it is unsafe. As a consequence, ordinary citizens withdraw from the streets. Instead, drunkards, beggars and, eventually, criminals start to frequent the area as they think that norms are not enforced there: '[S]erious street crime flourishes in areas in which disorderly behavior goes unchecked. The unchecked panhandler is, in effect, the first broken window.'[261]

Although several authors have convincingly demonstrated that there is no evidence for the alleged link between disorder and crime,[262] the *broken windows* thesis is one of the leading criminal justice theories today and has been extremely influential in policy circles. The police strategy employed in New York City in the 1990s was explicitly based on the work of Wilson and Kelling.[263] Often described as *zero tolerance* or *quality of life* initiative, this strategy focused on the proactive and aggressive enforcement of laws against anti-social behaviour such as loitering, public drinking, graffiti writing, begging and prostitution to make the downtown area as well as other neighbourhoods attractive again. Because of its assumed success, the strategy has not only been copied by countless police forces in the United States but has shaped policing strategies across the Western world,[264] including in the United Kingdom[265] and Switzerland.[266]

Emphasising the link between the appearance of a neighbourhood and crime, the *broken windows* approach reinforces the focus on space in control strategies. But beyond that, it also widens the scope of such strategies. It is no longer only criminal activity that must be prevented

259 Kelling/Coles, *Fixing Broken Windows* (1996).

260 For alleged evidence in support of the theory, see Skogan, *Disorder and Decline* (1992).

261 Wilson/Kelling, 'Broken Windows' (1982), 34.

262 See in particular Harcourt, *Illusion of Order* (2001).

263 New York City Police Department, Police Strategy No. 5: Reclaiming the Public Spaces of New York (1994), 6.

264 Wacquant, *Prisons of Poverty* (2009), pp. 7–54; Smith, 'Global Social Cleansing' (2001).

265 Wacquant, *Prisons of Poverty* (2009), pp. 7–54; Innes/Jones, *Neighbourhood Security and Urban Change* (2006); Bowling, 'The Rise and Fall of New York Murder' (1999).

266 Gamma, *Möglichkeiten und Grenzen der Privatisierung polizeilicher Gefahrenabwehr* (2000), p. 242. Specifically with regard to the City of Berne, see Gasser, *Kriminalpolitik oder City-Pflege?* (2004), pp. 42–4; with regard to the City of Geneva, see '"Theorie der eingeschlagenen Fensterscheibe": Wie Genf von New York in Sachen Sicherheit lernen kann', *Neue Zürcher Zeitung*, 16 September 2011.

but a wide range of what are variably called 'anti-social behaviours', 'incivilities' or 'quality-of-life offences': behaviours that used to be merely offensive or annoying but that are now understood to be the first steps to crime or, at the very least, signs of a dangerous 'community atomisation'.[267] More precisely, what needs to be countered is *the appearance* that such behaviours may be tolerated. Already the mere presence of a homeless person in a wealthy neighbourhood may undermine that appearance, whereas public urinating by a well-dressed man does not necessarily do so. Thus, 'order-maintenance policing', as this form of community policing is often called,[268] is concerned with how particular spaces appear and with conveying a sense of safety to those using these spaces.[269] It therefore not only involves the increased control and surveillance of public space but also regularly resorts to measures that are primarily intended to be symbolic – that are designed to send a signal that broken windows will not be tolerated. As sending someone away from somewhere has a high 'signal value', exclusion from public space is a typical tool of this kind of policing.[270]

2.5.3 Public space transformed

In the 'security society', public space is controlled to an unprecedented degree. New surveillance techniques, neighbourhood watches and similar community policing initiatives, access control and screening have made it almost impossible for people to move anonymously in public space. More and more forms of behaviour in public space are prohibited. Public space may thus be losing its character as the *space of liberty.*

The binary distinction between private and public space has been blurred. Instead, the contemporary urban landscape is fragmented into myriad different zones with different normative orders: shopping centres, gated communities, airport terminals, BIDs, train stations, town squares and so on. Different sets of norms apply to these different zones; they may be policed differently (through community policing, private security services or ordinary police forces); and the terms of accessibility and exclusion are different. The notion that significant parts of a city must be equally accessible for everyone is losing its force. Public space may thus be losing its character as the *space of equality.*

[267] Hale, 'The Structural Determinants of Fear of Crime' (1994). See Skogan, *Disorder and Decline* (1992).

[268] Harcourt, *Illusion of Order* (2001), p. 1.

[269] Gasser, *Kriminalpolitik oder City-Pflege?* (2004), pp. 43–4.

[270] See Section 3.2.

With the adaptation of public space to the ideal of semi-public space and with the new focus on order maintenance, behaviour in public space has become subject to increased regulation. Incivilities that previously were seen as merely offensive have been criminalised; public-order regulations that were hardly used have been resurrected. Public space may thus be losing its character as the *space of tolerance.*

The fragmentation of the urban landscape into different areas that are not equally accessible for everyone and the increased control of public places make it increasingly difficult for people to meet and develop a culture of sharing public space. As a consequence, the function of public space as an important facility for public discussion and political process is being undermined. Public space may thus be losing its character as the *space of democracy.*

It is against the backdrop of these developments that the adoption of the sort of exclusion measures described in this book must be understood. The remainder of the book aims to shed light on the role that these measures play in the current transformation of public space.

2.6 Conclusion

The key element of the concept of public space is general accessibility: what makes a space public is the fact that it is accessible to, and can be used by, the general public, that is, everyone. This understanding is reflected in the way terms such as 'public place' or 'public streets' are employed in laws regulating the use of public space in Switzerland, the United Kingdom and the United States. That the availability of publicly accessible space, and a clear separation between public and private space, is of crucial importance to a liberal democracy does not need much explanation and is largely uncontroversial. Despite the arrival of the information age and the corresponding emergence of the 'virtual space', the significance of physical public space remains undiminished.

Depending on the exact (federal) structure of a state, different public authorities will be in charge of regulating the use of public space. Today, it is recognised in all three states at issue that, even when they own the respective piece of land, public authorities do not have a free hand in doing so: they do not have complete discretion in controlling use of their property as a private landowner would. In particular, they must take account of the important role that the availability of publicly accessible places plays in a liberal democracy and may thus be prevented from restricting forms of use that are essential for the exercise of fundamental rights. What kinds of use may be prohibited, or otherwise regulated, depends to a considerable extent on the purpose that the piece of land in question is meant to fulfil, that is, its dedication.

Public space has undergone a fundamental transformation in recent years. Zygmunt Bauman has warned that, instead of the sort of public space as we know it, there may soon only be two types of urban public space left. First, 'temples of consumption': spaces that are designed to encourage city residents to consume, without engaging in any actual social interaction. And second, spaces like la Défense in Paris that are designed for people to merely pass through and discourage them from staying.[271] This may be a rather one-sided and pessimistic prediction. What can certainly be observed, however, is that people spend less and less time in commonly shared spaces, that public space is increasingly being adapted to the new ideal of semi-public space and that public space is controlled to an unprecedented degree. As a consequence, behaviour in public space has become subject to increased regulation: rules of behaviour that previously only applied in privately owned space, as well as powers to enforce these rules, have been extended to public space. The emergence of exclusion measures, which will be explored in the following chapter, must be understood as forming an important and characteristic aspect of this transformation of public space.

[271] Bauman, *Liquid Modernity* (2000), pp. 96–8. For a similar argument, see Augé, *Non-lieux: Introduction à une anthropologie de la surmodernité* (1992).

3

Exclusion from public space

Sending people away from a specified area for an extended period of time (or even for life) used to be a standard form of punishment, especially in the medieval period. This practice, commonly referred to as 'banishment'[1] (*Verbannung*),[2] symbolised exclusion from the community. Starting from the eighteenth century, banishment was gradually abolished. Since about the 1990s, however, there has been a noticeable rise of measures banning certain categories of people from parts of public space for extended periods of time. Increasingly, these measures primarily serve preventive rather than punitive purposes. In many ways they are reminiscent of banishment, not least insofar as those subject to these contemporary exclusion measures frequently experience them as a form of banishment – namely, as exclusion from the community.[3]

This chapter starts by retracing the history of banishment and its decline (Section 3.1). It then explores the reasons for the rise of the new forms of exclusion from public space (Section 3.2). Section 3.3 (together with Annex I) gives an overview of the plethora of exclusion measures adopted in the last few years in the United Kingdom, the United States and Switzerland, explaining what types of social problems they are designed to address. Finally, Section 3.4 (together with Annex II) provides a typology of the different ways in which people are excluded from public space in the three states at issue, categorising exclusion measures according to their (legal) mode of exclusion, the type of behaviour they prevent, their geographical scope and their temporal scope.

3.1 Historical background: the decline of banishment

The power of the state to send people away from a given place – one of the strongest possible symbolic representations of exclusion from the

[1] Black, *Black's Law Dictionary* (1951), p. 183.
[2] Holzhauer, 'Landesverweisung (Verbannung)' (1971–1998).
[3] See Beckett/Herbert, *Banished* (2010), pp. 11–12.

community – has a very long tradition. Already the Code of Hammurabi, created by the Babylonian king Hammurabi in the eighteenth century BC and one of the oldest known sets of laws, mentions banishment ('driving someone from the place') as one of the available forms of punishment.[4] Banishment or exile was also considered to be a useful means of punishment, as well as a convenient tool to get rid of political opponents, in ancient Greece[5] and Rome.[6]

Banishment was one of the standard criminal sanctions throughout the Middle Ages in Europe, and in some medieval cities exclusion from the city even became the main form of punishment.[7] The same holds true, in later centuries, for the colonial towns in America.[8] The reasons for the popularity of banishment were its convenience, (perceived) effectiveness, reversibility and strong symbolic power.[9] Unlike the other forms of punishment common at the time (such as the death penalty or corporal punishment), banishment was also very flexible in that it could be adapted to the seriousness of the offence. Its temporal scope could vary from a few weeks to lifelong and its geographical scope from a distance of one mile to the city to thirty miles or more.[10] In Basel, for instance, the exclusion zone could reach from the urban centre '*innerhalb der Kreuzsteine*' ('within the cross stones') to the whole region '*diesseits der Alpen*' ('on this side of the Alps').[11] Furthermore, banishment could be, and often was, combined with other forms of punishment such as corporal punishment, degradation or a fine.[12] Already at that time, however, banishment was used not only to punish criminal offenders but also as a preventive police measure to get rid of various sorts of undesirable people, especially vagrants.[13]

4 Johns, *The Oldest Code of Laws in the World* (2000), Section 154 ('If a man be guilty of incest with his daughter, he shall be driven from the place (exiled).').
5 Drapkin, *Crime and Punishment in the Ancient World* (1989), pp. 178, 194. See also Arendt, *The Human Condition* (1998), p. 221.
6 Drapkin, *Crime and Punishment in the Ancient World* (1989), pp. 239–40.
7 Schubert, *Räuber, Henker, arme Sünder* (2007), p. 122; Schwerhoff, 'Vertreibung als Strafe' (2006); Spierenburg, 'The Body and the State' (1995), 62; Holzhauer, 'Landesverweisung (Verbannung)' (1971–1998), col. 1443.
8 Rothman, 'Perfecting the Prison' (1995), 112–13.
9 Schubert, *Räuber, Henker, arme Sünder* (2007), p. 123; Schwerhoff, 'Vertreibung als Strafe' (2006), 55–60; Holzhauer, 'Landesverweisung (Verbannung)' (1971–1998), col. 1443.
10 Schubert, *Räuber, Henker, arme Sünder* (2007), p. 123; Schwerhoff, 'Vertreibung als Strafe' (2006), 56–8; Holzhauer, 'Landesverweisung (Verbannung)' (1971–1998), col. 1445.
11 Hagemann, Basler Rechtsleben im Mittelalter (1981), Vol. I, p. 189.
12 Holzhauer, 'Landesverweisung (Verbannung)' (1971–1998), col. 1444.
13 Holzhauer, 'Landesverweisung (Verbannung)' (1971–1998), col. 1443.

With the emergence of the territorial state between the fifteenth and seventeenth century, banishment from the city was extended to expulsion from the state. Banishment was now used more systematically and became an almost automatically imposed sentence.[14] However, with its wider use, it also became increasingly apparent that simply dislocating people from the cities, principalities or other new state forms was an unsuitable means of protecting the community and, in fact, even had counter-productive effects: banishment was not only difficult to enforce but also prevented social rehabilitation, creating a rapidly increasing number of homeless vagrants.[15] In addition, it had always been recognised that banishment for longer terms was a very harsh measure as it had serious economic and social implications for those concerned, especially if they came from the settled lower classes.[16] Thus, starting from the early eighteenth century, banishment was gradually replaced with imprisonment, which previously had not been a common form of punishment, and forced labour. By the nineteenth century, most states had either completely abolished banishment as a form of punishment or limited its use to the expulsion of foreign nationals.[17] However, states such as the United Kingdom, France and Russia continued to deport citizens to their colonies or, in the case of Russia, Siberia.[18] In addition, in most European states, it was still possible to send paupers and beggars who were not locals back to their home municipalities.[19]

By the twentieth century, banishment had become an exceptional measure that was now only employed against the most marginalised groups (such as vagrants, beggars and foreign nationals)[20] or in times

[14] Schubert, *Räuber, Henker, arme Sünder* (2007), p. 124; Schwerhoff, 'Vertreibung als Strafe' (2006); Holzhauer, 'Landesverweisung (Verbannung)' (1971–1998), col. 1444.

[15] Schubert, *Räuber, Henker, arme Sünder* (2007), pp. 124–6; Schwerhoff, 'Vertreibung als Strafe' (2006), 61–7; Holzhauer, 'Landesverweisung (Verbannung)' (1971–1998), cols 1446–7.

[16] Schubert, *Räuber, Henker, arme Sünder* (2007), pp. 123, 126; Schwerhoff, 'Vertreibung als Strafe' (2006), 61–3.

[17] Friedrich II of Prussia completely abolished banishment, including for foreign nationals, in 1743/44. Holzhauer, 'Landesverweisung (Verbannung)' (1971–1998), col. 1447. See also Schubert, *Räuber, Henker, arme Sünder* (2007), p. 126; Schwerhoff, 'Vertreibung als Strafe' (2006), 67–70.

[18] In the United Kingdom, the Transportation Act 1718 standardised the process by which criminals were sentenced and shipped to the colonies in America and the West Indies. See McLynn, *Crime and Punishment in Eighteenth-Century England* (1989), pp. 285–97.

[19] Komlosy, 'Der Staat schiebt ab' (2006).

[20] Spierenburg, 'The Body and the State' (1995), 63; Chambliss, 'A Sociological Analysis of the Law of Vagrancy' (1964).

of emergency (such as during the Second World War, when the US government excluded people of Japanese origin from certain areas on the West Coast).[21] And even these exceptional applications of banishment, which were now no longer called 'banishment' but 'exclusion' or 'expulsion', were increasingly looked upon with suspicion, not least by the courts.[22] The rule was now that everyone is free to access public space and to behave there as they please, as long as their behaviour is not covered by one of the criminal offences, including those set out in public-order statutes. Breach of these norms was now to be sanctioned, not with long-term exclusion, but with a prison sentence, which in the case of public-order offences would typically be rather short, or a fine. Once the punishment was completed, people were allowed to move freely again.

What did remain was the power of the police to order people to leave *a specific public place for a short period* where there is *an immediate threat*. However, this power only applied in very specific situations, in particular when people needed to be sent away for their own protection (for example, in case of a natural disaster) or because they were obstructing emergency services or the police in the execution of their duties. Granting the police such a power has generally been seen as unproblematic and it is, accordingly, common to most legal systems of the world. In Switzerland, the power of the police to send people away momentarily from limited geographical areas in these kinds of situations, generally referred to as *Wegweisung* (or less frequently, as in Germany,[23] as *Platzverweis*), was originally understood to be one aspect of their broadly defined power to maintain public safety and order under the *polizeiliche Generalklausel* ('general police clause').[24] In later years, it started to be codified as an explicit power in the police acts of most of the cantons.[25] In the United Kingdom, this power is generally understood to follow

[21] United States Executive Order 9066, 19 February 1942. See *Korematsu* v. *United States*, 323 US 214 (1944); *Hirabayashi* v. *United States*, 320 U.S. 81 (1943).

[22] See e.g. *Papachristou* v. *City of Jacksonville*, 405 U.S. 156 (1972).

[23] See e.g. Schucht, *Generalklausel und Standardmassnahme* (2010), pp. 144–70; Neuner, *Zulässigkeit und Grenzen polizeilicher Verweisungsmassnahmen* (2003), pp. 57–100; Schmitz, *Strassen- und polizeirechtliches Vorgehen gegen Randgruppen* (2003), pp. 228–32.

[24] Keller/Bürli, 'Überdenken der polizeilichen Generalklausel bei Vorliegen staatlicher Schutzpflichten' (2011), 1146–7; Strasser, *Polizeiliche Zwangsmassnahmen* (1981), pp. 93–7. On the *polizeiliche Generalklausel*, see Section 4.2.3.1.

[25] See e.g. for the Canton of St. Gallen, Polizeigesetz vom 10. April 1980 (sGS 451.1), Art. 29(1)(a)–(c). See also the identical provisions in the police acts of the Cantons of Nidwalden (Gesetz über das Polizeiwesen vom 26. April 1987 (NG 911.1), Art. 63) and Basel-Stadt (Gesetz betreffend die Kantonspolizei des Kantons Basel-Stadt (Polizeigesetz,

from the police's common law power (and duty) to preserve the peace.[26] In the United States, the police may take similar action to prevent one of the breach-of-the-peace or public-order offences that have been established by statutory law at state level.[27]

3.2 The resurgence of exclusion

Starting from about the 1990s, there has been a marked resurgence of exclusion from public space. The sheer quantity of exclusion measures described in the following section, all of them adopted in the last few years, is evidence of this trend. However, there has also been a change in the *quality* of exclusion from public space. Exclusion is no longer limited to a power of the police to send people away temporarily from a specific place to deal with an immediate threat, such as in case of a natural disaster. Instead, it is used to address a very wide range of problems; it may have preventive and punitive aspects; people may be excluded from large geographic areas; and people may be kept away from public places for extended periods of time or even permanently. In short, exclusion has returned in a form that is reminiscent of medieval banishment.

The resurgence of exclusion measures must be understood as part of the two broader developments that have fundamentally transformed public space, described in the previous chapter: first, the privatisation of public space and, second, its increased regulation and control due to the rise of the 'security society'.

The notion of a clear separation between private and public space was unknown until the end of the medieval period and only became a settled principle in the eighteenth and nineteenth centuries.[28] Today that distinction has started to become blurred again. As the functions of private and public space are increasingly overlapping, legal tools developed in the context of privately owned places have started to become used to regulate and govern public space. The extension of the power to exclude others from private to public space is one element of this broader process of privatisation of public space described in Section 2.5.1. The power to deny others access to a given space was originally thought of as the very essence of private property, as the defining element of *private* space.[29]

PolG, SG 510.100) vom 13. November 1996, § 42). For an overview of the situation in the different cantons, see Moeckli/Keller, 'Wegweisungen und Rayonverbote' (2012), 232–3.

[26] See e.g. *Duncan* v. *Jones* [1936] 1 KB 218 (Divisional Court); *Humphries* v. *Connor* (1864) 17 Ir. CLR 1.

[27] See Section 4.2.3.1. [28] See Section 2.2. [29] See Section 2.1.1.3.

Now this power is being transposed to *public* space: 'The exclusionary regime of private space is being extended to swallow up the inclusive regime of public space.'[30]

Exclusion from public space is also in many ways characteristic of the rise of the 'security society'. As explained in Section 2.5.2, criminal justice policies of the 'security society' focus on predicting, preventing and managing risks rather than prosecuting, punishing and rehabilitating offenders and, as everyone is regarded as a potential criminal, on the control of space rather than people. While some of these spatial strategies (such as CCTV or random police controls) involve the increased control of all, or at least most, parts of public space, others are about dislocating risks from one place to the other. An example of the latter sort of strategies is the setting up of drug injection rooms, a widely used policy in Switzerland that is now also being discussed in the United Kingdom: drug use is regarded as largely unavoidable and the focus is on preventing and managing the connected risks, including by displacing it from public streets and squares to other spaces.[31] The more explicit exclusion measures described below are equally about displacement of (alleged) risks.

Just as the other technocratic control strategies of the 'security society', exclusion measures are not concerned with retribution or rehabilitation. They do not attempt to induce a change in behaviour of those concerned but simply to keep them away from certain places. This makes them easier to administer and, it may seem, more effective than the traditional, criminal law measures. Exclusion measures are typically designed so as to require a lower level of evidence than a criminal conviction; they entail long-term exclusion for relatively minor offences which, under the criminal law, would only be sanctioned with a fine or a short prison sentence; and they are cheaper than incarceration. Furthermore, the resurgence of exclusion from public space has been facilitated by the development of technological tools that make it much easier to enforce exclusion measures: public space is monitored as closely as never before, thanks to CCTV, satellite surveillance and similar devices;[32] 'intelligent' CCTV cameras have been developed that can automatically detect 'atypical behaviour' such as loitering;[33] devices emitting a high-frequency sound

[30] von Hirsch/Shearing, 'Exclusion from Public Space' (2000), 86.
[31] Lindenberg/Schmidt-Semisch, 'Komplementäre Konkurrenz in der Sicherheitsgesellschaft' (2000), 311.
[32] Goold, *CCTV and Policing* (2004).
[33] ORF, Futurezone, ' "Indect": Werkzeuge für den Präventivstaat', available at www.fuzo-archiv.at/artikel/1631510v2.

that can only be heard by people below a certain age (so-called 'Mosquito' devices) may be used to deter juveniles from certain locations;[34] people can be asked to go away through 'talking' CCTV cameras;[35] modern communication technology and devices such as mobile fingerprint scanners make it easier to quickly identify individuals who may be subject to a ban from certain areas;[36] the movement of people can be monitored with electronic tagging and tracking devices;[37] and sophisticated IT systems allow the police to control large crowds of people and to prevent them from accessing or leaving certain areas.[38] The mere availability of these new possibilities serves as an important impetus for the increased resort to exclusion and similar control policies.[39]

Exclusion from public space is also characteristic of the 'security society' in that it is primarily concerned with the *appearance* of particular spaces. The *broken windows* approach emphasises the need to counter the appearance that anti-social behaviour may be tolerated, the need to make people feel safe. It does not aim to solve the underlying social problems: it is sufficient to remove their manifestations (the 'broken windows'). Exclusion measures fit this bill perfectly. Sending certain people away from public places may not only be a way of making these places appear more orderly and safer[40] but – just as medieval banishment – also has a strong symbolic power. As Adam Crawford has argued, exclusion measures have a particularly high 'signal value': they convey a strong message that certain behaviour (or rather the appearance of certain behaviour) will not be tolerated but will be met with drastic action symbolising exclusion from the community.[41] It is thus not surprising

[34] Antwort des Bundesrates vom 28. November 2007 auf die Interpellation Leutenegger Oberholzer Susanne 'Mosquito. Schallwellen in hohen Frequenzbereichen. Folgen für Mensch und Umwelt', Amtliches Bulletin Nationalrat 2007, p. 2011; Urteil des Verwaltungsgerichts des Kantons Graubünden U 07 83 vom 8. Januar 2008; S. Campbell, 'Now crime gadget can annoy us all', *BBC News*, 2 December 2008, available at http://news.bbc.co.uk/2/hi/uk_news/7759818.stm; Parliamentary Assembly of the Council of Europe, Recommendation 1930 (2010).

[35] ' "Talking" CCTV scolds offenders', *BBC News*, 4 April 2007, available at http://news.bbc.co.uk/2/hi/6524495.stm.

[36] O. Bowcott, 'Police will use new device to take fingerprints in street', *The Guardian*, 27 October 2008.

[37] Nellis, '24/7/365' (2008).

[38] M. Monroy, 'Situational Awareness für die Polizei', Telepolis, 12 February 2002, available at www.heise.de/tp/artikel/32/32066/1.html.

[39] See generally Aas/Oppen Gundhus/Monk Lomell (eds), *Technologies of Insecurity* (2008).

[40] See Gasser, *Kriminalpolitik oder City-Pflege?* (2004), pp. 43–4.

[41] Crawford, 'Dispersal Powers and the Symbolic Role of Anti-Social Behaviour Legislation' (2008).

that exclusion from public places was already part of the order-maintenance policing initiative carried out in New York City, which has influenced policing strategies all over the world.[42] Today, exclusion – of which spatial exclusion is only the most visible aspect – is arguably one of the main paradigms of policing and social control in general.[43]

3.3 The targets of exclusion

A plethora of exclusion measures have been introduced in the last few years in the United Kingdom, the United States and Switzerland. This section provides an overview of these measures and explains their purpose, that is, what kind of social problems (and thereby what kind of behaviour) they are designed to address. The section should be read together with Annex I, which reproduces the text of some of the most important legal norms authorising exclusion from public space. Annex II contains a table categorising these norms, including with regard to the behaviour they target. Especially in the United States and Switzerland, where such norms are typically found at the state/cantonal or municipal level, there are a very great number of norms authorising exclusion from public space. It is therefore impossible to cover all of them. Nevertheless, an attempt has been made to at least include examples of all the different types of exclusion measures.

Analysis of the exclusion measures adopted in recent years in the three states at issue shows that these have been designed, and used, to deal with mainly three types of behaviour: (future) crime, anti-social behaviour and political protest. Categorising exclusion measures according to these types of behaviour is not unproblematic for at least two reasons. First, the distinction between these types may itself not always be clear-cut. For example, behaviour that used to be regarded as 'only' anti-social may be criminalised; conversely, behaviour that previously had been treated as a crime may be decriminalised and become 'merely' anti-social; some forms of political protest may involve criminal behaviour; other forms of protest may be treated as anti-social behaviour.[44] Second, it may sometimes be difficult to identify exactly what type of behaviour an exclusion measure is actually designed to address. Often exclusion measures are

[42] Kelling/Coles, *Fixing Broken Windows* (1996), pp. 123–5; Wilson/Kelling, 'Broken Windows' (1982).

[43] Singelnstein/Stolle, *Die Sicherheitsgesellschaft* (2012), pp. 87–95; Wehrheim, *Die überwachte Stadt* (2012), pp. 49–52; Young, *The Exclusive Society* (1999).

[44] See e.g. *R.* v. *Jones*, [2006] EWCA Crim 2942.

directed against a wide range of different behaviours and, as a consequence, their scope of application is defined very broadly. For example, some exclusion norms are designed to remove and keep away anyone who 'threatens or disturbs public safety and order'.[45] These types of provisions can be used to counter any of the three types of behaviour referred to above. The exclusion powers existing under various Swiss cantonal police acts, for example, have been used to deal with criminal behaviour such as football hooliganism,[46] anti-social behaviour such as gatherings of alcoholics[47] as well as political protest.[48] Similarly, the dispersal powers under the British Anti-social Behaviour Act 2003 have not only been deployed against those engaging in behaviour that one would commonly expect to be defined as 'anti-social' but also against protesters.[49] In the United States, laws prohibiting sitting or lying on sidewalks have been used in the same way, that is, to remove protesters.[50] Even more narrowly defined exclusion norms, such as curfew laws, may be intended to achieve a number of different objectives (prevention of youth delinquency or disorder, for example), depending on the context.[51] Nevertheless, the categorisation is helpful to understand the basic objectives that contemporary exclusion measures are meant to serve.

3.3.1 *Criminal behaviour*

For certain types of crime, the traditional criminal law approach of investigating, prosecuting, trying and, finally, imprisoning offenders has come to be regarded as insufficient. Some offences, it is argued, are

45 See e.g. the Police Act of the Canton of Berne: Polizeigesetz vom 8. Juni 1997, Art. 29(1)(d) ('Die Kantonspolizei kann Personen von einem Ort vorübergehend wegweisen oder fern halten, wenn [. . .] der begründete Verdacht besteht, dass sie oder andere, die der gleichen Ansammlung zuzurechnen sind, die öffentliche Sicherheit und Ordnung gefährden oder stören').

46 BVR 2009, 385 (Verwaltungsgericht des Kantons Bern).

47 BGE 132 I 49 (2006); BVR 2005, 97 (Verwaltungsgericht des Kantons Bern).

48 M. Dütschler, 'Polizei hat Politiker unbegründet weggewiesen', *Der Bund*, 9 November 2011.

49 *R (Singh)* v. *Chief Constable of the West Midlands*, [2006] EWCA Civ 1118.

50 Global Justice Clinic (NYU School of Law) and Walter Leitner International Human Rights Clinic at the Leitner Center for International Law and Justice (Fordham Law School), 'Suppressing Protest' (2012), 118–19.

51 For Switzerland, see e.g. Urteil des Verwaltungsgerichts des Kantons Zürich VB.2009.00055 vom 30. April 2009, E. 4.3, 5.2.2; Gerber Jenni, 'Abendausgang Kinder' (2006), 845. For the United Kingdom, see Crawford, 'Dispersal Powers and the Symbolic Role of Anti-Social Behaviour Legislation' (2008), 767. For the United States, see *Bykofsky* v. *Borough of Middletown*, 401 F.Supp. 1242, 1255 (D.C. Pa. 1975).

so serious that it is not sufficient to rely on the 'general preventive effect' of the criminal law; instead, they need to be prevented by any means, including by resorting to measures that have not traditionally been part of the criminal law. This particularly applies to those types of crime that tend to attract a great deal of public attention, so that state authorities feel a particular urge to be seen to be taking strong action against them. Sex offences, terrorism, other forms of organised crime and football hooliganism belong to this category of crimes. As a consequence, special powers to exclude from public space those who may commit these types of offences have been created, be it to prevent these persons from re-offending, be it to prevent them from offending in the first place.

3.3.1.1 Convicted offenders

Exclusion from public space may be designed as a means of preventing already convicted criminal offenders from re-offending. In these cases, it is imposed as an additional restriction following a conviction in the normal criminal process.

In the United Kingdom, for example, under Section 14A of the Football Spectators Act 1989 (as amended by the Football Disorder Act 2000), any court that convicts a person of a football-related offence must, in addition to the sentence, issue a so-called banning order against that person if such an order would help prevent violence or disorder at or in connection with any football matches. Part of such an order may be a requirement not to be in certain places at certain times.[52] The Criminal Justice Act 2003 gives courts the power to impose similar exclusion requirements with regard to any offender sentenced to a suspended prison sentence, prohibiting them from entering a specified place for a specified period.[53] For example, a court may impose an exclusion order banning a convicted offender from accessing an area known for drug dealing for several years.[54] Under the Sexual Offences Act 2003 (as amended by the Anti-social Behaviour, Crime and Policing Act 2014), courts can issue a sexual harm prevention order (SHPO) against convicted sex offenders if this is necessary to protect the public or any particular members of the public from sexual harm.[55] Any restriction required for this purpose can be imposed as part of such an order, which may include prohibitions from being in certain areas.[56] Prohibitions

[52] Football Spectators Act 1989 (as amended by the Football Disorder Act 2000), s. 14G.
[53] Criminal Justice Act 2003, s. 190 in connection with s. 205.
[54] See *R.* v. *F (Philip)*, [2008] EWCA Crim 1558.
[55] Sexual Offences Act 2003, s. 103A.
[56] Ibid., s. 103C.

from going to specified places may also be imposed as part of a violent offender order, which magistrates' courts are authorised to issue under the Criminal Justice and Immigration Act 2008 against convicted violent offenders.[57]

Under the sex offender legislation of the US state of Georgia, convicted sex offenders are not allowed to loiter near any childcare facility, school or area where minors congregate[58] and may be prohibited, as part of their conditions of probation, from being in the vicinity of the victim.[59] In the state of Michigan, registered sex offenders are banned from loitering within any 'student safety zone', that is, an area that lies 1,000 feet or less from school property.[60] Similar laws exist in many other US states.[61] In addition, many cities and municipalities in the United States ban sex offenders from entering public parks.[62] The City of Atlanta, Georgia, has designated a number of commercial areas, areas around schools, recreational zones and certain residential areas as 'drug-free zones';[63] anyone convicted for possessing or distributing illegal drugs within such a zone can be banned from 'the public streets, sidewalks, and other public ways in all designated drug-free zones'.[64]

In Switzerland, the Swiss Criminal Code provides that when a court sentences a criminal offender to a suspended sentence, it can impose an order on him or her for the time of the probationary period, which may include a requirement to keep away from certain areas.[65] The correctional service authorities have the power to impose equivalent orders in the case of conditional releases of offenders.[66] Such orders imposing exclusion requirements may be used, for example, to keep

57 Criminal Justice and Immigration Act 2008, ss 98–106.

58 Official Code of Georgia, § 42-1-15. 59 Ibid., § 42-8-35.

60 Michigan Compiled Laws, ss 28.733-4.

61 See e.g. Bains, 'Next-Generation Sex Offender Statutes' (2007).

62 E.g. Woodfin, North Carolina, Code of Ordinance, § 130.03 (2005); Plainfield, Indiana, Ordinance No. 16-2002, s. 18. See also *Dowdell* v. *City of Jeffersonville*, 907 N.E.2d 559 (Ind. C.A. 2009).

63 Atlanta, Georgia, Code of Ordinances, ss 106-403, 106-421.

64 Ibid., s. 106-423. See also the respective provision in Atlanta, Georgia, Code of Ordinances, s. 106-405.

65 StGB, Art. 44(2) in connection with Art. 94. See also Militärstrafgesetz vom 13. Juni 1927 (SR 321.0) (Military Criminal Code) (MStG), Arts 38(2) and 47 in connection with Arts 34b(1) and 54; Bundesgesetz über das Jugendstrafrecht vom 20. Juni 2003 (Jugendstrafgesetz, SR 311.1) (Juvenile Criminal Code) (JStG), Art. 35(2) in connection with Art. 29(2). See also JStG, Art. 22(2).

66 StGB, Arts 62(3), 64a(1) and 87(2) in connection with Art. 94. See also MStG, Art. 47 in connection with Art. 54; JStG, Art. 29(2).

away sex offenders from (potential) victims or drug offenders from areas known for drug dealing.[67] In the case of persons sentenced to a suspended sentence for football-related offences, it is the common practice of courts to impose orders requiring them not to come within 1,000 metres of venues of football matches during the game or four hours before and after the game.[68] In 2013, the Federal Assembly (the federal parliament) adopted an amendment to the Swiss Criminal Code that gives the courts the power to impose on certain convicted offenders, primarily sex offenders, so-called *Rayonverbote/interdictions géographiques* (area bans), regardless of whether a probationary period applies or not.[69] According to the new provision, the convicting court can impose such an area ban on anyone who has committed a criminal offence directed against particular persons or persons belonging to a particular group, if there is a risk that he or she will commit another offence in case of contact with these persons.[70] The offender can be prohibited from approaching a person or their home and being in specified locations such as particular streets, squares or neighbourhoods.[71] The area bans can be imposed for renewable periods of up to five years.[72]

3.3.1.2 Potential offenders

Not only convicted offenders are the targets of exclusion measures. In the 'security society', exclusion from public space is also increasingly used against *potential* offenders, that is, as a means to prevent certain crimes from being committed in the first place. It is especially in the context of the fight against serious and organised crime that exclusion has been used in this manner.

As early as in the 1990s, the City of Chicago created a power for the police to disperse anyone they 'reasonably believe[d] to be a criminal street gang member loitering in any public place with one or more other persons'.[73] During the three years in which this Gang Congregation Ordinance was enforced in its original form, the police issued over

[67] Imperatori, 'Art. 94' (2013), 1882.

[68] Konferenz der Strafverfolgungsbehörden der Schweiz (KSBS), Empfehlungen betreffend Gewalt an Sportveranstaltungen vom 18. November 2010; Urteil des Kantonsgerichts St. Gallen vom 23. April 2011, Nr. ST2010.7891.

[69] StGB, Art. 67b. See also MStG, Art. 50(b); JStG, Art. 16(a)(2).

[70] StGB, Art. 67b(1).

[71] Ibid., Art. 67b(2)

[72] Ibid., Art. 67b(1), (5).

[73] Chicago Municipal Code, § 8-4-015 (original wording of 17 June 1992). The original version of the provision was declared unconstitutional by the US Supreme Court in *City of Chicago* v. *Morales*, 527 U.S. 41 (1999) and thereupon amended.

89,000 dispersal orders and arrested over 42,000 people for violating the ordinance.[74] Similarly, in the United Kingdom, in 2011, the police and local authorities were given the power to apply for injunctions in court against individuals who they believe are involved in gang-related violence.[75] The conditions that may be imposed as part of such gang injunctions include prohibitions of being in particular places or being with particular persons in particular places.[76]

Similar measures are used to counter drug trafficking. In the United States, the City of Chicago has created dispersal powers similar to the ones used against criminal street gangs to counter 'narcotics-related loitering'.[77] As explained in Chapter 1, the City of Cincinnati enacted an ordinance that banned all persons who had been arrested for a drug offence from returning to any area designated as a 'drug exclusion zone'.[78] The City of Portland has a similar scheme in place, authorising the Chief of Police to prohibit anyone arrested for a drug offence within a 'drug-free zone' from returning to such zones for three months; upon conviction that period can be extended to one year.[79]

In the United Kingdom, the Prevention of Terrorism Act 2005 gave the Home Secretary the power to make a so-called 'control order' against an individual 'if he ha[d] reasonable grounds for suspecting that the individual is or has been involved in terrorism-related activity'.[80] Any obligations deemed necessary to prevent involvement of the individual in terrorism-related activity could be imposed as part of a control order, including a prohibition on his or her being at specified places or in specified areas at specified times and a prohibition or restriction on his or her movements.[81] By the end of 2011, fifty-two individuals had been subject to terrorist control orders.[82] In December 2011, the Prevention of Terrorism Act 2005 was repealed and replaced with the Terrorism Prevention and Investigation Measures Act 2011, establishing a very similar system. According to this Act, the Home Secretary can impose

[74] *City of Chicago* v. *Morales*, 527 U.S. 41, 49 (1999).
[75] Policing and Crime Act 2009, ss 34–50. [76] Ibid., s. 35(2).
[77] Chicago Municipal Code, § 8–4–017.
[78] Cincinnati Municipal Code, § 755–5 (repealed). The relevant provisions are reproduced in *State* v. *Burnett*, 755 N.E.2d 857, 858–9 (Ohio 2001) and *Johnson* v. *City of Cincinnati*, 310 F.3d 484, 487–8 (6th Cir. 2002).
[79] Charter and Code of the City of Portland, Oregon, ss 14B.20.010 - 070.
[80] Prevention of Terrorism Act 2005, s. 2(1) (repealed).
[81] Ibid., ss 1(4)(f)–(g) (repealed).
[82] D. Anderson, Control Orders in 2011, Final Report of the Independent Reviewer on the Prevention of Terrorism Act 2005 (2012).

a Terrorism Prevention and Investigation Measure (TPIM) on an individual if she 'reasonably believes that the individual is, or has been, involved in terrorism-related activity'.[83] The measures that can be imposed include 'exclusion measures', that is, restrictions on the individual entering specified areas or places,[84] as well as night curfews.[85] Ten individuals have been subject to TPIMs.[86] A similar power is provided by the Serious Crime Act 2007 for a number of serious offences such as drug trafficking, people trafficking, prostitution and child sex, money laundering and so on.[87] The High Court can make a 'serious crime prevention order', which may include restrictions in relation to the places to which a person has access,[88] 'if it is satisfied that [that] person has been involved in serious crime' and that the order would protect the public.[89]

Also with regard to sex offences and football-related violence, exclusion powers are not limited to convicted offenders. In the United Kingdom, magistrates' courts can make a sexual risk order if they are satisfied that a person has done an act of a sexual nature that makes it necessary to protect the public or any particular member of the public.[90] Any prohibition necessary to achieve this purpose can be imposed as part of a sexual risk order.[91]

With regard to football-related violence, the Football Disorder Act 2000, passed as a response to the violence seen during Euro 2000, gave magistrates' courts the power to impose exclusion requirements as part of a football banning order against anyone who 'has at any time caused or contributed to any violence or disorder in the United Kingdom or elsewhere'.[92] Typically, a football banning order will prevent an individual from entering the town centre on designated match-days.[93] Around 500 to 1,000 football banning orders are imposed a year; by September 2014, a total of 2,273 orders were in force.[94] Switzerland

[83] Terrorism Prevention and Investigation Measures Act 2011, ss 2, 3(1).

[84] Ibid., Schedule 1, para. 3. [85] Ibid., Schedule 1, para. 1.

[86] D. Anderson, Terrorism Prevention and Investigation Measures in 2014, Third Report of the Independent Reviewer on the Operation of the Terrorism Prevention and Investigation Measures Act 2011 (2015), p. 5.

[87] Serious Crime Act 2007, Schedule 1. [88] Ibid., ss 1(3), 5. [89] Ibid., s. 1(1).

[90] Sexual Offences Act 2003, s. 122A(6). [91] Ibid., ss 122A(7), (9).

[92] Football Spectators Act 1989 (as amended by the Football Disorder Act 2000), s. 14B in conjunction with s. 14G.

[93] Pearson, 'Hybrid Law and Human Rights' (2006).

[94] Home Office, Statistics on football-related arrests and banning orders, Season 2013–14, 11 September 2014, available at www.gov.uk/government/statistics/football-related-arrests-and-banning-orders-season-2013-to-2014.

followed the British model in preparation of Euro 2008.[95] In 2006, the Federal Act Concerning Measures for the Protection of Internal Security was amended to create similar preventive powers to deal with violence related to sports events.[96] Most of the relevant provisions were later transferred into a concordat (Konkordat über Massnahmen gegen Gewalt anlässlich von Sportveranstaltungen (Hooligan Concordat)),[97] that is, a treaty between the cantons, as it was thought that this was a matter that should properly be regulated at the cantonal rather than the federal level.[98] According to the concordat, which has been ratified by all the cantons, the police can prohibit persons from entering specified zones surrounding sports events (*Rayonverbot/interdiction de périmètre*) if they have been previously involved in violence against persons or property in connection with sports events.[99] Previous involvement in such violence can be substantiated by other means than conviction by a court, including, for example, credible statements by the police or security personnel, stadium bans issued by sports clubs or reports by foreign authorities.[100] A revision of the concordat, which, among other things, extends the temporal and geographical scope of the area bans, was adopted in 2012 but has not (yet) been ratified by all cantons.[101] As of 31 July 2015, 412

[95] See Botschaft zur Änderung des Bundesgesetzes über Massnahmen zur Wahrung der inneren Sicherheit (Massnahmen gegen Gewaltpropaganda und gegen Gewalt anlässlich von Sportveranstaltungen) vom 17. August 2005, BBl 2005, 5613, pp. 5617, 5623–4, 5639. For comparisons of the Swiss measures to deal with football-related violence with those of the United Kingdom, see Wohlers/Trunz, 'Hooliganismus-Bekämpfung' (2011); Bichovsky, *Prévention de la violence commise par les spectateurs lors de manifestations sportives* (2009).

[96] BWIS, Art. 24a–Art. 24h (Änderung vom 24. März 2006: AS 2006 3703).

[97] Konkordat über Massnahmen gegen Gewalt anlässlich von Sportveranstaltungen vom 15. November 2007. See e.g. for the Canton of Zurich: Gesetz über den Beitritt zum Konkordat über Massnahmen gegen Gewalt anlässlich von Sportveranstaltungen vom 18. Mai 2009 (LS 551.19).

[98] Botschaft zur Änderung des Bundesgesetzes über Massnahmen zur Wahrung der inneren Sicherheit (Massnahmen gegen Gewaltpropaganda und gegen Gewalt anlässlich von Sportveranstaltungen) vom 17. August 2005, BBl 2005, 5613, pp. 5638–9.

[99] Konkordat über Massnahmen gegen Gewalt anlässlich von Sportveranstaltungen vom 15. November 2007, Art. 4(1).

[100] Ibid., Art. 3.

[101] Konkordat über Massnahmen gegen Gewalt anlässlich von Sportveranstaltungen vom 15. November 2007; Änderung vom 2. Februar 2012. For a list of the cantons that have ratified the revised version of the concordat, see the website of the Konferenz der Kantonalen Justiz- und Polizeidirektorinnen und -direktoren (KKJPD), at www.kkjpd.ch/?action=get_file&language=de&id=55&resource_link_id=6f8. For an overview of the revised concordat, see Müller, 'Das revidierte Konkordat über Massnahmen zur Bekämpfung der Gewalt an Sportveranstaltungen' (2013).

area bans in connection with sports events were in force in Switzerland.[102]

In addition, in all three states at issue, exclusion is also used as a means to protect people from violent or threatening behaviour, in particular in the context of domestic violence. In Switzerland, numerous cantonal police acts provide that persons who pose a danger or a serious threat to the physical or mental integrity of their partners may not only be expelled by the police from the shared home but also banned from accessing specific areas, which may include parts of public space.[103] In addition, the Swiss Civil Code authorises civil courts to issue orders prohibiting individuals from approaching the claimant, his or her home or specific streets, squares or districts, as far as this is necessary in order to protect the claimant from violence, threats or harassment.[104] In the United Kingdom, courts can, for similar purposes, issue exclusion orders relating to a defined area surrounding the home of the (former) spouse or a child under the Family Law Act 1996[105] and the Children Act 1989.[106] In most US states, courts can issue so-called 'stay away orders', which may relate not only to the home, place of employment or school of the (former) spouse or a child but also to any other location designated by the court.[107]

More generally, in Switzerland anyone reasonably suspected of having committed a criminal offence may, if certain conditions are met,[108] instead of being remanded into custody, be ordered by a court to comply with specific requirements.[109] These requirements may include a ban on accessing specified areas.[110]

[102] Fedpol, 'Medienmitteilung: Aktuelle Zahlen aus dem Informationssystem HOOGAN', 31 July 2015, available at www.fedpol.admin.ch/fedpol/de/home/aktuell/news/2015/2015-07-31.html.

[103] See e.g. for the Canton of Zurich: Gewaltschutzgesetz des Kantons Zürich vom 19. Juni 2006 (GSG, LS 351), § 3; for the Canton of Neuchâtel: Loi sur la police du 4 novembre 2014 (LPol, RSN 561.1), Art. 57–61. For an overview of the situation in all cantons, see Schwander, *Häusliche Gewalt* (2006).

[104] ZGB, Art. 28b(1). [105] Family Law Act 1996, s. 33(3)(g).

[106] Children Act 1989, ss 38A(3)(c), 44A(3)(c).

[107] See e.g. New York Family Court Act, § 842(a). For an overview of the situation in the other states, see American Bar Association Commission on Domestic Violence, 'Domestic Violence Civil Protection Orders (CPOs) by State', June 2009, available at www.americanbar.org/content/dam/aba/migrated/domviol/pdfs/dv_cpo_chart.authcheckdam.pdf.

[108] See Schweizerische Strafprozessordnung vom 5. Oktober 2007 (StPO) (SR 312.0) (Swiss Criminal Procedure Code), Art. 221.

[109] Ibid., Art. 237. [110] Ibid., Art. 237(2)(c).

3.3.2 *Anti-social behaviour*

A second group of exclusion measures target behaviour that, although not commonly regarded as criminal, is seen as contributing to the decline of public order and undermining the integrity of public space. As explained in Section 2.5.2, according to the predominant crime-fighting strategies, this kind of behaviour is one of the main contributing factors to crime and therefore must be tackled aggressively. Accordingly, a wide range of policies and laws designed to counter behaviour that, especially in the United Kingdom, has come to be generically described as 'anti-social' have been adopted in recent years. Of course, there have always been attempts by the state to prevent particular forms of conduct in public space that were seen as not criminal but still deserving of being suppressed. In many cases, however, the scope of such measures has now been considerably expanded to cover behaviour that is so vaguely defined that these measures can be used against almost anyone. In fact, in the case of some of these measures, their applicability has been delinked from behaviour completely: they can be applied to whole categories of people regardless of their behaviour or previous behaviour.

3.3.2.1 Vagrancy, loitering, begging

Forms of 'anti-social behaviour' in public space that have been suppressed for several centuries include vagrancy and begging. In the United Kingdom, vagrancy statutes, enacted to control wages and prevent idleness, date back to the fourteenth century.[111] In 1824, a Vagrancy Act, prohibiting peddling, begging and street prostitution, was created to deal with the social problems arising after the Napoleonic wars.[112] Despite criticisms, this Act remains in force until today. In Switzerland, begging bans, which originated in the fourteenth century, had almost completely disappeared by the twentieth century.[113] However, citing public-order concerns, many municipal and cantonal authorities started to reintroduce them around 2000. Today, most Swiss cantons and cities have prohibitions of begging in place.[114] In the United States, vagrancy and loitering laws have existed since the eighteenth century.[115] Following

[111] Adler, 'A Historical Analysis of the Law of Vagrancy' (1989); Chambliss, 'A Sociological Analysis of the Law of Vagrancy' (1964).

[112] Vagrancy Act 1824. [113] Moeckli, 'Bettelverbote' (2010), 539–42.

[114] Ibid., 537, 542–3.

[115] Adler, 'A Historical Analysis of the Law of Vagrancy' (1989); Chambliss, 'A Sociological Analysis of the Law of Vagrancy' (1964).

a number of legal challenges in the 1960s and the Supreme Court's ruling in *Papachristou* v. *City of Jacksonville* in 1972, which held Jacksonville's vagrancy ordinance to be unconstitutionally vague,[116] many states and cities redrafted their laws to direct them against loitering with a specific intent or loitering in particular public places. The New York Penal Code, for example, criminalises loitering in a public place 'for the purpose of gambling with cards, dice or other gambling paraphernalia'[117] and 'for the purpose of engaging, or soliciting another person to engage, in oral sexual conduct, anal sexual conduct, or other sexual behavior of a deviate nature',[118] while in Charleston it is prohibited to 'loiter or prowl in a place, at a time or in a manner not usual for law abiding individuals under circumstances that warrant alarm for the safety of persons or property in the vicinity'.[119] A survey conducted in 2009 found that 47 per cent of US cities prohibited loitering in particular public areas.[120]

As far as such measures are directed against forms of use of public space that are primarily *commercially motivated*, such as begging, street prostitution and gambling, they are, for the reasons set out in Section 1.3, not dealt with in this book.

3.3.2.2 Sitting, lying, spitting, drinking alcohol

In all three states at issue, legal provisions have been adopted in recent years that are directed against forms of behaviour that used to be regarded as legitimate but are now described as contributing to the decline of public order. Typically, the scope of these measures is very broadly defined. In the 1990s, many cities in the United States began to proscribe a wide range of allegedly anti-social behaviours, including to 'obstruct pedestrian or vehicular traffic',[121] to sleep in a street, a sidewalk, public parks or other public places,[122] to drink alcohol in a public place[123] and even simply to 'sit or lie down upon a public sidewalk'.[124] By 2009,

116 *Papachristou* v. *City of Jacksonville*, 405 U.S. 156 (1972).

117 New York Penal Code, s. 240.35(2). 118 Ibid., s. 240.35(3).

119 Charleston, South Carolina, Code of Ordinances, s. 21–108.

120 National Law Center on Homelessness & Poverty and National Coalition for the Homeless, 'Homes Not Handcuffs' (2009), 10.

121 Seattle Municipal Code, s. 12A.12.015. See also Code of the City of Phoenix, Arizona, s. 23–8.

122 Dallas, Texas Code of Ordinances, s. 31–13; Code of the City of Phoenix, Arizona, s. 23–48.01.

123 New York City Administrative Code, § 10–125.

124 City of Orlando, Code of Ordinances, s. 43.88. See also Seattle Municipal Code, s. 15.48.040; Reno, Nevada, Municipal Code, s. 8.12.015.

30 per cent of 235 US cities surveyed prohibited sitting or lying in certain parts of public space.[125] Similarly, in the Swiss City of Berne it is now prohibited to sit or lie down on the ground or on stairways in or near the train station.[126] Several Swiss towns have banned the consumption of alcohol in public places at night[127] or spitting in public.[128] In the United Kingdom, the Violent Crime Reduction Act 2006 gave the police the power to give a direction to anyone who may contribute to the occurrence of alcohol-related disorder, requiring them to leave and prohibiting them from returning for up to forty-eight hours.[129] The relevant provision was repealed by the Anti-social Behaviour, Crime and Policing Act 2014, which created more extensive exclusion powers.[130]

3.3.2.3 Juvenile curfews

All three states under consideration have also passed exclusion measures that are directed against children and juveniles who, apparently, are seen as a particularly significant source of 'anti-social behaviour'. While in the United States juvenile curfew laws have existed since the end of the nineteenth century,[131] the early 1990s witnessed a sharp increase in such laws.[132] By 1995, more than 146 of the largest 200 US cities had adopted some type of curfew,[133] and, in total, around 3,000 municipalities were estimated to have curfew laws.[134] For instance, the Dallas Juvenile Curfew Ordinance of 1991, which was upheld by the Court of Appeals for the Fifth Circuit[135] and has therefore become something like a blueprint for other curfew schemes, makes it an offence for any person under seventeen to be in any public place (or on the premises of any 'establishment') between 11 pm and 6 am on weekdays and between

[125] National Law Center on Homelessness & Poverty and National Coalition for the Homeless, 'Homes Not Handcuffs' (2009), 10.

[126] Stadt Bern, Reglement betreffend die Benützung des städtischen Teils des Bahnhofs Bern (Bahnhofreglement; BHR), Art. 2(2)(b).

[127] E.g. Polizeigesetz der Stadt Chur vom 24. Februar 2008 (PG, 411), Art. 14(5). See B. Grossrieder, 'Szenen einer disziplinierten Gesellschaft', *Neue Zürcher Zeitung*, 4 July 2011.

[128] E.g. Polizeiverordnung der Stadt Dübendorf vom 23. August 2012, Art. 16(1).

[129] Violent Crime Reduction Act 2006, s. 27 (repealed).

[130] See Section 3.3.2.4.

[131] 'Curfew Ordinances and the Control of Nocturnal Juvenile Crime' (1958), 66. See also Franz, *Ausgehverbot für Jugendliche* (2000), pp. 11–16.

[132] Franz, *Ausgehverbot für Jugendliche* (2000), pp. 21–7.

[133] Ruefle/Reynolds, 'Keep Them at Home' (1996), 76.

[134] Trollinger, 'The Juvenile Curfew' (1995), 975.

[135] *Qutb* v. *Strauss*, 11 F.3d 488 (5th Cir. 1993).

midnight and 6 am on weekends.[136] In 2009, the curfew ordinance was amended to also cover school times.[137] In New Orleans, persons under seventeen are not allowed to be in public places between 8 pm (during the summer months the curfew starts at 9 pm) and 6 am on weekdays and between 11 pm and 6 am on weekends.[138] Juvenile curfew laws are widely enforced in the United States.[139] In 2007, 109,815 persons aged under eighteen were arrested for violations of curfew and loitering laws;[140] in 2014 this number was at 41,741 persons.[141]

Juvenile curfews have now also become increasingly common in Europe. In Switzerland, several municipalities have adopted curfew laws that make it unlawful for children and youths to either assemble in public places[142] or simply to be in public places[143] at certain times. In the United Kingdom, the now repealed Section 14 of the Crime and Disorder Act 1998 gave local authorities and the police the power to ban children under sixteen from being in a public place at night. Section 30(6) of the Anti-social Behaviour Act 2003 authorised the police to remove to their home address any person under sixteen they found in a public place between 9 pm and 6 am. This power was replaced with the dispersal power under the Anti-social Behaviour, Crime and Policing Act 2014. According to Section 35(7) of this Act, a police constable may remove persons under sixteen who engage in anti-social behaviour to their home address.

136 Dallas, Texas Code of Ordinances, s. 31–33. For an overview of the curfew schemes in place in other cities, see e.g. U.S. Department of Justice, *Curfew: An Answer to Juvenile Delinquency and Victimization?* (April 1996).

137 Dallas, Texas Code of Ordinances, s. 31–33(a)(1)(C).

138 New Orleans, Louisiana Code of Ordinances, s. 54–414.

139 See Ruefle/Reynolds, 'Keep Them at Home' (1996), 79–81.

140 Federal Bureau of Investigation, *Crime in the United States: 2007*, Table 38, available at www2.fbi.gov/ucr/cius2007/data/table_38.html.

141 Federal Bureau of Investigation, *Crime in the United States: 2014*, Table 38, available at www.fbi.gov/about-us/cjis/ucr/crime-in-the-u.s/2014/crime-in-the-u.s.-2014/tables/table-38.

142 Polizeiverordnung der Gemeinde Dänikon vom 18. Juni 2008, Art. 27 (repealed; see Urteil des Verwaltungsgerichts des Kantons Zürich VB.2009.00055 vom 30. April 2009).

143 Ortspolizeireglement der Stadt Biel vom 21. November 2012 (SGR 552.1), Art. 27(1); Polizeireglement der Stadt Gossau vom 4. November 2008 (18.01), Art. 19 (Nachtrag vom 6. Dezember 2011); Polizeireglement der Gemeinde Visp vom 27. Mai 2009, Art. 12; Polizeireglement der Gemeinden Bad Zurzach, Baldingen, Böbikon, Böttstein, Döttingen, Endingen, Fisibach, Full-Reuenthal, Kaiserstuhl, Klingnau, Koblenz, Leibstadt, Lengnau, Leuggern, Mandach, Mellikon, Rekingen, Rietheim, Rümikon, Schneisingen, Siglistorf, Tegerfelden, Unterendingen und Wislikofen vom 1. April 2008, § 25(2); Gemeindepolizeireglement der Gemeinde Interlaken vom 5. Dezember 2006 (552.11), Art. 9(4); Gemeindepolizeireglement der Gemeinde Urtenen-Schönbühl vom 15. Mai 2006, Art. 6.

3.3.2.4 Blanket exclusion norms

Finally, a number of blanket exclusion norms have been introduced in recent years, encompassing forms of anti-social behaviour that are not already covered by the provisions described above. The British Crime and Disorder Act 1998 authorised magistrates' courts, on application from the police or local authorities, to issue an ASBO against anyone who has acted 'in an anti-social manner, that is to say, in a manner that caused or was likely to cause harassment, alarm or distress to one or more persons not of the same household as himself'.[144] Examples of behaviours for which ASBOs were imposed include drunkenness, swearing, spitting, harassment of neighbours, homelessness, begging and prostitution,[145] but also various forms of political protest[146] and criminal behaviour such as drug dealing.[147] Part of an ASBO could be a prohibition on accessing certain public areas.[148] For example, ASBOs have been used to ban a sixteen-year-old from entering any part of Manchester for ten years,[149] to prevent an animal rights activist from going within 500 yards of any animal research laboratory,[150] to prevent a man who had engaged in disorderly behaviour and had intimidated and harassed people from going into Birmingham city centre for a period of five years,[151] to ban a beggar from entering a certain part of the Birmingham city centre for an unlimited period,[152] to prohibit a thirteen-year-old from visiting the high street and other parts of the centre of his home town for two years,[153] and, as explained in Chapter 1, to prevent a seventeen-year-old from accessing Whitley Bay town centre for

144 Crime and Disorder Act 1998, s. 1(1)(a).

145 For overviews, see Macdonald, 'A Suicidal Woman, Roaming Pigs and a Noisy Trampolinist' (2006); Statewatch, 'ASBOwatch: Case Studies', available at www.statewatch.org/asbo/ASBOwatch.html.

146 See e.g. *R.* v. *Jones*, [2006] EWCA Crim 2942. For an overview, see Statewatch, 'ASBOwatch: Protesters', available at www.statewatch.org/asbo/asbowatch-protesters.htm.

147 *R. (on the application of Luke Kenny)* v. *Leeds Magistrates Court*, [2003] EWHC 2963 (Admin).

148 Crime and Disorder Act 1998, ss 1(4), (6).

149 'Young thug barred from Manchester', *Manchester Evening News*, 22 January 2004.

150 N. Fielding, 'British animal rights activists spread violence on Continent', *Sunday Times*, 2 October 2005.

151 *R* v. *Braxton (Curtis)*, [2003] EWCA Crim 1037.

152 *Samuda* v. *Director of Public Prosecutions*, [2008] EWHC 205 (Admin).

153 I. Mason, 'Asbo boy, 13, banned from Feltham town centre', *Richmond and Twickenham Times*, 8 January 2010; E. Saunt, 'Feltham ASBO yob banned from town centre', *Hounslow, Heston & Whitton Chronicle*, 6 January 2010.

two years.[154] By the end of 2013, a total of 24,427 ASBOs had been issued in England and Wales, although it is not clear how many of these included prohibitions on accessing parts of public space.[155] The ASBO regime was complemented by a blanket dispersal power under the Anti-social Behaviour Act 2003. Section 30 of this Act allowed the police to disperse groups of two or more persons if 'any members of the public have been intimidated, harassed, alarmed or distressed as a result of [their] presence [. . .] in public places'.[156]

In order to 'streamline the toolkit available to tackle anti-social behaviour',[157] the Anti-social Behaviour, Crime and Policing Act was passed in 2014, replacing the previous ASBO with the Injunction to Prevent Nuisance and Annoyance (IPNA) and the Criminal Behaviour Order (CBO). An IPNA can be granted by the High Court or the County Court upon application from the police, a local council or another government agency against anyone who has engaged or threatens to engage in anti-social behaviour, provided the court considers making such an injunction 'just and convenient'.[158] The definition of 'anti-social behaviour' is based on that of the Crime and Disorder Act 1998, although extending it in some respects.[159] An IPNA may prohibit the person concerned from doing anything described in the injunction, which may include accessing certain public places.[160] Breach of an IPNA is dealt with by a civil contempt of court, which is punishable by up to two years in prison and/or an unlimited fine.[161] A prohibition on accessing parts of public space can also be imposed as part of a CBO, which may be made by the convicting court against an offender if it considers that this will help prevent the offender from engaging in anti-social behaviour.[162] The Anti-social Behaviour, Crime and Policing Act 2014 has also reformed the dispersal power of the police, which can now be employed not only against groups of persons but also against individuals. Provided

[154] *R. v. Lamb (Christopher)*, [2005] EWCA Crim 3000.

[155] Home Office, Anti-Social Behaviour Order Statistics – England and Wales 2013, 18 September 2014, available at www.gov.uk/government/statistics/anti-social-behaviour-order-statistics-england-and-wales-2013.

[156] Anti-social Behaviour Act 2003, s. 30(1).

[157] Home Office, Putting Victims First: More Effective Responses to Anti-social Behaviour, May 2012, Cm 8367, p. 55.

[158] Anti-social Behaviour, Crime and Policing Act 2014, s. 1.

[159] Ibid., s. 2(1).

[160] Ibid., s. 1(4)(a).

[161] Home Office, Anti-social Behaviour, Crime and Policing Act 2014: Reform of Anti-social Behaviour Powers: Statutory Guidance for Frontline Professionals, July 2014, p. 26.

[162] Anti-social Behaviour, Crime and Policing Act 2014, s. 22.

use of this power is authorised by a police officer of at least the rank of inspector,[163] a constable in uniform may direct a person to leave a public place and not to return to it for an 'exclusion period' of up to forty-eight hours if the behaviour of that person has contributed or is likely to contribute to members of the public being harassed, alarmed or distressed.[164] Finally, the Act has given local authorities the power to make a Public Spaces Protection Order (PSPO) if activities in a public place have had, or are likely to have, a detrimental effect on the quality of life of those in the locality.[165] A PSPO may apply to all persons or certain categories of persons[166] and may be used to restrict access to parts of public space.[167] As breach of a CBO[168] or a dispersal order,[169] breach of a PSPO constitutes a criminal offence.[170] The new power to make PSPOs has already been employed by several local councils, including to prohibit behaviours such as sleeping in certain public places[171] and to prevent persons under the age of twenty-one from entering a Council estate.[172]

In Switzerland, paralleling a similar development in Germany since the 1990s,[173] several cantons have adopted new police acts in the last few years that give the police the power to remove (*wegweisen*) and keep away (*fernhalten*) from public places anyone who threatens or disturbs public safety and order and, in the case of some of the acts, anyone who harasses others or impedes them from using public space.[174] As explained in Section 3.1, originally, the police only had the power to exclude people for a short period from a specific public place for their own protection or to deal with an immediate threat, for example because people were obstructing emergency services or the police in the execution of their duties. A police power that is applicable whenever public safety and order

[163] Ibid., s. 34. [164] Ibid. s. 35. [165] Ibid., s. 59. [166] Ibid., s. 59(6)(a).

[167] Ibid., ss 59(4), 64–5. [168] Ibid., s. 30. [169] Ibid., s. 39. [170] Ibid., ss 67–8.

[171] H. Osborne, 'Charities Warn Councils against Criminalising Rough Sleepers', *The Guardian*, 22 May 2015. Following protest, Hackney Council later amended the PSPO: Hackney Council, Public Spaces Protection (Amendment) Order 2015 No.1, 5 June 2015, available at www.hackney.gov.uk/safer-communities-crime-community-safety.htm#.Vin8nGtJ2gg.

[172] Oxford City Council, Foresters Tower PSPO, 20 February 2015, available at www.oxford.gov.uk/PageRender/decC/PublicSpacesProtectionOrders.htm.

[173] Rachor, 'Polizeihandeln' (2012), 432–3; Schucht, *Generalklausel und Standardmassnahme* (2010), pp. 171–80; Finger, *Die offenen Szenen der Städte* (2006), pp. 114–17.

[174] Moeckli/Keller, 'Wegweisungen und Rayonverbote' (2012), 232–6; Trochsler-Hugentobler/Lobsiger, 'Polizeiliche Befugnisse und Handlungsformen' (2008), 312–13; Sauer, *Das Recht der Vollzugspolizeien von Bund und Kantonen in der Schweiz* (2007), pp. 293–307.

is threatened or disturbed and that is, accordingly, also much wider in its geographical and temporal scope was first introduced at the federal level in 1994. The then-Federal Act on the Sojourn and Residence of Foreign Nationals provided that all foreign nationals without leave to stay who threaten or disturb public safety and order may be ordered not to access (or leave) a specified area.[175] Such areas were intended to cover not only specific neighbourhoods but entire towns or even regions.[176] An upper time limit was not defined in the Act. Today, the provision authorising the exclusion of foreign nationals is found in the Federal Act on Foreign Nationals.[177] Until 2002, roughly 1,000 such exclusion orders were issued in Switzerland on average per year.[178] This number is, however, significantly on the rise now.[179] In the Canton of Zurich, for example, fifty-six exclusion orders were imposed in 2011, 286 in 2012 and 378 in the first five months of 2013.[180] In this canton alone, 554 orders were issued in the period from June 2012 until May 2013.[181]

The first canton to introduce a similar blanket exclusion norm that can be used to deal with a wide range of behaviours, but is not limited to foreign nationals, was the Canton of Berne. Article 29(1)(b) of the Police Act of the Canton of Berne, adopted in 1997, gives the police the power to remove and keep away from public places anyone 'for whom there is reasonable suspicion that they, or others who form part of the same assembly, pose a danger to or disturb public safety and order'.[182] The primary legislative intent underlying Article 29(1)(b) was to give the police a tool to deal with 'scenes' of drug and alcohol addicts, which were said to cause a great deal of littering and noise and to affect passers-by,

[175] Bundesgesetz über Aufenthalt und Niederlassung der Ausländer (ANAG) vom 26. März 1931, Art. 13e(1)(a), eingefügt durch das Bundesgesetz über Zwangsmassnahmen im Ausländerrecht vom 18. März 1994, AS 1995 146.

[176] Botschaft zum Bundesgesetz über Zwangsmassnahmen im Ausländerrecht, BBl 1994 I, 305, p. 317.

[177] AuG, Art. 74(1)(a).

[178] Botschaft zum Bundesgesetz über die Ausländerinnen und Ausländer vom 8. März 2002, BBl 2002, 3709, p. 3767.

[179] Widmer, 'Vereinbarkeit besonderer Zentren für renitente Asylbewerber mit der Bewegungsfreiheit und den Garantien beim Freiheitsentzug' (2013), 21.

[180] F. Baumgartner, '554 Rayonverbote gegen straffällige Asylsuchende in Zürich', *Neue Zürcher Zeitung*, 9 June 2013.

[181] Ibid.

[182] Polizeigesetz vom 8. Juni 1997 (BSG 551.1), Art. 29(1)(b) ('Die Kantonspolizei kann Personen von einem Ort vorübergehend wegweisen oder fern halten, wenn [. . .] der begründete Verdacht besteht, dass sie oder andere, die der gleichen Ansammlung zuzurechnen sind, die öffentliche Sicherheit und Ordnung gefährden oder stören.').

as well as the presence of other marginalised groups in inner-city areas.[183] Once this provision had been applied in practice for a few years, it began to serve as a model for the creation of similar police powers directed against anti-social behaviour in numerous further cantons as well as several municipalities. The Canton of Grisons introduced a similar provision into its Police Act in 2001,[184] followed by numerous other cantons, mainly (but not exclusively) from the German-speaking region, including Schaffhausen (2002),[185] Thurgau (2004),[186] Aargau (2005),[187] Zurich (2007),[188] Glarus (2007),[189] Solothurn (2007),[190] Schwyz (2007),[191] Lucerne (2008),[192] St. Gallen (2008),[193] Uri (2008),[194] Geneva (2009),[195] Appenzell Ausserrhoden (2009),[196] Obwalden (2010),[197] Fribourg (2010)[198] and Neuchâtel (2014).[199] Most of these more recent provisions define the respective police powers more narrowly than that contained in the Police Act of the Canton of Berne, in that they set an explicit time limit

[183] For a summary of the parliamentary debate, see BVR 2005, 97, pp. 106–8 (Verwaltungsgericht des Kantons Bern).

[184] The relevant provision was originally contained in Verordnung über die Kantonspolizei (BR 613.100), Art. 8a (geändert am 28. November 2001). Today a virtually identical provision is found in Polizeigesetz des Kantons Graubünden vom 20. Oktober 2004 (PolG, BR 613.000), Art. 12.

[185] Polizeiverordnung vom 22. Oktober 2002 (SHR 354.111), § 31.

[186] Dienstreglement der Kantonspolizei Thurgau vom 25. Mai 2004 (RB 551.21), § 52. Today the respective provisions are found in the new police act: Polizeigesetz vom 9. November 2011 (RB 551.1), §§ 44–5.

[187] Gesetz über die Gewährleistung der öffentlichen Sicherheit (Polizeigesetz) vom 6. Dezember 2005 (SAR 531.200), § 34(1)(a).

[188] Polizeigesetz vom 23. April 2007 (PolG, LS 550.1), §§ 33(a)–(b), 34.

[189] Polizeigesetz des Kantons Glarus vom 6. Mai 2007 (GS V A/11/1), Art. 15(a)–(b).

[190] Gesetz über die Kantonspolizei vom 23. September 1990 (BGS 511.11), § 37(1)(d), (2)–(3) (geändert am 15. Mai 2007).

[191] Verordnung über die Kantonspolizei (Polizeiverordnung) vom 22. März 2000 (SRSZ 520.110), § 19(c)–(d) (geändert am 28. Juni 2007).

[192] Gesetz über die Luzerner Polizei vom 27. Januar 1998 (SRL 350), § 19(1)(a)–(b), (2)–(4) (geändert am 28. April 2008).

[193] Polizeigesetz vom 10. April 1980 (sGS 451.1), Arts 29(1)(d), 29bis–29ter (eingefügt am 18. September 2008).

[194] Polizeigesetz vom 30. November 2008 (PolG, RB 3.8111), Art. 22.

[195] Loi sur la police du 26 octobre 1957 (LPol, RSG F 1 05), Arts 22A(a)–(b), 22B–22C (adopté le 19 février 2009).

[196] Polizeigesetz vom 13. Mai 2002 (bGS 521.1), Arts 22(1)(d), 22a–22b (eingefügt am 14. September 2009).

[197] Polizeigesetz vom 11. März 2010 (GDB 510.1), Art. 18(1)(b)–(c), (3)–(4).

[198] Loi du 15 novembre 1990 sur la Police cantonale (SGF 551.1), Art. 31d (adopté le 31 mai 2010).

[199] Loi sur la police du 4 novembre 2014 (LPol), Art. 62.

on the duration of exclusion orders. Several municipalities, such as the towns of Winterthur (2004)[200] and Chur (2008),[201] have adopted similar provisions in recent years. Finally, within their specific competencies, the military police and the traffic police also have such blanket exclusion powers at their disposal.[202]

The City of Berne has had a pioneering role in the development of blanket exclusion powers, so that its policy of employing such powers to deal with anti-social behaviour may serve as an illustrative example of how they are implemented in practice. The police have divided the inner-city area of Berne into five 'perimeters' from which people can be excluded.[203] All of these 'perimeters' are areas that are important to the image of Berne as a commercial centre with a high quality of life, but where drug and alcohol addicts and homeless people have tended to congregate.[204] Police officers have been issued with a leaflet that explains the various requirements that must be met so that they can impose an exclusion order under Article 29(1)(b) of the Police Act of the Canton of Berne.[205] Among other things, the leaflet contains a list of behaviours that are said to be sufficient for demonstrating that the person concerned poses a danger to, or disturbs, public safety and order. These behaviours include, for example, consumption of drugs, excessive consumption of alcohol, rude behaviour, littering in public places and harassment of others.[206] If a police officer thinks that the requirements are satisfied, he or she will issue an exclusion order by filling in on a form the personal details of the person concerned, an explanation of the facts justifying the exclusion and an indication of the prohibited 'perimeter'.[207] The form provides for a standard duration of the exclusion measure of three months and includes a map of the banned area. The form also informs the person concerned that the exclusion order is issued under threat of a criminal penalty according to Article 292 of the Swiss Criminal Code in case of non-compliance, meaning that its breach amounts to a criminal offence punishable with a fine, which in case of non-payment can be

200 Allgemeine Polizeiverordnung der Stadt Winterthur vom 26. April 2004, Art. 16.

201 Polizeigesetz der Stadt Chur vom 24. Februar 2008 (PG, 411), Art. 13.

202 Bundesgesetz über die Armee und die Militärverwaltung vom 3. Februar 1995 (Militärgesetz, SR 510.10) (Military Act) (MG), Art. 92(2)(a); Bundesgesetz über die Sicherheitsorgane der Transportunternehmen im öffentlichen Verkehr vom 18. Juni 2010 (SR 745.2) (Federal Act on the Security Units of Public Transport Companies) (BGST), Art. 4(1)(b).

203 Gasser, *Kriminalpolitik oder City-Pflege?* (2004), pp. 30, 46–8. 204 Ibid., pp. 44–63.

205 Ibid., pp. 37–44. 206 The leaflet is reproduced in ibid., pp. 102–3.

207 The form is reproduced in ibid., pp. 104–5.

transformed into a prison sentence.[208] A majority of those subject to exclusion orders do not comply with them. As they are regularly not in a position to pay the resulting fines, exclusion orders often eventually result in prison terms.[209]

Widely defined exclusion powers such as the one contained in the Police Act of the Canton of Berne have over the last few years become the main legal tool for the police to clear away 'scenes' of drug and alcohol addicts as well as, increasingly, other marginalised groups such as juveniles or beggars.[210] In the City of Berne, over the last ten years, between about 400 and 700 exclusion orders were issued by the police per year.[211] In the largest Swiss city, the City of Zurich, where exclusion orders started to be used with the entering into force of the new Police Act of the Canton of Zurich in 2009, 1,703 such orders were imposed in 2010, 5,770 in 2011 and 5,232 in 2012, which equals roughly fifteen exclusion orders per day.[212] Exclusion orders have been imposed on people simply for drinking alcohol in public parks.[213] Following some criticism, the annual number went down to 2,572 in 2013.[214] In the City of St. Gallen, a town with a population of around 73,000 without any large 'drug scene', the number of exclusion orders constantly rose from 54 in 2006 to 961 in 2011.[215] Since then, this number has decreased again, with 819 orders issued in 2012 and 438 in 2013.[216] Variations between the different cantons and municipalities are, however, considerable. In the Canton

[208] StGB, Art. 36. [209] Gasser, *Kriminalpolitik oder City-Pflege?* (2004), p. 33.

[210] See Litscher/Grossrieder/Mösch-Payot/Schmutz, *Wegweisung aus öffentlichen Stadträumen* (2011).

[211] Antwort des Gemeinderats auf die Interpellation Fraktion GB/JA!: Sisyphus-Wegweisungen: Wie viel kosten sie die Stadt?, 06.000044, 26 January 2006; Litscher/Grossrieder/Mösch-Payot/Schmutz, *Wegweisung aus öffentlichen Stadträumen* (2011), p. 78; Lorenz, 'Der Wegweisungsartikel im Sicherheitsdiskurs der Stadt Bern' (2011), 18.

[212] Stadt Zürich, Polizeidepartement, 'Medienmitteilung: Erste Erfahrungen mit Wegweisungen in der Stadt Zürich', 20 March 2013, available at www.stadt-zuerich.ch/content/pd/de/index/das_departement/medien/medienmitteilung/2013/maerz/130320a.html; M. Tribelhorn, '15 Wegweisungen pro Tag in der Stadt Zürich', *Neue Zürcher Zeitung*, 21 March 2013.

[213] L.-C. Vaudan, 'Wer Bier mitbringt, muss gehen', *Tages-Anzeiger*, 22 June 2012.

[214] Stadt Zürich, *Geschäftsbericht 2013* (April 2014), p. 102.

[215] Stadtpolizei St. Gallen, 'Medienmitteilung: Wegweisungen und Fernhaltungen 2011', 29 February 2012, available at www.stadt.sg.ch/content/applikationen/news/13/2012/02/29_februar_2012.html; Litscher/Grossrieder/Mösch-Payot/Schmutz, *Wegweisung aus öffentlichen Stadträumen* (2011), p. 79.

[216] Stadtpolizei St. Gallen, 'Medienmitteilung: Wegweisungen und Fernhaltungen 2013', 17 February 2014, available at www.stadt.sg.ch/news/13/2014/02/wegweisungen-und-fernhaltungen-2013-in-der-stadt-st-gallen.html.

of Lucerne, for example, the number of exclusion orders is – or at least used to be – significantly lower. In 2009, only twenty persons were subject to such an order, even though the City of Lucerne is a town of a similar size as St. Gallen. By 2012, however, this number had risen to 415.[217]

The Canton of Basel-Stadt amended its Police Act in 2008 by adding a norm that is atypical, in that it defines the targets of exclusion much more narrowly than the police acts referred to above. Instead of referring to the vague concept of public safety and order, the relevant provision only allows the police to remove a person from a specified public place if that person endangers or seriously threatens third persons or, through his or her behaviour, creates an immediate threat of a violent conflict.[218] The Police Act of the Canton of Zug, amended in 2011, now contains a similarly narrowly defined exclusion power, requiring a serious and immediate threat to public safety and order.[219]

3.3.3 *Political protest*

Mainly because of public safety and order concerns, states have, from very early on, tried to regulate the use of public ground for public assemblies, pickets, demonstrations, processions, parades and other forms of political protest. The traditional approach to such regulation has been not to completely prohibit the use of public ground for political protest but to impose permit or advance notice requirements. All three jurisdictions under consideration know such requirements. In Switzerland and the United States, where these matters are regulated mainly at the local level, most relevant laws require those organising a demonstration on public ground to apply for a written permit.[220] For spontaneous demonstrations it is generally sufficient to give advance notice.[221] In the United Kingdom,

[217] A. von Däniken, 'Noch nie so viele Personen weggewiesen', *Neue Luzerner Zeitung*, 12 January 2013.

[218] Gesetz betreffend die Kantonspolizei des Kantons Basel-Stadt vom 13. November 1996 (Polizeigesetz, PolG, SG 510.100), § 42a (eingefügt am 15. Oktober 2008).

[219] Polizeigesetz vom 30. November 2006 (BGS 512.1), § 16(1)(b) (geändert am 29. September 2011).

[220] For Switzerland, see for the City of Berne: Reglement der Stadt Bern über Kundgebungen auf öffentlichem Grund vom 20. Oktober 2005 (Kundgebungsreglement; KgR; SSSB 143.1), Art. 2; for the City of Zurich: Verordnung der Stadt Zürich über die Benutzung des öffentlichen Grundes vom 23. November 2011 (Benutzungsordnung, AS 551.210), Arts 2 and 21–2. See generally Gander, 'Sicherheit und Demonstrationen' (2008). For the United States, see e.g. New York City Administrative Code, § 10–110.

[221] See e.g. Reglement der Stadt Bern über Kundgebungen auf öffentlichem Grund vom 20. Oktober 2005 (Kundgebungsreglement; KgR; SSSB 143.1), Art. 2. In contrast, the law

advance notice must be given to the police for public processions, while for public assemblies there has generally been no permit or advance notice requirement.[222] As in Switzerland and the United States, the police can, however, impose certain conditions on public processions as well as assemblies[223] or prohibit public processions and 'trespassory assemblies' altogether.[224]

In recent years, state authorities have increasingly shifted their focus in controlling political protest from *what* is said to *where* it is said.[225] As a consequence, the general rule that all public places are open and accessible for protest activities has started to erode.

3.3.3.1 Creation of permanent protest-free zones

This has happened, first of all, through the introduction of laws that establish special rules for certain parts of public space, imposing additional restrictions or even complete bans on political protest for these special zones. The idea of such special zones (referred to as *Bannmeilen* or *befriedete Bezirke* in German terminology)[226] originates from Germany, where, during the Weimar Republic, a complete ban on demonstrations in front of the Reichstag was seen as the only way of dealing with the violent political clashes of the time.[227] Special zones have been created in all three states at issue.

In the Swiss capital of Berne, the ordinance regulating manifestations of 2006 provides that on the Bundesplatz (the public square in front of the parliament building) manifestations are only permitted in exceptional cases on days when parliament is sitting,[228] thus turning the usual authorisation requirement into an effective prohibition during parliamentary sessions (that is, about twelve weeks a year). General bans on political manifestations also apply, for example, to the square

regulating demonstrations of the Canton of Geneva requires a prior authorisation for any kind of demonstrations, including spontaneous ones. Loi sur les manifestations sur le domaine public du 26 juin 2008 (LMDPu, RSG F 3 10), Art. 3.

222 Public Order Act 1986, s. 11. 223 Ibid., ss 12, 14. 224 Ibid., ss 13, 14A.

225 See Mitchell, 'The Liberalization of Free Speech' (2003).

226 Richter, ' "Befriedete Bezirke" ' (2002); Breitbach, 'Für die Abschaffung der Bannmeile' (1998).

227 Gesetz über die Befriedung der Gebäude des Reichstags und der Landtage vom 8. Mai 1920. For today's regulation, see Gesetz über Versammlungen und Aufzüge vom 24. Juli 1953, § 16(1); Gesetz über befriedete Bezirke für Verfassungsorgane des Bundes vom 11. August 1999.

228 Reglement der Stadt Bern über Kundgebungen auf öffentlichem Grund vom 20. Oktober 2005 (Kundgebungsreglement; KgR; SSSB 143.1), Art. 6.

in front of the monastery of Einsiedeln[229] and the Landsgemeindeplatz in Zug.[230] On the Rütli, a publicly accessible meadow above Lake Lucerne, where the legendary Rütli oath, a defining moment in the founding of the Swiss Confederation, is said to have taken place, gatherings of more than fifty persons are subject to permission, which must be applied for several months in advance.[231] According to the constant and consistent practice of the public authority in charge, assemblies for political purposes are denied permission.[232]

In the United Kingdom, the SOCPA 2005 criminalised protest without prior authorisation in the vicinity of parliament. Any form of protest within a zone of up to one kilometre from Parliament Square, regardless of the number of participants, had to be authorised by the Commissioner of the Metropolitan Police.[233] The Police Reform and Social Responsibility Act 2011 repealed this ban and replaced it with limitations on the means of protest permitted in Parliament Square.[234] As a reaction to protests by animal rights activists, the United Kingdom has also imposed restrictions on demonstrations outside the houses of employees of relevant companies. The police have been given the power to direct protesters to 'leave the vicinity of the premises' if this is necessary to prevent harassment, alarm or distress to the resident.[235]

In the United States, several state and local legislatures have passed laws that prohibit protests outside abortion clinics. Massachusetts, for example, introduced a prohibition on entering any area 'within a radius of thirty-five feet of any portion of an entrance to, exit from, or driveway of a reproductive health care facility'.[236] Other states, as well as municipalities, have adopted laws that combine such 'fixed buffer zones' around clinics with 'floating buffer zones' or 'bubbles' around clinic employees. The relevant statute of the state of Colorado, for example, provides that '[n]o person shall knowingly approach another person within eight feet of such person, unless such other person consents, for the purpose of passing a leaflet or handbill to, displaying a sign to, or engaging in oral

[229] See BGE 124 I 267 (1998). [230] See BGE 100 Ia 392, 403 (1974).

[231] Schweizerische Gemeinnützige Gesellschaft, Benutzungsordnung: Reglement für die Nutzung der Anlage Rütli, Seelisberg, Kt. Uri, Art. 10, available at www.sgg-ssup.ch/sites/default/files/attachments/Benutzungsordnung.pdf.

[232] See 'Bundesrat will auf dem Rütli politische Versammlungen zulassen', *Neue Zürcher Zeitung*, 30 May 2012.

[233] SOCPA 2005, ss 132–8 (repealed).

[234] Police Reform and Social Responsibility Act 2011, ss 142–9.

[235] Criminal Justice and Police Act 2001, s. 42.

[236] Massachusetts General Laws, Chapter 266, s. 120E1/2 (repealed).

protest, education, or counseling with such other person in the public way or sidewalk area within a radius of one hundred feet from any entrance door to a health care facility'.[237]

3.3.3.2 New police strategies

In addition to the creation of permanent special zones where protest is severely restricted or even completely prohibited, recent years have witnessed a shift in strategy in the policing of protest from controlling and managing demonstrations towards denying demonstrators access to potential sites of protest.

In Switzerland, the new blanket police powers to remove and keep away persons who threaten or disturb public safety and order have been designed, and used, for exactly this purpose, among others. The revision of the relevant Police Act of the Canton of Grisons, for example, was justified by the government on the basis that there was a need for new legal tools, including powers to keep away people from certain parts of public space, to police large-scale events such as the annual WEF meeting in Davos or the skiing world championships.[238] As explained in Chapter 1, in the context of the WEF meeting it has been the general practice of the cantonal police of Grisons to establish checkpoints on the road and train line leading to the mountain resort of Davos and to turn back potential protesters.[239] Similarly, in the City of Zurich the police have repeatedly used the exclusion power contained in the cantonal Police Act to remove potentially violent protesters as well as bystanders during the May Day demonstrations.[240] On May Day 2011, 468 persons were issued with an exclusion order, banning them from accessing part of the city centre.[241] The police of the Canton of Schwyz regularly keep away potential demonstrators on 1 August, the Swiss national holiday, from the Rütli, the site where the official celebration takes place.[242] In Berne, the police have used their exclusion power to order thirty-seven individuals to keep away from the city centre for the duration of a political event organised by the Swiss People's Party.[243]

[237] Colorado Revised Statutes, § 18-9-122.

[238] Botschaften der Regierung an den Grossen Rat, Heft Nr. 7/2001–2002, p. 421.

[239] See BGE 130 I 369, 370–71 (2004); BGE 128 I 167, 168 (2002).

[240] Ch. Landolt, 'Der Gaffer ist der Komplize des Chaoten', *Tages-Anzeiger*, 29 April 2011.

[241] Urteile des Bundesgerichts 1C_350/2013, 1C_352/2013, 1C_354/2013 vom 22. Januar 2014, E. 2.2.

[242] See Entscheide 2007 der Gerichts- und Verwaltungsbehörden (EGV-SZ 2007), C.17.1, 206–22 (Regierungsrat Schwyz).

[243] M. Dütschler, 'Polizei hat Politiker unbegründet weggewiesen', *Der Bund*, 9 November 2011.

In the United Kingdom, the police have used similar tactics by invoking their common-law power to prevent a breach of the peace. For example, relying on this power, they intercepted and turned back coaches with demonstrators to prevent them from reaching their intended site of protest at a US air base in Gloucestershire.[244] In addition, as mentioned in Section 3.3.2.4, the police have repeatedly used ASBOs to keep (potential) protesters away from (potential) sites of protest.[245] Ahead of the Olympic Games 2012 in London, for example, several persons were served with ASBOs banning them from approaching any Olympic venue.[246] Thus, one individual was prohibited 'from going within 100 yards of any Olympic-related venue, route or the home of participants, officials or spectators, or approaching any road where the Olympic torch will pass that day'.[247]

In the United States, the police use similar strategies to control demonstrations. For the 2000 Democratic National Convention in the Staples Center in Los Angeles, for example, the Los Angeles Police Department (LAPD) designated a 'secured zone' of more than eight million square feet around the centre that was not accessible to the public. Some 260 yards from the entrance to the Staples Center, a small 'Official Demonstration Site' was established for use during the convention.[248] At the occasion of the 1999 WTO conference in Seattle, the mayor of Seattle even turned a large section of the downtown area into a 'no-protest zone' by imposing a curfew in that portion of the city.[249] The temporary establishment of such zones, to which only participants of the relevant event have access, has become a blueprint for dealing with protests against major international conferences.[250] As a geographically more limited measure, during the Occupy Wall Street protests of 2011 and 2012 in New York City, the police repeatedly 'closed' certain sidewalks and parks that are normally open to the public, without explaining what the legal basis for doing so was.[251]

244 *R (Laporte)* v. *Chief Constable of Gloucestershire Constabulary*, [2006] UKHL 55.

245 See e.g. *R.* v. *Jones*, [2006] EWCA Crim 2942.

246 M. Townsend, 'Olympic Games 2012: police plan pre-emptive arrests to stop disruption', *The Guardian*, 2 June 2012.

247 P. Walker, 'Protester receives Olympics asbo', *The Guardian*, 17 April 2012.

248 See *Service Employee International Union v. City of Los Angeles*, 114 F.Supp.2d 966 (C.D. Cal. 2000).

249 See *Menotti* v. *City of Seattle*, 409 F.3d 1113 (9th Cir. 2005).

250 Richter, ' "Befriedete Bezirke" ' (2002), 929–30.

251 Global Justice Clinic (NYU School of Law) and Walter Leitner International Human Rights Clinic at the Leitner Center for International Law and Justice (Fordham Law School), 'Suppressing Protest' (2012), 113–18.

Another common (and very recent) police strategy, known as 'kettling', is to contain demonstrators, often for several hours, within a small cordoned-off area and to thus deny them access to other potential sites of protest. 'Kettling' has been used repeatedly to control demonstrations in London, including during May Day, G20 and student protests.[252] Police forces in Switzerland have deployed the same practices against demonstrators during the WEF[253] and on May Day[254] (as well as against football supporters).[255] In the United States, the NYPD and other police forces used 'kettling' practices on several occasions in the context of the Occupy Wall Street protests in 2011 and 2012.[256]

3.4 A typology of exclusion measures

With so many new laws providing for exclusion from public space, it is important to be clear about the way they operate and about what exactly they involve. This section provides a typology of the different ways in which people are excluded from public space in the United Kingdom, the United States and Switzerland. Apart from the targeted behaviour (dealt with in the previous section), the main characteristics according to which exclusion measures can be categorised include the (legal) mode of exclusion they employ, the type of behaviour they prevent, their geographical scope and their temporal scope. Annex II provides an overview of that categorisation in the form of a table.

[252] See *Austin* v. *Commissioner for the Metropolis*, [2009] UKHL 5; *Austin and others* v. *The United Kingdom* [GC], nos 39692/09; 40713/09; 41008/09, 15 March 2012, ECHR 2012; Joint Committee on Human Rights, *Demonstrating Respect for Rights? Follow-up*, 28 July 2009, HL 141, HC 522; P. Walker and A. Gabbatt, 'Student protesters announce more marches and walkouts over tuition fees', *The Guardian*, 25 November 2010.

[253] On the 'Kessel von Landquart', see Entscheid der Beschwerdekammer des Kantonsgerichts von Graubünden BK 05 62 vom 16. November 2005.

[254] See Urteile des Bundesgerichts 1C_350/2013, 1C_352/2013, 1C_354/2013 vom 22. Januar 2014.

[255] On the 'Kessel von Altstetten', see ZR 107/2008 Nr. 75, 257 (Zürich, Obergericht); 'Kritik am Polizeieinsatz gegen FCB-Fans', *Neue Zürcher Zeitung*, 7 December 2004; P. Loser, 'Über hundert Fans wollen klagen', *Basler Zeitung*, 8 December 2004.

[256] Global Justice Clinic (NYU School of Law) and Walter Leitner International Human Rights Clinic at the Leitner Center for International Law and Justice (Fordham Law School), 'Suppressing Protest' (2012), 110–13.

3.4.1 *Mode of exclusion*

There are different modes by which the state can exclude people from public space, ranging from informal means such as urban design to granting the police explicit exclusion powers. Typically, the state can achieve a particular objective through more than one mode of exclusion. For example, if the aim is to remove homeless people from a city centre, this can be achieved through urban design measures, a prohibition of specified behaviours (such as sleeping, sitting and lying on public sidewalks and streets), creation of powers of the police to remove and keep away certain persons, or a combination of these different measures. The means used to achieve a particular aim is not a 'natural' choice but a political decision involving consideration of a number of factors. A general trend that can be observed over the last few years is that, in particular in Switzerland and the United Kingdom, there has been a marked increase in police powers to exclude people from public space. These powers are often very broadly defined and far-reaching and thus place considerable discretion in the hands of law enforcement agencies. In the United States, the most common mode of exclusion is prohibition of certain forms of behaviour.

3.4.1.1 Informal exclusion: urban design

People can be excluded from public space through manipulations of the urban environment that make it impossible, or at least more difficult, for them to access, or remain in, certain places. To some extent, such manipulations are part of a wider trend in modern urban planning to design public space as an area to *move through* rather than *be in.*[257] Some of these manipulations, however, are also specifically designed as 'situational crime prevention' measures. While 'situational crime prevention' has come to signify different things, in its broad meaning it refers to 'any attempt to manipulate the environment to reduce opportunities for crime',[258] encompassing measures such as strengthened coin boxes, fencing around car parks, improved street lighting, CCTV systems and so on. Such measures are not exclusively directed against behaviour that constitutes a criminal offence but are often also employed to prevent

[257] Sennett, *The Fall of Public Man* (1992), pp. 12–16. See also Bauman, *Liquid Modernity* (2000), pp. 96–8.

[258] Clarke, 'Situational Prevention, Criminology, and Social Values' (2000), 99. See also Clarke, 'Situational Crime Prevention' (1995), 91; Clarke, 'Situational Crime Prevention: Its Theoretical Basis and Practical Scope' (1983), 225.

various forms of anti-social behaviour such as sleeping in parks, sitting on pavements or drinking alcohol in public. Situational prevention that is designed to exclude people from certain public places – or at least to deter them from being there – includes, for example, locking the gates of public parks, installation of outdoor sprinklers and 'anti-homeless spikes', making benches and seats at bus stops and in parks as uncomfortable as possible, as well as removing bus shelters, public toilets and water fountains.[259] Such 'deterrence by design' may be used to enforce the formal exclusion measures described below. But often it is used irrespective of any formally adopted exclusion measures, raising the question as to the legitimacy of (and the need for a legal basis for) such informal state action.

3.4.1.2 Prohibitions

A more formal way of excluding people from public space is for the legislator to either prohibit certain categories of people from being in public space at all, regardless of their behaviour, or prohibit certain forms of behaviour in public places. With this mode of exclusion, the addressee of the respective legal norm is the individual. Individuals are bound by the prohibition, without there being a need for further specification of the obligation in an order or, in Swiss legal terminology, a *Verfügung/décision*.[260] If an individual breaches the prohibition, the authority of law enforcement agencies to intervene and enforce the prohibition, including by removing or arresting the offender, is triggered. The power to enforce the prohibition may be backed up by repressive sanctions. These may be very harsh. In the US state of Georgia, for example, all registered sex offenders are prohibited from loitering within 1,000 feet of any child care facility, church, school or area where minors congregate; those who violate the prohibition can be punished by imprisonment for between ten and thirty years.[261]

Typical examples of measures that prohibit the *mere presence* of certain categories of people in all, or certain, public places are the child and juvenile curfew laws that have been adopted in recent years. In the case of the juvenile curfews imposed in some Swiss municipalities, there is still

[259] Wehrheim, *Die überwachte Stadt* (2012), pp. 118–19; Matthews, 'Developing More Effective Strategies for Curbing Prostitution' (1990); Davis, *City of Quartz* (1990), pp. 233–5.

[260] Häfelin/Müller/Uhlmann, *Allgemeines Verwaltungsrecht* (2010), p. 193; Tanquerel, *Manuel de droit administratif* (2011), pp. 269–70.

[261] Code of Georgia, § 42-1-15(g).

a very tenuous link to behaviour, in that they 'only' prohibit juveniles from 'assembling' in public places at certain times.[262] The juvenile curfew laws adopted by most Swiss municipalities[263] and in major US cities,[264] however, have completely removed the link to behaviour: they prevent children and youths from simply being in public places at certain times, regardless of how they behave. These laws are, in other words, directed against the mere presence of children and youths in public space. Mere presence is also prohibited by, for example, the Cincinnati ordinance referred to in Chapter 1 that banned everyone previously arrested for drug offences from being in designated 'drug exclusion zones'[265] and a PSPO issued by the Oxford City Council that prevents persons under the age of twenty-one from entering a Council estate.[266]

Other measures exclude people from public space by prohibiting *specified forms of behaviour*. Examples include the bans on vagrancy, 'loitering' and sitting and lying on public sidewalks or streets as they exist in all three states under consideration.[267] These laws prohibit activities that are typical for certain groups of people and that are not normally regarded as criminal. The measures directed against protests in the vicinity of abortion clinics or in other parts of public space adopted in the United States also take the form of prohibitions.[268]

262 E.g. Polizeiverordnung der Gemeinde Dänikon vom 18. Juni 2008, Art. 27 (repealed; see Urteil des Verwaltungsgerichts des Kantons Zürich VB.2009.00055 vom 30. April 2009).

263 E.g. Polizeireglement der Stadt Gossau vom 4. November 2008 (18.01), Art. 19 (Nachtrag vom 6. Dezember 2011); Polizeireglement der Gemeinde Visp vom 27. Mai 2009, Art. 12; Polizeireglement der Gemeinden Bad Zurzach, Baldingen, Böbikon, Böttstein, Döttingen, Endingen, Fisibach, Full-Reuenthal, Kaiserstuhl, Klingnau, Koblenz, Leibstadt, Lengnau, Leuggern, Mandach, Mellikon, Rekingen, Rietheim, Rümikon, Schneisingen, Siglistorf, Tegerfelden, Unterendingen und Wislikofen vom 1. April 2008, § 25(2); Gemeindepolizeireglement der Gemeinde Interlaken vom 5. Dezember 2006 (552.11), Art. 9(4); Gemeindepolizeireglement der Gemeinde Urtenen-Schönbühl vom 15. Mai 2006, Art. 6.

264 E.g. Dallas, Texas Code of Ordinances, s. 31–33.

265 Cincinnati Municipal Code, § 755-5 (repealed).

266 Oxford City Council, Foresters Tower PSPO, 20 February 2015, available at www.oxford.gov.uk/PageRender/decC/PublicSpacesProtectionOrders.htm.

267 E.g. for Switzerland: Reglement der Stadt Bern betreffend die Benützung des städtischen Teils des Bahnhofs Bern (Bahnhofreglement; BHR), Art. 2. For the United Kingdom: Vagrancy Act 1824. For the United States: Dallas, Texas Code of Ordinances, s. 31–13; Code of the City of Phoenix, Arizona, s. 23–48.01; City of Orlando, Code of Ordinances, s. 43.88; Seattle Municipal Code, s. 15.48.040; Reno, Nevada, Municipal Code, s. 8.12.015.

268 Massachusetts General Laws, Chapter 266, s. 120E1/2 (repealed); Colorado Revised Statutes, § 18-9-122; *Service Employee International Union v. City of Los Angeles*, 114 F.Supp.2d 966 (C.D. Cal. 2000).

Of course, there are many legal norms that prohibit certain forms of behaviour in public space, violation of which may entail, at least indirectly, exclusion from public space. If someone kills another person on a public street, he or she may have to go to prison and will thus be prevented from accessing public space for some time. However, killing a human being is treated as a crime in all three states at issue and, indeed, in any legal system of the world.[269] The forms of behaviour referred to above (such as 'loitering' and sitting or lying on a public sidewalk), in contrast, are not normally characterised as crimes. Indeed, some of them, such as political protest, may even be regarded as desirable activities in a liberal democracy. Nor are these behaviours commercially motivated. Furthermore, some of the prohibited forms of behaviour (such as 'loitering' or sitting on a public street or pavement) are so broadly defined that they may prevent whole groups of people (for example, the homeless) from simply being present in public space. They serve to police the 'doing of nothing', the perceived harm said to result from the visible presence of certain groups in public.[270] Thus, in practice, such prohibitions of 'specified' behaviour may have the same effect as prohibitions of mere presence in public places. It would therefore be arbitrary not to deal with these measures for the purposes of the present study only because they are formulated as prohibitions of specified behaviour, rather than of mere presence, in public space.

3.4.1.3 Authorisation requirements

Instead of regulating the use of public space by prohibiting certain types of behaviour, the legislator may establish a system of preventive control by requiring people who wish to engage in a certain type of behaviour to apply for an authorisation or permit. It is then left to the executive branch, normally some local authority or the police, to decide in individual cases whether to allow the particular behaviour or not. Engaging in the behaviour without having been given authorisation will amount to an offence. There is, to put it the other way round, a general prohibition with the possibility of exceptions. The effect of this may be that people will refrain from making use of public places in the manner subject to authorisation.

A typical example of a form of use of public space that is commonly subject to authorisation is political protest. As explained in Section 3.3.3,

[269] Horder (ed.), *Homicide Law in Comparative Perspective* (2007).

[270] Levi, 'Making Counter-Law' (2009), 132.

there are in all three jurisdictions under consideration laws in force that require a permit or advance notice for certain forms of protest in public space. Authorisation requirements are normally justified on the basis that these forms of protest amount to what Swiss legal doctrine refers to as *gesteigerter Gemeingebrauch* ('increased common use'): they involve a more intense use of the respective public places than these were originally designed for and/or preclude others from using the public places for the intended purpose.[271]

3.4.1.4 Court powers

Instead of directly addressing itself to the individual, the legislator may also grant another branch of government the power to exclude people from public space. Although in recent years the trend has been towards granting more and more exclusion powers to the executive branch,[272] there are also some, mainly older, instances of *judicial* exclusion powers.

Thus, in the United Kingdom, convicting courts have the power to impose exclusion or curfew requirements on all types of criminal offenders;[273] in the United States, on sex offenders on probation.[274] In the United Kingdom, courts may also impose such requirements, for the time of the probationary period, when they sentence offenders to a suspended prison sentence.[275] In Switzerland, courts have the same power when they sentence criminal offenders to any kind of suspended sentence[276] and, in the case of sex offenders, regardless of whether the sentence is suspended or not.[277]

However, powers of courts to exclude people from public space are not limited to convicted offenders. As explained above, in the United Kingdom, the High Court, the County Court and magistrates' courts can also impose bans on accessing certain parts of public space as part of, for example, IPNAs and football banning orders, regardless of whether the persons concerned have been convicted of any offence.[278] Breach of an IPNA constitutes contempt of court, breach of a football banning

[271] See Section 2.4.1. [272] See Section 3.4.1.5.

[273] Powers of Criminal Courts (Sentencing) Act 2000, ss 37, 40A; Anti-social Behaviour, Crime and Policing Act 2014, s. 22.

[274] E.g. Code of Georgia, § 42-8-35. [275] Criminal Justice Act 2003, ss 190, 204, 205.

[276] StGB, Art. 44(2) in connection with Art. 94. [277] StGB, Art. 67b.

[278] Anti-social Behaviour, Crime and Policing Act 2014, s. 1; Football Spectators Act 1989 (as amended by the Football Disorder Act 2000), s. 14B in conjunction with s. 14G.

order a criminal offence.[279] In Switzerland, civil courts can issue orders prohibiting people from accessing parts of public space as far as this is necessary for the protection of third persons from violence, threats or harassment.[280]

3.4.1.5 Police powers

In recent years, it has been mainly the executive branch of government that has been granted new, and often very wide, powers to exclude people from public space. With this mode of exclusion, the addressees of the relevant legal norms are the police or other law enforcement authorities (such as immigration authorities or, in the United Kingdom, the Home Secretary). The legal basis for executive exclusion powers may be provided by either an explicit legal regulation or the general powers of the police to prevent a breach of the peace (corresponding to the concept of the *polizeiliche Generalklausel* in Switzerland). The distinction between these two legal bases is explored in more detail in Chapter 4 below.

Some of the explicit legal regulations authorising exclusion from public space have been adopted to deal with a limited set of problems and are, accordingly, quite specific as to the context in which law enforcement agencies are authorised to use the respective powers. Examples include the police powers adopted in Switzerland to deal with violence surrounding sports events,[281] the British TPIMs[282] or the Gang Congregation Ordinance of the City of Chicago.[283] On the other hand, there are norms that authorise the police to exclude persons from public space as part of their more general power (and duty) to protect public safety and order. Norms falling into this category tend to be much more broadly drafted. They include the dispersal powers under the British Anti-social Behaviour, Crime and Policing Act 2014, which can be used whenever members of the public feel harassed, alarmed or distressed,[284] and the police powers adopted by numerous Swiss cantons in the last few years to

279 Home Office, Anti-social Behaviour, Crime and Policing Act 2014: Reform of Anti-social Behaviour Powers: Statutory Guidance for Frontline Professionals, July 2014, p. 26; Football Spectators Act 1989 (as amended by the Football Disorder Act 2000), s. 14G.

280 ZGB, Art. 28b(1).

281 Konkordat über Massnahmen gegen Gewalt anlässlich von Sportveranstaltungen vom 15. November 2007. See e.g. for the Canton of Zurich: Gesetz über den Beitritt zum Konkordat über Massnahmen gegen Gewalt anlässlich von Sportveranstaltungen vom 18. Mai 2009 (LS 551.19).

282 Terrorism Prevention and Investigation Measures Act 2011, ss 2, 3(1).

283 Chicago Municipal Code, § 8-4-015.

284 Anti-social Behaviour, Crime and Policing Act 2014, s. 35.

remove and keep away from public places anyone who threatens or disturbs public safety and order.[285]

As will be explained in more detail in Section 4.2.3, in the absence of explicit exclusion powers, there may be the possibility for the executive branch to invoke other, more general powers to deal with exceptional situations. In Switzerland, the executive branch may, despite the lack of an explicit legal authority, take action based on the so-called *polizeiliche Generalklausel* (general police clause), if there is no other way of averting a serious and imminent danger to fundamental interests of the state or private actors. In the United Kingdom, the police may rely on their common-law power to prevent a breach of the peace. In the United States, there are in most states very broadly defined breach-of-the-peace or public-order statutes or emergency powers available that the police can invoke to justify exclusion measures.

As far as the enforcement of these different executive exclusion powers is concerned, one can distinguish between two approaches. In the case of short-term exclusion such as removals, dispersals or very short bans on access, law enforcement authorities will generally enforce their powers by simply asking people to leave and keep away and, if necessary, removing them by physical force. In the case of exclusion measures that prevent people from accessing certain public places for longer periods, it is common for law enforcement authorities to specify the terms of exclusion in a written order (*Verfügung/décision*). The Police Act of the Canton of Geneva, for example, explicitly provides that exclusion of up to twenty-four hours may be ordered orally, whereas for longer-term exclusion (of up to three months) the police must issue a written order.[286] As with prohibitions, authorisation requirements and judicial orders, breach of an executive order will generally constitute a criminal offence. In the United Kingdom, for example, breach of the terms of a TPIM is a criminal offence punishable by up to five years in prison.[287]

3.4.2 *Excluded behaviour*

Some of the exclusion measures described above prevent people from engaging in particular forms of behaviour in public space, others from simply being present in (certain) public places. The form of behaviour

285 E.g. for the Canton of Berne: Polizeigesetz vom 8. Juni 1997 (BSG 551.1), Art. 29(1)(b).

286 Loi sur la police du 26 octobre 1957 (LPol, RSG F 1 05), Art. 22B (adopté le 19 février 2009).

287 Terrorism Prevention and Investigation Measures Act 2011, s. 23.

that is excluded does not necessarily correspond to the targeted behaviour described in Section 3.3, but may be broader than that. For example, although the police powers under the Swiss Hooligan Concordat are designed to prevent violent behaviour in connection with sports events, those against whom these powers are used may be prevented not only from engaging in such behaviour in the specified area but from being present there at all. Whereas originally the focus of most exclusion measures had been on excluding quite clearly defined behaviour through criminal prohibitions, it is now increasingly on complete exclusion from (parts of) public space.

3.4.2.1 Exclusion of particular forms of behaviour

In the case of the traditional approach to exclusion from public space through criminalisation of particular forms of behaviour in public places (including vagrancy, 'loitering', sitting and lying on public sidewalks or streets etc.), the excluded behaviour corresponds to the targeted behaviour. Bans on lying on public sidewalks, for instance, target lying on public sidewalks and, accordingly, exclude all those who may want to do so. Police powers and court powers can also have the effect of only preventing people from engaging in certain specified behaviour. For instance, although the exclusion powers under the various Swiss cantonal police acts authorise complete exclusion, they can be (and have been) used not only to ban people from certain parts of public space completely, but also, in some cases, to prevent people from engaging in specified behaviour, such as 'assembling in groups that consume alcohol'.[288] Similarly, in the United Kingdom, an IPNA or a CBO may prohibit people from simply being present in certain places, but it may also instead impose a duty not to engage in certain behaviour.[289]

3.4.2.2 Complete exclusion

Some of the more recent exclusion measures in the form of prohibitions, foremost among them juvenile curfew laws, prevent certain categories of people from being in public space at all. The excluded behaviour corresponds to the targeted behaviour, which is in both cases the mere presence of children or juveniles in public places at certain times. However, also exclusion norms that are designed to prevent only a particular, specified behaviour may entail complete exclusion. TPIMs, for example,

[288] See e.g. BGE 132 I 49, 50 (2006).

[289] Anti-social Behaviour, Crime and Policing Act 2014, ss 1(4), 22(5).

are designed to prevent terrorist behaviour but may involve complete exclusion.[290] Similarly, even though the exclusion powers under the Swiss cantonal police acts are targeted against those who threaten or disturb public safety and order, they can be used to ban people from certain areas regardless of how they intend to behave there.[291]

3.4.3 Geographical scope

With regard to the geographical scope of exclusion measures, there has been a shift from excluding people from quite narrowly defined areas towards exclusion from larger areas or even from any part of public space.

3.4.3.1 Limited scope

Some exclusion norms define the geographical area from which people can be excluded in a precise manner. This is especially true for laws that ban political protest in certain areas. The Massachusetts legislation establishing 'buffer zones' around abortion clinics referred to above, for example, defined the banned area as any 'public way or sidewalk adjacent to a reproductive health care facility within a radius of 35 feet of any portion of an entrance to, exit from, or driveway of a reproductive health care facility, or within the area within a rectangle created by extending the outside boundaries of any entrance to, exit from, or driveway of, a reproductive health care facility in straight lines to the point where such lines intersect the sideline of the street in front of such entrance, exit or driveway'.[292] The respective Colorado law establishes protective 'bubbles' of eight feet around clinic employees when they are 'within a radius of one hundred feet from any entrance door to a health care facility'.[293] In Switzerland, the ordinance of the City of Berne regulating manifestations creates special authorisation requirements for the Bundesplatz, that is, the square in front of the parliament building,[294] as did in the United Kingdom SOCPA 2005 for Parliament Square and a zone of up to one kilometre around it.[295]

290 Terrorism Prevention and Investigation Measures Act 2011, Schedule 1, para. 3.

291 E.g. for the Canton of Berne: Polizeigesetz vom 8. Juni 1997 (BSG 551.1), Art. 29(1)(b).

292 Massachusetts General Laws, Chapter 266, s. 120E1/2(b) (repealed).

293 Colorado Revised Statutes, § 18-9-122(3).

294 Reglement der Stadt Bern über Kundgebungen auf öffentlichem Grund vom 20. Oktober 2005 (Kundgebungsreglement; KgR; SSSB 143.1), Art. 6.

295 SOCPA 2005, s. 138 (repealed).

Other legal regulations leave it to the executive branch to define the geographical scope of exclusion. They may impose certain limitations on the executive, as is the case with the Swiss Hooligan Concordat, which requires the police to specify 'a precisely defined area related to sports events' in their banning orders.[296] In contrast, other legal norms give the executive branch almost complete discretion. The exclusion norms contained in most Swiss cantonal police acts authorise the police to remove and keep away people from 'a location',[297] while at the federal level the norm authorising exclusion of foreign nationals refers to 'a specified area'.[298] In practice, that 'location' or 'specified area' often covers a certain area of a city. However, in many instances it also extends to the complete territory of a city – for example, in 2011, 645 out of 961 exclusion orders issued in the City of St. Gallen extended to the whole territory of the city.[299] In the case of the exclusion power directed against foreign nationals under federal law, the banned area often extends to a whole region or even a whole canton.[300] In the United Kingdom, neither the legislation relating to IPNAs and CBOs nor that relating to football banning orders contains any limitations with regard to the geographical scope of such orders.[301] Exclusion measures imposed as part of the previous ASBOs often covered whole town centres[302] or even

[296] Konkordat über Massnahmen gegen Gewalt anlässlich von Sportveranstaltungen vom 15. November 2007, Art. 2(1) ('in einem genau umschriebenen Gebiet im Umfeld von Sportveranstaltungen').

[297] See e.g. for the Canton of Berne: Polizeigesetz vom 8. Juni 1997 (BSG 551.1), Art. 29(1) ('von einem Ort'); for the Canton of Zurich: Polizeigesetz (PolG) vom 23. April 2007, § 33 ('von einem Ort'). A smaller number of provisions refer to 'a specified location or area'. See e.g. for the Canton of Uri: Polizeigesetz vom 30. November 2008, Art. 22(2)(a) ('einen bestimmten Ort oder ein bestimmtes Gebiet'); for the Canton of Geneva: Loi sur la police du 26 octobre 1957 (LPol, RSG F 1 05), Art 22A (adopté le 19 février 2009) ('d'un lieu ou d'un périmètre déterminé').

[298] AuG, Art. 74(1) ('ein bestimmtes Gebiet').

[299] Stadtpolizei St. Gallen, 'Medienmitteilung: Wegweisungen und Fernhaltungen 2011', 29 February 2012, available at www.stadt.sg.ch/content/applikationen/news/13/2012/02/29_februar_2012.html. For the exclusion power under the Federal Act on Foreign Nationals, see BGE 124 IV 280, 280 (1998) (relating to the identical Article 13e of the previous Federal Act on the Sojourn and Residence of Foreign Nationals (ANAG) of 1994).

[300] See BGE 126 IV 30, 31 (1999); BVR 2000, 145, p. 145 (Verwaltungsgericht des Kantons Bern) (relating to the identical Article 13e of the previous Federal Act on the Sojourn and Residence of Foreign Nationals (ANAG) of 1994).

[301] See Anti-social Behaviour, Crime and Policing Act 2014, ss 1, 22; Football Spectators Act 1989 (as amended by the Football Disorder Act 2000), ss 14A–14J.

[302] See *R.* v. *Lamb (Christopher)*, [2005] EWCA Crim 3000, para. 18; *R* v. *Braxton (Curtis)*, [2003] EWCA Crim 1037.

the entire territory of a city.[303] Similarly, the dispersal powers under the Anti-social Behaviour, Crime and Policing Act 2014 allow the police to ban people from 'the locality (or part of the locality)' specified in the authorisation by the police officer,[304] although the Act at least makes it clear that access to the home and the workplace must still be possible.[305]

It is quite common for the respective authorities to refer to maps to define the relevant exclusion zones. The standard form used by the police in the City of Berne to impose exclusion orders under the cantonal Police Act, for instance, includes a map identifying the perimeter(s) where the ban applies.[306] The Swiss Hooligan Concordat even explicitly provides that the banning order issued to the person in question must include a map identifying the areas where the ban applies.[307] Similarly, in the case of the curfew imposed during the WTO conference in Seattle, a map was attached to the emergency order to specify the 'no-protest zone'.[308]

3.4.3.2 Unlimited scope

Prohibitions of specified behaviour in public space, such as bans on vagrancy or 'loitering', are normally unlimited with regard to their geographical scope and thus apply in all public streets, squares, parks and so on. (There are, however, also a number of such prohibitions that have a limited geographical scope, such as the ordinance of the City of Berne that prevents people from sitting or lying down, which only applies in or near the train station.[309]) Curfews, including juvenile curfews, also typically involve exclusion from any part of public space.[310]

303 See 'Young thug barred from Manchester', *Manchester Evening News*, 22 January 2004.

304 Anti-social Behaviour, Crime and Policing Act 2014, s. 35(1).

305 Ibid., ss 36(2), (3).

306 The form is reproduced in Gasser, *Kriminalpolitik oder City-Pflege?* (2004), pp. 104–5.

307 Konkordat über Massnahmen gegen Gewalt anlässlich von Sportveranstaltungen vom 15. November 2007, Art. 5(1), sentence 2 ('Der Verfügung ist ein Plan beizulegen, der die vom Verbot erfassten Orte und die zugehörigen Rayons genau bezeichnet.'). The revised version of the Concordat removes this requirement and leaves it to the police how to inform the person concerned of the geographical scope of the ban. Konkordat über Massnahmen gegen Gewalt anlässlich von Sportveranstaltungen vom 15. November 2007; Änderung vom 2. Februar 2012, Art. 5(1), sentence 2 ('Der Verfügung sind Angaben beizufügen, die es der betroffenen Person erlauben, genaue Kenntnis über die vom Verbot erfassten Rayons zu erhalten').

308 See *Menotti* v. *City of Seattle* 409 F.3d 1113, 1125 and App. A (9th Cir. 2005).

309 Reglement der Stadt Bern betreffend die Benützung des städtischen Teils des Bahnhofs Bern (Bahnhofreglement; BHR), Art. 2(2)(b).

310 E.g. Dallas, Texas Code of Ordinances, s. 31–33(9); Gemeindepolizeireglement der Gemeinde Urtenen-Schönbühl vom 15. Mai 2006, Art. 6.

3.4.4 Temporal scope

To momentarily send people away from a specific place (including a public place) is one of the main tools available to the police to de-escalate an immediate conflict situation or to address other threats to public safety and order. Accordingly, the power of the police to order people to leave (and stay away for a short period) is a traditional police power common to most legal systems.[311] In contrast, the power of the state to exclude people from public places *for long periods* had, since the decline of banishment, been limited to very exceptional situations, such as times of war.[312] In recent years, however, more and more measures have been created that are designed to not only remove persons momentarily but keep them away from public places for longer periods or even permanently.

3.4.4.1 Short term

The long-established power of the police to ask people to go away has been expanded and strengthened through more explicit and broader powers, such as those contained in the police acts of different Swiss cantons that have been created or amended in the last few years. Some of these provisions put specific time limits on the police's power to remove (*wegweisen*) and keep away (*fernhalten*) people. In the case of the Police Act of the Canton of Lucerne, for example, the maximum period of exclusion is twenty-four hours, which may however be extended to one month if the person concerned objects to the exclusion order.[313] In the United Kingdom, the period for which the police may, under the Anti-social Behaviour, Crime and Policing Act 2014, prevent people from returning to a locality is limited to forty-eight hours.[314] Short-term exclusion is also often used to keep away demonstrators from potential sites of political protest.[315]

[311] See Section 3.1.

[312] See e.g. United States Executive Order 9066, 19 February 1942 and the resulting cases of *Hirabayashi* v. *United States*, 320 U.S. 81 (1943) and *Korematsu* v. *United States*, 323 U.S. 214 (1944).

[313] Gesetz über die Luzerner Polizei vom 27. Januar 1998 (SRL 350), § 19(1)–(2) (geändert am 28. April 2008).

[314] Anti-social Behaviour, Crime and Policing Act 2014, s. 35(4).

[315] See e.g. BGE 130 I 369, 371 (2004); *R (Laporte)* v. *Chief Constable of Gloucestershire Constabulary*, [2006] UKHL 55, para. 12 (Lord Bingham); *Menotti* v. *City of Seattle*, 409 F.3d 1113, 1124–5 (9th Cir. 2005).

3.4.4.2 Long term

Many of the police acts of the Swiss cantons allow for longer periods of exclusion. The Police Act of the Canton of Berne, as well as a number of other cantonal police acts, authorises the police to keep away people 'temporarily', without specifying a time limit.[316] The general practice of the Bernese police is to issue exclusion orders for three months.[317] In the United Kingdom, bans on protests outside a person's home under the Criminal Justice and Police Act 2001 can be imposed for up to ninety days.[318] In the case of the Cincinnati 'drug exclusion zones', the time limit was also ninety days and one year in case of a subsequent conviction.[319] Longer time limits apply in the case of exclusion orders directed against alleged football hooligans. In Switzerland, the Hooligan Concordat provides for a maximum period of one year.[320] The revised version of the concordat, which has been ratified by nearly all cantons, extends this time limit to three years and provides for a minimum period of one year.[321] In the United Kingdom, the football banning orders issued by magistrates' courts last for a minimum of two years and a maximum of three years.[322] Exclusion may be particularly long term when it is imposed by way of court orders: exclusion orders under the British Serious Crime Act 2007 may last for up to five years;[323] football banning orders issued by the convicting court even for three to ten years.[324]

[316] Polizeigesetz vom 8. Juni 1997 (BSG 551.1), Art. 29(1) ('Die Kantonspolizei kann Personen von einem Ort *vorübergehend* wegweisen oder fern halten') (emphasis added). See also the police acts of the following cantons: Aargau: Gesetz über die Gewährleistung der öffentlichen Sicherheit (Polizeigesetz) vom 6. Dezember 2005, § 34; Glarus: Polizeigesetz des Kantons Glarus vom 6. Mai 2007, Art. 15; Solothurn: Gesetz über die Kantonspolizei vom 23. September 1990, § 37 (geändert am 15. Mai 2007); Schwyz: Verordnung über die Kantonspolizei (Polizeiverordnung) vom 22. März 2000, § 19 (geändert am 28. Juni 2007); Fribourg: Loi du 15 novembre 1990 sur la Police cantonale, Art. 31d (adopté le 31 mai 2010).

[317] See the standard form used by the Bernese police to issue exclusion orders reproduced in Gasser, *Kriminalpolitik oder City-Pflege?* (2004), pp. 104–5. See also S. Bühler, 'Wer stört, hat in Bern nichts verloren', *NZZ am Sonntag*, 20 October 2002.

[318] Criminal Justice and Police Act 2001, s. 42(4)(b).

[319] Cincinnati Municipal Code, § 755-5 (repealed).

[320] Konkordat über Massnahmen gegen Gewalt anlässlich von Sportveranstaltungen vom 15. November 2007, Art. 4(2).

[321] Konkordat über Massnahmen gegen Gewalt anlässlich von Sportveranstaltungen vom 15. November 2007; Änderung vom 2. Februar 2012, Art. 4(2). The Federal Supreme Court has held that this minimum time limit violates the principle of proportionality and is therefore unconstitutional: BGE 140 I 2, 38–40 (2014).

[322] Football Spectators Act 1989 (as amended by the Football Disorder Act 2000), s. 14F(5).

[323] Serious Crime Act 2007, s. 16.

[324] Football Spectators Act 1989 (as amended by the Football Disorder Act 2000), s. 14F (3)–(4).

3.4.4.3 Permanent

Prohibitions of certain behaviour in public places, such as bans on vagrancy, 'loitering' and sitting and lying on public sidewalks or streets, are typically permanent measures, as are authorisation requirements for political protest and prohibitions of protest in specified areas. However, also exclusion imposed by way of a court order may be permanent. In the United Kingdom, IPNAs and CBOs may be imposed for a fixed period, which in the case of the latter must be not less than two years, or an indefinite period.[325] For SHPOs the minimum is five years, with no upper limit.[326] In some US municipalities, sex offenders are prohibited from entering public parks for their lifetime.[327] In Switzerland, even the police may impose permanent exclusion from public places. Neither the Police Acts of the Cantons of Grisons or Uri nor, at the federal level, the Federal Act on Foreign Nationals specify any time limits.[328] Finally, also exclusion by way of curfew is typically a permanent measure, though limited to certain times of the day. The juvenile curfews in force in many US cities typically apply from 10 pm or 11 pm (and 12 am on Friday and Saturday nights) until 5 am or 6 am,[329] though some cities have now started to extend them to school hours.[330]

3.5 Conclusion

While banishment had largely disappeared by, at the latest, the first half of the twentieth century, starting from about the 1990s there has been a marked resurgence of measures excluding people from parts of public space. These new forms of exclusion are mainly intended to address three types of social problems: criminal behaviour, 'anti-social behaviour' and political protest.

Convicted criminal offenders can be banned from accessing certain parts of public space in all three states at issue. This power is mainly deployed against those convicted of sexual offences, drug offences and

[325] Anti-social Behaviour, Crime and Policing Act 2014, ss 1(6), 25(5).

[326] Sexual Offences Act 2003, s. 103C(2).

[327] See *Dowdell* v. *City of Jeffersonville*, 907 N.E.2d 559 (Ind. Ct. App., 2009).

[328] For the Canton of Grisons: Polizeigesetz des Kantons Graubünden vom 20. Oktober 2004 (PolG, BR 613.000), Art. 12; for the Canton of Uri: Polizeigesetz vom 30. November 2008 (RB 3.8111), Art. 22; for the federal level: AuG, Art. 74.

[329] E.g. Indiana Code, s. 31–37-3–2; District of Columbia Code, § 2–1542(1); Charter and Code of the City of Portland, Oregon, s. 14A.80.010.

[330] E.g. Dallas, Texas Code of Ordinances, s. 31–33(a)(1)(C); San Diego Municipal Code, § 58.05(b)(1).

football-related offences. In addition, more and more powers have been adopted in recent years that also allow *potential criminal offenders* to be excluded from public space. In the United States, such exclusion measures were first introduced in the early 1990s to deal with suspected members of criminal street gangs; the United Kingdom later adopted the same model of preventing gang-related violence. Since then, similar preventive exclusion measures have been adopted in these two states to target those suspected of being involved in drug-related crime, sexual offences, terrorism and other forms of serious crime. The United Kingdom was also the first state to introduce football banning orders, extending their scope of application in 2000 to individuals who have not been convicted of a relevant offence. In 2006, Switzerland followed the British model by adopting preventive exclusion powers directed against violence related to sports events.

Also in the 1990s, numerous US cities began to proscribe a wide range of allegedly *anti-social behaviours*, including, for example, sleeping or drinking alcohol in a public place or even simply sitting or lying down on a public sidewalk. At the same time, there was a sharp increase in juvenile curfew laws, so that today young persons are banned from being in public places at night in the vast majority of US cities. Such juvenile curfews have also become increasingly common in the United Kingdom and Switzerland. In addition, in both of these states blanket exclusion powers have been adopted that can be deployed against all sorts of anti-social behaviours. Use of these powers is extensive and significantly on the rise. In the United Kingdom, the ASBO, now replaced by the IPNA and the CBO, and the blanket dispersal power of the police have become the main tools for dealing with anti-social behaviour and have influenced developments elsewhere. In Switzerland, the Police Act of the Canton of Berne, adopted in 1997, was the first police act to create a broadly defined power of the police to remove and keep away people from parts of public space. Nearly all other cantons have since followed the Bernese example by adding similar exclusion powers to their respective police acts. Within a few years, these blanket exclusion powers have become the standard instrument of the police to clear away ‘scenes’ of drug and alcohol addicts, juveniles and other marginalised groups.

In order to control *protest* activities, all three states have created permanent special zones where protest is severely restricted, most importantly around parliament buildings in Switzerland and the United Kingdom and around abortion clinics in the United States. On a more temporary basis, the police now regularly prevent demonstrators from protesting in certain parts of public space, either by denying them access to the respective sites or by containing them within small cordoned-off areas ('kettling').

As far as the mode of exclusion is concerned, there has been a marked increase in police powers in Switzerland and the United Kingdom in recent years. These are typically very broadly defined and far-reaching and thus give law enforcement agencies wide scope of discretion. In the United Kingdom, court powers are also of great significance as various courts can impose bans on accessing certain public places as part of IPNAs, CBOs and football banning orders. In the United States, in contrast, the main form of excluding people from public space is by way of prohibitions: either certain groups of people are prohibited from being present in (parts of) public space (as with juvenile curfews) or certain forms of behaviour in public space are prohibited. Often these forms of behaviour are so broadly defined (as with prohibitions of sitting or lying on public sidewalks) that they may be used against almost anyone.

What is common to all three states is that the focus with regard to the excluded behaviour is now increasingly on complete exclusion from public space (rather than exclusion of particular forms of behaviour), that there has been a shift from excluding people from quite narrowly defined areas towards exclusion from larger areas or even any part of public space and that more and more measures allow people not only to be sent away temporarily but to be kept away from parts of public space for extended periods of time or even permanently. It is due to these developments that the new forms of exclusion from public space are reminiscent of medieval forms of banishment.

4

Rule of law

Exclusion from public space is a typical tool of 'order-maintenance policing', which emphasises the importance of the appearance of particular spaces. As has been explained in the two previous chapters, in the 'security society' this form of policing has become more and more influential. It is widely recognised, however, that the task of maintaining order, if it is so broadly defined, is not compatible with narrow legal constraints, that is, that the police must be granted a wide scope of discretion to be able to perform it.[1] There is, therefore, an inherent tension between the new, preventive forms of policing, including the use of exclusion measures, on the one hand and the various requirements following from the rule of law on the other. It is this fundamental tension that underlies the particular problems discussed in the present chapter. While it is not possible to review each and every rule-of-law issue raised by exclusion from public space, the chapter aims to at least highlight the most important problems that exclusion measures raise from the perspective of the rule of law.

The chapter first briefly sets out the meaning of the rule of law in the United Kingdom and the United States and of the *Rechtsstaatsprinzip* in Switzerland, drawing out the common elements underlying, and requirements following from, these concepts (4.1). The following section is devoted to one of the most important principles implicit in the rule of law and the *Rechtsstaatsprinzip*: the 'principle of legality', that is the requirement for a legal basis of all government action. The section briefly reviews the various legal bases of exclusion from public space in the three states at issue and critically examines exclusion measures that are not based on any explicit legal authority but, instead, on breach-of-the-peace powers or, in Switzerland, the *polizeiliche Generalklausel* (4.2). Next, the legal norms authorising exclusion from public space are assessed for their conformity with another requirement following from the rule of law,

[1] E.g. Livingston, 'Police Discretion and the Quality of Life in Public Places' (1997).

namely that of sufficient precision (4.3). The final section highlights the most important problems that people subject to exclusion measures may face with regard to the availability of procedural safeguards and access to justice (4.4).

4.1 The rule of law/*Rechtsstaatsprinzip*

The rule of law is one of the defining characteristics of the Western political tradition and generally thought to be a fundamental value of any liberal political system. Even states that do not subscribe to Western notions of democracy and individual rights support the rule of law. The UN has repeatedly called on states and international bodies to comply with the rule of law and is engaged in various activities promoting the rule of law around the world.[2] The World Bank and the International Monetary Fund condition the provision of financial assistance on adherence to the rule of law, and various non-governmental organisations have built up a worldwide movement in its support.[3]

Yet, despite its recognition as a global ideal, there is little agreement on precisely what the rule of law means. In fact, some authors have argued that this lack of consensus is inevitable as the rule of law is what the philosopher W.B. Gallie has described as an 'essentially contested concept',[4] that is, a concept 'the proper use of which inevitably involves endless disputes about [its] proper uses on the part of [its] users'.[5] Accordingly, the rule of law has been given different meanings at different moments in time and in different legal traditions. The Anglo-American notion of the rule of law, for example, is based on the assumption of an antagonistic relationship between the state and law. It understands law as something that, independently from the state, constantly develops and thus focuses on procedural issues.[6] In contrast, the idea of the *Rechtsstaat* (which literally translates as 'the state of law'), according to the German legal tradition, is a more static

[2] See Section 4.1.5.

[3] See e.g. the websites of the World Justice Project (www.worldjusticeproject.org), the International Commission of Jurists (www.icj.org) and the American Bar Association Rule of Law Initiative (www.abanet.org/rol).

[4] Waldron, 'Is the Rule of Law an Essentially Contested Concept (in Florida)?' (2002); Fallon, ' "The Rule of Law" as a Concept in Constitutional Discourse' (1997), 7.

[5] Gallie, 'Essentially Contested Concepts' (1956), 169.

[6] See e.g. Rosenfeld, 'Rule of Law versus Rechtsstaat' (2000); Rosenfeld, 'The Rule of Law and the Legitimacy of Constitutional Democracy' (2000), 1307; Müller, 'Rule of Law – Rechtsstaat' (2000); Kriele, *Einführung in die Staatslehre* (1975), pp. 106–11.

concept that understands law as inextricably tied to the state and assumes a symbiotic relationship between the state and law.[7]

Nevertheless, even these two quite distinct concepts, rooted in different political and legal traditions, share important commonalities in that they incorporate a number of essentially identical principles.[8] In fact, it is quite uncontroversial that there are some basic, formal elements that inevitably form part of *any* conception of the rule of law. As the present inquiry focuses on these basic, uncontroversial aspects of the rule of law, there is no need to answer the difficult question as to the extent to which more substantive elements form, or should form, part of the rule of law.

4.1.1 Historical background

The idea that the power of the government needs to be curbed and controlled by subjecting it to the law goes back to at least the days of the Greek philosophers.[9] Both Plato and Aristotle thought that government by laws is superior to government by men.[10] In the words of Aristotle:

> And the rule of law, it is argued, is preferable to that of any individual. [. . .] Therefore he who bids the law rule may be deemed to bid God and Reason alone rule, but he who bids man rule adds an element of the beast; for desire is a wild beast, and passion perverts the minds of rulers, even when they are the best of men. The law is reason unaffected by desire.[11]

Medieval doctrine similarly maintained that rulers must be subject to law. The English Magna Carta, signed in 1215, confirmed in its famous clause 39 that citizens were protected by the law against the king and that they had to be afforded due process of law:

> No free man is to be taken or imprisoned or disseised or outlawed or exiled or in any way ruined, nor will we go or send against him, except by the lawful judgement of his peers or by the law of the land.[12]

[7] Ibid.

[8] Pech, 'The Rule of Law as a Constitutional Principle of the European Union' (2009); Weber, 'Rechtsstaatsprinzip als gemeineuropäisches Verfassungsprinzip' (2008); Carpano, *État de droit et droits européens* (2005); Fernandez Esteban, *The Rule of Law in the European Constitution* (1999), pp. 65–101; MacCormick, 'Der Rechtsstaat und die rule of law' (1984).

[9] For an overview, see Miller, 'The Rule of Law in Ancient Greek Thought' (2010).

[10] See Costa, 'The Rule of Law' (2007), 75–7; Tamanaha, *On the Rule of Law* (2004), pp. 7–10.

[11] Aristotle, *Politics* (1962), Book III, p. 1286.

[12] Holt, *Magna Carta* (2015), p. 389.

The idea of the rule of law was further strengthened as a consequence of the seventeenth-century struggle for power between the king and parliament in England. Both the Petition of Right of 1628 and the Bill of Rights of 1689 affirmed the principle that the monarch was subject to the law.[13]

However, it was only with the rise of liberalism, starting from the end of the seventeenth century, that the rule of law acquired the status it has today. Thinkers such as John Locke in England, Baron de Montesquieu in France and James Madison, Alexander Hamilton and John Jay in the United States helped to shape the notion of the rule of law as it exists in today's Western democracies by stressing its crucial function in preserving liberty. Locke's *Second Treatise of Government* (1690) argued that there could only be freedom if the power of the government was exercised by established and promulgated laws, although he failed to identify specific mechanisms for the protection of individual liberties.[14] In his *De l'esprit des lois* (1748), Montesquieu elaborated his famous scheme of a separation of powers with an independent judiciary as a safeguard against the abuse of governmental power.[15] In their *Federalist Papers* (1787–88), Hamilton, Madison and Jay advocated representative (rather than direct) democracy, the separation of powers and judicial review of legislation to curb the power of the majority for the protection of individual liberties.[16]

These liberal ideas deeply influenced political developments throughout the Western world. Depending on the exact national context, however, the common commitment to the rule of law was implemented through different normative and institutional structures.

4.1.2 The rule of law in the United Kingdom

The constitutional history of the United Kingdom is characterised by a sequence of struggles over the composition and influence of the different organs of the state. Thus, the English notion of the rule of law developed as part of the contest between king and parliament. The common law, understood to be the product of custom from time immemorial and reflecting basic legal principles, was thought to set limits

[13] Bradley/Ewing, *Constitutional and Administrative Law* (2011), pp. 91–2.
[14] Locke, *Two Treatises of Government* (1998), ss 136–7.
[15] De Montesquieu, *De l'esprit des lois* (1950–1961), especially Livre XI, Chapitre 6.
[16] Federalist Papers, Nos 10, 51 and 78. The Federalist Papers are available on the website of the Library of Congress, at http://thomas.loc.gov/home/histdox/fedpapers.html.

to all government conduct.[17] Originally, there was a view that even acts of parliament can be declared void by the judiciary for being in violation of the common law.[18] However, since (at the latest) the end of the seventeenth century, judges started to accept the legislative omnipotence of parliament.[19] Law came to be seen as the product of sovereign legislative will rather than the reflection of a timeless body of legal principles, and so judicial review of legislation was repudiated.[20] Apart from judicial review of legislation, the constitutional set-up of the United Kingdom also lacks other features that are generally understood to be characteristic of a liberal state subscribing to the rule of law, such as a written constitution or an explicit bill of rights. Nevertheless, it is widely acknowledged that the United Kingdom is a state based on the rule of law – and even its birthplace. The explanation for this is that the common law continues to 'live' in the decisions of judges whose position is independent from the executive and legislative branches and that there is a widespread commitment to the rule of law. Government officials, policy-makers and the wider public do not question that the executive and legislative branches must operate within the restraints of certain fundamental legal principles. Even the legislator, whose powers are in theory unlimited, feels bound by the rule of law. Thus, in the United Kingdom, it has been argued, the rule of law exists not due to some elaborate constitutional mechanism but due to it being 'a common ideal shared and unquestioningly accepted by the majority'.[21]

The term 'rule of law' started to be used in the second half of the nineteenth century.[22] In his authoritative and highly influential work *Introduction to the Study of the Law of the Constitution*, first published in 1885, Albert Venn Dicey provided the first prominent formulation of the rule of law. Dicey identified three aspects of the rule of law. First, the rule of law means 'the absolute supremacy or predominance of regular law as opposed to the influence of arbitrary power', excluding 'the existence of arbitrariness, of prerogative, or even of wide discretionary authority on the part of the government'.[23] Thus, 'a man may with us be punished for

[17] See Santoro, 'The Rule of Law and the "Liberties of the English"' (2007).

[18] *Dr Bonham's Case*, (1610) 8 Co Rep 113b, 118a (Coke, CJ) ('[I]n many Cases, the Common Law doth controll Acts of Parliament, and sometimes shall adjudge them to be void.')

[19] See Bradley/Ewing, *Constitutional and Administrative Law* (2011), p. 58.

[20] Tamanaha, *On the Rule of Law* (2004), p. 57.

[21] Von Hayek, *The Constitution of Liberty* (1960), p. 206.

[22] Zolo, 'The Rule of Law' (2007), 7.

[23] Dicey, *An Introduction to the Study of the Law of the Constitution* (1959), p. 202.

a breach of law, but he can be punished for nothing else'.[24] Second, the rule of law requires 'equality before the law, or the equal subjection of all classes to the ordinary law of the land administered by the ordinary law courts'.[25] This implies that no one is above the law and that public officials do not have special immunities or privileges. Third, Dicey thought that the rule of law expresses the fact that the constitutional law is 'the result of the judicial decisions determining the rights of private persons in particular cases brought before the courts'.[26] According to Dicey, the rights of the individual are protected not by a written constitution or a bill of rights but by decisions of the courts – the common law.

Although Dicey's formulation of the rule of law has been criticised for seeking to promote an individualistic political theory[27] and for being based on wrong (or no longer valid) assumptions about different systems of government,[28] it has had a great influence on British legal doctrine and is still regarded as the classic definition today. The values underlying Dicey's rule of law – legality, certainty, predictability, consistency, accountability as well as due process and access to justice – remain at the heart of modern conceptions of the rule of law.[29] Even in the absence of a power of the courts to strike down legislation, '[a]s a constitutional principle, the Rule of Law serves as a basis for the evaluation of all laws and provides a critical focus for public debate'.[30] The practical implementation of the rule of law occurs primarily through judicial review of the actions of public officials: the most important grounds of judicial review all rest in some way on the rule of law.[31] Lord Hope has even gone as far as to claim that '[t]he rule of law enforced by the courts is the ultimate controlling factor on which our constitution is based'.[32]

4.1.3 The rule of law in the United States

Aware of the danger that a democracy can turn into a tyranny of the majority or the powerful, Hamilton, Madison and Jay sought ways to control democracy for the protection of individual liberties. As explained in Section 4.1.1, in their *Federalist Papers*, they identified three mechanisms for this purpose: representative (rather than direct) democracy,

[24] Ibid. [25] Ibid. [26] Ibid., p. 195.
[27] Jennings, *The Law and the Constitution* (1933), pp. 309–11.
[28] Arthurs, 'Rethinking Administrative Law' (1979).
[29] See Jowell, 'The Rule of Law' (2015). [30] Ibid., 17. [31] Ibid., 18–21.
[32] *Jackson* v. *Her Majesty's Attorney General*, [2005] UKHL 56, para. 107.

a clear separation of powers and judicial review of legislation. The first two postulates were implemented in the US Constitution of 1787. The third, judicial review of legislation, was not mentioned in the Constitution. Nevertheless, in 1803, in the landmark case of *Marbury* v. *Madison*, the Supreme Court held that the courts do have the power to review actions of the legislative branch for their constitutionality.[33] Without judicial review, Chief Justice Marshall declared, the US government would not deserve to be called 'a government of laws, and not of men'.[34] Thus, unlike in the United Kingdom, the power of the courts to strike down legislation is regarded as an essential element of the rule of law.

A further element, commonly regarded as an aspect of a *substantive* conception of the rule of law but not originally advocated in the *Federalist Papers*, was added in 1791 by way of amendment of the Constitution: the Bill of Rights.[35] As with the power of the courts to strike down legislation, the rationale for its adoption was the protection of individual liberties from the majority. As the Supreme Court observed, '[t]he very purpose of a Bill of Rights was to withdraw certain subjects from the vicissitudes of political controversy, to place them beyond the reach of majorities and officials and to establish them as legal principles to be applied by the courts'.[36]

Thus, whereas in the United Kingdom the protection of individual liberties is seen as arising from a long common law tradition, the US system relies on the normative superiority of the Constitution and an institutional system of checks and balances with a strong judiciary. *Marbury* v. *Madison* allowed the judiciary to take over the role of protector of individual rights and interpreter of the Constitution. The Supreme Court used the interpretative scope offered by the vagueness of some of the constitutional clauses to develop considerable activism in defence of individual rights. The powerful position of the Supreme Court was further strengthened through the introduction of the Fourteenth Amendment in 1868, giving the court the opportunity to extend most of the fundamental guarantees of the Bill of Rights from the federal level to the states.[37]

The main instrument that the Supreme Court has used to interfere with political decisions is the due process of law requirement of the Fifth

[33] *Marbury* v. *Madison*, 5 U.S. 137 (1803). [34] Ibid., 163.
[35] US Constitution, Amendments I–X.
[36] *West Virginia State Board of Education* v. *Barnette*, 319 U.S. 624, 638 (1943).
[37] See Tribe, *American Constitutional Law* (1988), pp. 546–86.

Amendment (applicable to the federal government) and the Fourteenth Amendment (applicable to the states), which provides that no one 'shall [. . .] be deprived of life, liberty, or property, without due process of law'.[38] The concept of due process of law has its origins in clause 39 of the Magna Carta, quoted above.[39] It operates as a limitation not only upon the executive but also upon the legislative branch of government, preventing any governmental action that is 'unreasonable', 'unnecessary' or 'arbitrary'.[40] Governments must operate within the limits of those 'principles of liberty and justice lying at the foundation of our civil and political institutions which no State can violate consistently with that due process of law required by the Fourteenth Amendment in proceedings involving life, liberty, or property'.[41]

This vague standard has been concretised in a rich case law that has developed over several decades. Two types of due process of law can be distinguished: procedural and substantive. *Procedural* due process refers to the way in which government acts, that is, the manner in which a law or ordinance is enforced. When government takes action that may deprive persons of their life, liberty or property, it must afford them some kind of 'process'. The nature of the process that is due is situation-specific and depends on a number of factors, including the private interest affected, the risk of an erroneous decision and the government's interest.[42] Generally speaking, the minimum guarantees of a fair decision-making process include the right to reasonable notice of charges or proceedings, the opportunity to be heard and the right to a neutral decision-maker.[43]

Substantive due process, a concept that was only embraced by the Supreme Court during the second half of the nineteenth century, refers to the substance of government action: it imposes limitations upon governmental authority with regard to the content of legislation rather than merely the mode of procedure. As far as socio-economic regulation is concerned, legislation or government action will be upheld as constitutional as long as there is a rational relationship between the regulation

38 US Constitution, Amendment V. Amendment XIV states: 'nor shall any State deprive any person of life, liberty, or property, without due process of law'.

39 Corwin, 'The Doctrine of Due Process of Law Before the Civil War' (1911), 368.

40 See *Lochner* v. *People of State of New York*, 198 U.S. 45, 56 (1905).

41 *Hurtado* v. *California*, 110 U.S. 516, 546 (1884) (Harlan, J., dissenting).

42 See e.g. *Mathews* v. *Eldridge*, 424 U.S. 319, 335 (1976).

43 For overviews, see Chemerinsky, *Constitutional Law* (2009), pp. 1197–204; Nowak/Rotunda, *Constitutional Law* (2004), pp. 633–40; Tribe, *American Constitutional Law* (1988), pp. 718–49.

and a legitimate governmental interest.[44] When the regulation restricts the exercise of a fundamental right, however, this lenient 'rational basis test' is forsaken in favour of a heightened standard of review. Although the standard employed is not always uniform, the Supreme Court commonly states that a regulation impairing a fundamental right will be invalid unless the government demonstrates that it is narrowly tailored to promote a compelling or overriding interest.[45] The basis upon which a right is treated as a 'fundamental right' triggering this exacting judicial scrutiny remains quite unclear. What is clear is that, apart from the guarantees explicitly listed in the Bill of Rights, the concept of 'fundamental rights' also includes non-enumerated rights such as the freedom of association, the right to interstate travel and the right to privacy.[46]

4.1.4 The Rechtsstaatsprinzip *in Switzerland*

The term *Rechtsstaat* was first introduced into constitutional law by the German scholar Robert von Mohl in 1829.[47] Heavily influenced by the liberal ideas of Immanuel Kant, early conceptions of the *Rechtsstaat* referred to a state based on rational principles whose central aim was the promotion of the good of its citizens, in particular by guaranteeing their liberty, security and property. Thus, citizens in the *Rechtsstaat* were to be granted individual liberties (such as personal liberty, freedom of thought, freedom of expression and economic freedoms), equality before the law and protection of property; they had the right to political participation; there had to be an independent judiciary; and, crucially, all actions of the state had to be authorised by general, abstract laws.[48] Yet in the course of the nineteenth century, this decidedly political, liberal conception of the *Rechtsstaat* was increasingly detached from any reference to ethical values and political content and reduced to a formal conception, which focused exclusively on the primacy of the law and legal redress.[49] Thus, as opposed to the United Kingdom and the United States, in Germany the protection

[44] *United States* v. *Carolene Products Co.*, 304 U.S. 144, 152 (1938).

[45] See e.g. *Reno* v. *Flores*, 507 U.S. 292, 302 (1993).

[46] See Nowak/Rotunda, *Constitutional Law* (2004), pp. 467–74; Fallon, *The Dynamic Constitution* (2004), pp. 138–54.

[47] See Böckenförde, 'Entstehung und Wandel des Rechtsstaatsbegriffs' (1969), 54.

[48] Gozzi, 'Rechtsstaat and Individual Rights in German Constitutional History' (2007), 240–4; Böckenförde, 'Entstehung und Wandel des Rechtsstaatsbegriffs' (1969), 55–9.

[49] Heuschling, *État de droit, Rechtsstaat, Rule of Law* (2002), pp. 73–108; Stolleis, 'Rechtsstaat' (1971–1998), 370–2; Böckenförde, 'Entstehung und Wandel des Rechtsstaatsbegriffs' (1969), 59–66.

of individual liberties was thought to be provided, not primarily by the courts or a bill of rights, but by the principle that the executive is bound by the law (*Gesetzmässigkeit der Verwaltung*). As part of this shift, the idea of the *Rechtsstaat* came to be viewed as compatible with constitutional monarchy as a compromise between liberalism and conservatism.[50] The failure of the positivist understanding of law to serve as a barrier against the terror of the Nazi regime, however, nurtured the view that the *Rechtsstaat* cannot be reduced to its formal elements.[51] As a consequence, the conception of the *Rechtsstaat* prevailing in Germany today is that of a material/substantive (instead of a formal) and a social (instead of a purely liberal) *Rechtsstaat*,[52] placing human dignity at its heart.[53]

In Switzerland, due to the different political context – in particular the absence of an authoritarian police state against which the concept was to be deployed – the idea of the *Rechtsstaat/état de droit* developed somewhat differently and had, at least originally, less purchase.[54] Nevertheless, the influence that the original, liberal German conception of the *Rechtsstaat* had at that time is manifest in the Federal Constitution of the Swiss Confederation of 1848.[55] Although it lacked the grand references to the ideals of liberty and law that were characteristic of other constitutional documents of those days, the Constitution contained several elements that reflected central postulates of the *Rechtsstaat*, including guarantees of a number of individual liberties, the principle of equality before the law and the 'principle of legality' (*Legalitätsprinzip/principe de la légalité*).[56] The same elements had already been part of the constitutions that some of the Swiss cantons had enacted in earlier years.[57] The complete revision of

[50] Gozzi, 'Rechtsstaat and Individual Rights in German Constitutional History' (2007), 245–50; Zolo, 'The Rule of Law' (2007), 11–13.

[51] Grote, 'Rule of Law, Rechtsstaat and "Etat de droit"' (1999), 285; Stolleis, 'Rechtsstaat' (1971–1998), 373–4.

[52] Böckenförde, 'Entstehung und Wandel des Rechtsstaatsbegriffs' (1969), 66–75.

[53] Grundgesetz für die Bundesrepublik Deutschland vom 23. Mai 1949 (BGBl I 1), Art. 1(1).

[54] See Schindler, '100 Jahre Verwaltungsrecht in der Schweiz' (2011), 342; Biaggini, 'Grundlagen und Grundzüge staatlichen Verfassungsrechts: Schweiz' (2007), 590–1; Bäumlin, 'Der schweizerische Rechtsstaatsgedanke' (1965).

[55] For an overview of the theories of the *Rechtsstaat* developed by Swiss constitutional lawyers at the time, see Garzoni, *Die Rechtsstaatsidee im schweizerischen Staatsdenken des 19. Jahrhunderts* (1952).

[56] See Kölz, *Neuere schweizerische Verfassungsgeschichte* (1992), pp. 583–9; Kägi, 'Zur Entwicklung des Schweizerischen Rechtsstaates seit 1848' (1952), 182–7.

[57] See e.g. Kölz, *Neuere schweizerische Verfassungsgeschichte* (1992), pp. 320–42, 477–9, 508–10, 537–8; Fleiner, *Entstehung und Wandlung moderner Staatstheorien in der Schweiz* (1916), pp. 20–1.

the Federal Constitution in 1874, partial revisions in following decades, important decisions of the Federal Supreme Court and a number of legislative changes further strengthened the idea of the *Rechtsstaat*: the list of guaranteed individual liberties was expanded, the principle of equality before the law was further developed, a clearer separation of powers emerged and the position of the Federal Supreme Court was strengthened.[58]

Today, the idea of the *Rechtsstaat* is described as a 'structural principle',[59] a 'general principle'[60] or a 'fundamental value'[61] underlying the Federal Constitution of the Swiss Confederation. The completely revised Federal Constitution of 1999 explicitly refers to the concept of the *Rechtsstaat* in its Article 5, entitled '*Grundsätze rechtsstaatlichen Handelns*' ('principles of state action according to the rule of law'). Article 5(1) states that the law is the basis as well as the limit of any state action ('Grundlage und Schranke staatlichen Handelns ist das Recht'), thus guaranteeing the 'principle of legality'. A number of other constitutional norms further specify the principle of legality.[62] Article 5(4) makes it clear that the federal government and the cantons have to observe international law, Article 5(2) that any state action must be in the public interest and proportionate. The Federal Constitution implements a further postulate of the *Rechtsstaat*, the separation of powers, by establishing in detail the respective competencies of the three branches of the federal government.[63] Further norms of the Constitution provide for procedural guarantees,[64] the right of access to a court[65] and the independence of the courts.[66] Finally, the Federal Constitution implements the central aspect of a substantive conception of the rule of law by stipulating a comprehensive list of guarantees of individual rights, which starts with the fundamental guarantee of human dignity.[67] However, there is also an important limitation to the principle of the *Rechtsstaat* in Switzerland in that, unlike in the United States, courts (as well as other law-applying

58 Kölz, *Neuere schweizerische Verfassungsgeschichte* (2004), pp. 797–861; Kägi, 'Zur Entwicklung des Schweizerischen Rechtsstaates seit 1848' (1952), 187–208.

59 Tschannen, *Staatsrecht der Schweizerischen Eidgenossenschaft* (2011), p. 77 ('Strukturprinzip'). For a detailed explanation of the term, see Mastronardi, *Strukturprinzipien der Bundesverfassung?* (1988).

60 Schmid/Uhlmann, 'Idee und Ausgestaltung des Rechtsstaates' (2001), 226 ('allgemeiner Grundsatz').

61 Häfelin/Haller/Keller, *Schweizerisches Bundesstaatsrecht* (2012), p. 51 ('tragender Grundwert').

62 See Section 4.2.1. 63 BV, Arts 143–191c. 64 BV, Art. 29. 65 BV, Art. 29a.

66 BV, Arts 30 and 191c. 67 BV, Arts 7–34.

bodies) are bound to apply acts of the Federal Assembly even if they are incompatible with the Constitution.[68] In other words, there exists no constitutional review at the federal level. Courts can, however, disapply federal acts if they conflict with international norms guaranteeing human rights.[69] Furthermore, in contrast to federal acts, *cantonal* and *municipal* legislation can be invalidated for being unconstitutional.

4.1.5 The rule of law in international law

Due to the distinctive characteristics of the international legal system, such as the requirement of state consent and the lack of a central law-making authority, easy analogies between the national and the international level should be avoided.[70] Nevertheless, it can be observed that most of the essential elements of the rule of law as it has developed at the national level in different states are reflected in the basic features of the contemporary international legal system. To name only the most important of these features: there is a substantial, and growing, body of international norms that are regarded as authoritative (and thus as proper law), providing for certainty, predictability and stability and limiting discretionary power; this body of international law applies, as a matter of principle, equally to all legal subjects; and there is a growing number of independent international courts and tribunals that are accessible to legal subjects for the adjudication of disputes.[71] Based on these features, it can be argued that there is, at the very least, an 'emerging international rule of law'.[72]

Importantly, not only the international legal system bears the most important characteristics of a system based on the rule of law, but numerous international commitments have been made that the rule of law must be complied with and promoted, both nationally and internationally. Already the Universal Declaration of Human Rights (UDHR) of 1948 stated in its preamble that 'it is essential, if man is not to be compelled to have recourse, as a last resort, to rebellion against tyranny and oppression, that human rights should be protected by the rule of law'.[73] In 1959, judges

[68] BV, Art. 190. However, this does not prevent the Federal Supreme Court from examining and criticising acts of the Federal Assembly. See e.g. BGE 129 II 249, 263 (2003).
[69] BGE 125 II 417, 424–6 (1999). See Section 5.1.4.
[70] See Waldron, 'The Rule of International Law' (2006).
[71] See Beaulac, 'The Rule of Law in International Law Today' (2009).
[72] Zangl, 'Is there an Emerging International Rule of Law?' (2005).
[73] Universal Declaration of Human Rights (UDHR) (General Assembly Resolution 217A (III), 10 December 1948, UN Doc. A/810), preamble, para. 3.

and lawyers from all over the world gathered in New Delhi and solemnly declared their commitment to promote the rule of law through the work of the International Commission of Jurists.[74] At the 2005 World Summit, the community of states repeatedly affirmed their commitment to the rule of law[75] and recognised 'the need for universal adherence to and implementation of the rule of law at both the national and international levels'.[76] The main organs of the UN, the General Assembly[77] and the Security Council,[78] have adopted various resolutions calling on states and international bodies to comply with the rule of law, and its Secretary-General has produced several reports on the issue.[79] Finally, different agencies of the UN undertake a vast array of activities to promote the rule of law worldwide.[80]

4.1.6 Common elements of the rule of law and the Rechtsstaatsprinzip

Modern theoretical formulations of the rule of law and the *Rechtsstaatsprinzip* are commonly divided into two basic categories: formal and substantive versions.[81] *Formal* conceptions focus on the procedure in which law is made, the form it must take and its temporal

[74] International Congress of Jurists, Declaration on the Rule of Law, Conference at New Delhi, India, 10 January 1959, (1959) 2 *Journal of International Commission of Jurists* 7.

[75] GA Resolution 60/1, 24 October 2005, UN Doc. A/RES/60/1, paras 11, 16, 21, 24(b), 25(a), 119, 134.

[76] Ibid., para. 134.

[77] E.g. GA Resolution 64/116, 15 January 2010, UN Doc. A/RES/64/116; GA Resolution 63/128, 15 January 2009, UN Doc. A/RES/63/128; GA Resolution 62/70, 8 January 2008, UN Doc. A/RES/62/70; GA Resolution 61/39, 18 December 2006, UN Doc. A/RES/61/39. See also the Declaration of the High-level Meeting of the General Assembly on the Rule of Law at the National and International Levels, 19 September 2012, UN Doc. A/67/L.1.

[78] E.g. SC Resolution 1888 (2009), 30 September 2009, UN Doc. S/RES/1888 (2009), para. 8; SC Resolution 1674 (2006), 28 April 2006, UN Doc. S/RES/1674 (2006).

[79] E.g. Report of the Secretary-General, Annual report on strengthening and coordinating United Nations rule of law activities, 17 August 2009, UN Doc. A/64/298; Report of the Secretary-General, Strengthening and coordinating United Nations rule of law activities, 6 August 2008, UN Doc. A/63/226; Report of the Secretary-General, Uniting our strengths: Enhancing United Nations support for the rule of law, 14 December 2006, UN Doc. S/2006/980; Report of the Secretary-General, The rule of law and transitional justice in conflict and post-conflict societies, 23 August 2004, UN Doc. S/2004/616.

[80] For an overview, see Report of the Secretary-General, The rule of law at the national and international levels, 12 March 2008, UN Doc. A/63/64. See also the UN website 'United Nations Rule of Law', at www.unrol.org.

[81] Craig, 'Formal and Substantive Conceptions of the Rule of Law' (1997); Bäumlin, *Die rechtsstaatliche Demokratie* (1954), pp. 43–53.

dimension. However, they are not concerned with the content of the law, that is, whether a law is 'good' or 'bad'. Within this category of formal conceptions, 'thinner' and 'thicker' versions can be distinguished, depending on the exact requirements.[82] The thinnest formal version only requires that government act through law ('rule by law'), while thicker versions require the law to have certain qualities – for instance, to be prospective, general, clear, relatively stable and applied by an independent judiciary. The thickest formal version adds as a further requirement that law be passed in a democratic process.[83] Famous examples of formal conceptions of the rule of law include those of Dicey, discussed above, Lon Fuller[84] and Joseph Raz.[85] *Substantive* conceptions of the rule of law and the *Rechtsstaat* also incorporate these formal elements but add to them requirements about the content of the law. According to the most common substantive version, the rule of law requires the guarantee of individual rights. Ronald Dworkin,[86] Trevor Allan[87] and, in Switzerland, Werner Kägi[88] are some of the principal advocates of such substantive rule-of-law conceptions. The thickest substantive version requires not only the advancement of individual rights but also the establishment of 'social, economic, educational and cultural conditions under which [the individual's] legitimate aspirations and dignity may be realized'.[89]

As is apparent from the account in the previous sections, elements of these different theoretical conceptions of the rule of law and the *Rechtsstaat* have been realised to different extents at different historical periods in different political systems. It is true that today's German and Swiss notion of the *Rechtsstaat* with its emphasis on human dignity is more substantively grounded than the Anglo-American concept of the rule of law with its focus on procedural safeguards. However, as is demonstrated by the different phases that the idea of the *Rechtsstaat* itself has gone through, this has not always been the case. In that sense, there is little point in trying to work out fundamental distinctions between the concept of the rule of law and that of the *Rechtsstaat*. Both concepts refer

82 See Tamanaha, *On the Rule of Law* (2004), pp. 91–101.
83 For such a thick version, see e.g. Habermas, *Faktizität und Geltung* (1992).
84 Fuller, *The Morality of Law* (1969), Chapter 2.
85 Raz, 'The Rule of Law and Its Virtue' (1977).
86 Dworkin, 'Political Judges and the Rule of Law' (1978).
87 Allan, 'The Rule of Law as the Rule of Reason' (1999).
88 Kägi, 'Zur Entwicklung des Schweizerischen Rechtsstaates seit 1848' (1952), 174–80.
89 International Congress of Jurists, Declaration on the Rule of Law, Conference at New Delhi, India, 10 January 1959, (1959) 2 *Journal of International Commission of Jurists* 7.

to the same basic idea which, depending on the historical and political context, may be (and has been) implemented in different ways, either focusing more on formal requirements or, in addition, emphasising material elements.[90]

The basic idea underlying the rule of law in the United Kingdom and the United States as well as the *Rechtsstaatsprinzip* in Switzerland is that the power of the state and its officials needs to be limited by law to prevent arbitrariness. There is broad consensus today, therefore, that any concept of the rule of law must incorporate, at the very least, a number of fundamental formal elements. These minimal requirements, or principles, can be found in all three legal systems at issue. They include the principle of legality; the requirement that laws be public, prospective, general, clear and stable; the principle of formal equality; due process guarantees; and access to justice. Some of these principles are of particular relevance for the present context and are therefore discussed in more detail below.

4.1.7 Link to fundamental rights and democracy

It is widely acknowledged that the rule of law is a prerequisite for upholding fundamental guarantees of liberty and equality. The link between the rule of law and fundamental rights is stressed in the preambular passage of the UDHR quoted above, according to which 'human rights should be protected by the rule of law'.[91] By requiring authorities to act in accordance with laws declared publicly in clear terms in advance, the rule of law enables people to plan and act as autonomous rational beings and thus to exercise their liberties. As Montesquieu put it, 'liberty is a right of doing whatever the laws permit'.[92] Furthermore, the rule of law forces those in power to articulate their claims in terms of rules that are equally applicable to everyone, both the powerful and the powerless, and, as E.P. Thompson understood, thus renders them 'prisoners of their own rhetoric'.[93] In this way, the very form of law functions as a crucial

[90] See also Pech, 'The Rule of Law as a Constitutional Principle of the European Union' (2009); Weber, 'Rechtsstaatsprinzip als gemeineuropäisches Verfassungsprinzip' (2008); Carpano, *État de droit et droits européens* (2005); Fernandez Esteban, *The Rule of Law in the European Constitution* (1999), pp. 65–101; MacCormick, 'Der Rechtsstaat und die rule of law' (1984).

[91] UDHR, preamble, para. 3.

[92] De Montesquieu, *De l'esprit des lois* (1950–1961), Livre XI, Chapitre III ('La liberté est le droit de faire tout ce que les lois permettent.').

[93] Thompson, *Whigs and Hunters* (1990), p. 263.

inhibition on state power. As the Frankfurt-school jurist Franz Neumann observed, '[t]he generality and the abstractness of law together with the independence of the judge guarantee a minimum of personal and political liberty'.[94] It has therefore been rightly claimed that liberal political systems cannot exist without the rule of law.[95] However, the converse is not true. The rule of law, at least if understood in a strictly formal sense, can exist in illiberal systems that do not respect fundamental rights. As explained above, there existed what can be described as forms of the rule of law in ancient Greece and the Middle Ages. Today, illiberal states such as China[96] and Iran[97] claim to comply with the requirements of a formal conception of the rule of law. Only if a substantive conception that understands fundamental rights as forming part and parcel of the rule of law is adopted, can it be maintained that the latter depends on the former.

There is an equally close link between the rule of law and democracy.[98] The Swiss constitutional lawyer Werner Kägi even argued that the *Rechtsstaat* and democracy have a 'common destiny', that there is a need for a synthesis of the two concepts.[99] Writing in the wake of the Second World War, Kägi had in mind the dangers of a tyranny of the majority.[100] He was of the view that democracy can only survive if its power is channelled and limited through the rule of law.[101] The view that democracy cannot exist without the rule of law is shared by many[102] and has, as explained in the previous sections, shaped the constitutional arrangements in the three states under examination, although in different ways. Again, the converse is not necessarily true.[103] Although Gustav Radbruch argued that only democracy can secure the *Rechtsstaat*,[104] the

94 Neumann, *Behemoth* (1942), pp. 362–3.
95 Tamanaha, *On the Rule of Law* (2004), p. 33.
96 See Peerenboom, *China's Long March Toward Rule of Law* (2002).
97 E.g. R. Worth and N. Fathi, 'Ahmadinejad, Rejecting Strife, Hints of Arrests', *New York Times*, 14 June 2009.
98 See generally Maravall and Przeworski (eds), *Democracy and the Rule of Law* (2003); Bäumlin, *Die rechtsstaatliche Demokratie* (1954).
99 Kägi, 'Rechtsstaat und Demokratie (Antinomie und Synthese)' (1953), 107–8.
100 Ibid., 107.
101 Ibid., 137–8. See also Kägi, 'Zur Entwicklung des Schweizerischen Rechtsstaates seit 1848' (1952), 179.
102 See e.g. Auer, 'Direkte Demokratie und Rechtsstaat' (2009), 32–4. For an overview and critique, see Hutchinson/Monahan, 'Democracy and the Rule of Law' (1987).
103 See Auer, 'Direkte Demokratie und Rechtsstaat' (2009), 33.
104 Radbruch, 'Gesetzliches Unrecht und übergesetzliches Recht' (1946), 108. See also Bäumlin, *Die rechtsstaatliche Demokratie* (1954), pp. 95–6.

political reality would seem to prove otherwise: China and other non-democratic states arguably meet all the requirements of a *strictly formal* conception of the rule of law. Joseph Raz has even argued that '[a] non-democratic legal system [. . .] may, in principle, conform to the requirements of the rule of law better than any of the legal systems of the more enlightened western democracies'.[105]

In summary, then, compliance with the rule of law is a prerequisite for the protection of fundamental rights and upholding a democratic system: a liberal democracy without the rule of law is unthinkable.

4.2 Principle of legality

One of the most fundamental principles implicit in the rule of law and the *Rechtsstaatsprinzip* is the requirement for a legal basis of all government action. This 'principle of legality', in turn, implies a number of further requirements, in particular that of sufficient precision, discussed in Section 4.3.

4.2.1 The need for legal authority

Since the rule of law aims to secure 'a government of laws, and not of men',[106] it implies as its perhaps most basic and central principle that the government is bound by law and that all of its actions must be authorised by law.[107]

At least as far as limitations of human rights are concerned, this principle, often referred to as the 'principle of legality', is firmly established in international law, including in treaties ratified by the states under consideration. The UDHR, in Article 11(2), the International Covenant on Civil and Political Rights (ICCPR),[108] in Article 15, and the ECHR, in Article 7, all guarantee the principle of *nullum crimen, nulla poena sine lege*.[109] The requirement for a clear legal basis is, however, not limited to the criminal law context. The UDHR, the ICCPR and the ECHR require that – as far as limitations are permissible at all – any

105 Raz, 'The Rule of Law and Its Virtue' (1977), 196.
106 *Marbury* v. *Madison*, 5 U.S. 137, 163 (1803).
107 Raz, 'The Rule of Law and Its Virtue' (1977), 196.
108 International Covenant on Civil and Political Rights (ICCPR) (adopted 16 December 1966, entered into force 23 March 1976) 999 UNTS 171.
109 On this principle, see Gallant, *The Principle of Legality in International and Comparative Criminal Law* (2009).

limitation of the rights they guarantee must be 'determined by law',[110] 'prescribed by law'[111], 'provided by law',[112] 'in conformity with the law'[113] or 'in accordance with the law'.[114] All these formulations refer to essentially the same requirement: namely, that the state must be able to point to some specific legal rule that authorises the interference. This legal rule must be adequately accessible and sufficiently precise to enable citizens to regulate their conduct.[115] It does not, however, need to be written down in legislation but can also be part of unwritten law, as in the case of common law in the Anglo-American tradition.[116]

The principle that all government action must be authorised by law underlies the legal systems of all liberal democracies, although the specific form it takes and the description that is attached to it may differ.[117] The requirement is of particularly great importance in the German legal tradition. Described in Switzerland as *Legalitätsprinzip* or *Prinzip der Gesetzmässigkeit* in German and as *principe de la légalité* in French ('principle of legality'),[118] it is at the heart of the formal conception of the *Rechtsstaat*. In the Anglo-American legal tradition, the emphasis is more on the requirement that government must not act unlawfully, and the terms 'principle of legality' and 'legality' are used in a rather inconsistent manner.

Given that the *Legalitätsprinzip* is at the heart of the idea of the *Rechtsstaat*, it is not surprising that it constitutes one of the fundamental principles of Swiss constitutional law. As explained above, Article 5(1) of the Federal Constitution explicitly guarantees the principle, stating that the law is the basis as well as the limit of any state action. This provision requires, among other things, any action of the state to be based on legal rules, a requirement traditionally described as *Gesetzesvorbehalt/réserve de la loi* ('authorisation by law').[119] These

110 UDHR, Art. 29(2). 111 ICCPR, Arts 18(3), 22(2); ECHR, Arts 9(2), 10(2), 11(2).

112 ICCPR, Arts 12(3), 19(3). 113 ICCPR, Art. 21. 114 ECHR, Art. 8(2).

115 For the ICCPR, see UNESCO, Siracusa Principles on the Limitation and Derogation Provisions in the International Covenant on Civil and Political Rights, UN Doc. E/CN.4/1985/4, Annex (1985), Principles 5 and 15–18. For the ECHR, see *The Sunday Times* v. *The United Kingdom (No. 1)*, no. 6538/74, 26 April 1979, Series A no. 30, para. 49. On the requirement of sufficient precision, see Section 4.3.

116 For the ECHR, see *The Sunday Times* v. *The United Kingdom (No. 1)*, no. 6538/74, 26 April 1979, Series A no. 30, para. 47.

117 For an overview of the European states, see Schwarze, *Europäisches Verwaltungsrecht* (2005), pp. 198–218.

118 E.g. Auer/Malinverni/Hottelier, *Droit constitutionnel suisse* (2013), Vol. I, p. 609; Biaggini, *Kommentar BV* (2007), p. 76.

119 E.g. Auer/Malinverni/Hottelier, *Droit constitutionnel suisse* (2013), Vol. I, p. 618; Biaggini, *Kommentar BV* (2007), p. 76; Mahon, 'Art. 5' (2003), 44.

legal rules must be general (that is, addressed to an indeterminate number of legal subjects), abstract (that is, regulating an indeterminate number of recurring situations), published in advance as well as sufficiently precise so that citizens can regulate their conduct accordingly and foresee the consequences that a given action may entail.[120] These requirements relating to the quality of a legal authority apply to any type of state action,[121] helping to ensure equality before the law and legal certainty.[122] With regard to certain types of state action, heightened requirements apply: they must be based on law that, in addition to having the qualities listed above ('law in the material sense'), has been passed in a democratic process. Thus, these types of state action must be based on an act that has been passed by parliament and, at least at the federal level, is subject to a referendum ('law in the formal sense').[123] Which state actions require such an explicit basis in a law in the formal sense may differ between the federal and the cantonal level and between different cantons.[124] This is not the place to review the complex case law determining exactly what the principle of legality entails in different fields.[125] What is important to note for the present context is that the requirements regarding the legal basis of state action are particularly stringent as far as there is an interference with fundamental rights. Article 36(1) of the Federal Constitution provides not only that there must be a legal basis for any interference with fundamental rights – be it by a federal, cantonal or municipal authority – but, in its second sentence, also that any 'serious' interference must be prescribed by

120 Häfelin/Haller/Keller, *Schweizerisches Bundesstaatsrecht* (2012), p. 100; Häfelin/Müller/Uhlmann, *Allgemeines Verwaltungsrecht* (2010), pp. 86–9; Biaggini, *Kommentar BV* (2007), p. 76; Moor, 'Principes de l'activité étatique et responsabilité de l'Etat' (2001), 269–70.

121 See BGE 103 Ia 369, 380–81 (1977).

122 BGE 130 I 1, 5 (2003). See Auer/Malinverni/Hottelier, *Droit constitutionnel suisse* (2013), Vol. I, pp. 619–20; Häfelin/Haller/Keller, *Schweizerisches Bundesstaatsrecht* (2012), pp. 52, 100; Häfelin/Müller/Uhlmann, *Allgemeines Verwaltungsrecht* (2010), p. 85; Biaggini, *Kommentar BV* (2007), p. 76; Mahon, 'Art. 5' (2003), 44.

123 Tschannen/Zimmerli/Müller, *Allgemeines Verwaltungsrecht* (2014), pp. 138–9; Häfelin/Müller/Uhlmann, *Allgemeines Verwaltungsrecht* (2010), pp. 89–91; Zimmerli, 'Zum Gesetzmässigkeitsprinzip im Verwaltungsrecht' (1984). On the distinction between 'law in the material sense' and 'law in the formal sense', see Cottier, *Die Verfassung und das Erfordernis der gesetzlichen Grundlage* (1983), pp. 7–17, 248–53.

124 For the federal level, see BV, Arts 36(1) and 127(1) and the list contained in Art. 164(1).

125 For good overviews, see Tschannen/Zimmerli/Müller, *Allgemeines Verwaltungsrecht* (2014), pp. 144–53; Auer/Malinverni/Hottelier, *Droit constitutionnel suisse* (2013), Vol I, pp. 626–31; Häfelin/Müller/Uhlmann, *Allgemeines Verwaltungsrecht* (2010), pp. 86–97; Zimmerli, 'Zum Gesetzmässigkeitsprinzip im Verwaltungsrecht' (1984), 73.

a law in the formal sense.[126] Generally speaking, the more serious the interference is, the more stringent the requirements as to its democratic legitimacy are.[127] For less serious interferences it is sufficient for them to be based on a law in the material sense such as a regulation issued by the executive branch, as long as that regulation in turn has a sufficient legislative basis, that is, as long as there is a sufficient delegating norm in a law in the formal sense.[128] Standards are also relaxed as far as the regulation of 'extended common use' (*gesteigerter Gemeingebrauch*) of public goods is concerned. In its older jurisprudence, the Federal Supreme Court suggested that authorisation requirements for such use of public goods could be imposed even in the absence of any legal basis for doing so.[129] This view has been heavily criticised.[130] In recent relevant cases, the Federal Supreme Court has neither confirmed nor overturned its previous position, instead leaving the issue open.[131]

As far as the United Kingdom is concerned, it is well established that the first element of Dicey's rule of law requires public authorities and officials to act according to the law and within the powers that have been conferred upon them.[132] This requirement is often described as the 'principle of legality',[133] although use of the term is inconsistent.[134] The main instrument to ensure compliance with this requirement is the *ultra vires* doctrine, empowering courts to invalidate acts of public

[126] BV, Art. 36(1), sentence 2 ('Schwerwiegende Einschränkungen müssen im Gesetz selbst vorgesehen sein.').

[127] Häfelin/Haller/Keller, *Schweizerisches Bundesstaatsrecht* (2012), p. 101; Kiener/Kälin, *Grundrechte* (2013), p. 102.

[128] Auer/Malinverni/Hottelier, *Droit constitutionnel suisse* (2013), Vol. I, p. 628; Kiener/Kälin, *Grundrechte* (2013), pp. 103–4; Häfelin/Haller/Keller, *Schweizerisches Bundesstaatsrecht* (2012), p. 101.

[129] E.g. BGE 105 Ia 91, 93 (1979); BGE 100 Ia 392, 398 (1974).

[130] Tschannen/Zimmerli/Müller, *Allgemeines Verwaltungsrecht* (2014), pp. 486–7; Auer/Malinverni/Hottelier, *Droit constitutionnel suisse* (2013), Vol I, pp. 635–6; Kiener/Kälin, *Grundrechte* (2013), pp. 112, 214–15; Gächter, 'Allgemeine Grundrechtslehren' (2011), 434; Häfelin/Müller/Uhlmann, *Allgemeines Verwaltungsrecht* (2010), p. 547; Malinverni, 'L'exercice des libertés idéales sur le domaine public' (2004), 30–1; Weber-Dürler, 'Grundrechtseingriffe' (2000), 137–8.

[131] BGE 135 I 302, 307–8 (2009); Urteil des Bundesgerichts 2P.191/2004 vom 10. August 2005, in 107 (2006) *Schweizerisches Zentralblatt für Staats- und Verwaltungsrecht* 254, 267. For a detailed discussion, see Moser, *Der öffentliche Grund und seine Benützung* (2011), pp. 255–61.

[132] Alder, *Constitutional and Administrative Law* (2013), p. 118; Bradley/Ewing, *Constitutional and Administrative Law* (2011), p. 96.

[133] Bradley/Ewing, *Constitutional and Administrative Law* (2011), pp. 95–6.

[134] Compare e.g. the meaning just referred to with that given to the term by Lord Hoffmann in *R* v. *Secretary of State for the Home Department, ex parte Simms*, [2000] 2 AC 115, 131.

authorities that are beyond their legal powers.[135] However, at least traditionally, the obligation on the part of public authorities has been primarily understood as an obligation not to act unlawfully, rather than, as in Switzerland, as an obligation to have legal authority for all their actions.[136] So the rule is that, just as with private actors, public officials can do whatever is not prohibited. It is true that Chief Justice Lord Camden held as early as 1765, in the leading case of *Entick* v. *Carrington*, that public officials must have legal authority in a statute or common law for their actions.[137] Similarly, leading constitutional lawyers have argued that 'the government must be able to point to some basis for its action that is regarded as valid by the relevant legal system'[138] and that '[a]ll decisions and acts of public officials should generally therefore be legally authorized'.[139] Nevertheless, the general view is that the government only needs to be able to point to formal legal authority when it interferes with established personal or property rights of the individual[140] – as was the case in *Entick* v. *Carrington* where there had been a trespass. William Wade aptly summarised the prevailing position: '[E]very government authority which does some act which would otherwise be a wrong (such as taking a man's land), or which infringes a man's liberty (as by refusing him planning permission), must be able to justify its action as authorised by law'.[141] With the incorporation of the ECHR into UK law by the Human Rights Act 1998, the scope of government action requiring explicit legal authority has been expanded to all areas where Convention rights are concerned.[142]

In US legal discourse, the term 'principle of legality' is used rather haphazardly – it 'has tended to function as a more or less convenient catch-all label attached to a more or less random collection of doctrines, rules, and maxims'.[143] Most commonly, its use is restricted to the criminal law context, in other words, it is reduced to the principle *nullum*

135 Barnett, *Constitutional and Administrative Law* (2013), pp. 60–2, 594–7; Craig, *Administrative Law* (2012), pp. 4–16; Bradley/Ewing, *Constitutional and Administrative Law* (2011), pp. 671–3.
136 See *Malone* v. *Commissioner of Police of the Metropolis (No.2)*, [1979] Ch. 344.
137 *Entick* v. *Carrington*, [1765] EWHC KB J98.
138 Craig, 'Appendix 5: The Rule of Law' (2006–2007), 98.
139 Jowell, 'The Rule of Law' (2015), 20.
140 Ewing/Gearty, *The Struggle for Civil Liberties* (2000), p. 14. See e.g. *R.* v. *Lord Chancellor, ex parte Witham*, [1998] Q.B. 575.
141 Wade/Forsyth, *Administrative Law* (2014), p. 15.
142 E.g. Amos, *Human Rights Law* (2006), pp. 80–4.
143 Dubber, 'The Legality Principle in American and German Criminal Law' (2010), 8.

crimen, nulla poena sine lege, in particular the prohibition of retroactive criminal laws.[144] This is reflective of the fact that there is in the United States no general requirement for an explicit legal authority for all government actions. It is true that according to the so-called non-delegation doctrine the legislature cannot delegate its power to the executive branch, unless it provides some 'intelligible principle' or prescribed standard to guide the latter.[145] However, the requirements established by the Supreme Court in this regard are very modest; it is generally seen as sufficient that a public authority can point to some broadly framed legal power.[146] Instead, in keeping with the process-oriented Anglo-American conception of the rule of law, the focus is primarily on the provision of procedural safeguards.[147] With regard to the present context, for example, the states have an extremely broadly defined police power (that is, an inherent power to protect the health, safety, morals and general welfare of the society), which they can in turn delegate to other entities.[148] As in the United Kingdom, the crucial question is therefore normally whether public authorities act unlawfully or not, rather than whether there is an explicit legal basis for their actions. In particular, of course, any government action as well as any legislation at whatever level – be it federal, state or municipal – must not violate constitutional guarantees. Of particular importance in this regard is the void-for-vagueness doctrine (or vagueness doctrine) developed in the context of the due process clauses of the Fifth and Fourteenth Amendments as well as of the First Amendment.[149] According to this doctrine, all laws limiting fundamental constitutional rights must define the prohibited conduct 'with sufficient definiteness that ordinary people can understand what conduct is prohibited and in a manner that does not encourage arbitrary and discriminatory enforcement'.[150] Thus, the vagueness doctrine is

[144] See *Calder* v. *Bull*, 3 U.S. 386, 390 (1798) (limiting the prohibition of retroactive legislation of US Constitution, Art. I (9)(3) and Art. I (10)(1) to criminal law); Dubber, 'Comparative Criminal Law' (2006), 1313–18.

[145] *J.W. Hampton, Jr., & Co.* v. *United States*, 276 U.S. 394, 406, 409 (1928). See Fleiner, *Die Delegation als Problem des Verfassungs- und Verwaltungsrechts* (1972), pp. 24–38.

[146] See e.g. *Mistretta* v. *United States*, 488 U.S. 361, 371–4 (1989); *Lichter* v. *United States*, 334 U.S. 742 (1948); *Yakus* v. *United States*, 321 U.S. 414 (1944). In view of this lenient approach to delegation, Oliver Lepsius has argued that the non-delegation doctrine has effectively been given up. Lepsius, *Verwaltungsrecht unter dem Common Law* (1997), pp. 184–9.

[147] See Davis, 'A New Approach to Delegation' (1968), 713–33.

[148] See Section 4.2.2.

[149] The classic account is 'The Void-for-Vagueness Doctrine in the Supreme Court' (1960).

[150] *Kolender* v. *Lawson*, 461 U.S. 352, 357 (1983).

designed to enforce the rule-of-law values of legal certainty and prevention of arbitrariness and has been described as 'the operational arm of legality'.[151]

In sum, while there are important differences with regard to the 'principle of legality' between the three legal systems under consideration, one basic requirement applies in all of them: at the very least when a public authority interferes with fundamental rights, it must be able to point to a formal legal authority for doing so. In practice, most legal disputes will turn around the question of whether that legal authority is sufficiently precise. This question is discussed in Section 4.3.

4.2.2 Exclusion from public space based on explicit legal authority

As will be explained in detail in Chapter 5, measures excluding people from public space interfere with (a range of) fundamental rights. Therefore, they are only compatible with the principle of legality if there is a legal basis for them. This section briefly reviews the legal bases of the various exclusion measures explained in Chapter 3 and set out in Annex I.

Switzerland and the United States are federal states so that the legal basis of exclusion measures may be found at different levels, namely that of the federal state, that of the cantons/states or that of the municipalities. In the United Kingdom, in contrast, only the central government can create the legal authority for exclusion from public space.

A wide range of public authorities may be involved in the administration and enforcement of legal norms authorising exclusion from public space, including courts, government ministers, immigration authorities, different police forces or other law enforcement agencies and various local authorities. The majority of exclusion measures are enforced by the police.[152] The way the police is organised in the states at issue differs widely. Briefly stated, in Switzerland there are a number of federal law enforcement agencies (which are only of minor relevance for the context of exclusion measures), the police forces of every canton and various police forces at the municipal level.[153] Similarly, in the United States the federal government maintains several law enforcement agencies (which,

151 Jeffries, 'Legality, Vagueness, and the Construction of Penal Statutes' (1985), 196.

152 On the definition of the term 'police', see Section 1.4.

153 Mohler, *Grundzüge des Polizeirechts in der Schweiz* (2012), pp. 71–89; Sauer, *Das Recht der Vollzugspolizeien von Bund und Kantonen in der Schweiz* (2007), pp. 82–103; Reinhard, *Allgemeines Polizeirecht* (1993), pp. 44–50.

again, are not of relevance for the present context); every state has a police force (state police); and, finally, there are, depending on the state, different types of police forces at the local level: the county police, sheriff's departments and the municipal (or city) police.[154] The institutional structure of the police is more straightforward in the United Kingdom where, apart from a few special police forces at the national level with a non-regional jurisdiction (such as the British Transport Police), all police officers are organised into a number of territorial police forces, each covering a 'police area'.[155]

4.2.2.1 Switzerland

In Switzerland, protection of public safety and order – the main justification for exclusion from public space – lies primarily in the competence of the cantons.[156] The scope for federal authorities to provide for, or enforce, exclusion measures is thus limited. Federal law does, however, provide for a power of exclusion from public space as far as immigration – a typical matter falling within the competence of the Swiss federation[157] – is concerned. As explained in Section 3.3.2.4, under the Federal Act on Foreign Nationals, foreign nationals without leave to stay who threaten or disturb public safety and order can be ordered not to leave or not to access a specified area.[158] Enforcement of this power is a matter for the cantonal authorities.[159] Furthermore, there are norms authorising exclusion from public space in federal law in the Swiss Criminal Code,[160] the Military Criminal Code,[161] the Juvenile Criminal Code,[162] the Swiss Criminal Procedure Code,[163] the Military Act[164] and the Swiss Civil Code.[165] Finally, as explained in Section 3.3.1.2, in a concordat (an intercantonal treaty) ratified by all cantons, cantons have agreed to create exclusion powers to deal with violence related to sports events.[166]

154 Langworthy/Travis III, *Policing in America* (1994), pp. 8–9, 93–115, 137–58; Walker, *The Police in America* (1992), pp. 42–50.

155 See, for England and Wales, Police Act 1996, s. 1 and Schedule 1.

156 See BV, Arts 3, 42, 57(1); Botschaft über eine neue Bundesverfassung vom 20. November 1996, BBl 1997 I, 1, p. 237; Mohler, *Grundzüge des Polizeirechts in der Schweiz* (2012), pp. 71–2; Linsi, 'Verfassungsrechtliche Zuständigkeit des Bundes für den Erlass von Polizeirecht' (2008); Lienhard/Häsler, 'Verfassungsrechtliche Grundlagen des Sicherheitsrechts' (2008), 114–20.

157 BV, Art. 121. 158 AuG, Art. 74(1). 159 AuG, Art. 74(2).

160 StGB, Arts 44, 62, 67b, 87, 94. 161 MStG, Art. 50(b). 162 JStG, Art. 16(a)(2).

163 StPO, Art. 237. 164 MG, Art. 92. 165 ZGB, Art. 28b.

166 Konkordat über Massnahmen gegen Gewalt anlässlich von Sportveranstaltungen vom 15. November 2007. See also Konkordat über Massnahmen gegen Gewalt anlässlich von

Apart from this, the legal basis for exclusion measures is to be found at the cantonal level or – as far as cantons have delegated their powers to the municipalities – at the municipal level. Most importantly, as explained in Section 3.3.2.4, most cantonal police acts authorise the police to exclude people from public space for reasons of public safety and order. Older police acts did not typically specify the various measures the police could resort to. Instead, the police would rely on their broadly defined power to maintain public safety and order under the 'general police clause' (*polizeiliche Generalklausel/clause générale de police*),[167] raising concerns with regard to the principle of legality.[168] Not least because of these concerns, beginning from the 1980s and, in the case of most cantons, the 1990s, many cantons started to revise their relevant legislation.[169] These new police acts not only specify the tasks of the police (protection of public safety and order, criminal prosecution etc.),[170] but normally also list the various measures the police are authorised to employ.[171] The power to remove (*wegweisen*) and keep away (*fernhalten*) from public places anyone who threatens or disturbs public safety and order is included as one of the available measures in nearly all of the recently revised cantonal police acts.[172] Depending on how the police in the respective canton is organised, this power may be exercised by the cantonal police force and the police forces of the towns or municipalities.

Municipal authorities may not only have the authority to enforce cantonal legislation but also to legislate on certain matters as such. As explained in Section 2.4.1 above, regulation of the use of smaller, local roads and squares typically falls within the competence of the municipalities. As far as exclusion measures are concerned, it is, for example, normally left to municipalities to pass legislation regulating the holding of demonstrations and other forms of political protest on

Sportveranstaltungen vom 15. November 2007; Änderung vom 2. Februar 2012 (not (yet) ratified by all cantons).

167 See Section 4.2.3.

168 See already Huber, 'Grundrechte und Polizeigewalt' (1952), 238. See also Keller/Bürli, 'Überdenken der polizeilichen Generalklausel bei Vorliegen staatlicher Schutzpflichten' (2011), 1146–7; Strasser, *Polizeiliche Zwangsmassnahmen* (1981), pp. 26, 95.

169 See Sauer, *Das Recht der Vollzugspolizeien von Bund und Kantonen in der Schweiz* (2007), pp. 37–40; Schweizer, 'Entwicklungen im Polizeirecht von Bund und Kantonen' (1997).

170 See e.g. for the Canton of Zurich: Polizeigesetz vom 23. April 2007 (PolG, LS 550.1), §§ 3–7.

171 Ibid., §§ 16–17, 21–44.

172 See Section 3.3.2.4. For an overview in the form of a table, see Moeckli/Keller, 'Wegweisungen und Rayonverbote' (2012), 233.

their public ground[173] or to impose juvenile curfews within their respective territory.[174]

4.2.2.2 United States

Just like Switzerland, the United States is a federal state and exclusion from public space is a matter primarily falling within the competence of the equivalent to the Swiss cantons, the states. The federal government 'is acknowledged by all to be one of enumerated powers' and therefore can only act based on the powers specifically granted to it by the US Constitution.[175] As is made clear by the Tenth Amendment to the Constitution, all powers not delegated to the federal government are retained by the states. In particular, the states have an extremely broadly defined power, understood as an inherent attribute of sovereignty, to protect the health, safety, morals and welfare of their citizens.[176] Based on this 'police power', states can subject individual rights to reasonable regulation for the general welfare.[177] As can be seen from the norms authorising exclusion from public space listed in Annex I, some of these, such as restrictions of demonstrations or measures directed against sex offenders, are part of legislation passed at the state level.

However, a state may also delegate the police power to the municipalities throughout the state.[178] In this regard, the situation varies from state to state and depending on the subject matter. While in some cases the powers delegated to the municipalities are precisely specified in the respective state constitutions or legislation, states may also grant municipalities a broadly defined power to legislate, for instance, in matters

[173] See e.g. for the City of Zurich: Verordnung über die Benutzung des öffentlichen Grundes (Benutzungsordnung) vom 23. November 2011 (AS 551.210), Arts 21–4.

[174] See e.g. Gemeindepolizeireglement der Gemeinde Interlaken vom 5. Dezember 2006 (552.11), Art. 9(4). For other examples, see Section 3.3.2.3.

[175] *McCulloch* v. *Maryland*, 17 U.S. 316, 405 (1819).

[176] E.g. *U.S.* v. *Morrison*, 529 U.S. 598, 617–18 (2000); *City of El Paso* v. *Simmons*, 379 U.S. 497, 508 (1965); *Queenside Hills Realty Co.* v. *Saxl*, 328 U.S. 80, 83 (1946); *Lochner* v. *New York*, 198 U.S. 45, 53 (1905) ('There are [. . .] certain powers, existing in the sovereignty of each state in the Union, somewhat vaguely termed police powers, the exact description and limitation of which have not been attempted by the courts. Those powers [. . .] relate to the safety, health, morals, and general welfare of the public.'); *Mugler* v. *Kansas*, 123 U.S. 623, 661 (1887). See Tribe, *American Constitutional Law* (1988), pp. 405–6.

[177] See Dubber and Valverde (eds), *Police and the Liberal State* (2008); Dubber, *The Police Power* (2005); Wickersham, 'The Police Power, a Product of the Rule of Reason' (1914); Freund, *The Police Power* (1904).

[178] *Zucht* v. *King*, 260 U.S. 174 (1922).

relating to public safety and order.[179] As is evident from the exclusion measures listed in Annex I, many states have delegated to cities, towns and municipalities the power to regulate matters such as juvenile curfews or prohibitions of sleeping in public places or of lying or sitting on public sidewalks.

As explained in Section 4.2.1, unlike in Switzerland, public authorities such as the police must not necessarily be able to point to explicit legal authority for all their actions. Accordingly, while relevant pieces of legislation might refer in broad terms to the various duties of police forces (such as prevention of crime, detection and arrest of offenders, preservation of order, etc.),[180] they will not normally explicitly specify the powers and measures that are at the disposal of the police, such as the power to exclude people from public space. Instead, the legal basis for exclusion may be provided by legislation that prohibits the presence of certain people or of certain behaviour in public places, triggering the general power (and duty) of the police to enforce the law. The main issue with regard to police action, then, is whether it is in accordance with the general body of law, in particular whether it is within the limits set by the US Constitution (as well as the respective state constitution). Importantly in the present context, the legal basis of an exclusion measure must comply with the requirements of the vagueness doctrine.[181]

4.2.2.3 United Kingdom

Unlike in federal states such as Switzerland or the United States, in the United Kingdom, as a unitary state, the legal basis of all exclusion measures is to be found at the level of the central government. The parliament of the United Kingdom, sitting at Westminster, has full legislative supremacy. Of course, there are, as explained above, different regional police forces and local authorities that may be involved in the enforcement of exclusion measures. However, they must be able to point to some higher legal authority to justify their actions.

As explained in Section 4.2.1, unlike in Switzerland, government officials, including police officers, can, as a general rule, do whatever is not prohibited; in this regard they are treated much like private actors. However, whenever they interfere with someone's rights, they must be able to point to a specific legal authority that justifies their action.

[179] See e.g. Illinois Compiled Statutes, ch. 65, ss 5/11-1-1, 5/11-1-5.

[180] See e.g. New York City Charter, Chapter 18, § 435 (for the NYPD).

[181] See Section 4.3.

The tasks or duties of the police are not spelled out in legislation and they cannot derive any special powers from the mere fact that they are acting in the execution of their duties.[182] Instead, there must be a specific legal basis justifying police action, which may be provided either by a statute passed by parliament or by the common-law power to keep the peace. Annex I gives an overview of the wide range of statutory provisions authorising various public authorities (typically the police, but also other authorities such as courts or the Home Secretary) to exclude people from public space. As explained in Section 3.4, these provisions may take the form of police powers, court powers, prohibitions or authorisation requirements. The other potential legal basis for exclusion, the common-law power to prevent a breach of the peace, is discussed in the following section.

4.2.3 *Exclusion from public space without explicit legal authority*

4.2.3.1 *Breach-of-the-peace powers and* polizeiliche Generalklausel

In all three states under consideration it is accepted that, under certain circumstances, the police are empowered to take action – and interfere with fundamental rights – even in the absence of a specific legal authority if this is necessary for the protection of public order.

Switzerland In Switzerland, it has been acknowledged since the nineteenth century that certain police action may be taken based on the legal concept of the so-called *polizeiliche Generalklausel/clause générale de police* ('general police clause') instead of a specific legislative authority.[183] The federal constitutions of 1848[184] and 1874[185] provided

[182] See *Halsbury's Laws of England* (1988–2008), Vol. 36(1), para. 478 ('However a constable is himself subject to the law, and he cannot claim immunity from it by reason only that he is acting in pursuance of his duty; indeed a constable who flouted the law (whether civil or criminal) could scarcely be said to be acting in the execution of his duty as such.'); *Morris* v. *Beardmore*, [1981] AC 446.

[183] However, it should be noted that the concept was originally understood in a broader manner than it is today and that the term *polizeiliche Generalklausel* was only introduced in the middle of the twentieth century. Kaufmann/Walti, 'Die polizeiliche Generalklausel' (2011), 61–5.

[184] Bundesverfassung der Schweizerischen Eidgenossenschaft vom 12. September 1848, Art. 90 No. 10 (reprinted in Kölz, *Quellenbuch: Band I* (1992), p. 473).

[185] Bundesverfassung der Schweizerischen Eidgenossenschaft vom 29. Mai 1874, Art. 102 Nos 8–10 (reprinted in Kölz, *Quellenbuch: Band II* (1996), p. 179).

for a broadly framed power of the executive branch to maintain public order, as did older cantonal constitutions.[186] Most legal scholars of the time held that the *polizeiliche Generalklausel* formed part of customary law and so applied even if there was no constitutional basis for it.[187] The Federal Supreme Court acknowledged as early as 1894 that the police can take action even in the absence of a specific legal basis if this is necessary to protect public safety.[188] It spelled out the exact requirements for applying the *polizeiliche Generalklausel* for the first time in 1957.[189]

Today, the Federal Constitution refers to the *polizeiliche Generalklausel* in two of its provisions.[190] Of particular relevance for the present context is Article 36(1), sentence 3, which establishes an exception to the requirement of a specific legal basis for interferences with fundamental rights by providing that 'in cases of serious and immediate danger where no other course of action is possible', limitations of fundamental rights need not be prescribed by law.[191] Many cantonal constitutions[192] and police acts contain similar provisions.[193] In legal doctrine, the *polizeiliche Generalklausel* is described as an unwritten constitutional principle that applies even if it is not codified in constitutional or statutory texts.[194]

According to the established case law of the Federal Supreme Court, four requirements must be met for the *polizeiliche Generalklausel* to be applicable.[195] First, there must be a danger to 'public order' ('*öffentliche Ordnung*') and 'fundamental interests' ('*fundamentale Rechtsgüter*') of the state or private actors. However, these terms have never been precisely defined. They have often been interpreted quite widely as a reference to the broad concept of 'public safety and order' ('*öffentliche Sicherheit und Ordnung*'), which includes, for example, the functioning

186 Dürr, *Die Polizeiliche Generalklausel* (1967), p. 58.

187 See Dürr, *Die Polizeiliche Generalklausel* (1967), pp. 59–60.

188 BGE 20 790, 796–7 (1894).

189 BGE 83 I 111, 117 (1957).

190 BV, Art. 36(1), sentence 3; BV, Art. 185(3).

191 BV, Art. 36(1), sentence 3 ('Ausgenommen sind Fälle ernster, unmittelbarer und nicht anders abwendbarer Gefahr.').

192 E.g. Verfassung des Kantons Bern vom 6. Juni 1993 (SR 131.212), Art. 28(1); Verfassung des Kantons Appenzell Ausserrhoden vom 30. April 1995 (SR 131.224.1), Art. 23(3).

193 E.g. for the Canton of Zurich: Polizeigesetz vom 23. April 2007 (LS 550.1), § 9; for the Canton of Berne: Polizeigesetz vom 8. Juni 1997 (BSG 551.1), Art. 22.

194 Tschannen/Zimmerli/Müller, *Allgemeines Verwaltungsrecht* (2014), p. 538; Häfelin/Müller/Uhlmann, *Allgemeines Verwaltungsrecht* (2010), p. 565; Reinhard, *Allgemeines Polizeirecht* (1993), p. 158. See also BGE 103 Ia 310, 312 (1977).

195 For the standard formula, setting out these requirements, as it tends to be repeated by the court, see e.g. BGE 126 I 112, 118 (2000).

of public institutions and transport, the protection of public morals and the inviolability of the legal order.[196] Second, the danger to 'public order' and 'fundamental interests' must be serious and imminent. If there is sufficient time to deal with a situation through the ordinary legislative process, the threat cannot be said to be imminent. Third, the *polizeiliche Generalklausel* can only be invoked as a last resort, that is, only if the measures provided for by law are not sufficient to deal with the danger. Fourth, there must be a real and unforeseeable emergency. The *polizeiliche Generalklausel* cannot be invoked if the legislator, despite being aware of a dangerous situation, failed to address it. In other words, it cannot be invoked to deal with situations that are predictable as they typically tend to repeat themselves.[197] In three recent decisions, however, the Federal Supreme Court has suggested that this last requirement does not apply where there is a threat to fundamental interests that the state is under a duty to protect,[198] such as a person's life or physical integrity.[199] According to the court, the requirement of unforeseeability is only one element among others that may need to be weighed against other interests.[200] If these four (or, according to the Federal Supreme Court's recent jurisprudence, in some cases three) requirements are satisfied, the executive branch of government can take action despite the lack of a specific legal authority. The Strasbourg institutions have held that an interference with one of the rights guaranteed by the ECHR that is based on the *polizeiliche Generalklausel* as provided in the Federal Constitution or in cantonal constitutions can, in principle, be regarded as 'prescribed by law' in the sense of the ECHR.[201]

[196] For critical assessments with regard to this requirement, see Kaufmann/Walti, 'Die polizeiliche Generalklausel' (2011), 71–4; Müller/Jenni, 'Die polizeiliche Generalklausel' (2008), 12–14, 18.

[197] BGE 130 I 369, 381–3 (2004); BGE 126 I 112, 118 (2000).

[198] BGE 137 II 431, 445 (2011); BGE 136 IV 97, 114–16 (2010); Urteil des Bundesgerichts 2C_166/2009 vom 30. November 2009, E. 2.3.2.1, in (2010) 111 *Schweizerisches Zentralblatt für Staats- und Verwaltungsrecht* 469, 474. See Keller/Bürli, 'Überdenken der polizeilichen Generalklausel bei Vorliegen staatlicher Schutzpflichten' (2011); Zünd/Errass, 'Die polizeiliche Generalklausel' (2011), 289–91.

[199] Urteil des Bundesgerichts 2C_166/2009 vom 30. November 2009, E. 2.3.2.1, in (2010) 111 *Schweizerisches Zentralblatt für Staats- und Verwaltungsrecht* 469, 474.

[200] BGE 137 II 431, 445 (2011).

[201] *Gsell c. Suisse*, no. 12675/05, 8 October 2009, paras 54–6 (only available in French) (concerning BV, Art. 36(1)); *Schneiter c. Suisse* (dec.), no 63062/00, 31 March 2005 (only available in French) (concerning Verfassung des Kantons Bern, Art. 28(1)); *Rassemblement jurassien et Unité jurasienne c. Suisse*, Commission decision of 10 October 1979, DR 17, 93, 105–6 (concerning the old version of the Verfassung des Kantons Bern, Art. 39).

United Kingdom A similar function to that of the *polizeiliche Generalklausel* is served in the Anglo-American legal tradition by the common-law concept of 'breach of the peace'. Historically, the Queen's (or King's) Peace describes the protection from violence that the monarch provides to her (or his) subjects. The concept refers not so much to a power as to a duty on the part of public officials as well as all citizens to preserve the peace.[202] 'Peace' in this context is defined more narrowly than the notion of 'public safety and order' on which the Swiss concept of the *polizeiliche Generalklausel* is founded: not every public disturbance constitutes a breach of the peace, only violence to the person or the threat of such violence. According to the generally accepted definition set forth by the Court of Appeal in *R* v. *Howell*, 'there is a breach of the peace whenever harm is actually done or is likely to be done to a person or in his presence to his property or a person is in fear of being so harmed'.[203] The inclusion in this definition of harm to property in the owner's presence is apparently due to the attendant risk of a violent reaction by the owner and not meant as a general extension to crimes against property.[204] As with the *polizeiliche Generalklausel*, the European Court of Human Rights has held that the common-law concept of breach of the peace constitutes a sufficient legal basis for imposing limitations on Convention rights. In *Steel and others* v. *United Kingdom* it concluded that, given that the concept had been clarified by the English courts over the years, including in *Howell*, it was now sufficiently precise and provided adequate guidance to meet the 'prescribed by law' standard of Articles 5(1), 10(2) and 11(2) of the ECHR.[205]

While prevention of a breach of the peace is a duty imposed on all citizens, police officers have a special responsibility in this area.[206] They may take any reasonable action to stop a breach of the peace that is occurring or to prevent one that is imminent, that is, one that they reasonably believe is about to take place.[207] For that purpose they may be justified in committing what would otherwise be a trespass to person and property.[208] In particular, the powers attached to the duty to prevent

202 Feldman, *Civil Liberties and Human Rights in England and Wales* (2002), pp. 1017–18.

203 *R* v. *Howell (Errol)*, [1982] QB 416, 427.

204 Feldman, *Civil Liberties and Human Rights in England and Wales* (2002), p. 1019.

205 *Steel and others* v. *The United Kingdom*, no. 24838/94, 23 September 1998, ECHR 1998-VII, 2719, paras 54–5, 94, 113.

206 Stone, 'Breach of the Peace' (2001).

207 *Albert* v. *Lavin*, [1982] AC 546, 553. See Feldman, *Civil Liberties and Human Rights in England and Wales* (2002), p. 1033; Stone, 'Breach of the Peace' (2001), 3.

208 Feldman, *Civil Liberties and Human Rights in England and Wales* (2002), p. 1021.

or stop breaches of the peace include those to impose restrictions on the freedom of movement, to enter premises and to arrest those who are in the process of committing a breach of the peace and those who will commit one in the immediate future.[209] The scope of powers of public officials is thus narrower than that under the Swiss *polizeiliche Generalklausel*: it is limited to measures taken 'on the spot' to deal with a breach of the peace that is already occurring or imminent and does not extend to the sort of preventive or legislative measures that may be taken based on the equivalent concept in Switzerland.

The common-law powers to keep the peace have not been replaced by statute and so continue to apply, although there is an overlap with certain statutory powers, especially those of the Public Order Act 1986. However, breach of the peace *per se* is, at least in England,[210] not an *offence* at common law[211] and the concept is no longer used as part of the definition of criminal offences, although more specific offences such as affray and riot are considered to be breaches of the peace.[212]

United States In the United States, on the other hand, breach of the peace is regarded as a common-law offence.[213] The common-law notion of 'breach of the peace' refers to essentially the same as in the United Kingdom, namely, violent conduct or conduct likely to incite violence.[214] However, since in the United States codification of criminal law is the rule, this meaning of 'breach of the peace' has been expanded through the creation of numerous statutes by states that prohibit a wide variety of behaviour that might constitute a threat to public order. In some cases, these statutory offences are specifically entitled 'breach of the peace' (or

209 Feldman, *Civil Liberties and Human Rights in England and Wales* (2002), pp. 1020–33; Stone, 'Breach of the Peace' (2001), 5–14.

210 Breach of the peace is a common-law offence in Scotland. See *Smith* v. *Donnelly*, [2002] JC 65.

211 *R (Laporte)* v. *Chief Constable of Gloucestershire Constabulary*, [2006] UKHL 55, para. 28 (Lord Bingham).

212 Law Commission, Criminal Law: Offences Relating to Public Order, Report No. 123 (HC85) (1983) 7–8.

213 E.g. *State* v. *Jones*, 88 Ohio St.3d 430, 727 N.E.2d 886 (2000); *State* v. *Runner*, 172 W.Va. 720, 310 S.E.2d 481 (1983); *Commonwealth* v. *Jarrett*, 359 Mass. 491, 269 N.E.2d 657 (1971).

214 See e.g. *Cantwell* v. *Connecticut*, 310 U.S. 296, 308 (1940) ('[The offense of breach of the peace] includes not only violent acts but acts and words likely to produce violence in others.'); Restatement (Second) of Torts § 116 (1965) ('A breach of the peace is a public offense done by violence, or one causing or likely to cause an immediate disturbance of public order'.).

'disturbance of the peace'), in others they are called 'disorderly conduct', 'vagrancy', 'loitering' or 'public intoxication'.[215] While in one state a particular form of behaviour may be a 'breach of the peace', the same behaviour may in another state be classified as 'disorderly conduct' or 'loitering'.[216] In addition to the plethora of state statutes, it is common for municipalities to proscribe public disorder in local ordinances.[217] As will be explained in Section 4.3.2, these prohibitions tend to be so broadly defined as to cover all sorts of conduct in public space. As a result, the police have a whole arsenal of – often very widely defined – public-order offences at their disposal, giving them broad legal authority to take action against actual or threatened public disorder. In fact, it has been argued that the very purpose of these breach-of-the-peace or public-order statutes is to provide legal authority for the police to intervene for apparent violations of these statutes.[218] Given this broad legal authority in statute law, there is not normally reason for the police to rely on enforcement of the common-law offence of breach of the peace.

4.2.3.2 Exclusion from public space based on breach-of-the-peace powers and the *polizeiliche Generalklausel*

In Switzerland and in the United Kingdom, the police have often invoked the *polizeiliche Generalklausel* and breach-of-the-peace powers, respectively, to justify exclusion measures in the absence of explicit legislative authority. In the United States, as explained in the previous section, there is normally some broadly defined legal authority in statute law available that the executive branch can invoke to justify exclusion measures. During the WTO conference in Seattle in 1999, for example, the Mayor of Seattle declared a civil emergency and invoked his emergency powers pursuant to the Seattle Municipal Code 'to protect the public peace, safety and welfare'.[219] Based on this broad legal authority, he banned people from entering a section of downtown Seattle.[220]

In Switzerland, the creation of explicit legal powers of the police to remove (*wegweisen*) and keep away (*fernhalten*) people from public places for reasons of public safety and order is a relatively recent phenomenon. As explained in Sections 3.3.2.4 and 4.2.2.1, cantonal police acts did not originally specify the powers at the disposal of the police. It was only from about the late 1990s that most cantons, including the

[215] For a good overview, see Force, 'Decriminalization of Breach of the Peace Statutes' (1972), 383–4, 461–7.
[216] Ibid., 369–70. [217] Ibid., 384. [218] Ibid., 373.
[219] *Menotti* v. *City of Seattle*, 409 F.3d 1113, 1124 (9th Cir. 2005). [220] Ibid., 1125.

larger ones, started to adopt 'modern' police acts that explicitly authorise the police to exclude people from public space.[221] Before then, and still today in those cantons that have not (yet) created an explicit legislative basis, the police would instead rely on the *polizeiliche Generalklausel* to, for example, disperse demonstrators or remove people who obstruct investigations.[222]

In the United Kingdom, the common-law power to prevent breaches of the peace has always been one of the most important legal authorities for justifying police action, including action short of arrest such as restricting people's freedom of movement. It is especially in the context of protests and demonstrations that the police have invoked their breach-of-the-peace powers to prevent people from accessing certain parts of public space. To list only a few examples, breach-of-the-peace powers have been relied upon to ask a speaker to move a protest meeting from one street to another to avoid a disturbance by political opponents,[223] to stop striking miners on their way to a pit to prevent a clash with working miners[224] and to corral demonstrators at a May Day demonstration into a small area of the city centre to prevent outbreak of public disorder.[225]

This raises the question of whether – and, if yes, under what circumstances and to what extent – it is permissible for the police to resort to exclusion measures in the absence of an explicit legal basis. Several recent key cases concerning the control of demonstrations provide important guidance on this question: the judgements of the Swiss Federal Supreme Court and the European Court of Human Rights in *Gsell*, that of the UK House of Lords in *Laporte* and that of the Court of Appeal in *Austin*.

Gsell The Swiss case concerned that of the journalist Mario Gsell, which has already been briefly referred to in Chapter 1. Gsell was on his way to the ski resort of Davos to report on the 2001 WEF and the conference Public Eye on Davos. Activists from the anti-globalisation movement had announced a demonstration for that day, which had not been authorised. The bus Gsell was travelling on was stopped by the

[221] See the chronological list in Section 3.3.2.4.

[222] See generally Strasser, *Polizeiliche Zwangsmassnahmen* (1981), pp. 93–7. For an example of a denial of access to a site of protest based on the *polizeiliche Generalklausel*, see BGE 130 I 369, 370–71 (2004), for one of 'kettling', see ZR 107/2008 Nr. 75, 257 (Zürich, Obergericht).

[223] *Duncan* v. *Jones*, [1936] 1 KB 218. [224] *Moss* v. *McLachlan*, [1985] IRLR 76.

[225] *Austin* v. *Commissioner of Police of the Metropolis*, [2009] UKHL 5.

police shortly before Davos. Despite presenting his press card, Gsell, as all other passengers, was ordered to turn back.[226]

The cantonal authorities and, finally, the Federal Supreme Court dismissed his appeal against the order. While the fundamental rights issues raised by this important case will be considered in more detail in Chapter 5, what is of particular interest for the present context is the Federal Supreme Court's reasoning with regard to the *polizeiliche Generalklausel*. It was undisputed that there was no explicit legislative basis for the order preventing Gsell from travelling to Davos. As the order amounted to an interference with his fundamental rights, most importantly his freedom of expression, the decisive question was whether the police could invoke the *polizeiliche Generalklausel* as provided by Article 36(1), sentence 3 of the Federal Constitution.[227] As explained above, this provision states that 'in cases of serious and immediate danger where no other course of action is possible', fundamental rights can be restricted even in the absence of an explicit legal basis. The court examined the requirements for applicability of the *polizeiliche Generalklausel* described in Section 4.2.3.1. It was not contested that, considering the expected protests, holding the WEF entailed a serious danger to public order. Instead, the main argument centred on whether this risk really had been unforeseeable or whether the legislator could and should have taken action in advance. Pointing to the fast-changing nature of the anti-globalisation movement and the escalation of violence at recent similar meetings of global leaders, the court argued that the risk situation surrounding an event such as the WEF was unique and complex and therefore very difficult to predict in advance. Therefore, the court held, the legislator could not be blamed for not having addressed the problem and it was permissible for the police to invoke the *polizeiliche Generalklausel*.[228] As to the *scope* of the police's exclusion power under the *polizeiliche Generalklausel*, the court concluded that it could be used even against persons who had not been clearly identified as posing a risk: given the dangerous situation and the great number of persons travelling to Davos, it was very difficult for police officers to distinguish peaceful demonstrators from those intent on causing trouble.[229]

The European Court of Human Rights, in *Gsell c. Suisse*, came to a different conclusion.[230] The key question the European Court had to

[226] BGE 130 I 369, 370–71 (2004). [227] See ibid., 381. [228] Ibid., 381–3.
[229] Ibid., 384–7.
[230] *Gsell c. Suisse*, no. 12675/05, 8 October 2009 (only available in French).

answer was whether the *polizeiliche Generalklausel* according to Article 36(1), sentence 3 of the Federal Constitution was a sufficient legal basis for the limitation of Gsell's freedom of expression so that the limitation could be said to be 'prescribed by law' as required by Article 10(2) of the ECHR. The court held that it was not, because the requirements for invoking the *polizeiliche Generalklausel*, as set forth in the case law of the Federal Supreme Court, were not fulfilled.[231] In particular, the court was not convinced that it had been impossible for the cantonal authorities to anticipate the risks arising in connection with the WEF 2001. The court argued that, given that there had already been militant demonstrations in Davos in the two previous years, as well as violent incidents at similar conferences elsewhere, the authorities could and should have reacted earlier to create an explicit legal basis for the type of police intervention at issue.[232] Finally, the European Court observed that according to the Federal Supreme Court's own jurisprudence, any police action had to be directed against those posing a threat to public order. This requirement was not met in the present case as the police failed to distinguish between peaceful and potentially violent demonstrators.[233] As a result, the order prohibiting Gsell from entering Davos was not prescribed by law and therefore in violation of Article 10 of the ECHR.[234]

Laporte The UK House of Lords was faced with a similar set of facts in *R (Laporte)* v. *Chief Constable of Gloucestershire Constabulary*.[235] Jane Laporte was a passenger on a coach travelling from London to a demonstration against the Iraq war at an air base in Gloucestershire. The coach was stopped by the police a few kilometres from the air base. The police searched the passengers and concluded that some, but not necessarily all of them were intent on causing trouble. The passengers were ordered to get back on the coach and the police escorted the coach back to London, preventing passengers from disembarking until they arrived there.[236]

As in *Gsell*, it was uncontested that there had been an interference with fundamental rights (in this case freedom of expression and freedom of assembly). The House of Lords found that there clearly was no statutory basis for the interference,[237] and so the key issue was whether the common-law power to prevent a breach of the peace provided legal

[231] Ibid., para. 59. [232] Ibid., paras 58–9. [233] Ibid., para. 60. [234] Ibid., paras 61–2.
[235] *R (Laporte)* v. *Chief Constable of Gloucestershire Constabulary*, [2006] UKHL 55.
[236] Ibid., paras 2–13. [237] Ibid., para. 44.

authority for the police intervention. The police authorities argued that it did: they had a power at common law to do whatever they judged to be reasonable to prevent a breach of the peace.[238] The House of Lords rejected this argument. Lord Bingham pointed, first of all, to the closely defined powers and duties to control demonstrations conferred on police officers by the Public Order Act 1986 and stated that it would be 'surprising' if, alongside these powers, there continued to exist a common-law power of rather uncertain scope.[239] Furthermore, their Lordships held that the test established by case law is one of imminence and not, as suggested by the police authorities, one of general reasonableness.[240] As a consequence, whether a given police intervention is by arrest or by action short of arrest, the breach of the peace must always be imminent, that is, it must reasonably appear to be about to be committed.[241] The majority of their Lordships thought that in the present case there was nothing to suggest that a breach of the peace was imminent[242] – even the police officer in charge himself had noted shortly before the intervention that he did not consider there to be an imminent breach of the peace.[243] Finally, Lord Bingham emphasised that if it was really thought to be necessary to extend the power of the police to control demonstrations to this kind of intervention, then this should be done by legislative enactment, not judicial decision.[244]

The case of *Laporte* also raised the question of whether the police may take action against persons who are not themselves committing or about to commit a breach of the peace. As the House of Lords came to the conclusion that, in any event, the requirements for invoking the breach-of-the-peace powers were not satisfied, it did not have to conclusively answer this question, although some of their Lordships suggested that the answer was yes.[245]

Austin The question as to the *scope* of the breach-of-the-peace powers arose again in *Austin* v. *Commissioner of Police of the Metropolis.*[246]

238 Ibid., para. 40. 239 Ibid., para. 46.

240 Ibid., paras 47 (Lord Bingham), 66 (Lord Rodger), 101 (Lord Carswell), 141 (Lord Mance).

241 Ibid., paras 50 (Lord Bingham), 66 (Lord Rodger).

242 Ibid., paras 50 (Lord Bingham), 118 (Lord Brown), 142 (Lord Mance). Lords Rodger (para. 71) and Carswell (para. 104) left the point open.

243 Ibid., para. 10. 244 Ibid., para. 52.

245 Ibid., paras 72–84 (Lord Roger), para. 123 (Lord Brown) ('perhaps in extreme and exceptional circumstances').

246 *Austin* v. *Commissioner of Police of the Metropolis*, [2008] 2 WLR 415.

The case concerned the 2001 May Day demonstration in London. The police had good reason to anticipate serious violence and property damage. Demonstrators in Oxford Circus were surrounded by a police cordon and not allowed to leave for up to seven hours, despite the fact that the police were aware that some of the demonstrators would not cause a breach of the peace. Based on the finding by the High Court that a breach of the peace was imminent, the Court of Appeal held that the common-law powers to prevent a breach of the peace *can* be used against innocent third parties, but only as the last resort where it is strictly necessary, a test which the court thought 'can only be justified in truly extreme and exceptional circumstances'.[247] The court found that in the instant case that test was met as there was no realistic alternative to deal with the imminent threat other than to contain all demonstrators, including peaceful ones.[248] Although appeal was made to the House of Lords, the findings of the Court of Appeal on the scope of the common-law power to prevent a breach of the peace were not appealed,[249] nor was this issue explicitly addressed by the European Court of Human Rights in its judgment in the case of *Austin* of 2012.[250]

Result The issues the various courts had to address in the decisions described above are of striking similarity. Several principles can be drawn from the case law, imposing important limitations on the use of exclusion measures in the absence of an explicit legal basis.

First, it must be emphasised that in all situations described above there was a quite serious threat to public-order and fundamental interests. The cases concerned demonstrations relating to major occasions (WEF, Iraq War, May Day) where large numbers of participants, some of them militant, were expected. It was therefore beyond dispute in all cases that it was reasonable for the police to anticipate public disorder of a level serious enough to trigger, in principle, the applicability of the *polizeiliche Generalklausel* and the breach-of-the-peace powers, respectively. However, resort to exclusion measures in situations involving a threat of this seriousness is clearly the exception. As is apparent from the overview in Section 3.3, it is much more common for exclusion from public space to be used to deal with rather minor public-order problems. In these latter

[247] Ibid., 430–31. [248] Ibid., 440–41.

[249] *Austin* v. *Commissioner of Police of the Metropolis*, [2009] UKHL 5, para. 11.

[250] *Austin and others* v. *The United Kingdom* [GC], nos 39692/09; 40713/09; 41008/09, 15 March 2012, ECHR 2012. For a discussion of the European Court's judgment, see Section 5.2.4.2.

kinds of situations, already the threshold requirement of serious danger to public-order and fundamental interests (in the case of the *polizeiliche Generalklausel*) or threat of violence to the person (in the case of the breach-of-the-peace powers) will not be satisfied, so that, without an explicit legislative basis, exclusion measures will not be permissible.[251]

Second, especially the House of Lords decision in *Laporte* demonstrates that, today, courts will scrupulously insist on the imminence requirement and will not be easily satisfied that it is met. *Laporte* stands in stark contrast to earlier cases such as *Moss* v. *McLachlan*.[252] In *Moss*, decided in 1985, striking miners were stopped by the police on their way to a demonstration at a pit when they were a few miles away from their destination. The Divisional Court applied a test of 'close proximity both in place and time' and concluded that a breach of the peace was imminent.[253] While it may be true that in *Laporte* the police intervention occurred (slightly) further away from the site of the planned demonstration and while it was certainly of relevance that the police officer in charge himself seemed to think that a breach of the peace was not imminent, the facts of the two cases are nevertheless very similar. Therefore, it seems not far-fetched to conclude from *Laporte* that courts will now be more attentive to calls made earlier in the literature that a more stringent approach to the imminence requirement should be applied.[254] In fact, at least some of their Lordships in *Laporte* suggested that *Moss* might be decided differently today.[255]

Third, especially *Gsell* highlights the crucial importance of the requirement of unforeseeability and the strict standards to be applied in this regard. In Switzerland, it is widely accepted that the principle of legality serves an important democratic function and that any exceptions to this principle by way of the *polizeiliche Generalklausel* may only be permissible where it was impossible for the legislator to address a problem itself. But also Lord Bingham in *Laporte* thought that the imposition of exclusion measures 'calls in the first instance for the wide consultation and inquiry and democratic consideration which should characterise the legislative process'.[256] In addition, as is made clear by the judgment of the European Court of Human Rights in *Gsell*, the requirement

[251] See also Müller/Jenni, 'Die polizeiliche Generalklausel' (2008), 12.

[252] *Moss* v. *McLachlan*, [1985] IRLR 76. [253] Ibid., para. 20.

[254] Feldman, *Civil Liberties and Human Rights in England and Wales* (2002), pp. 1021–2.

[255] *R (Laporte)* v. *Chief Constable of Gloucestershire Constabulary*, [2006] UKHL 55, paras 118 (Lord Brown), 150 (Lord Mance).

[256] Ibid., para. 52.

contributes to legal certainty and predictability: citizens should not have to expect to be faced with restrictions imposed by the police on the spot if the details of these restrictions could have been spelled out in advance in legislation.[257] The European Court was therefore right to make it clear that it is not enough for the requirement of unforeseeability to be satisfied that, as the Swiss Federal Supreme Court would have had it, the authorities are faced with a complex situation involving a difficult risk assessment. Instead, the requirement of an explicit legal basis for exclusion measures can only be waived where such measures are employed to deal with a threat that simply could not have been anticipated. It may be true, for example, that major demonstrations are difficult to police. However, it is well known that international gatherings such as the WEF in Davos attract a large number of demonstrators. In addition, as the cases discussed here show, the problems with regard to the control of such demonstrations tend to repeat themselves over and over again. It is therefore for the legislator to decide whether – and, if so, under what conditions – the police should be granted the power to keep away demonstrators from certain parts of public space. The same applies even more so with regard to exclusion measures that are used to deal with the kind of minor public disorders that occur on an almost daily basis. Not only is it perfectly possible for the legislator to anticipate these issues, but there are also numerous possible ways of addressing them. It must be up to the legislator, not the police, to choose the appropriate course of action and to set out the relevant criteria and procedures.

Some scholars have suggested that the requirement of unforeseeability should be abandoned. They argue that today pretty much any risk can be said to be predictable and yet there may nevertheless be situations not regulated in law that need to be dealt with by the executive branch on an urgent basis.[258] Similarly, as explained above, the Swiss Federal Supreme Court, in a string of decisions issued after the European Court's judgment in *Gsell*, has suggested that the requirement of unforeseeability should, in certain cases, not be applied in too strict a manner.[259]

[257] *Gsell c. Suisse*, no. 12675/05, 8 October 2009, paras 52–3, 59 (only available in French).

[258] E.g. Tschannen/Zimmerli/Müller, *Allgemeines Verwaltungsrecht* (2014), pp. 539–40; Kiener/Kälin, *Grundrechte* (2013), pp. 110–11; Lienhard/Zielniewicz, 'Zum Anwendungsbereich des bundesrätlichen Notrechts' (2012), 134; Müller/Jenni, 'Die polizeiliche Generalklausel' (2008), 15–18.

[259] BGE 137 II 431, 445 (2011); BGE 136 IV 97, 114–16 (2010); Urteil des Bundesgerichts 2C_166/2009 vom 30. November 2009, E. 2.3.2.1, in (2010) 111 *Schweizerisches Zentralblatt für Staats- und Verwaltungsrecht* 469, 474.

However, to simply abandon the requirement would increase the incentive for parliaments to leave difficult decisions to the executive branch. If it is really true that all risks have become predictable, then the legislator can be expected to address them. Therefore, it should be insisted that the police and other law enforcement agencies make do with the measures put at their disposal by the legislative branch. Only in the most extreme of circumstances, where the executive branch has a positive duty to protect fundamental rights of third persons, there is a serious threat to these fundamental rights and there is absolutely no alternative measure provided by the law to deal with that threat, can there be an exception to this requirement.[260]

Fourth and finally, the decisions referred to above provide some guidance on the *scope* of the powers available to the police under the *polizeiliche Generalklausel* and the concept of breach of the peace, respectively. The *polizeiliche Generalklausel* has traditionally been understood as being capable of justifying a rather wide range of measures, including those of a preventive and regulatory nature. Accordingly, in the *Gsell* case, the Federal Supreme Court found that, given the scale of the WEF, it was legitimate for the police to deny access to Davos to anyone not clearly identified as posing no risk. The European Court of Human Rights, however, disagreed and imposed very narrow limits on the powers available under the *polizeiliche Generalklausel.* The court rightly insisted that any police action be directed against those who pose a threat to public order, a requirement that is, in fact, well established in Swiss law as a crucial aspect of the principle of proportionality.[261] Given that the police intervention occurred not 'in the heat of the moment' but on a road leading to Davos, it was certainly not unreasonable to expect the police to apply a more targeted approach than to turn back busloads of people. In the case of *Austin*, in contrast, the European Court concluded that there was no interference with any of the rights guaranteed by the ECHR in the first place, so that there was no reason for it to consider the issue of the scope of the breach-of-the-peace powers.[262] The question as

[260] For a similar argument, see Egli, 'Grundrechte' (2012), 199; Keller/Bürli, 'Überdenken der polizeilichen Generalklausel bei Vorliegen staatlicher Schutzpflichten' (2011).

[261] On the so-called *Störerprinzip/principe du perturbateur*, see e.g. BGE 122 II 65, 70 (1996); BGE 118 Ib 407, 414–15 (1992); BGE 101 Ib 410, 414–21 (1975); Moor/Flückiger/Martenet, *Droit administratif I* (2012), pp. 827–31; Häfelin/Müller/Uhlmann, *Allgemeines Verwaltungsrecht* (2010), pp. 569–73; Thürer, 'Das Störerprinzip im Polizeirecht' (1983); Mathys, *Zum Begriff des Störers im Polizeirecht* (1974).

[262] *Austin and others* v. *The United Kingdom* [GC], nos 39692/09; 40713/09; 41008/09, 15 March 2012, ECHR 2012.

to the proportionality of police interventions, be they based on an explicit legal basis or not, will be revisited in more detail in Chapter 5.

4.3 Requirement of sufficient precision

4.3.1 In general

As explained above, the principle of legality requires not only that government action, at least as far as it interferes with fundamental rights, must be authorised by law, but also that that law must be of a certain quality: it must be published in advance, adequately accessible and sufficiently precise. These requirements are designed to ensure legal certainty, the central concern of a formal conception of the rule of law. While it is normally not very difficult to assess whether a given law meets the first two requirements, the requirement of sufficient precision may pose a number of problems, not least with regard to norms authorising exclusion from public space.

The requirement of a sufficiently precise legal basis is part of international law as far as government action interferes with human rights. According to both the ICCPR and the ECHR, any limitations of the rights guaranteed by these treaties must be based on a law that is sufficiently precise to enable citizens to regulate their conduct. For the ECHR, the European Court of Human Rights stated this principle as early as in the *Sunday Times* case of 1979, the leading decision on the quality of law:

> [A] norm cannot be regarded as a 'law' unless it is formulated with sufficient precision to enable the citizen to regulate his conduct: he must be able – if need be with appropriate advice – to foresee, to a degree that is reasonable in the circumstances, the consequences which a given action may entail.[263]

The court has since then provided additional guidance on what 'sufficient precision' entails. It has accepted that absolute precision is unattainable and has pointed out that the level of precision required of domestic legislation depends to a considerable degree on the content of the instrument in question, the field it is designed to cover and the number and status of those to whom it is addressed.[264] Especially in matters where the

[263] *The Sunday Times* v. *The United Kingdom (No. 1)*, no. 6538/74, 26 April 1979, Series A no. 30, para. 49.

[264] *Rekvény* v. *Hungary*, no. 25390/94, 20 May 1999, ECHR 1999-III, 423, para. 34.

situation may change depending on the prevailing views of society, such as with obscenity laws, the degree of precision may be relaxed.[265] On the other hand, serious interferences must be based on a law that is particularly precise, containing clear and detailed rules.[266] Importantly, where a law confers discretion, it must also indicate with sufficient clarity the limits of that discretion,[267] that is, the scope and manner of its exercise.[268] As the European Court has confirmed:

> It would be contrary to the rule of law for the legal discretion granted to the executive in areas affecting fundamental rights to be expressed in terms of an unfettered power. Consequently, the law must indicate the scope of any such discretion conferred on the competent authorities and the manner of its exercise with sufficient clarity, having regard to the legitimate aim of the measure in question, to give the individual adequate protection against arbitrary interference.[269]

Especially where the law bestows on the executive wide discretionary powers, there must be safeguards, including procedural safeguards, to ensure that the discretion left to the executive is exercised in accordance with the law and without abuse.[270] Consequently, any measures affecting fundamental human rights must be subject to some form of adversarial proceedings before an independent body competent to review the reasons for the decision and relevant evidence.[271] The relative vagueness of legislative provisions may be compensated for by strong procedural safeguards, in particular judicial control.[272]

While the case law under the ICCPR on this issue is not as rich as that under the ECHR, the UN Human Rights Committee has interpreted the requirement of sufficient precision in essentially the same manner. In its General Comments on the rights to privacy and freedom of movement, for example, it has pointed out that legislation authorising interferences with these rights 'must specify in detail the precise circumstances in

265 *Müller and others* v. *Switzerland*, no. 10737/84, 24 May 1988, Series A no. 133, para. 29.
266 *Kruslin* v. *France*, no. 11801/85, 24 April 1990, Series A no. 176-A, para. 33.
267 See e.g. *Silver and others* v. *The United Kingdom*, nos 5947/72; 6205/73; 7052/75; 7061/75; 7107/75; 7113/75; 7136/75, 25 March 1983, Series A no. 61, para. 88.
268 E.g. *Kruslin* v. *France*, no. 11801/85, 24 April 1990, Series A no. 176-A, para. 36.
269 *Al-Nashif* v. *Bulgaria*, no. 50963/99, 20 June 2002, para. 119.
270 See e.g. *Gillan and Quinton* v. *The United Kingdom*, no. 4158/05, 12 January 2010, ECHR 2010, para. 79; *Al-Nashif* v. *Bulgaria*, no. 50963/99, 20 June 2002, para. 122; *Silver and others* v. *The United Kingdom*, nos 5947/72; 6205/73; 7052/75; 7061/75; 7107/75; 7113/75; 7136/75, 25 March 1983, Series A no. 61, para. 90.
271 *Al-Nashif* v. *Bulgaria*, no. 50963/99, 20 June 2002, para. 123.
272 Grabenwarter/Pabel, *Europäische Menschenrechtskonvention* (2012), p. 127.

which such interferences may be permitted'[273] and 'should use precise criteria and may not confer unfettered discretion on those charged with their execution'.[274] In its case law it has emphasised that very broadly framed legislative provisions may not provide satisfactory protection against arbitrary application.[275]

These requirements established by international law as to the quality of laws authorising limitations of human rights are reflected in, and indeed originate from, corresponding principles in domestic law, including that of the three states at issue.

In Switzerland, one of the central postulates of the principle of legality guaranteed by Article 5(1) and, as far as limitations of fundamental rights are concerned, Article 36(1) of the Federal Constitution is that all government action must be based on legal rules that are sufficiently precise.[276] This requirement serves legal certainty and equality of treatment.[277] According to the standard formula of the Federal Supreme Court, which is virtually identical to that of the European Court of Human Rights, norms must be formulated precisely enough for citizens to be able to regulate their conduct and to foresee, to a degree that corresponds to the circumstances, the consequences of a given action.[278] Swiss legal doctrine often uses the term 'normative density' (*Normdichte/densité normative*) in this context, which makes it clear that the requirement of sufficient precision is not simply about the clarity of legal terms but about the openness or density of a law, that is, the degree

[273] UN Human Rights Committee, General Comment No. 16, UN Doc. HRI/GEN/1/Rev.1, 21 (1994), para. 8.

[274] UN Human Rights Committee, General Comment No. 27, UN Doc. CCPR/C/21/Rev.1/Add.9 (1999), para. 13.

[275] E.g. *Pinkney* v. *Canada*, Communication No. 27/1978, 29 October 1981, UN Doc. CCPR/C/OP/1 (1985), para. 34.

[276] On the requirement of sufficient precision (*Bestimmtheitsgebot*), see e.g. Moor/Flückiger/Martenet, *Droit administratif I* (2012), pp. 674–7; Häfelin/Müller/Uhlmann, *Allgemeines Verwaltungsrecht* (2010), pp. 87–9; Moor, 'Principes de l'activité étatique et responsabilité de l'Etat' (2001), 270–1; Cottier, *Die Verfassung und das Erfordernis der gesetzlichen Grundlage* (1983), especially pp. 144–9, 162–3, 186–206; Rhinow, *Rechtsetzung und Methodik* (1979), pp. 262–8; Müller, *Inhalt und Formen der Rechtssetzung als Problem der demokratischen Kompetenzordnung* (1979), pp. 86–95; Dubs, 'Die Forderung der optimalen Bestimmtheit belastender Rechtsnormen' (1974).

[277] Häfelin/Müller/Uhlmann, *Allgemeines Verwaltungsrecht* (2010), p. 87; Ritter, *Das Erfordernis der genügenden Bestimmtheit* (1994), pp. 161–5; Cottier, *Die Verfassung und das Erfordernis der gesetzlichen Grundlage* (1983), pp. 146–7.

[278] E.g. BGE 125 I 361, 364 (1999) ('Die Rechtsnorm soll so präzise formuliert sein, dass der Bürger sein Verhalten danach richten bzw. die Folgen eines bestimmten Verhaltens mit einem den Umständen entsprechenden Grad an Gewissheit voraussehen kann.').

to which the authorities applying a law are restricted by it.[279] Just as the European Court, the Swiss Federal Supreme Court has accepted that it may be unavoidable for the legislator to use general terms and thus to give the authorities applying the law some scope of discretion.[280] Use of open norms may be especially difficult to avoid where the situations to be regulated are multifaceted, the decisions to be taken in the particular case are complex or future developments are hard to predict.[281] The degree of precision may also be relaxed as far as authorisation for 'increased common use' (*gesteigerter Gemeingebrauch*) of public goods is concerned, as the permissible forms of use are already determined to a large extent by the purpose of the public good in question.[282] However, the requirement of sufficient precision applies to all types of government action and the rule is that the legislator must always be as precise as it can.[283] Norms authorising an interference with fundamental rights must be particularly precise. The more serious the interference is, the stricter the requirements as to the density of the norm authorising the interference are.[284] Lack of legal certainty due to the openness of a norm can be compensated for by strict compliance with the constitutional principles of public interest and proportionality as well as by the provision of procedural safeguards.[285] Therefore, where a degree of imprecision in a law is unavoidable, the procedure regulating the application of the law must be strengthened accordingly.[286]

[279] Auer/Malinverni/Hottelier, *Droit constitutionnel suisse* (2013), Vol. I, pp. 624–6; Moor/Flückiger/Martenet, *Droit administratif I* (2012), pp. 674–7; Schindler, *Verwaltungsermessen* (2010), pp. 296–7; Ritter, *Das Erfordernis der genügenden Bestimmtheit* (1994), pp. 171–4; Cottier, *Die Verfassung und das Erfordernis der gesetzlichen Grundlage* (1983), pp. 144–9; Müller, *Inhalt und Formen der Rechtssetzung als Problem der demokratischen Kompetenzordnung* (1979), p. 87; Dubs, 'Die Forderung der optimalen Bestimmtheit belastender Rechtsnormen' (1974), 223.

[280] BGE 125 I 361, 364 (1999); BGE 109 Ia 273, 284 (1983).

[281] BGE 136 I 87, 90 (2009); BGE 131 II 13, 29–30 (2004); BGE 128 I 327, 340 (2002).

[282] Moser, *Der öffentliche Grund und seine Benützung* (2011), pp. 259–61; Häfelin/Müller/Uhlmann, *Allgemeines Verwaltungsrecht* (2010), p. 547.

[283] Schweizer/Müller, 'Zwecke, Möglichkeiten und Grenzen der Gesetzgebung im Polizeibereich' (2008), 384; Dubs, 'Die Forderung der optimalen Bestimmtheit belastender Rechtsnormen' (1974), 243.

[284] Kiener/Kälin, *Grundrechte* (2013), p. 102; Reinhard, *Allgemeines Polizeirecht* (1993), p. 152.

[285] BGE 136 I 87, 90–91 (2009); Moor/Flückiger/Martenet, *Droit administratif I* (2012), pp. 683–5; Cottier, *Die Verfassung und das Erfordernis der gesetzlichen Grundlage* (1983), pp. 194–6, 206–14; Dubs, 'Die Forderung der optimalen Bestimmtheit belastender Rechtsnormen' (1974), 244–5.

[286] BGE 109 Ia 273, 284 (1983).

As far as the United Kingdom is concerned, the requirement of sufficient precision follows from Dicey's first element of the rule of law, 'the absolute supremacy or predominance of regular law as opposed to the influence of arbitrary power'.[287] For Dicey this was the very essence of the rule of law: law should be clear so that people are able to predict the scope of their obligations.[288] Dicey was fundamentally opposed to granting the executive branch discretion and went as far as to claim that the rule of law excludes 'wide discretionary authority on the part of the government'.[289] Today, it is widely accepted that, as the state regulates life in multifarious ways, discretionary authority in many spheres of government is inevitable.[290] However, it is equally recognised that legislation must be drafted as clearly as possible.[291] As Lord Hoffmann put it, 'the principle of legality means that Parliament must squarely confront what it is doing and accept the political cost. Fundamental rights cannot be overridden by general or ambiguous words.'[292] Legislation must give guidance on, and adequately constrain, the circumstances in which powers granted to the government may be used and the ways in which these powers may be exercised.[293] Where the government *is* granted discretionary powers, judicial review serves to control that discretion: the courts have the power to ensure that acts of public authorities conform to the purpose of the relevant piece of legislation.[294] In addition to these requirements derived from the concept of the rule of law and

287 Dicey, *An Introduction to the Study of the Law of the Constitution* (1959), p. 202.

288 See Jowell, 'The Rule of Law' (2015), 21; Ewing/Gearty, *The Struggle for Civil Liberties* (2000), pp. 14–15; Raz, 'The Rule of Law and Its Virtue' (1977), 198–9.

289 Dicey, *An Introduction to the Study of the Law of the Constitution* (1959), p. 202.

290 Bradley/Ewing, *Constitutional and Administrative Law* (2011), p. 93; Jowell, 'The Rule of Law and Its Underlying Values' (2007), 15; Galligan, *Discretionary Powers* (1986), pp. 56–107.

291 See e.g. *Merkur Island Shipping Corp* v. *Laughton (The Hoegh Anapa)*, [1983] 2 AC 570, 594 (Sir John Donaldson, M.R.) ('The judges of this court are all skilled lawyers of very considerable experience, yet it has taken us hours to ascertain what is and what is not "offside", even with the assistance of highly experienced counsel. This cannot be right. [...] My plea is that Parliament, when legislating in respect of circumstances which directly affect the "man or woman in the street" or the "man or woman on the shop floor" should give as high a priority to clarity and simplicity of expression as to refinements of policy.').

292 *R.* v. *Secretary of State for the Home Department Ex p. Simms*, [2000] 2 AC 115, 131 (Lord Hoffmann).

293 Ewing/Gearty, *The Struggle for Civil Liberties* (2000), pp. 15–16.

294 See e.g. Craig, *Administrative Law* (2012), pp. 4–16; Bradley/Ewing, *Constitutional and Administrative Law* (2011), pp. 669–86; Galligan, *Discretionary Powers* (1986), pp. 219–65, 290–313.

established in case law, the principles developed by the European Court of Human Rights to determine the required precision of a law apply whenever government action amounts to an interference with one of the Convention rights.

In the United States, it is through the void-for-vagueness doctrine (or simply vagueness doctrine), developed by the Supreme Court in the context of the due process clauses of the Fifth and Fourteenth Amendments and of the First Amendment, that important requirements with regard to the quality of laws have been established.[295] The vagueness doctrine serves the rule-of-law values of legal certainty and prevention of arbitrariness and, accordingly, has two aspects. First, laws must be drawn with sufficient clarity so that ordinary people can tell precisely what is expected from them: 'a statute which either forbids or requires the doing of an act in terms so vague that men of common intelligence must necessarily guess at its meaning and differ as to its application, violates the first essential of due process of law'.[296] Laws that are unclear may deter people from engaging in an activity that is perfectly legitimate, that is, they may have a 'chilling effect'.[297] The requirement for laws to be precise is therefore particularly important, and is applied with particular stringency by the courts, when the regulated activity relates to expression.[298] Second, laws must 'establish minimal guidelines to govern law enforcement'.[299] To prevent arbitrary and discriminatory enforcement of the law, those applying the law must not be given too much discretion.[300] Thus, as in Switzerland and the United Kingdom, it is recognised that the requirement of sufficient precision means more than simply that laws must be clear: a law can be perfectly clear but still be so generally worded as to grant those enforcing it virtually complete discretion. Accordingly, the Supreme Court has stated that this second aspect of the vagueness doctrine, the limitation of discretion, is the more important one.[301]

[295] See 'The Void-for-Vagueness Doctrine in the Supreme Court' (1960).

[296] *Connally* v. *General Construction Co.*, 269 U.S. 385, 391 (1926).

[297] See *Baggett* v. *Bullitt*, 377 U.S. 360, 372 (1964). The 'chilling effect' doctrine has been taken up by the European Court of Human Rights: *Goodwin* v. *The United Kingdom* [GC], no. 17488/90, 27 March 1996, ECHR 1996-II, 483, para. 39. See Harris/O'Boyle/Bates/Buckley, *Law of the ECHR* (2014), p. 630; Grabenwarter/Pabel, *Europäische Menschenrechtskonvention* (2012), p. 320.

[298] *Smith* v. *California*, 361 U.S. 147, 151 (1959).

[299] *Smith* v. *Goguen*, 415 U.S. 566, 574 (1974).

[300] See *Kolender* v. *Lawson*, 461 U.S. 352, 357 (1983).

[301] Ibid., 358.

4.3.2 *Norms authorising exclusion from public space and the requirement of sufficient precision*

It is recognised in all jurisdictions under consideration that it is difficult to regulate police action in a precise manner. As the police must deal with various sorts of threats that may emanate or change rapidly, their tasks and powers cannot all be set out in detail in advance but may need to be adapted to the concrete circumstances of the situation.[302] In addition, in the case of certain types of police operations, it is *not desirable* that police action is predictable as otherwise it would become ineffective.[303] While some degree of imprecision of the relevant laws is thus unavoidable, it is still striking how vaguely and broadly drafted many of the legal norms authorising or facilitating exclusion from public space set out in Annex I are. The reason for this is that, as mentioned in the introduction to this chapter, exclusion measures form a key part of the sort of 'order-maintenance policing' or 'community policing' that has become increasingly influential in the 'security society'.[304] This model of policing involves the granting of a very wide scope of discretion to the police to deal with a broad range of problems: police officers are turned into 'street corner politicians'.[305] As a consequence, exclusion norms raise particular concerns with regard to the requirement of sufficient precision in terms of the definition of, first, their scope of application and, second, the measures available to the police.

4.3.2.1 Scope of application

As has been shown in Section 3.3, exclusion measures are employed to deal with a wide range of social problems and it is not always easy to tell exactly what aim is pursued by adoption of a given exclusion measure. Typically, such measures are primarily meant to make public places look more orderly and safe, to restore the 'integrity of public space'.[306] They are concerned with *the appearance* of public space and are accordingly

302 For Switzerland, see e.g. BGE 136 I 87, 90 (2009); Egli, 'Grundrechte' (2012), 197; Schindler, *Verwaltungsermessen* (2010), pp. 332–3; Reinhard, *Allgemeines Polizeirecht* (1993), pp. 155–7. For the ECHR, and thus for the United Kingdom, see e.g. *Landvreugd* v. *The Netherlands*, no. 37331/97, 4 June 2002, paras 60–61 and *Olivieira* v. *The Netherlands*, no. 33129/96, 4 June 2002, ECHR 2002-IV, 193, paras 53–4. For the United States, see Livingston, 'Police Discretion and the Quality of Life in Public Places' (1997), 591–5.

303 Schindler, *Verwaltungsermessen* (2010), p. 332.

304 See Sections 2.5.2 and 3.2.

305 The term was coined by Muir, *Police* (1979). See also Legnaro, 'Konturen der Sicherheitsgesellschaft' (1997), 276–7.

306 See Volkmann, 'Die Rückeroberung der Allmende' (2000).

also intended to convey a symbolic message.[307] Yet given this broad, partially symbolic, aim, it is difficult to pinpoint the danger that is allegedly undermining the integrity of public space and to identify those responsible for this danger. This vagueness with regard to the objectives pursued and the targets of exclusion is reflected in the scope of application of the relevant provisions, making them difficult to reconcile with the concept of the rule of law.

Exclusion of those posing a danger to 'public safety and order' Most of the new cantonal police acts adopted in Switzerland in the last few years give the police a broadly defined power to remove and keep away from public places anyone posing a danger to 'public safety and order' ('*öffentliche Sicherheit und Ordnung*'). The relevant norm of the Police Act of the Canton of Grisons, for example, authorises the police to take all the necessary measures, including preventing people from being present in certain areas,[308] 'to maintain safety and order and to avert a danger'.[309] The Police Act of the Canton of Berne gives the police the power to remove and keep away from public places those 'for whom there is reasonable suspicion that they, or others who form part of the same assembly, pose a danger to or disturb public safety and order'.[310] Almost identical provisions are contained in the Police Acts of the Cantons of Aargau,[311] Zurich,[312] Glarus,[313] Schwyz,[314] Lucerne,[315] Uri,[316] Geneva,[317] Obwalden,[318] and Fribourg.[319] Federal law provides for a similarly broad exclusion power with regard to foreign nationals: the

[307] See Section 3.2.

[308] Polizeigesetz des Kantons Graubünden vom 20. Oktober 2004 (BR 613.000), Art. 12(2).

[309] Ibid., Art. 12(1) ('Die Kantonspolizei kann zur Wahrung der Sicherheit und Ordnung sowie zur Gefahrenabwehr ereignisbezogen die notwendigen Massnahmen anordnen.').

[310] Polizeigesetz vom 8. Juni 1997 (BSG 551.1), Art. 29(1)(b) ('Die Kantonspolizei kann Personen von einem Ort vorübergehend wegweisen oder fern halten, wenn [. . .] der begründete Verdacht besteht, dass sie oder andere, die der gleichen Ansammlung zuzurechnen sind, die öffentliche Sicherheit und Ordnung gefährden oder stören.').

[311] Gesetz über die Gewährleistung der öffentlichen Sicherheit (Polizeigesetz) vom 6. Dezember 2005 (SAR 531.200), § 34(1).

[312] Polizeigesetz vom 23. April 2007 (LS 550.1), § 33(a).

[313] Polizeigesetz des Kantons Glarus vom 6. Mai 2007 (GS V A/11/1), Art. 15(a).

[314] Verordnung über die Kantonspolizei (Polizeiverordnung) vom 22. März 2000 (SRSZ 520.110), § 19(c).

[315] Gesetz über die Luzerner Polizei vom 27. Januar 1998 (SRL 350), § 19(1)(a).

[316] Polizeigesetz vom 30. November 2008 (RB 3.8111), Art. 22(1).

[317] Loi sur la police du 26 octobre 1957 (RSG F 1 05), Art. 22A(a).

[318] Polizeigesetz vom 11. März 2010 (GDB 510.1), Art. 18(1)(b).

[319] Loi du 15 novembre 1990 sur la Police cantonale (SGF 551.1), Art. 31d(b).

Federal Act on Foreign Nationals allows for the imposition of area bans on all foreign nationals without leave to stay who disturb, or pose a threat to, public safety and order, although specifying that such area bans serve, in particular, the fight against drug trafficking.[320] Relevant laws in the United Kingdom and the United States do not normally include such broad references to 'public safety and order' or equivalent concepts to trigger the applicability of exclusion measures.

This raises the question of whether broadly framed norms authorising the exclusion from public space of all those who 'pose a danger to or disturb public safety and order' or 'contribute to disorder' are compatible with the requirement of sufficient precision. The question had to be answered by a number of Swiss courts, including the Federal Supreme Court, as the exclusion provisions of the Cantons of Grisons and Berne referred to above were challenged. These cases are reviewed here to illustrate and analyse the problems raised by this type of exclusion norms.

Its legislative history shows that the exclusion norm of the Canton of Grisons[321] was adopted in 2001 with the primary intention of giving the police a tool to deal with demonstrations at the occasion of large-scale events such as the WEF.[322] However, as is clear from the wording of the provision, its scope of application is much more broadly defined. Several persons challenged the provision before the Federal Supreme Court, claiming, among other things, that it was completely indeterminate and, considering that it authorised interference with fundamental rights, did not meet the requirement of sufficient precision. It was beyond dispute that the norm, by authorising exclusion from public space 'to maintain safety and order and to avert a danger', included vague terms and did not specify in any way the local and personal scope of application.[323] However, the Federal Supreme Court recognised that as far as the regulation of the police is concerned, it is very difficult to draft precise norms. Given the variety and fast-changing nature of the dangerous situations to be addressed by the police, the court argued, it is inevitable for the legislator to refer to indeterminate concepts such as 'safety and order'. This term had to be understood in a comprehensive way and could not be defined more precisely in advance. Thus, the court

320 AuG, Art. 74(1)(a).

321 The relevant provision at the time was contained in Verordnung über die Kantonspolizei (BR 613.100), Art. 8a. Today, a virtually identical provision is contained in Polizeigesetz des Kantons Graubünden vom 20. Oktober 2004 (BR 613.000), Art. 12.

322 Botschaften der Regierung an den Grossen Rat, Heft Nr. 7/2001–2002, 421.

323 BGE 128 I 327, 339 (2002).

concluded that the legislator could not be reproached with having defined the requirements for the use of exclusion measures too vaguely.[324]

In the case of the exclusion provision contained in the Police Act of the Canton of Berne, the historical background is somewhat different; this provision was primarily introduced to deal with 'scenes' of drug and alcohol addicts and the presence of other marginalised groups in inner city areas.[325] A group of persons banned from congregating in a central part of the City of Berne for three months challenged their exclusion orders. They argued, among other things, that the provision of the Police Act on which the orders were based failed to clearly distinguish those forms of conduct that fall within its scope of application from those that do not. By including all those 'posing a danger to or disturbing public safety and order', they argued, the list of impermissible forms of behaviour was almost limitless.[326] The Administrative Court of the Canton of Berne rejected this argument. As the Federal Supreme Court in the case of the exclusion norm of the Canton of Grisons, the court acknowledged that the provision at issue included vague terms[327] and that it was not clear from the text itself exactly what forms of conduct could entail exclusion from public space.[328] However, interpreted in light of its purpose, the provision was sufficiently precise and it was reasonably foreseeable in what circumstances the police would intervene. Furthermore, the court maintained that the police had to comply with the principle of proportionality when excluding people from public space and were thus prevented from applying the exclusion power too extensively.[329] The Administrative Court's finding was upheld by the Federal Supreme Court.[330] Referring extensively to its previous holding regarding the Police Act of the Canton of Grisons, the Federal Supreme Court again highlighted the difficulties of precisely regulating police action.[331] As the cantonal court before it, it argued that, interpreted in light of its purpose and of the principle of proportionality and also given that the interference was not serious, the norm at issue was sufficiently precise.[332] In addition, it pointed out that there were legal remedies available to challenge exclusion measures and held that these procedural safeguards compensated for the lack of precision of the norm at issue.[333]

324 Ibid., 340–2.

325 For a summary of the discussions in parliament, see BVR 2005, 97, pp. 106–8 (Verwaltungsgericht des Kantons Bern).

326 Ibid., pp. 118–19. 327 Ibid., p. 120. 328 Ibid., p. 122. 329 Ibid., pp. 122–3.

330 BGE 132 I 49 (2006). 331 Ibid., 59. 332 Ibid., 59–60. 333 Ibid., 60.

The Federal Supreme Court has applied a similarly lenient standard with regard to the exclusion power under the Federal Act on Foreign Nationals. It has held that a broad interpretation of the terms 'disturbance of, or threat to, public safety and order' corresponds to the legislator's intent. According to the court, there is no requirement for a criminal offence to have been committed for the exclusion power to be triggered. Instead, it is sufficient that there are 'concrete indications of a suspicion of criminal actions', that the foreign national 'has contacts to extremist circles' or that he or she 'quite generally breaches unwritten rules of social life in a serious manner'.[334]

The European Court of Human Rights had to deal with similarly broadly worded norms in *Landvreugd* v. *the Netherlands*.[335] The Burgomaster of Amsterdam had prohibited a drug abuser from entering a particular area of Amsterdam for fourteen days based on his authority 'in case of a riotous movement, of other serious disorders or of calamities, as well as in case of a well-founded fear of the development thereof' to issue all orders deemed 'necessary for the maintenance of public order or the limitation of general danger'.[336] The majority of the court acknowledged that this power was 'admittedly rather general in terms' but argued that, on the other hand, the circumstances requiring the Burgomaster to intervene were 'so diverse that it would scarcely be possible to formulate a law to cover every eventuality'.[337] As, in addition, in the instant case the applicant had been warned that an exclusion order could be issued against him, the majority concluded that the requirement of foreseeability was met.[338] A minority of three judges, in contrast, held that to grant such 'broad and unspecified discretionary powers to an executive authority is not compatible with the very idea of the rule of law which is the cornerstone of the Convention'.[339]

Of course, the Swiss courts and the European Court of Human Rights are right to indicate that, as far as the regulation of police action is concerned, use of indeterminate terms such as 'public safety and order' and 'danger' is unavoidable. This point has also been made by various

[334] Urteil des Bundesgerichts 2A.347/2003 vom 24. November 2003, E. 2.2 ('Vielmehr genügt es bereits, dass konkrete Anhaltspunkte für den Verdacht der Begehung strafbarer Handlungen – etwa im Drogenmilieu – bestehen, der Ausländer Kontakte zu extremistischen Kreisen unterhält oder dass er ganz allgemein in grober Weise gegen ungeschriebene Regeln des sozialen Zusammenlebens verstösst.').

[335] *Landvreugd* v. *The Netherlands*, no. 37331/97, 4 June 2002. See also the almost identical case of *Olivieira* v. *The Netherlands*, no. 33129/96, 4 June 2002, ECHR 2002-IV, 193.

[336] Ibid., para. 91. [337] Ibid., paras 60–1. [338] Ibid., paras 62–5.

[339] Ibid., Joint Dissenting Opinion of Judges Gaukur Jörundsson, Türmen and Maruste.

scholars who have correctly emphasised that the legislator cannot predict all potential dangers for public safety and order and provide detailed regulations for all of them – one of the very purposes of a police force, after all, is to deal with extraordinary and unexpected situations.[340]

Nevertheless, it must be stressed, first of all, that, as was explained in the previous section and is recognised by the Swiss Federal Supreme Court itself, an openly formulated norm can never constitute a sufficient legal basis for a *serious* interference with fundamental rights. As the courts have come to recognise in recent years, depending on the specific circumstances of a given case, an exclusion measure based on one of the norms at issue here may well amount to a serious interference.[341]

Furthermore, the fact that the police must have legal powers to deal with unexpected situations does not explain why it would not be possible for the legislator to at least indicate the broad context in which exclusion powers are supposed to be used. The now repealed Section 27 of the British Violent Crime Reduction Act 2006, for example, did exactly this by making it clear that the exclusion measures it created were only available to deal with alcohol-related violence. Similarly, if the legislator creates exclusion powers as a means of dealing with 'scenes' of drug and alcohol addicts, the scope of application could and should be defined accordingly in the relevant piece of legislation. Thus, in Switzerland, some cantonal police acts explicitly list specific forms of behaviour (such as 'creating public nuisance under the influence of alcohol or other intoxicants'[342] or drug trafficking[343]) that will trigger application of the respective exclusion powers.

Another way of clarifying the scope of application of exclusion measures is to specify exactly which aspects of public safety and order these measures are meant to protect. Are they designed to protect the physical integrity of individuals, their health, their liberty, their property, their honour, certain state institutions or other interests? As is demonstrated by the Police Act of the Canton of Basel-Stadt, it is perfectly feasible for a law to be more specific with regard to the protected interests: this Act

340 Ritter, *Das Erfordernis der genügenden Bestimmtheit* (1994), p. 79; Reinhard, *Allgemeines Polizeirecht* (1993), pp. 156–7.

341 See Section 5.2.

342 Canton of Appenzell Ausserrhoden: Polizeigesetz vom 13. Mai 2002 (bGS 521.1), Art. 22(1)(d) (eingefügt am 14. September 2009) ('unter Einfluss von Alkohol oder anderer Mittel mit berauschender Wirkung öffentliches Ärgernis erregen').

343 Canton of Geneva: Loi sur la police du 26 octobre 1957 (LPol, RSG F 1 05), Art. 22A(d) (adopté le 19 février 2009); Canton of Fribourg: Loi du 15 novembre 1990 sur la Police cantonale (SGF 551.1), Art. 31d(d) (adopté le 31 mai 2010).

limits the scope of application of exclusion powers to those who pose a danger to, or seriously threaten, *other persons* or through their behaviour cause an immediate danger of a *violent altercation*.[344] Finally, an exclusion norm may also specify the degree and/or the immediacy of the danger to public safety and order that is required so that the exclusion power becomes applicable. The Police Act of the Canton of Zug, for example, makes it clear that people can only be excluded from public space if they pose a *serious* and *immediate* danger to public safety and order.[345] Limitations of the scope of application of exclusion powers such as these make it possible for citizens to foresee to a reasonable degree what forms of behaviour will entail exclusion from public space.

The exclusion norms of the Cantons of Grisons and Berne, in contrast, do not contain any such specifications. While the original intention of the legislator can be gathered to some extent from the parliamentary debates, the way these norms have been drafted allows them to be applied far beyond their original focus. The exclusion powers of the Police Act of the Canton of Grisons, for example, are in no way limited to the policing of large-scale events but, as was acknowledged by the Federal Supreme Court, can be used to address all sorts of dangerous situations.[346] This makes it very difficult for citizens to foresee whether a given action will entail exclusion measures or not. This is all the more true considering that, as explained before, hidden behind the reference to 'public safety and order' is, in this context, increasingly the idea of ensuring that public space *appears* clean, orderly and safe, that is, of creating a public space where people not only *are* safe but also *feel* safe. However, if this is the real aim of these measures, then it becomes impossible for people to foresee what types of conduct will trigger their application, as an almost limitless number of behaviours can be said to undermine the appearance of orderliness and safety.

Finally, it is worth emphasising that if it is true, as it is argued here, that the exclusion norms at issue *could be* drafted more precisely, the mere

[344] Gesetz betreffend die Kantonspolizei des Kantons Basel-Stadt vom 13. November 1996 (Polizeigesetz, PolG, SG 510.100), § 42(a)(1) (eingefügt am 15. Oktober 2008) ('Die Kantonspolizei kann eine Person von einem bestimmten öffentlichen Ort für höchstens 72 Stunden wegweisen, wenn diese Person 1. Dritte gefährdet oder Dritten mit einer ernsthaften Gefährdung droht; 2. durch ihr Verhalten die unmittelbare Gefahr einer gewalttätigen Auseinandersetzung schafft.').

[345] Polizeigesetz vom 30. November 2006 (BGS 512.1), § 16(1)(b) (geändert am 29. September 2011) ('begründeter Verdacht besteht, sie werde die öffentliche Sicherheit und Ordnung ernsthaft und unmittelbar gefährden oder stören').

[346] BGE 128 I 327, 341 (2002).

fact that there are safeguards in the form of the principle of proportionality and legal remedies does not help. A lack of precision can only be compensated for if it is *impossible* for the legislator to draft a given norm more precisely. If, in contrast, there are, as a in the present context, practicable and sensible ways of drafting the relevant norms in a precise manner, the legislator is under an obligation to do so.[347] Furthermore, as will be pointed out in Section 4.4, procedural safeguards tend to be afforded only to a very limited extent with regard to exclusion measures, and legal remedies are often only available, if at all, after the interference has already occurred.

Exclusion of those 'causing harassment or distress to others' Another type of exclusion norms is somewhat more specific with regard to the intended target but still problematic in that it gives the police the power to exclude from public space 'those who cause harassment to others' or some similar wording. In Switzerland, the Police Act of the Canton of Geneva, for example, contains a provision authorising the exclusion of those, among others, who 'seriously harass others'.[348] The Police Act of the Canton of Zurich contains a virtually identical exclusion power,[349] as do the relevant Acts of the Cantons of Glarus,[350] Lucerne,[351] St. Gallen[352] and Obwalden.[353] In the case of the Police Acts of the Cantons of Solothurn[354] and Appenzell Ausserrhoden[355] there is not even a need to show that the harassment was 'serious', mere harassment is sufficient.

[347] See Schweizer/Müller, 'Zwecke, Möglichkeiten und Grenzen der Gesetzgebung im Polizeibereich' (2008), 384.

[348] Loi sur la police du 26 octobre 1957 (LPol, RSG F 1 05), Art. 22A(b) (adopté le 19 février 2009) ('La police peut éloigner une personne d'un lieu ou d'un périmètre déterminé, si [. . .] elle-même ou un rassemblement de personnes auquel elle participe importune sérieusement des tiers.').

[349] Polizeigesetz vom 23. April 2007 (PolG, LS 550.1), § 33(b) ('Die Polizei darf eine Person von einem Ort wegweisen oder für längstens 24 Stunden fernhalten, [. . .] wenn die Person oder eine Ansammlung von Personen, der sie angehört, Dritte erheblich belästigt.').

[350] Polizeigesetz des Kantons Glarus vom 6. Mai 2007 (GS V A/11/1), Art. 15(b).

[351] Gesetz über die Luzerner Polizei vom 27. Januar 1998 (SRL 350), § 19(1)(b) (geändert am 28. April 2008).

[352] Polizeigesetz vom 10. April 1980 (sGS 451.1), Art. 29(1)(d)(Ziff. 1) (eingefügt am 18. September 2008).

[353] Polizeigesetz vom 11. März 2010 (GDB 510.1), Art. 18(1)(c).

[354] Gesetz über die Kantonspolizei vom 23. September 1990 (BGS 511.11), § 37(1)(d) (geändert am 15. Mai 2007).

[355] Polizeigesetz vom 13. Mai 2002 (bGS 521.1), Art. 22(1)(d) (eingefügt am 14. September 2009).

The British anti-social behaviour legislation provides for similar exclusion powers. The Anti-social Behaviour, Crime and Policing Act 2014 has largely taken over the definition of 'anti-social behaviour' from the previous Crime and Disorder Act 1998 and the Anti-social Behaviour Act 2003. It allows for people to be banned from public places as part of IPNAs and CBOs if their behaviour 'has caused, or is likely to cause, harassment, alarm or distress to any person'.[356] To be subject to a dispersal direction it is sufficient that the person 'has contributed or is likely to contribute' to members of the public being harassed, alarmed or distressed.[357]

The exclusion norm of the Police Act of the Canton of Geneva was challenged before the Federal Supreme Court in 2009. With regard to a passage of the provision that authorised exclusion measures against anyone 'who prevents without reason the normal use of public space'[358] the court concluded that it was not clear what the terms 'without reason' and 'normal use' were meant to refer to. Therefore, the court held that this passage was too vague for the police and citizens to be able to tell what forms of conduct would fall within its scope and was, as a result, not compatible with the requirement of sufficient precision guaranteed by Article 36(1) of the Federal Constitution.[359] In contrast, the Federal Supreme Court held that the passage referred to above, which authorises exclusion of those who 'seriously harass others', was of sufficient normative density. The court acknowledged that the provision does neither provide a definition of the term 'seriously harass others' nor refer to examples of behaviour that fall within its scope. Nevertheless, it thought that it was clear that the norm is meant to encompass forms of conduct that are below the threshold of endangering public safety and order but still of a sufficient gravity to 'seriously' inconvenience others. Therefore, and because the police would have to comply with the principle of proportionality when applying the provision, it could be precluded that the exclusion power would be used to deal with innocuous forms of behaviour or only temporary minor disturbances.[360] As in its previous decisions dealing with this issue, the court emphasised how difficult it

356 Anti-social Behaviour, Crime and Policing Act 2014, ss 2(1)(a), 22(3).

357 Ibid., s. 35(2)(a).

358 See Urteil des Bundesgerichts 1C_226/2009 vom 16. Dezember 2009, E. 4.2 ('La police peut éloigner une personne d'un lieu ou d'un périmètre déterminé, si elle-même ou un rassemblement de personnes auquel elle participe [. . .] empêche sans motif l'usage normal du domaine public.')

359 Ibid., E. 4.2.2.

360 Ibid., E. 4.2.1.

was for the legislator to regulate police action[361] and held that, in view of the great variety of behaviours that could potentially harass others, the relative vagueness of the norm at issue was justified.[362] Finally, the court argued that the lack of precision of the norm was compensated for by the availability of legal remedies against exclusion measures.[363]

Similarly, the European Court of Human Rights, although not in a decision concerning exclusion measures, seems to have suggested that a provision that criminalises harassing conduct may be regarded as sufficiently precise. *Chorherr* v. *Austria* concerned two protesters who caused a commotion at a military ceremony by carrying placards that blocked the view of some of the spectators.[364] After having refused to comply with instructions by the police to cease their demonstration, they were arrested. The European Court held that there was nothing to suggest that the wording of the relevant Austrian law, which made it an offence to 'cause a breach of the peace by conduct likely to cause annoyance',[365] 'creates a situation incompatible with legal certainty'.[366] Therefore, the applicant (only one of the protesters had lodged an application in Strasbourg) had been able to foresee to a reasonable extent the risks inherent in his conduct.[367] It is not clear from the court's very summary reasoning on this point whether it thought that the phrase 'conduct likely to cause annoyance' as such met the test for legal certainty[368] or whether it was only due to the combination with the breach-of-the-peace requirement that the norm was regarded as sufficiently precise.

In the United Kingdom, to my knowledge, the courts have not had to deal with the question of whether the exclusion norms under the anti-social behaviour legislation meet the requirement of sufficient precision.[369] However, the vagueness of these provisions has been widely criticised in the academic literature.[370] The definition of 'anti-social

361 Ibid., E. 4.1.1. 362 Ibid., E. 4.2.1. 363 Ibid.

364 *Chorherr* v. *Austria*, no. 13308/87, 25 August 1993, Series A no. 266-B.

365 Ibid., para. 12. 366 Ibid., para. 25. 367 Ibid.

368 In *Hashman and Harrup* v. *The United Kingdom* [GC], no. 25594/94, 25 November 1999, ECHR 1999-VIII, 1, para. 38, the court seemed to suggest as much.

369 Whilst in *R (Singh)* v. *Chief Constable of the West Midlands*, [2006] EWCA Civ 1118, the Court of Appeal did discuss the scope of application of Section 30 of the Anti-Social Behaviour Act 2003, this discussion was limited to the question of whether or not protests were covered.

370 See generally with regard to the Crime and Disorder Act 1998 von Hirsch and Simester (eds), *Incivilities: Regulating Offensive Behaviour* (2006); Macdonald, 'A Suicidal Woman, Roaming Pigs and a Noisy Trampolinist' (2006); with regard to the Anti-Social Behaviour Act 2003 Crawford, 'Dispersal Powers and the Symbolic Role of Anti-Social Behaviour Legislation' (2008).

behaviour' of section 1(1) of the Crime and Disorder Act 1998 (having acted 'in a manner that caused or was likely to cause harassment, alarm or distress to one or more persons not of the same household as himself'), which is virtually identical to that of the new Anti-social Behaviour, Crime and Policing Act 2014, has been described as intolerably 'sweeping and vague'.[371] The 'huge scope'[372] of this provision is said to give police and local authority officials a 'vast power' to 'bring people into the grasp of the criminal law on a discretionary basis'.[373] Even the Home Office itself has admitted that the definition 'is broad', 'lacks specificity' and 'can encompass a range of behaviours', depending on local context and individual perception: 'what may be considered anti-social behaviour to one person can be seen as acceptable behaviour to another'.[374]

The scope of discretion is particularly wide in the case of the dispersal powers according to Section 35 of the Anti-social Behaviour, Crime and Policing Act 2014 as it is sufficient for these powers to be triggered that a person 'has contributed or is likely to contribute' to members of the public being harassed, alarmed or distressed. In *R (Singh)* v. *Chief Constable of the West Midlands*, Lady Justice Hallett in the Court of Appeal acknowledged that '[o]ne or two particularly sensitive members of the public may be alarmed or distressed by conduct that would not or should not offend others'.[375] Therefore, she held, it is important that police officers use the dispersal powers sensibly and they are not allowed to 'act on a whim'.[376] However, research carried out by Adam Crawford shows that in practice police officers found it very difficult to answer questions about what behaviour might trigger the power of dispersal. Many young people (the main targets of these powers), in turn, were keen to know from the police what the parameters of acceptable behaviour were as they wanted to 'know where we stand' with regard to the law; they felt that dispersal powers provided too much scope for the police to base their judgments on stereotypes.[377]

371 Ashworth/Gardner/Morgan/Smith/von Hirsch/Wasik, 'Neighbouring on the Oppressive' (1998), 9.
372 Ramsay, 'The Theory of Vulnerable Autonomy and the Legitimacy of the Civil Preventative Order' (2008), 6.
373 Ashworth/Gardner/Morgan/Smith/von Hirsch/Wasik, 'Neighbouring on the Oppressive' (1998), 9.
374 Home Office, Defining and Measuring Anti-Social Behaviour, Home Office Development and Practice Report (2004), 3.
375 *R (Singh)* v. *Chief Constable of the West Midlands*, [2006] EWCA Civ 1118, para. 89.
376 Ibid., para. 90.
377 Crawford, 'Dispersal Powers and the Symbolic Role of Anti-Social Behaviour Legislation' (2008), 770–2.

This highlights the crucial problem posed by exclusion norms that are directed against conduct causing harassment or alarm or distress. Such norms may have a narrower scope of application and therefore appear, at first sight, to be more precise than those containing a general reference to 'public safety and order'. Yet, as largely symbolic measures designed to counter perceptions of insecurity,[378] they inevitably include – even more so than the latter category of norms – a very strong subjective element.[379] Whether a person feels harassed or distressed by someone else's behaviour depends to a large extent on the sensitivity of this person. For example, while some will consider the noise of playing children perfectly acceptable, others might find it distressing. The 'absence of any objective standard of sensitivity of [the] "victim"'[380] means that perfectly legitimate or even praiseworthy conduct could, in theory, be covered by these provisions. For example, a racist may feel harassed by a person with a different colour of skin sitting next to him on the bus or onlookers might find it alarming or distressing to witness a house owner using physical force in self-defence against a burglar.[381]

The Crime and Disorder Act 1998 at least provided for an exception by exempting from its scope 'any act of the defendant which he shows was reasonable in the circumstances'.[382] The new British anti-social behaviour legislation and the police acts of the Swiss cantons do not contain similar exceptions. It could be argued, however, that most of the Swiss police acts set a higher threshold by covering only 'serious' harassment. Yet even with this qualification the test remains a primarily subjective one: behaviour considered to be seriously harassing by some will be experienced as simply harassing or not harassing at all by others. As a consequence of this inherently subjective character of the relevant test, it becomes virtually impossible for citizens to tell where the threshold lies between acceptable behaviour, harassment and serious harassment. Is swearing at someone, asking for money or a man whistling at

378 See Section 3.2.

379 See the comment on ASBOs in Council of Europe, *Report by Mr Alvaro Gil-Robles, Commissioner for Human Rights, on his visit to the United Kingdom*, 8 June 2005, CommDH(2005)6, para. 110: 'This inevitably results in a very broad, and occasionally, excessive range of behaviour falling within their scope as the determination of what constitutes anti-social behaviour becomes conditional on the subjective views of any given collective.'

380 Ramsay, 'The Theory of Vulnerable Autonomy and the Legitimacy of the Civil Preventative Order' (2008), 9.

381 See Roberts, 'Penal Offence in Question' (2006), 28.

382 Crime and Disorder Act 1998, s. 1(5) (repealed).

a woman serious harassment, harassment or no harassment at all? If it is not possible for citizens to foresee whether a given action will be covered by a norm, this norm cannot be said to be sufficiently precise.

Interestingly, unlike the Swiss Federal Supreme Court, the US Supreme Court recognised this problem as early as 1971, in *Coates* v. *City of Cincinnati*.[383] The City of Cincinnati had passed an ordinance that made it a criminal offence for 'three or more persons to assemble [. . .] on any of the sidewalks, street corners, vacant lots, or mouths of alleys, and there conduct themselves in a manner annoying to persons passing by'.[384] The Supreme Court observed that the city was free to take measures against clearly specified forms of anti-social behaviour. However, the way the ordinance was drafted, the court held, did not specify any objective standard of conduct whatsoever: 'Conduct that annoys some people does not annoy others.'[385] As a consequence, it was impossible for ordinary people to tell precisely what the scope of application of the provision was. Thus, the court concluded that the provision was in violation of the due process standard of vagueness.[386]

What makes exclusion norms targeting unspecified 'harassing behaviour' particularly troublesome is that, in practice, it is left to those enforcing these norms (in most cases the police) to decide what amounts to harassment. In fact, affording the police wide discretion in dealing with various forms of behaviour may often be the very rationale for the adoption of such exclusion norms. The police may welcome such discretionary powers.[387] Thus, a police officer in Leeds stated that, even though anti-social behaviour was not a major problem in the city, 'a dispersal order gives us a really effective tool which we can use at our discretion to ensure that the very small minority who involve themselves in behaviour which spoils everyone else's enjoyment of the city centre can be ordered to leave'.[388] The US Supreme Court made it clear in *Coates* v. *City of Cincinnati* that it is incompatible with the requirement of sufficient precision to grant the police such wide discretion: the city, the court held, cannot prevent anti-social behaviour 'through the enactment and

[383] *Coates* v. *City of Cincinnati*, 402 U.S. 611 (1971).

[384] Code of Ordinances of the City of Cincinnati (1956), s. 901–L6.

[385] *Coates* v. *City of Cincinnati*, 402 U.S. 611, 614 (1971). [386] Ibid., 614–15.

[387] See Crawford, 'Dispersal Powers and the Symbolic Role of Anti-Social Behaviour Legislation' (2008), 768.

[388] BBC News, 'Dispersal order granted in Leeds city centre', 24 July 2010, available at www.bbc.co.uk/news/uk-england-leeds-10749759.

enforcement of an ordinance whose violation may entirely depend upon whether or not a policeman is annoyed'.[389]

Prohibitions of vaguely defined behaviour As explained in Section 3.4.1.2, instead of granting the police explicit exclusion powers, another way of excluding people from public space is for the legislator to prohibit certain forms of behaviour in public places. Breach of such a prohibition then triggers the authority of the police to intervene and take enforcement action, including by removing (or arresting) the offender. This approach is particularly common in the United States. While the scope of such prohibitions naturally tends to be much narrower than that of the sort of blanket police powers common in Switzerland and, to a lesser extent, in the United Kingdom, they may nevertheless raise serious problems with regard to the requirement of sufficient precision.

Until about the 1960s and 1970s, many US states and municipalities had public-order laws that prohibited a wide range of broadly defined behaviours in public places (such as loitering, vagrancy, breaches of the peace and disorderly conduct) and thus had the effect of conferring a great amount of discretion on the police.[390] As William J. Stuntz observed, '[p]rior to the 1960s, vagrancy and loitering laws made it possible for police to arrest pretty much anyone, or at least anyone on the street: the laws were so broad as to plausibly cover anything anyone might do in public'.[391] As with some of the exclusion powers described above, these prohibitions were intentionally framed in an imprecise manner 'so as to allow the net to be cast at large, to enable men to be caught who are vaguely undesirable in the eyes of police and prosecution, although not chargeable with any particular offense'.[392]

In the late 1960s and early 1970s many of these public-order statutes were declared unconstitutional by the courts for, among other reasons, being too vague.[393] This case law, and in particular the leading decision of the Supreme Court in *Papachristou* v. *City of Jacksonville* of 1972,[394] established important standards, which are valid to this day, to determine whether prohibitions entailing exclusion from public space are

389 *Coates* v. *City of Cincinnati*, 402 U.S. 611, 614 (1971).

390 See e.g. Foote, 'Vagrancy-Type Law and Its Administration' (1956).

391 Stuntz, 'Crime Talk and Law Talk' (1995), 157.

392 *Winters* v. *New York*, 333 U.S. 507, 540 (1948) (Frankfurter, J., dissenting).

393 For an overview, see Livingston, 'Police Discretion and the Quality of Life in Public Places' (1997), 595–608.

394 *Papachristou* v. *City of Jacksonville*, 405 U.S. 156 (1972).

sufficiently precise. *Papachristou* concerned a vagrancy ordinance of the City of Jacksonville that prohibited behaviours such as 'being a vagabond', 'disorderly conduct', 'common nightwalking' and 'wandering or strolling around from place to place without any lawful purpose or object'. Citing from one of its previous decisions, the Supreme Court declared that '[l]iving under a rule of law entails various suppositions, one of which is that "[all persons] are entitled to be informed as to what the State commands or forbids"'.[395] The Jacksonville ordinance, however, was so unclear that it failed to give fair notice to people of what conduct was prohibited. The court put even more emphasis on the second aspect of its vagueness doctrine: the prevention of arbitrary enforcement. As there were no standards governing the exercise of the discretion granted by the ordinance, the court observed that the discretion of the police was almost unfettered, thus permitting and encouraging arbitrary and discriminatory enforcement of the law: 'Where the list of crimes is so all-inclusive and generalized as the one in this ordinance, those convicted may be punished for no more than vindicating affronts to police authority.'[396] As a result, the Supreme Court held that the ordinance was void for vagueness.

Using the same reasoning, the Supreme Court declared a number of similar provisions unconstitutional in later years. In *Kolender* v. *Lawson*, for instance, it invalidated a provision of the California Penal Code that required persons who loiter or wander on the streets to identify themselves and to account for their presence when requested to do so by a police officer.[397] Again, the Supreme Court stressed that the crucial element of its vagueness doctrine was the requirement for the legislator to establish sufficient guidelines to govern law enforcement.[398] As the provision at issue contained no standard for determining how people could identify themselves, it vested 'virtually complete discretion in the hands of the police to determine whether the suspect has satisfied the statute and must be permitted to go on his way',[399] thus encouraging arbitrary enforcement.[400] As a result, the court found that the provision was too vague and therefore in violation of the due process clause of the Fourteenth Amendment. Various federal and state courts have also held statutes prohibiting behaviours such as 'loitering' or 'wandering in or about a place without apparent reason' to be unconstitutional for vagueness, arguing that these prohibitions were so indefinite that it was

[395] Ibid., 162. [396] Ibid., 166–7. [397] *Kolender* v. *Lawson*, 461 U.S. 352 (1983).
[398] Ibid., 358. [399] Ibid. [400] Ibid., 361.

impossible for people to discern whether they risked criminal responsibility and that they could be abused by the police for pretextual arrests.[401] For the same reasons, the US Court of Appeals for the Ninth Circuit held that San Diego's juvenile curfew ordinance, which made it unlawful for minors to 'loiter, idle, wander, stroll or play' in public places during curfew hours, was unconstitutionally vague. The court thought that while this phrase seemed to mean something different than just presence in public places, it remained unclear what the difference was.[402]

The Supreme Court case of *Chicago* v. *Morales* concerned a 'Gang Congregation Ordinance' enacted by the Chicago City Council, which authorised the police to order persons reasonably believed to be 'criminal street gang members' who are 'loitering' in a public place to disperse.[403] Anyone not promptly obeying such an order was in violation of the ordinance. The majority of the Supreme Court concluded that the ordinance was unconstitutionally vague. A plurality of the court held that the term 'loiter' as it was defined by the ordinance ('to remain in any one place with no apparent purpose') was unclear: it was impossible for citizens to tell whether they have an 'apparent purpose' for being in a public place or not. Therefore, the ordinance left the public uncertain as to the prohibited conduct.[404] The majority found the ordinance to be unconstitutionally vague for the further reason that it did not contain sufficient guidelines to govern law enforcement. As a consequence of its broad definition of the term 'loiter', it provided police officers too much discretion to determine what activities constitute 'loitering'.[405] Thus, the result of the ordinance was, in the words of Justice O'Connor, that '[an]y police officer in Chicago is free [. . .] to order at his whim any person standing in a public place with a suspected gang member to disperse'.[406]

It is, admittedly, no easy task for courts to determine whether a given prohibition entailing exclusion from public space is defined precisely enough or not. In the United States, different state courts have often come to different conclusions with regard to public-order laws that prohibited almost identically defined behaviours.[407] Nevertheless, the

401 E.g. *Bullock* v. *City of Dallas*, 248 Ga. 164, 281 S.E.2d 613 (Ga. 1981); *U.S. ex rel. Newsome* v. *Malcolm*, 492 F.2d 1166 (2nd Cir. 1974); *People* v. *Berck*, 32 N.Y.2d 567, 300 N.E.2d 411 (N.Y. 1973).

402 *Nunez* v. *City of San Diego*, 114 F.3d 935, 942 (9th Cir. 1997).

403 *Chicago* v. *Morales*, 527 U.S. 41 (1999). See Strosnider, 'Anti-Gang Ordinances after City of Chicago v. Morales' (2002).

404 *Chicago* v. *Morales*, 527 U.S. 41, 56–60 (1999). 405 Ibid., 60–4. 406 Ibid., 66.

407 See Livingston, 'Police Discretion and the Quality of Life in Public Places' (1997), 605.

Supreme Court in the case law described above has provided important guidance as to how that distinction must be drawn. Importantly, it has made it clear that it is not enough for a statute to use clear legal terms so that citizens will be able to understand which behaviours are covered by it and which are not. Just as is acknowledged in the other jurisdictions, the requirement of sufficient precision is also about the degree to which the authorities applying a law are restricted by it. At the very least, provisions that may entail exclusion from public space must provide minimal guidance on how the discretion they afford should be exercised to prevent arbitrary enforcement. Thus, even a prohibition that is clear may be too imprecise because it is so openly worded as to grant those enforcing it virtually unfettered discretion.

4.3.2.2 Available exclusion measures

Exclusion norms not only tend to be vague in terms of their scope of application but also with regard to the consequences they entail, that is, with regard to the measures at the disposal of the police. The relevant provision of the Police Act of the Canton of Grisons referred to above simply states that the police 'may take the necessary measures to deal with an event' for purposes of maintaining safety and order[408] and refers, by way of example, to ordering people to leave an area and preventing them from accessing it or being present there.[409] Similarly, the Police Act of the Canton of Berne does not in any way specify the exclusion power of the police but simply states that the police 'may temporarily remove or keep away persons from a location'.[410] The same is true for the Police Acts of the Cantons of Aargau,[411] Glarus,[412] Schwyz,[413] Uri[414] and

[408] Polizeigesetz des Kantons Graubünden vom 20. Oktober 2004 (BR 613.0000), Art. 12(1) ('Die Kantonspolizei kann zur Wahrung der Sicherheit und Ordnung sowie zur Gefahrenabwehr ereignisbezogen die notwendigen Massnahmen anordnen.').

[409] Ibid., Art. 12(2) ('Insbesondere kann sie (a) Personen anweisen, einen bestimmten Ort oder ein bestimmtes Gebiet zu verlassen; (b) das Betreten von Objekten, Grundstücken oder Gebieten untersagen; (c) den Aufenthalt in Objekten, Grundstücken oder Gebieten untersagen.').

[410] Polizeigesetz vom 8. Juni 1997 (BSG 551.1), Art. 29(1) ('Die Kantonspolizei kann Personen von einem Ort vorübergehend wegweisen oder fern halten.').

[411] Gesetz über die Gewährleistung der öffentlichen Sicherheit (Polizeigesetz) vom 6. Dezember 2005 (SAR 531.200), § 34(1).

[412] Polizeigesetz des Kantons Glarus vom 6. Mai 2007 (GS V A/11/1), Art. 15.

[413] Verordnung über die Kantonspolizei (Polizeiverordnung) vom 22. März 2000 (SRSZ 520.110), § 19 (geändert am 28. Juni 2007).

[414] Polizeigesetz vom 30. November 2008 (RB 3.8111), Art. 22.

Fribourg.[415] As a final example, the Chicago Gang Congregation Ordinance, in its original version, authorised the police to 'order all such persons [loitering criminal street gang members] to disperse and remove themselves from the area', without indicating the terms of the order such as its duration or geographical scope.[416]

The Swiss Federal Supreme Court has not objected to the vague definition of the exclusion measures available under the cantonal police acts. In respect of the Police Act of the Canton of Grisons, it acknowledged that the relevant provision did not in any way specify what type of exclusion measures the police could and should adopt or what their geographical scope should be.[417] However, as with regard to the scope of application, the court satisfied itself with pointing out that it was difficult to draft precise norms when it comes to the regulation of police action; the police had to address a variety of dangerous situations that could quickly change, so that it was impossible to define the measures required to deal with them in a more precise manner.[418] With regard to the Police Act of the Canton of Berne, the Federal Supreme Court thought that the wording 'temporarily remove or keep away persons from a location' limited the temporal scope of the available exclusion measures and was therefore actually quite precise.[419] In view of the difficulties of predicting what measures may be required in a given situation, the large number of people potentially subject to the exclusion power and the fact that the interference with fundamental rights was not very serious, the court came to the conclusion that the provision was sufficiently precise.[420] Finally, it argued that any imprecision with regard to the definition of the available exclusion measures was compensated for by the requirement to comply with the principle of proportionality and the availability of legal remedies.[421]

The US Supreme Court has applied a much stricter approach with regard to the definition of exclusion measures available to the police. One of the reasons why, in *Chicago* v. *Morales*, it found the Chicago Gang Congregation Ordinance to be void for vagueness was that the wording 'shall order all such persons to disperse and remove themselves from the area' left open too many questions as to the duration and features of the dispersal orders to be issued under the ordinance: 'After such an order

[415] Loi du 15 novembre 1990 sur la Police cantonale (SGF 551.1), Art. 31d (adopté le 31 mai 2010).
[416] Chicago Municipal Code, § 8-4-015(a) (added 17 June 1992).
[417] BGE 128 I 327, 336–7 and 339 (2002). [418] Ibid., 340–2.
[419] BGE 132 I 49, 59 (2006). [420] Ibid. [421] Ibid., 60.

issues, how long must the loiterers remain apart? How far must they move? If each loiterer walks around the block and they meet again at the same location, are they subject to arrest or merely to being ordered to disperse again?'[422] Similarly, the US Court of Appeals for the Second Circuit struck down a juvenile curfew ordinance as unconstitutionally vague because it only specified the time at which the night curfew started but not the hour at which it ended.[423] In the case of *Landvreugd* v. *the Netherlands* before the European Court of Human Rights, described above, the dissenting judges criticised that the nature of the orders the Burgomaster could issue was not specified at all so that citizens were not given any guidance as to the possible consequences of their behaviour. Accordingly, they concluded that the requirement of foreseeability was not met.[424]

This strict approach is to be preferred over the rather lax standard used by the Swiss Federal Supreme Court. It is, of course, true that it may be difficult to predict what sort of exclusion measure will be required and adequate to deal with a given situation in a given case; the legislator cannot be required to exactly define in advance each and every situation where exclusion measures may be used and to set out in detail the terms of the corresponding measures. This, however, does not mean that it is impossible for the legislator to circumscribe the scope of exclusion measures. As has been correctly pointed out in Swiss legal scholarship, the different measures that are available to deal with different dangers are, as a rule, not only known in advance but also often already part of police routine and/or the subject of internal police guidelines, so that there is no reason why they could not be regulated by the legislator.[425]

Therefore, relevant legislation should define, first, the geographical scope of exclusion measures, indicating, at the very least, the maximum extension of exclusion zones. None of the Swiss cantonal police acts does this at the moment. Second, it should define the temporal scope of exclusion measures, at the very least setting an upper time limit. There is no reason why the legislator, instead of using indeterminate terms such as 'temporarily' (or not setting an upper time limit at all), could and should not prescribe a maximum period. In fact, new (or newly revised)

422 *Chicago* v. *Morales*, 527 U.S. 41, 59 (1999).

423 *Naprstek* v. *City of Norwich*, 545 F.2d 815 (2nd Cir. 1976).

424 *Landvreugd* v. *The Netherlands*, no. 37331/97, 4 June 2002, Joint Dissenting Opinion of Judges Gaukur Jörundsson, Türmen and Maruste.

425 Egli, 'Grundrechte' (2012), 197; Schweizer/Müller, 'Zwecke, Möglichkeiten und Grenzen der Gesetzgebung im Polizeibereich' (2008), 385–6.

police acts of Swiss cantons now tend to include upper time limits.[426] Third, relevant legislation should clearly set out the sanctions that are available in case of a violation of exclusion orders.

4.3.2.3 Result

Vague exclusion norms may have a 'chilling effect' not only on forms of behaviour that are completely legitimate, such as meeting friends in a public square, but also on those that are, in addition, crucial to the functioning of a democracy, such as political protest.[427] This makes it all the more important that exclusion norms are drafted in a way that enables people to clearly foresee under what circumstances these norms may be applied and that precludes too much discretion on the part of those enforcing them. It is this function of the requirement of sufficient precision that makes it an effective safeguard for fundamental rights: precisely formulated norms help ensure that people can plan and act as autonomous rational beings and thus exercise their liberties, including those that contribute to democratic discourse.

Therefore, it is not enough, as the Swiss Federal Supreme Court tends to do, to stress how difficult it is to create precise legislation when it comes to the regulation of police action. As the review of the case law above demonstrates, the Federal Supreme Court has only invalidated an exclusion provision where that provision was so unclear that it was simply impossible to understand what it meant. In contrast, the court has refrained from intervening on grounds that too much discretion is afforded to the police. The US Supreme Court, on the other hand, has rightly emphasised that this second aspect of the requirement of sufficient precision is just as important as, if not even more important than, clarity of the law. Exclusion norms should be drafted so as to grant the police as little discretion to decide against whom to employ them as is required in the circumstances and should provide clear guidelines to prevent arbitrary enforcement. In addition, relevant legislation should set out in as much detail as possible the terms of exclusion measures, establishing specific limitations on their geographical and temporal scope.

426 See e.g. for the Canton of Zurich: Polizeigesetz vom 23. April 2007 (LS 550.1), §§ 33–4 (24 hours and, in certain cases, 14 days); for the Canton of Geneva: Loi sur la police du 26 octobre 1957 (LPol, RSG F 1 05), Art. 22B (adopté le 19 février 2009) (24 hours and, in certain cases, three months); for the Canton of Obwalden: Polizeigesetz vom 11. März 2010 (GDB 510.1), Art. 18 (24 hours and, in certain cases, one month).

427 See Section 3.3.3.

4.4 Procedural safeguards and access to justice

As explained in Section 4.1, a crucial element of any conception of the rule of law is the provision of procedural safeguards and access to justice. Given the differences between the legal procedures applicable in the three states at issue (and, indeed, in the case of the federal systems of Switzerland and the United States, the differences within these states), it is impossible to review here each and every procedural safeguard guaranteed by the legal systems at issue or to discuss in detail all the problems that exclusion measures raise with regard to these safeguards. For example, as is apparent from Annex I, even the procedural rules relating to exclusion measures under the different Swiss cantonal police acts vary considerably. The purpose of this final section of the chapter is merely to highlight that exclusion measures have a general tendency to undermine existing procedural guarantees, a point that will be illustrated by reference to a few specific examples. Indeed, the very impetus for the adoption of schemes of exclusion from public space is often the desire to avoid the level of due process applicable under the ordinary legal system. This is particularly problematic in view of the fact that, as explained in the previous section, exclusion norms are often very vaguely drafted, which would make it all the more important that there are strong procedural safeguards.

4.4.1 Circumvention of procedural safeguards

As explained in Section 3.2, most exclusion measures have a pre-emptive logic: they are designed to *prevent* certain behaviours from occurring in the first place by banning certain people from accessing (certain) public places. Typically, they have been introduced out of a certain discontent with criminal law and procedure, which is concerned with holding people accountable for *past* behaviour. Due to its retrospective focus, criminal law and procedure has come to be regarded not only as an ineffective means of tackling these behaviours but, by providing for certain standards and procedures, as creating unnecessary obstacles.[428]

[428] See e.g. *Clingham* v. *Royal Borough of Kensington and Chelsea; R (McCann and Others)* v. *Crown Court at Manchester and Another*, [2002] UKHL 39, paras 16 (Lord Steyn explaining the rationale for introducing the ASBO powers as follows: 'There appeared to be a gap in the law. The criminal law offered insufficient protection to communities. Public confidence in the rule of law was undermined by a not unreasonable view in some communities that the law failed them.') and 42 (Lord Hope: 'The social disruption which their behaviour creates is unacceptable. So too is the apparent inability of the criminal law to restrain their activities.').

As opposed to criminal prohibitions enforced through the criminal justice system, preventive exclusion measures normally take the form of discretionary police powers. Where, as is especially the case in the United Kingdom, the police (or local authorities) are required to apply for a court order to impose an exclusion measure, the respective proceedings are normally characterised as civil rather than criminal.

Nevertheless, for people subject to them, preventive exclusion measures typically entail consequences that are equally burdensome as those under criminal law. It has therefore been rightly observed that schemes of preventive exclusion from public space are often adopted as a means of imposing restrictions that have a punitive effect and are backed up by draconian sanctions but at the same time avoid the criminal process and its safeguards.[429]

The prime example of this circumvention of the criminal process are so-called 'two-step'[430] or 'hybrid' prohibitions,[431] as they are particularly widely used in the United Kingdom. With these prohibitions, the police (or local authorities) can apply for a civil order against persons who have engaged in, or are likely to engage in, undesired conduct, prohibiting them, for example, from accessing certain parts of public space or re-engaging in similar conduct. Breach of the order constitutes contempt of court or a criminal offence that is punishable, depending on the type of order, with a serious penalty of up to several years of imprisonment; for breach of an IPNA, for instance, the maximum penalty is imprisonment for two years[432] and for breach of a CBO, five years.[433] Thus, as the case of Christopher Lamb described in Chapter 1 illustrates, a person may be banned, for example, from entering a town centre by civil order. If he disobeys the order, he may be sentenced to a long prison sentence. Key examples of such prohibitory orders include, apart from IPNAs, CBOs and the previous ASBOs, football banning orders,[434] sexual risk orders,[435] serious crime prevention orders,[436] gang injunctions[437] as

[429] Zedner, 'Seeking Security by Eroding Rights' (2007); Simester/von Hirsch, 'Regulating Offensive Conduct through Two-Step Prohibitions' (2006).
[430] Simester/von Hirsch, 'Regulating Offensive Conduct through Two-Step Prohibitions' (2006).
[431] Pearson, 'Hybrid Law and Human Rights' (2006).
[432] Home Office, Anti-social Behaviour, Crime and Policing Act 2014: Reform of Anti-social Behaviour Powers: Statutory Guidance for Frontline Professionals, July 2014, p. 26.
[433] Anti-social Behaviour, Crime and Policing Act 2014, s. 30(2).
[434] Football Spectators Act 1989 (as amended by the Football Disorder Act 2000), s. 14B.
[435] Sexual Offences Act 2003, s. 122A.
[436] Serious Crime Act 2007, s. 1.
[437] Policing and Crime Act 2009, s. 34.

well as some of the previous terrorist control orders.[438] The new TPIMs, in contrast, are issued by the Home Secretary herself, although she has to seek permission from the High Court.[439]

In Switzerland, the preventive exclusion powers under the cantonal police acts and under the Hooligan Concordat similarly authorise the police to issue far-reaching orders requiring people not to access specified areas for extended periods of time (up to three years in the case of the revised concordat).[440] While the relevant proceedings are characterised as administrative (rather than criminal) in nature,[441] those subject to such an order regularly experience it as punitive.[442] In addition, non-compliance with such an order can be made a criminal offence by issuing it under threat of a criminal penalty according to Article 292 of the Swiss Criminal Code,[443] meaning that its breach amounts to a criminal offence punishable with a fine, which in case of non-payment can be transformed into a prison sentence.[444] As many of those subject to exclusion orders are not in a position to pay the resulting fines, such orders often eventually result in prison terms.[445]

Finally, to also refer to an example from the United States, the revised Chicago Gang Congregation Ordinance authorises the police to order suspected criminal gang members loitering in a public place 'to disperse and remove themselves' from the area.[446] Failure to obey such a dispersal order constitutes a criminal offence punishable by up to six months of imprisonment.[447]

There is nothing wrong as such with dealing with certain forms of behaviour through other means than the criminal process. However, the burdens imposed on people as a consequence of the sort of exclusion measures described above may be even more draconian than

[438] Prevention of Terrorism Act 2005, ss 1, 4.

[439] Terrorism Prevention and Investigation Measures Act 2011, ss 2–3, 6.

[440] E.g. for the Canton of Berne: Polizeigesetz vom 8. Juni 1997 (BSG 551.1), Art. 29; Konkordat über Massnahmen gegen Gewalt anlässlich von Sportveranstaltungen vom 15. November 2007, Art. 4; Konkordat über Massnahmen gegen Gewalt anlässlich von Sportveranstaltungen vom 15. November 2007; Änderung vom 2. Februar 2012, Art. 4.

[441] For area bans in connection with sports events, see BGE 137 I 31, 40 and 43–4 (2010); for the exclusion power under the police act of the Canton of Zurich, see Urteil des Verwaltungsgerichts des Kantons Zürich vom 3. Dezember 2009, VB.2009.00523, E. 3.2.

[442] See e.g. Hensler, 'Strafe ohne Strafrecht' (2011), 41–2; Litscher/Grossrieder/Mösch-Payot/Schmutz, *Wegweisung aus öffentlichen Stadträumen* (2011), pp. 96–9.

[443] See e.g. for the Canton of Zurich, explicitly: Polizeigesetz (PolG) vom 23. April 2007 (LS 550.1), § 34(2).

[444] StGB, Art. 36. [445] E.g. Gasser, *Kriminalpolitik oder City-Pflege?* (2004), p. 33.

[446] Chicago Municipal Code, § 8-4-015(a)(ii). [447] Ibid., § 8-4-015(e).

criminal sanctions, and dealing with these behaviours through civil or administrative proceedings may undermine the due process safeguards that would apply in the criminal process.[448] It is a generally accepted principle that in criminal cases higher standards of due process must apply than in civil or administrative proceedings. This principle is reflected in international human rights law: for those charged with a criminal offence, the fair trial provisions of human rights instruments guarantee the presumption of innocence[449] and a number of additional due process rights not applicable in civil or administrative proceedings.[450] The novel hybrid measures contribute to the blurring of the distinction between criminal and civil law[451] and allow for the circumvention of the criminal due process standards. For example, in the United Kingdom, begging is a criminal offence but not one that carries a prison sentence.[452] Under the Anti-social Behaviour, Crime and Policing Act 2014, however, a person can be required not to beg as part of a CBO,[453] and breach of such an order then constitutes a criminal offence with a maximum penalty of five years of imprisonment.[454] Such exclusion measures may thus ultimately result in the establishment of a parallel system of justice for certain categories of people (such as those engaging in anti-social behaviour or suspected sexual offenders) where a lower standard of due process but equally (or even more) draconian sanctions apply.

The following paragraphs briefly highlight some of the ways in which exclusion of people from public space through preventive, hybrid measures may conflict with the due process aspect of the rule of law.

First, these measures often involve what Adam Crawford has called a 'de-juridification of decision-making': decisions that used to be taken by courts (or the legislator) are increasingly being taken elsewhere, as considerable discretion is ceded to non-judicial officers, notably the

448 See Zedner, 'Seeking Security by Eroding Rights' (2007), 266.

449 ICCPR, Art. 14(2); ECHR, Art. 6(2); ADHR, Art. 26(1). The presumption of innocence is also guaranteed by the domestic law of the three states at issue. For the British common law, see *Woolmington* v. *DPP*, [1935] UKHL 1. For the United States, see *Coffin* v. *United States*, 156 U.S. 432 (1895). For Switzerland, see BV, Art. 32(1).

450 ICCPR, Art. 14(3); ECHR, Art. 6(3); ADHR, Art. 26(2).

451 See, generally, Steiker, 'Punishment and Procedure' (1997).

452 Vagrancy Act 1824, s. 3.

453 Under the previous ASBO system, ASBOs prohibiting begging were in fact issued. Macdonald, 'A Suicidal Woman, Roaming Pigs and a Noisy Trampolinist' (2006), 199–201.

454 Anti-social Behaviour, Crime and Policing Act 2014, s. 30.

police and staff of local authorities.[455] Under the Anti-social Behaviour, Crime and Policing Act 2014, for example, the powers to authorise an area for use of dispersal powers, to issue dispersal directions and to enforce the directions are – despite the serious consequences they may have for those affected by them – all placed in the hands of police officers, and judicial oversight and review are severely limited.[456] Similarly, the exclusion powers under most cantonal police acts and the Hooligan Concordat allow police officers to take measures that have so far-reaching consequences for those affected by them (namely, being prevented from accessing possibly very large areas of a town for several years or even permanently)[457] that they traditionally would probably have been seen as properly belonging to the domain of a court. Obviously, this shift may raise concerns with regard to the independence and impartiality of the relevant decision-makers.

Second, since they treat the respective proceedings as non-criminal, the relevant legal regimes often fail to guarantee to those affected by an exclusion measure a right to a fair hearing, or they even explicitly restrict this right. The British Prevention of Terrorism Act 2005, for example, provided that the proceedings for the issuance of a control order could be conducted 'in the absence of any person, including a relevant party to the proceedings and his legal representative'[458] and that the Secretary of State did not have to disclose the relevant evidence.[459] The Terrorism Prevention and Investigation Measures Act 2011 similarly provides that the respective proceedings can take place in the absence of a party to the proceedings (or his or her legal representative)[460] and 'without full particulars of the reasons for the decisions to which the proceedings relate being given to a party to the proceedings'.[461] In *Secretary of State*

[455] Crawford, 'Dispersal Powers and the Symbolic Role of Anti-Social Behaviour Legislation' (2008), 780–1.

[456] Anti-Social Behaviour Act 2003, ss 34–42. See Crawford, 'Dispersal Powers and the Symbolic Role of Anti-Social Behaviour Legislation' (2008), 778–80.

[457] Area bans according to the revised Concordat may last for up to three years. Konkordat über Massnahmen gegen Gewalt anlässlich von Sportveranstaltungen vom 15. November 2007; Änderung vom 2. Februar 2012, Art. 4(2). Exclusion orders under the Police Act of the Canton of Grisons may be imposed permanently. Polizeigesetz des Kantons Graubünden vom 20. Oktober 2004 (BR 613.000), Art. 12.

[458] Prevention of Terrorism Act 2005, Schedule, para. 4(2)(b); Civil Procedure (Amendment No. 2) Rules 2005, Schedule, Rule 76.22.

[459] Prevention of Terrorism Act 2005, Schedule, para. 4(3)(b); Civil Procedure (Amendment No. 2) Rules 2005, Schedule, Rules 76.2(2), 76.26, 76.28.

[460] Terrorism Prevention and Investigation Measures Act 2011, Schedule 4, para. 2(2)(e).

[461] Ibid., Schedule 4, para. 2(2)(d).

for the Home Department v. *MB* the House of Lords confirmed that control orders did not involve the determination of a criminal charge: the purpose of the control order regime was preventative, not punitive.[462] As a consequence, according to the House of Lords, the presumption of innocence guaranteed by Article 6(2) of the ECHR and the additional safeguards for criminal proceedings of Article 6(3) of the ECHR did not apply. Nevertheless, their Lordships found that Article 6(1) of the ECHR at least demands a 'measure of procedural protection as is commensurate with the gravity of the potential consequences'[463] or 'a substantial measure of procedural justice'.[464] The majority of their Lordships concluded that those subject to control orders in the case at issue did not even enjoy such a minimum degree of procedural justice as they were not told what allegations were made against them.[465]

In Switzerland, the Hooligan Concordat, which authorises the police to impose bans on accessing certain designated areas in connection with sports events (*Rayonverbote*), similarly does not explicitly provide for a right of those affected to be heard. The District Court of Zurich, however, ruled that, despite the absence of a specific guarantee, those subject to such an area ban should be heard before it is imposed. The court argued that such a ban constitutes a considerable interference with fundamental rights and that granting a hearing allows for the specific situation of those affected to be taken into account, making the ban more compliant with the principle of proportionality.[466] In 2010, also the Federal Supreme Court concluded that, according to Article 29(2) of the Federal Constitution, a person subject to such a ban has a right to be heard before the ban is imposed.[467]

However, even where people *are* given the opportunity to be heard or if they can later bring an appeal or complaint against an exclusion measure, they may in practice face serious difficulties in effectively defending themselves. Because of the great number of exclusion measures such as dispersal orders, exclusion orders under the Swiss cantonal police acts or football banning orders, the respective authorities tend to

462 *Secretary of State for the Home Department* v. *MB*, [2007] UKHL 46, paras 23–4 (Lord Bingham).

463 Ibid., para. 24 (Lord Bingham).

464 Ibid., paras 32, 41 (Lord Bingham), 66 (Lady Hale).

465 Ibid., paras 41–3 (Lord Bingham). Lord Hoffmann dissented on this issue: ibid., para. 54.

466 Verfügung des Bezirksgerichts Zürich vom 5. Dezember 2007, cited after Soòs/Vögeli, 'BWIS-Massnahmen gegen Gewalt an Sportveranstaltungen' (2008), 158 (the case concerned the predecessor of the Concordat, the BWIS).

467 Urteil des Bundesgerichts 1C_453/2009 vom 12. Januar 2010, E. 2.3.

issue these orders on standard forms, often using text modules.[468] In many cases in Switzerland and the United Kingdom, the explanations of the reasons for imposing an exclusion measure have been so summary as to simply make it impossible for those concerned to understand what they were alleged to have done (or what they were prohibited from doing in the future).[469]

Third, as a consequence of the fact that these measures are treated as non-criminal, and accordingly the presumption of innocence is regarded as inapplicable, the applicable rules of evidence and the required standard of proof will generally be considerably less stringent than those in criminal proceedings. In Switzerland, the above-mentioned area bans under the Hooligan Concordat, for example, can be imposed on any person who has been previously involved in violence against persons or property in connection with sports events.[470] Previous involvement in such violence can be substantiated by various means, including, for example, existence of a criminal complaint, a credible statement by the police or private security personnel, stadium bans issued by sports clubs or associations and reports by foreign authorities.[471] Thus, the police can themselves contribute to the creation of evidence justifying an area ban by producing statements of police officers[472] or by recommending sports clubs to issue stadium bans,[473] against which no legal remedies are available.[474] In a case brought before the Administrative Court of the

[468] For the practice of issuing exclusion orders in the City of Berne, see Section 3.3.2.4. For an illustrative case, see BVR 2009, 385, pp. 394–7, 400 (Verwaltungsgericht des Kantons Bern).

[469] E.g. Rekursgericht im Ausländerrecht, Kanton Aargau, Urteil 1-PO.2010.1 vom 14. Oktober 2010, in: Jusletter, 6. Dezember 2010, available at http://jusletter.weblaw.ch/it/juslissues/2010/596/_8878.html (concerning an area ban imposed in connection with a football game that not only failed to explain the actions the applicant was alleged to have engaged in and to specify the time and place of the alleged incident but also did not clearly define the terms of the ban); *Sierney* v. *DPP*, [2006] EWHC 716 (Admin) (concerning an authorisation for the use of dispersal orders under Section 30 of the Anti-social Behaviour Act 2003 that failed to give any information regarding the grounds on which the authorisation was given).

[470] Konkordat über Massnahmen gegen Gewalt anlässlich von Sportveranstaltungen vom 15. November 2007, Art. 4(1).

[471] Ibid., Art. 3.

[472] For such a case, see e.g. Urteil des Verwaltungsgerichts des Kantons Zürich vom 5. Oktober 2009, VB.2009.00368, E. 4.

[473] Konkordat über Massnahmen gegen Gewalt anlässlich von Sportveranstaltungen vom 15. November 2007, Art. 10.

[474] See Bichovsky, *Prévention de la violence commise par les spectateurs lors de manifestations sportives* (2009), pp. 261–2.

Canton of Zurich, a person who had been subject to an area ban because he was allegedly involved in football-related disorder complained that, by merely requiring a criminal complaint or a credible statement by the police for the imposition of a ban, the relevant norm violated the presumption of innocence.[475] The court rejected this argument. It held that the presumption of innocence only applies in criminal proceedings and that the area ban at issue was an administrative law measure, not a criminal law sanction.[476] Adopting essentially the same reasoning as the House of Lords with regard to control orders, the Administrative Court explained that the purpose of the area ban was preventative, not punitive.[477] The Federal Supreme Court reached the same conclusion when it reviewed the relevant norm of the concordat as part of a so-called *abstrakte Normenkontrolle*, that is, as part of a direct challenge to the piece of legislation itself.[478]

The question as to the applicable rules of evidence and standard of proof was also addressed by the House of Lords with regard to ASBOs. In *Clingham* v. *Royal Borough of Kensington and Chelsea; R (McCann)* v. *Crown Court at Manchester*, it held that the proceedings leading to the making of an ASBO are civil, not criminal.[479] Their Lordships argued that the Crown Prosecution Service is not involved in the proceedings, no breach of the criminal law needs to be proved, no criminal conviction results and the purpose of the proceedings is preventative.[480] As a consequence, the House of Lords held that, first, unlike as is generally the case in criminal proceedings, the use of hearsay evidence is permissible and therefore the right to examine witnesses guaranteed by Article 6(3)(d) of the ECHR does not apply.[481] Second, it concluded that the civil standard of proof (the balance of probabilities) applies. However, their Lordships did acknowledge that this standard of proof should be applied in such a way as to take account of 'the seriousness of the matters to be proved and the implications of proving them', which for all practical purposes means

475 Urteil des Verwaltungsgerichts des Kantons Zürich vom 19. Juni 2008, VB.2008.00237. While this case related to Article 21b of the Verordnung über Massnahmen zur Wahrung der inneren Sicherheit (VWIS), which is no longer in force, the Konkordat über Massnahmen gegen Gewalt anlässlich von Sportveranstaltungen vom 15. November 2007 contains an identical provision in Article 3.

476 Ibid., para. 4.3.

477 Ibid. See also BGE 134 I 125, 136 (2008).

478 BGE 137 I 31, 43–4 (2010).

479 *Clingham* v. *Royal Borough of Kensington and Chelsea; R (McCann)* v. *Crown Court at Manchester*, [2002] UKHL 39.

480 Ibid., paras 22 (Lord Steyn), 68–77 (Lord Hope).

481 Ibid., paras 35 (Lord Steyn), 113 (Lord Hutton).

that the applicable standard is indistinguishable from the criminal standard.[482] The Anti-social Behaviour, Crime and Policing Act 2014, however, effectively obviates the decision of the House of Lords as it explicitly provides that IPNAs can be issued on the balance of probabilities.[483] Essentially, the same approach is used in the case of football banning orders. The Court of Appeal has held that the procedure to impose such orders is civil rather than criminal.[484] As a consequence, there is no right to examine witnesses and the civil standard of proof applies, although that standard should, according to the court, be a strict one.[485]

These are just some of many examples demonstrating that those subject to most types of exclusion measures will generally enjoy a lower degree of due process protection than those charged with a criminal offence. The European Court of Human Rights has recognised the danger that states may simply re-label proceedings as non-criminal to circumvent the safeguards applicable in criminal proceedings. In *Engel* v. *Netherlands*[486] and a number of subsequent decisions[487] it held that the term 'criminal charge' of Article 6 of the ECHR has an autonomous meaning. Thus, whether proceedings are criminal in the sense of the ECHR depends not simply on the domestic classification but also on the nature of the offence and the severity of the possible punishment.[488] The European Court has not yet ruled on the question of whether proceedings leading to exclusion measures as part of a civil preventive order are criminal in the sense of Article 6 of the ECHR or not, although the previous European Commission of Human Rights did hold that the (considerably less severe) requirement to register as a sex offender is not a criminal penalty (in the sense of Article 7 of the ECHR) as the purpose of the measure is preventative and mere registration is not sufficiently onerous to amount to a penalty.[489] Thus, the possibility remains that

482 Ibid., paras 37 (Lord Steyn), 83 (Lord Hope).

483 Anti-social Behaviour, Crime and Policing Act 2014, s. 1(2).

484 *Gough* v. *Chief Constable of the Derbyshire Constabulary*, [2002] EWCA Civ 351, para. 89.

485 Ibid., paras 90–91, 102.

486 *Engel and others* v. *The Netherlands*, nos 5100/71; 5101/71; 5102/71; 5354/72; 5370/72, 8 June 1976, Series A no. 22.

487 E.g. *Ezeh and Connors* v. *The United Kingdom* [GC], nos 39665/98; 40086/98, 9 October 2003, ECHR 2003-X, 101; *Weber* v. *Switzerland*, no. 11034/84, 22 May 1990, Series A no. 177.

488 *Engel and others* v. *The Netherlands*, nos 5100/71; 5101/71; 5102/71; 5354/72; 5370/72, 8 June 1976, Series A no. 22, para. 82.

489 *Ibbotson* v. *The United Kingdom*, no. 40146/98, admissibility decision of 21 October 1998; (1999) 27 EHRR CD 332.

exclusion measures could be resorted to as a means to water down standards of due process protection. On the other hand, as is clear from the examples referred to above, Swiss and UK courts have insisted that, despite characterisation of a given exclusion measure as non-criminal, at least a minimum degree of due process must apply. However, given the lack of explicit guarantees in this respect, they have had to be rather inventive to justify this finding.

4.4.2 Right to an effective remedy

The question as to the availability of a legal remedy against exclusion from public space is relatively unproblematic if exclusion is imposed in the form of a written order issued by the police (or some other authority), if it is ordered by a court or if it follows from a criminal conviction for breach of a relevant prohibition. In these cases, the legal systems of the three states at issue will normally explicitly provide for a legal remedy such as an appeal, a *Beschwerde/recours* (complaint) or an application for judicial review. Often, however, exclusion measures are imposed in a more informal way: a police officer may simply ask a person to leave and keep away for some time, or he may remove her by physical force, or (as is often the case with demonstrations) barriers or cordons may be erected, blocking people from accessing parts of public space. Typically, there is no written documentation with regard to these actions by the police or other public authorities. It is especially with regard to these informal ways of exclusion that it may be difficult for people to gain access to justice.

Again, due to the diversity of the procedural systems, it is not possible to review here all possible legal remedies against exclusion measures in each of the jurisdiction at issue. Instead, the purpose of this section is much more modest. It will use an actual situation already discussed in Chapter 1 (and earlier in this chapter) to briefly illustrate some of the problems that people seeking remedy against exclusion measures may face: the denial of access to the resort of Davos to all potential protesters at the occasion of the WEF of 2001. Several demonstrators and journalists who had been stopped by the police on their way to Davos and ordered to turn back tried to take legal action. A crucial issue in all of these proceedings was whether a legal remedy against the actions of the police was available at all. For, under the Swiss system of administrative law (of which the law regulating police action forms part), the availability of a legal remedy has traditionally depended on a so-called

Verfügung/décision,[490] that is, a (normally written) order directed at an individual addressee (or individual addressees) that regulates in a legally binding way a concrete situation and establishes, changes or abrogates rights or duties of private actors.[491]

In a case that eventually reached the Federal Supreme Court, several persons asked the court to declare the operational directives for the police operation which led to their denial of access to Davos to be unlawful.[492] The court held that the directives did not constitute a *Verfügung* as they were not addressed to the complainants and did not directly touch upon their rights and duties.[493] Nor did the directives constitute a piece of cantonal legislation (in which case a legal remedy would also have been available) as they were of a purely internal nature and were not intended to regulate rights and duties of citizens.[494] Finally, the court argued that the directives as such could not be challenged as the complainants had legal remedies at their disposal to challenge the specific actions of the police that had followed from the directives. The court acknowledged that it may often be difficult to identify the appropriate legal remedy to challenge police measures such as controls or denials of access to a public place, as these regularly did not involve a *Verfügung* but constituted so-called *Realakte* (informal actions).[495] Nevertheless, the court speculated that it might have been possible for the complainants to bring an action in tort or some other legal remedy after the event.[496] Therefore, no legal remedy existed to challenge the directives for the police operation.

In the case of *Gsell*, which has already been touched upon in the context of the *polizeiliche Generalklausel*,[497] Gsell did try to directly challenge the specific police action, that is, his denial of access to Davos.[498] The lower cantonal instances rejected his legal challenge on the basis that the police measure constituted a *Realakt* against which no remedy was available, even if it involved an interference with fundamental rights. The highest cantonal authority and the Federal Supreme Court

[490] Kiener/Rütsche/Kuhn, *Öffentliches Verfahrensrecht* (2012), pp. 281–2; Richli, 'Zum Rechtsschutz gegen verfügungsfreies Staatshandeln in der Totalrevision der Bundesrechtspflege' (1998).

[491] Kiener/Rütsche/Kuhn, *Öffentliches Verfahrensrecht* (2012), pp. 88–95; Moor/Poltier, *Droit administratif II* (2011), pp. 179–208; Tanquerel, *Manuel de droit administratif* (2011), pp. 269–81; Häfelin/Müller/Uhlmann, *Allgemeines Verwaltungsrecht* (2010), pp. 193–6.

[492] BGE 128 I 167 (2002). [493] Ibid., 170. [494] Ibid., 171–3.

[495] Ibid., 173–6. See also Urteil des Bundesgerichts 1C_226/2009 vom 16. Dezember 2009, E. 5.3.

[496] BGE 128 I 167, 173–6 (2002). [497] See Section 4.2.3.2. [498] BGE 130 I 369 (2004).

disagreed. They held that Gsell could rely on Article 13 of the ECHR, as he was claiming that there had been a violation of his ECHR rights. Accordingly, he had a right to be afforded with some sort of effective remedy at the domestic level. As the cantonal law did not explicitly provide for a remedy against informal police actions, Gsell was to be granted an effective remedy *sui generis*, in analogous application of the cantonal administrative procedural law.[499]

Gsell had challenged his exclusion from Davos before the cantonal *administrative authorities*. In a third case concerning the WEF 2001, a journalist claimed that he was entitled to have his exclusion reviewed by *a court*.[500] Yet the Federal Supreme Court confirmed the decision of the cantonal administrative court not to consider the application brought by the journalist. It rejected the journalist's claim that there was a constitutional right to judicial review following from the *Rechtsstaatsprinzip* and the guarantee of fundamental rights.[501] Nor did such a right, according to the Federal Supreme Court, follow from Article 6 of the ECHR. The denial of access to Davos, the court held, did not involve a determination of the journalist's 'civil rights and obligations' in the sense of this provision. There had been no interference with his right to exercise his profession, and while he might have been restricted in his rights to freedom of movement and expression, these did not constitute 'civil rights'. As a result, the journalist only had a right to an effective remedy according to Article 13 of the ECHR, but not a right to review by a court.[502]

Two years after the Federal Supreme Court's decision a new provision of the Federal Constitution, Article 29a, entered into force, according to which, in case of a 'legal dispute' (*Rechtsstreitigkeit/cause*), everyone has a right to have their case determined by a *judicial* authority. Whether and, if yes, to what extent this new constitutional norm guarantees judicial review of police actions such as informal exclusion measures is, however, contentious. On the one hand, as is evident from the debates in the Federal Assembly, the term 'legal dispute' was clearly not intended to cover all informal administrative action.[503] Accordingly, it has been argued that it is largely left to the cantons to define what constitutes a 'legal dispute' in the sense of this provision and there is no constitutional requirement to provide judicial review of informal actions.[504]

499 Ibid., 376–9. 500 BGE 130 I 388 (2004). 501 Ibid., 391–4. 502 Ibid., 394–400.
503 Amtliches Bulletin Ständerat, Verfassungsreform, p. 106. See Kley, 'Art. 29a' (2014), 681–2.
504 Müller, 'Die Rechtsweggarantie' (2004), 173–4.

On the other hand, it has been maintained that the term 'legal dispute' encompasses all disputes concerning the legal position of individuals and, therefore, access to a court must be granted whenever rights and duties of individuals are at issue, including when the state acts informally.[505] With many types of police action this will regularly be the case, so that judicial review must be available.[506]

While the specific procedural issues will of course differ from jurisdiction to jurisdiction, it can nevertheless be generally observed that – as is illustrated by the cases concerning the protest against the WEF in Davos – people seeking to challenge exclusion measures imposed in an informal way will face several major hurdles. First, they may not have standing to challenge directives, guidelines or operational instructions of the police or other public authorities as they are said to be not directly affected by them. Second, a legal system may not provide for a legal remedy against actions of the police that are characterised as merely informal. Third, where a remedy against such actions *is* available, the individuals concerned may not be aware of its availability since they are not issued with a written order explaining them the legal situation. Fourth, the available remedy may only be a remedy before a non-judicial body. Fifth, legal remedies against informal exclusion measures are only available after the event, that is, once a – possibly unlawful – interference with fundamental rights has already occurred. Retrospective remedies, however, cannot effectively counteract the 'chilling effect' that exclusion measures tend to have. (This would make it all the more important that norms authorising exclusion from public space strictly adhere to the requirement of sufficient precision. As has been pointed out in Section 4.3.2, this is often not the case.) Sixth, the available legal remedies may be of limited effectiveness for other reasons, for example, because the only form of possible redress is some internal disciplinary measure or financial compensation. Seventh, and finally, informal exclusion measures are regularly only poorly documented or not documented

[505] E.g. Kiener/Rütsche/Kuhn, *Öffentliches Verfahrensrecht* (2012), pp. 54–5; Mohler, *Grundzüge des Polizeirechts in der Schweiz* (2012), pp. 478–80; Uhlmann, 'Verfahrensgrundrechte' (2011), 528; Biaggini, *Kommentar BV* (2007), p. 221; Fleiner/Ivanov, *Die Umsetzung der Rechtsweggarantie gemäss Art. 29a BV im interkantonalen Recht* (2007), pp. 21–2; Hangartner, 'Recht auf Rechtsschutz' (2002), 146. See now also Urteil des Bundesgerichts 2C_272/2012 vom 9. Juli 2012, E. 4.3.

[506] Mohler, *Grundzüge des Polizeirechts in der Schweiz* (2012), pp. 285–6, 294–5, 480–5; Schindler, 'Rechtsschutz im Polizeirecht' (2012), 218; Mohler, 'Zur Anfechtbarkeit polizeilicher intervenierender Realakte unter dem Gesichtspunkt der Rechtsweggarantie gemäss Art. 29a BV' (2007).

at all, making it extremely difficult for those subject to them to adduce evidence when bringing a legal challenge.

4.5 Conclusion

The new, preventive forms of 'order maintenance policing', of which exclusion measures form an integral part, tend to operate with a minimum of legal constraints and, in some instances, completely outside of the ordinary legal system. As a consequence, they regularly conflict with various requirements that follow from the rule of law.

According to the principle of legality the police and other public authorities may, as a general rule, only exclude people from (parts of) public space if there is an explicit legal rule that authorises them to do so. That they may, instead, invoke the *polizeiliche Generalklausel* or breach-of-the-peace powers to justify exclusion measures will be the rare exception. The vast majority of exclusion measures are designed to deal with minor public-order problems that are perfectly predictable (and can thus be addressed by the legislator), rather than serious, imminent threats that simply cannot be anticipated. Only in the most extreme of circumstances, where there is a serious threat to the fundamental rights of third persons and there is absolutely no alternative measure provided by the law to deal with this threat, can an exclusion measure be justified by resort to the *polizeiliche Generalklausel* or breach-of-the-peace powers.

It is admittedly difficult to regulate police action in a detailed, precise manner. Yet even if one takes into account the inevitability of a degree of imprecision, some of the norms authorising exclusion from public space reviewed here fail to meet the requirement of sufficient precision. Exclusion norms must be drafted so as to grant the police as little discretion to decide against whom to employ them as is required in the circumstances and must provide clear guidelines to prevent arbitrary enforcement. Thus, instead of simply authorising exclusion of all those posing a danger to 'public safety and order', the relevant legislation must at least give an indication of the forms of behaviour that will trigger application of the respective powers and/or specify which aspects of public safety and order these measures are meant to protect. Similarly, norms authorising exclusion of those 'causing harassment or distress to others' are not precise enough if they are based on a purely subjective standard of sensitivity of the victim and thus leave it completely to those enforcing these norms to decide what amounts to harassment or distress. Finally, prohibitions of certain forms of behaviour in public places must not be so openly worded as to grant those enforcing them virtually unfettered discretion. As far as the available exclusion measures are concerned, relevant legislation must set out in as much detail as possible their terms, including, at the very least, the maximum geographical extension of exclusion zones, the upper time limit of exclusion measures and the sanctions available in case of a violation of exclusion orders.

Exclusion measures also raise concerns with regard to the procedural aspects of the rule of law. Even though preventive exclusion measures typically entail consequences that are equally burdensome as those under the criminal law and are in fact experienced as punitive, those subject to them will generally enjoy a lower degree of due process protection than those charged with a criminal offence. There is therefore a danger that such measures may be used to circumvent the safeguards applicable in criminal proceedings. In addition, people seeking to challenge exclusion measures imposed in an informal way often face a number of major hurdles in gaining access to an effective remedy.

Even when exclusion measures comply with the various requirements following from the rule of law, this does not necessarily mean that they are lawful. As will be explained in the following two chapters, even exclusion measures that are based on legal schemes that are perfectly clear and precise and provide for sufficient procedural safeguards may be impermissible because they are incompatible with guarantees of fundamental rights.

5

Fundamental rights: liberty

Private space protects one sphere of liberty: the freedom to be left alone. Yet there is more to liberty than the right to be left alone. As is more clearly apparent from the English term '*civil* liberties' than the German counterpart *Freiheitsrechte*, as social beings, virtually all our freedoms have a social dimension: they 'are necessarily tied up with our engagement with persons outside ourselves'.[1] Accordingly, they depend on the existence of, and access to, places where we can meet and reach others, places that are accessible to everyone, that is, *public* space. Without access to public space, none of the freedoms (or civil liberties) dealt with in this chapter can be meaningfully exercised. For those who have no private space available (such as homeless people), denial of access to public space even results in complete unfreedom. As Jeremy Waldron has put it, 'no one is free to perform an action unless there is somewhere he is free to perform it'.[2] Since space is a social product,[3] it is, conversely, the existence of these legally guaranteed freedoms that turns a given space into a *public* space: rights produce space.

As the central forum for the exercise of various freedoms, public space is inevitably a locus where different interests collide. As a general rule, if I claim certain freedoms in public space, I have to tolerate that others exercise theirs, even if it is in a controversial or confrontational manner. This is the flipside to the characteristic of public space as the space of liberty: as a logical consequence it must also be the space of tolerance.[4] However, as has been explained before, this is only the general rule and does not mean that public space is, or should be, a completely unregulated space.[5] Some form of regulation to coordinate the conflicting interests and preserve the nature of public space as a truly communal space is inevitable. The state may provide such regulation not only by

[1] Gearty, *Civil Liberties* (2007), p. 17.
[2] Waldron, 'Homelessness and the Issue of Freedom' (1991). [3] See Section 2.1.1.1.
[4] See Section 2.3.3. [5] See Section 2.4.

completely prohibiting particular forms of behaviour in public space but, since the conflict is often about the exact *location* where a freedom is exercised, also by, for example, prohibiting certain forms of behaviour in certain parts of public space, preventing certain people from accessing certain parts of public space or requiring a permit or authorisation for certain activities in certain parts of public space.[6] Such state interventions obviously reduce the degree of liberty that the persons concerned enjoy. This chapter explains exactly which legally guaranteed freedoms may be engaged by exclusion measures and assesses whether these interferences are compatible with the respective legal guarantees.

The chapter starts with a brief explanation of how fundamental rights are protected in the three states at issue and under international law (Section 5.1). It then explores which guarantees of liberty may be engaged by exclusion measures (Section 5.2). The final and most substantial section sets out the requirements for the limitation of these legally guaranteed freedoms in the three jurisdictions and assesses exclusion measures for their compliance with these requirements (Section 5.3).

5.1 Fundamental and human rights

Ideas related to fundamental and human rights can be traced back to ancient civilisations such as Babylonia and various religious codes; similarly, documents such as the Magna Carta of 1215 can be interpreted as early legal efforts to protect the rights of the individual.[7] However, it was in the Age of the Enlightenment that the concept of fundamental rights which came to shape the constitutional systems of most modern states, including the United Kingdom, the United States and Switzerland, was developed. The great thinkers of the Enlightenment such as the Englishman John Locke,[8] the French Baron de Montesquieu,[9] the Swiss Jean-Jacques Rousseau[10] and the German Immanuel Kant[11] put the individual, endowed with reason, at the heart of their theories. They advocated the idea that all human beings are born equal and with a set

6 See Section 3.4. 7 Ishay, *The History of Human Rights* (2008), pp. 16–61.

8 Locke, *Two Treatises of Government* (1998).

9 De Montesquieu, *De l'esprit des lois* (1950–1961).

10 Rousseau, *Du contrat social* (2007).

11 Kant, *Gesammelte Schriften: IV: Grundlegung zur Metaphysik der Sitten* (1900–); Kant, *Groundwork of the Metaphysics of Morals* (1998); Kant, *Gesammelte Schriften: VI: Die Metaphysik der Sitten* (1900–); Kant, *The Metaphysical Elements of Justice* (1965).

of natural, inalienable rights; the purpose of the state is to protect these rights, and it derives its authority from the consent of the governed.

These ideas were the intellectual force behind the great political transformations at the end of the eighteenth century. The first constitutional documents based on them were drafted in the United States, leading Henry Steele Commager to claim that 'the Old World imagined the Enlightenment and the New World realized it'.[12] The Virginia Bill of Rights of 1776, the first 'proper' bill of rights setting forth a comprehensive catalogue of individual rights,[13] and the US Declaration of Independence of the same year contained proclamations that were unmistakably directly influenced by the great Enlightenment thinkers.[14] In the 'Old World' it was, of course, the French Revolution and its aftermath that fundamentally reshaped the political landscape. The French Declaration of the Rights of Man and Citizen of 1789 transformed Enlightenment philosophy into positive law by providing guarantees of liberty and equality in place of the pre-revolutionary absolute monarchical system based on class distinctions and privileges of the nobility.[15] New constitutional arrangements with similar guarantees of individual rights emerged throughout Europe, including Switzerland, during the nineteenth century. All of these were profoundly influenced by the American and French models.[16]

It took much longer for the idea that all human beings should be guaranteed certain fundamental rights to take hold at the international level. In the nineteenth century, fundamental rights were still mainly understood to be constitutional guarantees for citizens. International law, with some exceptions such as conventions prohibiting slave trade and the treaty system for the protection of minorities adopted after the First World War, had nothing to say about the way states could treat individuals.[17] It was only after the horrors of the Second World War that the protection of individual rights became a subject of concern at the

[12] Commager, 'America and the Enlightenment' (1988), 247.
[13] See Rutland, *The Birth of the Bill of Rights* (1955), pp. 24–40.
[14] See, especially, the opening words of the US Declaration of Independence of 4 July 1776.
[15] The original text of the declaration is available on the website of the French Ministry of Justice, at www.textes.justice.gouv.fr/textes-fondamentaux-10086/droits-de-lhomme-et-libertes-fondamentales-10087/declaration-des-droits-de-lhomme-et-du-citoyen-de-1789-10116.html. An English translation is available on the website of the Avalon Project, at http://avalon.law.yale.edu/18th_century/rightsof.asp.
[16] For Switzerland, see Kölz, *Der Weg der Schweiz zum modernen Bundesstaat* (1998), pp. 15–84; Kölz, *Neuere schweizerische Verfassungsgeschichte* (1992), p. 618.
[17] For an overview, see Bates, 'History' (2014), 23–8.

international level. Thus, in the UN Charter of 1945 member states committed themselves to promoting human rights,[18] and with the UDHR of 1948 the General Assembly of the UN adopted the first international document setting out the rights to which every human being is entitled to, simply by virtue of being human. The UDHR is drafted in language that is strikingly similar to that of the constitutional documents of the eighteenth century,[19] reflecting a strong influence of Enlightenment thinking.[20]

5.1.1 International law

While the UDHR sets forth a comprehensive catalogue of human rights guarantees, many of which are relevant for the present context,[21] it is not a treaty and was not originally thought to give rise to international legal obligations. Nevertheless, substantial parts of it are now widely regarded as customary international law binding on all states.[22] In any event, the human rights listed in the UDHR did finally become part of treaty law when the two covenants were adopted in 1966. The covenant that is at the centre of attention for present purposes, the ICCPR, has been ratified by all three states at issue.[23] However, none of these states has recognised the competence of the UN Human Rights Committee to receive and consider individual communications alleging a violation of the ICCPR by becoming a party to the First Optional Protocol to the ICCPR.[24]

18 Charter of the United Nations (UN Charter) (adopted 26 June 1945, entered into force 24 October 1945) 892 UNTS 119, Arts 55(c) and 56.

19 Compare, for example, Article 1, sentence 1 of the French Declaration of the Rights of Man and Citizen of 1789 ('Men are born and remain free and equal in rights.') with Article 1, sentence 1 of the UDHR ('All human beings are born free and equal in dignity and rights.').

20 See e.g. UDHR, Art. 1, sentence 2 ('They [all human beings] are endowed with reason and conscience [. . .]').

21 UDHR, Arts 1, 2, 7, 9, 12, 13, 19, 20.

22 See Vienna Declaration and Programme of Action, adopted at the World Conference on Human Rights, 25 June 1993, UN Doc A/CONF157/23, in particular preambular paras 3, 8; Final Act of the International Conference on Human Rights, held in Teheran in 1968, UN Doc A/CONF32/41 (1968), para. 2 (proclaiming unanimously that the UDHR 'constitutes an obligation for the members of the international community'); Lillich, 'Civil Rights' (1984), 116–17; Sohn, 'The Human Rights Law of the Charter' (1977), 133; Humphrey, 'The International Bill of Rights' (1976), 529.

23 The United Kingdom signed 16 September 1968 and ratified 20 May 1976; the United States signed 5 October 1977 and ratified 8 June 1992; Switzerland acceded 18 June 1992.

24 First Optional Protocol to the ICCPR (adopted 16 December 1966, entered into force 23 March 1976) 999 UNTS 302.

The International Covenant on Economic, Social and Cultural Rights (ICESCR) is of less interest here; it has been ratified by Switzerland and the United Kingdom, but not the United States.[25] Further human rights guarantees of relevance for the present context are contained in the International Convention on the Elimination of All Forms of Racial Discrimination (ICERD), ratified by all three states,[26] and the Convention on the Rights of the Child (CRC), ratified by the United Kingdom and Switzerland.[27]

As far as regional human rights treaties are concerned, the most influential instrument is the ECHR. Together with the rich jurisprudence developed under it by the European Court of Human Rights, it has had a profound impact on the formation of human rights standards on the international level and in other regions.[28] The ECHR has been ratified by both the United Kingdom and Switzerland.[29] Therefore, and due to its outstanding international importance, it is accorded a relatively great degree of attention in this study. The United States has signed but not ratified the American Convention on Human Rights (ACHR).[30] However, important human rights guarantees are also set forth by the American Declaration of the Rights and Duties of Man (ADHR).[31] The Inter-American Court of Human Rights and the Inter-American Commission on Human Rights have both held that, since the ADHR

[25] International Covenant on Economic, Social and Cultural Rights (ICESCR) (adopted 16 December 1966, entered into force 3 January 1976) 993 UNTS 3. The United Kingdom signed 16 September 1968 and ratified 20 May 1976; Switzerland acceded 18 June 1992. The United States signed 5 October 1977.

[26] International Convention on the Elimination of All Forms of Racial Discrimination (ICERD) (adopted 21 December 1965, entered into force 4 January 1969) 660 UNTS 195. The United Kingdom signed 11 October 1966 and ratified 7 March 1969; the United States signed 28 September 1966 and ratified 21 October 1994; Switzerland acceded 29 November 1994.

[27] Convention on the Rights of the Child (CRC) (adopted 20 November 1989, entered into force 2 September 1990) 1577 UNTS 3. The United Kingdom signed 19 April 1990 and ratified 16 December 1991; Switzerland signed 1 May 1991 and ratified 24 February 1997. The United States signed 16 February 1995 but has not yet ratified.

[28] See e.g. Merrills, *The Development of International Law by the European Court of Human Rights* (1993).

[29] The United Kingdom signed 4 November 1950 and ratified 8 March 1951; Switzerland signed 21 December 1972 and ratified 28 November 1974.

[30] American Convention on Human Rights (ACHR) (adopted 22 November 1969, entered into force 18 July 1978) 1144 UNTS 123. The United States signed 1 June 1977.

[31] American Declaration of the Rights and Duties of Man (ADHR) (OAS Resolution XXX, reprinted in Basic Documents Pertaining to Human Rights in the Inter-American System, OAS/Ser.L/V/I.4 Rev 9 (2003)).

defines the human rights referred to in the Charter of the Organization of American States (OAS),[32] it is a source of international legal obligations for all member states of the OAS, including the United States.[33]

With regard to the United Kingdom, in some (rather rare) instances EU law may be applicable. The Charter of Fundamental Rights of the EU guarantees a wide range of fundamental rights.[34] However, according to its Article 51(1), the Charter is primarily addressed to the institutions and bodies of the EU, whereas the member states are only bound by it when they are implementing Union law. The Charter is therefore of hardly any relevance to the issues examined here and will not be considered further. In addition, the Treaty on the Functioning of the European Union (TFEU) guarantees a number of fundamental rights to citizens of the EU, most importantly for present purposes the right to freedom of movement within the territory of the member states of Articles 20(2)(a) and 21(1).[35] With regard to Switzerland, according to the Agreement on the Free Movement of Persons concluded between the EC and Switzerland,[36] citizens of EU states in Switzerland (as well as Swiss citizens in an EU state such as the United Kingdom) enjoy a number of rights, including the right to occupational and geographical mobility.[37]

[32] Charter of the OAS (adopted 30 April 1948, entered into force 13 December 1951) 119 UNTS 3. The United States signed 30 April 1948 and ratified 15 June 1951.

[33] *Interpretation of the American Declaration of the Rights and Duties of Man Within the Framework of Article 64 of the American Convention on Human Rights*, Advisory Opinion OC-10/89, 14 July 1989, Inter-American Court of Human Rights (Series A) No. 10 (1989), paras 35–45; *Roach and Pinkerton* v. *United States*, Case 9647, 22 September 1987, Inter-American Commission on Human Rights Resolution No. 3/87, paras 46–9.

[34] Charter of Fundamental Rights of the EU, 7 December 2000, [2010] OJ C 83/389.

[35] Treaty on the Functioning of the European Union, [2008] OJ C 115/47.

[36] Agreement between the European Community and its Member States, of the one part, and the Swiss Confederation, of the other, on the free movement of persons, 21 June 1999, OJ L 114 (SR 0.142.112.681); Protocol to the Agreement between the European Community and its Member States, of the one part, and the Swiss Confederation, of the other, on the free movement of persons regarding the participation, as contracting parties, of the Czech Republic, the Republic of Estonia, the Republic of Cyprus, the Republic of Latvia, the Republic of Lithuania, the Republic of Hungary, the Republic of Malta, the Republic of Poland, the Republic of Slovenia and the Slovak Republic pursuant to their accession to the European Union, 26 October 2004, OJ L 089 (AS 2006 995); Protocol to the Agreement between the European Community and its Member States, of the one part, and the Swiss Confederation, of the other, on the free movement of persons, regarding the participation, as contracting parties of the Republic of Bulgaria and Romania pursuant to their accession to the European Union, 27 May 2008, OJ L 124 (SR 0.142.112.681.1).

[37] Ibid., Art. 7(b) and Annex I, Art. 8.

5.1.2 United Kingdom

What are sometimes described as the first fundamental rights documents emerged in the United Kingdom: the Magna Carta of 1215, the Petition of Right of 1628, the Habeas Corpus Act of 1679 and the Bill of Rights of 1689. However, these early documents were not bills of rights in the modern sense as they were designed to protect the interests of powerful groups against the monarch rather than to guarantee the rights of every human being.[38] In fact, until 1998, the United Kingdom was one of the very few Western states that did not have an explicit guarantee of the fundamental rights of individuals, be it as part of a written constitution or in the form of a bill of rights or a similar document. According to the traditional British approach, which was greatly influenced by Dicey, the common law was seen as sufficient to protect fundamental rights.[39] Under the common law, people are free to do whatever they please unless it is expressly prohibited by law.[40] Therefore people already enjoy rights such as the freedom of expression and the freedom of assembly and any interference with these rights has to be authorised by statute or common law. According to this system of 'residual liberty' only parliament, elected by the people, can impose restrictions on fundamental rights, which was thought to be a sufficient safeguard.

However, as the power of parliament started to decline and that of the executive to grow, it became increasingly obvious that the traditional system failed to give effective protection from misuse of power by the state. A long campaign to achieve formal recognition of fundamental rights in the United Kingdom finally culminated in the adoption of the Human Rights Act 1998.[41] The Human Rights Act incorporates the ECHR with its comprehensive catalogue of civil and political rights, ratified by the United Kingdom as the very first state in 1951, into domestic law. Importantly, it does so in a way that leaves parliamentary sovereignty, together with the rule of law, the most fundamental principle of the British constitution,[42] intact. Section 3 of the Act places an

[38] Bates, 'History' (2014), 16.

[39] Bradley/Ewing, *Constitutional and Administrative Law* (2011), pp. 397–9.

[40] *Beatty* v. *Gillbanks*, (1882) 9 QBD 308; *Entick* v. *Carrington*, [1765] EWHC KB J98. See also *R (Laporte)* v. *Chief Constable of Gloucestershire Constabulary*, [2006] UKHL 55, para. 34.

[41] For a history of the Human Rights Act, see Klug, *Values for a Godless Age* (2000).

[42] Alder, *Constitutional and Administrative Law* (2013), pp. 152–7; Barnett, *Constitutional and Administrative Law* (2013), pp. 112–17; Bradley/Ewing, *Constitutional and Administrative Law* (2011), pp. 49–59.

obligation on courts to interpret legislation in a way which is compatible with the Convention rights 'so far as it is possible to do so'. Where a particular law cannot be interpreted in such a way, courts can make a 'declaration of incompatibility'.[43] However, courts do not have the power to strike down a piece of legislation which conflicts with the ECHR. Furthermore, parliament is not bound by the provisions of the Human Rights Act.[44]

In addition to the ECHR, the United Kingdom has ratified a number of further human rights instruments, including the ICCPR, the ICERD and the CRC. In the United Kingdom, the relationship between domestic and international law follows a broadly dualist model: domestic and international law are treated as two separate systems.[45] As a consequence, implementing legislation would be needed for the obligations created by these human rights treaties to become rules of domestic law.[46] In contrast, rules of customary international law generally form part of domestic law automatically, without the need for legislation.[47]

5.1.3 United States

Only a few individual rights, notably the writ of habeas corpus,[48] the prohibition of bills of attainder or *ex post facto* laws[49] and the right to trial by jury,[50] were incorporated in the original text of the Constitution of the United States adopted in 1787. The majority of the delegates at the Philadelphia Constitutional Convention thought that inclusion of a bill of rights was not necessary. After all, all the states had adopted their own bills of rights protecting individual rights.[51] Nevertheless, only two years later, the first ten Amendments to the Constitution were approved by the first US Congress, and by 1791 the required number of states had ratified them.[52] Inspired in particular by the English Bill of Rights of 1689 and the Virginia Bill of Rights of 1776, these Amendments guarantee a set of fundamental rights and liberties and accordingly came to be described as the US Bill of Rights.

[43] Human Rights Act, s. 4. [44] Ibid., s. 6(3).
[45] Shaw, *International Law* (2014), pp. 99–101. [46] Ibid., pp. 148–57.
[47] Ibid., pp. 141–8. [48] US Constitution, Art. I (9)(2). [49] Ibid., Art. I (9)(3).
[50] Ibid., Art. III (2)(3).
[51] See Levy, 'The Bill of Rights' (1988), 296; Rutland, *The Birth of the Bill of Rights* (1955), pp. 106–25.
[52] See Rutland, *The Birth of the Bill of Rights* (1955), pp. 190–218.

In an early decision the Supreme Court ruled that the first ten Amendments were only applicable to the federal government but not to the states.[53] After the passage of the Fourteenth Amendment in 1868, the argument was made that its wording ('No State shall make or enforce any law which shall abridge the privileges or immunities of citizens of the United States; nor shall any State deprive any person of life, liberty, or property, without due process of law.') made the US Bill of Rights also applicable to the states.[54] In 1873 the Supreme Court rejected the argument that the first clause of the Amendment, the privileges or immunities clause, obliged the states to protect the rights guaranteed by the Bill of Rights.[55] However, starting with the freedom of speech guarantee of the First Amendment in 1925,[56] the Supreme Court began to make selected provisions of the Bill of Rights applicable to the states through the second clause of the Fourteenth Amendment, the due process clause. According to the Supreme Court's doctrine of selective incorporation, the states are bound by those provisions of the Bill of Rights that are 'fundamental to the American scheme of justice'.[57] By today, the Supreme Court has characterised nearly all of the principal guarantees of the Bill of Rights as fundamental and thus applicable to the states.[58]

Guarantees of fundamental rights also arise from the human rights treaties that have been ratified by the United States. These include the ICCPR and the ICERD, but not the CRC. In addition, as explained above, the ADHR, although not initially adopted as a legally binding treaty, now imposes legal obligations on the United States as a signatory of the OAS Charter. The US system regulating the relationship between international and domestic law can be described as a hybrid between monism and dualism.[59] Treaties that enjoy self-executing status take effect as domestic law immediately upon ratification, whereas other treaties are characterised as not self-executing and thus require implementing legislation

[53] *Barron* v. *Mayor and City Council of Baltimore*, 32 U.S. (7 Pet.) 243, 8 L.Ed. 672 (1833).

[54] See Abraham/Perry, *Freedom and the Court* (2003), pp. 36–48.

[55] *Slaughter-House Cases*, 83 U.S. 36 (1872).

[56] See *Gitlow* v. *New York*, 268 U.S. 652 (1925).

[57] *Duncan* v. *Louisiana*, 391 U.S. 145, 149 (1968).

[58] For an overview, see Sullivan/Feldman, *Constitutional Law* (2013), pp. 446–65; Abraham/Perry, *Freedom and the Court* (2003), pp. 54–95.

[59] Keller, *Rezeption des Völkerrechts* (2003), pp. 125–7; Jackson, 'Status of Treaties in Domestic Legal Systems' (1992), 320; Henkin, 'Plenary Session' (1991), 191; Steinhardt, 'The Role of International Law as a Canon of Domestic Statutory Construction' (1990), 1104–6; Jackson, 'United States' (1987).

to become part of domestic law.[60] With regard to the most important human rights treaties, the United States has made 'not self-executing' declarations upon ratification, that is, it has declared that the respective human rights norms are not self-executing and thus not enforceable in US courts until implemented by congressional legislation.[61] Such declarations have also been made with regard to Articles 1 to 27 of the ICCPR[62] and the provisions of the ICERD.[63] However, the legal validity of these declarations is disputed.[64] Even if legally valid, it is not clear how they should be interpreted. While courts have tended to dismiss claims based on the respective human rights treaties,[65] it has been argued that 'not self-executing' declarations do in fact not preclude courts from directly applying human rights treaty provisions in all cases.[66] In any event, such declarations cannot affect the obligations of the United States under international law, and a presidential executive order has declared that '[i]t shall be the policy and practice of the Government of the United States [. . .] fully to respect and implement its obligations under the international human rights treaties to which it is a party'.[67] As far as the hierarchy between international treaties and federal law is concerned, the former are subject to constitutional limitations[68] but equal to acts of Congress, meaning that in case of conflict the more recent

60 *Whitney* v. *Robertson*, 124 U.S. 190, 194 (1888); *Foster and Elam* v. *Neilson*, 27 U.S. (2 Pet.) 253, 314–15 (1829).

61 For overviews, see Keller, *Rezeption des Völkerrechts* (2003), pp. 402–7; Sloss, 'The Domestication of International Human Rights' (1999), 139–42.

62 138 Congressional Record S4781-84 (1992); Multilateral Treaties Deposited with the Secretary-General (UN Doc. ST/LEG/SER/E/), available at http://treaties.un.org/Pages/ViewDetails.aspx?src=TREATY&mtdsg_no=IV-4&chapter=4&lang=en.

63 140 Congressional Record S7634–35 (1994); Multilateral Treaties Deposited with the Secretary-General (UN Doc. ST/LEG/SER/E/), available at http://treaties.un.org/Pages/ViewDetails.aspx?src=TREATY&mtdsg_no=IV-2&chapter=4&lang=en#EndDec.

64 See e.g. Henkin, 'U.S. Ratification of Human Rights Conventions' (1995); 'Symposium: The Ratification of the International Covenant on Civil and Political Rights' (1993); Dearborn, III, 'The Domestic Legal Effect of Declarations That Treaty Provisions Are Not Self-Executing' (1979), 233–4.

65 E.g. *White* v. *Paulsen*, 997 F.Supp. 1380, 1387 (E.D. Wash., 1998); *Igartua De La Rosa* v. *United States*, 32 F.3d 8, 10, footnote 1 (1st Cir., 1994). For an overview, see Sloss, 'The Domestication of International Human Rights' (1999), 197–203.

66 Sloss, 'The Domestication of International Human Rights' (1999).

67 Executive Order No. 13107: Implementation of Human Rights Treaties, 10 December 1998, Fed. Reg. 68,991 (1998), reprinted in (1999) 38 *International Legal Materials* 493.

68 *Reid* v. *Covert*, 354 U.S. 1, 15–18 (1957); *The Cherokee Tobacco*, 78 U.S. (11 Wall.) 616, 620–1 (1870).

prevails.[69] More importantly for our purposes, however, international treaties always prevail over contrary state law, be it state constitutions or acts of state legislatures.[70]

As explained in Section 4.1.3, a key element for the enforcement of guarantees of fundamental rights is the power of the courts to review actions of the other branches of government for their constitutionality. In *Marbury* v. *Madison* the Supreme Court held that it has the power to invalidate actions of the federal executive and laws passed by Congress.[71] A number of subsequent decisions established federal judicial power over state actions.[72] Over the decades, the Supreme Court has made increasingly extensive use of its power of judicial review to protect fundamental rights. As part of its selective incorporation doctrine it has invalidated a growing number of acts of individual states for infringing guarantees of the Bill of Rights, and almost all of its rulings against actions of the federal government have been due to violations of individual rights.[73] Whereas in the 1935–1936 term only two out of 160 cases decided by the Supreme Court concerned 'basic human freedoms' (that is, personal liberties other than property rights), that ratio had risen to eighty out of 149 by 1979–1980. This trend has since continued unabated.[74]

5.1.4 Switzerland

Through the 'medium' of the French Revolution the concept of fundamental rights made its way from the United States to Switzerland.[75] The first constitution for the country as a whole (as opposed to the individual cantons) – indeed the first written constitution introduced anywhere on Swiss territory – was adopted in 1798 upon pressure from France.[76] The so-called First Helvetic Constitution was, accordingly,

[69] *Breard* v. *Greene*, 523 U.S. 371, 376 (1998); *Chinese Exclusion Case*, 130 U.S. 581, 600–11 (1889); *Whitney* v. *Robertson*, 124 U.S. 190, 193–4 (1888).

[70] US Constitution, Art. VI (2). See *United States* v. *Pink*, 315 U.S. 203, 230–1, 233–4 (1942); *United States* v. *Belmont*, 301 U.S. 324, 327–32 (1937); *Nielsen* v. *Johnson*, 279 U.S. 47, 52 (1929); *Hauenstein* v. *Lynham*, 100 U.S. 483, 488–90 (1879); *Ware* v. *Hylton*, 3 U.S. (3 Dall.) 199, 237 (1796).

[71] *Marbury* v. *Madison*, 5 U.S. (1 Cranch) 137 (1803).

[72] *Cohens* v. *Commonwealth of Virginia*, 19 U.S. (6 Wheat.) 264 (1821); *Martin* v. *Hunter's Lessee*, 14 U.S. (1 Wheat.) 304 (1816); *Fletcher* v. *Peck*, 10 U.S. (6 Cranch) 87 (1810).

[73] Abraham/Perry, *Freedom and the Court: Civil Rights and Liberties in the United States* (2003), p. 5.

[74] Ibid. [75] Kölz, *Der Weg der Schweiz zum modernen Bundesstaat* (1998), p. 6.

[76] Verfassung der helvetischen Republik vom 12. April 1798.

based on the ideas of the French Revolution and modelled after the French constitutional documents of the time, in particular the Constitution of 1795.[77] It established a unitary state based on the principles of representative democracy and separation of powers and, in the spirit of the Enlightenment,[78] guaranteed equality and a number of fundamental rights, including the right to citizenship, the right to vote, freedom of the press, freedom of religion and the right to property.[79] The Helvetic Republic, however, was only to last five years. Whilst the return to a confederation of cantons through the Act of Mediation of 1803[80] brought about the enactment of written constitutions also at the cantonal level, these, just as the new federal constitution, were largely based on pre-revolutionary values and did not contain guarantees of fundamental rights.[81] Only during the so-called *Regeneration*, a period marked by the resurgence of liberal ideas lasting from 1830 to 1848, did some of the cantons adopt constitutions that included guarantees of individual freedoms and equality following the model of the French constitutional documents.[82]

The first Federal Constitution of 1848 transformed Switzerland into a federal state and a liberal democracy based on the rule of law.[83] However, as was also the case for the completely revised second Federal Constitution of 1874,[84] it provided for a rather fragmented system of fundamental rights protection: it guaranteed only those rights that were seen as insufficiently protected at the cantonal level, that were of relevance to the whole federation or that were particularly contentious.[85] This incomplete catalogue of protected rights was compensated for by

[77] Kölz, *Neuere schweizerische Verfassungsgeschichte* (1992), pp. 98–123; Kölz, 'Die Bedeutung der Französischen Revolution für das schweizerische öffentliche Recht und politische System' (1989); His, *Geschichte des neuern schweizerischen Staatsrechts: Band 1, 1798–1813* (1920), pp. 24–42.

[78] See Verfassung der helvetischen Republik vom 12. April 1798, Art. 4: 'Die zwei Grundlagen des öffentlichen Wohls sind die Sicherheit und Aufklärung. Aufklärung ist besser als Reichthum und Pracht.' ('The two foundations of public welfare are security and Enlightenment. Enlightenment is better than abundance and glory.').

[79] Ibid., Arts 5–9, 19–22.

[80] Vermittlungsacte des Ersten Consuls der fränkischen Republik zwischen den Parteien, in welche die Schweiz getheilt ist ('Mediationsverfassung') vom 19. Februar 1803.

[81] Kölz, *Neuere schweizerische Verfassungsgeschichte* (1992), pp. 143–53.

[82] Ibid., pp. 320–42.

[83] Bundesverfassung der Schweizerischen Eidgenossenschaft vom 12. September 1848 (reprinted in Kölz, *Quellenbuch: Band I* (1992), pp. 447 ff.).

[84] Bundesverfassung der Schweizerischen Eidgenossenschaft vom 29. Mai 1874 (reprinted in Kölz, *Quellenbuch: Band II* (1996), pp. 151 ff.).

[85] Kölz, *Neuere schweizerische Verfassungsgeschichte* (1992), pp. 583–94.

cantonal guarantees and, importantly, also by the case law of the Federal Supreme Court, which developed the guarantees of the Federal Constitution in an innovative way and even recognised unwritten guarantees of fundamental rights.[86]

The Federal Constitution in force today,[87] which has undergone a process of complete revision finished in 1999, contains a comprehensive catalogue of protected fundamental rights (Articles 7 to 34) as well as provisions on the realisation (Article 35) and limitation (Article 36) of these rights. The drafting of this part on fundamental rights of the new Federal Constitution was influenced, not least, by the ECHR and US case law and doctrine.[88] With regard to the cantonal constitutions, older constitutions normally only guarantee a limited range of fundamental rights, whereas those that have been revised in recent years contain exhaustive lists of guarantees similar to that of the Federal Constitution.[89] As federal law prevails over cantonal law,[90] cantonal guarantees of fundamental rights can only be of relevance as far as they provide protection that goes beyond that already provided by the Federal Constitution.[91] Since the new Federal Constitution contains a very detailed catalogue of fundamental rights, the practical significance of cantonal constitutional guarantees is very limited nowadays.[92]

A further important source of fundamental rights guarantees is constituted by the international human rights treaties ratified by Switzerland, which include the ICERD, the CRC and, most importantly for the present context, the ICCPR and the ECHR. Switzerland has a monist system: treaties become part of domestic law immediately upon ratification, without there being a need for implementing legislation.[93] For an international norm to be directly applicable, however, it must be of a self-executing character. A norm is self-executing if it meets the following

[86] Kölz, *Neuere schweizerische Verfassungsgeschichte* (2004), pp. 806–20.

[87] Bundesverfassung der Schweizerischen Eidgenossenschaft vom 18. April 1999 (BV; SR 101).

[88] Müller, 'Geschichtliche Grundlagen, Zielsetzung und Funktionen der Grundrechte' (2007), 23–4, 27–8.

[89] See Kiener/Kälin, *Grundrechte* (2013), p. 12.

[90] BV, Art. 49(1).

[91] BGE 93 I 130, 137 (1967).

[92] Kiener/Kälin, *Grundrechte* (2013), p. 12.

[93] BGE 127 II 177, 181 (2001); BGE 122 II 234, 237 (1996); BGE 94 I 669, 672 (1968); Bericht des Bundesrates zum Verhältnis von Völkerrecht und Landesrecht vom 5. März 2010, BBl 2010, 2263, pp. 2302–3; Bundesamt für Justiz/Direktion für Völkerrecht, Verhältnis zwischen Völkerrecht und Landesrecht im Rahmen der schweizerischen Rechtsordnung, VPB 53 (1989) Nr. 54, p. 403; Ziegler, *Einführung in das Völkerrecht* (2011), pp. 116–17; Thürer, 'Verfassungsrecht und Völkerrecht' (2001), 186–7.

requirements: first, it regulates the rights and duties of individuals; second, it is justiciable, that is, sufficiently clear and precise to form the basis of a decision in an individual case; and third, it is addressed to the authorities applying the law (that is, the executive and the judicial branches) rather than the legislature.[94] All the human rights guarantees of the ICCPR and the ECHR are self-executing and thus directly applicable.[95] The ICERD and the CRC contain norms that are addressed to the legislature as well as self-executing norms. Therefore, it must be decided with regard to each norm individually whether it is directly applicable or not.[96] Human rights guarantees contained in international treaties that are directly applicable have the same status as the fundamental rights guarantees of the federal and cantonal constitutions. However, their practical relevance is limited to cases where the protection they provide goes beyond that already provided by the latter.[97] Given that in the course of the recent revision of the Federal Constitution care was taken to ensure that the text reflects Switzerland's obligations under international human rights law, these cases will be rare.[98]

Both at the federal and the cantonal level, courts can review actions of the legislative and executive branches for their conformity with the fundamental rights guarantees set forth in the Federal Constitution, the respective cantonal constitution and international law. The only limit to this judicial power is Article 190 of the Federal Constitution, which provides that courts (as well as any other law-applying authorities) are bound to apply acts of the Federal Assembly. Whilst this norm prevents courts from disapplying a federal act on the ground that it violates constitutional rights, the same does not hold true for a conflict between a federal act and international law. Rather, the general rule is that international law prevails over federal acts.[99] A federal act may only then prevail over international law if it was passed after the respective

[94] BGE 126 I 240, 242 (2000); BGE 124 III 90, 91 (1997). See Hangartner, 'Unmittelbare Anwendbarkeit völker- und verfassungsrechtlicher Normen' (2007).

[95] For the ICCPR, see BGE 122 I 109, 114 (1996); BGE 120 Ia 247, 254–5 (1994); BGE 120 Ia 1, 12 (1994). For the ECHR, see Häfelin/Haller/Keller, *Schweizerisches Bundesstaatsrecht* (2012), p. 76; Villiger, *Handbuch der Europäischen Menschenrechtskonvention (EMRK)* (1999), p. 47 and case law cited there.

[96] See e.g. BGE 133 I 286, 291–2 (2007); BGE 124 III 90, 91–2 (1997).

[97] BGE 101 Ia 67, 69 (1975). [98] See Kiener/Kälin, *Grundrechte* (2013), p. 20.

[99] For the most recent decision of the Federal Supreme Court reaffirming this general rule, see BGE 139 I 16, 28–9 (2012). For a summary of the relevant case law, see Bericht des Bundesrates zum Verhältnis von Völkerrecht und Landesrecht vom 5. März 2010, BBl 2010, 2263, pp. 2310–13.

international norm had come into force and if it was parliament's intention to pass an act that violates international law.[100] International norms guaranteeing human rights, however, are afforded a special status: according to the Federal Supreme Court they prevail even over federal acts that were passed by parliament in the knowledge that they violate international law.[101] Most norms authorising exclusion from public space are, in any event, cantonal rather than federal norms.[102] Cantonal norms can be disapplied or invalidated by the courts in case of a conflict with constitutional rights.

5.2 Scope of protection

In order to determine whether a given exclusion measure is compatible with the guarantees of fundamental rights as they exist in the three states at issue, one must first consider whether one of the guaranteed rights provides protection with regard to the situation concerned and, if this is the case, whether the measure amounts to an interference with that right.[103]

As far as the first question is concerned, it makes intuitive sense that the scope of protection of fundamental rights should extend to situations where the state orders people to leave, and not return to, a public place. After all, as already indicated in the introduction to this chapter and as will also become clear from the following discussion, fundamental rights are about the rights of people conceived as social beings living in community with others rather than isolated individuals: they protect not only the freedom to be left alone (in one's private space) but also the freedom to appear in public and engage with others. Exactly what rights are engaged by an exclusion measure depends on the particular nature of that measure and on the catalogue of protected rights in the respective legal system. Generally speaking, exclusion from public space may engage the rights to personal liberty, respect for private life, freedom of movement, freedom from arbitrary detention, freedom of assembly, freedom of expression, respect for family life as well as a number of other rights such as those to freedom of association and freedom of

[100] BGE 99 Ib 39, 43–5 (1973). [101] BGE 125 II 417, 424–6 (1999).

[102] See Section 4.2.2.1.

[103] For short overviews of the general structure of the fundamental rights test, see e.g. for Switzerland: Kiener/Kälin, *Grundrechte* (2013), pp. 93–4; for the ECHR (and thus also the United Kingdom): Harris/O'Boyle/Bates/Buckley, *Law of the ECHR* (2014), p. 521; for the United States: Chemerinsky, *Constitutional Law* (2009), pp. 946–9.

religion. This section explains the respective scope of protection of these rights and explores whether exclusion measures fall within that scope. In addition, exclusion measures raise problems with regard to the right to equality and non-discrimination. That issue is explored in Chapter 6.

The personal scope of these rights extends to all human beings. They constitute *human* rights and as such they protect, as a general rule, citizens and non-citizens alike and also extend to children. In the United States, courts, including the Supreme Court, have sometimes suggested that the rights of children may be subject to greater restrictions than is the case for the rights of adults.[104] Although it is undoubtedly true that the specific vulnerabilities and needs of children may in some cases demand special treatment in the form of greater protection by the state, it is for the state to justify any restrictions.[105] The presumption must be that children are protected by fundamental rights to the same extent as adults. A different issue is whether children and juveniles can *personally exercise* their rights and so bring themselves, without representation, a claim in court. The answer to this question depends on the procedural rules applicable in the respective judicial system.[106]

If the scope of protection of a guaranteed right is engaged, the second question that needs to be answered is whether the particular exclusion measure amounts to an interference with that right. Any restriction of a protected interest that is attributable to the state constitutes an interference, irrespective of the form in which the interference occurs. As will be seen from the cases discussed below, in the present context the interference may, for example, take the form of a prohibition, a written order, a criminal conviction or informal state action such as the closing off of an area by the police. The only difference between these various forms of interference concerns the available legal remedy. As explained in Section 4.4.2, in the case of informal exclusion measures it may be more difficult for those affected by them to gain access to justice.

The following sections will also discuss whether an interference with the respective rights through exclusion measures should be qualified as serious or not. The general rule in all jurisdictions at issue is that the more serious an interference, the more difficult it is for the government to show

[104] E.g. *Ginsberg* v. *New York*, 390 U.S. 629 (1968); *Prince* v. *Massachusetts*, 321 U.S. 158 (1944).

[105] See 'Assessing the Scope of Minors' Fundamental Rights' (1984).

[106] In Switzerland, Article 11(2) of the Federal Constitution explicitly provides that children and juveniles may personally exercise their rights to the extent that their power of judgement allows them to do so.

that the limitation requirements discussed in Section 5.3 are satisfied.[107] The question as to the intensity of the interference is of particular relevance in Switzerland where, as explained in Section 4.2.1, there is the additional requirement that any serious interference must be based on a 'law in the formal sense'. The seriousness of an interference depends on the impact it has on the individual(s) in the case at hand, on the number of persons affected by it and on how important the protective function of the right is that is affected by it.[108]

5.2.1 Human dignity

5.2.1.1 The guarantee of human dignity

What underlies the guarantees of specific rights discussed in the following sections is the fundamental notion of human dignity. Human dignity is the foundational axiom on which the international system of human rights protection is built. The UDHR guarantees human dignity in its very first article ('All human beings are born free and equal in dignity and rights'); the UN Charter and the two Covenants invoke it in their preambles;[109] and various international guarantees of specific rights refer, explicitly or implicitly, to the concept.[110] Numerous national constitutions incorporate human dignity, albeit in various forms.[111]

The Swiss Federal Constitution contains an explicit guarantee of human dignity, placed at the very beginning of the list of fundamental rights. Article 7 provides that '[h]uman dignity must be respected and protected',[112] thus guaranteeing recognition of every human being's intrinsic value and singularity.[113] The Federal Supreme Court has described this norm as the highest constitutional principle and

107 For the ECHR, see Harris/O'Boyle/Bates/Buckley, *Law of the ECHR* (2014), p. 518. For the United Kingdom, see e.g. *A* v. *Secretary of State for the Home Department*, [2004] UKHL 56, para. 192 (Lord Walker). For the United States, see Nowak/Rotunda, *Constitutional Law* (2004), pp. 691–2; Tribe, *American Constitutional Law* (1988), pp. 777–80. For Switzerland, see Schefer, *Die Beeinträchtigung von Grundrechten* (2006), pp. 29–30.

108 Schefer, *Die Beeinträchtigung von Grundrechten* (2006), pp. 26–9.

109 UN Charter, preambular para. 2; ICESCR, preambular para. 1; ICCPR, preambular para. 1.

110 E.g. ICCPR, Arts 7, 10; CRC, Arts 23, 37, 40.

111 For good overviews, see Cohn/Grimm, '"Human Dignity" as a Constitutional Doctrine' (2013); Mahlmann, 'Human Dignity and Autonomy in Modern Constitutional Orders' (2012); Rao, 'Three Concepts of Dignity in Constitutional Law' (2011).

112 BV, Art. 7 ('Die Würde des Menschen ist zu achten und zu schützen.').

113 BGE 127 I 6, 14 (2001).

a guideline for the interpretation of the other fundamental rights.[114] Although the guarantee of Article 7 is an independent, justiciable right, it is only rarely invoked as such since its content is normally realised through one (or several) of the more specific fundamental rights.[115] Accordingly, it has been characterised as an *Auffanggrundrecht/garantie subsidiaire* ('subsidiary fundamental right').[116]

There are no corresponding norms that would explicitly protect human dignity in the US Constitution (although there are references to human dignity in several state constitutions)[117] or in the constitutional framework of the United Kingdom.[118] Nevertheless, there have been repeated references to human dignity, including as a right or fundamental principle of constitutional law, in the jurisprudence of the US Supreme Court.[119] In the United Kingdom, the concept has also become increasingly significant over the last few years, especially since the entry into force of the Human Rights Act.[120] The main functions that the concept of human dignity serves in the three jurisdictions are those of helping to define a minimum core of fundamental rights and contributing to the interpretation and contextualisation of these more specific rights.[121]

5.2.1.2 Exclusion from public space and human dignity

Exclusion from public space as such will normally not amount to a violation of human dignity. In the case concerning the exclusion orders issued in the City of Berne already discussed in Section 4.3.2.1, those subject to these orders had been prohibited from assembling, within a certain area, in groups that consume alcohol.[122] They claimed that

114 Ibid.

115 Kiener/Kälin, *Grundrechte* (2013), p. 131; Haller, 'Menschenwürde, Recht auf Leben und persönliche Freiheit' (2007), pp. 206–7.

116 BGE 132 I 49, 54 (2006); BGE 127 I 6, 14 (2001); Mahon, 'Art. 7' (2003), 70.

117 Constitution of the State of Montana, Art. II (4); Constitution of the State of Louisiana, Art. I (3); Constitution of the State of Illinois, Art. I (20).

118 See Wilms, 'Der Menschenwürdebegriff in der neuen schweizerischen Bundesverfassung' (2002).

119 For the first reference to human dignity, see *In re Yamashita*, 327 U.S. 1, 29 (1946) (Murphy, J., dissenting). For an overview, see Rao, 'Three Concepts of Dignity in Constitutional Law' (2011); Goodman, 'Human Dignity in Supreme Court Constitutional Jurisprudence' (2006); Neuman, 'Human Dignity in United States Constitutional Law' (2000); Paust, 'Human Dignity as a Constitutional Right' (1984).

120 Feldman, 'Human Dignity as a Legal Value: Part 1' (1999); Feldman, 'Human Dignity as a Legal Value: Part 2' (2000).

121 See McCrudden, 'Human Dignity and Judicial Interpretation of Human Rights' (2008); Neuman, 'Human Dignity in United States Constitutional Law' (2000), 270–71.

122 BGE 132 I 49, 50 (2006).

their exclusion violated Article 7 of the Swiss Federal Constitution. The Federal Supreme Court rejected the claim, holding that the exclusion orders in themselves did not amount to a humiliation of the complainants or their devaluation as human beings and that their complaint had to be considered under the headings of the more specific fundamental rights such as the right to liberty, the freedom of assembly and the prohibition of discrimination.[123]

Although the reasoning of the Federal Supreme Court on this point is rather cursory, the conclusion it reaches appears to be the right one. Of course, as will be explained in detail in Chapter 6, there is a danger that exclusion measures may be employed against individuals simply because they belong to a particular category of people, typically some marginalised group. In the case at hand, the Federal Supreme Court too readily dismissed the possibility that those subject to the exclusion orders might have been targeted because they were alcohol addicts.[124] Clearly, exclusion from public space that is based on stereotypical prejudice against particular groups of people may be said to involve a disregard for a human being's intrinsic value and singularity and is, in fact, regularly experienced as an attack on human dignity.[125] Nevertheless, the right to non-discrimination already provides protection against this aspect of exclusion measures, so that there is normally no need to consider the issue separately under the heading of human dignity.[126] Similarly, exclusion from public space can be said to be linked to issues of dignity in that people develop as human beings through their contact with others: they can only realise their human potential if they are allowed to participate in activities with others and take part in public life. Yet these aspects of human dignity are covered by more specific rights such as those to personal liberty, respect for private life, freedom of assembly and freedom of expression. When it comes to the interpretation of these specific rights as well as of the right to non-discrimination, however, human dignity may serve as a useful guiding principle.

5.2.2 *The general guarantee: personal liberty/respect for private life*

5.2.2.1 The right to personal liberty/respect for private life

Two of the states discussed here, Switzerland and the United States, each have a general constitutional guarantee that protects a very broad range of liberties. At the international level, the guarantee of the right to respect

[123] Ibid., 55. [124] See Section 6.2.2.2. [125] See Section 6.2. [126] See ibid.

for private life of Article 8 of the ECHR, which has become part of the domestic law of the United Kingdom, also has a very wide scope of protection, although it is not quite as comprehensive as that of the Swiss and US guarantees. Further guarantees of the right to private life and privacy in international human rights instruments relevant for the present context include Article 12 of the UDHR, Article 17 of the ICCPR, Article 16 of the CRC and Article 5 of the ADHR, which is binding on the United States. With regard to the ICCPR, the UN Human Rights Committee has given the concept of 'privacy' a similarly broad meaning as the European Court of Human Rights has done with regard to that of 'private life'.[127]

As far as Switzerland is concerned, Article 10(2) of the Federal Constitution provides that 'everyone has the right to personal liberty, in particular to physical and mental integrity and to freedom of movement'.[128] The guarantee of personal liberty protects all elementary freedoms that are indispensable for a person's development and that all human beings must be entitled to as a protection of their dignity against state interference.[129] Apart from physical and mental integrity and freedom of movement, this also includes the right to choose one's way of life, to organise one's leisure time and to entertain contacts with others.[130] Given this broad scope, Article 10(2) has been characterised by the Federal Supreme Court as a general and subsidiary guarantee that can be referred to when the fundamental rights invoked in a particular case are not covered by one of the more specific constitutional guarantees.[131] The right to respect for private life of Article 13(1) of the Federal Constitution equally protects the right to decide on the elementary aspects of one's life, including the right 'to be left alone'.[132] There is an overlap between the respective scopes of these two constitutional

[127] See e.g. *Coeriel and Aurik* v. *The Netherlands*, Communication No. 453/1991, 31 October 1994, UN Doc. CCPR/C/52/D/453/1991, para. 10.2 ('The Committee considers that the notion of privacy refers to the sphere of a person's life in which he or she can freely express his or her identity, be it by entering into relationships with others or alone.').

[128] BV, Art. 10(2) ('Jeder Mensch hat das Recht auf persönliche Freiheit, insbesondere auf körperliche und geistige Unversehrtheit und auf Bewegungsfreiheit.').

[129] BGE 133 I 110, 119 (2007).

[130] BGE 103 Ia 293, 295 (1977). For an overview of the rich case law, see e.g. Baumann, *Das Grundrecht der persönlichen Freiheit in der Bundesverfassung* (2011), pp. 43–62; Müller/Schefer, *Grundrechte in der Schweiz* (2008), pp. 138–63.

[131] BGE 123 I 112, 118 (1997).

[132] Müller/Schefer, *Grundrechte in der Schweiz* (2008), p. 140.

guarantees, so that it may not always be clear which one of them should be applied in a particular case.[133]

In the United States, a comparable general guarantee exists in the form of the due process clause of the Fifth and Fourteenth Amendments. As explained in Section 4.1.3, according to the substantive due process test, the requirement of these two Amendments that no one 'shall [...] be deprived of [...] liberty [...] without due process of law' imposes substantive limitations on government action, whatever the nature of the liberty interest involved may be. The Supreme Court has explained that the 'liberty' that is guaranteed 'denotes not merely freedom from bodily restraint but also the right of the individual to contract, to engage in any of the common occupations of life, to acquire useful knowledge, to marry, establish a home and bring up children, to worship God according to the dictates of his own conscience, and generally to enjoy those privileges long recognized at common law as essential to the orderly pursuit of happiness by free men'.[134] The standard employed to review governmental interference with liberty, however, varies. If there is not a restriction of a 'fundamental right', the Supreme Court will uphold the government action as long as it is rationally related to a legitimate governmental interest. In contrast, when there is a restriction of a 'fundamental right', the government action will be subject to strict scrutiny: the government must demonstrate that it is narrowly tailored to promote a compelling or overriding interest.[135] The Supreme Court has stated that the category of 'fundamental rights' embraces those rights that are 'implicit in the concept of ordered liberty'[136] or 'so rooted in the traditions and conscience of our people as to be ranked as fundamental'.[137] However, since the qualification of liberty interests as 'fundamental rights' has been approached on a case-by-case basis, the criteria for making the decision are not quite clear. The category includes not only the rights that are explicitly listed in the Constitution or its Amendments but also further freedoms. One such fundamental element of personal liberty is the freedom 'to enter into and maintain certain intimate human relationships'.[138]

[133] Kiener/Kälin, *Grundrechte* (2013), pp. 166, 181–2; Baumann, *Das Grundrecht der persönlichen Freiheit in der Bundesverfassung* (2011), pp. 97, 98–101, 107–9.

[134] *Meyer* v. *Nebraska*, 262 U.S. 390, 399 (1923).

[135] See generally Tribe, *American Constitutional Law* (1988), pp. 769–84, 1436–66.

[136] *Palko* v. *Connecticut*, 302 U.S. 319, 325 (1937).

[137] *Snyder* v. *Massachusetts*, 291 U.S. 97, 105 (1934).

[138] *Roberts* v. *United States Jaycees*, 468 U.S. 609, 617–18 (1984).

The scope of Article 8 of the ECHR is defined very broadly and has been interpreted by the European Court of Human Rights in a dynamic and extensive fashion.[139] The guarantee of Article 8 requires, among other things, respect for private life and thus 'secure[s] to the individual a sphere within which he can freely pursue the development and fulfilment of his personality'.[140] In particular, it protects the right to lead one's life according to one's own ideas without state interference.[141] In addition to the explicitly mentioned right to respect for family life, Article 8(1) protects, more generally, respect for all personal relationships.[142] The European Court has refused to limit the concept of private life to an 'inner circle', that is, to the right 'to be left alone'. Instead, according to the court, individuals must also have the opportunity to establish and develop relationships with other human beings.[143] This freedom to associate with others is not limited to the private context but extends to the public context,[144] including the business context.[145]

5.2.2.2 Exclusion from public space and personal liberty/respect for private life

These broad guarantees of personal liberty and respect for private life will regularly be engaged by exclusion from public space and may be invoked when the more specific guarantees described in the following sections fail to provide protection. Furthermore, they may also be used in combination with one (or several) of these more specific rights.

Guarantees of personal liberty and respect for private life are applicable to all those situations where an exclusion measure interferes with a person's freedom to lead their life according to their own ideas. This is the case whenever access to public space is denied to persons for whom, for

[139] See Feldman, 'The Developing Scope of Article 8 of the European Convention on Human Rights' (1997).

[140] *Brüggemann and Scheuten* v. *Germany*, report of the European Commission of Human Rights of 12 July 1977, DR 10, p. 115, para. 55. See also *Deklerck* v. *Belgium*, judgment of 11 July 1980, DR 21, p. 120. See Breitenmoser, *Der Schutz der Privatsphäre gemäss Art. 8 EMRK* (1986), p. 40.

[141] Grabenwarter/Pabel, *Europäische Menschenrechtskonvention* (2012), p. 233; Meyer-Ladewig, *Europäische Menschenrechtskonvention* (2011), p. 194; Villiger, *Handbuch der Europäischen Menschenrechtskonvention (EMRK)* (1999), p. 358.

[142] See generally Harris/O'Boyle/Bates/Buckley, *Law of the ECHR* (2014), pp. 525–6; Grabenwarter/Pabel, *Europäische Menschenrechtskonvention* (2012), pp. 233–4.

[143] *Niemietz* v. *Germany*, no. 13710/88, 16 December 1992, Series A no. 251-B, para. 29.

[144] *P.G. and J.H.* v. *The United Kingdom*, no. 44787/98, 25 September 2001, ECHR 2001-IX, 195, para. 56.

[145] *Niemietz* v. *Germany*, no. 13710/88, 16 December 1992, Series A no. 251-B, para. 29.

whatever reason, spending time in public places is an important aspect of their way of life. For certain marginalised groups such as alcoholics, drug addicts or vagrants, access to public space is a precondition for key aspects of their private life. Public streets and squares may offer them the most important, or even the only, opportunity for social contact and may thus feel like home to them.[146] Similarly, juveniles tend to spend a large part of their free time in public places to meet with others of their age. As research in developmental psychology has shown, this constitutes for them an essential aspect of developing their own sense of identity and their social skills.[147] For those who are homeless it can even be said that it becomes completely impossible for them to lead an autonomous life if they are denied access to public space.[148]

The Swiss Federal Supreme Court was therefore right to conclude that the exclusion orders issued in the City of Berne amounted to an interference with the personal liberty guarantee of Article 10(2) of the Federal Constitution. Those subject to these orders were prevented from assembling, within a certain area, in groups that consume alcohol.[149] Since such get-togethers combined with the consumption of alcohol had been part of the routine of these people, the court found that they constituted an aspect of their personal development protected by Article 10(2).[150] For the same reason, most juvenile curfews amount to an interference with guarantees of personal liberty and respect for private life: especially for young people it is crucial to be able to meet friends and get to know new people in public places. Accordingly, several US courts have recognised that juvenile curfews amount to restrictions of the liberty protected by the due process clause.[151] The US District Court for the District of Columbia, for instance, held that the liberty restricted by the curfew in question was a fundamental one, so that a strict standard of review had to be applied.[152] It explained:

146 See e.g. the interviews with people banned from public places in Seattle in Beckett/Herbert, *Banished* (2010), pp. 103–39.

147 E.g. Flammer/Alsaker, *Entwicklungspsychologie der Adoleszenz* (2002), pp. 194–8.

148 See Waldron, 'Homelessness and the Issue of Freedom' (1991).

149 BGE 132 I 49, 50 (2006) ('Obgenannten Personen wird verboten, sich am oben bezeichneten Ort in Personensammlungen aufzuhalten, in welchen Alkohol konsumiert wird.').

150 Ibid., 56.

151 *Bykofsky* v. *Borough of Middletown*, 429 U.S. 964, 964 (1976) (Marshall, J., dissenting from denial of certiorari); *Waters* v. *Barry*, 711 F.Supp. 1125, 1134 (D.D.C. 1989); *Johnson* v. *City of Opelousas*, 658 F.2d 1065, 1072 (5th Cir. 1981); *Bykofsky* v. *Borough of Middletown*, 401 F.Supp. 1242, 1254–5 (D.C. Pa. 1975).

152 *Waters* v. *Barry*, 711 F.Supp. 1125, 1134–5 (D.D.C. 1989).

> The right to walk the streets, or to meet publicly with one's friends for a noble purpose or for no purpose at all – and to do so whenever one pleases – is an integral component of life in a free and ordered society. [. . .] This right is rooted in the First Amendment's protection of expression and association, as well as (in this case) the Fifth Amendment's protection of fundamental liberty interests under the doctrine of substantive due process.[153]

The US Supreme Court has ruled that also an ordinance that prohibits loitering in public places amounts to an interference with the liberty protected by the due process clause.[154]

Guarantees of personal liberty and respect for private life are also engaged whenever exclusion measures interfere with a person's right to establish and develop relationships with others. For certain marginalised groups, public places may be the only locations where they can freely meet with other people. The right to develop contacts with others thus may be particularly at risk if exclusion measures are directed against members of such groups. This aspect of personal liberty cannot always be clearly separated from the right to lead one's life according to one's own ideas: in the cases just referred to above, for example, an important aspect of the way of life that is protected consists exactly of associating with others in public places.

In summary, guarantees of personal liberty and respect for private life are engaged by all those exclusion measures that interfere with essential aspects of a person's development or the right to establish and develop relationships with others.

The broad scope of protection of Article 8 of the ECHR is of particular relevance in the present context. As will be explained in the following section, the ECHR, unlike Swiss and US constitutional law, does not contain a specific guarantee of freedom of movement. Article 8 of the ECHR can, at least to some extent, fill this gap: as the European Court of Human Rights has made explicit, restrictions of free movement that affect a person's right to develop his or her personality or to develop personal ties with others fall within its scope.[155]

Guarantees of personal liberty and respect for private life will only be engaged in the first place if some essential aspect of a person's private life is involved. An interference with these guarantees will therefore almost inevitably be a *serious* one. It can only then be qualified as not serious if the degree of interference is very minor. Such an exceptional case was, for example, that of the Bernese exclusion orders. Those subject to the orders

[153] Ibid., 1134. [154] *City of Chicago* v. *Morales*, 527 U.S. 41, 54 (1999).

[155] See *İletmiş* v. *Turkey*, no. 29871/96, 6 December 2005, ECHR 2005-XII, 155, paras 42, 50.

were only prevented from assembling in groups *that consume alcohol* and so were still allowed to meet in the relevant area as long as there was no alcohol consumption involved, to drink there on their own or to meet and drink somewhere else. Given these exceptional circumstances, the Federal Supreme Court was right to qualify the interference with the guarantee of personal liberty as not serious.[156]

5.2.3 *Freedom of movement*

5.2.3.1 The right to freedom of movement

The liberty of every person 'to go where he pleases' is a fundamental value in all three states examined and has also been recognised in international law. Article 13(1) of the UDHR guarantees everyone's 'right to freedom of movement [. . .] within the borders of each State'. The same guarantee is contained in Article 12(1) of the ICCPR. Accordingly, 'persons are entitled to move from one place to another' and states are precluded from 'preventing the entry or stay of persons in a defined part of the territory'.[157] At the regional level, the ECHR itself does not expressly enshrine the right to freedom of movement, but Article 2(1) of Protocol No. 4 to the ECHR does,[158] in exactly the same words as Article 12(1) of the ICCPR. This Protocol, however, has not been signed by Switzerland; the United Kingdom has signed but not ratified it. The ADHR, binding on the United States, guarantees the right to freedom of movement in its Article 8, although it restricts its scope to citizens of the respective state. The TFEU grants, in Articles 20(2)(a) and 21(1), all citizens of the EU (and not only 'workers' in the sense of Article 45) the right to free movement within the territory of the member states, including the United Kingdom. Finally, according to the Agreement on the Free Movement of Persons between the EC and Switzerland, citizens of EU states present in Switzerland (and Swiss citizens present in EU states) enjoy 'the right to occupational and geographical mobility which enables nationals of the Contracting Parties to move freely within the territory of the host state'.[159]

156 BGE 132 I 49, 63–4 (2006).

157 UN Human Rights Committee, General Comment No. 27, UN Doc. CCPR/C/21/Rev.1/Add.9 (2 November 1999), paras 5, 7.

158 Protocol No. 4 to the ECHR (adopted 16 September 1963, entered into force 2 May 1968) ETS 46.

159 Agreement between the European Community and its Member States, of the one part, and the Swiss Confederation, of the other, on the free movement of persons, 21 June 1999, OJ L 114 (SR 0.142.112.681), Art. 7(b). See also ibid., Annex I, Art. 8.

Switzerland is the only one of the three states with an explicit constitutional guarantee of the right to freedom of movement. As explained in the previous section, the guarantee of personal liberty of Article 10(2) of the Federal Constitution specifically refers to the right of freedom of movement. The Federal Supreme Court has described this freedom as 'the freedom to come and go' ('la liberté d'aller et venir').[160] This means that everyone has the right to freely change their location.[161] Freedom of movement includes, first, the right to go away from a particular place.[162] Even short police stops of only a few minutes amount to an interference with this right.[163] Second, freedom of movement means that everyone has the right to go to any place of their choice that is publicly accessible,[164] though not necessarily by any means of transport of their choice.[165] Third, apart from the right to go to a particular place and to leave it, freedom of movement also protects the right to a minimum degree of physical movement as such.[166] The Federal Supreme Court has highlighted the importance of freedom of movement by pointing out that personal liberty is the prerequisite for the exercise of all other constitutionally guaranteed liberties[167] and by stating that the freedom of citizens to circulate at will without prior authorisation is the element that distinguishes best a state based on the rule of law from a police state.[168]

Notwithstanding the fact that it is not explicitly mentioned in the text of the US Constitution, freedom of movement is also recognised as a constitutional right in the United States. The Supreme Court has never clearly established what the source of this right – often also referred to as the 'right to travel' – is. It has sometimes suggested that it is

160 BGE 103 Ia 293, 295 (1977); BGE 90 I 29, 34 (1964).

161 Baumann, *Das Grundrecht der persönlichen Freiheit in der Bundesverfassung* (2011), p. 23; Baumann, 'Inhalt und Tragweite der Bewegungsfreiheit' (2004), 508; Spoendlin, *Die verfassungsmässige Garantie der persönlichen Freiheit* (1945), pp. 37–8.

162 Baumann, *Das Grundrecht der persönlichen Freiheit in der Bundesverfassung* (2011), p. 23; Baumann, 'Inhalt und Tragweite der Bewegungsfreiheit' (2004), 508–9.

163 BGE 109 Ia 146, 149–50 (1983).

164 Baumann, *Das Grundrecht der persönlichen Freiheit in der Bundesverfassung* (2011), p. 23; Baumann, 'Inhalt und Tragweite der Bewegungsfreiheit' (2004), 509; Spoendlin, *Die verfassungsmässige Garantie der persönlichen Freiheit* (1945), pp. 37–8.

165 Urteil des Bundesgerichts 2P.113/1999 vom 17. April 2000, E. 3a; BGE 108 Ia 59, 61 (1982).

166 Baumann, 'Inhalt und Tragweite der Bewegungsfreiheit' (2004), 509–10.

167 BGE 97 I 45, 49 (1971).

168 Urteil des Bundesgerichts 1C_226/2009 vom 16. Dezember 2009, E. 3.2; BGE 109 Ia 146, 150 (1983) ('La liberté des citoyens de circuler à leur gré dans le pays sans autorisation préalable [. . .] est sans doute l'élément qui caractérise le mieux l'Etat de droit par rapport a l'Etat policier.').

a 'sourceless' right.[169] At other times the court has relied on various constitutional clauses, including the privileges and immunities clause of Article IV,[170] the privileges and immunities clause of the Fourteenth Amendment,[171] the commerce clause,[172] the equal protection clause of the Fourteenth Amendment[173] and the due process clause of the Fifth Amendment and the Fourteenth Amendment.[174] In any event, it has consistently characterised the right to travel as a 'fundamental' or 'basic right',[175] restrictions of which are thus subject to a strict standard of review. Just as the Swiss Federal Supreme Court, the US Supreme Court has stressed the importance of freedom of movement by pointing out that it is this freedom that makes all other rights meaningful.[176] While it is clear that the right to travel protects travel between states, the Supreme Court has never explicitly ruled on whether it also encompasses movement within a state. However, it has repeatedly *implied* that a right to intrastate travel does exist. In *United States* v. *Wheeler*, for example, it observed that '[i]n all the states, from the beginning down to the adoption of the Articles of Confederation, the citizens thereof possessed the fundamental right, inherent in citizens of all free governments, peacefully to dwell within the limits of their respective states, to move at will from place to place therein, and to have free ingress thereto and egress therefrom.'[177] More recently, in *City of Chicago* v. *Morales*, the court held that 'it is apparent that an individual's decision to remain in a public place of his choice is as much a part of his liberty as the freedom of movement inside frontiers that is "a part of our heritage" [. . .] or the right to move "to whatsoever place one's own inclination may direct" identified in Blackstone's Commentaries'.[178] Furthermore, numerous federal

[169] *Shapiro* v. *Thompson*, 394 U.S. 618, 630 (1969); *United States* v. *Guest*, 383 U.S. 745, 758–9 (1966).

[170] E.g. *Ward* v. *Maryland*, 79 U.S. 418, 430 (1871).

[171] *Saenz* v. *Roe*, 526 U.S. 489, 502–4 (1999).

[172] *Edwards* v. *California*, 314 U. S. 160, 172–4 (1941).

[173] E.g. *Zobel* v. *Williams*, 457 U.S. 55, 66–7 (1982) (Brennan, J., concurring); *Memorial Hosp.* v. *Maricopa County*, 415 U.S. 250, 253–70 (1974).

[174] *Sosna* v. *Iowa*, 419 U.S. 393, 409–10 (1975); *Aptheker* v. *Secretary of State*, 378 U.S. 500, 505–6 (1964); *Kent* v. *Dulles*, 357 U.S. 116, 125–7 (1958).

[175] *United States* v. *Guest*, 383 U.S. 745, 757–8 (1966); *Kent* v. *Dulles*, 357 U.S. 116, 126 (1958).

[176] *Aptheker* v. *Secretary of State*, 378 U.S. 500, 520 (1964) (Douglas, J., concurring).

[177] *States* v. *Wheeler*, 254 U.S. 281, 293 (1920).

[178] *City of Chicago* v. *Morales*, 527 U.S. 41, 54 (1999). See also *Kolender* v. *Lawson*, 461 U.S. 352, 358 (1983); *Papachristou* v. *City of Jacksonville*, 405 U.S. 156, 164 (1972); *Smith* v. *Turner*, 48 U.S. (7 How.) 283, 492 (1849) (Taney, C.J., dissenting) ('We are all citizens

and state courts have recognised that the US Constitution also protects the right to intrastate travel.[179] In so finding, courts have argued that freedom of movement is of great practical significance for all sorts of daily activities[180] and that it would be absurd to describe the right to interstate travel as a fundamental aspect of personal liberty and not to recognise a corresponding right to travel within a state.[181]

As far as the United Kingdom is concerned, already the Magna Carta guaranteed some aspects of free movement[182] and Blackstone's *Commentaries on the Laws of England* identified a right to move 'to whatsoever place one's own inclination may direct, without imprisonment or restraint'.[183] However, there is no specific, positive guarantee of the freedom of movement in common law. Instead, following the traditional, negative approach of 'residual liberty', the contours of this freedom are defined by that which is not prohibited by statute or common law. Unlike as with other rights, where positive guarantees have been created by way of incorporation of the ECHR into domestic law, the ECHR itself does not provide for a right to freedom of movement. As noted above, Protocol No. 4 to the ECHR, which guarantees this right, has not been ratified by the United Kingdom. It should be noted,

of the United States, and, as members of the same community, must have the right to pass and repass through every part of it without interruption, as freely as in our own State.').

179 E.g. *Johnson* v. *City of Cincinnati*, 310 F.3d 484, 493–8 (6th Cir. 2002) ('[W]e find that the right to travel locally through public spaces and roadways enjoys a unique and protected place in our national heritage.'); *State* v. *Burnett*, 755 N.E.2d 857, 865 (Ohio 2001) ('Much like the right to interstate travel, the right to intrastate travel has a long, historical recognition in the conscience and traditions of our people.'); *Spencer* v. *Casavilla*, 903 F.2d 171, 174 (2d Cir. 1990) ('[T]he Constitution also protects the right to travel freely within a single state.'); *Lutz* v. *City of York*, 899 F.2d 255, 268 (3rd Cir. 1990) (holding that 'the right to move freely about one's own neighborhood or town' is a fundamental liberty interest protected by the due process clause); *Bykofsky* v. *Borough of Middletown*, 401 F. Supp. 1242, 1254, 1261 (M.D. Pa. 1975) ('The rights of locomotion, freedom of movement, to go where one pleases, and to use the public streets in a way that does not interfere with the personal liberty of others are basic values "implicit in the concept of ordered liberty" protected by the due process clause of the fourteenth amendment.'); *Eggert* v. *City of Seattle*, 505 P.2d 801, 804 (Wash. 1973) ('Rights, such as the right to travel, which involve personal liberty are not dependent on state lines. Both travel within and between states is protected.').

180 *Johnson* v. *City of Cincinnati*, 310 F.3d 484, 498 (6th Cir. 2002).

181 *Eggert* v. *City of Seattle*, 505 P.2d 801, 804 (Wash. 1973); *King* v. *New Rochelle Mun. Hous. Auth.*, 442 F.2d 646, 648 (2d Cir. 1971).

182 Magna Carta 1215, Chs 41 and 42, reprinted in McKechnie, *Magna Carta* (2000), pp. 398–411.

183 Blackstone, *Commentaries on the Laws of England* (1967), Vol. I, p. 134.

however, that the European Court of Human Rights has held that restrictions of the right to freedom of movement may amount to a violation of the right to respect for private life guaranteed by Article 8 of the ECHR, as freedom of movement may be considered essential to the full development of a person's private life.[184] While the court has not given any detailed guidance as to when this will be the case, it will probably be limited to situations where far-reaching restrictions of the freedom of movement that seriously affect the applicant's close personal ties are imposed.[185] The only explicit positive guarantee of the freedom of movement in the United Kingdom, in addition to that of the TFEU, is thus that of Article 12(1) of the ICCPR, which has not been incorporated into domestic law.

5.2.3.2 Exclusion from public space and freedom of movement

Exclusion from public space will regularly involve restrictions of the freedom of movement. That there is an interference with the freedom of movement is perhaps most obvious with those measures that confine people to a specific place, be it private or public, in order to keep them away from (other) public places.

These measures include, for example, curfews, which may be imposed on a whole category of people by way of a prohibition (such as night curfews for juveniles) or on particular persons through an individual order (such as a TPIM). That night curfews for juveniles as they exist in all three states at issue amount to an interference with the freedom of movement is rather uncontroversial in the literature[186] and has been confirmed by a number of US courts.[187] The European Commission of Human Rights has equally held that a night curfew – although imposed on a suspected Mafia member rather than juveniles – constitutes

184 *İletmiş* v. *Turkey*, no. 29871/96, 6 December 2005, ECHR 2005-XII, 155, paras 47, 50.

185 In *İletmiş* v. *Turkey* the state authorities confiscated the passport of the applicant, who had family and professional ties in several countries, for more than seven years. Ibid., paras 14, 30–1, 42, 50.

186 For the United States, see e.g. 'Juvenile Curfews and Gang Violence' (1994), 1701; Horowitz, 'A Search for Constitutional Standards' (1991). For Switzerland, see Gerber Jenni, ' "Abendausgang Kinder" ' (2006), 849.

187 *Bykofsky* v. *Borough of Middletown*, 429 U.S. 964, 964 (Marshall, J., dissenting from denial of certiorari); *Waters* v. *Barry*, 711 F.Supp. 1125, 1134 (D.D.C. 1989); *McCollester* v. *City of Keene*, 586 F.Supp. 1381, 1384–5 (D.N.H. 1984); *Johnson* v. *City of Opelousas*, 658 F.2d 1065, 1072 (5th Cir. 1981); *Bykofsky* v. *Borough of Middletown*, 401 F.Supp. 1242, 1254–5 (D.C. Pa., 1975).

a restriction of the freedom of movement.[188] A curfew will only then *not* amount to an interference with the freedom of movement if it is framed as a prohibition of specified behaviour, rather than of mere presence, in public places. For example, the Swiss municipality of Dänikon introduced a Police Ordinance that made it unlawful for children of compulsory school age *to assemble in groups* in public places after 10 pm.[189] Arguably, such a prohibition does not interfere with the freedom of movement, as children are still allowed to leave home at night and circulate as they please as long as they do not meet in groups.[190]

While in the case of curfews people are excluded from public space by confining them to private places, there are also exclusion measures that confine people to limited parts of public space. Orders that prevent foreign nationals from leaving a specified province or area, as they also exist in Switzerland,[191] are one example of such restrictions that clearly engage the freedom of movement.[192] Another example is the police strategy known as 'kettling' that is now regularly used in all three states under consideration to control demonstrators and football supporters. The strategy basically consists of containing people, often for several hours, within a small cordoned-off area such as a square in order to keep them away from other parts of public space.[193] Such police strategies involve a restriction of the right to leave a particular place and thus clearly interfere with the freedom of movement.[194] Depending on the specific circumstances of the case, they may even amount to a deprivation of liberty.[195]

188 *Ciancimino* v. *Italy*, no. 12541/86, admissibility decision of 27 May 1991, 70 DR 103, pp. 123–4.

189 Polizeiverordnung der Gemeinde Dänikon vom 18. Juni 2008, Art. 27 (repealed; see Urteil des Verwaltungsgerichts des Kantons Zürich VB.2009.00055 vom 30. April 2009).

190 The Administrative Court of the Canton of Zurich, which was called upon to review this provision, did not address this particular issue as it concluded that, in any event, the provision was in violation of the guarantee of freedom of assembly of Article 22 of the Federal Constitution. Urteil des Verwaltungsgerichts des Kantons Zürich VB.2009.00055 vom 30. April 2009, E. 5.1. See Section 5.2.5.2.

191 See Section 3.3.2.4.

192 With regard to the Swiss Federal Constitution, see e.g. Urteil des Bundesgerichts 2A.148/2003 vom 30. Mai 2003, E. 2.3. With regard to the ICCPR, see *Karker* v. *France*, Communication No. 833/1998, 26 October 2000, UN Doc. CCPR/C/70/D/833/1998; *Celepli* v. *Sweden*, Communication No. 456/1991, 18 July 1994, UN Doc. CCPR/C/51/D/456/1991.

193 See Section 3.3.3.2.

194 See *Austin* v. *Commissioner for the Metropolis*, [2009] UKHL 5, para. 16 (Lord Hope); ZR 107/2008 Nr. 75, 257, p. 259 (Zürich, Obergericht).

195 See Section 5.2.4.2.

Guarantees of the freedom of movement may not only be engaged when people are confined to a specific place but also when they are denied access to certain parts of public space. For, as pointed out above, freedom of movement does not only include the right to leave a particular place or area but also the right to access any place or area that is normally publicly accessible. In fact, it can be argued that these two aspects of freedom of movement are congruent, that is, that they protect the same. Every prohibition to leave area A can instead be formulated as a prohibition to access area B, and the other way round – it only depends on how the respective areas are defined.

That bans on access to parts of public space amount to an interference with the freedom of movement has been recognised by key international human rights bodies. The UN Human Rights Committee has found that a prohibition of entering a specific district of a country falls within the scope of protection of Article 12 of the ICCPR.[196] The European Court of Human Rights has adopted a similar approach. For example, in the almost identical cases of *Landvreugd* v. *The Netherlands* and *Olivieira* v. *The Netherlands*, the municipal authorities of Amsterdam had prohibited the applicants from entering a particular area of the city centre known for attracting persons addicted to, and/or dealing in, hard drugs for fourteen days. The court found that there was an interference with Article 2 of Protocol No. 4 to the ECHR, a fact that the Dutch government had not even tried to dispute.[197] In an admissibility decision concerning an injunction that prohibited the applicant from being within 250 meters of a particular abortion clinic, the court equally found that there was an interference with the freedom of movement, despite the very limited scope of the banned area.[198]

As a consequence, all the various measures described in Section 3.3 that prevent people from accessing parts of public space amount to an interference with the freedom of movement. This applies, for example, to the area bans that under Swiss law can be imposed on foreign nationals and in connection with sports events. The Federal Supreme Court has held with regard to both of these measures that they interfere with Article

[196] *Ackla* v. *Togo*, Communication No. 505/1992, 25 March 1996, UN Doc. CCPR/C/51/D/505/1992, para. 10.

[197] *Landvreugd* v. *The Netherlands*, no. 37331/97, 4 June 2002, para. 46; *Olivieira* v. *The Netherlands*, no. 33129/96, 4 June 2002, ECHR 2002-IV, 193, para. 39.

[198] *Van den Dungen* v. *The Netherlands*, no. 22838/93, admissibility decision of 22 February 1995, para. 3.

10(2) of the Federal Constitution.[199] Similarly, US courts have found that drug-exclusion zones, such as that in Cincinnati referred to in Chapter 1, amount to a restriction on the freedom of movement.[200] The same holds true for measures that deny all potential demonstrators access to (potential) sites of protest, such as the creation of 'secured zones' or 'no-protest zones' in the United States or the setting up of road blocks where nearly everyone is turned back at the occasion of major demonstrations in Switzerland and the United Kingdom.[201] The Swiss Federal Supreme Court was therefore right to conclude in the case of *Gsell*, the facts of which have been set out in detail in Section 4.2.3.2, that the order preventing the complainant from travelling to Davos 'clearly' amounted to an interference with his freedom of movement guaranteed by Article 10(2) of the Federal Constitution.[202] Axel Tschentscher has criticised this finding, arguing that the case only involved denial of access to a narrowly defined area and that, otherwise, Gsell was not restricted in his movement. According to Tschentscher, the main concern for Gsell, as a journalist, was not the restriction of his movement as such but the fact that, as a result, he was not able to conduct research and report on the events.[203] Of course, Tschentscher is right to point out that the primary right at issue in the particular case of Gsell was freedom of expression rather than freedom of movement. Accordingly, the Federal Supreme Court did, in fact, examine the access ban also under the heading of freedom of expression.[204] However, contrary to what Tschentscher seems to suggest, it is not the case that geographically narrowly defined access bans do not amount to an interference with the freedom of movement. As pointed out above, there is no distinction in kind between a prohibition to leave a particular area and a prohibition to access a certain area. The applicability of guarantees of freedom of movement cannot be avoided simply by framing a prohibition to leave area A as

[199] For the former type of measure, see Urteil des Bundesgerichts 2A.501/2005 vom 30. August 2005, E. 2.1; Urteil des Bundesgerichts 2A.347/2003 vom 24. November 2003, E. 2.2, 4.2; Urteil des Bundesgerichts 2A.148/2003 vom 30. Mai 2003, E. 2.3. For the latter type of measure, see BGE 137 I 31, 45 and 48–9 (2010).

[200] *Johnson* v. *City of Cincinnati*, 310 F.3d 484, 498 (6th Cir. 2002); *State* v. *Burnett*, 755 N.E. 2d 857, 867 (Ohio 2001).

[201] See Section 3.3.3.2.

[202] BGE 130 I 369, 373 (2004) ('Dadurch ist er klarerweise in seiner Bewegungsfreiheit im Sinne von Art. 10 Abs. 2 BV beeinträchtigt worden.').

[203] Kälin/Kiener/Müller/Tschannen/Tschentscher, 'Die staatsrechtliche Rechtsprechung des Bundesgerichts in den Jahren 2004 und 2005' (2005), 655.

[204] BGE 130 I 369, 374–5 (2004).

a prohibition to access area B. Furthermore, the European Court of Human Rights has made it clear in its case law referred to above that even bans on accessing very small areas may amount to an interference with the freedom of movement. What matters is not the geographical extension of the area concerned but rather whether that area is otherwise publicly accessible and so only particular persons (or groups of persons) are denied access to it.[205]

As explained in Sections 3.3 and 3.4, the police (and courts) are often granted broadly defined powers to issue orders that may involve exclusion from public space. The British pieces of legislation authorising, for example, football banning orders, SHPOs, TPIMs or IPNAs, just as the police acts of the Swiss cantons that authorise exclusion orders for reasons of public safety and order, typically grant the authorities wide discretion to define the terms of the order, including the definition of the prohibited behaviour. As a consequence, one will have to look at the exact terms of the particular order at issue to determine whether it involves an interference with the freedom of movement or not. For example, an order issued under one of the Swiss cantonal police acts will constitute an interference with the freedom of movement if a person is prevented from merely being present in specified public places for a certain period. On the other hand, such orders sometimes prohibit specified behaviour instead of mere presence in public space. In the case of the exclusion orders in the City of Berne referred to before, for example, those concerned were ordered not to assemble, within a certain area, in groups that consume alcohol.[206] The Federal Supreme Court, unlike the Administrative Court of the Canton of Berne before it,[207] rightly concluded that the order did not amount to an interference with the freedom of movement as those subject to it were not prevented from moving around in the designated area.[208]

In summary, generally speaking, all types of exclusion measures that prevent people from merely being in public space or parts of it, or from being there at certain times, amount to an interference with the freedom of movement. The only exclusion measures that do not fall within the scope of protection of this freedom are those that prohibit certain behaviour, rather than mere presence, in public places. Even

205 See also Kiener/Kälin, *Grundrechte* (2013), pp. 154–5.

206 BGE 132 I 49, 50 (2006) ('Obgenannten Personen wird verboten, sich am oben bezeichneten Ort in Personensammlungen aufzuhalten, in welchen Alkohol konsumiert wird.').

207 BVR 2005, 97, p. 116 (Verwaltungsgericht des Kantons Bern).

208 BGE 132 I 49, 56 (2006).

a prohibition of certain behaviour may, however, interfere with the freedom of movement if the behaviour is very widely defined. For example, a prohibition of 'loitering' in public places effectively amounts to a ban on simply being there and thus constitutes a restriction of the freedom of movement.[209]

As far as the question of the *seriousness* of the interference with fundamental rights is concerned, there is a general tendency of courts and commentators to qualify restrictions of the freedom of movement as not particularly grave. The Swiss Federal Supreme Court and various cantonal courts have characterised exclusion measures such as the area bans applicable to foreign nationals,[210] exclusion orders based on cantonal police acts[211] and bans on accessing certain locations,[212] including the denial of access to Davos,[213] as not very serious. With regard to access bans, for example, the Federal Supreme Court has held that as a general rule these cannot be qualified as serious restrictions.[214]

The observation that restrictions of free movement do not generally amount to a serious interference may be true for temporary restrictions applicable to narrowly defined areas. However, as pointed out in Chapter 3, exclusion from public space has in recent years been turned from a short-term measure limited to narrowly defined places into a long-term, or even permanent, measure covering ever larger areas or even all public places.[215]

In view of this development, the assumption that, as a general rule, exclusion measures are not to be qualified as a serious interference with the freedom of movement is no longer tenable. That banning a sixteen-year old from entering any part of a city for ten years, as has happened in Manchester,[216] amounts to a very serious interference is obvious. However, also area bans covering large parts of an inner city area that are imposed for several months have a serious impact on the daily lives of those concerned. In addition to simply restricting spatial mobility, such

[209] See *Chicago* v. *Morales*, 527 U.S. 41, 53–4 (1999); *Kolender* v. *Lawson*, 461 U.S. 352, 358 (1983).

[210] Urteil des Bundesgerichts 2A.501/2005 vom 30. August 2005, E. 2.1; Urteil des Bundesgerichts 2A.347/2003 vom 24. November 2003, E. 2.2; Urteil des Bundesgerichts 2A.148/2003 vom 30. Mai 2003, E. 2.3; BVR 2002, 97, p. 99 (Verwaltungsgericht des Kantons Bern); BVR 2000, 145, p. 151 (Verwaltungsgericht des Kantons Bern).

[211] BVR 2005, 97, pp. 127–8 (Verwaltungsgericht des Kantons Bern).

[212] BGE 128 I 327, 344 (2002).

[213] BGE 130 I 369, 385–6 (2004).

[214] BGE 128 I 327, 344 (2002).

[215] See especially Sections 3.2, 3.4.3 and 3.4.4.

[216] 'Young thug barred from Manchester', *Manchester Evening News*, 22 January 2004.

area bans often inhibit interaction with family members and other social contacts and reduce access to basic goods and services such as work, education or training opportunities, social services, health or drug treatment programmes and shopping opportunities.[217] Courts seem to increasingly have come to recognise the seriousness of these impacts. In the case concerning Patricia Johnson described in Chapter 1, the US Court of Appeals for the Sixth Circuit found that banning her from returning to the respective 'drug exclusion zone' constituted a severe restriction, which had to be reviewed with strict scrutiny, as the relevant zone comprised an entire neighbourhood of Cincinnati.[218] In a decision concerning an area ban imposed on a football supporter, the Administrative Court of the Canton of Zurich held that, given the temporal scope of the ban (every match day six hours before and after the game) and the size of the banned area (large parts of the inner city area), the ban amounted to an interference with the freedom of movement that, contrary to the claims of the police, was more than just marginal.[219] Similarly, as has been rightly pointed out in the literature, night curfews that are not only in force for a limited period such as during an emergency but apply throughout someone's childhood and adolescence cannot be qualified as only a minor interference with the freedom of movement.[220]

A further reason why exclusion measures may amount to a serious interference is the impact that restrictions of movement regularly have on the enjoyment of other fundamental rights. Freedom of movement is inextricably linked to other freedoms, as is made clear by the following passage from a decision of the Supreme Court of Wisconsin concerning a municipal night-time curfew:

> If, for any reason, people cannot walk or drive to their church, their freedom to worship is impaired. If, for any reason, people cannot walk or drive to the meeting hall, freedom of assembly is effectively blocked. If, for any reason, people cannot safely walk the sidewalks or drive the streets of a community, opportunities for freedom of speech are sharply limited.[221]

[217] See Beckett/Herbert, *Banished* (2010), pp. 103–39 (setting out the results of interviews conducted with people subject to area bans in Seattle).

[218] *Johnson* v. *Cincinnati*, 310 F.3d 484, 502 (6th Cir. 2002).

[219] Urteil des Verwaltungsgerichts des Kantons Zürich VB.2009.00019 vom 26. Februar 2009, E. 4.2.

[220] Gerber Jenni, ' "Abendausgang Kinder" ' (2006), 853; Baumann, 'Inhalt und Tragweite der Bewegungsfreiheit' (2004), 523.

[221] *Ervin* v. *State*, 41 Wis.2d 194, 200, 163 N.W.2d 207, 210 (Wis. 1968).

5.2.4 *Freedom from arbitrary detention*

5.2.4.1 The right to freedom from arbitrary detention

'Mere' restrictions of movement must be distinguished from deprivations of liberty in the sense of arrest or detention. For the latter both international law and the domestic law of the three states at issue establish additional, mainly procedural, requirements. Such additional requirements are explicitly provided by Article 9 of the UDHR, Article 9 of the ICCPR, Article 5 of the ECHR, Article 25 of the ADHR and Article 31 of the Swiss Federal Constitution. They include, for example, the requirements that people may only be detained based on specific grounds that are prescribed by law and that they must be informed promptly of the reasons for the arrest. Similarly, in the United States, under the Fourth Amendment to the Constitution, any deprivation of liberty requires, depending on its extent, probable cause or reasonable suspicion, and under the Fifth Amendment any person deprived of their liberty must be informed about their rights to remain silent and legal assistance.[222]

The distinction between freedom of movement and freedom from arbitrary detention is of particular relevance with regard to the United Kingdom where only the latter freedom enjoys effective protection, thanks to the incorporation of Article 5 of the ECHR into domestic law. In contrast, as explained above, since the United Kingdom has not ratified Protocol No. 4 to the ECHR, the only explicit, positive guarantee of freedom of movement applicable to the United Kingdom is that of the ICCPR, which has not been incorporated. The distinction between restrictions of movement falling under Article 2(1) of Protocol No. 4 to the ECHR and deprivations of liberty falling under Article 5 of the ECHR is, as the European Court of Human Rights held in the leading case of *Guzzardi* v. *Italy*, not one of nature or substance but of degree and intensity.[223] Article 5 applies when a person is confined 'in a particular restricted space for a not negligible length of time' and he or she has not validly consented to the confinement.[224] To determine whether there is a deprivation of liberty, the starting point must always be the concrete situation 'and account must be taken of a whole range of criteria such as

222 See *Miranda* v. *Arizona*, 384 U.S. 436 (1966).

223 *Guzzardi* v. *Italy*, no. 7367/76, 6 November 1980, Series A no. 39, para. 93.

224 *Storck* v. *Germany*, no. 61603/00, 16 June 2005, ECHR 2005-V, 111, para. 74.

the type, duration, effects and manner of implementation of the measure in question'.[225]

5.2.4.2 Exclusion from public space and freedom from arbitrary detention

Exclusion from public space will generally not be of a sufficient degree and intensity to qualify as detention. Measures that prevent people from accessing certain places or zones,[226] or from leaving rather large areas,[227] do therefore not trigger the applicability of the heightened requirements set out in the provisions referred to above. Nevertheless, particular forms of exclusion from public space may amount to a deprivation of liberty. Because of the particular practical importance of the distinction between freedom of movement and freedom from arbitrary detention in the United Kingdom, it is especially there that courts have had to address the issue. Accordingly, the focus of this section is on the case law of UK courts and the European Court of Human Rights.

Austin v. *Commissioner of Police of the Metropolis*, which has already been touched upon in Section 4.2.3.2, concerned the 'kettling' or containment of a group of people by the police on public-order grounds. During the 2001 May Day demonstration in London, the police surrounded demonstrators in Oxford Circus with a cordon and did not allow them to leave for up to seven hours. While the High Court judge found that this amounted to a deprivation of liberty within the meaning of Article 5(1) of the ECHR,[228] the Court of Appeal held that it did not.[229] The House of Lords agreed with the Court of Appeal, holding that 'measures of crowd control that are undertaken in the interests of the community' do not fall

225 *Guzzardi* v. *Italy*, no. 7367/76, 6 November 1980, Series A no. 39, para. 92. See also *Engel and others* v. *The Netherlands*, nos 5100/71; 5101/71; 5102/71; 5354/72; 5370/72, 8 June 1976, Series A no. 22, para. 59.

226 See e.g. BGE 134 I 140, 144 (2008) (holding that prohibiting a violent husband from coming within a certain distance of his wife's flat constitutes a restriction of movement but not a deprivation of liberty in the sense of Article 5 of the ECHR and Article 31 of the Federal Constitution); BGE 130 I 369, 374 (2004) (holding the same with regard to Gsell's denial of access to Davos).

227 See e.g. *Karker* v. *France*, Communication No. 833/1998, 26 October 2000, UN Doc. CCPR/C/70/D/833/1998; *Celepli* v. *Sweden*, Communication No. 456/1991, 18 July 1994, UN Doc. CCPR/C/51/D/456/1991 (both holding that orders that require foreign nationals not to leave a certain province or municipality do not engage Article 9 of the ICCPR).

228 *Austin* v. *Commissioner of Police of the Metropolis*, [2005] HRLR 20, paras 501–12.

229 *Austin* v. *Commissioner of Police of the Metropolis*, [2008] 2 WLR 415, paras 100–7.

under Article 5 of the ECHR as long as they are resorted to in good faith and are proportionate to the situation.[230]

In 2012, the Grand Chamber of the European Court of Human Rights, in its first judgment addressing the police strategy of 'kettling', upheld the decision of the House of Lords.[231] The court started with the general observation that it could not be excluded 'that the use of containment and crowd control techniques could, in particular circumstances, give rise to an unjustified deprivation of liberty' in breach of Article 5(1) of the ECHR.[232] With regard to the case at hand, it observed that according to its previous case law the aim of a given measure is not one of the factors to be taken into account when deciding whether there has been a deprivation of liberty.[233] Nevertheless, it thought that 'the requirement to take account of the "type" and "manner of implementation" of the measure in question [. . .] enables it to have regard to the specific context and circumstances surrounding types of restriction other than the paradigm of confinement in a cell'.[234] With regard to the specific context of the case at hand, the court found that it was important to note that 'the measure was imposed to isolate and contain a large crowd, in volatile and dangerous conditions', that the imposition of an absolute cordon was the least intrusive and most effective means available to the police and that 'the police kept the situation constantly under close review'.[235]

This finding is, at the very least, highly questionable. As the court acknowledged itself, according to its own constant case law, the purpose or aim of a deprivation of liberty is not a relevant consideration for determining whether Article 5 of the ECHR is *engaged* (or not), nor are issues concerning the proportionality of the measure at hand. Instead, the purpose is relevant only in assessing whether the deprivation of liberty is *justified* (or not) based on one of the grounds listed in subparagraphs (a)-(f) of Article 5(1). By taking into account that the police imposed the cordon to control a large crowd in difficult conditions under the headings of 'type' and 'manner of implementation', the court seems to introduce considerations regarding the purpose of the measure through the backdoor. Yet, as a minority of three judges

[230] *Austin* v. *Commissioner of Police of the Metropolis*, [2009] UKHL 5, para. 34 (Lord Hope). For a thorough, critical discussion of the decision of the House of Lords, see Mead, 'Of Kettles, Cordons and Crowd Control' (2009).

[231] *Austin and others* v. *The United Kingdom* [GC], nos 39692/09; 40713/09; 41008/09, 15 March 2012, ECHR 2012.

[232] Ibid., para. 60. [233] Ibid., para. 58. [234] Ibid., para. 59. [235] Ibid., paras 66–7.

correctly observed in their dissenting opinion, there is no reason to treat such public-order motivated deprivations of liberty differently from any other kinds of deprivation of liberty.[236] As is clear from the statements of the European Court referred to in the previous section, what must be focused on is not the purpose of the measure but the concrete situation of those detained. In this regard, the minority was right to point out that where, as happened in the case at hand, people are held against their will for six to seven hours in a relatively small area together with some 3,000 other people, without access to toilet facilities, food or water, a compelling case can be made that there is a deprivation of liberty.[237] Indeed, even the majority of the court had to concede that 'the coercive nature of the containment within the cordon; its duration; and its effect on the applicants, in terms of physical discomfort and inability to leave Oxford Circus, point towards a deprivation of liberty'.[238] Accordingly, the majority did not seem to be completely at ease with its own findings. It stressed that its conclusion was 'based on the specific and exceptional facts of this case' and that '[h]ad it not remained necessary for the police to impose and maintain the cordon in order to prevent serious injury or damage, the "type" of the measure would have been different, and its coercive and restrictive nature might have been sufficient to bring it within Article 5'.[239] Remarkably, the Swiss Federal Supreme Court, also in a case concerning 'kettling', has explicitly rejected the notion propounded in *Austin* that the dangerousness of the situation is a relevant consideration for determining whether there is a deprivation of liberty.[240] In summary, for the reasons set out above, the correct conclusion would have been to hold that there *was* a deprivation of liberty in the case at hand and then to consider whether that deprivation could be justified based on one of the grounds listed in Article 5(1) of the ECHR.

The question as to the distinction between restrictions of movement and deprivations of liberty may also arise in the case of curfews. Also in this case it is important to consider the concrete situation of

[236] Ibid., dissenting opinion of judges Tulkens, Spielmann and Garlicki, para. 5.
[237] Ibid., dissenting opinion of judges Tulkens, Spielmann and Garlicki, para. 14.
[238] Ibid., para. 64. [239] Ibid., para. 68.
[240] See Urteile des Bundesgerichts 1C_350/2013, 1C_352/2013, 1C_354/2013 vom 22. Januar 2014, E. 3.6.2 ('Die spezifische Gefahrenlage ist bei der Beurteilung des öffentlichen Interesses und der Verhältnismässigkeit einer Freiheitsbeschränkung von Bedeutung, kann aber nicht dazu führen, dass bereits das Vorliegen einer Freiheitsbeschränkung von vornherein verneint wird.').

the person who is subject to the curfew. In *R (Lonergan)* v. *Lewes Crown Court* the Divisional Court held that an ASBO requirement that prevented the applicant from leaving, or travelling between, specified premises between the hours of 11.30 pm and 6.00 am is a restriction on movement but not a deprivation of liberty in the sense of Article 5 of the ECHR.[241] Given the duration and intensity of this particular curfew, this would seem to be the correct conclusion. In contrast, more draconian curfews, as they have often been imposed as part of terrorist control orders (or as they are now imposed as part of TPIMs), may engage Article 5, although courts have struggled to define the exact threshold. *Secretary of State for the Home Department* v. *JJ* concerned six suspected terrorists who, among other restrictions, were required to remain within their flats from 4.00 pm to 10.00 am (so for eighteen hours a day) and, outside of these hours, were not allowed to leave a pre-defined geographical area. The majority of the House of Lords found that the cumulative effect of these restrictions was that those subject to them found themselves in a situation akin to detention in an open prison and that there was thus a deprivation of liberty in the sense of Article 5.[242] In *Secretary of State for the Home Department* v. *MB*, on the other hand, their Lordships held that a fourteen-hour curfew (from 6.00 pm to 8.00 am) does not fall under Article 5.[243] It is difficult to define an exact time limit above which a curfew will amount to a deprivation of liberty. Lord Brown has suggested that the limit should be set at sixteen hours a day.[244] However, as pointed out above, the assessment must take account of all the individual features of the situation in which a person finds himself or herself and should therefore not only depend on the time a person is required not to leave the house, but also on factors such as the nature of the confined area or house, the degree of social isolation of the person, the restrictions that apply during the curfew period, the control imposed outside the curfew period, the effects of the curfew on the person and so on.[245]

241 *R (Lonergan)* v. *Lewes Crown Court*, [2005] 1 WLR 2570, para. 6.

242 *Secretary of State for the Home Department* v. *JJ*, [2007] UKHL 45, paras 24 (Lord Bingham), 62–3 (Baroness Hale), 105–6 (Lord Brown).

243 *Secretary of State for the Home Department* v. *MB*, [2007] UKHL 46, paras 11 (Lord Bingham), 78 (Lord Carswell), 89 (Lord Brown).

244 *Secretary of State for the Home Department* v. *JJ*, [2007] UKHL 45, para. 105.

245 For an overview of the case law of the European Court of Human Rights regarding curfews, see Harris/O'Boyle/Bates/Buckley, *Law of the ECHR* (2014), pp. 289–92.

5.2.5 Freedom of assembly

5.2.5.1 The right to freedom of assembly

The right to freedom of assembly is firmly established in international law. Article 20(1) of the UDHR and Article 21 of the ICCPR both guarantee the freedom of 'peaceful assembly', as does Article 15 of the CRC with regard to children. The right to freedom of assembly is also part of the key human rights instruments at the regional level, including the ADHR (Article 21) and the ECHR (Article 11).

Due to the incorporation of Article 11 of the ECHR into its domestic law, the United Kingdom now has a specific, positive guarantee of the freedom of assembly, rather than, as previously, only a 'residual freedom' encompassing that which had not been prohibited by the various Public Order Acts and other relevant legislation.[246] The scope of Article 11 of the ECHR is wide: it protects assemblies whether their purpose is of a political, religious or spiritual, cultural, social or some other nature and regardless of their form.[247] Even an assembly that 'may annoy or give offence to persons opposed to the ideas or claims that it is seeking to promote' is covered by it.[248] The only limitation is that, as is the case with the guarantees of the other human rights treaties, the assembly must be 'peaceful'. However, neither an assembly that involves a breach of domestic law, even if it is a flagrant one,[249] nor a public procession involving a real risk that it will result in disorder is automatically 'unpeaceful'.[250] Only those assemblies where the organisers and participants have violent intentions fall outside the scope of Article 11.[251] Freedom of assembly includes the freedom to organise an assembly according to one's wishes and to choose its content, time and place.[252] Although there is, in general, no right to use a particular public place for an assembly, such a right may

[246] On the historical development of the freedom of assembly in the United Kingdom, see e.g. Mead, *The New Law of Peaceful Protest* (2010), pp. 4–6, 26–9; Thurnheer, *Demonstrationsfreiheit in England und der Schweiz* (2010), pp. 83–92.

[247] For good summaries of the Strasbourg case law, see Harris/O'Boyle/Bates/Buckley, *Law of the ECHR* (2014), p. 711; Peters/Altwicker, *Europäische Menschenrechtskonvention* (2012), pp. 105–6; Mead, *The New Law of Peaceful Protest* (2010), pp. 63–76.

[248] *Plattform Ärzte für das Leben* v. *Austria*, no. 10126/82, 21 June 1988, Series A no. 139, para. 32.

[249] See *Cissé* v. *France*, no. 51346/99, 9 April 2002, ECHR 2002-III, 19, paras 35–40.

[250] See *Christians against Racism and Fascism* v. *United Kingdom*, no. 8440/78, admissibility decision of 16 July 1980, 21 DR 138, p. 148.

[251] *Stankov and the United Macedonian Organisation Ilinden* v. *Bulgaria*, nos 29221/95; 29225/95, 2 October 2001, ECHR 2001-IX, 273, para. 77.

[252] Barendt, *Freedom of Speech* (2005), p. 272.

arise if the location of the assembly is crucial to its purpose.[253] The Strasbourg institutions have stressed that the freedom of assembly is a foundational element of a democratic society.[254] Especially for members of smaller political groups who lack direct access to the mass media, marches, demonstrations, sit-ins and other public meetings may be a crucial – and possibly the only – tool to attract public attention.[255]

The Swiss Federal Constitution contains in Article 22 a guarantee of the freedom of assembly that largely corresponds to the respective guarantees of the ECHR and the ICCPR.[256] According to the Federal Supreme Court, Article 22 protects gatherings of persons, in all their various forms, which have a certain degree of organisation and serve the purpose of exchanging, expressing or forming ideas, understood in a broad sense.[257] Thus, a random gathering of people, such as a crowd of onlookers at the site of an accident or a group of persons happening to eat out in the same restaurant, does not qualify as an assembly in the sense of Article 22.[258] However, as long as there is a minimal degree of organisation, which will generally already follow from the fact that a common objective is pursued, even very spontaneous meetings are protected.[259] The requirement that there must be some communicative purpose excludes from the scope of Article 22 events that are purely commercial or only meant to entertain people, such as sports events.[260] In line with the wording of the respective international guarantees, the Federal Supreme Court limits the scope of Article 22 to 'peaceful' assemblies.[261] Thus, assemblies can be prohibited if there are direct calls for violence and there is a concrete threat to public order.[262] In practice, the court has been rather easily satisfied that these

253 *United Macedonian Organisation Ilinden and Ivanov* v. *Bulgaria*, no. 44079/98, 20 October 2005, para. 103; *Stankov and the United Macedonian Organisation Ilinden* v. *Bulgaria*, nos 29221/95; 29225/95, 2 October 2001, ECHR 2001-IX, 273, para. 109.

254 *Güneri et autres c. Turquie*, nos 42853/98; 43609/98; 44291/98, 12 July 2005, para. 76 (only available in French); *Rassemblement jurassien & Unité jurasienne* v. *Switzerland*, no. 8191/78, admissibility decision of 10 October 1979, 17 DR 93, p. 119.

255 For an example see *Cissé* v. *France*, no. 51346/99, 9 April 2002, ECHR 2002-III, 19.

256 See BGE 127 I 164, 172–4 (2001).

257 Ibid., 168 ('verschiedenste Formen des Zusammenfindens von Menschen im Rahmen einer gewissen Organisation mit einem weit verstandenen gegenseitig meinungsbildenden oder meinungsäussernden Zweck').

258 See Kiener/Kälin, *Grundrechte* (2013), p. 251; Malinverni, *La liberté de réunion* (1981), pp. 9–11.

259 Errass, 'Art. 22' (2014), 506; Zimmerli, 'Versammlungsfreiheit' (2007), 477.

260 See Kiener/Kälin, *Grundrechte* (2013), p. 251–2; Zimmerli, 'Versammlungsfreiheit' (2007), 477; Malinverni, *La liberté de réunion* (1981), pp. 11–12.

261 BGE 132 I 256, 259 (2006); BGE 127 I 164, 170 (2001); BGE 111 Ia 322, 322 (1985).

262 BGE 127 I 164, 170 (2001); BGE 58 I 84, 90–91 (1932).

requirements for prohibitions are met.[263] The freedom of assembly implies a right to have access to a part of public space that can accommodate for the assembly's possible need for publicity.[264] Although there is no right to hold an assembly at a place of one's choosing,[265] in some cases the communicative purpose of the assembly may require that it be held in a specific location.[266] Just as the Strasbourg institutions, the Federal Supreme Court has emphasised the crucial importance of the freedom of assembly for a democratic society.[267] It has pointed out explicitly that minorities that do not have the possibility to make themselves sufficiently heard through the existing democratic channels and that lack the means to reach the broad public are particularly reliant on the possibility to hold demonstrations in public places in order to draw public attention to an issue.[268] According to the court, political demonstrations, as assemblies with a specific expressive function, fall within the scope of protection of both the freedom of assembly and the freedom of expression.[269]

The First Amendment to the US Constitution guarantees 'the right of the people peaceably to assemble'. Despite this wording, the freedom of assembly is in the United States often also described, rather confusingly, as 'freedom of association'.[270] As in the other jurisdictions, a broad range of forms of assembly, including marches, demonstrations, picketing and so on, fall within the scope of this guarantee.[271] The freedom of assembly is not limited to gatherings that have a political objective but extends to gatherings for almost any purpose, be it social, economic, educational or cultural.[272] However, there must be some expressive element and a degree of organisation involved for the gathering to fall within the scope of the First Amendment.[273] Thus, 'chance encounters in dance-halls' are not protected.[274] Nor does the freedom of assembly extend to assemblies that are not 'peaceable', that is, assemblies that incite to violence or advocate unlawful methods.[275] The Supreme Court has

263 See BGE 127 I 164, 176 (2001). For criticism of the Federal Supreme Court's approach, see Kiener/Kälin, *Grundrechte* (2013), p. 253; Müller/Schefer, *Grundrechte in der Schweiz* (2008), pp. 584–5; Wyss, 'Appell und Abschreckung' (2002), 402–4.

264 BGE 124 I 267, 271–2 (1998). 265 Ibid., 272. 266 BGE 132 I 256, 260–61 (2006).

267 BGE 96 I 219, 223–4 (1970). 268 BGE 100 Ia 392, 400 (1974).

269 BGE 132 I 256, 258–60 (2006); 127 I 164, 167–8 (2001). See on this point Malinverni, *La liberté de réunion* (1981), pp. 26–8.

270 See Sullivan/Feldman, *Constitutional Law* (2013), p. 1345. 271 Ibid., pp. 1279–92.

272 *Roberts* v. *United States Jaycees*, 468 U.S. 609, 622 (1984); *Griswold* v. *Connecticut*, 381 U.S. 479, 482 (1965).

273 *City of Dallas* v. *Stanglin*, 490 U.S. 19, 24–5 (1989). 274 Ibid., 25.

275 *De Jonge* v. *State of Oregon*, 299 U.S. 353, 363–5 (1937).

pointed out that it is by upholding the freedom of assembly that resort to violence can be prevented in the first place:

> The greater the importance of safeguarding the community from incitements to the overthrow of our institutions by force and violence, the more imperative is the need to preserve inviolate the constitutional rights of free speech, free press and free assembly in order to maintain the opportunity for free political discussion, to the end that government may be responsive to the will of the people and that changes, if desired, may be obtained by peaceful means. Therein lies the security of the Republic, the very foundation of constitutional government.[276]

The guarantee of the First Amendment includes a right to freely use 'traditional public fora' such as streets, sidewalks, squares and parks for communicative purposes.[277]

5.2.5.2 Exclusion from public space and freedom of assembly

Some exclusion measures do not prevent the presence of people, as individuals, in public space, but instead are specifically directed against *gatherings* in public places. It is in these cases that guarantees of the freedom of assembly are especially relevant. In fact, depending on the particular circumstances of the case and the jurisdiction, the right to freedom of assembly may be the only right providing protection in such situations. Accordingly, courts have focused on the issue of freedom of assembly to review, for example: dispersal orders issued under the British Anti-social Behaviour Act 2003 on the basis that members of the public were 'intimidated, harassed, alarmed or distressed as a result of the presence or behaviour of groups of two or more persons in public places';[278] the ordinance of the City of Cincinnati that made it unlawful for three or more persons to assemble on the streets and conduct themselves in a manner annoying to persons passing by;[279] the curfew introduced by the Swiss municipality of Dänikon that prevented children of compulsory school age from assembling in groups in public places after 10 pm;[280] and the exclusion orders issued in the City of Berne preventing those concerned from assembling in groups that consume alcohol.[281]

[276] Ibid., 365. [277] *Hague* v. *CIO*, 307 U.S. 496, 515 (1939).

[278] *R (Singh)* v. *Chief Constable of the West Midlands*, [2006] EWCA Civ 1118.

[279] *Coates* v. *City of Cincinnati*, 402 U.S. 611 (1971). See Section 4.3.2.1.

[280] Urteil des Verwaltungsgerichts des Kantons Zürich VB.2009.00055 vom 30. April 2009, E. 5.1. See Section 5.2.3.2.

[281] BGE 132 I 49, 56–7 (2006). See Sections 4.3.2.1 and 5.2.2.2.

The perhaps most typical examples of exclusion measures falling into this category, however, are those that prohibit demonstrations in certain parts of public space. The effective ban on manifestations on the square in front of the parliament building in Berne during paraliamentary sessions, for example, specifically targets assemblies of people: only events attended by several persons fall under the relevant definition of 'manifestation'.[282] Other similar measures, such as the 'buffer zones' around abortion clinics in the United States,[283] are directed more broadly against any form of political protest, be it by individuals or groups. All of these measures amount to an interference with the freedom of assembly insofar as they prevent people from holding demonstrations that are not intended to incite to violence. In addition, they engage the freedom of expression.[284]

However, also measures that prohibit mere presence in (parts of) public space may interfere with the freedom of assembly. Since such measures also indirectly prevent people from assembling in the relevant area with others, guarantees of the freedom of assembly are engaged by any exclusion measure that prevents access to this area and is imposed on someone who wants to peacefully meet there with others. This will regularly be the case for juvenile (or other) curfews, area bans imposed on football supporters and drug-exclusion zones. In these cases, the right to freedom of assembly may be invoked alongside the right to freedom of movement.

It is important to note that the scope of protection of the freedom of assembly extends beyond assemblies that support some political cause or raise some issue of public concern. Therefore, also juvenile curfews or exclusion orders directed against anti-social behaviour constitute interferences with the freedom of assembly. The Swiss Federal Supreme Court, in the case of the exclusion orders in the City of Berne, explicitly held that it was sufficient that those subject to these orders met to entertain themselves and to maintain their personal relationships; this made their assembly more than just a random gathering or a crowd of onlookers. Article 22 of the Federal Constitution, the court concluded, applied even if there was no political objective and no intention to approach third persons.[285] In line with this reasoning, the Administrative Court of the Canton of Zurich held that the curfew

[282] Reglement der Stadt Bern über Kundgebungen auf öffentlichem Grund vom 20. Oktober 2005 (Kundgebungsreglement; KgR; SSSB 143.1), Art. 1(3).

[283] See Section 3.3.3.1. [284] See Section 5.2.6. [285] BGE 132 I 49, 57 (2006).

introduced in Dänikon amounted to an interference with the freedom of assembly, even if the meetings of the juveniles were not organised in advance and only served to entertain.[286] Several US courts have similarly concluded that juvenile curfews engage the freedom of assembly guaranteed by the First Amendment. The US Court of Appeals for the Fifth Circuit, for instance, stated that 'the right to associate freely [. . .] is not limited to political associations but includes associations for social, legal, or economic purposes'.[287] As the curfew at issue effectively prevented juveniles from attending 'associational activities' such as religious or school meetings, theatre or sporting events and organised dances, the court found that there was an interference with the freedom of assembly.[288] Similarly, a district court held that a juvenile curfew constitutes a restriction of the freedom of assembly guaranteed by the First Amendment, even if the youths are 'on the street simply to socialize or talk with other youths'.[289] Finally, the UN Committee on the Rights of the Child has expressed its concern that the British juvenile curfew powers may be incompatible with Article 15 of the CRC, guaranteeing children's freedom of peaceful assembly.[290] Even exclusion measures directed against football supporters may infringe on the freedom of assembly if the supporters do not just happen to attend the same game but attend it as a group. Accordingly, the Swiss Federal Supreme Court has acknowledged that area bans imposed on football supporters may engage the freedom of assembly if they meet to attend together a sports event, possibly travel there together and there is thus some element of organisation involved.[291]

The *seriousness* of an interference with the freedom of assembly through exclusion from public space will depend on all the specific factors relating to the case at hand, including the duration of the measure, its geographical scope, its exact terms and so on. As already explained above in the context of the guarantee of personal liberty, in the case of the Bernese exclusion orders the Federal Supreme Court correctly characterised the interference as not serious as the prohibition of assembly had a narrowly defined geographical scope and was limited to gatherings that

[286] Urteil des Verwaltungsgerichts des Kantons Zürich VB.2009.00055 vom 30. April 2009, E. 5.1.

[287] *Johnson* v. *City of Opelousas*, 658 F.2d 1065, 1072 (5th Cir. 1981). [288] Ibid.

[289] *Bykofsky* v. *Borough of Middletown*, 401 F.Supp. 1242, 1258 and 1260 (D.C. Pa. 1975).

[290] UN Committee on the Rights of the Child, Concluding observations: United Kingdom, 3 October 2008, UN Doc. CRC/C/GBR/CO/4, paras 34–5.

[291] BGE 137 I 31, 44–5 (2010).

involved consumption of alcohol.[292] A typical juvenile night-time curfew, in contrast, must be qualified as a serious interference with the freedom of assembly if it covers all public places and is in force for several years.[293] Again, the exact terms of the curfew have to be taken into account in making this determination. A US district court came to the conclusion that a curfew ordinance that contained an exception, allowing juveniles to exercise their rights of assembly, association and free expression provided they give advance notice to the authorities, 'restricts only slightly' the freedom of assembly.[294]

5.2.6 *Freedom of expression*

5.2.6.1 The right to freedom of expression

Article 19 of the UDHR, Article 19(2) of the ICCPR and Article 13 of the CRC all guarantee the right to freedom of expression. The ICCPR defines the freedom of expression as 'freedom to seek, receive and impart information and ideas of all kinds, regardless of frontiers, either orally, in writing or in print, in the form of art, or through any other media of his choice'. The freedom of expression is also guaranteed by all the major regional human rights instruments, including Article 10 of the ECHR and Article 4 of the ADHR.

Again, due to its incorporation into the domestic law of the United Kingdom, the guarantee of the ECHR is particularly relevant for the present context. According to the text of Article 10(1), the freedom of expression includes 'freedom to hold opinions and to receive and impart information and ideas without interference by public authority and regardless of frontiers'. The European Court of Human Rights characterises freedom of expression as 'one of the essential foundations of [a democratic] society' and thus attaches central importance to it.[295] This sentiment is reflected in the case law of English courts. Lord Steyn, for example, has described freedom of expression as 'the lifeblood of democracy'.[296] Accordingly, its scope of protection is defined

[292] BGE 132 I 49, 63–4 (2006).
[293] See also Gerber Jenni, ' "Abendausgang Kinder" ' (2006), 853.
[294] *Bykofsky* v. *Borough of Middletown*, 401 F.Supp. 1242, 1258 (D.C. Pa. 1975).
[295] *Handyside* v. *The United Kingdom*, no. 5493/72, 7 December 1976, Series A no. 24, para. 49.
[296] *R* v. *Secretary of State for the Home Department, ex parte Simms*, [2000] 2 AC 115, 126.

broadly.[297] All forms and means of expression are protected,[298] including symbolic actions.[299] Not only ideas and opinions fall within the scope of Article 10 but also 'information', meaning that also mere statements of fact are covered.[300] Nor does the nature of the content matter: Article 10 is not limited to political expression but extends to artistic and commercial expression.[301] However, political expression and expression designed to contribute to public debate attract particularly strong protection.[302] Furthermore, Article 10 is applicable 'not only to information or ideas that are favourably received or regarded as inoffensive or as a matter of indifference, but also to those that offend, shock or disturb the State or any sector of the population'.[303] Even expressions that may incite to violence fall within the scope of protection of Article 10, so that any restrictions have to meet the limitation requirements of Article 10(2).[304]

The Federal Constitution of Switzerland contains a general guarantee of the freedom of expression, defined as the freedom to form, express and impart opinions without interference, in Articles 16(1) and 16(2). In addition, there is a specific guarantee of the freedom of information, that is, the freedom to receive, gather and disseminate information, in Articles 16(1) and 16(3). Article 17 guarantees the freedom of the media, in particular the press, radio and television. These guarantees are largely congruent with Article 10 of the ECHR.[305] Just as the European Court of Human Rights, the Federal Supreme Court has stressed that freedom of expression is the foundation of any democratic state and that it therefore deserves to be given 'a privileged treatment' by the authorities.[306] Any

[297] See e.g. *Nilsen and Johnsen* v. *Norway*, no. 23118/93, 25 November 1999, ECHR 1999-VIII, 57, para. 43; *Markt Intern Verlag GmbH and Klaus Beermann* v. *Germany*, no. 10572/83, 20 November 1989, Series A no. 165, para. 26.

[298] See *Sokolowski* v. *Poland*, no. 75955/01, 29 March 2005, para. 44.

[299] See *Hashman and Harrup* v. *The United Kingdom* [GC], no. 25594/94, 25 November 1999, ECHR 1999-VIII, 1, para. 28; *Steel and others* v. *The United Kingdom*, no. 24838/94, 23 September 1998, ECHR 1998-VII, 2719, para. 92.

[300] *Barthold* v. *Germany*, no. 8734/79, 25 March 1985, Series A no. 90, para. 42.

[301] For an overview of the different categories of expression, see Harris/O'Boyle/Bates/Buckley, *Law of the ECHR* (2014), pp. 629–39.

[302] E.g. *Stoll* v. *Switzerland* [GC], no. 69698/01, 10 December 2007, ECHR 2007-V, 267, para. 106; *Castells* v. *Spain*, no. 11798/85, 23 April 1992, Series A no. 236, para. 42.

[303] *Handyside* v. *The United Kingdom*, no. 5493/72, 7 December 1976, Series A no. 24, para. 49.

[304] For a summary of the relevant case law of the European Court, which mainly relates to Turkey, see Harris/O'Boyle/Bates/Buckley, *Law of the ECHR* (2014), pp. 626–9.

[305] See Urteil des Bundesgerichts vom 17. Februar 1987, in: (1988) 44 *Schweizerisches Jahrbuch für internationales Recht* 335. See also BGE 108 Ia 172, 175 (1982).

[306] BGE 96 I 586, 592 (1970).

forms of expression and means of communication are protected.[307] The term 'opinion' of Articles 16(1) and 16(2) is interpreted broadly to include, for example, rather thoughtless or emotional comments.[308] As in the case of the ECHR, expressions are protected regardless of the nature of their content, although particularly strong protection is afforded to discussion of political questions and issues of public concern.[309] The Federal Supreme Court has held that also extreme and provocative ideas that may be shocking to many deserve to be protected.[310] Unlike Article 10 of the ECHR, however, according to the court Article 16 of the Federal Constitution only protects non-commercial expression, whereas expressions with a commercial content falls within the scope of Article 27, the guarantee of economic freedom.[311]

The First Amendment to the US Constitution guarantees the 'freedom of speech' and the freedom of the press. As courts in the other jurisdictions, US courts have highlighted the crucial role that freedom of expression plays in a democratic society. The Supreme Court has proclaimed that 'freedom to think as you will and to speak as you think are means indispensable to the discovery and spread of political truth'.[312] Therefore, these freedoms, the court has suggested, enjoy 'a preferred position'.[313] Even though the First Amendment does not use the term 'expression' but the narrower term 'speech', the US courts have interpreted its scope broadly, so as to give protection to a similarly wide range of conduct as that under the ECHR and Swiss law. In particular, also a diverse variety of non-verbal expressions, referred to as 'symbolic speech', are protected by the First Amendment.[314] In principle, all expressions, whatever their content, fall within the scope of the First Amendment, including speech that is offensive, provocative or even racist.[315] However, the Supreme Court has developed a complex system of different categories of speech to

[307] Kiener/Kälin, *Grundrechte* (2013), p. 204; Malinverni, 'Meinungs-, Medien- und Informationsfreiheit' (2007), 387–8.

[308] See Müller/Schefer, *Grundrechte in der Schweiz* (2008), p. 358.

[309] See e.g. BGE 131 IV 23, 28 (2004).

[310] Urteil des Bundesgerichts 1C_9/2012 vom 7. Mai 2012, E. 2.1; BGE 131 IV 23, 28 (2004); BGE 116 Ib 37, 48 (1990).

[311] BGE 128 I 295, 308 (2002); BGE 125 I 417, 420 (1999).

[312] *Whitney* v. *California*, 274 U.S. 357, 375 (1927).

[313] *Murdock* v. *Pennsylvania*, 319 U.S. 105, 115 (1943).

[314] See e.g. *Texas* v. *Johnson*, 491 U.S. 397 (1989) (burning of the US flag); *Clark* v. *Community for Creative Non-Violence*, 468 U.S. 288 (1984) (sleeping in a park); *United States* v. *O'Brien*, 391 U.S. 367 (1968) (burning of a military draft card).

[315] *R.A.V.* v. *St. Paul*, 505 U.S. 377, 383 (1992) (stating that no 'categories of speech [are] entirely invisible to the Constitution').

which it applies different tests to evaluate the permissibility of restrictions. For example, political expression and 'pure speech' are given particularly strong protection, whereas commercial speech, 'symbolic conduct' and inflammatory speech are protected less strictly.[316]

5.2.6.2 Exclusion from public space and freedom of expression

Section 3.3.3 describes numerous exclusion measures that are specifically directed against political protest. All of these measures essentially prevent people from protesting where they would like to protest. Since, as explained in Sections 2.1 and 2.4, people in all three states examined have, as a general rule, the right to access and use public streets and squares for a range of activities, including communicating their views to others, these measures amount to an interference with the freedom of expression. Thus, for example, the US Supreme Court has confirmed that the establishment of 'buffer zones' prohibiting protest outside abortion clinics constitutes a restriction of the freedom of expression,[317] as has the European Commission of Human Rights.[318] The Swiss Federal Supreme Court has come to the same conclusion with regard to a ban on political manifestations on the square in front of a monastery.[319] If the protest, or planned protest, at issue is a common endeavour of several persons rather than a protest by an individual actor, then guarantees of the freedom of assembly will be engaged in addition to the freedom of expression.

The right to freedom of expression will also be engaged if exclusion from public space prevents the gathering or dissemination of information. This was the case in *Gsell*. As explained before, Gsell was a journalist who wanted to observe, and report on, the 2001 WEF. The Swiss Federal Supreme Court held that there could be no doubt that by denying him access to Davos, the police infringed on Gsell's rights to freedom of information according to Articles 16(1) and 16(3) and freedom of the press according to Article 17 of the Federal Constitution. The court

316 For an overview, see e.g. Cohen/Danelski/Yalof, *Constitutional Law* (2007), pp. 355, 413–51, 273–309, 310–54; Nowak/Rotunda, *Constitutional Law* (2004), pp. 1130–43, 1176–9, 1227–62, 1283–92, 1349–59.

317 *McCullen* v. *Coakley*, 573 U.S. _ (2014), Docket No. 12-1168; *Hill* v. *Colorado*, 530 U.S. 703 (2000); *Schenck* v. *Pro-Choice Network of Western New York*, 519 U.S. 357 (1997); *Madsen* v. *Women's Health Center*, 512 U.S. 753 (1996).

318 *Van den Dungen* v. *The Netherlands*, no. 22838/93, admissibility decision of 22 February 1995, para. 2.

319 BGE 124 I 267, 269 (1998).

found that, in addition, there was an interference with Article 10 of the ECHR and Article 19 of the ICCPR.[320] The European Court of Human Rights came to the same conclusion; it observed that even though Gsell was not singled out because he was a journalist, the general ban of access to Davos nevertheless prevented him from covering the events there and therefore amounted to an interference with Article 10 of the ECHR.[321]

This, of course, holds true for *any* exclusion measure: it is not necessary for the right to freedom of expression to be engaged that the authorities *intended* to suppress free expression. Any exclusion measure will amount to an interference with this right if its effect, even if only indirectly, is to inhibit the free expression of ideas or gathering or dissemination of information. For example, curfews that completely prohibit persons below a certain age from being on the streets after a certain hour make it impossible for them to attend council meetings, marches, prayer vigils or other political events that last longer than the starting time of the curfew. An Ohio court pointed out that 'a minor could not even attend the city council meetings if they ran past 10:30 (which they frequently do) to express his views on the necessity to repeal the curfew ordinance'.[322] Several courts in the United States have therefore correctly concluded that juvenile curfews that do not provide for relevant exceptions amount to an interference with the freedom of speech guaranteed by the First Amendment.[323]

Exclusion measures that prevent people from protesting where they would like to protest will regularly have to be qualified as *serious* interferences with the freedom of expression. First, the exact location of a political protest is a crucial factor determining the degree of attention it attracts and thus the impact it has.[324] In the case of events such as the WTO conference in Seattle, the WEF in Davos or the Olympic Games in London, for example, protest activities must be visible to those attending these events and the media present there to serve their purpose, namely, to draw the attention of the attendees and the public to the viewpoints of the protesters. In such cases, preventing demonstrations from taking

320 BGE 130 I 369, 374–5 (2004).

321 *Gsell c. Suisse*, no. 12675/05, 8 October 2009, para. 49 (only available in French).

322 *In re Mosier*, 394 N.E.2d 368, 372 (Ohio C.P. 1978).

323 *Hodgkins* v. *Peterson*, 355 F.3d 1048, 1057–9 (7th Cir. 2004); *Nunez* v. *City of San Diego*, 114 F.3d 935, 949–51 (9th Cir. 1997); *Maquoketa* v. *Russell*, 484 N.W.2d 179, 185–6 (Iowa 1992); *In re Mosier*, 394 N.E.2d 368, 372 (Ohio C.P. 1978); *Bykofsky* v. *Borough of Middletown*, 401 F.Supp. 1242, 1258 (D.C. Pa. 1975).

324 Parkinson, *Democracy and Public Space* (2012), pp. 42–4.

place in the vicinity of the venues may have an almost equally inhibiting effect as completely banning them. In contrast, a narrowly circumscribed 'buffer zone' of no more than a few meters around an abortion clinic may still allow protesters to convey their message to patients and clinic employees as well as the wider public. Second, exclusion measures directed against political protest often affect a very significant number of persons. Several tens of thousands people wanted to demonstrate against the WTO in Seattle, for example. Third and finally, as explained above, it is recognised in all three states at issue that political expression plays a crucial function in a democratic society and therefore deserves particularly strong protection.

The last point also applies to exclusion measures that interfere with the ability of journalists to follow, and report on, political events. Nevertheless, in the case of *Gsell* the Swiss Federal Supreme Court qualified the order denying him access to Davos as a 'not very grave' interference.[325] While the court acknowledged that the access ban had more serious consequences for Gsell than, for example, a tourist (who would only be restricted in his or her freedom of movement), it argued that he was not denied access to Davos for the whole duration of the WEF and so could have travelled there at a later time to report on the events.[326] This is not a convincing argument. The freedom of the press includes the freedom of journalists to decide which events, or which aspects of an event, they want to follow because they consider them as newsworthy.[327] An interference is not automatically less serious only because a journalist has the opportunity to cover an event at a different point in time not chosen by him or her. In fact, given the speed of today's media, a delay in journalistic research and, as a consequence, reporting may render publication of the relevant news item almost completely worthless.

5.2.7 *Respect for family life*

5.2.7.1 The right to respect for family life

The right to respect for family life is guaranteed by Article 12 of the UDHR, Articles 17 and 23 of the ICCPR, Article 16 of the CRC, Article 8 of the ECHR and Article 5 of the ADHR. The concept of 'family'

325 BGE 130 I 369, 386 (2004) ('lassen diese Umstände den konkreten Eingriff in die Meinungsfreiheit doch als wenig gravierend erscheinen').

326 Ibid., 385–6.

327 See *Dammann c. Suisse*, no. 77551/01, 25 April 2006, para. 52 (only available in French).

according to Article 8 of the ECHR includes more than the traditional family of husband, wife and children: not only does it extend to other formal relationships such as those between siblings and grandparents and grandchildren, it also covers de facto unions between, for example, unmarried partners.[328] Thus, the existence of family life needs to be determined based on the substance and reality of the relationships, though cohabitation is not essential.[329] Article 8 protects the right of the members of the family defined in this way to 'lead a normal family life'[330] and 'enjoy each other's company'.[331]

In Switzerland, an almost identically worded guarantee of respect for family life is found in Article 13(1) of the Federal Constitution. The scope of protection of this provision largely corresponds to that of Article 8 of the ECHR and thus covers a broadly defined concept of 'family life'.[332]

In the United States, according to the Supreme Court, one fundamental element of personal liberty protected by the due process clause is the freedom 'to enter into and maintain certain intimate human relationships'.[333] At the core of this so-called 'freedom of intimate association' is the freedom to maintain family relationships without undue interference by the state.[334] While the Supreme Court has not exactly defined the concept of 'family' or the degree of protection different family relationships will receive, it has suggested that protection extends beyond the nuclear family to grandparents, uncles, aunts and cousins.[335]

5.2.7.2 Exclusion from public space and respect for family life

The most obvious way in which exclusion from public space may interfere with the right to respect for family life is by preventing those concerned from visiting their family members. As explained in Section 3.3, football supporters, drug addicts, sex offenders and those who allegedly have engaged in anti-social behaviour, among others, can

[328] *Johnston* v. *Ireland*, no. 9697/82, 18 December 1986, Series A no. 112, paras 55–6. See generally Rainey/Wicks/White, *The European Convention on Human Rights* (2014), pp. 335–8; Grabenwarter/Pabel, *Europäische Menschenrechtskonvention* (2012), pp. 235–7; Peters/Altwicker, *Europäische Menschenrechtskonvention* (2012), pp. 205–6; Meyer-Ladewig, *Europäische Menschenrechtskonvention* (2011), pp. 207–9.

[329] *Berrehab* v. *The Netherlands*, no. 10730/84, 21 June 1988, Series A no. 138, para. 21.

[330] *Marckx* v. *Belgium*, no. 6833/74, 13 June 1979, Series A no. 31, para. 31.

[331] *Olsson* v. *Sweden (No. 1)*, no. 10465/83, 24 March 1988, Series A no. 130, para. 59.

[332] See e.g. Müller/Schefer, *Grundrechte in der Schweiz* (2008), pp. 234–8; Schweizer, 'Recht auf Ehe und Familie' (2007), 339–45.

[333] *Roberts* v. *United States Jaycees*, 468 U.S. 609, 617–18 (1984). [334] Ibid., 618–20.

[335] *Moore* v. *City of East Cleveland*, 431 U.S. 494, 504 (1976).

be banned from accessing what are often quite large zones, typically in inner-city areas. If those subject to these measures happen to have family members in the respective zones, they may be prevented from 'enjoying their company' and maintaining contact with them. For example, as explained in Chapter 1, Patricia Johnson was ordered not to enter the 'drug-exclusion zone' of Over-the-Rhine, a Cincinnati neighbourhood of 10,000 residents, for three months.[336] One of her daughters and her grandchildren, two of which she regularly took to school, lived in the zone. The US Court of Appeals for the Sixth Circuit held that Johnson 'has a fundamental freedom of association right to participate in the upbringing of her grandchildren', which constitutes a fundamental liberty protected by the due process clause of the Fourteenth Amendment, and that the drug-exclusion order prevented her from exercising this right.[337] Similar issues may be raised by exclusion orders issued under the Swiss Federal Act on Foreign Nationals. Since these orders often extend to the territory of a whole city or even to the whole of a canton,[338] they may prevent those subject to such orders from living with their family.[339] Sexual risk orders, football banning orders, IPNAs and CBOs as they exist in the United Kingdom may have similar effects. In Leeds, for instance, an ASBO was imposed on a man with a drinking problem, prohibiting him from accessing a certain zone in order to stop him from harassing and intimidating his neighbours. As that exclusion zone included the home of his partner, the Court of Appeal acknowledged that there was an interference with his right to respect for family life guaranteed by Article 8 of the ECHR.[340] The converse problem, as it were, arises when an exclusion measure effectively prevents family members from visiting the person subject to that measure. This may be the case, for example, with a curfew imposed as part of a terrorist control order or TPIM.[341]

5.2.8 *Other fundamental rights*

The fundamental rights discussed in the previous sections are those that are most typically engaged by exclusion from public space. However, spatial exclusion may infringe on a wide range of further rights. This

[336] *Johnson* v. *Cincinnati*, 310 F.3d 484 (6th Cir. 2002). [337] Ibid., 500–2.
[338] See Section 3.4.3.1.
[339] See e.g. Urteil des Kantonsgerichts Graubünden vom 7. April 2011, SK2 11 12.
[340] *Leeds City Council* v. *Fawcett*, [2008] EWCA Civ 597.
[341] See *Secretary of State for the Home Department* v. *AP*, [2010] UKSC 24.

section highlights some of these additional potential infringements, without discussing them in detail as they are less relevant in practice.

Juvenile curfews may make it impossible for those below the relevant age to attend religious services that end after the curfew hour, an issue that has been raised repeatedly before US courts.[342] The same problem has arisen in the United Kingdom in connection with curfews imposed as part of terrorist control orders.[343] Similarly, people who are banned from certain areas may be prevented from attending activities of their religious communities if these take place within the banned area. In such cases, there will be an infringement with the right to freedom of religion, which is guaranteed by international law[344] as well as the domestic law of Switzerland,[345] the United States[346] and the United Kingdom[347] and which includes the freedom to manifest one's religion in public and in community with others.

In a similar way, the imposition of exclusion zones and curfews may prevent people from taking part in the activities of associations, of which they are members. This amounts to an interference with the right to freedom of association, which is also guaranteed by relevant international legal instruments[348] as well as the domestic law of all three states at issue.[349]

Moreover, exclusion from certain parts of public space may make it impossible for people to access particular educational institutions, to get to their place of work or to engage in certain professional activities.[350] Such restrictions may amount to interferences with the right to education guaranteed by international law,[351] including Protocol No. 1 to the ECHR,[352] which has been ratified by the United Kingdom,[353] economic liberties as they are guaranteed by the domestic law of Switzerland[354] and

342 *Hodgkins* v. *Peterson*, 355 F.3d 1048, 1058 (7th Cir. 2004); *Maquoketa* v. *Russell*, 484 N.W.2d 179, 185 (Iowa 1992); *Waters* v. *Barry*, 711 F.Supp. 1125, 1134 (D.D.C. 1989); *Johnson* v. *City of Opelousas*, 658 F.2d 1065, 1072–3 (5th Cir. 1981); *In re Mosier*, 394 N.E.2d 368, 372 (Ohio C.P. 1978).

343 *Secretary of State for the Home Department* v. *AP*, [2008] EWHC 2001 (Admin), para. 98; *AF* v. *Secretary of State for the Home Department*, [2007] EWHC 2001 (Admin).

344 UDHR, Art. 18; ICCPR, Art. 18; CRC, Art. 14; ADHR, Art. 3; ECHR, Art. 9.

345 BV, Art. 15. 346 US Constitution, First Amendment. 347 ECHR, Art. 9.

348 UDHR, Art. 20; ICCPR, Art. 22; CRC, Art. 15; ADHR, Art. 22; ECHR, Art. 11.

349 BV, Art. 23; US Constitution, First Amendment; ECHR, Art. 11.

350 See e.g. Beckett/Herbert, *Banished* (2010), p. 121.

351 UDHR, Art. 26; ICESCR, Art. 13; CRC, Art. 28; ADHR, Art. 12.

352 Protocol No. 1 to the ECHR, Art. 2.

353 The United Kingdom signed 20 March 1952 and ratified 3 November 1952.

354 BV, Art. 27.

the United States[355] or the right to work guaranteed by international law.[356]

Finally, even political rights[357] may be engaged if exclusion measures prevent people from attending and thus voting in, for example, city council meetings or caucuses.[358]

5.2.9 Result

In Switzerland and the United States, where the respective constitutions contain comprehensive catalogues of protected rights that include broadly defined guarantees of personal liberty, almost any exclusion measure will constitute an interference with at least one of these rights. The question then is less whether there is an interference, but more which rights exactly are engaged. In the United Kingdom, it is more difficult to obtain effective protection against exclusion measures as it must be demonstrated that one of the guarantees contained in the more limited rights catalogue of the ECHR is engaged. In particular, there is no effective protection of the freedom of movement in the United Kingdom, as the only explicit positive guarantee of this freedom is that of Article 12(1) of the ICCPR, which has not been incorporated into domestic law. However, Article 8 of the ECHR can, at least to some extent, compensate for this lack of protection: its scope has been defined very broadly and will thus encompass any exclusion measure that affects a person's right to develop his or her personality or to develop personal ties with others.

Many instances of exclusion from public space fall within the scope of protection of several fundamental rights. A juvenile curfew, for example, may engage the rights to personal liberty, freedom of movement and freedom of assembly; the blocking of access to a site of a demonstration those to freedom of movement, freedom of assembly and freedom of expression; and a drug-exclusion zone those to freedom of movement and respect for family life. As a general rule, the more general guarantees, including the guarantee of human dignity and the right to personal

[355] US Constitution, Fifth and Fourteenth Amendments.

[356] UDHR, Art. 23; ICESCR, Art. 6; ADHR, Art. 14; European Social Charter (adopted 18 October 1961, entered into force 26 February 1965) ETS 35 (the United Kingdom signed 18 October 1961 and ratified 11 July 1962), Art. 1.

[357] Guaranteed at the international level by: UDHR, Art. 21; ICCPR, Art. 25; ADHR, Art. 20. Guaranteed in Switzerland by BV, Art. 34.

[358] See *Maquoketa* v. *Russell*, 484 N.W.2d 179, 185 (Iowa 1992).

liberty, are treated as subsidiary rights that are only invoked if protection is not already provided by one of the more specific rights. In contrast, several specific rights may be engaged at the same time if they protect different spheres of liberty.[359]

5.3 Limitations

That a given exclusion measure interferes with one of the fundamental rights listed above does not necessarily mean that there is also a *violation* of that right. Except for the guarantee of human dignity, all these rights are rights that are not absolute but that can be limited, provided certain requirements are met. Human dignity, in contrast, is an absolute right, meaning that – as, for example, with the freedom from torture – any interference will automatically constitute a violation. As explained in Section 5.2.1, however, that exclusion from public space amounts to an interference with human dignity will be the very rare exception. The requirements that a limitation of a protected fundamental right must meet for it to be justified are essentially the same under international law and the domestic law of the three states at issue.

In the case of the ICCPR, the CRC and the ECHR these requirements are set out individually in separate paragraphs (so-called 'limitation clauses') of the norms guaranteeing the respective rights.[360] The UDHR and the ADHR, on the other hand, each contain a provision that sets out in general terms the limitation requirements for all the rights guaranteed by the respective instrument.[361] With regard to the rights associated with citizenship of the EU, the TFEU contains both a general limitation provision and specific limitation clauses.[362] Finally, the Agreement on the Free Movement of Persons between the EC and Switzerland contains, in its Annex, a general limitation provision.[363]

[359] With regard to Switzerland, see e.g. Auer/Malinverni/Hottelier, *Droit constitutionnel suisse* (2013), Vol. II, pp. 118–25; Kiener/Kälin, *Grundrechte* (2013), pp. 73–7; Gächter, 'Allgemeine Grundrechtslehren' (2011), 428–9; Hottelier, 'Grundrechtskonkurrenzen und Grundrechtskollisionen' (2007), 130–4. With regard to the other jurisdictions, there are no established doctrines as to how to proceed when several fundamental rights are engaged at the same time and courts decide on a case-by-case basis.

[360] With regard to the rights that are most relevant for the present context, see ICCPR, Arts 12(3), 19(3), 21; CRC, Arts 13(2), 15(2); ECHR, Arts 8(2), 10(2), 11(2).

[361] UDHR, Art. 29(2); ADHR, Art. 28.

[362] TFEU, Art. 20(2); e.g. TFEU, Art. 21(1).

[363] Agreement between the European Community and its Member States, of the one part, and the Swiss Confederation, of the other, on the free movement of persons, 21 June 1999, OJ L 114 (SR 0.142.112.681), Annex I, Art. 5.

While the limitation requirements are essentially the same for all international instruments, the focus here will be on the ECHR as, due to its incorporation into UK law, its limitation test is now also that applicable in the United Kingdom. According to the second paragraphs of Articles 8 to 11 of the ECHR, three elements must be given for a limitation to be justified. First, the limitation must be 'prescribed by law' (or 'in accordance with the law' in the wording of Article 8(2)), that is, it must be authorised by a legal rule that is adequately accessible and sufficiently precise to enable citizens to regulate their conduct.[364] This is a substantiation of the principle of legality discussed in Section 4.2.1. Second, the limitation must be intended to achieve one of the legitimate aims that are listed in the respective limitation clause. Third, the limitation must be 'necessary in a democratic society', meaning that it must be 'proportionate to the legitimate aim pursued'.[365]

The Federal Constitution of Switzerland contains in Article 36 a provision establishing in general terms the limitation requirements for all fundamental rights – or at least for all freedoms: although Article 36 refers to 'fundamental rights' in general, it is in fact designed to be applied to those rights that guarantee a sphere of freedom (rather than equality rights, procedural rights or economic and social rights).[366] The test is virtually the same as under the ECHR. First, Article 36(1) specifies the principle of legality by providing that there must be a legal basis for any limitation of fundamental rights.[367] As under the ECHR, this legal basis must be precise enough so that citizens can regulate their conduct accordingly.[368] The second sentence of Article 36(1) establishes the additional requirement that any 'serious' interference must be prescribed by an act passed by parliament ('law in the formal sense').[369] Second, there must be a legitimate aim: Article 36(2) provides that the limitation must be justified in the public interest or for the protection of

[364] *The Sunday Times* v. *The United Kingdom (No. 1)*, no. 6538/74, 26 April 1979, Series A no. 30, para. 49.

[365] *Olsson* v. *Sweden (No. 1)*, no. 10465/83, 24 March 1988, Series A no. 130, para. 67.

[366] See e.g. Kiener/Kälin, *Grundrechte* (2013), pp. 89–90; Weber-Dürler, 'Grundrechtseingriffe' (2000), 133–4. Schefer, however, argues that Article 36 – or at least certain elements of it – may be applied to any fundamental right: Schefer, *Die Beeinträchtigung von Grundrechten* (2006), pp. 9–10; Schefer, *Die Kerngehalte von Grundrechten* (2001), pp. 62–72.

[367] See Section 4.2.1. [368] BGE 117 Ia 472, 480 (1991).

[369] For the definition of the term 'law in the formal sense', see BGE 132 I 157, 159 (2006). See also Section 4.2.1.

fundamental rights of others. Third, according to Article 36(3), any limitation must be proportionate.

In the United States, the Supreme Court has developed different tests to review interferences with different categories of rights. Therefore, the exact limitation requirements will depend on the standard of review that is applied in a given case. Three basic standards can be distinguished.[370] First, as a minimum standard applicable in all cases that do not qualify for one of the stricter standards (mainly cases concerning economic and social welfare), the 'rational basis' test applies, requiring that the limitation must be rationally related to a legitimate government purpose.[371] Second, in cases involving 'content-neutral' regulation of speech (that is, restrictions on speech imposed not because of its content), 'intermediate scrutiny' applies. Such limitations are justified if they further an important or substantial government interest and are 'no greater than is essential to the furtherance of that interest'.[372] Third, if there is an interference with a 'fundamental right' protected by the due process clause, which, as explained above, will regularly be the case for exclusion measures, 'strict scrutiny' applies. Such an interference can only be justified if it is 'narrowly tailored to serve a compelling state interest'.[373] As can be seen from the short descriptions of these tests, they all turn around two limitation requirements, although these are defined varyingly: first, the existence of some legitimate aim for the interference and, second, an appropriately close relationship between the interference and that aim, in other words, a varyingly strict degree of proportionality.

The three key limitation requirements in all three jurisdictions are thus: a clear legal basis for the limitation, a legitimate aim justifying the limitation and proportionality. Issues relating to the first requirement, which is explicitly established by international law (including, with particular relevance for the United Kingdom, the ECHR) and Swiss constitutional law and is implicit in the US vagueness doctrine,[374] have already been discussed in Chapter 4. There, it has been pointed out that exclusion measures raise concerns in this regard: they are often not based on an explicit legislative authority but, instead, on breach-of-the-peace powers or the *polizeiliche Generalklausel*, respectively, and, insofar as relevant norms do exist, these tend to lack sufficient precision. Many exclusion measures may thus already fail to take this first hurdle of the

[370] See generally Tribe, *American Constitutional Law* (1988), pp. 769–84, 1436–66.

[371] *United States* v. *Carolene Products Co.*, 304 U.S. 144, 152 (1938).

[372] *United States* v. *O'Brien*, 391 U.S. 367, 377 (1968).

[373] *Reno* v. *Flores*, 507 U.S. 292, 302 (1993). [374] See Section 4.2.1.

limitation test. The following sections discuss the other two requirements: legitimate aim and proportionality.

The Federal Constitution of Switzerland establishes in Article 36(4) the additional requirement that limitations may not interfere with the 'core content' (*Kerngehalt/essence)* of fundamental rights. Thus, even where the three limitation requirements are satisfied, the inviolable core of a right may never be interfered with. These core contents can be conceptualised as substantiations of the guarantee of human dignity according to Article 7, which itself can never be limited.[375] The ECHR as well as other human rights treaties (including the ICCPR) similarly provide that certain guarantees may never be derogated from, not even in time of war or other public emergency.[376] These core or non-derogable aspects of rights include, for instance, the prohibition of torture, the freedom from slavery, the freedom of thought and the prohibition of systematic prior censorship.[377] While exclusion from public space may in certain cases raise general issues with regard to the guarantee of human dignity,[378] it will hardly ever amount to an interference with the core content of specific rights.

Finally, it should be noted that a different set of limitation requirements applies in the case of the guarantee of freedom from arbitrary detention. Therefore, if an exclusion measure amounts to a deprivation of liberty (which, as explained in Section 5.2.4, will only be the case in exceptional situations), the specific requirements of the respective guarantees must be met, including, for example, that those detained must be informed promptly of the reasons for the arrest.[379]

5.3.1 Legitimate aim

In the case of the ECHR, the limitation clauses of Articles 8 to 11 contain exhaustive lists of the aims that may be invoked to justify an interference with a Convention right. The lists of these four articles are largely identical; the main difference is that Article 10 (freedom of expression) refers to some additional aims that are, however, not of relevance for the present context.[380] To cite a typical example, Article 11(2) allows

375 See Schefer, *Die Kerngehalte von Grundrechten* (2001), pp. 5–145.

376 ECHR, Art. 15(2); ICCPR, Art. 4(2).

377 For an overview, see Schefer, *Die Kerngehalte von Grundrechten* (2001), pp. 403–560.

378 See Section 5.2.1. 379 See Section 5.2.4.

380 See generally Greer, *The Exceptions to Articles 8 to 11 of the European Convention on Human Rights* (1997). For a comparison of the different limitation clauses in the form of

restrictions on the freedom of assembly 'in the interests of national security or public safety, for the prevention of disorder or crime, for the protection of health or morals or for the protection of the rights and freedoms of others'. All the limitation clauses define the legitimate aims so broadly that states will usually not find it difficult to show that a restriction was imposed for one of these reasons.[381]

Article 36(2) of the Federal Constitution of Switzerland lists as legitimate aims justifying the restriction of fundamental rights 'a public interest' and 'the protection of fundamental rights of others'. Only those interests that, as a result of public deliberation (that is, democratic processes), have crystallised as particularly important concerns to society as a whole can qualify as 'public interests'. Thus, a 'public interest' is more than just the sum of individual interests.[382] At the same time, not every interest that is reflected in a law passed by the democratic legislator automatically constitutes a 'public interest': that a law has gone through the democratic process does not necessarily mean that there is a legitimate aim behind it.[383] Furthermore, not any public interest can justify the restriction of fundamental rights: what qualifies as a sufficient interest needs to be assessed specifically with regard to each fundamental right.[384] The most important – and for the present context particularly relevant – public interest justifying interferences with fundamental rights is the protection of the so-called *Polizeigüter/valeurs de police* ('police interests'), which include, above all, public safety, public order, public health, public peace and public morals.[385] Often these various interests are summarised under the generic term *öffentliche Sicherheit und*

a table, see Rainey/Wicks/White, *The European Convention on Human Rights* (2014), p. 315.

381 Harris/O'Boyle/Bates/Buckley, *Law of the ECHR* (2014), pp. 509–10; Rainey/Wicks/White, *The European Convention on Human Rights* (2014), p. 314; Grabenwarter/Pabel, *Europäische Menschenrechtskonvention* (2012), p. 128; Frowein/Peukert, *Europäische Menschenrechtskonvention* (2009), p. 283.

382 Schefer, *Die Beeinträchtigung von Grundrechten* (2006), p. 76; Müller, 'Allgemeine Bemerkungen zu den Grundrechten' (2001), 637–8.

383 Kiener/Kälin, *Grundrechte* (2013), p. 117; Wyss, *Öffentliche Interessen* (2001), pp. 215–29.

384 Auer/Malinverni/Hottelier, *Droit constitutionnel suisse* (2013), Vol. II, p. 98; Weber-Dürler, 'Grundrechtseingriffe' (2000), 139–40.

385 Tschannen/Zimmerli/Müller, *Allgemeines Verwaltungsrecht* (2014), pp. 514–19; Moor/Flückiger/Martenet, *Droit administratif I* (2012), pp. 766–70; Mohler, *Grundzüge des Polizeirechts in der Schweiz* (2012), pp. 45–6; Häfelin/Müller/Uhlmann, *Allgemeines Verwaltungsrecht* (2010), pp. 558–9; Reinhard, *Allgemeines Polizeirecht* (1993), pp. 59–94.

Ordnung/ordre public (public safety and order).[386] Only 'police interests' can justify restrictions of the use of public ground that does not go beyond *Gemeingebrauch* ('common use'), whereas more intense use can be restricted for any public interest.[387] As far as the second legitimate aim referred to by Article 36(2) is concerned, 'protection of fundamental rights of others', it is debatable whether this extends to more than what is already covered by 'public interest'.[388] For where the rights of a great number of third persons are at stake, there normally is also a public interest for the interference.[389] In addition, the protection of legal interests of the individual such as life, health, liberty, property and reputation is already included in the public interest of 'public safety'.[390] Therefore, at least in the present context, where the focus is on restrictions of fundamental rights designed to protect 'police interests', the concepts of 'public interest' and 'protection of fundamental rights of others' are largely congruent.[391] As for the European Court of Human Rights with regard to the ECHR, it is very rare for Swiss courts to overturn a state measure interfering with fundamental rights on the sole basis that it lacked a legitimate aim.[392]

Although, because of the reliance on a case-by-case approach of US courts, it is difficult to make general assertions, basically all the objectives listed above also qualify as legitimate aims in the United States.[393] At least in those cases where the rational basis test applies, it is, in any event, easy for the state to justify an interference: all a court needs to be satisfied with in such a case is that the interference rationally relates to any 'legitimate government purpose'. Courts start from the

[386] Tschannen/Zimmerli/Müller, *Allgemeines Verwaltungsrecht* (2014), pp. 515–17; Auer/Malinverni/Hottelier, *Droit constitutionnel suisse* (2013), Vol. II, p. 99; Moor/Flückiger/Martenet, *Droit administratif I* (2012), p. 767; Mohler, *Grundzüge des Polizeirechts in der Schweiz* (2012), pp. 36–45; Häfelin/Müller/Uhlmann, *Allgemeines Verwaltungsrecht* (2010), p. 558; Schweizer/Sutter/Widmer, 'Grundbegriffe' (2008), 73; Reinhard, *Allgemeines Polizeirecht* (1993), pp. 59–63.

[387] See Section 2.4.1.

[388] See Schweizer, 'Art. 36' (2014), 838; Weber-Dürler, 'Grundrechtseingriffe' (2000), 141.

[389] Wyss, *Öffentliche Interessen* (2001), pp. 204–5.

[390] Tschannen/Zimmerli/Müller, *Allgemeines Verwaltungsrecht* (2014), p. 516; Häfelin/Müller/Uhlmann, *Allgemeines Verwaltungsrecht* (2010), p. 558.

[391] On the difficulty of distinguishing between public and private interests, see Wyss, *Öffentliche Interessen* (2001), pp. 5–8; Häfelin/Müller/Uhlmann, *Allgemeines Verwaltungsrecht* (2010), p. 560.

[392] Wyss, *Öffentliche Interessen* (2001), pp. 206–8.

[393] See e.g. for public safety *Heffron* v. *International Society for Krishna Consciousness*, 452 U.S. 640, 649–50 (1981).

presumption that the state measure is constitutional and give great deference to the legislator in defining the scope of legitimate government ends, so that virtually any interest can qualify as such.[394] The legitimate aim test does, however, present a significant hurdle where intermediate scrutiny or strict scrutiny applies. In these cases the interference is only justified if it is supported by a state interest that is, in the case of intermediate scrutiny, 'important' or 'substantial' or, in the case of strict scrutiny, 'compelling'.[395] Even though it is far from impossible for the government to demonstrate a 'compelling' public interest,[396] courts, including the Supreme Court, have repeatedly found interferences to be unconstitutional because this demonstration had not been made.[397]

As explained in Section 3.3, exclusion measures are mainly designed to deal with three types of behaviour: criminal behaviour, anti-social behaviour and political protest. The remainder of this section explores whether there are legitimate aims for excluding from public space those who engage in these types of behaviour.

5.3.1.1 Criminal behaviour

Some exclusion measures are designed to reduce the risk of criminal behaviour by keeping away from (certain) public places those who may commit particular types of offences. These include measures intended to prevent people from re-offending, such as the British SHPOs, the sex offender laws of various US states and cities or, in Switzerland, the orders imposed on those convicted to a suspended sentence for the time of their probationary period or the area bans for convicted sex offenders,[398] as

[394] *FCC* v. *Beach Communications, Inc.*, 508 U.S. 307, 315 (1993) ('[T]hose attacking the rationality of the legislative classification have the burden "to negative every conceivable basis which might support it" [. . .]. Moreover, because we never require a legislature to articulate its reasons for enacting a statute, it is entirely irrelevant for constitutional purposes whether the conceived reason for the challenged distinction actually motivated the legislature.') (concerning an equal protection challenge). See Farrell, 'Successful Rational Basis Claims in the Supreme Court' (1999).

[395] E.g. *Shapiro* v. *Thomson*, 394 U.S. 618, 634 (1969); *Bates* v. *Little Rock*, 361 U.S. 516, 524 (1960).

[396] See Winkler, 'Fatal in Theory and Strict in Fact' (2006).

[397] E.g. *Sherbert* v. *Verner*, 374 U.S. 398, 406–9 (1963) (holding that the prevention of fraudulent claims is not a compelling state interest for denying unemployment compensation benefits to persons who refuse to work on Saturdays for religious reasons); *NAACP* v. *Alabama*, 357 U.S. 449 (1958) (holding that the state of Alabama had failed to show a compelling interest for forcing the NAACP to disclose its membership lists). For an overview, see Siegel, 'The Origin of the Compelling State Interest Test and Strict Scrutiny' (2006).

[398] See Section 3.3.1.1.

well as measures intended to prevent crimes from being committed in the first place, such as the TPIMs, serious crime prevention orders, football banning orders and sexual risk orders in the United Kingdom, the drug-exclusion zones and gang congregation ordinances in the United States or the area bans imposed in connection with sports events in Switzerland.[399]

Clearly, in being aimed at the prevention of crime through the control of space, these measures pursue a legitimate objective. In the case of the ECHR with its exhaustive lists of legitimate aims, Articles 8(2), 10(2) and 11(2) explicitly refer to the 'prevention of disorder or crime' as one of the aims justifying limitations. (Article 9(2) instead refers to the equivalent concept of 'protection of public order'). Thus, in the cases concerning the drug-exclusion zone in Amsterdam, the European Court of Human Rights found that, by targeting the traffic and use of hard drugs in public, the respective restriction of the freedom of movement 'pursued the legitimate aims of maintenance of *ordre public* and prevention of crime'.[400] 'Public safety', listed in all the limitation clauses of the ECHR, is another legitimate aim such measures may be said to pursue. As far as exclusion from public space is designed to prevent forms of crime that are directed against the state itself, 'national security', which is listed in Articles 8(2), 10(2) and 11(2) of the ECHR, can also be invoked. Accordingly, British courts have found restrictions on Convention rights imposed as part of terrorist control orders to be justified on national security grounds.[401]

In Switzerland, the prevention of crime is characterised as a central aspect of the protection of *Polizeigüter* ('police interests'), the most important public interest justifying the limitation of fundamental rights.[402] As mentioned above, the generic term 'public safety and order' is typically invoked in this context. When proposing the piece of legislation that authorises bans on accessing designated areas in connection with sports events (*Rayonverbote*), for example, the federal government argued that hooliganism at football and ice hockey matches was a major problem, posing a serious threat to public safety and order.[403]

399 See Section 3.3.1.2.

400 *Landvreugd* v. *The Netherlands*, no. 37331/97, 4 June 2002, para. 68; *Olivieira* v. *The Netherlands*, no. 33129/96, 4 June 2002, ECHR 2002-IV, 193, para. 61.

401 E.g. *Abu Rideh* v. *Secretary of State for the Home Department*, [2007] EWHC 2237 (Admin).

402 E.g. Tschannen/Zimmerli/Müller, *Allgemeines Verwaltungsrecht* (2014), pp. 516–17; Mohler, *Grundzüge des Polizeirechts in der Schweiz* (2012), pp. 36–45.

403 Botschaft zur Änderung des Bundesgesetzes über Massnahmen zur Wahrung der inneren Sicherheit (Massnahmen gegen Gewaltpropaganda und gegen Gewalt anlässlich von

The Federal Supreme Court confirmed that there is a weighty public interest in preventing violent incidents at sports events. In addition to invoking 'public order', the court found that the interference with the rights to freedom of assembly and freedom of movement was also justified for the protection of the fundamental rights of others, namely those attending and organising these events.[404] Similarly, area bans for sex offenders may be said to pursue the objective of protecting the integrity of children and juveniles, guaranteed by Article 11 of the Federal Constitution.[405]

In the United States, exclusion measures designed to prevent crime will equally have no problems passing the legitimate aim test. This holds true even where courts apply strict scrutiny, as the prevention of crime is invariably characterised as a 'compelling' public interest.[406] For example, in the case concerning the drug-exclusion zone in Cincinnati, the US Court of Appeals for the Sixth Circuit observed that the city introduced the zone to protect the safety of citizens living in drug-plagued neighbourhoods, as well as their health and welfare. According to the court, this represented 'a compelling government interest'.[407]

5.3.1.2 Anti-social behaviour

Identifying the aims A second group of exclusion measures are those that target behaviours such as vagrancy, loitering, obstructing pedestrian traffic, sleeping, sitting, spitting or drinking alcohol in public places,[408] those that are directed against the presence of juveniles in public places at certain times,[409] as well as the various blanket exclusion norms that can be employed against these and further forms of 'anti-social behaviour'.[410]

The first difficulty with assessing the legitimacy of the objectives pursued by exclusion measures directed against anti-social behaviour is to establish what exactly they are actually designed to achieve. Typically,

Sportveranstaltungen) vom 17. August 2005, BBl 2005, 5613, pp. 5617–18, 5638–9. See also Thaler, 'Hooliganismus und Sport' (2006), 287–9.

404 BGE 137 I 31, 46–7 (2010).

405 See Botschaft zur Volksinitiative 'Pädophile sollen nicht mehr mit Kindern arbeiten dürfen' sowie zum Bundesgesetz über das Tätigkeitsverbot und das Kontakt- und Rayonverbot (Änderung des Strafgesetzbuchs, des Militärstrafgesetzes und des Jugendstrafgesetzes) als indirektem Gegenvorschlag vom 10. Oktober 2012, BBl 2012, 8819, p. 8875.

406 E.g. *In re Gault*, 387 U.S. 1, 69 (1967) (Harlan, J., concurring in part and dissenting in part).

407 *Johnson* v. *Cincinnati*, 310 F.3d 484, 502 (6th Cir. 2002).

408 See Sections 3.3.2.1 and 3.3.2.2. 409 See Section 3.3.2.3. 410 See Section 3.3.2.4.

a mix of diverse reasons is adduced in their support. A good example is an ordinance of the City of Reno, Nevada, which prohibits sitting or lying down on public sidewalks in the downtown area. The preamble to the relevant provision explains the reasons for the prohibition as follows:

> In some circumstances people sitting or lying on the sidewalks deter many members of the public from frequenting the downtown area, which contributes to undermining the essential economic vitality of this area. Business failures and relocations can cause vacant buildings which contribute to a spiral of deterioration and blight which harms the public health, safety and welfare. An important factor in protecting public safety is attracting people to the streets and sidewalks of the city's downtown redevelopment district, because the presence of many law abiding citizens serves as a deterrent to crime and increases the public's sense of security and the safety of all.[411]

The two main developments that have transformed public space and led to the resurgence of exclusion measures – the hybridisation of public and private space and the new focus on order maintenance[412] – are clearly discernible in this sort of justification. As explained above, order maintenance policing does no longer just focus on crime but, much more broadly, on a wide range of 'anti-social behaviours' or 'incivilities' that are thought to contribute to the deterioration of public space, which, in turn, will allegedly give rise to all sorts of social ills.[413] It is concerned with how particular spaces appear and with conveying a sense of safety to those using these spaces and therefore relies on tools that have a high 'signal value', such as exclusion from public space.[414] It is also on this basis that the blanket exclusion norms contained in many cantonal police acts in Switzerland, which are mainly directed against 'scenes' of alcohol and drug addicts and demonstrators,[415] have been justified. They were needed, it has been explained, not only for reasons of public safety understood in a narrow sense, but also to prevent the littering, noise, obstruction of pedestrians and aggressive begging that are allegedly linked to the presence of certain groups of people in public places as well as to protect members of the public from encounters that they may experience as offending or even intimidating, thus making them avoid the relevant areas.[416] In this sense, reasons of, on the one hand, public

[411] Reno, Nevada, Municipal Code, s. 8.12.015(a)(6). [412] See Sections 2.5 and 3.2.

[413] See Section 2.5.2. [414] See Sections 2.5.2 and 3.2.

[415] See Sections 3.3.2.4 and 4.3.2.1.

[416] See Urteil des Bundesgerichts 1C_247/2008 vom 21. Januar 2009, E. 3.4; BGE 132 I 49, 61–2 (2006).

safety and, on the other, public order and cleanliness of public places are, according to the Federal Supreme Court, closely intertwined and it is impossible to clearly distinguish between the preventive and repressive elements of these exclusion measures.[417]

Unlike exclusion measures intended to prevent and counter criminal behaviour, exclusion measures directed against anti-social behaviour can thus not be justified on the basis that they prevent crime, at least not in any direct way. In the case of the blanket exclusion norms in Switzerland, for example, it is clear from their legislative history that in most cases prevention of crime was not among the primary reasons cited in their support.[418] In their decisions concerning the exclusion orders issued in the City of Berne, the Cantonal Administrative Court and the Federal Supreme Court explicitly acknowledged that there were no suggestions that those subject to the orders might have been involved in criminal conduct.[419] Instead, the Federal Supreme Court observed, the banning orders were imposed because those concerned had assembled in groups in the train station, consumed alcohol, left litter behind, made noise and thus engaged in behaviour that numerous passers-by had taken offence at. This sort of behaviour could, in addition, cause feelings of insecurity and fear, making people avoid the relevant parts of the station. All of this meant that there was a threat to public safety and order.[420] Importantly, the court explicitly stated that the fact that there was a subjective element to this understanding of public safety and order did not alter the conclusion that the exclusion orders were in the public interest: behaviour that caused offence or even intimidation to several pedestrians could, from an objective point of view, be understood as a threat to public safety and order.[421] As will be explained below, this is a highly problematic argument. In a later decision dealing with the exclusion norm contained in

[417] Urteil des Bundesgerichts 1C_247/2008 vom 21. Januar 2009, E. 3.4.

[418] For the Canton of Berne, see Botschaften der Regierung an den Grossen Rat, Heft Nr. 7/2001–2002, p. 421. See also BVR 2005, 97, pp. 123–5 (Verwaltungsgericht des Kantons Bern); Gasser, *Kriminalpolitik oder City-Pflege?* (2004), pp. 41–2.

[419] BVR 2005, 97, pp. 124–5 (Verwaltungsgericht des Kantons Bern); BGE 132 I 49, 61 (2006).

[420] BGE 132 I 49, 61–2 (2006).

[421] Ibid., 62 ('An der Bejahung des öffentlichen Interesses an den umstrittenen Massnahmen ändert auch der Umstand nichts, dass dem Begriff der Gefährdung und Störung der öffentlichen Ordnung und Sicherheit eine subjektive Komponente anhaftet. Was wie im vorliegenden Fall bei mehreren Passanten Anstoss erregte oder gar zu Verunsicherung und Angstgefühlen führt, kann bei objektivierter Betrachtung als Beeinträchtigung der öffentlichen Ordnung und Sicherheit verstanden werden, der zu begegnen im öffentlichen Interesse liegt.').

the Police Act of the Canton of Geneva, the Federal Supreme Court simply observed that it was 'obvious that there is a public interest in preventing citizens from being seriously harassed'.[422] In this case, however, the court apparently assumed that public safety and order was not engaged: contradicting its previous decision concerning the Bernese exclusion orders, it explicitly stated that 'serious harassment' was conduct that was below the threshold of endangering public safety and order.[423] Nevertheless, it failed to explain where the alleged public interest could be derived from, if not from public safety and order.

An equally subjective approach underlies the British anti-social behaviour legislation. The Anti-social Behaviour, Crime and Policing Act 2014 provides that an IPNA, part of which may be an exclusion order, can be imposed on any person who has engaged or threatens to engage in anti-social behaviour,[424] defined as 'conduct that has caused, or is likely to cause, harassment, alarm or distress to any person'.[425] Similarly, the Act allows the police to disperse people from public places if their behaviour 'has contributed or is likely to contribute to members of the public in the locality being harassed, alarmed or distressed'.[426] These powers have also been used against persons who clearly cannot be said to pose a threat to public safety and order, if this concept is conceived objectively. In a town in northern England, for example, dispersal powers were deployed against a group of so-called 'moshers', an alternative teenage subcultural group whose members wear black clothes and tend to look depressed, who used to gather in a public place around the entrance to a shopping arcade. The police readily admitted that the dispersals were prompted, not by any actual misbehaviour, but mainly by the concern that the image of the area as conducive to business could suffer from the group's presence: 'Actually, in terms of their involvement in crime and such, [there are] no issues at all, but they do cause, by their behaviour and the fact that they are gathering in very large groups up and around the [shopping arcade], a great deal of concern for certain groups of people.'[427]

As is clear from the above, exclusion measures directed against anti-social behaviour are designed to achieve a range of aims that are only very

[422] Urteil des Bundesgerichts 1C_226/2009 vom 16. Dezember 2009, E. 5 ('Il est cependant manifeste qu'il existe un intérêt public à éviter que les citoyens ne soient sérieusement importunés.').

[423] Ibid., E. 4.2. [424] Anti-social Behaviour, Crime and Policing Act 2014, s. 1(2).

[425] Ibid., s. 2(1)(a). [426] Ibid., s. 35(2)(a).

[427] Crawford, 'From the Shopping Mall to the Street Corner' (2011), 505–6.

broadly and vaguely defined. This in itself is problematic from a fundamental rights perspective in that the proportionality of a restriction can only be assessed if it is clear what it is meant to achieve. This problem is exacerbated by the fact that, insofar as these measures are designed to protect against feelings of insecurity and fear and the causing of offence, harassment and distress, they have a highly subjective element. As pointed out in Section 4.3.2.1, this subjective element makes it questionable whether the norms authorising these exclusion measures can be said to be sufficiently precise. Yet even if this first requirement of the limitation test was held to be satisfied, there is the further question of whether the protection of feelings can constitute a legitimate aim justifying the restriction of fundamental rights.

Protection from feelings of insecurity as a legitimate aim? As explained above, the Swiss Federal Supreme Court seems to have answered this question in the affirmative in its decisions concerning the exclusion powers contained in the cantonal police acts, even though it remains unclear exactly what sort of public interest it thinks is engaged. This corresponds to the court's recent jurisprudence relating to a different context where, quoting a remark from an academic comment on one of its own decisions, it held that the population's subjective need for security is a fact that can and must influence the legislator if it is ascertained through surveys.[428] In the United Kingdom, to my knowledge, no ASBOs, IPNAs, CBOs or dispersal orders have ever been challenged on the grounds that the prevention of harassment, alarm or distress was not a legitimate aim justifying the restriction of human rights, so the issue has not been addressed in any detail.[429] However, courts generally seem to have assumed that exclusion zones imposed as part of the previous ASBOs did have a legitimate aim, namely that of 'the protection of the rights and freedoms of others' as provided by the various ECHR limitation clauses.[430] The European Court of Human Rights has sent out rather conflicting signals regarding the question as to whether the protection of feelings can constitute a legitimate aim. In the case of *Chorherr* v. *Austria*, discussed in Section 4.3.2.1, it held that the arrest of two protesters

[428] BGE 136 I 1, 11 (2010) ('Das Sicherheitsgefühl der Bevölkerung stellt ein Faktum dar, das die Rechtssetzung legitimerweise beeinflussen darf und muss, wenn es aufgrund von Erhebungen festgestellt wird (dazu Yvo Hangartner, Besprechung von BGE 132 I 7, AJP 2006, S. 740 ff., 742).'). See also BGE 133 I 249, 256–7 (2007); BGE 132 I 7, 12 (2005).

[429] See also Ramsay, *The Insecurity State* (2012), p. 116.

[430] See e.g. *Leeds City Council* v. *Fawcett*, [2008] EWCA Civ 597, paras 14, 22, 26.

against a military ceremony based on a provision that made it an offence to 'cause a breach of the peace by conduct likely to cause annoyance' pursued the legitimate aim of prevention of disorder.[431] It should be noted, however, that the breach-of-the-peace requirement might have provided an objective element in this case, although it is not clear whether the court in fact considered this a decisive factor for holding that the legitimate aim requirement was met. In contrast, in *Vajnai* v. *Hungary* the European Court held that the applicant's conviction for wearing a red star violated Article 10 of the ECHR. The mere fact that members of the public may find the display of this symbol disrespectful, the court held, did not constitute a sufficient reason to restrict the applicant's right to freedom of expression if there was no rational basis for this public feeling.[432]

There are several reasons why it is problematic to justify the existence of a legitimate aim on the mere basis of subjective factors.

First, it is difficult to establish the existence of feelings, let alone to measure them. Whether a person feels offended, harassed, distressed or even intimated by someone else's behaviour depends on the sensibility of that person. Behaviour that some might find harassing or distressing may be regarded as perfectly acceptable by others. A situation in which some people may feel insecure will appear to be completely safe to others. As pointed out by the Swiss Federal Supreme Court, in some cases it may be possible to ascertain, at least to some extent, the population's subjective insecurity through surveys. So it may be true that, as the court observed in the respective case, the majority of the Swiss population experiences pit bulls and dogs of several other dog breeds as particularly intimidating.[433] However, as far as the present context is concerned, there is, in general, hardly any evidence that would establish what types of behaviour, or the presence of what types of persons, is considered as particularly offensive, harassing or intimidating. In the case concerning the Bernese exclusion orders, the only evidence that the Federal Supreme Court could cite to support its finding that the presence of the respective group of people drinking alcohol in public 'evidently' caused offence were some complaints of passers-by.[434] No evidence whatsoever was

431 *Chorherr* v. *Austria*, no. 13308/87, 25 August 1993, Series A no. 266-B, para. 28.

432 *Vajnai* v. *Hungary*, no. 33629/06, 8 July 2008, ECHR 2008, paras 57–8.

433 BGE 136 I 1, 6–7 and 10–11 (2010).

434 BGE 132 I 49, 61 (2006) ('Ausschlaggebend ist vielmehr, dass sich die Beschwerdeführer in Gruppen zusammengefunden haben, die dem Alkohol erheblich zugesprochen haben, mit Abfall und Unrat grosse Unordnung hinterlassen, grossen Lärm verursacht und

quoted to support the conclusion that their presence would not only provoke offence but even feelings of insecurity and fear. Often such observations about the feelings of 'the public' may simply reflect the attitudes of a particularly vocal or influential minority rather than those of the 'silent majority'. At least in the case of blanket exclusion norms, such as those contained in the Swiss cantonal police acts or the British Anti-social Behaviour, Crime and Policing Act 2014, this problem is not mitigated by the fact that they have been passed in a democratic process: it is not clear from them exactly what behaviours the democratic legislator would regard as causing offence or distress or as undermining the subjective security of the population.

Second, even if it was practically possible to establish and measure feelings, it is questionable whether it would be legally permissible for the state to do so. A serious and comprehensive evaluation of, for instance, the degree of existing subjective insecurity among the population would require the collection of large amounts of sensitive personal information,[435] amounting to an interference with the right to respect for private life that could only be justified if there was a legitimate aim for it and it was proportionate.

Third, even if it was practically and legally possible to demonstrate the degree of, say, existing subjective *insecurity*, there is still the problem of establishing the required degree of subjective *security*. Again, the degree of subjective security that is needed is something highly individual. It may be possible to define a desirable degree of *objective* public safety (for example, by setting crime rates that are to be regarded as (un) acceptable) but, at least in a liberal democratic state, it is not possible to take account of everyone's feelings at the same time and define a desirable degree of *subjective* security that would be equally applicable to everyone.[436] Where one person feels protected by the state, the other feels controlled. If an interest cannot be generalised, however, it cannot constitute a public interest.

Fourth, even if it was possible to define in a general way the desirable degree of protection of feelings and to agree on how such protection of

damit ein Verhalten an den Tag gelegt haben, an welchem zahlreiche Passanten Anstoss genommen haben. Solche Erscheinungen sind geeignet, die öffentliche Ordnung und Sicherheit zu gefährden oder zu stören. Sie wirken sich direkt auf das den öffentlichen Raum benützende Publikum aus und beeinträchtigen die Passanten in einer Weise, die offensichtlich Anstoss erregt.') See also BVR 2005, 97, p. 127 (Verwaltungsgericht des Kantons Bern).

[435] See Gusy, 'Der öffentliche Raum' (2009), 221. [436] See ibid., pp. 221–2.

feelings should be achieved, this does not necessarily mean that the relevant measure is in the public interest. Not all measures supported by the majority are in the public interest.[437] The majority of a population may take offence at red-haired people sitting on the same park bench as them or even at just meeting them in public streets. Perhaps the majority of the population is even afraid of red-haired people. Does that mean that there is a public interest in banning all red-haired people from public space? 'Red-haired' in this scenario could be replaced with a number of characteristics that seem less far-fetched, and the answer would still be 'no'. The example shows that, even if it was possible to demonstrate and measure the existence of subjective anxieties, there must be certain limits to taking these into account, as there is an important difference between the subjective state of feeling offended or afraid and the objective moral appraisal of these feelings.[438] In other words, as is even acknowledged by those who support state intervention to protect feelings,[439] the legitimate aim test cannot rely on subjective factors alone but must include some objective element to ensure a degree of reasonableness.[440] As the European Court of Human Rights observed in *Vajnai* v. *Hungary*, 'a legal system which applies restrictions on human rights in order to satisfy the dictates of public feeling – real or imaginary – cannot be regarded as meeting the pressing social needs recognised in a democratic society, since that society must remain reasonable in its judgement'.[441] It is for this reason that the British Crime and Disorder Act 1998 provided that in determining whether an ASBO should be imposed, courts 'shall disregard any act of the defendant which he shows was reasonable in the circumstances'.[442] It is especially with regard to subjective anxieties relating to public space that such a limitation would be crucial. For it is in the nature of public space that people experience it as less safe than their private spaces: the more alien an environment is, the more dangerous it appears, even if statistically the contrary is true. In other words, as numerous studies have demonstrated, the degree of subjective security

437 See Kiener/Kälin, *Grundrechte* (2013), p. 117. See also Waechter, 'Rechtsgütergewichtung und wahre sowie eingebildete Bedrohungen' (1999), 813.

438 Roberts, 'Penal Offence in Question' (2006), 13–20; Simester/von Hirsch, 'Rethinking the Offense Principle' (2002).

439 Ramsay, 'The Theory of Vulnerable Autonomy and the Legitimacy of the Civil Preventative Order' (2008), 24.

440 See also Waechter, 'Rechtsgütergewichtung und wahre sowie eingebildete Bedrohungen' (1999).

441 *Vajnai* v. *Hungary*, no. 33629/06, 8 July 2008, ECHR 2008, para. 57.

442 Crime and Disorder Act 1998, s. 1(5) (repealed).

experienced in public space depends on a whole range of factors such as gender, age, degree of social integration, reporting by the media and so on; it is only to a limited extent that it is related to the actual, objective safety of public space.[443]

All of this is in no way to suggest that the state should not be concerned with people's feelings. In a liberal democracy, where the needs of human beings must be at the centre of attention, the authorities can and should care about whether citizens feel safe or not.[444] There is therefore a public interest in carrying out educational campaigns informing citizens about existing and non-existing dangers, improving street lightning, designing less intimidating subways, building female-friendly car parks, deploying social workers on the streets to support marginalised groups and prevent conflicts and similar measures to increase people's subjective security.[445] Where the problem to be addressed is mainly of a symbolic nature, it makes sense for the state to react by protecting people's feelings through the adoption of symbolic measures.

In contrast, because of the problems set out above, it is highly questionable whether the protection of mere feelings such as subjective security can ever justify *an interference with fundamental rights.* Feelings as such are not, to refer to the concepts used by the ECHR and in US terminology, part of 'public safety' or 'the prevention of disorder or crime' and they are not, to use Swiss terminology, 'police interests' (*Polizeigüter*). Contrary to what the Swiss Federal Supreme Court has suggested, the mere fact that several members of the public may feel offended or perhaps even intimidated by a certain behaviour does not automatically mean that the interest of public safety is engaged. This would boil down to a purely subjective conception of public safety, which, as explained above, raises insurmountable problems with regard to proof, democratic legitimacy and reasonableness.

Nor do feelings such as these qualify as 'rights and freedoms of others' or 'fundamental rights of others'. Already the existence of a 'right to security', understood in a comprehensive way as going beyond the

[443] See Killias/Kuhn/Aebi, *Grundriss der Kriminologie* (2011), pp. 353–60; Sessar/Herrmann/Keller/Weinrich/Breckner, *Insecurities in European Cities* (2004), pp. 91–3; Albrecht, 'Kriminalitätsumfang, Opferrisiken und Kriminalitätsfurcht' (1997); Boers, *Kriminalitätsfurcht* (1991); Garofalo, 'Victimization and the Fear of Crime' (1979), 80. For a good overview, see Schewe, *Das Sicherheitsgefühl und die Polizei* (2008), pp. 93–131 , especially pp. 106–7.

[444] Gusy, 'Der öffentliche Raum' (2009), 221; Hangartner, 'Besprechung des Bundesgerichtsentscheides BGE 132 I 7' (2006), 742.

[445] Schewe, *Das Sicherheitsgefühl und die Polizei* (2008), pp. 274–91.

context of physical liberty, is highly contentious.[446] Even if such a right did exist, it would not include a right *to feel* secure or a right *not to feel* offended, annoyed or distressed. Since fundamental and human rights are based on values that are universal, they cannot protect feelings such as insecurity, which, as explained above, are highly individual. Just as the right to food does not include a right *to feel* well-fed and the right to personal liberty does not include a right *to feel* free, none of the legal systems at issue guarantees a right *to feel* secure.[447]

That the protection of feelings is not a legitimate aim justifying the restriction of fundamental rights is well established in the case law of the US Supreme Court. In *Coates* v. *City of Cincinnati* it held that the relevant ordinance of the City of Cincinnati that made it a criminal offence for 'three or more persons to assemble [. . .] on any of the sidewalks, street corners, vacant lots, or mouths of alleys, and there conduct themselves in a manner annoying to persons passing by' was not only, as explained in Section 4.3.2.1, unconstitutionally vague, but also too broad and thus in violation of the right to freedom of assembly. Whilst the city could, according to the court, prohibit behaviours such as blocking sidewalks, obstructing traffic, littering streets or other forms of 'anti-social conduct', it was not allowed 'to make criminal the exercise of the right of assembly simply because its exercise may be "annoying" to some people'.[448] '[M]ere public intolerance or animosity', the court succinctly summarised its case law in this regard, 'cannot be the basis for abridgment of these constitutional freedoms.'[449]

It is worth noting that until quite recently the Swiss Federal Supreme Court's position on this issue used to be quite similar. In 1999 the court had to review a new cantonal norm that, among other things, authorised the police to take action against those who approach others on public ground in a manner that causes unacceptable annoyance to passers-by. The court found that the mere fact that people may find it annoying to be approached about a particular cause was not a sufficient reason for prohibiting such approaches, regardless of how unpopular the cause was.[450] The court stressed that the definition of what amounted to

[446] For a comprehensive treatment, see Lazarus, 'Mapping the Right to Security' (2007). See also Lienhard/Häsler, 'Verfassungsrechtliche Grundlagen des Sicherheitsrechts' (2008), 139–41; Mohler, 'Vernetzung von Sicherheit' (2008), 542–4, 600.

[447] See, however, Ramsay, *The Insecurity State* (2012), pp. 113–31.

[448] *Coates* v. *City of Cincinnati*, 402 U.S. 611, 615 (1971).

[449] Ibid.

[450] BGE 125 I 369, 387 (1999) ('Die blosse Tatsache, dass Personen es als lästig empfinden, auf der Allmend angesprochen zu werden, um sie von einer Sache zu überzeugen, darf

annoying behaviour could not solely depend on the subjective views of those who felt annoyed, even if these were the views of a majority.[451] The relevant norm was only upheld because of its limitation to the causing of *unacceptable* annoyance, which, the court thought, would ensure the application of an objective standard.[452] Similarly, a proposed provision that would have authorised the police to issue exclusion orders against anyone whose behaviour 'causes offence or fear to the public' was eventually dropped from the bill for the new Police Act of the Canton of Zurich. There was a need to refer to objective criteria rather than the purely subjective standard of the public's perception, the government observed in its report on the bill.[453] Such a requirement of an objective standard does not appear in the Federal Supreme Court's recent decisions concerning cantonal exclusion norms, which, for the reasons explained above, is highly problematic.

In sum, a restriction of fundamental rights can only be said to pursue a legitimate aim if it is designed to protect either a public interest that is objectively conceived or the rights of others, rather than only feelings. Therefore, any exclusion measures directed against anti-social behaviour have to be examined closely and on an individual basis to assess whether there is, in the case at hand, a legitimate aim defined in this way or whether the measure merely serves to protect from feelings such as annoyance, distress or fear.

Objectively conceived legitimate aims There are several ways in which exclusion measures directed against anti-social behaviour may be said to pursue an objectively conceived public interest. For example, such measures may be in the interest of public safety and the prevention of disorder because the respective forms of behaviour, such as gatherings of drug or alcohol addicts, may lead to the obstruction of traffic, because they involve threats to or (not only subjectively experienced) harassment of passers-by or because there is a real danger that they may provoke violent reactions. In some rare cases, exclusion measures directed against anti-social behaviour may also be justified on the basis that they directly

nicht als Belästigung ausgelegt werden, unabhängig davon, wie unbeliebt diese Sache in der Öffentlichkeit ist.').

451 Ibid. ('Es kann nicht allein auf das subjektive Empfinden der Belästigten ankommen, auch wenn es sich um das Empfinden einer Mehrheit des Publikums handeln sollte.').

452 Ibid.

453 Antrag und Weisung des Regierungsrates zum Polizeigesetz (PolG) vom 5. Juli 2006, ABl 2006, 856, p. 901.

prevent crime rather than just to increase subjective security. In Switzerland and the United States, for example, some municipalities have justified their juvenile curfews by arguing that, apart from ensuring the juveniles' own safety and protecting the public 'from nocturnal mischief by minors', these also served to reduce nocturnal juvenile crime.[454] Similarly, laws that prohibit sleeping in public places have been defended on the basis that they were adopted, among other reasons, to respond to an increase in criminal behaviour in the relevant areas.[455] Insofar as exclusion measures directed against anti-social behaviour are also designed to prevent crime by keeping certain groups of people off the streets, they pursue, as explained in Section 5.3.1.1, an aim that is legitimate and, indeed, compelling.[456] The more difficult question is then whether banning from public space all juveniles or all those who sleep outside is a suitable, necessary and proportionate means to achieve this aim. This question is explored in Section 5.3.2.

Furthermore, some forms of anti-social behaviour, such as congregations of juveniles or of people drinking alcohol, may result in high levels of noise, including at night.[457] To impose restrictions on such behaviour may thus serve the interest of public peace (*öffentliche Ruhe/ tranquillité*), which is often characterised as an aspect of public health.[458] Prohibitions of sleeping in public parks or streets, bans on drinking alcohol in public places and the prevention of open assemblies of drug addicts, in turn, may be justified on the basis that there is a public interest in keeping the respective parts of public space clean and orderly.[459] While the prevention of noise and littering are undoubtedly legitimate aims, they will not, in general, qualify as particularly strong, or in US terminology 'compelling', public interests.[460] This may

454 Urteil des Verwaltungsgerichts des Kantons Zürich VB.2009.00055 vom 30. April 2009, E. 4.3, 5.2.2; *Bykofsky* v. *Borough of Middletown*, 401 F.Supp. 1242, 1255 (D.C. Pa. 1975). See also *Nunez* v. *City of San Diego*, 114 F.3d 935, 946 (9th Cir. 1997); *Qutb* v. *Strauss*, 11 F.3d 488, 492 (5th Cir. 1993); *Johnson* v. *City of Opelousas*, 658 F.2d 1065, 1073 n. 9 (5th Cir. 1981).

455 See Ades, 'The Unconstitutionality of "Antihomeless" Laws' (1989), 625.

456 E.g. *Qutb* v. *Strauss*, 11 F.3d 488, 492 (5th Cir. 1993).

457 One of the objectives of the juvenile curfew introduced in the municipality of Dänikon, for example, was the reduction of noise. See Urteil des Verwaltungsgerichts des Kantons Zürich VB.2009.00055 vom 30.April 2009, E. 4.3, 5.2.2.

458 E.g. Häfelin/Müller/Uhlmann, *Allgemeines Verwaltungsrecht* (2010), p. 558.

459 For an example, see Ades, 'The Unconstitutionality of "Antihomeless" Laws' (1989), 625.

460 *Clark* v. *Community for Creative Non-Violence*, 468 U.S. 288, 299 (1984) (qualifying the state interest in banning sleeping in public parks as 'substantial'); *Schneider* v. *State of New Jersey (Town of Irvington)*, 308 U.S. 147, 162 (1939) (holding 'that the purpose to

be different, however, in cases where the litter left behind amounts to a serious threat to public health, as may be the case, for example, with used syringes of drug addicts.

In some cases, economic reasons are adduced to support the adoption of exclusion measures directed against anti-social behaviour. As explained above, one of the justifications for the ordinance of the City of Reno, Nevada, which prohibits sitting or lying down on public sidewalks in the downtown area, was that such behaviour undermines the economic vitality of the area. After all, the city argued, '[p]ublic sidewalks in the downtown redevelopment district are created and maintained for the primary purposes of enabling pedestrians to safely and efficiently move about from place to place, facilitating deliveries of goods and services, and providing convenient access to entertainment, goods and services'[461] and '[t]he public welfare is promoted by an economically healthy downtown area which attracts people to shop, recreate, work and be entertained'.[462] The City of Seattle equally referred to economic vitality to defend an anti-sitting ordinance in its downtown area, as individuals blocking the public sidewalks could cause 'a steady cycle of decline as residents and tourists go elsewhere to meet, shop and dine'.[463] In the United Kingdom, as the example with the youths dispersed from the entrance of a shopping arcade shows, exclusion from public space has also been used to maintain the attractiveness of city centres for consumers. However, where exclusion measures interfere with fundamental rights that are of crucial importance to a democratic society, such as the freedom of assembly, purely economic reasons can, at least under the ECHR and Swiss law, never be a sufficient justification.[464] In any event, even under US law, economic reasons, just as the prevention of noise and littering, will certainly not constitute a particularly strong or 'compelling' public interest for the adoption of the sort of measures at issue here.[465]

Other public interests that exclusion measures directed against anti-social behaviour could be said to pursue are the protection of '(public)

keep the streets clean and of good appearance is insufficient to justify an ordinance which prohibits a person rightfully on a public street from handing literature to one willing to receive it').

461 Reno, Nevada, Municipal Code, s. 8.12.015(a)(1). 462 Ibid., s. 8.12.015(a)(5).

463 *Roulette* v. *City of Seattle*, 97 F.3d 300, 306 (9th Cir. 1996).

464 See ECHR, Article 11(2); Weber-Dürler, 'Grundrechtseingriffe' (2000), 139.

465 See *Roulette* v. *City of Seattle*, 97 F.3d 300, 308–9 (9th Cir. 1996) (Pregerson, CJ, dissenting) (describing the interest of the City of Seattle in preserving the economic vitality of its commercial areas as, at best, 'substantial').

morals' (*öffentliche Sittlichkeit/moralité publique*)[466] or the protection of 'public order' (*öffentliche Ordnung/ordre public*), understood in a broad sense as including all those social rules that are generally recognised as being essential for the peaceful coexistence of individuals but that have not yet become binding legal norms. Such a broad understanding of 'public order' has sometimes been adopted in Swiss legal doctrine.[467] However, this understanding has also rightly been criticised, as it should primarily be for the democratic legislator to decide which social rules deserve to be protected by the state.[468] Therefore, the invocation of such a notion of 'public order' should be limited to very exceptional cases.[469] In addition, the protection of 'morals' or of 'public order' as broadly conceived as described above is difficult to square with the concept of fundamental rights.[470] The notion of fundamental rights is neutral with regard to moral issues and thus incompatible with attempts by the state to enforce a particular moral order: fundamental rights require that the decision of whether or not to comply with mere social conventions is left to the individual.[471] In a tolerant and pluralist society, individuals may exercise the freedom protected by fundamental rights guarantees in a way that the majority may regard as pointless or even objectionable. In fact, one of the very key functions of fundamental rights is to protect the freedom of those in the minority to behave in a non-conformant manner. It is thus difficult to see how, in the context of the forms of anti-social behaviour at issue here, the protection of morals or social conventions could ever constitute a sufficient reason to justify the restriction of fundamental rights.

Finally, in addition to these public interests, exclusion measures directed against anti-social behaviour may pursue the objective of protecting the rights of others, an aim that is explicitly recognised as legitimate by the limitation clauses of the ECHR and Article 36(2) of the Swiss Federal Constitution. This aim may be relevant in cases where the form

466 The limitation clauses of Articles 8(2)–11(2) of the ECHR all list 'the protection of morals' as one of the legitimate aims.

467 See Tschannen/Zimmerli/Müller, *Allgemeines Verwaltungsrecht* (2014), p. 517; Häfelin/Müller/Uhlmann, *Allgemeines Verwaltungsrecht* (2010), p. 558.

468 Tschannen, ' "Öffentliche Sittlichkeit" ' (2005), 564–5; Reinhard, *Allgemeines Polizeirecht* (1993), p. 83.

469 Schweizer/Sutter/Widmer, 'Grundbegriffe' (2008), 77–80.

470 Schweizer/Sutter/Widmer, 'Grundbegriffe' (2008), 78; Tschannen, ' "Öffentliche Sittlichkeit" ' (2005), 566.

471 See Nowlin, 'The Protection of Morals Under the European Convention for the Protection of Human Rights and Fundamental Freedoms' (2002); Volkmann, 'Die Rückeroberung der Allmende' (2000), 367.

of anti-social behaviour at issue is of such intensity as to make it impossible for others to exercise their rights in the respective part of public space. For example, if a group of drug or alcohol addicts 'takes over' a small public square on a nearly permanent basis, others may be prevented from, say, meeting friends, staging a political protest or making other legitimate use of that square. As already pointed out above, the practical relevance of the protection of the rights of others as a separate aim is, however, rather limited. In nearly all situations where the rights of others are at stake, it will also be possible for the state to invoke a public interest for taking action. In our example, depending on the specific circumstances, the adoption of exclusion measures against the drug or alcohol addicts could just as well be justified by reference to the protection of public safety or the prevention of disorder. Finally, it should be noted that, as explained in Section 5.3.1.2, the aim of the protection of the rights of others cannot be invoked to protect from mere *subjective* insecurity or offence: there are no rights to feel secure or not to feel offended, annoyed or distressed.

5.3.1.3 Political protest

As explained in Section 3.3.3, all three states at issue have in recent years adopted measures that are designed to prevent political protest from taking place in particular parts of public space. These measures include, first, the adoption of laws that create special zones where protest is severely restricted or even completely prohibited[472] and, second, the introduction of policing strategies that aim at denying demonstrators access to potential sites of protest.[473]

As far as the first category of restrictions is concerned, the creation of special zones is often intended to protect third persons from being harassed or threatened by protesters. A classic example are the 'buffer zones' around abortion clinics that several states and municipalities in the United States have established to ensure patients' and employees' access to such clinics. The US Supreme Court has held that such zones serve a number of governmental interests, including 'ensuring public safety and order, promoting the free flow of traffic on streets and sidewalks, protecting property rights, and protecting a woman's freedom to seek pregnancy-related services', and has qualified these interests as 'significant'.[474] The restrictions on demonstrations outside the houses of employees of companies engaged

[472] See Section 3.3.3.1. [473] See Section 3.3.3.2.

[474] *Schenck* v. *Pro-Choice Network of Western New York*, 519 U.S. 357, 376 (1997). See also *Hill* v. *Colorado*, 530 U.S. 703, 715 (2000); *Madsen* v. *Women's Health Center, Inc.*, 512 U.S. 753, 767–8 (1994).

in animal testing that the United Kingdom has introduced as a reaction to protests by animal rights activists serve a similar purpose.[475] These kinds of zones clearly pursue several legitimate aims, including the prevention of crime, the protection of public safety and the protection of the rights of others (such as the right to seek an abortion or the right to enjoy one's private space without interference).

It is somewhat more difficult to understand what legitimate aims the severe restrictions of protest on Parliament Square in London and the Bundesplatz in Berne are meant to serve. In the case of the ban on the Bundesplatz during parliamentary sessions, one of the reasons cited in support was to allow parliamentarians 'to deliberate in freedom and without pressure'.[476] The underlying assumption of this argument is that the democratic will of the people is expressed solely through the election of parliament and that, once parliament is elected, it should be left to work in peace. This notion of parliamentary representation is antithetical to any modern concept of democracy and all the more so to the Swiss model of (semi-)direct democracy.[477] In a democratic state, isolation of parliamentarians from the views of the public cannot qualify as a legitimate interest.[478] Both with regard to Parliament Square and the Bundesplatz, a number of more practical reasons were also referred to, including ensuring the unimpeded access of parliamentarians and emergency services to the parliament building, preventing sessions of parliament from being disturbed by outside noise and reducing the risk of explosives being placed in the vicinity of the parliament building.[479] Undoubtedly, all of these are legitimate objectives. The crucial question is then whether an effective ban on demonstrations covering the whole square is a proportionate means to achieve these rather specific aims; this question will be explored in Section 5.3.2.2.

A rather peculiar interest was invoked by the Swiss Federal Supreme Court to uphold a general prohibition of political manifestations on the square in front of the monastery of Einsiedeln. The ban, the court held,

475 Criminal Justice and Police Act 2001, s. 42.

476 Votum Laubacher Otto, Amtliches Bulletin Nationalrat 2007, p. 635 ('Ziel dieses Verbotes ist es, den eidgenössischen Räten, den gewählten Vertretern des Souveräns, die Möglichkeit zu geben, in aller Freiheit und ohne Druck zu tagen.').

477 On the different concepts of democracy, see Section 7.1.

478 See also Parkinson, *Democracy and Public Space* (2012), pp. 122–72; Richter, ' "Befriedete Bezirke" ' (2002), 908–11, 969–70; Breitbach, 'Für die Abschaffung der Bannmeile' (1998), 242–3.

479 Votum Laubacher Otto, Amtliches Bulletin Nationalrat 2007, p. 635; Hansard, HC vol. 430 col. 1289–91 (7 February 2005).

was justified because of the special status the square had due to its function and location: not only did it serve as the way of access to a frequently visited place of pilgrimage but it also allowed visitors to enjoy the view of the monastery complex.[480] What the court thus seemed to be referring to in this case is not just the protection of the special character of this particular public place (which, in itself, would not appear to be a particularly strong public interest), but the protection of the rights of others through the creation of a 'zone free from disturbances for pilgrims and other visitors to the monastery'.[481]

The second category of measures, policing strategies aimed at denying demonstrators access to potential sites of protest, do not normally raise any problems with regard to the legitimacy of the aim pursued. The Swiss Federal Supreme Court has confirmed repeatedly that the blocking of access to Davos during the WEF served not only the legitimate aim of preserving public safety and order in Davos during the meeting but also that of protecting the rights of others, in particular those who would like to make use of public ground to organise, or participate in, events there.[482] In the United Kingdom, the House of Lords has similarly found that preventing demonstrators from reaching their intended site of protest at a US air base in Gloucestershire served the aim of 'prevention of disorder' according to Articles 10(2) and 11(2) of the ECHR.[483] US courts have found that there is a 'significant' government interest in protecting public safety by not letting demonstrators within a certain distance from a political convention.[484] Once a demonstration is underway, 'crowd control' measures such as 'kettling' (that is, containing demonstrators within a small cordoned-off area)[485] may be justified 'to protect people and property from injury' and 'to prevent serious public disorder'.[486]

480 BGE 124 I 267, 270 (1998) ('Zunächst kommt dem Platz vor dem Kloster Einsiedeln aufgrund seiner Funktion und Lage ein besonderer Stellenwert zu. Er dient nicht nur als Zugang zur Klosterkirche als sakraler Stätte und Wallfahrtsort für viele Pilger, weshalb er sich als auf Störungen besonders empfindlich erweist. Der Klosterplatz lädt auch zum Verweilen und Betrachten der gesamten kunsthistorisch wertvollen Klosteranlage ein.').

481 Ibid., 272 ('beabsichtigte Funktion des Klosterplatzes als störungsfreie Zone für die Pilger und die übrigen Klosterbesucher').

482 BGE 130 I 369, 383–4 (2004); BGE 128 I 327, 343–4 (2002); BGE 127 I 164, 174–6 (2001).

483 *R (Laporte)* v. *Chief Constable of Gloucestershire Constabulary*, [2006] UKHL 55, para. 85 (Lord Rodger).

484 *Service Employee International Union* v. *City of Los Angeles*, 114 F.Supp.2d 966, 970–71 (C.D. Cal. 2000).

485 See Section 3.3.3.2.

486 *Austin* v. *Commissioner for the Metropolis*, [2009] UKHL 5, paras 57–8 (Lord Neuberger).

5.3.2 *Proportionality*

5.3.2.1 The principle of proportionality as a universal criterion of constitutionality

The final requirement of the limitation test is proportionality. The principle of proportionality has become a standard for assessing interferences with fundamental rights that is so widely accepted that, as Alec Stone Sweet and Jud Mathews have shown, proportionality analysis can now be described as 'a dominant technique of rights adjudication in the world': virtually every effective constitutional justice system in the world has embraced its main tenets.[487] The principle of proportionality – and the requirement of balancing it implies – is, according to Robert Alexy, even 'unavoidable, since there is no other rational way in which the reason for the limitation can be put in relation to the constitutional right'[488] and, according to David Beatty, '[t]he only conceptual apparatus judges have, and all that they need, to harmonize the autonomy of each person with the general will of the community'.[489] Accordingly, Beatty has gone as far as to characterise proportionality as 'a universal criterion of constitutionality'[490] and 'the ultimate rule of law'.[491] There is also nearly universal agreement that proportionality consists of three main components, although there is some inconsistency in the terminology used to describe these components: suitability (or rational connection), necessity (or least restrictive means test) and proportionality in the narrow sense (or balancing).[492]

Although not specifically mentioned in the text of the ECHR, proportionality is one of the central principles governing the application of the rights guaranteed therein.[493] Articles 8(2)–11(2) of the ECHR not only

487 Stone Sweet/Mathews, 'Proportionality Balancing and Global Constitutionalism' (2008), 72. See also Möller, *The Global Model of Constitutional Rights* (2012), pp. 13–15, 178–205; Schlink, 'Proportionality (1)' (2012), 731–2; Barak, *Proportionality* (2012), pp. 181–210, 457.

488 Alexy, *A Theory of Constitutional Rights* (2002), p. 74. See also Kumm, 'The Idea of Socratic Contestation and the Right to Justification' (2010), 141.

489 Beatty, *The Ultimate Rule of Law* (2004), p. 116.

490 Ibid., p. 162.

491 Ibid. For a critique of Beatty's claim, see Jackson, 'Being Proportional About Proportionality' (2004), 803.

492 See e.g. Barak, *Proportionality* (2012), pp. 303–70; Klatt/Meister, *The Constitutional Structure of Proportionality* (2012), pp. 8–10; Gardbaum, 'The Structure and Scope of Constitutional Rights' (2011), 390.

493 McBride, 'Proportionality and the European Convention on Human Rights' (1999); Eissen, 'The Principle of Proportionality in the Case-Law of the European Court of Human Rights' (1993).

require that any limitation must serve a legitimate aim but also that it must be 'necessary in a democratic society'. This phrase, according to the European Court of Human Rights, 'implies that the interference corresponds to a pressing social need and, in particular, that it is proportionate to the legitimate aim pursued'.[494] In assessing the proportionality of an interference, the European Court concedes to states a 'margin of appreciation' as '[b]y reason of their direct and continuous contact with the vital forces of their countries, State authorities are in principle in a better position than the international judge to give an opinion [...] on the "necessity" of a "restriction" or "penalty" '.[495] Nevertheless, this margin of appreciation is limited as it 'goes hand in hand with a European supervision'.[496] Assessing proportionality is a complex inquiry that may require the court to consider a variety of factors.[497] For example, the proportionality requirement will not be satisfied where the aim pursued cannot be achieved by the means employed (that is, by the interference).[498] An interference will also be disproportionate if it is not necessary in the sense that there is a less restrictive measure available to achieve the aim[499] or if the state fails to provide evidence for the necessity of the interference.[500] Finally, assessing proportionality involves some element of balancing between the legitimate aim pursued by the state and the enjoyment of Convention rights by the individual.[501] In the United Kingdom, following the introduction of the Human Rights Act, courts started to apply the proportionality test in cases where Convention rights are concerned. Proportionality involves a somewhat greater intensity of review than the grounds of judicial review traditionally known in the United Kingdom do.[502] According to the decision of the House of Lords in *R (Daly)* v. *Secretary of State for the Home Department*, in assessing

494 *Olsson* v. *Sweden (No. 1)*, no. 10465/83, 24 March 1988, Series A no. 130, para. 67.

495 *Handyside* v. *The United Kingdom*, no. 5493/72, 7 December 1976, Series A no. 24, para. 48.

496 Ibid., para. 49.

497 See Harris/O'Boyle/Bates/Buckley, *Law of the ECHR* (2014), pp. 510–12; McBride, 'Proportionality and the European Convention on Human Rights' (1999).

498 E.g. *Observer and Guardian* v. *The United Kingdom*, no. 13585/88, 26 November 1991, Series A no. 216, paras 68–69.

499 E.g. *Informationsverein Lentia and others* v. *Austria*, nos 13914/88; 15041/89; 15717/89; 15779/89; 17207/90, 24 November 1993, Series A no. 276, para. 39.

500 E.g. *Kokkinakis* v. *Greece*, no. 14307/88, 25 May 1993, Series A no. 260-A, para. 49.

501 E.g. *Hatton and others* v. *The United Kingdom* [GC], no. 36022/97, 8 July 2003, ECHR 2003-VIII, 189, para. 122.

502 *R (Daly)* v. *Secretary of State for the Home Department*, [2001] UKHL 26, in particular paras 23, 27. See Rivers, 'Proportionality and Variable Intensity of Review' (2006); Jowell,

proportionality courts should consider 'whether: (i) the legislative objective is sufficiently important to justify limiting a fundamental right; (ii) the measures designed to meet the legislative objective are rationally connected to it; and (iii) the means used to impair the right or freedom are no more than is necessary to accomplish the objective'.[503] In a later decision, it added as a further requirement that the judgment on proportionality 'must always involve the striking of a fair balance between the rights of the individual and the interests of the community'.[504]

It is a recognised general legal principle in Switzerland that pursuance of a legitimate aim cannot justify every state measure. The Swiss concept of proportionality has its historical origins in that area of law that is directly relevant to exclusion measures, namely the law regulating police action.[505] The scope of application of the principle of proportionality was later gradually extended,[506] and today's Federal Constitution requires in its Article 5(2) that *any* state action must be proportionate. Article 36, the limitation clause, explicitly restates this general rule in its third paragraph with regard to interferences with fundamental rights. According to the established case law of the Federal Supreme Court,[507] and as is recognised in legal doctrine,[508] the proportionality test consists of three elements. First, the state measure must be a *suitable* means to achieve the aim pursued.[509] Second, the interference must be *necessary* to achieve that aim, that is, there must be no less intrusive measure available.[510] Thus, the personal, geographical and temporal scope of the measure may not extend beyond what is required for achieving the aim and the interference may not be more intense than necessary.[511] Third, there must be

'Beyond the Rule of Law' (2000); Feldman, 'Proportionality and the Human Rights Act 1998' (1999).

503 *R (Daly)* v. *Secretary of State for the Home Department*, [2001] UKHL 26, para. 27.

504 *R (Razgar)* v. *Secretary of State for the Home Department*, [2004] UKHL 27, para. 20.

505 Zimmerli, 'Der Grundsatz der Verhältnismässigkeit im öffentlichen Recht' (1978), 9–10; Muller, 'Le principe de la proportionnalité' (1978), 209–10; Huber, 'Über den Grundsatz der Verhältnismässigkeit im Verwaltungsrecht' (1977), 4, 9.

506 Zimmerli, 'Der Grundsatz der Verhältnismässigkeit im öffentlichen Recht' (1978), 10–11; Huber, 'Über den Grundsatz der Verhältnismässigkeit im Verwaltungsrecht' (1977), 9–16. See also already Imboden, *Schweizerische Verwaltungsrechtsprechung* (1960), 121–2.

507 E.g. BGE 129 I 173, 181 (2003); BGE 117 Ia 472, 483 (1991); BGE 112 Ia 65, 70 (1986).

508 See Schefer, *Die Beeinträchtigung von Grundrechten* (2006), p. 82 and further references cited there. See also Kiener/Kälin, *Grundrechte* (2013), p. 119.

509 BGE 130 I 369, 384–5 (2004); BGE 116 Ia 355, 358 (1990).

510 E.g. BGE 128 I 3, 16–17 (2001).

511 E.g. BGE 126 I 112, 119–20 (2000); BGE 124 I 40, 44–5 (1998).

a *reasonable relationship* between the aim pursued and the interference: the burden imposed on the individual must not be disproportionate to the importance of the public interest (or of the rights of others).[512] This third element, often referred to as 'proportionality in the narrow sense',[513] requires a careful balancing between the interests of the individual and those of the state (or of third persons).[514]

In US law, the term 'proportionality' is explicitly used only in limited areas. Nevertheless, at least implicitly, courts have applied the principle of proportionality in many different contexts to review government measures.[515] In fact, it arguably was the US Supreme Court that first developed the 'least restrictive means' test, which is now so central to proportionality analysis in numerous other jurisdictions.[516] Today, it has been argued, proportionality analysis is emerging as a general standard of review in the United States, and the differences between the US approach of reviewing government measures and that of other, including European, jurisdictions have become largely semantic.[517] As far as the present context of interferences with fundamental rights is concerned, the different elements of proportionality as required under the ECHR (and thus UK law) and Swiss law are clearly reflected in the case law of the Supreme Court. As explained above, the court requires different degrees of means-end relationships, depending on the applicable standard of review.[518] Under all US standards of review, the interference must serve – or at the very least be rationally related to – a government interest, corresponding to the first element of proportionality under the ECHR and Swiss law: suitability.[519] Second, the 'least restrictive means' test, which is an important test in US constitutional law,[520] is analogous to the necessity requirement of the ECHR and Swiss law.[521] Finally, although the two concepts have different historical origins, the balancing doctrine

512 BGE 116 Ia 420, 423–25 (1990); BGE 115 Ia 207, 210–12 (1989).

513 Häfelin/Haller/Keller, *Schweizerisches Bundesstaatsrecht* (2012), p. 105 ('Verhältnismässigkeit im engeren Sinn').

514 BGE 128 I 327, 342–5 (2002).

515 See Mathews/Stone Sweet, 'All Things in Proportion?' (2011); Sullivan/Frase, *Proportionality Principles in American Law* (2009).

516 *Shelton* v. *Tucker*, 364 U.S. 479, 493 (1960).

517 Sullivan/Frase, *Proportionality Principles in American Law* (2009).

518 See Section 5.3. 519 See Section 5.3.

520 See Wormuth/Mirkin, 'The Doctrine of the Reasonable Alternative' (1964).

521 For an example, see *United States* v. *O'Brien*, 391 U.S. 367, 377 (1968) (the interference must be 'no greater than is essential to the furtherance of [a governmental] interest').

of US constitutional law[522] resembles the balancing requirement under the ECHR and Swiss law in important respects, equally requiring the weighing of individual rights against the interests of the public.[523] As Justice Breyer of the Supreme Court has explained,

> [W]here a law significantly implicates competing constitutionally protected interests in complex ways, the Court has closely scrutinized the statute's impact on those interests, but refrained from employing a simple test that effectively presumes unconstitutionality. Rather, it has balanced interests. And in practice that has meant asking whether the statute burdens any one such interest in a manner out of proportion to the statute's salutary effects upon the others.[524]

5.3.2.2 Proportionality of exclusion measures

What needs to be examined under the heading of proportionality is whether, considering all the circumstances of the case at hand, the legitimate aim invoked by the state can justify the particular interference with fundamental rights. It is therefore difficult to make general statements about the proportionality of exclusion measures – whether a particular measure is proportionate or not depends on the nature of the aim pursued, the importance of the protected right (or the relevant aspect of that right), the personal, geographical and temporal scope of the interference, the seriousness of the interference and a variety of other factors. As a consequence, for example, a particular type of exclusion measure may be a proportionate means to deal with one sort of situations but not necessarily with another, or the same exclusion power may be applied in a proportionate way in one case and in a disproportionate manner in another. This also means that legal challenges against exclusion norms themselves, where these are possible at all, will normally fail as it is almost always possible to think of a scenario where the respective norm could be applied in a proportionate way.[525]

522 See Aleinikoff, 'Constitutional Law in the Age of Balancing' (1987).

523 Cohen-Eliya/Porat, 'American Balancing and German Proportionality' (2010).

524 *Nixon* v. *Shrink Missouri Government PAC*, 528 U.S. 377, 402 (2000) (Breyer, J., concurring). See also Justice Breyer's more recent remarks in *District of Columbia* v. *Heller*, 554 U.S. 570, 689–91 (2008) (Breyer, J., dissenting).

525 See e.g. BGE 128 I 327, 345 (2002) (pointing out that, given the manifold possible scenarios and threat situations in which an exclusion norm contained in a cantonal police act could be applied, it is nearly impossible to come to a conclusive assessment of its proportionality in the abstract.). See also *Doe* v. *Town of Plainfield*, 893 N.E.2d 1124, 1129 (Ind. C.A. 2008) (explaining that 'a facial challenge to the constitutionality of an ordinance requires the challenging party to demonstrate that there are no set of circumstances under which the [ordinance] can be constitutionally applied').

One general statement that can be made, however, is that one form of exclusion from public space will normally be unproblematic in terms of its proportionality: namely, police measures ordering people to leave a specific public place for a short period to defuse a dangerous or volatile situation. As explained in Section 3.1, such a police power to deal with an immediate threat to public safety and order has since long been part of many legal systems of the world. For example, it is not subject to serious doubt that the police must have the power to ask onlookers to leave the site of an accident, send away people who are impeding the fire or emergency services or the police in the execution of their duties, close off part of a road in case of a traffic accident, prohibit people (not least for their own protection) from being within a certain distance of a nuclear power plant after an accident or evacuate them from the site of a natural catastrophe.[526] All of these police interventions are narrowly circumscribed, and thus proportionate, responses to an immediate threat to public safety and order and/or public health. In contrast, the focus of what follows is on measures that apply to larger geographical areas, for longer periods and regardless of whether there is an immediate threat to public safety and order – in other words, on the sort of exclusion measures that, as explained in Chapter 3, have become increasingly common in recent years.

Criminal behaviour As explained before, some exclusion measures are imposed as an additional restriction to prevent re-offending following a conviction in the normal criminal process. This is the case, for instance, in the United Kingdom, with SHPOs and those football banning orders that are imposed under Section 14A of the Football Spectators Act 1989, in the United States, with state and municipal laws that prohibit convicted sex offenders from loitering near schools or other areas where minors congregate or from entering public parks and, in Switzerland, with orders imposed on those convicted to a suspended sentence for the time of their probationary period and the area bans for convicted sex offenders that apply regardless of a probationary period.[527] Especially where, as in the case of the Swiss measures or in that of the British SHPOs and football banning orders, such measures are imposed following an

[526] See BGE 128 I 327, 336, 342 (2002). For an example of such a narrowly defined police power, see the Police Act of the Canton of Basel-Stadt: Gesetz betreffend die Kantonspolizei des Kantons Basel-Stadt vom 13. November 1996 (Polizeigesetz, PolG, SG 510.100), § 42.

[527] See Section 3.3.1.1.

individualised assessment, carried out by a court, of the threat that the convicted person poses to society, they will normally not raise major problems with regard to their proportionality. Such an assessment is not only an important safeguard to ensure that there is sufficient evidence that the respective measure is necessary in the circumstances of the particular case, but it also allows the court to comprehensively balance the various interests at stake and to tailor the terms of the measure to the specific requirements of the situation. Having said this, there must, of course, always be a reasonable relationship of proportionality between, on the one hand, the terms of the exclusion measure imposed and, on the other, the public interest to be achieved through imposition of the measure.

The various US sex offender laws are more problematic in this regard as the exclusion measures they provide for automatically apply to everyone who, because he or she has been convicted of one of a number of listed offences, is registered as a sex offender. Thus, although there will have been a conviction by a court for a relevant offence at some stage in the past, there is no individualised assessment as to whether the exclusion measure is a suitable, necessary and proportionate means to prevent crime. Instead, there is a blanket assumption that everyone convicted of certain offences poses a threat to public safety. This broad personal scope raises problems with regard to the proportionality – in particular the necessity – of the relevant exclusion measures. After all, past conviction of a particular type of offence is not necessarily a significant determinant of future dangerousness. For example, it is not clear why it should be necessary for reasons of public safety to ban a girl convicted for having oral sex with a fifteen-year-old boy when she was eighteen from entering public parks or being in the vicinity of schools, as would be the case under the relevant legislation of the state of Georgia.[528] This sort of legislation will almost inevitably lead to disproportionate outcomes in that people will be subject to exclusion from public space despite the fact that this is not necessary for the prevention of crime. In addition, the burden imposed on individuals through such measures is often very significant and may thus be disproportionate to the importance of the aim pursued. Most of the exclusion measures directed against sex offenders apply for lifetime. The Indiana Appeals Court made the following observation in the case

[528] Official Code of Georgia, s. 42-1-12. See Bains, 'Next-Generation Sex Offender Statutes' (2007), 489, 492–3.

of a man who had been convicted of sexual battery eleven years earlier and was, as a consequence, banned from entering Jeffersonville's parks and thereby prevented from attending his son's baseball games: 'Much of a community's social life occurs in public parks – youth and adult sporting events, picnics, community celebrations and events, to name but a few – and an ordinance that fully and forever prohibits one from taking part in such activities – or from taking a walk in the park – is a real and significant restraint'.[529] The imbalance between the aim pursued and the burden imposed on the individual is often aggravated by the severity of the sentence that may be imposed if the exclusion measure is breached. In the case of the sex offender legislation of Georgia, for example, a violation of the loitering prohibition is punishable by imprisonment for ten to thirty years.[530]

Even more problematic are those exclusion measures that do not require a previous conviction for a criminal offence by a court, that is, measures that are imposed on *potential* offenders. Such measures intended to prevent crimes from being committed include the terrorism control orders and TPIMs, serious crime prevention orders, football banning orders imposed under Section 14B of the Football Spectators Act 1989 and sexual risk orders in the United Kingdom, the drug-exclusion zones and gang congregation ordinances in the United States and the area bans imposed in connection with sports events in Switzerland.[531] As will now be explained in detail, it may be questionable whether these measures satisfy the tests of suitability, necessity and proportionality in the narrow sense.

Suitability

Courts often tend to affirm the suitability of exclusion measures to prevent crime without undertaking a proper, thorough examination of the issue. In a case concerning the area bans imposed in connection with sports events in Switzerland, for example, the Administrative Court of the Canton of Zurich devoted only one sentence of its opinion to the question of suitability, simply stating that it was obvious that the respective area ban was a suitable means to protect public safety as it kept the applicant away from sports events.[532] When the area bans were introduced in Switzerland, the alleged success of the UK banning orders was

[529] *Dowdell v. City of Jeffersonville*, 907 N.E.2d 559, 566 (Ind. C.A. 2009).

[530] Official Code of Georgia, s. 42-1-15(g). [531] See Section 3.3.1.2.

[532] Urteil des Verwaltungsgerichts des Kantons Zürich VB.2008.00237 vom 19. Juni 2008, E. 6.2.

cited in support of this measure.[533] Yet an important body of research on the football banning orders in the United Kingdom questions whether the banning orders have played any significant role in reducing crime and disorder caused by football supporters.[534] Those subject to football banning orders, it seems, are often not the 'real' hooligans.[535] In addition, control and enforcement of such orders presupposes that the police are aware of who is subject to them, which may not always be the case.[536]

The Swiss Federal Supreme Court has acknowledged that, rather than to solve the problem of violence around sports events, area bans may simply lead to a displacement of violent incidents to other areas or to lower leagues. Nevertheless, it found that such bans were still a suitable means as they at least kept away potentially violent persons from those areas where experience shows violent incidents are particularly frequent.[537] Whilst – assuming enforcement is indeed possible – this is true, it still puts into perspective the effectiveness of area bans in preventing crime. Furthermore, it is questionable whether mere displacement is a suitable means to address other forms of crime than football-related violence. In the case of drug-exclusion zones, for example, it may make sense to keep away 'drug scenes' from heavily frequented locations in city centres. Apart from this, however, it is subject to serious doubt whether anything is gained by moving 'drug scenes' away from one part of town to another. In Portland, Oregon, an ordinance creating a drug-exclusion zone was not renewed because it did not lead to a reduction in drug-related crime but merely resulted in the criminal activity moving to another location.[538]

Necessity

With many of the exclusion measures intended to prevent crime it is questionable whether they are the least restrictive means available to achieve this aim. It is primarily the broad personal scope of many of these measures that is of concern in this regard. As explained before, for

[533] Botschaft zur Änderung des Bundesgesetzes über Massnahmen zur Wahrung der inneren Sicherheit (Massnahmen gegen Gewaltpropaganda und gegen Gewalt anlässlich von Sportveranstaltungen) vom 17. August 2005, BBl 2005, 5613, p. 5624.

[534] See Stott/Pearson, 'Football Banning Orders, Proportionality, and Public Order Policing' (2006).

[535] See ibid., 244–5.

[536] Soòs/Vögeli, 'BWIS-Massnahmen gegen Gewalt an Sportveranstaltungen' (2008), 160.

[537] BGE 137 I 31, 47–8 (2010).

[538] 'Portland's 'drug free zone' laws to end October 1st', Katu.com, 27 September 2007, available at www.katu.com/news/10068071.html.

none of the exclusion measures at issue here is a previous conviction for a criminal offence a prerequisite. In fact, the threshold is generally rather low. For example, in the United Kingdom it is sufficient for the making of a serious crime prevention order that the High Court 'is satisfied that a person has been involved in serious crime [. . .] and [. . .] it has reasonable grounds to believe that the order would protect the public by preventing, restricting or disrupting involvement by the person in serious crime'.[539] The Swiss area bans surrounding sports events can be imposed by the police against anyone who has been previously involved in violence against persons or property in connection with sports events;[540] previous involvement can be substantiated by other means than conviction by a court,[541] including, for example, credible statements by the police or security personnel, stadium bans issued by sports clubs or associations and reports by foreign authorities.[542] As a final example, in the case of the ban from drug-exclusion zones in the US City of Cincinnati the only requirement was that the respective person 'has been arrested or otherwise taken into custody within any drug-exclusion zone for drug abuse or any drug abuse-related activities'.[543] The 'drug-free zone' scheme of the City of Portland establishes a similar threshold.[544]

Measures such as drug-exclusion zones, which do not require any individualised assessment whatsoever of the threat posed by the individual to public safety or of the need for excluding that individual from public space, are particularly problematic. The US Court of Appeals for the Sixth Circuit correctly observed that the Cincinnati ordinance relied only on general evidence that those arrested for drug activity in the relevant zone typically return there and repeat their offences. The court found that reliance on such general evidence meant that the ban from drug-exclusion zones was not narrowly tailored enough to address the public interest, that is, prevention of crime. Instead, the court held, there must be some individualised consideration and a particularised finding that the arrested individual is likely to repeat his or her drug crime.[545]

[539] Serious Crime Act 2007, s. 1(1).
[540] Konkordat über Massnahmen gegen Gewalt anlässlich von Sportveranstaltungen vom 15. November 2007, Art. 4(1).
[541] See Urteil des Bundesgerichts 1C_88/2011 vom 15. Juni 2011, E. 3.5.
[542] Konkordat über Massnahmen gegen Gewalt anlässlich von Sportveranstaltungen vom 15. November 2007, Art. 3.
[543] Cincinnati Municipal Code, § 755-5 (repealed).
[544] Charter and Code of the City of Portland, Oregon, s. 14B.20.030(A).
[545] *Johnson* v. *City of Cincinnati*, 310 F.3d 484, 503–4 (6th Cir. 2002).

Even where there is an individualised assessment of the threat to public safety, exclusion measures designed to prevent crime raise concerns because this assessment is often not undertaken by a court. Of the measures listed above, only the legal regimes of the United Kingdom relating to the sexual risk orders and the serious crime prevention orders provide for a judicial assessment, whereas in the other instances the assessment is carried out by the police or some other government authority. There is accordingly a danger that these broadly defined exclusion powers may be used in a disproportionate manner, that is, in cases where this is not warranted for the prevention of crime. At least with some of these measures, the evidence seems to suggest that this is indeed the case. For example, in the City of Zurich, by 2013, seventy-nine appeals had been brought against area bans in connection with sports events. In only six of these cases did the courts confirm the area bans imposed by the police. In forty-seven cases the appeal was upheld or partially upheld, in twenty-three cases the courts had to define more precisely the area bans that had been imposed by the police.[546] In one case, for instance, the police imposed an area ban on a football supporter who had caused minor material damage (to a seat) during a game but had not threatened others, had apologised to the club and had no previous criminal conviction. The Administrative Court of the Canton of Zurich found that the area ban was disproportionate as the risk that the supporter would become violent again was minimal.[547] Another exclusion measure where figures concerning its enforcement suggest that it may have been applied in a disproportionate manner is the Gang Congregation Ordinance of the City of Chicago. During the three years of its enforcement, the police issued over 89,000 dispersal orders and arrested over 42,000 people for violating the ordinance.[548]

In other cases, the particular terms imposed as part of an exclusion measure may be more restrictive than is required by the situation. It was for this reason that the Administrative Court of the Canton of Zurich overturned an area ban that prevented the applicant from being in five specified zones of the City of Zurich six hours before and six hours after any football or ice hockey game for a year. The court held that it was in no way necessary for the ban to apply with regard to all sports events, which,

[546] Information provided to the author by the Bezirksgericht Zürich with message of 10 July 2013 (statistics on file with author).

[547] Urteil des Verwaltungsgerichts des Kantons Zürich VB.2009.00019 vom 26. Februar 2009, E. 4.2.

[548] *City of Chicago* v. *Morales*, 527 U.S. 41, 49 (1999).

given the sheer number of sports events held in Zurich, would make it impossible for the applicant to identify the times when he would be allowed to enter the specified zones and when not.[549] Instead, the court reduced the ban to first league and international football matches as these were the only events where there was a danger of disorder and it was undisputed that the applicant did not attend ice hockey games; the territorial scope of the ban was also limited accordingly.[550] In other cases, Swiss courts have found the temporal duration of area bans imposed on football supporters to be excessive.[551]

Finally, all the measures at issue here allow for the prohibition of mere presence in the respective parts of public space, raising the question of whether such a broad definition of the scope of prohibited conduct is necessary for the prevention of crime. As both the US Court of Appeals for the Sixth Circuit and the Supreme Court of Ohio highlighted with regard to the Cincinnati drug-exclusion zones, the zones prevented those concerned not only from engaging in drug-related activity but also from engaging in conduct that was completely innocent and, indeed, socially beneficial.[552] Thus, the zones made it impossible for Patricia Johnson to care for her grandchildren and walk them to school, while another complainant was prevented from meeting with his lawyer.[553] Both courts concluded that the Cincinnati ordinance targeted more than the source of the drug problem and was therefore not narrowly tailored to achieve the – compelling – interest in reducing drug-related activity.[554]

As with the other limitation requirements, it is up to the state to show that the measure interfering with an individual's fundamental rights is necessary to achieve the aim pursued. In the case of the Cincinnati drug-exclusion zones, for example, the US Court of Appeals for the Sixth Circuit laid great stress on the fact that it was the city that bore the burden of identifying potential alternatives. The court was not satisfied with its assertion that other attempts to reduce drug-related crime in the relevant areas, in particular through an increase in police patrols, had failed; the city, the court held, would have had to put forth concrete

549 Urteil des Verwaltungsgerichts des Kantons Zürich VG.2008.00237 vom 19. Juni 2008, E. 6.

550 Ibid., E. 7.

551 E.g. Urteil des Verwaltungsgerichts des Kantons St. Gallen B 2009/81 vom 22. September 2009, E. 4.2.

552 *Johnson* v. *City of Cincinnati*, 310 F.3d 484, 503 (6th Cir. 2002); *State* v. *Burnett*, 755 N.E. 2d 857, 866–7 (Ohio 2001).

553 *Johnson* v. *City of Cincinnati*, 310 F.3d 484, 503 (6th Cir. 2002).

554 Ibid., 503–504; *State* v. *Burnett*, 755 N.E.2d 857, 866–7 (Ohio 2001).

evidence demonstrating that these efforts were ineffective.[555] As this example shows, exclusion measures designed to prevent crime raise the general question of why the instruments that have traditionally been available to the police to protect public safety (such as police patrols or the identification and apprehension of offenders with a view to prosecuting them) are no longer seen as sufficient for this task. Of course, there may be good reasons why it may be necessary to introduce new tools to prevent criminal behaviour. However, mere *claims* that exclusion measures are more effective than forms of police action that interfere less with fundamental rights are not enough for the state to meet the necessity requirement.

Proportionality in the narrow sense

As far as proportionality in the narrow sense is concerned, it is important to take into account that exclusion measures designed to prevent crime typically amount to rather serious interferences. Terrorist control orders or TPIMs, for instance, may involve curfews and thus restrictions of movement that are so serious as to amount to a deprivation of liberty in the sense of Article 5 of the ECHR;[556] in addition, they often infringe on a number of further rights such as the right to respect for family life.[557] The 'drug exclusion zone' at issue in *Johnson* v. *City of Cincinnati* comprised a whole neighbourhood and was thus correctly qualified as a severe restriction.[558] The Swiss area bans in connection with sports events prevent people from accessing large parts of inner city areas for several hours on match days over a period of up to one year (and, under the revised Hooligan Concordat, up to three years) and have thus been held to be, at the very least, more than just marginal interferences.[559] More fundamentally, since those concerned are effectively prevented from associating with their fellow supporters for several months or even years, such area bans, as well as the British football banning orders, often entail exclusion from a social group. Finally, as explained at the beginning of this section, exclusion measures directed against sex offenders in the United States may prevent them from participating in an important part of a community's social life for the rest of their lives.

[555] *Johnson* v. *City of Cincinnati*, 310 F.3d 484, 504–5 (6th Cir. 2002).

[556] *Secretary of State for the Home Department* v. *JJ*, [2007] UKHL 45, paras 24 (Lord Bingham), 62–3 (Baroness Hale), 105–6 (Lord Brown).

[557] See *Secretary of State for the Home Department* v. *AP*, [2010] UKSC 24.

[558] *Johnson* v. *Cincinnati*, 310 F.3d 484, 502 (6th Cir. 2002).

[559] Urteil des Verwaltungsgerichts des Kantons Zürich VB.2009.00019 vom 26. Februar 2009, E. 4.2.

On the other hand, the effectiveness of many exclusion measures designed to prevent crime (such as 'drug exclusion zones' or area bans in connection with sports events) is, as also explained above, contentious and, at best, limited. Thus, where the benefit of exclusion measures in preventing crime is minimal as compared to other forms of police intervention, the requirement of a reasonable relationship between the interests of the individual and those of the state will not be satisfied. Only a real gain in public safety can justify imposing such a heavy burden on individuals.

Anti-social behaviour The various blanket exclusion norms that primarily target anti-social behaviour[560] as well as the more specific exclusion measures directed against the presence of juveniles,[561] vagrancy, loitering,[562] obstructing pedestrian traffic, sleeping, sitting, spitting and drinking alcohol in public places[563] are based on the notion that the appearance of particular parts of public space needs to be improved. They are designed to create a sense of orderliness and safety for those using these spaces and to convey a strong message that behaviour that may undermine this sense will not be tolerated but will be met with drastic action.[564] That such an approach of meeting relatively minor disorder and incivilities with a resolute reaction containing a strong symbolic element will clash with the principle of proportionality is almost inevitable.[565] As explained in Section 5.3.1.2, exclusion measures based on this approach may already fail to satisfy the legitimate aim test if they are purely about the protection of feelings. Instead, they must serve some objectively conceived public interest, and it is this objective standard that must be referred to when assessing their proportionality. The relevant legitimate aims thus include the protection of public order and safety, understood in an objective sense, the protection of public health, in particular the prevention of noise and littering, and, with the reservations explained above,[566] economic reasons.

Suitability

The suitability of exclusion measures directed against anti-social behaviour has rarely been subjected to critical analysis. Both with regard to

[560] See Section 3.3.2.4. [561] See Section 3.3.2.3. [562] See Section 3.3.2.1.

[563] See Section 3.3.2.2. [564] See Sections 2.5.2 and 3.2.

[565] See also Volkmann, 'Die Rückeroberung der Allmende' (2000), 364–5; Volkmann, 'Broken Windows, Zero Tolerance und das deutsche Ordnungsrecht' (1999), 230–31.

[566] See Section 5.3.1.2.

blanket exclusion norms[567] and to more specific exclusion measures such as juvenile curfews,[568] courts have concluded that these were clearly suitable means to prevent anti-social behaviour, as they kept the groups of people that are seen as its main source off the streets. Although a US district court acknowledged in a case concerning a juvenile curfew that, in the absence of relevant statistical data, it was impossible to ascertain the effectiveness of such curfews with scientific certainty, it still thought that it was 'apparent' that they had some positive effect.[569]

The most obvious objection that can be made to the suitability of measures banning alcoholics, homeless people, vagrants, drug addicts or unruly juveniles from parts of public space is that they merely lead to a displacement of 'the problem', be it a geographical displacement or, in the case of juvenile curfews, also a displacement in time.[570] This is, however, not necessarily a strong objection. Depending on the nature of the aim pursued, displacing the respective groups of people may be a perfectly suitable and sufficient means for achieving the aim. Moving away alcoholics from an inner-city shopping area may be a suitable means of improving the cleanliness of that area, keeping away drug addicts from a residential neighbourhood with families may be an effective way of protecting public health and banning juveniles from the streets after a certain hour may be a suitable means of preventing – or at least reducing – noise at night. That a measure fails to solve the root problem does not automatically mean that it does not meet the suitability test.

That exclusion measures are an effective means of at least displacing the groups of people that are allegedly responsible for anti-social behaviour is, however, not as obvious as it often seems to be assumed. Whilst there are no comprehensive studies on the effectiveness of exclusion measures directed against anti-social behaviour, anecdotal evidence suggests that such measures tend not to be complied with. A large part of those who have been subject to exclusion orders based on the cantonal Police Act in the City of Berne (mainly alcohol and drug addicts), have

567 Urteil des Bundesgerichts 1C_226/2009 vom 16. Dezember 2009, E. 5.1; BGE 132 I 49, 63 (2006).

568 *Bykofsky* v. *Borough of Middletown*, 401 F.Supp. 1242, 1256 (D.C. Pa. 1975).

569 Ibid., 1256.

570 Several empirical studies of juvenile curfew laws in the United States have concluded that such curfews are ineffective and may lead to a displacement in time and place. Cole, 'The Effect of a Curfew Law on Juvenile Crime in Washington, D.C.' (2003); Reynolds/Seydlitz/Jenkins, 'Do Juvenile Curfew Laws Work?' (2000) and references cited there.

persistently refused to leave the parts of public space from which they had been banned. As a consequence, many of them have been sentenced to fines and short prison terms and issued with new exclusion orders, which, in turn, they have refused to comply with.[571] Some individuals in Berne have apparently received up to thirty-eight exclusion orders.[572] In the United Kingdom, of a total of 24,427 ASBOs issued between 1999 and the end of 2013, 58 per cent were breached at least once,[573] leading the government to the conclusion 'that ASBOs are not always effective in tackling anti-social behaviour'[574] and, eventually, to a reconsideration of its policy of dealing with anti-social behaviour.[575] Research carried out in Seattle showed that only a third of respondents (mainly homeless people and alcohol and drug addicts) who had been served with exclusion orders complied with their orders.[576] The respondents explained their lack of compliance with the fact that the places they had been banned from (mainly parks and drug-exclusion zones) were the only place where they felt at home and safe and which offered them opportunities for social contact. As a consequence, in their view, there was simply no other place for them to go.[577]

Necessity

Exclusion measures designed to counter anti-social behaviour raise concerns with regard to their broad personal scope. As in the 'security society' the attention has shifted from individuals and their concrete acts to segments of the population that are categorised according to their levels of dangerousness and to the appearance of particular spaces; it is no longer individuals that are the focus of policing strategies but broadly defined collectives.[578] Accordingly, for example, juvenile curfews cover everyone below a certain age, regardless of whether they have given

571 Gasser, *Kriminalpolitik oder City-Pflege?* (2004), pp. 32–3.

572 C. Weber, 'Wegweisungen in der Stadt Bern: ein untaugliches Polizeimittel', Medienorientierung Grüne/AL, 11 November 2004.

573 Home Office, Anti-Social Behaviour Order Statistics – England and Wales 2013, 18 September 2014, available at www.gov.uk/government/statistics/anti-social-behaviour-order-statistics-england-and-wales-2013.

574 Home Office, Criminal Behaviour Order, Injunction and Dispersal Powers Impact Assessment, 9 May 2013, p. 5, available at www.gov.uk/government/uploads/system/uploads/attachment_data/file/197611/ReformingASBtools_and_powers__CBO-CPIand Dispersal130509.pdf.

575 See Home Office, Fact Sheet: Anti-social Behaviour Reforms Overview, 9 May 2013, available at www.gov.uk/government/uploads/system/uploads/attachment_data/file/201072/Fact_sheet_ASB_Overview.pdf.

576 Beckett/Herbert, *Banished* (2010), p. 109.

577 Ibid., pp. 103–16.

578 See Section 2.5.2.

any cause for complaint or, indeed, how likely they are ever to give cause for complaint. Similarly, blanket exclusion norms such as the one contained in the Police Act of the Canton of Berne can be used, not only against those who threaten or disturb public safety and order themselves, but also against anyone who assembles with others who do so.[579]

This de-coupling from the risk posed by individuals runs counter to the principle that measures interfering with fundamental rights must be limited to those who have given cause for the interference, that is, in the context of police actions, to those who disturb or pose a threat to public safety and order. This principle, referred to as *Störerprinzip/principe du perturbateur* in Swiss legal doctrine, is closely linked to the necessity requirement of the principle of proportionality and is well-established in all three jurisdictions at issue.[580] Therefore, it is up to the police to identify the individuals who pose such a threat and to take action against them. The fact that this may not always be easy to achieve is not a sufficient justification for adopting measures that extend to forms of behaviour that are unproblematic from the perspective of the legitimate aim pursued.

It is for this reason that several courts in the United States and Switzerland have held that juvenile curfews fail to meet the necessity requirement. The Administrative Court of the Canton of Zurich, for instance, found that the Police Ordinance of the municipality of Dänikon, which made it unlawful for children of compulsory school age to assemble in public places after 10 pm,[581] was overly broad in its personal scope.[582] The court rejected the argument of the municipality that it was inevitable that measures such as curfews also have an impact on those who did not cause any problems as it was difficult to identify the real culprits. The court observed that there already existed

[579] Polizeigesetz vom 8. Juni 1997 (BSG 551.1), Art. 29(1)(b).

[580] For Switzerland, see e.g. BGE 122 II 65, 70 (1996); BGE 118 Ib 407, 414–15 (1992); BGE 101 Ib 410, 414–21 (1975); Moor/Flückiger/Martenet, *Droit administratif I* (2012), pp. 827–31; Häfelin/Müller/Uhlmann, *Allgemeines Verwaltungsrecht* (2010), pp. 569–73; Thürer, 'Das Störerprinzip im Polizeirecht' (1983); Mathys, *Zum Begriff des Störers im Polizeirecht* (1974). For the United Kingdom, see *Redmond-Bate v. Director of Public Prosecutions*, (1999) 163 JP 789; *Beatty* v. *Gillbanks*, (1882) 9 QBD 308. For the United States, see *Gregory* v. *Chicago*, 394 U.S. 111 (1969); *Feiner* v. *New York*, 340 U.S. 315, 321–31 (1951) (Black, Douglas and Minton, JJ, dissenting); *Wolin* v. *Port of New York Authority*, 392 F. 2d 83 (2nd Cir. 1968).

[581] Polizeiverordnung der Gemeinde Dänikon vom 18. Juni 2008, Art. 27 (repealed; see Urteil des Verwaltungsgerichts des Kantons Zürich VB.2009.00055 vom 30. April 2009).

[582] Urteil des Verwaltungsgerichts des Kantons Zürich VB.2009.00055 vom 30.April 2009, E. 5.2.3.

prohibitions of disturbing the peace and vandalism and that it was up to the authorities to enforce these prohibitions; it was impermissible to instead create a new measure that also encompasses persons who have not given any cause for complaint, solely because this may be an easier solution for the authorities.[583] While in the United States the Supreme Court has never addressed the issue, several lower courts have overturned juvenile curfews based on the same reasoning as that of the Administrative Court of the Canton of Zurich.[584] Thus, the US District Court for the District of Columbia observed with regard to a curfew statute of the district that made it illegal for persons below the age of eighteen to be on the streets between 11 pm and 6 am: 'The Act subjects the District's juveniles to virtual house arrest each night without differentiating either among those juveniles likely to embroil themselves in mischief, or among those activities most likely to produce harm. The Act is a bull in a china shop of constitutional values.'[585] Although other courts have upheld more targeted juvenile curfews,[586] courts have generally agreed that, at the very least, curfews that also apply to *adults* are overbroad.[587]

The same applies to exclusion norms, the scope of which is not limited to those who threaten or disturb public safety and order themselves, such as the one of the Police Act of the Canton of Berne. By also covering persons who merely associate with others who pose a threat to public safety and order, such provisions overshoot their objective. That this makes it easier for the police to take action is not a sufficient justification for broadening the scope of the respective provisions to cover forms of behaviour that do not themselves undermine public safety and order. In its decision concerning the Bernese exclusion orders, the Federal Supreme Court did not directly address this issue, apparently assuming that those subject to the orders in the case at hand had themselves disturbed public safety and order through their own behaviour.[588] In practice, however, there have been several cases in Berne where exclusion orders were issued against persons who clearly did not pose

583 Ibid.

584 *Nunez* v. *City of San Diego*, 114 F.3d 935, 949 (9th Cir. 1997); *Waters* v. *Barry*, 711 F. Supp. 1125, 1134 (D.D.C. 1989).

585 *Waters* v. *Barry*, 711 F.Supp. 1125, 1134 (D.D.C. 1989).

586 E.g. *Bykofsky* v. *Borough of Middletown*, 401 F.Supp. 1242 (D.C. Pa. 1975).

587 E.g. *Ruff* v. *Marshall*, 438 F. Supp. 303 (M.D. Ga. 1977). See Horowitz, 'A Search for Constitutional Standards' (1991), 384–5.

588 BGE 132 I 49, 63 (2006).

a threat to public safety and order themselves, including two street workers who were giving medical support to alcoholics.[589]

That it must be shown in each and every case that a given person poses a threat to public safety and order in a way that makes it necessary to ban them from public space is a general rule that applies to *any* kind of exclusion measure. The Administrative Court of the Canton of Berne has accordingly stressed that the police must be able to demonstrate in each case why imposing an exclusion order on the person concerned is necessary for reasons of public safety and order and has warned against the use of standard formulations and text modules in exclusion orders.[590]

As far as exclusion measures *are* targeted at those who pose a threat to public safety and order or to public health, an assessment of their necessity will depend on several factors, such as the availability of less restrictive measures, the geographical and temporal scope of the exclusion measure and the form of behaviour that is prohibited in the relevant area (that is, whether specified behaviour or mere presence is prohibited). These factors need to be examined with regard to each and every exclusion measure individually. With regard to ASBOs, the English Court of Appeal has correctly made the following observation: '[E]ach separate order prohibiting a person from doing a specified thing must be necessary to protect persons from further anti-social acts by him. Any order should therefore be tailor-made for the individual offender, not designed on a word processor for use in every case.'[591] As is highlighted by the court's last remark, there is a danger that in the case of measures directed against anti-social behaviour, which often tend to be imposed in great numbers, the necessity test with regard to *the terms* of the measure imposed may not be carried out with the required attention to the specific circumstances of the individual case.

Thus, it must be explored with regard to each and every exclusion measure whether there is not a less restrictive means available to achieve the aim pursued. For example, it may be sufficient for the police to simply ask people who are engaging in anti-social behaviour to move on, rather than to issue a formal exclusion order, which will normally apply for an extended period.[592]

With regard to the temporal scope of exclusion, the relevant pieces of legislation often fail to specify any time limits.[593] This is the case, for

589 Gasser, *Kriminalpolitik oder City-Pflege?* (2004), p. 30.

590 BVR 2009, 385, p. 394 (Verwaltungsgericht des Kantons Bern).

591 *R* v. *Boness (Dean)*, [2005] EWCA Crim 2395, para. 28.

592 See Urteil des Bundesgerichts 1C_226/2009 vom 16. Dezember 2009, E. 5.1.

593 See Section 3.4.4.3.

example, with some of the cantonal police acts in Switzerland (such as those of the Cantons of Grisons and Uri)[594] or the British Anti-social Behaviour, Crime and Policing Act 2014, which neither for IPNAs nor CBOs sets an upper time limit.[595] The authorities applying these provisions thus have wide discretion in determining the period of exclusion. It will normally only be necessary to resort to longer-term exclusion measures once measures of a shorter duration have proved fruitless.[596] In addition, once in place, an exclusion measure such as, for example, a curfew imposed as part of an ASBO (or, today, an IPNA or a CBO) may have to be reduced in duration to adapt it to a change in the factual situation.[597] As with exclusion measures designed to prevent crime, it is often only once cases are brought before the courts that exclusion measures directed against anti-social behaviour are limited in time. In the case of the exclusion orders in the City of Berne, for example, the police had to reduce the standard period for exclusion from one year to three months following legal proceedings.[598] In the United Kingdom, the courts have often corrected the periods of exclusion measures imposed as part of ASBOs because they were held to be 'manifestly excessive' in the particular circumstances.[599]

The geographical scope of exclusion measures directed against anti-social behaviour is often very extensive, raising the question of whether a narrower definition of the banned areas would not be sufficient for achieving the respective objective. As with the temporal scope, the relevant norms normally give the executive branch almost complete discretion in defining the geographical scope of exclusion.[600] In the United Kingdom, people have been banned as part of ASBOs from entering large areas of towns[601] or, as in the case of Christopher Lamb referred to in Chapter 1, city centres for extended periods of time[602]

[594] For the Canton of Grisons: Polizeigesetz des Kantons Graubünden vom 20. Oktober 2004 (PolG, BR 613.000), Art. 12; for the Canton of Uri: Polizeigesetz vom 30. November 2008 (RB 3.8111), Art. 22.

[595] Anti-social Behaviour, Crime and Policing Act 2014, ss 1(6), 25(5) (upper time limits only apply if the person concerned is below eighteen).

[596] See Urteil des Bundesgerichts 1C_226/2009 vom 16. Dezember 2009, E. 5.1.

[597] *R (Lonergan)* v. *Lewes Crown Court*, [2005] 1 WLR 2570, para. 13.

[598] Gasser, *Kriminalpolitik oder City-Pflege?* (2004), p. 31.

[599] E.g. *R* v. *Boness (Dean)*, [2005] EWCA Crim 2395, paras 84, 97.

[600] See Section 3.4.3.

[601] E.g. *Clingham* v. *Royal Borough of Kensington and Chelsea; R (McCann and Others)* v. *Crown Court at Manchester and Another*, [2002] UKHL 39, para. 12;

[602] *R.* v. *Lamb (Christopher)*, [2005] EWCA Crim 3000, para. 2.

and, in one case, even any part of Manchester for ten years.[603] In Switzerland, exclusion orders issued under the cantonal police acts typically cover certain zones or 'perimeters' defined by the police, normally extending to large inner city areas,[604] while those imposed on foreign nationals under federal legislation may cover as much as the complete territory of a city[605] or even of an entire canton.[606] When it comes to anti-social behaviour, zones of exclusion tend to be defined in standardised procedures applicable in a great number of cases, so that it will often be questionable whether in a given case there really is a need for the banned area to extend to the respective pre-defined zone. Finally, juvenile curfews typically apply on the whole territory of the respective city or municipality – despite the fact that, if the aim is the prevention of night time disturbance, it may be sufficient to restrict them to residential areas.

In terms of the behaviour that is prohibited in the relevant areas, exclusion measures directed against anti-social behaviour typically prohibit people from simply being present there. This is problematic with regard to the necessity requirement in that a prohibition of engaging in specified behaviour would constitute a less serious interference. For example, a prohibition of making noise at night (which, in any event, already exists by virtue of general regulations in pretty much every municipality and city) is a less restrictive means of preventing night time disturbance than a juvenile curfew, and a prohibition of harassing passers-by is a less restrictive means of protecting public safety and order than an exclusion order applicable for several months. The main concern raised by measures prohibiting mere presence in certain parts of public space is that they prevent people from engaging in activities that may not only be perfectly legitimate but, indeed, desirable in a liberal democracy. Anti-social behaviour orders, exclusion orders, dispersal orders and juvenile curfews may prevent those subject to them from, for example, demonstrating, picketing, attending community, cultural or political events, taking part in associational activities such as school meetings or exercising their political rights. It is for this reason that courts in the United States have concluded in several cases that the juvenile curfews at

603 'Young thug barred from Manchester', *Manchester Evening News*, 22 January 2004.

604 See e.g. for Berne, Gasser, *Kriminalpolitik oder City-Pflege?* (2004), pp. 30, 44–61.

605 E.g. Urteil des Bundesgerichts 2A.514/2006 vom 23. Januar 2007; Urteil des Bundesgerichts 2A.347/2003 vom 24. November 2003; BGE 124 IV 280, 280 (1998).

606 E.g. BGE 126 IV 30, 31 (1999); BVR 2000, 145, p. 145 (Verwaltungsgericht des Kantons Bern).

issue were overbroad.[607] As one court observed with regard to the curfew under review, it 'sweeps within its ambit a number of innocent activities which are constitutionally protected' and '[t]he stifling effect upon these legitimate activities is overt and is both real and substantial'. Since the curfew could be tailored more narrowly, the court concluded, 'less drastic means are available'.[608] Accordingly, today, juvenile curfew ordinances in the United States normally contain a number of exceptions exempting official school and religious activities and the exercise of First Amendment rights.[609] Similarly, the British Anti-social Behaviour, Crime and Policing Act 2014 provides that dispersal directions may not be used in respect of persons who are picketing or taking part in public processions.[610] However, even where the respective pieces of legislation do provide for exceptions, they may still have a 'chilling effect' as often it may only be possible for the persons concerned to show that they were engaged in an exempted activity once they have already been arrested.[611] Furthermore, the necessity test may not always be met because there may be a less restrictive means available in the form of a prohibition of specified behaviour. In addition, especially as far as marginalised groups or children and juveniles are concerned, protective and supportive measures may be sufficient, and indeed more effective, means to prevent anti-social behaviour than exclusion from public space.[612]

Proportionality in the narrow sense

The interests that the state pursues through the adoption of exclusion measures directed against anti-social behaviour cannot be qualified as particularly weighty. The threat posed to public safety and order by incivilities such as sleeping or drinking alcohol in public places or by the presence of potentially disorderly juveniles at night time is generally not particularly serious; nor are the other aims served by such measures – the prevention of noise and littering and, potentially, the protection of the image of commercial areas as attractive places for shopping and leisure – very compelling.

607 *Hodgkins* v. *Peterson*, 355 F.3d 1048, 1064 (7th Cir. 2004); *Nunez* v. *City of San Diego*, 114 F.3d 935, 949 (9th Cir. 1997); *Maquoketa* v. *Russell*, 484 N.W.2d 179, 185–6 (Iowa 1992); *In re Mosier*, 394 N.E.2d 368, 372 (Ohio C.P. 1978).

608 *Johnson* v. *City of Opelousas*, 658 F.2d 1065, 1074 (5th Cir. 1981).

609 E.g. Dallas, Texas Code of Ordinances, s. 31-33(c)(1)(G)–(H); District of Columbia Code, § 2-1543(b)(1)(G)–(H).

610 Anti-social Behaviour, Crime and Policing Act 2014, s. 36(4).

611 See e.g. *Hodgkins* v. *Peterson*, 355 F.3d 1048, 1060–65 (7th Cir. 2004).

612 See Gerber Jenni, ' "Abendausgang Kinder" ' (2006), 853–4.

On the other hand, the impact that exclusion measures designed to prevent anti-social behaviour have on the interests of the individuals concerned is often also described as relatively minor. The Swiss Federal Supreme Court, for example, characterised the interference with fundamental rights caused by the exclusion orders issued in the City of Berne as 'not serious'.[613] It must be noted, however, that it came to this conclusion due to the fact that the orders had a narrowly defined geographical scope and only prohibited gatherings that involved the consumption of alcohol. In contrast, where measures against anti-social behaviour prevent people from merely being present in large parts of public space, the conclusion must be a different one. As pointed out in Section 5.2.2.2, for socially marginalised groups (the main targets of measures directed against anti-social behaviour), public places may be the only location where they can freely meet with other people. Thus, if they are excluded from large inner city areas or even from entire towns, they are thereby also prevented from establishing and developing social contacts. The same applies to juveniles who tend to spend a large part of their free time in public places to meet with others of their age. Night-time curfews that cover all public places thus interfere with an essential aspect of juveniles' development of their own sense of identity and must therefore be qualified as serious restrictions.[614]

Another reason why exclusion measures designed to prevent anti-social behaviour will often have to be characterised as serious interferences is that, beyond the ban from a particular part of public space, they may entail very severe restrictions in case of a breach-of-the-exclusion terms. In the United Kingdom, breach of an ASBO was punishable with up to five years imprisonment,[615] in case of the new IPNA and CBO the maximum penalty is imprisonment for two years[616] and five years, respectively.[617] Christopher Lamb, for example, was sentenced to twenty-two months in a young offender institution, simply because he breached his ASBO by entering the prohibited area (that is, the town centre of Whitley Bay).[618] In Switzerland, exclusion orders can be issued under threat of a criminal penalty according to Article 292 of the Swiss Criminal

613 BGE 132 I 49, 63–4 (2004) ('Dieser kann nicht als schwerwiegend eingestuft werden.').

614 See Section 5.2.2.2. 615 Crime and Disorder Act 1998, s. 1(10)(b).

616 Home Office, Anti-social Behaviour, Crime and Policing Act 2014: Reform of Anti-social Behaviour Powers: Statutory Guidance for Frontline Professionals, July 2014, p. 26.

617 Anti-social Behaviour, Crime and Policing Act 2014, s. 30(2).

618 *R. v. Lamb (Christopher)*, [2005] EWCA Crim 3000, para. 10.

Code in case of non-compliance;[619] breach-of-the-exclusion order is then a criminal offence punishable with a fine, which in case of non-payment can be transformed into a prison sentence.[620] As those subject to exclusion orders are regularly not in a position to pay the fines, such orders often eventually result in prison terms.[621]

In sum, the approach of meeting a wide range of behaviours qualified as 'anti-social' with drastic action by the state raises important concerns with regard to the requirement of proportionality in the narrow sense. Whereas the public interest in preventing rather minor disorder and incivilities is not particularly weighty, exclusion measures directed against anti-social behaviour affect a great number of individuals, often entailing serious consequences for them. Given that there is no real evidence supporting the effectiveness of this approach, the burden imposed on individuals through such measures will often have to be considered to be disproportionate to the importance of the public interest. The lack of a reasonable relationship between the aim pursued and the interference is particularly striking in those cases where anti-social behaviour eventually leads to substantial prison sentences.

Political protest Location is crucial to political protest. Protest activities against major international conferences, for example, are only effective if they occur in locations where they are visible to those attending these events and the media present there; anti-abortion demonstrations only serve their purpose if they can be held in places where women who intend to have an abortion become aware of them; members of parliament may be reached best through protest held in front of the parliament building. As a consequence, protest can be silenced not only by prohibiting it but, more subtly, by dislocating it. Preventing protest from being held in the vicinity of conference locations, anti-abortion clinics or parliaments may have an almost equally inhibiting effect as banning it completely.[622] The UN Special Rapporteur on the rights to freedom of peaceful assembly and of association has accordingly warned against the practice of allowing a demonstration to take place but only in a part of public space where its impact will be muted.[623]

619 E.g. explicitly for the Canton of Zurich: Polizeigesetz vom 23. April 2007 (LS 550.1), § 34(2).
620 StGB, Art. 36.
621 For the City of Berne, see Gasser, *Kriminalpolitik oder City-Pflege?* (2004), p. 33.
622 See Section 5.2.6.2.
623 Report of the Special Rapporteur on the rights to freedom of peaceful assembly and of association, 21 May 2012, UN Doc. A/HRC/20/27, para. 40.

This needs to be kept in mind when measures designed to prevent political protest from being held in particular parts of public space are assessed for their proportionality. As explained above, these measures include, first, the adoption of laws that create special zones where protest is severely restricted[624] and, second, the introduction of policing strategies that aim at denying demonstrators access to potential sites of protest.[625] One crucial issue that needs to be explored is thus whether such exclusion measures leave intact the possibility for protesters 'to reach the minds of willing listeners' and 'to win their attention'[626] or whether the publicity effect of the protest will be lost.[627]

Suitability

Exclusion from public space is, in general, a suitable means to achieve the aims listed in Section 5.3.1.3. The establishment of special zones where protest is prohibited is undoubtedly an effective means of protecting third persons from being harassed or threatened and of upholding public safety and order. Similarly, the creation of protest-free zones near parliament buildings serves the aims of ensuring the unimpeded access of parliamentarians and emergency services to the parliament building and preventing sessions of parliament from being disturbed by outside noise. Finally, as the Swiss Federal Supreme Court confirmed in the *Gsell* case, denying access to a potential site of demonstration to everyone except those who clearly do not pose a risk is an effective means of preventing disorder.[628] Furthermore, as opposed to exclusion measures directed against criminal and anti-social behaviour, measures that prevent political protest in certain public places will not normally lead to a mere displacement: since the location of the protest is of crucial importance, exclusion measures will often result in the protest not being held at all.

The situation is different, however, when exclusion measures are deployed against protests that are already underway. In this case, denying protesters access to parts of public space may result in an escalation of the situation and thus not only be an unsuitable means to prevent disorder but actually be counter-productive. For example, the available evidence suggests that in some instances the police method of 'kettling' caused frustration and aggressiveness on the part of demonstrators and thus

[624] See Section 3.3.3.1. [625] See Section 3.3.3.2.
[626] *Hill* v. *Colorado*, 530 U.S. 703, 728 (2000). [627] See BGE 127 I 164, 180 (2001).
[628] BGE 130 I 369, 384–5 (2004).

contributed to disorder.[629] Where this could be shown to be the case, an exclusion measure would fail the proportionality test already at this stage.

Necessity

The proportionality of exclusion measures directed against political protest will typically turn on the question of whether or not there is a less restrictive means available. From this perspective, as well as with regard to the requirement of proportionality in the narrow sense, the creation of zones where protest is severely restricted or even completely prohibited raises serious concerns. Since blanket bans of assemblies or protest in particular locations do not allow the specific circumstances of each particular case to be taken into account, they are much more problematic than restrictions on particular forms of protest. The OSCE/ODIHR Panel of Experts on the Freedom of Assembly has therefore concluded that they should only be used as a measure of last resort.[630] The same concerns apply to the creation of zones where protest activities, such as demonstrations, are only allowed if they are authorised. International human rights bodies have stated that, as a general rule, protest activities should not be subject to prior authorisation but, at most, to an advance notification requirement and have requested states in which an authorisation is required to amend their laws accordingly.[631]

Therefore, exclusion measures in the form of complete bans on protest in particular zones may only be used as a last resort and if they are so limited in scope to still allow for protesters to make their point in an effective manner. Only if these requirements are met, can a less restrictive alternative be said not to exist. For example, the creation of very narrowly defined 'buffer zones' around abortion clinics may be considered a proportionate means of protecting the rights of women to have a lawful operation and of medical staff to enter their place of work, free from harassment and intimidation, and of upholding public safety and order.

[629] See e.g. Her Majesty's Chief Inspector of Constabulary, Adapting to Protest (2009), 31–2, available at www.hmic.gov.uk/media/adapting-to-protest-20090705.pdf.

[630] OSCE/ODIHR Panel of Experts on the Freedom of Assembly, Guidelines on Freedom of Peaceful Assembly, 2nd ed., Strasbourg/Warsaw (2010), p. 59.

[631] Report of the Special Rapporteur on the rights to freedom of peaceful assembly and of association, 21 May 2012, UN Doc. A/HRC/20/27, paras 28, 90; OSCE/ODIHR Panel of Experts on the Freedom of Assembly, Guidelines on Freedom of Peaceful Assembly, 2nd ed., Strasbourg/Warsaw (2010), p. 65.

In *Madsen* v. *Women's Health Center*[632] and *Schenck* v. *Pro-Choice Network of Western New York*[633] the US Supreme Court confirmed that 'fixed buffer zones', which prohibited demonstrations within thirty-six and, respectively, fifteen feet of entrances to abortion clinics, were justifiable restrictions on the right to free speech. These zones, the court held, were essential to allow patients and staff to enter and leave the building freely. At the same time, they still allowed protesters to be heard from a short distance.[634] In contrast, the 'floating buffer zones' prohibiting protesters from coming within a certain distance of people trying to access the clinics that had also been created in both cases were found to impose a greater burden than was required to protect the interests in public safety and free traffic flow.[635] In 2000, in *Hill* v. *Colorado*, the Supreme Court upheld a more narrowly defined 'floating buffer zone' that made it unlawful, within 100 feet of a health care facility, to approach within eight feet of a person to hand that person a leaflet, to display a sign or to engage in verbal protest, education or counselling.[636] The court held that such a zone only imposed a minor restriction on the manner and place of communication: it was still possible for pedestrians to read the signs displayed by demonstrators and for demonstrators to make themselves heard at a 'normal conversational distance'.[637] Therefore, the court concluded, the 'floating buffer zone' was narrowly tailored to serve the interest of protecting those who wish to enter health care facilities and left open ample alternative channels for communication.[638] In contrast, in 2014, in *McCullen* v. *Coakley*, the Supreme Court held that the previously mentioned Massachusetts statute that made it a crime to stand on a public sidewalk within thirty-five feet of an abortion clinic was not narrowly tailored enough and therefore violated the First Amendment. According to the court, the state had failed to show that it had seriously explored less intrusive alternatives to the 'fixed buffer zone', such as injunctions.[639]

The US Supreme Court's jurisprudence on 'buffer zones' to regulate anti-abortion demonstrations displays a remarkable awareness of the importance of location for political protest. The court correctly observes

632 *Madsen* v. *Women's Health Center*, 512 U.S. 753 (1994).
633 *Schenck* v. *Pro-Choice Network of Western New York*, 519 U.S. 357 (1997).
634 *Schenck* v. *Pro-Choice Network of Western New York*, 519 U.S. 357, 380–2 (1997); *Madsen v. Women's Health Center*, 512 U.S. 753, 769–70 (1994).
635 *Schenck v. Pro-Choice Network of Western New York*, 519 U.S. 357, 376–9 (1997); *Madsen v. Women's Health Center*, 512 U.S. 753, 773–4 (1994).
636 *Hill* v. *Colorado*, 530 U.S. 703 (2000). 637 Ibid., 726–8. 638 Ibid., 728–30.
639 *McCullen* v. *Coakley*, 573 U.S. _ (2014), Docket No. 12-1168.

that such zones may be a suitable and necessary means of protecting important public interests. Yet at the same time it acknowledges the interest of anti-abortion protesters to hold their protests in the close vicinity of respective clinics. Accordingly, the court sensibly concludes that 'buffer zones' may only be used as a last resort, that they must not extend beyond what is strictly required to achieve their objectives and that it must still be possible for protests to be held in locations where they can be seen and heard.

It is more difficult to see the need for protest-free zones near parliament buildings. As explained in Section 5.3.1.3, allowing parliamentarians to deliberate without being exposed to the 'pressure of the streets' cannot qualify as a legitimate aim. The remaining, more practical, aims of ensuring the unimpeded access of parliamentarians and emergency services to the parliament building, preventing sessions of parliament from being disturbed by outside noise and reducing the risk of terrorist attacks can be achieved through less drastic means than protest bans extending to entire squares. The Swiss Federal Supreme Court held in a case concerning a cantonal parliament that an authorisation requirement for the distribution of leaflets to parliamentarians within the parliament building or at the entrance is a proportionate restriction of the freedom of expression,[640] but has not had to deal with the sort of bans at issue here. In the United Kingdom, the parliamentary Joint Committee on Human Rights acknowledged that the maintenance of access to parliament is a persuasive reason to impose restrictions on protest.[641] However, it (successfully) called for the repeal of the provisions of the SOCPA 2005 that criminalised protest without prior authorisation within a zone of up to one kilometre from Parliament Square, as they were not necessary to ensure access or prevent noise.[642] Even a ban on protest on specific areas of the road and pavement would, according to the committee, have been disproportionate. Instead, it was sufficient to impose conditions on protesters to ensure that access for parliamentarians is maintained at all times.[643] Clearly, this is the correct approach. Bans covering large areas

640 BGE 110 Ia 47 (1984).

641 Joint Committee on Human Rights, Demonstrating Respect for Rights? A Human Rights Approach to Policing Protest: Seventh Report of Session 2008–2009, HL Paper 47-I, HC 320-1, para. 126.

642 Ibid., para. 127. See also Mead, *The New Law of Peaceful Protest* (2010), pp. 153–5.

643 Joint Committee on Human Rights, Demonstrating Respect for Rights? A Human Rights Approach to Policing Protest: Seventh Report of Session 2008–2009, HL Paper 47-I, HC 320-1, paras 130–1.

around parliament could only be qualified as necessary if the aim was assumed to be the isolation of parliamentarians from the views of the public. In contrast, they are not required to achieve the more limited aims referred to above.

Police strategies aimed at denying demonstrators access to potential sites of protest, in turn, raise concerns with regard to their broad personal and geographical scope. They prevent even entirely peaceful protesters from demonstrating where they would like to demonstrate and often cover very extensive areas. In contrast to 'buffer zones', their large geographical scope also regularly makes it impossible for protesters to make themselves heard. Some of the problems raised by such police strategies have been discussed in the context of the breach-of-the-peace powers and the *polizeiliche Generalklausel* in Section 4.2.3.2. They are revisited here from the perspective of the principle of proportionality.

Despite the concerns raised by them, the Swiss Federal Supreme Court has upheld police strategies implementing access bans. Already in 1977 it had shown itself to be not very protective of demonstrations when it found that a ban of political assemblies on the entire territory of a municipality was a proportionate means of maintaining public safety and order, when it was feared that there would be violent clashes between two opposing political factions.[644] Seized of the matter, the European Commission of Human Rights equally came to the conclusion that, considering the ban was limited to a municipality where the risk of clashes was particularly high and was also limited in time, the interference with the freedom of assembly was proportionate.[645] In its decision in the *Gsell* case of 2004, the Federal Supreme Court then upheld the police strategy of denying access to Davos to all potential protesters against the WEF meeting. The court observed that, given the dangerous situation and the great number of persons travelling to Davos, it was very difficult for police officers to distinguish peaceful demonstrators from those intent on causing trouble. Therefore, the police could not be blamed for adopting a rather schematic and rigorous approach to controls: to turn back everyone who has not been clearly identified as not posing a risk was, according to the court, a proportionate means of protecting public safety and order.[646]

[644] BGE 103 Ia 310, 315–17 (1977).

[645] *Rassemblement jurassien & Unité jurasienne v. Switzerland*, no. 8191/78, admissibility decision of 10 October 1979, 17 DR 93, 121.

[646] BGE 130 I 369, 384–7 (2004).

In an almost identical case, the British House of Lords came to the opposite conclusion. In *R (Laporte)* v. *Chief Constable of Gloucestershire Constabulary*[647] the police stopped three coaches with people who wanted to demonstrate against the Iraq war a few kilometres before the intended site of the demonstration, an air base in Gloucestershire. The police prevented the coaches and passengers from continuing their journey and escorted them back to London. The House of Lords held that the police action was a disproportionate interference with the rights to freedom of expression and freedom of assembly of Ms Laporte, one of the passengers. Their Lordships correctly observed that it was up to the police to establish that their action was the least restrictive means available.[648] As they turned the coaches back 'without considering any less drastic alternative',[649] they had not discharged that burden.[650] The House of Lords explicitly rejected the schematic, indiscriminate approach that the Swiss Federal Supreme Court had upheld in the *Gsell* case. According to their Lordships, the police should have tried to ascertain the intentions and affiliations of the individual passengers and the latter should have been given the opportunity to explain their positions.[651] Accordingly, it should have been, and indeed was, clear to the police that there was no reason for classifying all passengers indiscriminately as potentially violent demonstrators: the large majority of them were entirely peaceful. In particular, just as with Mr Gsell, there was nothing about Ms Laporte that would have suggested any violent intentions.[652] The mere fact that a small minority of the passengers might have become violent at the demonstration, the House of Lords concluded, did not make it necessary to turn back everyone.[653]

In the United States, the Supreme Court has not so far considered a comparable case, while lower courts have come to different conclusions on the issue. A Californian district court had to consider a case in which the LAPD had blocked off from public access an area of more than eight million square feet around the Staples Center in Los Angeles at the occasion of the 2000 Democratic National Convention. Some 260 yards from the entrance to the centre, a small 'Official Demonstration Site' was established for use during the convention.[654] The court held that

647 *R (Laporte)* v. *Chief Constable of Gloucestershire Constabulary*, [2006] UKHL 55.

648 Ibid., para. 106 (Lord Carswell). 649 Ibid., para. 88 (Lord Roger).

650 Ibid., para. 106 (Lord Carswell). 651 Ibid., para. 154 (Lord Mance). 652 Ibid.

653 Ibid., paras 55 (Lord Bingham), 90 (Lord Roger), 106 (Lord Carswell), 155 (Lord Mance).

654 *Service Employee International Union* v. *City of Los Angeles*, 114 F.Supp.2d 966 (C.D. Cal. 2000).

the area that had been cordoned off from public access was much larger than necessary to protect public safety, in particular to ensure that delegates could enter and exit the centre.[655] The temporal scope of the ban also extended beyond what was strictly required as the area had been blocked off three days before the start of the conference and applied twenty-four hours a day.[656] Finally, the 'Official Demonstration Site' was so far from the entrance that it was impossible for protesters to be seen or heard by those attending the convention. Therefore, the court found that the police action did not provide sufficient alternative means of communication.[657]

On the other hand, a majority of the US Court of Appeals for the Ninth Circuit thought that denying access to a large section of the downtown area of Seattle to everyone except conference delegates, employees and shoppers during the 1999 WTO conference was a proportionate means of maintaining public order.[658] The court stressed that the city authorities faced an exceptional situation in that violent demonstrators were hiding in a crowd of tens of thousands of peaceful protesters.[659] In these circumstances, the court found, it was impossible for the police to distinguish on an individualised basis between peaceful protesters and those with violent intentions.[660] Furthermore, the court thought that the restricted zone was narrowly tailored as it covered only enough territory for the WTO delegates to move from their hotels to the conference facilities and only lasted during the conference.[661] Finally, it argued that the ban may have made it more difficult for protesters to make themselves heard to the delegates, but not impossible.[662] Judge Paez filed a partial dissent in which he concluded that the blocking of access to the relevant zone was not a proportionate interference with the right to free speech. He argued that the zone was geographically larger than required,[663] that it would have been possible for the police to make case-by-case determinations as to who to allow in the restricted area[664] and that the ban prevented demonstrators from reaching their intended audience.[665]

The soundest approach to reviewing the sort of bans on accessing extensive parts of public space discussed in this section is the one adopted by the British House of Lords. As their Lordships correctly observed, it is the state that bears the burden of establishing that an access ban was the

[655] Ibid., 971. [656] Ibid., 971–2. [657] Ibid.
[658] *Menotti* v. *City of Seattle* 409 F.3d 1113 (9th Cir. 2005). [659] Ibid., 1132–3.
[660] Ibid., 1134–5. [661] Ibid., 1133–4. [662] Ibid., 1138–43. [663] Ibid., 1168.
[664] Ibid., 1169. [665] Ibid., 1173–4.

least restrictive means available. It is not sufficient for the police to discharge this burden – as the Swiss Federal Supreme Court assumed – that they simply point to the fact that they had to assess a great number of people for the risk posed by them.[666] Just as in *Laporte*, the police in *Gsell* were faced by a coach full of potential demonstrators.[667] To indiscriminately turn back everyone on the coach who is not clearly identified as posing no risk – including a journalist displaying his press card – may be the easiest way for the police to deal with such a situation, but it is manifestly not the only possible way; it is not clear from the judgment whether, and if yes, why, the Federal Supreme Court thought that it was. The European Court of Human Rights was therefore right to disagree with the Federal Supreme Court on this point. It took the view that the Federal Supreme Court's finding contradicted the principle it had established itself in its case law, according to which any police action had to be directed against those posing the threat to public order – that is, the *Störerprinzip* referred to above, which forms a central aspect of proportionality.[668] According to the European Court, this requirement was not met in the present case as the police failed to distinguish between peaceful and potentially violent demonstrators.[669]

A deviation from the principle that police action must be directed against those posing a threat to public order can only be permissible in very exceptional situations, such as the one in Seattle during the WTO conference where the police were faced by tens of thousands of demonstrators. It should be noted, however, that even in Seattle the police were able to implement individualised access controls, although these were carried out on the rather questionable basis of denying access to everyone who appeared to intend to demonstrate in the relevant zone.[670]

Finally, as far as the police strategy of 'kettling' is concerned,[671] it has been pointed out in Section 5.2.4.2 that, depending on the concrete situation of those contained in this manner, 'kettling' may amount to a deprivation of liberty (in the sense of Article 5 of the ECHR and Article 31 of the Swiss Federal Constitution). The key question in this regard is not whether the containment is proportionate or not but whether there is a legal ground justifying the deprivation of liberty and whether the respective procedural requirements have been complied with.[672] Even if

[666] See also Mead, *The New Law of Peaceful Protest* (2010), pp. 341, 343–5, 347–8.
[667] BGE 130 I 369, 371 (2004). [668] See Section 5.3.2.2.
[669] *Gsell c. Suisse*, no. 12675/05, 8 October 2009, para. 60 (only available in French).
[670] *Menotti* v. *City of Seattle* 409 F.3d 1113, 1126, 1162 (9th Cir. 2005).
[671] See Section 3.3.3.2. [672] See Section 5.2.4.1.

'kettling' is not implemented in a manner that amounts to a deprivation of liberty, it will still normally constitute an interference with the rights to freedom of movement, freedom of assembly and freedom of expression, so that the issue of proportionality needs to be addressed. In this regard, similar principles as the ones just set out above apply. This means that 'kettling' may only be used as a tactic when and as long as it is required to deal with forms of protest that are particularly difficult to police. Thus, the High Court of England and Wales held that '[t]he police may only take such preventive action as a last resort catering for situations about to descend into violence'.[673] In addition to this overall assessment, the need for 'kettling' must also be examined in relation to each individual contained. Therefore, as the British Joint Committee on Human Rights has explained, 'individual officers policing the perimeter of the contained area [must] consider whether, in an individual case, it is appropriate to maintain that cordon for that individual, given his or her particular circumstances'.[674] It would be disproportionate, the committee correctly pointed out, to operate a blanket ban on individuals leaving the contained area.[675] The UN Special Rapporteur on the rights to freedom of peaceful assembly and of association even thinks there is no scope for using the practice of 'kettling' whatsoever, stating in general terms that he is opposed to this practice.[676]

Proportionality in the narrow sense

Since location is so important to the impact of political protest and dislocating protest can have almost the same effect as completely banning it, exclusion measures directed against political protest will, as explained in Section 5.2.6.2, regularly have to be qualified as serious interferences with fundamental rights (normally the rights to freedom of expression and/or freedom of assembly). Further reasons supporting the conclusion that such measures must be qualified as serious interferences are the great number of people affected by them (in the case of the Seattle demonstration, for example, several tens of thousands) and the fact that in all three states at issue political expression enjoys particularly strong

[673] *R (Moos)* v. *Commissioner of Police of the Metropolis*, [2011] EWHC 957 (Admin), para. 56.

[674] Joint Committee on Human Rights, Demonstrating Respect for Rights? Follow-up: Twenty-second Report of Session 2008–2009, HL Paper 141, HC 522, para. 28.

[675] Ibid.

[676] Report of the Special Rapporteur on the rights to freedom of peaceful assembly and of association, 21 May 2012, UN Doc. A/HRC/20/27, para. 37.

protection.[677] Seen in this light, the approach of the Swiss Federal Supreme Court, which has suggested that temporary bans on accessing a potential site of a demonstration do not in general amount to a serious interference as the persons concerned can reach their destination at a later time,[678] appears too sweeping.

On the other hand, the public interests that are pursued through adoption of the sort of measures discussed here may be very weighty. Especially high-profile political meetings attracting demonstrators from across the globe may pose a considerable threat to public safety and order.[679] States hosting such meetings have an obligation under customary international law to take all appropriate steps to ensure the personal protection of visiting heads of state, heads of government and other senior state officials.[680] Importantly, as pointed out in Section 5.3.1.3, political protests also regularly have an impact on the fundamental rights of 'ordinary' third persons. A large-scale demonstration in a town centre, for example, affects the rights of those who would like to make use of public ground themselves (for instance to organise, or participate in, an event there) and, as far as these are protected in the respective legal system, the economic liberties of shop owners. Similarly, protests in front of abortion clinics and the homes of animal researchers have an impact on the rights of women to have an abortion and the rights of researchers to enjoy their private space free from interferences, respectively, which are both protected as part of the right to respect for private life.

Any exclusion measure must thus strike a proper balance between these various, significant interests. As will have become clear from the discussion of the necessity of such measures, the main argument proposed here is that narrowly defined zones where protest is prohibited

[677] See Section 5.2.6.1. [678] BGE 128 I 327, 344 (2002); BGE 130 I 369, 385–7 (2004).

[679] See e.g. BGE 130 I 369, 383–4 (2004); BGE 128 I 327, 342–4 (2002); BGE 127 I 164, 175–6 (2001); *Menotti v. City of Seattle* 409 F.3d 1113, 1121–4, 1131–2 (9th Cir. 2005).

[680] Watts, 'The Legal Position in International Law of Heads of States, Heads of Governments and Foreign Ministers' (1994), 35–40, 48–51, 104–5. For relevant treaty law, see Convention on the Prevention and Punishment of Crimes against Internationally Protected Persons, including Diplomatic Agents (adopted 14 December 1973, entered into force 20 February 1977) 1035 UNTS 167. The United Kingdom signed 13 December 1974 and ratified 2 May 1979. The United States signed 28 December 1973 and ratified 26 October 1976. Switzerland acceded 5 March 1985. See also Convention on Special Misssions (adopted 8 December 1969, entered into force 21 June 1985) 1400 UNTS 231, Arts 21(2), 25(2), 29, 30(1). The United Kingdom signed 17 December 1970 but has not ratified. The United States has not signed. Switzerland signed 31 July 1970 and ratified 3 November 1977.

may be a sensible way of accommodating the different interests at stake. Narrowly defined 'buffer zones', for example, strike a fair balance between, on the one hand, the rights of anti-abortion protesters and, on the other, the rights of persons trying to gain access to hospitals (who are often in particularly vulnerable physical and emotional conditions) and the interests of public safety: they are an effective means of protecting women from harassment, while still allowing protesters to be visible and to be heard. For the same reason, giving the police the power to order protesters not to come within a certain distance of people's homes is a proportionate means of protecting the latter's rights to enjoy their private space.

In contrast, whether prohibitions of protest extending to entire squares or the temporary blocking of access to a city centre or even the whole territory of a municipality or town can be said to strike a fair balance between the various interests at stake is questionable. Even where such measures meet the necessity requirement (which, as pointed out above, will be the exception), they tend to attach too much weight to interests of public safety and order, while often rendering the respective protest completely ineffective: they regularly make it impossible for protesters to reach their intended audience. It is all the more problematic when such extensive bans are adopted, not on a temporary basis to address immediate public safety concerns, but permanently to protect some other interests. This is the case, for example, with the general prohibition of political manifestations on the square in front of the monastery of Einsiedeln in Switzerland. As explained in Section 5.3.1.3, the Federal Supreme Court has upheld this ban on the basis that it protects the interests of pilgrims and other visitors in enjoying the square's atmosphere free from disturbances. Yet the court failed to explain why these interests should generally prevail over the rights of those who would like to demonstrate on the square. That the ban imposes a disproportionate burden on demonstrators is all the more obvious when one considers that political manifestations are far from the only potential source of disturbance for visitors to the monastery.[681]

5.3.3 *Result*

Many exclusion measures designed to prevent *criminal behaviour* will meet the requirements of the limitation test. Such forms of exclusion

[681] See also Richter, ' "Befriedete Bezirke" ' (2002), 951–4.

from public space clearly pursue legitimate, and indeed compelling, aims. Where they are imposed by a court as an additional restriction to prevent re-offending following a conviction in the normal criminal process, they will not normally raise problems with regard to the principle of proportionality. More problematic are those exclusion measures that automatically apply to everyone who has committed a particular type of offence and those that do not require a previous conviction for a criminal offence at all, that is, measures that are imposed on *potential* offenders. The personal scope of these measures is typically very wide and some of them do not require any individualised assessment of the threat posed by the individual to public safety or of the need for excluding that individual from public space. As a consequence, they may be employed in a disproportionate manner, that is, in cases where this is not warranted for the prevention of crime, or terms of exclusion may be imposed that are more restrictive than is required by the situation.

Exclusion measures directed against *political protest* equally do not normally raise concerns with regard to the legitimacy of the aims they serve. As far as the proportionality requirement is concerned, the establishment of narrowly defined zones around particular critical locations where protest is prohibited will typically satisfy this requirement: this may be the least restrictive means of protecting public safety and the rights of others and may, in addition, be a sensible way of accommodating the different interests at stake. In contrast, prohibitions of protest extending to entire squares as well as the temporary blocking of access to a city centre or the whole territory of a municipality or town will frequently constitute disproportionate restrictions of fundamental rights. Instead of resorting to indiscriminate strategies that interfere with the rights of all protesters, the police must focus their actions on those who are potentially violent. Furthermore, as such measures often render it completely impossible for protesters to reach their intended audience, they fail to strike a fair balance between the legitimate aims pursued by the state and the enjoyment of fundamental rights by the individual.

The most problematic exclusion measures from a fundamental rights perspective are those that are directed against *anti-social behaviour*. Instead of being designed to promote an objectively conceived public interest, many of these measures serve to protect from mere feelings such as annoyance, distress or fear. Where this is the case, such measures already fail to meet the legitimate aim test. Furthermore, what underlies exclusion measures directed against anti-social behaviour is the basic notion that the state must meet relatively minor disorder and incivilities with a resolute reaction containing a strong symbolic element. This approach almost inevitably leads to conflicts with the principle of proportionality. Instead of focusing on those who actually pose a threat to public safety and order, the scope of exclusion measures directed against anti-social behaviour regularly extends to everyone who shares certain personal characteristics with them or associates with them. To define the personal scope of exclusion measures in such a broad manner runs counter to the principle that measures interfering with fundamental rights must be limited to those who have given cause for the interference, forming an important aspect of the necessity requirement. In addition, exclusion measures directed against anti-social behaviour tend to have a broader temporal and geographical scope than is required to achieve the aims pursued and they typically prohibit mere presence in public space, thus preventing those subject to them from engaging in behaviour that may not only be perfectly legitimate but, indeed, desirable. Finally, such measures raise important concerns with regard to the requirement of proportionality in the narrow sense: whereas the public interest in preventing rather minor disorder and incivilities is not particularly weighty, exclusion from public places and streets for long periods of time constitutes – especially for members of socially marginalised groups – a serious interference.

Given the great variety of situations in which exclusion from public space may be used, it is impossible to make general statements as to which exclusion measures will, or will not, meet the limitation test. Nevertheless, it may be helpful to conclude this section by referring to a police power authorising exclusion from public space that may be described as an example of good practice in terms of the objectives it pursues and its proportionality: § 42a of the Police Act of the Canton of Basel-Stadt in Switzerland, which came into force in 2009.[682] Instead of referring to public safety and order or similarly vague notions, as comparable norms do,[683] § 42a makes it clear that exclusion from public space may only be resorted to if there is an actual danger or a serious threat to persons: it provides that the police can ban a person from a specified public place if that person (1) endangers or seriously threatens third persons or (2) through his or her behaviour creates an immediate threat of a violent

[682] Gesetz betreffend die Kantonspolizei des Kantons Basel-Stadt (Polizeigesetz, PolG) vom 13. November 1996 (SG 510.100), § 42a (eingefügt am 15. Oktober 2008).

[683] See e.g. for the Canton of Berne: Polizeigesetz vom 8. Juni 1997 (BSG 551.1), Art. 29(1)(b).

conflict.[684] The temporal scope of these exclusion orders is limited to seventy-two hours.[685] They can be extended to a maximum of one month in grave cases, in particular if a person (1) violates the physical integrity of others, (2) carries dangerous objects or weapons or (3) actively participates in a violent conflict, or when a person has been issued with an exclusion order before.[686] This temporal gradation ensures that the duration of the exclusion order is in an appropriate relationship to the aim pursued. Geographically, the scope of an exclusion order must cover a specified public place. § 42a requires that, in addition to the banned location and the duration, the exclusion order must also specify the reasons for the exclusion.[687] Finally, it provides that the police must inform the excluded person about advice and support facilities, thus ensuring that in its practical implementation the measure is not exclusively repressive.[688]

5.4 Conclusion

Liberty cannot be reduced to the freedom to be left alone. The fundamental rights that constitute the focus of this chapter protect the liberty, not of isolated individuals, but of social beings living in community with others. As such, they can only be meaningfully exercised if their right-holders have access to public space: to places where they can meet and reach others, where they can be present, and participate, in public life. The freedom to access and be present in public space includes the freedom to behave there in a way that may not conform to the majority's idea of a good life. Public space can only be the space of liberty if it is, at the same time, also the space of tolerance: people have to tolerate that others exercise their liberties, even if it is in a controversial or confrontational manner, and they have to be prepared to be confronted with manifestations of social or economic problems that they might prefer to avoid.[689]

Of course, this does not mean that there is complete and unlimited freedom in public space. There are legitimate aims that may justify restrictions on access to public space. In particular, some restrictions are inevitable in order to coordinate the different interests that collide in public space and to preserve its nature as a truly communal space. Where,

[684] Gesetz betreffend die Kantonspolizei des Kantons Basel-Stadt (Polizeigesetz, PolG) vom 13. November 1996 (SG 510.100), § 42a(1).
[685] Ibid., § 42a(1). [686] Ibid., § 42a(3). [687] Ibid., § 42a(3). [688] Ibid., § 42a(4).
[689] See Section 2.3.3.

for example, groups of drug or alcohol addicts harass and threaten passers-by so that certain parts of public space can no longer be used by large sections of the population, the state may have to interfere to protect public safety. In contrast, the protection of third persons from mere feelings such as annoyance, distress or fear does not constitute a legitimate aim for excluding people from public space.

Any restrictions of access to public space must be proportionate to the aim pursued. Many exclusion measures reviewed in this study, especially those directed against political protest and, even more so, those directed against anti-social behaviour, raise concerns in this regard. Enabling the preventive exclusion from public space of all those who may engage in certain, often very vaguely defined, forms of behaviour, they affect large groups of people who have not been convicted of any criminal offence. Instead of this preventive approach, it would be preferable to establish, first of all, a coherent set of rules for the use of public space that precisely sets out what is allowed and what is not, and to only impose prohibitions on accessing parts of public space once it has been shown that someone has violated these rules. Doubts regarding the proportionality of exclusion from public space are reinforced by the fact that this instrument has been transformed from a short-term measure limited to narrowly defined places into a long-term, or even permanent, measure covering ever larger, or even all, parts of public space and thus regularly amounts to a serious interference. Finally, what makes exclusion measures all the more problematic are the cumulative effects they have combined with other measures adopted in recent years to increase control of public space. In today's 'security society', the freedom to use public space is subject to an unprecedented number of restrictions.[690]

In fact, in many instances exclusion from public space may be an instrument that is not only disproportionate but even counterproductive. As one element of the broader process of privatisation of public space, it contributes to the fragmentation of the urban landscape into different segments, which are subject to locally differentiated strategies of control.[691] This spatial segregation fosters suspicion and mistrust as people become increasingly unfamiliar with the behaviour of others. As a result, public space is transformed from an open, common space

[690] See Section 2.5.2. [691] See Section 2.5.

into a space that appears alien and dangerous[692] – the exact opposite of what exclusion measures are actually intended to achieve.

Exclusion measures may undermine the idea of fundamental rights understood as the rights of social beings to participate in public life free from state interference. Only if public space remains truly public, that is, freely accessible to all, can the freedoms discussed in this chapter be exercised meaningfully and effectively.

[692] See Wehrheim, *Die überwachte Stadt* (2012), p. 236; Volkmann, 'Die Rückeroberung der Allmende' (2000), 366; Frug, 'The Geography of Community' (1996).

6

Fundamental rights: equality

What makes a given place public and distinguishes it from private space is the fact that it is accessible to, and can be used by, the public, that is, everyone.[1] Equality is thus immanent to the concept of public space. The rule is that everyone has the same rights to access and use public space. Accordingly, various legal instruments at both the international and domestic levels aim to ensure that vulnerable groups of people have access to public space on an equal basis with others. For example, the Convention on the Rights of Persons with Disabilities (CRPD) as well as national legislation in the three states at issue to the same effect require public authorities to eliminate any obstacles that persons with disabilities face in accessing public streets, squares, buildings, facilities and so on.[2]

Just as equality is inbuilt in the concept of public space, unequal treatment is inherent to that of exclusion from public space. Virtually all exclusion measures are intended to prevent *certain members* of the public from accessing public space, to make it inaccessible to *particular groups* of people. That *everyone* is excluded from a part of public space is the rare exception.[3] Thus, each time an exclusion measure is imposed, this can be said to undermine the nature of public space as the space that is equally accessible to everyone. This does not mean that exclusion measures *per se* constitute a violation of the right to equality and

[1] See Section 2.1.1.3.

[2] Convention on the Rights of Persons with Disabilities (CRPD) (adopted 13 December 2006, entered into force 3 May 2008) 2515 UNTS 3, Art. 9. The United Kingdom signed the CRPD 30 March 2007 and ratified 8 June 2009. Switzerland acceded 15 April 2014. The United States signed 30 July 2009 but has not yet ratified. For domestic legislation in the United Kingdom, see Equality Act 2010, especially ss 20 and 29. For the federal level in Switzerland, see Bundesgesetz über die Beseitigung von Benachteiligungen von Menschen mit Behinderungen vom 13. Dezember 2002 (SR 151.3) (Federal Act on the Elimination of Discrimination against People with Disabilities) (BehiG), Arts 3 and 7. For the United States, see 42 U.S.C. §§ 12181–3 (introduced by the Americans with Disabilities Act of 1990).

[3] An example would be the complete evacuation of an area following a catastrophe.

non-discrimination. As will be explained below, unequal treatment is compatible with this right as long as there is a sufficient justification for it. This chapter aims to demonstrate that there are, however, several types of exclusion measures with regard to which it is questionable whether such a justification exists.

The chapter first explains how the right to equality and non-discrimination is protected in international law and the three jurisdictions at issue and what its content is (Section 6.1). Then, it reviews a number of exclusion measures that are particularly problematic with regard to this right, examining their conformity with the obligations that follow from it (Section 6.2).

6.1 The right to equality and non-discrimination

The claim that all human beings are equal and therefore deserve to be treated equally has a powerful intuitive appeal. Just as liberty,[4] equality is inherently linked to the fundamental value of human dignity.[5] It is one of the central ideals of the Enlightenment and at the heart of liberal theories of the state.[6] Already the US Declaration of Independence of 1776 famously stated that 'all men are created equal'. Today, equality is a fundamental rule of international human rights law, reflected in the fact that it is proclaimed in the very first article of the UDHR. In fact, the right to equality and non-discrimination gives concrete expression to the basic idea on which *any* system for the protection of fundamental rights is founded: that all human beings, regardless of their status or membership of a particular group, are entitled to the same minimal set of basic rights. As the great international lawyer Hersch Lauterpacht put it:

> The claim to equality before the law is in a substantial sense the most fundamental of the rights of man. It occupies the first place in most written constitutions. It is the starting point of all other liberties.[7]

While the right to equality and non-discrimination is codified in numerous legal sources and its fundamental importance is largely undisputed, its precise content and practical application are less clear. Nevertheless, in all three jurisdictions at issue, a set of legal standards and tests has been developed that helps distinguish lawful from wrongful

[4] See Section 5.2.1.1.
[5] E.g. Waldron, *Dignity, Rank, and Rights* (2012); Baer, 'Dignity, Liberty, Equality' (2009).
[6] Moeckli, 'Equality and Non-discrimination' (2014), 157.
[7] Lauterpacht, *An International Bill of the Rights of Man* (1945), p. 115.

differences in treatment. With regard to their most important aspects, these legal standards and tests are largely identical in all three states.

6.1.1 *Sources*

The idea of equality can be traced back to the work of Aristotle, who formulated the classical maxim that equals must be treated equally or, more precisely, likes must be treated alike.[8] However, as with the concept of fundamental rights as such,[9] modern notions of individual equality did not emerge until the dissolution of feudalism and the rise of Enlightenment thinking.[10] They were developed by philosophers such as Thomas Hobbes and John Locke, who believed that men (women did not feature in their theories) were equally free in the state of nature and thus endowed with the same natural rights.[11] In the words of Locke: 'Men [are] by Nature all free, equal and independent.'[12] Likewise, in Immanuel Kant's view, each human being is owed, 'by virtue of his humanity', the right to equal individual liberties.[13] It is in this 'innate right'[14] that Kant grounded his categorical imperative, requiring that every person should be treated 'as an end, never merely as a means',[15] and, as he also put it, that everyone should '[a]ct only in accordance with that maxim through which [they] can at the same time will that it become a universal law'.[16] Thus, according to Kant, the right to equal individual liberties implies the

[8] Aristotle, *The Nicomachean Ethics of Aristotle* (1911), Book V3, paras 1131a–1131b.

[9] See Section 5.1. [10] See Fredman, *Discrimination Law* (2011), pp. 4–5.

[11] Hobbes, *Leviathan* (1998), Ch. 13, paras 1–2; Locke, *Two Treatises of Government* (1998), Second Treatise, paras 4–5.

[12] Locke, *Two Treatises of Government* (1998), Second Treatise, para. 95.

[13] Kant, *The Metaphysical Elements of Justice* (1965), p. 38; Kant, *Gesammelte Schriften: VI: Die Metaphysik der Sitten* (1900–), p. 237 ('Freiheit (Unabhängigkeit von eines Anderen nöthigender Willkür), sofern sie mit jedes Anderen Freiheit nach einem allgemeinen Gesetz zusammen bestehen kann, ist dieses einzige, ursprüngliche, jedem Menschen kraft seiner Menschheit zustehende Recht. Die angeborne Gleichheit, d. i. die Unabhängigkeit nicht zu mehrerem von Anderen verbunden zu werden, als wozu man sie wechselseitig auch verbinden kann').

[14] Kant, *The Metaphysical Elements of Justice* (1965), p. 38; Kant, *Gesammelte Schriften: VI: Die Metaphysik der Sitten* (1900–), p. 237 ('Das angeborne Recht').

[15] Kant, *Groundwork of the Metaphysics of Morals* (1998), p. 38; Kant, *Gesammelte Schriften: IV: Grundlegung zur Metaphysik der Sitten* (1900–), p. 429 ('Handle so, dass du die Menschheit sowohl in deiner Person, als in der Person eines jeden anderen jederzeit zugleich als Zweck, niemals bloss als Mittel brauchst.').

[16] Kant, *Groundwork of the Metaphysics of Morals* (1998), p. 31; Kant, *Gesammelte Schriften: IV: Grundlegung zur Metaphysik der Sitten* (1900–), p. 421 ('Handle nur nach derjenigen Maxime, durch die du zugleich wollen kannst, dass sie ein allgemeines Gesetz werde.').

establishment of a legal system that is based on the principles of universality and generality, and it is this universality that gives the law its legitimacy. As Jürgen Habermas has summarised the Kantian position, 'the form of a general law legitimates the distribution of liberties, because it implies that a given law has passed the universalization test and been found worthy in the court of reason'.[17] The fundamental importance of the principle of equality is also emphasised in contemporary liberal philosophy. Equality with regard to basic liberties is the first principle of John Rawls's theory of justice[18] and, indeed, the very precondition of his 'original position', the hypothetical starting point from which a fair agreement on principles of political justice can be reached.[19] Equality is also at the heart of Ronald Dworkin's rights thesis. For Dworkin, the fundamental right to be treated with the same respect and concern as anyone else forms the foundation of individual rights[20] and constitutes the 'sovereign virtue of political community'.[21]

Equality is thus one of the key principles on which liberal theories of the state are founded.[22] Today, virtually every liberal democracy includes a guarantee of the right to equality and non-discrimination in its constitution.[23] Equality and non-discrimination has gained a similarly important status in international law. It is included in the key human rights instruments, and the Vienna Declaration and Programme of Action, adopted at the World Conference on Human Rights in 1993, describes it as a 'fundamental rule of international human rights law'.[24]

6.1.1.1 International law

As is emphasised in Article 1(3) of the UN Charter, one of the basic purposes of the UN is the promotion of the guarantee of human rights for

[17] Habermas, *Between Facts and Norms* (1996), p. 120; Habermas, *Faktizität und Geltung* (1992), p. 153 ('[D]ie Form des allgemeinen Gesetzes legitimiert die Verteilung subjektiver Handlungsfreiheiten, weil sich in ihr ein erfolgreich bestandener Verallgemeinerungstest der gesetzesprüfenden Vernunft ausdrückt.').

[18] Rawls, *A Theory of Justice* (1999), p. 266.

[19] Rawls, 'Reply to Alexander and Musgrave' (2000), 33.

[20] Dworkin, *Taking Rights Seriously* (1977), pp. 272–3.

[21] Dworkin, *Sovereign Virtue* (2000), p. 1.

[22] See Moeckli, *Human Rights and Non-discrimination in the 'War on Terror'* (2008), pp. 59–61.

[23] According to David Law and Mila Versteeg, by 2006, 97 per cent of the world's constitutions included an equality guarantee. Law/Versteeg, 'The Evolution and Ideology of Global Constitutionalism' (2011), 1200.

[24] Vienna Declaration and Programme of Action, adopted at the World Conference on Human Rights, 25 June 1993, UN Doc. A/CONF.157/23, para. 15.

all without any distinction. Numerous instruments have been adopted under the auspices of the UN to realise this idea. The general human rights instruments guarantee the right to equality and non-discrimination in several of their provisions: the UDHR in Articles 1, 2(1) and 7; the ICCPR in Articles 2, 3, 24(1) and 26; and the ICESCR in Articles 2(2) and 3. The two specialised human rights treaties most relevant for present purposes also provide protection against discrimination: the ICERD stipulates a specific prohibition of discrimination on the grounds of race or national or ethnic origin;[25] the CRC contains several provisions guaranteeing the right to equality and non-discrimination of children.[26]

The right to equality and non-discrimination is also guaranteed by all major regional human rights instruments. Of those of relevance in the present context, the ECHR includes prohibitions of discrimination in its Article 14 as well as in Protocol No. 12, while the ADHR contains a guarantee of equality and non-discrimination in Article 2. With regard to citizens of the EU, Article 18 of the TFEU prohibits discrimination on grounds of nationality, as does the Agreement on the Free Movement of Persons between the EC and Switzerland with regard to nationals of one contracting party who are lawfully resident in the territory of another contracting party.[27]

Beyond treaty law, it is now widely acknowledged that, at the very least, the right to non-discrimination on the grounds of race, sex and religion binds all states, irrespective of their ratification of human rights treaties, because it constitutes a rule of customary international law and/or a general principle of law in the sense of Article 38(1)(c) of the Statute of the International Court of Justice (ICJ Statute).[28] The Inter-American

25 ICERD, in particular Arts 1(1), 2(1)(a), 5. 26 CRC, Arts 2 and 28.

27 Agreement between the European Community and its Member States, of the one part, and the Swiss Confederation, of the other, on the free movement of persons, 21 June 1999, OJ L 114 (SR 0.142.112.681), Arts 2 and 7(a).

28 Statute of the International Court of Justice (ICJ Statute) (adopted 26 June 1945, entered into force 24 October 1945) 33 UNTS 993. For race, see e.g. *Legal Consequences for States of the Continued Presence of South Africa in Namibia (South West Africa) notwithstanding Security Council Resolution 276 (Advisory Opinion)*, [1971] ICJ Reports 16, 130; *Barcelona Traction (Second Phase)*, [1970] ICJ Reports 3, 32; *South-West Africa Cases (Second Phase)*, [1966] ICJ Reports 6, 293 and 299–300 (Tanaka, J., dissenting); UNESCO Declaration on Race and Racial Prejudice, adopted by the UNESCO General Conference (20th Sess.), 27 November 1978, Art. 9 (reaffirming that 'the principle of equality in dignity and rights of all human beings and all peoples, irrespective of race, colour and origin, is a generally accepted and recognized principle of international law'.); Shaw, *International Law* (2014), pp. 208–9; Crawford, *Brownlie's Principles of Public*

Court of Human Rights has gone further than this and held that also the guarantee against discrimination on other grounds, including language, political or other opinion, national, ethnic or social origin, nationality, age, economic situation, property, civil status, birth or any other status, forms part of general international law and, indeed, is a norm of *jus cogens* that cannot be set aside by treaty or acquiescence.[29]

Non-discrimination provisions are commonly subdivided into subordinate (or parasitic) and autonomous (or free-standing) norms.[30] *Subordinate norms* prohibit discrimination only in the enjoyment of the rights guaranteed in the respective instrument. An example is Article 2(1) of the ICCPR, which provides:

> Each State Party to the present Covenant undertakes to respect and to ensure to all individuals within its territory and subject to its jurisdiction the rights recognized in the present Covenant, without distinction of any kind, such as race, colour, sex, language, religion, political or other opinion, national or social origin, property, birth or other status.

Of the other non-discrimination provisions of relevance here, Article 2(1) of the UDHR, Article 2(1) of the CRC and Article 14 of the ECHR[31] are also subordinate norms. Since the ECHR itself does not contain an autonomous norm in addition to its subordinate provision of Article 14,[32] the jurisprudence of the European Court of Human Rights interpreting it is of particular importance. The European Court has held that, in order to invoke Article 14, an applicant must show that the facts of the case fall 'within the ambit' of another substantive ECHR right.[33] However, there is no need to show that there has been *a violation* of that right. A measure that in itself is in conformity with the requirements of a given Convention right, but is of a discriminatory nature, will violate that right when read in conjunction

International Law (2012), p. 645. For the other grounds, see Shaw, *International Law* (2014), p. 209 and references cited there; Crawford, *Brownlie's Principles of Public International Law* (2012), pp. 645–6.

29 OC/18, *Juridical Condition and Rights of the Undocumented Migrants*, IACtHR Series A No. 18 (2003), paras 100–101 and 173.4.

30 See Moeckli, 'Equality and Non-discrimination' (2014), 161–3; Bayefsky, 'The Principle of Equality or Non-discrimination in International Law' (1990), 3.

31 Article 14 of the ECHR reads: 'The enjoyment of the rights and freedoms set forth in this Convention shall be secured without discrimination on any ground such as sex, race, colour, language, religion, political or other opinion, national or social origin, association with a national minority, property, birth or other status.'

32 On Protocol No. 12 to the ECHR, see further below in this section.

33 E.g. *Rasmussen* v. *Denmark*, no. 8777/79, 28 November 1984, Series A no. 87, para. 29.

with Article 14.[34] As is evident from the analysis in Section 5.2, most measures excluding people from public space fall within the scope of protection of one (or several) of the substantive ECHR rights, so that Article 14 is applicable in these cases.

On the other hand, Article 7 of the UDHR, Article 26 of the ICCPR, Articles 2 and 5 of the ICERD and Article 2 of the ADHR are *autonomous norms*: they guarantee non-discrimination not only in the context of other rights but in general. For example, Article 26 of the ICCPR states:

> All persons are equal before the law and are entitled without any discrimination to the equal protection of the law. In this respect, the law shall prohibit any discrimination and guarantee to all persons equal and effective protection against discrimination on any ground such as race, colour, sex, language, religion, political or other opinion, national or social origin, property, birth or other status.

The UN Human Rights Committee held in *Broeks* v. *The Netherlands* that it does not matter whether the subject matter to which a complaint relates is covered by the ICCPR or some other international instrument.[35] It stressed that 'Article 26 does not merely duplicate the guarantees already provided for in Article 2' but instead 'prohibits discrimination in law or in practice in any field regulated and protected by public authorities'.[36] The Committee confirmed this finding in its General Comment 18. Thus, state parties to the ICCPR have a general obligation neither to enact legislation with a discriminatory content nor to apply laws in a discriminatory way.[37] Switzerland, however, has entered a reservation concerning Article 26 of the ICCPR to the effect that its guarantee of equality shall only apply in connection with other ICCPR rights, meaning that the protection it provides does not go beyond what is already guaranteed by the subordinate provision of Article 2 of the ICCPR.[38] While, as explained above, the ECHR itself only contains a subordinate norm in the form of Article 14, Protocol No. 12 to the ECHR, which entered into force in 2005, contains a non-

[34] Harris/O'Boyle/Bates/Buckley, *Law of the ECHR* (2014), pp. 786–7; Meyer-Ladewig, *Europäische Menschenrechtskonvention* (2011), p. 282.

[35] *Broeks* v. *The Netherlands*, Communication No. 172/1984, 9 April 1987, UN Doc. CCPR/C/29/D/172/1984, paras 12.1–12.2.

[36] Ibid., para. 12.3.

[37] UN Human Rights Committee, General Comment No. 18, UN Doc. HRI/GEN/1/Rev.9 (Vol. I) 195, para. 12.

[38] Bundesbeschluss betreffend den internationalen Pakt über bürgerliche und politische Rechte vom 13. Dezember 1991, BBl 1991 IV, 1105, p. 1106. See BGE 121 V 229, 234 (1995).

discrimination guarantee that is not limited to the enjoyment of Convention rights.[39] However, neither Switzerland nor the United Kingdom has signed Protocol No. 12.

6.1.1.2 United Kingdom

As explained in Section 4.1.2, Dicey took the view that equality before the law is one of three components of the rule of law, which, in turn, is one of the most fundamental principles of the British constitutional system.[40] The Privy Council has similarly observed that the principle of equality 'is one of the building blocks of democracy and necessarily permeates any democratic constitution'.[41] And in the view of the House of Lords, it is a 'fundamental principle of justice [. . .] that people should be treated equally and like cases treated alike', any exception requiring sound justification.[42] Equality has therefore been characterised as a fundamental principle of the British constitution.[43] As has been made clear by the House of Lords, the equality guarantee applies to everybody within the United Kingdom, including foreign citizens.[44] However, the Diceyan conception of equality before the law has been criticised for not being concerned with the content of the law but only with its enforcement and application.[45] According to these critics, the constitutional principle of equality goes in fact further and forbids not only the unequal application of equal laws, but also unequal laws – even though, legally speaking, parliament as the sovereign authority cannot be prevented from passing unequal laws.[46]

Whatever the precise content of the original constitutional principle of equality, the Human Rights Act 1998 now 'give[s] further effect' to the rights guaranteed by the ECHR.[47] These include Article 14 of the

[39] Protocol No. 12 to the Convention for the Protection of Human Rights and Fundamental Freedoms (adopted 4 November 2000, entered into force 1 April 2005) ETS 177, Art. 1.

[40] Dicey, *An Introduction to the Study of the Law of the Constitution* (1959), p. 202.

[41] *Matadeen* v. *Pointu*, [1999] 1 AC 98, 109 (Lord Hoffmann).

[42] *Arthur JS Hall* v. *Simons*, [2002] 1 AC 615, 688 (Lord Hoffmann).

[43] Jowell, 'Is Equality a Constitutional Principle?' (1994). See also Feldman, *Civil Liberties and Human Rights in England and Wales* (2002), p. 133.

[44] *Khawaja* v. *Secretary of State for the Home Department*, [1984] AC 74, 111 (Lord Scarman) (holding that '[e]very person within the jurisdiction enjoys the equal protection of our laws. There is no distinction between British nationals and others.').

[45] E.g. Jowell, 'Is Equality a Constitutional Principle?' (1994), 4; Jennings, *The Law and the Constitution* (1933), p. 49.

[46] Jowell, 'Is Equality a Constitutional Principle?' (1994), 7; Allan, *Law, Liberty, and Justice* (1993), pp. 39–47, 163–82.

[47] Human Rights Act 1998, preamble.

ECHR,[48] which precludes any kind of differential treatment with regard to the Convention rights. Legislation must be interpreted in a way that is compatible with Article 14,[49] and courts can make a declaration of incompatibility if they think that a particular provision cannot be interpreted in such a way.[50] In contrast, the other non-discrimination provisions binding the United Kingdom under international law, including those of the ICCPR, the ICERD and the CRC, have not been incorporated into domestic law. However, in addition to the Human Rights Act, on 1 October 2010 the Equality Act 2010 entered into force. This Act prohibits discrimination based on a number of specified characteristics by anyone exercising a public function, including, for example, the police and local authorities.[51] The Equality Act 2010 also requires public authorities to have due regard to the need to eliminate discrimination.[52]

6.1.1.3 United States

The equal protection clause of the Fourteenth Amendment to the US Constitution provides that '[n]o State shall [. . .] deny to any person within its jurisdiction the equal protection of the laws'. Passed in 1868, it was primarily intended to provide equal protection for the recently freed slaves.[53] Originally the Supreme Court was therefore reluctant to bring other groups within the scope of the equal protection clause,[54] and even with regard to racial discrimination it applied a very lenient standard of review, only rarely striking down government policies.[55] It was only from 1938 onwards that the Court began to develop its 'strict scrutiny' jurisprudence, subjecting racial classifications to a heightened standard of review, and only from about the 1960s did it start to seriously question classifications based on other grounds than race.[56]

The equal protection clause guarantees that similar individuals will be dealt with in a similar manner by the government and prohibits unreasonable classifications.[57] The Supreme Court recognised already very

[48] Ibid., s. 1. [49] Ibid., s. 3. [50] Ibid., s. 4. [51] Equality Act 2010, ss 4–12, 29(6).
[52] Ibid., s. 149.
[53] TenBroek, *Equal Under Law* (1965). See also Chemerinsky, *Constitutional Law* (2009), pp. 748–54.
[54] See e.g. *Slaughterhouse Cases*, 83 U.S. 36, 81 (1873).
[55] See e.g. *Plessy* v. *Ferguson*, 163 U.S. 537 (1896).
[56] For a helpful overview of the Supreme Court's jurisprudence, see Kommers/Niehaus, 'An Introduction to American Equal Protection Law' (2003). See also Sullivan/Feldman, *Constitutional Law* (2013), pp. 601–767.
[57] See the classic treatise on the equal protection clause: Tussman/tenBroek, 'The Equal Protection of the Laws' (1949), 344.

early on that the clause not only requires equal enforcement of the laws but also demands that legislation itself be equal.[58]

Although the equal protection clause of the Fourteenth Amendment by its own terms only applies to *state* governments, the Supreme Court has interpreted the due process clause of the Fifth Amendment to test *federal* classifications under the same standard of review.[59] The guarantees of both the Fourteenth and the Fifth Amendments extend to all 'persons' rather than being confined to 'citizens'. Accordingly, the Supreme Court has recognised that the equal protection clause is applicable 'to all persons within the territorial jurisdiction, without regard to any differences of race, of color, or of nationality'[60] and, in the case of a non-citizen, '[w]hatever his status under the immigration laws'.[61] Likewise, the Court has held that 'the Due Process Clause applies to all "persons" within the United States, including aliens, whether their presence here is lawful, unlawful, temporary, or permanent'.[62]

Furthermore, under international law, the United States is bound to comply with the non-discrimination norms of the ICCPR, the ICERD and the ADHR. As explained in Section 5.1.3, it has, however, declared that the provisions of the ICCPR and the ICERD are not self-executing and thus not enforceable in US courts until implemented by congressional legislation.

6.1.1.4 Switzerland

The idea of equality made its way to Switzerland from revolutionary France at the end of the eighteenth century,[63] and equality before the law was subsequently among the central principles on which the first Swiss Federal Constitution of 1848 was based.[64] Already in its earliest case law,

[58] *Yick Wo* v. *Hopkins*, 118 U.S. 356, 369 (1886).

[59] E.g. *Bolling* v. *Sharpe*, 347 U.S. 497 (1954).

[60] *Yick Wo* v. *Hopkins*, 118 U.S. 356, 369 (1886).

[61] *Plyler* v. *Doe*, 457 U.S. 202, 210 (1982).

[62] *Zadvydas* v. *Davis*, 533 U.S. 678, 693 (2001). See also *Kwong Hai Chew* v. *Colding*, 344 U.S. 590, 596–7, footnote 5 (1953) (holding that the Fifth Amendment does not allow 'any distinction between citizens and resident aliens').

[63] See Grisel, *Egalité* (2009), p. 30; Weber-Dürler, 'Rechtsgleichheit' (2001), 658; Haefliger, *Alle Schweizer sind vor dem Gesetze gleich* (1985), pp. 13–16; His, *Geschichte des neuern schweizerischen Staatsrechts: Band 1*(1920), pp. 321–59.

[64] Bundesverfassung der Schweizerischen Eidgenossenschaft vom 12. September 1848, Art. 4 (reprinted in Kölz, *Quellenbuch: Band I* (1992), p. 448). See Haefliger, *Alle Schweizer sind vor dem Gesetze gleich* (1985), pp. 18–20; His, *Geschichte des neuern schweizerischen Staatsrechts: Band 3* (1938), pp. 497–532. For a more critical assessment, see Kölz, *Neuere schweizerische Verfassungsgeschichte* (1992), pp. 583–9. The Federal Constitution of 1874

the Federal Supreme Court characterised the principle of equality as a demand of justice and a general axiom underlying the entire legal system.[65] The Federal Constitution in force today guarantees equality in its Article 8(1), which provides that 'all human beings are equal before the law'.[66] Unlike the equality provisions of the older versions of the Constitution, which referred to 'Swiss citizens',[67] the wording of the new Article 8(1) makes it clear that also foreign nationals are protected by the equality guarantee.

In addition to the general equality clause of paragraph 1, Article 8 of the Federal Constitution contains in its further paragraphs several specific equality requirements directed against particularly serious forms of unequal treatment. Most importantly for present purposes, Article 8(2) prohibits discrimination based on a (non-exhaustive) list of grounds, including origin, race, sex, age, language, social status, way of life, religious, ideological or political conviction, or because of a physical, mental or psychological disability.[68] Furthermore, Article 8(3) provides for a number of guarantees intended to ensure equality between women and men, while Article 8(4) requires the state to take positive action to eliminate discrimination against persons with disabilities.

As in the other jurisdictions, the principle of equality has been interpreted to imply that equals must be treated equally and unequals unequally and, thus, that any difference in treatment must be based on objective and reasonable grounds.[69] Distinctions based on one of the grounds listed in Article 8(2) of the Federal Constitution, the prohibition of discrimination, must meet a higher threshold: there is a presumption that such distinctions are unlawful and this presumption can only be

contained an identical provision, also in Article 4. Bundesverfassung der Schweizerischen Eidgenossenschaft vom 29. Mai 1874, Art. 4 (reprinted in Kölz, *Quellenbuch: Band II* (1996), p. 152). See Kägi, 'Zur Entwicklung des Schweizerischen Rechtsstaates seit 1848' (1952), 184, 193–5.

65 BGE 6 171, 173. 66 BV, Art. 8(1) ('Alle Menschen sind vor dem Gesetz gleich.').

67 Nevertheless, the Federal Supreme Court accepted already early on that the scope of protection of the equality guarantee extends to foreign nationals. E.g. BGE 14 489, 493 (1888).

68 BV, Art. 8(2) ('Niemand darf diskriminiert werden, namentlich nicht wegen der Herkunft, der Rasse, des Geschlechts, des Alters, der Sprache, der sozialen Stellung, der Lebensform, der religiösen, weltanschaulichen oder politischen Überzeugung oder wegen einer körperlichen, geistigen oder psychischen Behinderung.').

69 Kiener/Kälin, *Grundrechte* (2013), pp. 413–22; Häfelin/Haller/Keller, *Schweizerisches Bundesstaatsrecht* (2012), pp. 235–8; Müller/Schefer, *Grundrechte in der Schweiz* (2008), pp. 654–73; Oesch, *Differenzierung und Typisierung* (2008), pp. 29–30, 31–42; Martenet, *Géométrie de l'égalité* (2003), pp. 260–86; Weber-Dürler, 'Rechtsgleichheit' (2001), 661–5.

rebutted if it is demonstrated that there is a 'qualified justification', that is, that there are serious and cogent reasons for making the respective distinction.[70] Despite the fact that the text of Article 8(1) merely refers to equality *before* the law, it is undisputed that the general equality clause binds not only those organs of the state that apply the law (thus requiring equal enforcement of the laws) but also the legislator (thus requiring that laws themselves be equal).[71]

Finally, Switzerland is bound by the equality and non-discrimination norms of the ICERD, the CRC and, most importantly, the ICCPR and the ECHR, which, as a consequence of its monist system, have become part of the domestic law of Switzerland.[72] As explained in Section 6.1.1.1, the reservation entered by Switzerland with regard to Article 26 of the ICCPR means that the guarantee of equality and non-discrimination under that treaty is limited to the scope of protection provided by the subordinate provision of Article 2 of the ICCPR.

6.1.2 Content

As can be seen from the short review above, Aristotle's classical equality maxim according to which equals must be treated equally (and unequals unequally) is central to all guarantees of equality and non-discrimination. This simple definition of equality, however, is tautological and turns equality into an 'empty idea': it does not answer the questions of who (or what) are equals and what constitutes equal treatment.[73] External normative standards, not derivable from the concept of equality, are needed to answer these questions and thus to determine which differences in treatment are legitimate and which ones are not. The abstract notion of equality must therefore be given substance by translating it into concrete legal formulations that make clear which forms of unequal

70 BGE 134 I 49, 53–4 (2008). See Kiener/Kälin, *Grundrechte* (2013), pp. 430–34; Grisel, *Egalité* (2009), pp. 85–90; Peters, 'Diskriminierungsverbote' (2007), 257–8, 282–3; Waldmann, *Das Diskriminierungsverbot* (2003), pp. 318–38; Martenet, *Géométrie de l'égalité* (2003), pp. 287–306.

71 This was acknowledged by the Federal Supreme Court as early as 1880 in BGE 6 171, 173. See generally Kiener/Kälin, *Grundrechte* (2013), p. 414; Grisel, *Egalité* (2009), pp. 45–8; Weber-Dürler, 'Rechtsgleichheit' (2001), 660–61.

72 See Section 5.1.4.

73 Westen, 'The Empty Idea of Equality' (1982). See also Altwicker, *Menschenrechtlicher Gleichheitsschutz* (2011), pp. 13–14; Grisel, *Egalité* (2009), p. 49; Oesch, *Differenzierung und Typisierung* (2008), pp. 22–4; Weber-Dürler, 'Gleichheit' (2007), 233; Müller, 'Der Gleichheitssatz' (1989), 40, 45.

treatment are legitimate because they are based on morally acceptable criteria and which ones are wrongful. As will be demonstrated in this section, the legal standards and tests that have been developed for this purpose in the jurisdictions at issue are, with regard to their most important aspects, very similar.

6.1.2.1 General issues

While some of the norms listed in the previous section are framed as general guarantees of equality, others prohibit discrimination based on particular personal characteristics. With regard to the scope of protection, the difference between these two types of norms should not be overplayed: prohibitions of discrimination are, in the end, negative, more detailed formulations of the general guarantee of equality, specifying its substance.[74] Especially, prohibitions of discrimination that include an open-ended list of prohibited grounds provide, in their practical operation, the same degree of protection as general equality guarantees.[75] Article 14 of the ECHR, for example, prohibits 'discrimination on *any* ground *such as* sex, race, colour, language, religion, political or other opinion, national or social origin, association with a national minority, property, birth *or other status*',[76] leading the European Court of Human Rights to hold that it precludes any kind of differential treatment of persons that has no objective and reasonable justification.[77] Sometimes the Court does not even find it necessary to state the particular ground of distinction involved when considering a case under Article 14.[78] At least for the present context, where the focus is on differences in treatment based on personal characteristics, it does, from a practical point of view, therefore not matter whether a general equality guarantee or a prohibition of discrimination applies to a given situation.

Some of the legal instruments of relevance for present purposes, including the ICCPR and the Swiss Federal Constitution, contain both

[74] See e.g. Grisel, *Egalité* (2009), pp. 49–50; Waldmann, *Das Diskriminierungsverbot* (2003), pp. 92–193; Martenet, *Géométrie de l'égalité* (2003), p. 1; Bayefsky, 'The Principle of Equality or Non-discrimination in International Law' (1990), 1; Explanatory report to Protocol No. 12 to the Convention for the Protection of Human Rights and Fundamental Freedoms, ETS No. 177, para. 15.

[75] See also Grabenwarter/Pabel, *Europäische Menschenrechtskonvention* (2012), p. 526; Nolte, 'Gleichheit und Nichtdiskriminierung' (2003), 251.

[76] Emphases added.

[77] E.g. *Zarb Adami* v. *Malta*, no. 17209/02, 20 June 2006, ECHR 2006-VIII, 305, para. 71.

[78] E.g. *Žičkus* v. *Lithuania*, no. 26652/02, 7 April 2009, para. 28; *Rasmussen* v. *Denmark*, no. 8777/79, 28 November 1984, Series A no. 87, para. 34.

a general guarantee of equality and a prohibition (or several prohibitions) of discrimination (with a non-exhaustive list of prohibited grounds).[79] The equal protection clause of the Fourteenth Amendment to the US Constitution provides, at least according to its wording, for a general guarantee of equality. In the United Kingdom, Article 14 of the ECHR, incorporated into domestic law through the Human Rights Act, prohibits discrimination on the basis of an open-ended list of grounds. There is an additional statutory guarantee of non-discrimination in the form of the Equality Act 2010, which prohibits discrimination on the basis of an exhaustive list of personal characteristics (including age, disability, gender reassignment, marriage and civil partnership, pregnancy and maternity, race, religion or belief, sex, and sexual orientation).[80]

As has been pointed out above, it is well established in international as well as in the national law of the three states under consideration that the respective equality and non-discrimination norms require, first, that laws be equal ('equality in law') and, second, that laws be applied and enforced equally ('equality before the law' or 'equality in fact').

The test used to determine whether there is a violation of the right to equality and non-discrimination consists of essentially the same elements in all jurisdictions at issue. First, it must be considered whether there is a difference in treatment or whether, although there is no difference in treatment, a rule or measure has a disproportionate impact on particular groups (Section 6.1.2.2). Second, one must determine whether the persons who are treated differently are in comparable situations (Section 6.1.2.3). Third, it must be decided whether there is a justification for the difference in treatment or outcome (Section 6.1.2.4). Furthermore, this section explores the intensity of review that courts apply to assess the existence of a justification (Section 6.1.2.5) and considers matters concerning evidence and proof (Section 6.1.2.6).

One element that must generally *not* be demonstrated to establish a violation of the right to equality and non-discrimination is *discriminatory intention*. It is well established that under international law both intended and unintended discrimination are prohibited. This is apparent, for example, from the explicit definition of discrimination contained in the ICERD[81] as well as that adopted by the UN Human Rights Committee,

[79] ICCPR, Arts 2(1) and 26; BV, Arts 8(1) and (2). [80] Equality Act 2010, s. 4.

[81] Article 1(1) of the ICERD defines discrimination as any distinction based on one of the listed grounds 'which has the purpose *or effect* of nullifying or impairing the recognition,

in its General Comment on non-discrimination, for the purposes of the ICCPR.[82] In addition, both the Human Rights Committee and the European Court of Human Rights have repeatedly made it clear in their jurisprudence that discriminatory intention is not a necessary element of discrimination; instead, discrimination may also relate to the *effects* of a given measure.[83] In the United Kingdom, the House of Lords has similarly held that the reason why someone has been treated less favourably is irrelevant: discrimination can be established regardless of the alleged discriminator's intention.[84] The Swiss Federal Supreme Court as well as legal doctrine equally take the position that discriminatory intention is not required.[85] In the United States, in contrast, the Supreme Court has held that the equal protection principle of the Fourteenth and Fifth Amendments only prohibits intentional governmental discrimination.[86] However, according to the court, the discriminatory purpose must not necessarily be express or appear on the face of the law but may also be inferred from, for example, the discriminatory impacts shown to exist in fact or the historical background of a law or a government action.[87] Moreover, all express discrimination is by definition considered intentional.[88] Therefore, in its practical operation, the US equal protection guarantee is not as different from the respective norms under international, UK and Swiss law as might appear at first sight.

enjoyment or exercise, on an equal footing, of human rights and fundamental freedoms' (emphasis added).

[82] UN Human Rights Committee, General Comment No. 18, UN Doc. HRI/GEN/1/Rev.9 (Vol. I) 195, para. 7.

[83] For the UN Human Rights Committee, see e.g. *Althammer* v. *Austria*, Communication No. 998/2001, 8 August 2003, UN Doc. CCPR/C/78/D/998/2001, para. 10.2; *Adam* v. *the Czech Republic*, Communication No. 586/1994, 23 July 1996, UN Doc. CCPR/C/57/D/586/1994, para. 12.7; *Simunek et al* v. *The Czech Republic*, Communication No. 516/1992, 19 July 1995, UN Doc. CCPR/C/54/D/516/1992, para. 11.7. For the European Court of Human Rights, see e.g. *Hugh Jordan* v. *United Kingdom*, no. 24746/94, 4 May 2001, ECHR 2001-III, para. 154; *Case Relating to Certain Aspects of the Laws on the Use of Languages in Education in Belgium (Belgian Linguistics Case) (No. 2)*, (1968) 1 EHRR 252, para. 10.

[84] *R (European Roma Rights Centre)* v. *Immigration Officer at Prague Airport*, [2004] UKHL 55, para. 82 (Baroness Hale) (relating to the Race Relations Act).

[85] E.g. BGE 127 III 207, 216 (2001); Kiener/Kälin, *Grundrechte* (2013), p. 435; Biaggini, *Kommentar BV* (2007), p. 103; Peters, 'Diskriminierungsverbote' (2007), 266–7; Waldmann, *Das Diskriminierungsverbot* (2003), pp. 318, 364; Martenet, *Géométrie de l'égalité* (2003), p. 104.

[86] The leading case is *Washington* v. *Davis*, 426 U.S. 229 (1976).

[87] *Arlington Heights* v. *Metropolitan Housing Corp.*, 429 U.S. 252, 264–8 (1977); *Washington* v. *Davis*, 426 U.S. 229, 241–2 (1976).

[88] Sedler, 'The Role of "Intent" in Discrimination Analysis' (1999), 91–2.

6.1.2.2 Difference in treatment or outcome

According to the consistent case law of international human rights bodies and national courts, persons claiming a violation of the right to equality and non-discrimination must, first of all, show that there is a difference in treatment.[89] Thus, the complainant must demonstrate that he or she is treated less favourably than someone else who is in a comparable position. If this less favourable treatment occurs on account of one or more of the grounds listed in a norm prohibiting discrimination, it is described as *direct discrimination*[90] or, in the United States, *express discrimination.*[91]

However, international human rights law as well as the domestic law of the three states at issue prohibit not only direct but also *indirect discrimination*. Indirect discrimination occurs when a practice, rule or requirement that is outwardly 'neutral', that is, not based on one of the prohibited grounds of distinction, has a disproportionate impact on particular groups defined by reference to one of these grounds. Thus, although there is no difference in treatment, due to structural biases, treating unequals equally leads to unequal results.[92] The concept of indirect discrimination is well established in US law where, in fact, it was shaped at the beginning of the 1970s.[93] It then made its way to the United Kingdom where prohibitions of indirect discrimination were included in the anti-discrimination acts passed in the mid-1970s.[94] The relevant statute in force today, the Equality Act 2010, contains

[89] For the ECHR, see e.g. Harris/O'Boyle/Bates/Buckley, *Law of the ECHR* (2014), pp. 788–90; Meyer-Ladewig, *Europäische Menschenrechtskonvention* (2011), p. 283. For the United Kingdom, see Amos, *Human Rights Law* (2006), pp. 454–5. For the United States, see Chemerinsky, *Constitutional Law* (2009), p. 718. For Switzerland, see Kiener/Kälin, *Grundrechte* (2013), p. 415.

[90] For international human rights law, see e.g. Moeckli, 'Equality and Non-discrimination' (2014), 164–5; Altwicker, *Menschenrechtlicher Gleichheitsschutz* (2011), pp. 255–66. For the United Kingdom, see the definition contained in Article 13 of the Equality Act 2010 and Amos, *Human Rights Law* (2006), p. 455. For Switzerland, see BGE 126 II 377, 392–3 (2000); Kiener/Kälin, *Grundrechte* (2013), pp. 435–7; Waldmann, *Das Diskriminierungsverbot* (2003), pp. 308–25.

[91] See e.g. Sarine, 'Regulating the Social Pollution of Systemic Discrimination Caused by Implicit Bias' (2012), 1371; Fallon, *The Dynamic Constitution* (2004), p. 122.

[92] Moeckli, 'Equality and Non-discrimination' (2014), 165.

[93] The leading case of the US Supreme Court is *Griggs* v. *Duke Power Co.*, 401 U.S. 424 (1971) (concerning the Civil Rights Act). See also *Washington* v. *Davis*, 426 U.S. 229 (1976) (concerning the constitutional equal protection principle). See Rieder, *Form oder Effekt?* (2003), pp. 110–47; Selmi, 'Indirect Discrimination' (1999).

[94] Sex Discrimination Act 1975, s. 1(1)(b); Race Relations Act 1976, s. 1(1)(b). See Fredman, *Discrimination Law* (2011), pp. 178–9.

an explicit definition and prohibition of indirect discrimination.[95] In the 1990s, via EC law, the notion of indirect discrimination also found its way to Switzerland.[96] It has been recognised by the Swiss Federal Supreme Court, as well as in legal doctrine, that Article 8(2) of the Federal Constitution prohibits not only direct but also indirect discrimination.[97] In international human rights law, recognition of the concept of indirect discrimination is an even more recent phenomenon.[98] Although the UN Human Rights Committee acknowledged the possibility of indirect discrimination already in its earlier case law,[99] it did not expressly refer to the concept until 2003.[100] Similarly, it was only in 2007 that the European Court of Human Rights, in its groundbreaking ruling in *D.H. and others* v. *Czech Republic*, came up with an explicit definition of indirect discrimination. Referring to the definition of indirect discrimination in EC law, the Grand Chamber confirmed in this case that 'a difference in treatment may take the form of disproportionately prejudicial effects of a general policy or measure which, though couched in neutral terms, discriminates against a group'.[101] In the same year, the Inter-American Commission on Human Rights made it clear that the Inter-American system of human rights prohibits not only direct but also indirect discrimination.[102]

6.1.2.3 Comparability

For a violation of the right to equality and non-discrimination to be established, it must be shown that the persons who are treated differently are in a comparable position. Thus, under Article 14 of the ECHR it must

[95] Equality Act 2010, s. 19.

[96] See Waldmann, *Das Diskriminierungsverbot* (2003), pp. 338–44.

[97] BGE 126 II 377, 393–4 (2000); Auer/Malinverni/Hottelier, *Droit constitutionnel suisse* (2013), Vol. II, p. 515; Kiener/Kälin, *Grundrechte* (2013), pp. 437–9; Peters, 'Diskriminierungsverbote' (2007), 285–7; Waldmann, *Das Diskriminierungsverbot* (2003), pp. 344–8; Rieder, *Form oder Effekt?* (2003), pp. 98–107, 209–35.

[98] See Moeckli, 'Equality and Non-discrimination' (2014), 165–6; Altwicker, *Menschenrechtlicher Gleichheitsschutz* (2011), pp. 266–72.

[99] *Singh Bhinder* v. *Canada*, Communication No. 208/1986, 9 November 1989, UN Doc. CCPR/C/37/D/208/1986.

[100] *Althammer* v. *Austria*, Communication No. 998/2001, 8 August 2003, UN Doc. CCPR/C/78/D/998/2001, para. 10.2.

[101] *D.H. and others* v. *The Czech Republic* [GC], no. 57325/00, 13 November 2007, ECHR 2007-IV, 241, para. 184.

[102] Inter-American Commission on Human Rights, Access to justice for women victims of violence in the Americas, 20 January 2007, OEA/Ser.L/V//II. Doc. 68, paras 89–99.

be demonstrated that persons in 'analogous'[103] or 'relevantly similar'[104] situations, under the US Constitution that persons who are 'similarly situated'[105] and under the Swiss Constitution that persons who are 'in comparable situations'[106] are treated differently, while under the British Equality Act 2010 'there must be no material difference between the circumstances relating to each case'.[107] In assessing the issue of comparability, regard must be had, in particular, to the nature and purpose of the law or measure under consideration.[108] If no comparable situations exist, there is normally no need to proceed in the analysis of the case. Some scholars have criticised the separate requirement of a comparability test, since the issue of comparability could not be assessed without having regard to the justification of a difference in treatment.[109] Accordingly, in practice courts often tend to merge the comparability test with the assessment as to whether a justification for the difference in treatment exists.[110]

6.1.2.4 Justification

Once it is established that there has been a difference in treatment or outcome, the next question that needs to be answered is whether there is a justification for it. It is to some extent inevitable that laws and government actions classify people into groups that are treated differently. The crucial question is whether there is an objective and reasonable justification for these distinctions.

[103] *Lithgow and others* v. *The United Kingdom*, nos 9006/80; 9262/81; 9263/81; 9265/81; 9266/81; 9313/81; 9405/81, 8 July 1986, Series A no. 102, para. 177.

[104] *Fredin* v. *Sweden (No. 1)*, no. 12033/86, 18 February 1991, Series A no. 192, para. 60.

[105] Tussman/tenBroek, 'The Equal Protection of the Laws' (1949), 345.

[106] BGE 126 II 377, 393 (2000) ('Personen in vergleichbaren Situationen').

[107] Equality Act 2010, s. 23(1).

[108] For the ECHR, see e.g. *Weller* v. *Hungary*, no. 44399/05, 31 March 2009, para. 30. For the United Kingdom, see *A v. Secretary of State for the Home Department*, [2004] UKHL 56, para. 235. For the United States, see Tussman/tenBroek, 'The Equal Protection of the Laws' (1949), 346. For Switzerland, see Oesch, *Differenzierung und Typisierung* (2008), pp. 33–8; Martenet, *Géométrie de l'égalité* (2003), p. 30.

[109] E.g. Peters/Altwicker, *Europäische Menschenrechtskonvention* (2012), p. 245; Altwicker, *Menschenrechtlicher Gleichheitsschutz* (2011), pp. 174–7; Peters, 'Diskriminierungsverbote' (2007), 282; Waldmann, *Das Diskriminierungsverbot* (2003), pp. 70–71, 319–22.

[110] For the UN Human Rights Committee, see Choudhury, 'Interpreting the Right to Equality under Article 26 of the International Covenant on Civil and Political Rights' (2003), 34–5. For the European Court of Human Rights, see Livingstone, 'Article 14 and the Prevention of Discrimination in the European Convention on Human Rights' (1997), 30.

As far as international law is concerned, the test that must be applied to distinguish between justified and unjustified distinction has now taken on quite clear contours. For the purposes of the ICCPR, the UN Human Rights Committee has stressed that 'not every differentiation of treatment will constitute discrimination, if the criteria for such differentiation are reasonable and objective and if the aim is to achieve a purpose which is legitimate under the Covenant'.[111] It is, however, the European Court of Human Rights that has most clearly articulated the elements of the justification test. The Court interpreted Article 14 of the ECHR for the first time in the *Belgian Linguistics Case* and has since repeatedly confirmed those conclusions:

> [T]he Court, following the principles which may be extracted from the legal practice of a large number of democratic states, holds that the principle of equality of treatment is violated if the distinction has no objective and reasonable justification. The existence of such a justification must be assessed in relation to the aim and effects of the measure under consideration, regard being had to the principles which normally prevail in democratic societies. A difference of treatment in the exercise of a right laid down in the Convention must not only pursue a legitimate aim: Article 14 is likewise violated when it is clearly established that there is no reasonable relationship of proportionality between the means employed and the aim sought to be realised.[112]

This two-limb test, requiring that any difference in treatment must (1) pursue a legitimate aim and (2) be proportionate, is very similar to the test used in the context of other fundamental rights to assess the permissibility of limitations, described in Section 5.3. The test formulated by the European Court has been adopted, explicitly or implicitly, by most other human rights bodies. Most importantly for the present context, the UN Committee on the Elimination of Racial Discrimination has essentially embraced the same approach.[113] While the UN Human Rights Committee had originally failed to provide a clear and consistent

[111] UN Human Rights Committee, General Comment No. 18, UN Doc. HRI/GEN/1/Rev.9 (Vol. I) 195, para. 13.

[112] *Case Relating to Certain Aspects of the Laws on the Use of Languages in Education in Belgium (Belgian Linguistics Case) (Merits)*, nos 1474/62; 1677/62; 1691/62; 1769/63; 1994/63; 2126/64, Series A no. 6, para. 10. See also e.g. *Salgueiro da Silva Mouta* v. *Portugal*, no. 33290/96, 21 December 1999, ECHR 1999-IX, 309, para. 29; *Van Raalte* v. *The Netherlands*, no. 20060/92, 21 February 1997, ECHR 1997-I, 29, para. 39.

[113] UN CERD, Concluding observations: Australia, 14 April 2005, UN Doc. CERD/C/AUS/CO/14, para. 24; UN CESCR, General Comment No. 20, UN Doc. E/C.12/GC/20, para. 13.

explanation of what it means by 'reasonable and objective criteria', it later also started to interpret these terms as requiring a legitimate aim and proportionality.[114]

As a result of incorporation of the ECHR, the jurisprudence of the European Court of Human Rights is directly relevant to UK law. Accordingly, as explained in Section 5.3.2.1, courts in the United Kingdom have shifted their focus from the traditional grounds of judicial review to a means-end analysis expressed in terms of proportionality in cases where Convention rights are concerned. This also holds true with regard to cases brought under Article 14 of the ECHR. Thus, according to the House of Lords, 'a difference in treatment can be justified only if it pursues a legitimate aim and there is a reasonable relationship of proportionality between the means employed and the aim sought to be realised'.[115] The proportionality approach is also reflected in the Equality Act 2010, which provides with regard to, for example, age discrimination that 'A does not discriminate against B if A can show A's treatment of B to be a proportionate means of achieving a legitimate aim.'[116]

The two elements of legitimate aim and proportionality are also reflected in US jurisprudence concerning the equal protection principle. As with interferences with individual freedoms,[117] the US Supreme Court has elaborated a system of three different, fairly fixed standards to review equal protection challenges.[118] Under the first standard, the 'rational relationship' or 'rational basis' test, applicable to most distinctions, the court only invalidates the classification if it has no rational relationship to any legitimate interest of government.[119] Thus, the distinction is accorded a strong presumption of legality.[120] Under the 'intermediate scrutiny' test, the distinction must have a substantial relationship to the promotion of an important interest of

[114] E.g. UN Human Rights Committee, *Gillot* v. *France*, Communication No. 932/2000, 15 July 2002, UN Doc. A/57/40, para. 13.2.

[115] *Ghaidan* v. *Godin-Mendoza*, [2004] UKHL 30, para. 18 (Lord Nicholls). See also e.g. *A* v. *Secretary of State for the Home Department*, [2004] UKHL 56, para. 50 (Lord Bingham); *R (ex parte LS)* v. *Chief Constable of South Yorkshire*, [2004] UKHL 39, paras 54–5 (Lord Steyn).

[116] Equality Act 2010, s. 13(2). [117] See Section 5.3.

[118] For summaries of the Supreme Court's relevant jurisprudence, see e.g. Chemerinsky, *Constitutional Law* (2009), pp. 719–21; Nowak/Rotunda, *Constitutional Law* (2004), pp. 680–92; Martenet, *Géométrie de l'égalité* (2003), pp. 202–8; Polyviou, *The Equal Protection of the Laws* (1980), pp. 177–298.

[119] E.g. *FCC* v. *Beach Communications, Inc.*, 508 U.S. 307, 313 (1993). See Chemerinsky, *Constitutional Law* (2009), pp. 723–48.

[120] *Heller* v. *Doe*, 509 U.S. 312, 319 (1993).

government.[121] Finally, distinctions affecting fundamental individual interests and distinctions based on certain suspect criteria entail 'strict scrutiny': the classification must be necessary (or narrowly tailored) to advance a compelling government interest.[122] In sum, a difference in treatment is justified if there is an appropriately close relationship between the distinction and the aim pursued, depending on the applicable standard of review.

Also in Switzerland it is well established that differences in treatment may be justified. According to the Federal Supreme Court and the majority of legal scholars, equality cases are not to be considered under Article 36 of the Federal Constitution, which sets out the requirements (legal basis, legitimate aim, proportionality) for the limitation of fundamental rights in general, but is in fact designed to be applied only to freedoms.[123] Instead, a different test applies: for a given difference in treatment to be compatible with the general equality guarantee of Article 8(1) of the Federal Constitution, it must be demonstrated that it is based on 'objective and reasonable grounds' (*'sachliche und vernünftige Gründe'/'une justification objective et raisonnable'*).[124] A minority of scholars, in contrast, argue that Article 36 is also applicable in equality cases.[125] In any event, even scholars who reject the direct application of Article 36 recognise that the existence of 'objective and reasonable grounds' depends to a large extent on the legitimacy of the aim pursued by a given measure and its proportionality.[126] Similarly, the Federal Supreme Court has referred to the principle of proportionality to assess whether a distinction is objective and reasonable and thus compatible

[121] E.g. *United States* v. *Virginia*, 518 U.S. 515, 533 (1996); *Graig* v. *Boren*, 429 U.S. 190, 197 (1976). See Nowak/Rotunda, *Constitutional Law* (2004), pp. 688–90; Polyviou, *The Equal Protection of the Laws* (1980), pp. 221–4.

[122] E.g. *Adarand Constructors, Inc.* v. *Peña*, 515 U.S. 200, 227 (1995). See Sullivan/Feldman, *Constitutional Law* (2013), pp. 616–809.

[123] See Section 5.3.

[124] E.g. BGE 136 I 121, 127 (2010); BGE 125 I 173, 178 (1999); Auer/Malinverni/Hottelier, *Droit constitutionnel suisse* (2013), Vol. II, pp. 481–3; Kiener/Kälin, *Grundrechte* (2013), pp. 415–18; Häfelin/Haller/Keller, *Schweizerisches Bundesstaatsrecht* (2012), pp. 236–8; Müller/Schefer, *Grundrechte in der Schweiz* (2008), pp. 654–73; Waldmann, *Das Diskriminierungsverbot* (2003), p. 184; Martenet, *Géométrie de l'égalité* (2003), pp. 260–86; Weber-Dürler, 'Rechtsgleichheit' (2001), 661–5.

[125] Müller/Schefer, *Grundrechte in der Schweiz* (2008), pp. 693–4; Oesch, *Differenzierung und Typisierung* (2008), pp. 307–98; Peters, 'Diskriminierungsverbote' (2007), 281; Martenet, *Géométrie de l'égalité* (2003), pp. 182–8, 307–51.

[126] Keller, 'Rechtsgleichheit und Diskriminierungsverbot' (2011), 511; Müller/Schefer, *Grundrechte in der Schweiz* (2008), p. 663; Biaggini, *Kommentar BV* (2007), p. 102.

with Article 8(1) of the Federal Constitution.[127] A stricter standard applies with regard to distinctions that affect fundamental rights and those that are based on one of the grounds listed in Article 8(2) of the Federal Constitution, the prohibition of discrimination.[128] Such distinctions are only lawful if there is a 'qualified justification'.[129] In the case of differences in treatment based on one of the grounds listed in Article 8(2), this means that they are presumed to be unlawful and this presumption can only be rebutted if it is demonstrated that there are serious and cogent reasons for making the respective distinction.[130] The majority of scholars agree that this inquiry as to the existence of a 'qualified justification' equates to a proportionality test, that is, it must be assessed whether the measure in question pursues a legitimate aim and whether, in view of this aim, the distinction is proportionate.[131] In a recent decision, the Federal Supreme Court adopted the same position, holding that for there to be a 'qualified justification', it must be demonstrated that the measure complained of pursues 'a weighty and legitimate public interest' in a proportionate manner.[132]

6.1.2.5 Intensity of review

As should already have become clear from the previous section, not all distinctions are reviewed with the same degree of intensity. Instead, the stringency with which courts review the existence of a justification for a difference in treatment or outcome will vary according to a number of factors.

[127] BGE 131 I 205, 215 (2005).

[128] See already BGE 106 Ib 182, 188–9 (1980) (relating to the situation prior to the adoption of the Federal Constitution in force today and its Article 8(2)). See also Kiener/Kälin, *Grundrechte* (2013), pp. 418–19, 433–4; Müller/Schefer, *Grundrechte in der Schweiz* (2008), pp. 662–4, 693–4, 697; Martenet, *Géométrie de l'égalité* (2003), pp. 287–300.

[129] E.g. BGE 126 II 377, 393 (2000) ('sich daraus ergebende Ungleichbehandlungen sind infolgedessen "qualifiziert zu rechtfertigen"').

[130] E.g. BGE 134 I 49, 53–4 (2008). See Auer/Malinverni/Hottelier, *Droit constitutionnel suisse* (2013), Vol. II, p. 505; Kiener/Kälin, *Grundrechte* (2013), pp. 430–31, 433; Grisel, *Egalité* (2009), p. 88; Peters, 'Diskriminierungsverbote' (2007), 282–3; Martenet, *Géométrie de l'égalité* (2003), pp. 289–94; Waldmann, *Das Diskriminierungsverbot* (2003), p. 325.

[131] E.g. Kiener/Kälin, *Grundrechte* (2013), pp. 433–4; Keller, 'Rechtsgleichheit und Diskriminierungsverbot' (2011), 514; Waldmann, *Das Diskriminierungsverbot* (2003), pp. 322–5.

[132] BGE 135 I 49, 59 (2008) ('Unter diesem Gesichtswinkel ist daher zu prüfen, ob die beanstandete Massnahme ein gewichtiges und legitimes öffentliches Interesse verfolgt, als geeignet und erforderlich betrachtet werden kann und sich gesamthaft als verhältnismässig erweist.').

Suspect grounds of distinction Most importantly, in all jurisdictions at issue, certain grounds of distinction are regarded as inherently suspect and therefore require particularly strict scrutiny. Under international human rights law, the distinctions attracting the greatest degree of attention and most likely to be declared unjustified are those based on race, ethnic origin, sex and religion.[133] These grounds are also treated as suspect by the European Court of Human Rights,[134] which, for example, has stressed that 'where [a] difference in treatment is based on race, colour or ethnic origin, the notion of objective and reasonable justification must be interpreted as strictly as possible'[135] and that 'no difference in treatment which is based exclusively or to a decisive extent on a person's ethnic origin is capable of being objectively justified in a contemporary democratic society built on the principles of pluralism and respect for different cultures'.[136] In addition to the grounds referred to above, the European Court also subjects to heightened scrutiny distinctions based on birth status, sexual orientation and nationality.[137] With regard to the latter ground, it has held that 'very weighty reasons would have to be put forward before the Court could regard a difference of treatment based exclusively on the ground of nationality as compatible with the Convention'.[138] These lists of suspect classifications are by no means fixed but can change as international law on these matters develops. Given the recent emergence of new international norms against discrimination on grounds such as disability[139] and old age,[140] it seems likely that also these classifications may soon be regarded as suspect by courts, if they are not already.

133 See Moeckli, 'Equality and Non-discrimination' (2014), 168–9.

134 For an overview of the case law, see Harris/O'Boyle/Bates/Buckley, *Law of the ECHR* (2014), pp. 796–803; Grabenwarter/Pabel, *Europäische Menschenrechtskonvention* (2012), pp. 528–35.

135 *D.H. and others* v. *The Czech Republic* [GC], no. 57325/00, 13 November 2007, ECHR 2007-IV, 241, para. 196.

136 *Timishev* v. *Russia*, nos 55762/00; 55974/00, 13 December 2005, ECHR 2005-XII, 169, para. 58.

137 See Harris/O'Boyle/Bates/Buckley, *Law of the ECHR* (2014), pp. 797–806; Grabenwarter/Pabel, *Europäische Menschenrechtskonvention* (2012), pp. 530, 532–4.

138 *Gaygusuz v Austria*, no. 17371/90, 16 September 1996, Reports 1996-IV, Vol. 14, para. 42. See also e.g. *Andrejeva* v. *Latvia* [GC], no. 55707/00, 18 February 2009, ECHR 2009, para. 87.

139 See CRPD.

140 See UN Principles for Older Persons, UN General Assembly Resolution 46/91, 16 December 1991, UN Doc. A/RES/46/91 (1991).

The British courts largely follow the European Court of Human Rights' approach and subject differential treatment to intense scrutiny if the ground of distinction is race, sex, sexual orientation or nationality, only accepting 'cogent reasons' as sufficient justification in these cases.[141] These grounds of distinction share in common that they are all closely related to a person's dignity.[142]

According to the analytical model of the US Supreme Court, distinctions based on race and nationality are reviewed under the 'strict scrutiny' test.[143] Classifications based on race, ethnic origin and national origin are subjected to the 'most rigid scrutiny',[144] calling for 'the most exacting judicial examination',[145] and can only be upheld if they are shown to be necessary to promote a 'compelling' or 'overriding' government interest.[146] Since racial classifications are hardly ever sustained by the Supreme Court, the 'strict scrutiny' test has been described as '"strict" in theory and fatal in fact'.[147] Similarly, distinctions based on nationality and non-citizenship are, as a general rule, 'inherently suspect and subject to close judicial scrutiny', since '[a]liens as a class are a prime example of a "discrete and insular" minority for whom such heightened judicial solicitude is appropriate'.[148] As far as decisions in the areas of immigration and naturalisation are concerned, however, the Supreme Court applies a more lenient standard of review.[149] Distinctions based on sex and birth status, finally, attract 'intermediate scrutiny' and must thus be substantially related to the achievement of an important interest of government.[150]

141 *Ghaidan* v. *Godin-Mendoza*, [2004] UKHL 30, para. 19 (Lord Nicholls); *R. (on the application of Morris)* v. *Westminster City Council (No. 3)*, [2004] EWHC 2191 (Admin), para. 32.

142 Fredman, 'From Deference to Democracy' (2006), 73–6.

143 See e.g. Chemerinsky, *Constitutional Law* (2009), pp. 748–878; Nowak/Rotunda, *Constitutional Law* (2004), pp. 687–8, 734–866; Ely, *Democracy and Distrust* (1980), pp. 145–70.

144 *Loving* v. *Virginia*, 388 U.S. 1, 11 (1967).

145 *Wygant* v. *Jackson Board of Education*, 476 U.S. 267, 273 (1986).

146 E.g. *Adarand Constructors, Inc* v. *Peña*, 515 U.S. 200, 227 (1995); *McLaughlin* v. *Florida*, 379 U.S. 184, 196 (1964).

147 Gunther, 'The Supreme Court 1971 Term' (1972), 8.

148 *Graham* v. *Richardson*, 403 U.S. 365, 372 (1971). See Chemerinsky, *Constitutional Law* (2009), pp. 917–33.

149 See *Mathews* v. *Diaz*, 426 U.S. 67 (1976).

150 E.g. *United States* v. *Virginia*, 518 U.S. 515, 533 (1996); *Graig* v. *Boren*, 429 U.S. 190, 197 (1976). See Nowak/Rotunda, *Constitutional Law* (2004), pp. 688–90; Polyviou, *The Equal Protection of the Laws* (1980), pp. 221–4.

In Switzerland, all distinctions based on one of the grounds listed in Article 8(2) of the Federal Constitution (origin, race, sex, age, language, social status, way of life, religious, ideological or political conviction, and physical, mental or psychological disability) require, as explained above, a 'qualified justification'. The reason for this is that these characteristics form important components of a person's identity that cannot (or can hardly) be changed – and that are thus linked to human dignity – and that groups defined by reference to them have historically been disadvantaged and excluded.[151] Any difference in treatment or outcome based on one of these criteria will therefore be reviewed with particular scrutiny by courts. However, not all grounds listed in Article 8(2) are equally suspect. While differences in treatment based on race can, as a general rule, never be permissible,[152] there may well be a justification for a distinction based on, for instance, age.[153]

Other factors Apart from the ground of distinction, the intensity of review may also depend on a number of other factors. Most importantly for present purposes, it is recognised in all jurisdictions at issue that distinctions that affect fundamental individual interests must be reviewed with stricter scrutiny. Thus, the European Court of Human Rights is less likely to afford the state a broad margin of appreciation when a particularly important aspect of an individual's existence is in issue.[154] Similarly, in the United Kingdom, the House of Lords has held that, where fundamental rights are at stake, the intensity of review must be greater than, for example, in matters of social or economic policy.[155] The US Supreme Court subjects to strict scrutiny not only classifications based on suspect criteria but also those that create inequalities with regard to fundamental rights.[156] Finally, in Switzerland, it is recognised

[151] BGE 132 I 49, 65–6 (2006).

[152] E.g. Biaggini, *Kommentar BV* (2007), p. 105; Waldmann, *Das Diskriminierungsverbot* (2003), p. 592; Weber-Dürler, 'Rechtsgleichheit' (2001), 669.

[153] Keller, 'Rechtsgleichheit und Diskriminierungsverbot' (2011), 513; Peters, 'Diskriminierungsverbote' (2007), 284.

[154] See e.g. *Dudgeon* v. *The United Kingdom*, no. 7525/76, 22 October 1981, Series A no. 45, para. 52.

[155] E.g. *A* v. *Secretary of State for the Home Department*, [2004] UKHL 56, paras 39 (Lord Bingham), 80–1 (Lord Nicholls), 107–8 (Lord Hope), 196 (Lord Walker).

[156] E.g. *City of Cleburne* v. *Cleburne Living Ctr.*, 473 U.S. 432, 440 (1985); *Shapiro* v. *Thompson*, 394 U.S. 618, 627–33 (1969); *Skinner* v. *Oklahoma*, 316 U.S. 535, 541 (1942). See Kommers/Niehaus, 'An Introduction to American Equal Protection Law' (2003), 40–47; Tribe, *American Constitutional Law* (1988), pp. 1454–65.

that the requirements for establishing the existence of a justification are heightened as far as differential treatment occurs in an area protected by fundamental rights.[157]

On the other hand, there are areas where, typically, a lenient standard will be used to review differences in treatment or outcome. This is especially true for matters of social or economic policy[158] and other areas where, for practical reasons, it may be difficult for the state to avoid schematic classifications.[159] Finally, it will generally be more difficult to justify direct discrimination than indirect discrimination.[160]

As explained in Section 5.2, measures excluding people from public space interfere with a range of fundamental rights. Already for this reason, differences in treatment or outcome with regard to such measures should be reviewed with strict scrutiny. The standard of review must be particularly intense where a given distinction is based on one of the grounds that are treated as inherently suspect.

6.1.2.6 Evidence and proof

In all jurisdictions at issue it is generally up to the individual complaining of discrimination to establish a difference in treatment or outcome, the ground of distinction and the existence of comparably situated groups. Having done so, the burden of proof shifts to the government to show that there is a justification for the distinction.[161] This onus of proof will

157 BGE 106 Ib 182, 188–9 (1980). See Kiener/Kälin, *Grundrechte* (2013), p. 419; Müller/Schefer, *Grundrechte in der Schweiz* (2008), pp. 662–6; Martenet, *Géométrie de l'égalité* (2003), pp. 298–9.

158 See e.g. *James and others* v. *The United Kingdom*, no. 8793/79, 21 February 1986, Series A no. 98, para. 46 (stating that 'the margin of appreciation available to the legislature in implementing social and economic policies should be a wide one'); *A* v. *Secretary of State for the Home Department*, [2004] UKHL 56, paras 39 (Lord Bingham), 108 (Lord Hope); Sullivan/Feldman, *Constitutional Law* (2013), pp. 602–16.

159 See Kiener/Kälin, *Grundrechte* (2013), pp. 419–20.

160 For example, the Declaration of Principles on Equality, an important but non-binding document signed by numerous human rights and equality experts, states that 'direct discrimination may be permitted only very exceptionally'. Equal Rights Trust, Declaration of Principles on Equality, 2 October 2008, Principle 5, available at www.equalrightstrust.org/ertdocumentbank/Pages%20from%20Declaration%20perfect%20principle.pdf.

161 For international law, see e.g. *South-West Africa Cases (Second Phase)*, [1966] ICJ Reports 6, 309 (Tanaka, J., dissenting) ('Equality being a principle and different treatment an exception, those who refer to the different treatment must prove its *raison d'être* and its reasonableness.'). For the ECHR, see *Timishev* v. *Russia*, nos 55762/00; 55974/00, 13 December 2005, ECHR 2005-XII, 169, para. 57 ('Once the applicant has shown that there has been a difference in treatment, it is then for the respondent Government to

be especially difficult to meet in cases that are subject to close judicial scrutiny, in particular those involving suspect grounds of distinction and classifications affecting fundamental interests.

In cases of alleged *indirect* discrimination, complainants may find it very difficult to prove that a neutral measure has a disproportionate impact on particular groups. Therefore, it is generally recognised by international human rights bodies as well as domestic courts that less strict evidential rules should apply in these cases and that complainants only need to adduce *prima facie* evidence. In particular, credible statistics that point to a disproportionate impact may be sufficient to shift the burden of proof to the respondent.[162] Importantly for present purposes, the European Court of Human Rights, in the highly significant Grand Chamber judgment in *D.H. and others* v. *Czech Republic*, observed that 'the courts of many countries and the supervisory bodies of the United Nations treaties habitually accept statistics as evidence of indirect discrimination in order to facilitate the victims' task of adducing prima facie evidence' and held that 'statistics which appear on critical examination to be reliable and significant will be sufficient to constitute the prima facie evidence the applicant is required to produce [to shift the burden of proof to the respondent state]'.[163] Even though the statistical figures submitted by the applicants in this case were contentious, the court still thought that they revealed a dominant trend and thus accepted them as sufficient to establish a presumption of disproportionate numbers of Roma children being placed in 'special schools'. As a consequence, the burden of proof shifted to the government to show that there was a justification for the disparate impact of the legislation.[164] In many cases, the statistical data required to establish a presumption that a measure has a discriminatory effect may, unlike in *D.H. and others* v. *Czech Republic*, only be available

show that the difference in treatment could be justified.'). For Switzerland, see Waldmann, *Das Diskriminierungsverbot* (2003), pp. 367–72; Martenet, *Géométrie de l'égalité* (2003), p. 163. For the United States (where, in addition, the complainant must prove discriminatory intent or purpose), see *Hunter* v. *Underwood*, 471 U.S. 222, 227–8 (1985).

162 Harris/O'Boyle/Bates/Buckley, *Law of the ECHR* (2014), pp. 809–10; Meyer-Ladewig, *Europäische Menschenrechtskonvention* (2011), p. 286; Martenet, *Géométrie de l'égalité* (2003), pp. 137–41; Waldmann, *Das Diskriminierungsverbot* (2003), pp. 367–71.

163 *D.H. and others* v. *The Czech Republic* [GC], no. 57325/00, 13 November 2007, ECHR 2007-IV, 241, paras 187–8. See also *Zarb Adami* v. *Malta*, no. 17209/02, 20 June 2006, ECHR 2006-VIII, 305, paras 77–8.

164 *D.H. and others* v. *The Czech Republic* [GC], no. 57325/00, 13 November 2007, ECHR 2007-IV, 241, paras 191–5.

to state authorities. It is therefore generally recognised that state authorities are obliged to produce the figures they have,[165] and the UN treaty bodies often stress in their concluding observations that states have a duty to collect and analyse relevant statistical data, disaggregated by grounds of distinction.[166]

6.2 Exclusion from public space and the right to equality and non-discrimination

In the contemporary 'security society', in which prevention is accorded the highest priority, the focus of criminal justice policies has shifted from individuals to large groups of people, which are categorised and controlled according to their levels of dangerousness. Based on certain characteristics that are deemed indicative of future (mis)behaviour, whole segments of the population are classified as, for example, having a tendency to anti-social behaviour.[167] As is the case with other preventive measures, exclusion from public space is thus deployed on the basis of assumptions about the behaviour of certain groups and targeted at those who meet the relevant group characteristics. In some cases it is already the legislator who defines, at least to some extent, the intended targets of exclusion measures, limiting the scope of application of these measures to particular categories of persons, such as (certain) foreign nationals, juveniles or people attending sports events. In other cases, norms authorising exclusion from public space are neutral (that is, equally applicable to everyone), but in practice the respective measures are used exclusively (or almost exclusively) against particular societal groups, such as ethnic minorities, homeless people, alcoholics or drug addicts, or the measures have a disproportionate impact on these groups. This raises concerns with regard to the right to equality and non-discrimination, which are especially pronounced where exclusion from public space is used as a standard police measure that is deployed against great numbers of people. Considerably less problematic from the perspective of the right to equality and non-discrimination are exclusion

[165] Waldmann, *Das Diskriminierungsverbot* (2003), p. 368.

[166] See e.g. UN CEDAW Committee, Concluding observations: Brazil, 7 July 2003, UN Doc. A/58/38 (part II), para. 134. See also Equal Rights Trust, Declaration of Principles on Equality, 2 October 2008, Principle 24, available at www.equalrightstrust.org/ertdocumentbank/Pages%20from%20Declaration%20perfect%20principle.pdf.

[167] See Section 2.5.2.

measures that are imposed in an individualised procedure, especially if it is a judicial procedure.

As has been pointed out repeatedly in Section 6.1, a central value underlying the right to equality and non-discrimination is, as with the guarantees of liberty described in Chapter 5, human dignity. Forms of exclusion from public space that may be experienced by those concerned as an attack on their dignity must therefore be reviewed with particular scrutiny for their conformity with the right to equality and non-discrimination. This applies, for example, to the use of the so-called 'Mosquito' youth dispersal device, which emits an irritating (or even painful) acoustic signal that is audible to almost everyone under the age of twenty years but is barely discernible to those older than twenty-five. This device is used by public authorities, schools and shopkeepers in several European states, including the United Kingdom and Switzerland, to deter juveniles from assembling in certain locations.[168] Teenagers exposed to the sound feel victimised, offended and alienated.[169] The Parliamentary Assembly of the Council of Europe has rightly observed that these devices treat young people 'as if they were unwanted birds or pests' and may thus result in a degrading treatment prohibited by Article 3 of the ECHR.[170] At the very least, the Parliamentary Assembly has held, their use is in breach of the prohibition of discrimination of Article 14 (in conjunction with Articles 8 and 11) of the ECHR, as all those below a certain age are treated as potential troublemakers, regardless of their behaviour.[171]

Also other forms of exclusion from public space may be experienced as an attack on one's dignity. As interviews in Seattle demonstrated, people who had been subject to exclusion measures felt particularly insulted when they believed that their exclusion was based on stereotypical prejudice, in this case against the homeless.[172] However, not only the *ground* of exclusion but also the mere *fact* that one is being sent away from a public place is often experienced as being directed against one's dignity: because of their visibility and high 'signal value',[173] exclusion measures are regularly perceived as embarrassing.[174] In fact, stigmatisation and

[168] See Section 3.2; Parliamentary Assembly of the Council of Europe, Recommendation 1930 (2010), para. 2.

[169] Parliamentary Assembly of the Council of Europe, Recommendation 1930 (2010), para. 6.

[170] Ibid., para. 11. [171] Ibid., paras 6, 9–10.

[172] Beckett/Herbert, *Banished* (2010), p. 124. [173] See Section 3.2.

[174] Beckett/Herbert, *Banished* (2010), p. 124.

discrimination may be the very purpose of an exclusion measure. In the United States, for instance, measures directed against sex offenders are often clearly intended to stigmatise the persons concerned, for example through publication of their personal details. As the Court of Appeals of Indiana observed with regard to an ordinance which prohibited convicted sex offenders from entering public parks, there are clear elements of banishment, shunning and shaming to such a prohibition.[175] This close link to human dignity must be kept in mind when exclusion measures are reviewed for their compatibility with the right to equality and non-discrimination.

While space does not allow a comprehensive review covering each and every exclusion measure, the following sections explore the problems raised with regard to the right to equality and non-discrimination by a number of selected exclusion measures designed to deal with, first, criminal behaviour (Section 6.2.1), second, anti-social behaviour (Section 6.2.2) and, third, political protest (Section 6.2.3).

6.2.1 Criminal behaviour

That it is often those who are regarded as 'alien' who are identified as particularly dangerous and, as a consequence, banned from being in parts of public space has a long tradition. The perhaps most famous instance was the executive order issued by the US government during the Second World War that banned all persons of Japanese descent from the West Coast.[176] Although the Supreme Court, in the landmark cases of *Hirabayashi* v. *United States* and *Korematsu* v. *United States*, acknowledged that 'distinctions between citizens solely because of their ancestry are by their very nature odious to a free people whose institutions are founded upon the doctrine of equality',[177] it nonetheless upheld the exclusion order as compatible with this doctrine.[178] It is difficult to imagine that exclusion measures that are so overtly discriminatory could be adopted today. Nevertheless, also contemporary exclusion measures adopted for the protection of public safety and order involve differences in treatment that raise concerns with regard to the right to equality and non-discrimination. By way of example, this section deals

175 *Dowdell* v. *City of Jeffersonville*, 907 N.E.2d 559, 569 (Ind. C.A. 2009).

176 See *Korematsu* v. *United States*, 323 U.S. 214, 216–17 (1944).

177 *Hirabayashi* v. *United States*, 320 U.S. 81, 100 (1943).

178 *Korematsu* v. *United States*, 323 U.S. 214, 223–4 (1944); *Hirabayashi* v. *United States*, 320 U.S. 81, 100–2 (1943).

with exclusion measures that involve two types of distinctions: those based on citizenship status and those based on race, ethnic origin or religion.

6.2.1.1 Unequal laws: distinctions based on citizenship and residence permit status

According to Article 74 of the Swiss Federal Act on Foreign Nationals, foreign nationals can be ordered not to leave or not to enter a specified area.[179] Such orders can be imposed on two categories of foreign nationals: first, according to Article 74(1)(b) and (c), on those who have been ordered to leave the country to ensure that expulsion orders can be enforced; and second, and more pertinently in this context, according to Article 74(1)(a), on those without a short-stay, residence or permanent residence permit who disturb, or pose a threat to, public safety and order, in particular those engaged in illegal drug trafficking. As explained in Section 4.3.2.1, the terms 'disturb, or pose a threat to, public safety and order' are interpreted very broadly. According to the Federal Supreme Court, there is no need for a criminal offence to have been committed. Instead, it is sufficient that there are 'concrete indications of a suspicion of criminal actions', that the foreign national 'has contacts to extremist circles' or that he or she 'quite generally breaches unwritten rules of social life in a serious manner'.[180] Exclusion orders issued under the Federal Act on Foreign Nationals may extend to the complete territory of a city[181] or even of an entire canton.[182] The Act does not set a maximum time period for exclusion orders, so that they could be imposed permanently.

This means that a particular category of foreign nationals (in particular asylum-seekers, tourists and those staying in the country illegally)[183] can be excluded for long periods (or even permanently) from large parts of public space for reasons of public safety and order. With regard to Swiss

[179] AuG, Art. 74.

[180] Urteil des Bundesgerichts 2A.347/2003 vom 24. November 2003, E. 2.2 ('Vielmehr genügt es bereits, dass konkrete Anhaltspunkte für den Verdacht der Begehung strafbarer Handlungen – etwa im Drogenmilieu – bestehen, der Ausländer Kontakte zu extremistischen Kreisen unterhält oder dass er ganz allgemein in grober Weise gegen ungeschriebene Regeln des sozialen Zusammenlebens verstösst.').

[181] E.g. Urteil des Bundesgerichts 2A.514/2006 vom 23. Januar 2007; Urteil des Bundesgerichts 2A.347/2003 vom 24. November 2003; BGE 124 IV 280, 280 (1998).

[182] E.g. BGE 126 IV 30, 31 (1999); BVR 2000, 145, p. 145 (Verwaltungsgericht des Kantons Bern).

[183] Hugi Yar, 'Zwangsmassnahmen im Ausländerrecht' (2009), 507.

citizens and foreign nationals who hold a short-stay, residence or permanent residence permit, in contrast, federal law does not provide for an equivalent exclusion power. Under cantonal law, this category of persons can only be subject to exclusion orders if the police legislation of the respective canton actually provides for a power of exclusion and, as far as this is the case, only for a much shorter period of time and a more limited geographical area.[184] Is this difference in treatment established by the Federal Act on Foreign Nationals compatible with the right to equality and non-discrimination? Is there a justification for it?

As far as the situation according to domestic law is concerned, the question arises as to whether this difference in treatment must be tested under the general equality guarantee of Article 8(1) of the Federal Constitution or the prohibition of discrimination of Article 8(2). If the latter applies, there would have to be a *qualified* justification for the difference in treatment. Among the suspect grounds of distinction explicitly listed in Article 8(2) is that of 'origin' (*Herkunft/origine*), which refers to characteristics that shape a person's identity such as their national, ethnic, geographical or cultural origin.[185] Thus, distinctions between different categories of non-citizens according to their nationality fall under Article 8(2).[186] The Federal Supreme Court has suggested in at least one case that also distinctions between Swiss citizens on the one hand and foreign nationals on the other may be covered by the prohibition of discrimination based on origin,[187] whereas according to the majority of legal scholars they are not, since such distinctions do not involve a danger of discrimination against members of particular ethnic or cultural groups.[188]

In the present case, the difference in treatment is based on a person's leave to stay in Switzerland. The category of persons accordingly treated

[184] See the definitions of the geographical and temporal scope of the exclusion powers under the various cantonal police acts in Annex I.

[185] See e.g. Müller/Schefer, *Grundrechte in der Schweiz* (2008), pp. 712–13; Biaggini, *Kommentar BV* (2007), p. 105; Kälin, 'Ausländerdiskriminierung' (1998), 572–4.

[186] Kiener/Kälin, *Grundrechte* (2013), pp. 431–2; Müller/Schefer, *Grundrechte in der Schweiz* (2008), pp. 713–14.

[187] BGE 129 I 392, 398–9 (2003) (' "Herkunft" im Sinne von Art. 8 Abs. 2 BV zielt vor allem auf Menschen, die unter anderem wegen ihrer nationalen Herkunft von Diskriminierung bedroht sind. [. . .] Ausländer sollen gegenüber Schweizern oder auch unter sich nicht diskriminiert werden.').

[188] Kiener/Kälin, *Grundrechte* (2013), p. 432; Müller/Schefer, *Grundrechte in der Schweiz* (2008), pp. 713–16; Waldmann, *Das Diskriminierungsverbot* (2003), pp. 579, 584; Kälin, 'Ausländerdiskriminierung' (1998).

less favourably is a heterogeneous group of foreign nationals, including asylum-seekers and tourists who may come from very different parts of the world, rather than a homogenous group of persons sharing the same national, ethnic, geographical or cultural origin. Thus, it cannot be said that the characteristics on which the distinction is based form an important component of a person's identity or that the group concerned has historically been disadvantaged and excluded.[189] As a consequence, it is sufficient for the difference in treatment to be justified that it meets the more lenient requirements of Article 8(1), that is, there must (only) be 'objective and reasonable grounds' (rather than 'cogent reasons') for it. Nevertheless, as the differential treatment occurs in an area protected by fundamental rights, the existence of objective and reasonable grounds must be reviewed with heightened scrutiny.

As far as international law is concerned, the prohibitions of discrimination of the ECHR are, in most cases, not applicable to exclusion orders imposed under the Federal Act on Foreign Nationals. As explained in Section 6.1.1.1, Switzerland has not ratified Additional Protocol No. 12 to the ECHR with its autonomous non-discrimination guarantee. The subordinate provision of Article 14 of the ECHR, in turn, only prohibits discrimination in the enjoyment of the rights otherwise set forth in the ECHR. As explained in Section 5.2, certain restrictions on free movement, including certain exclusion orders imposed under the Federal Act on Foreign Nationals, may amount to an interference with the right to respect for private life guaranteed by Article 8 of the ECHR or other substantive rights such as the right to freedom of assembly guaranteed by Article 11 of the ECHR. In these cases, Article 14 of the ECHR becomes applicable. Numerous such exclusion orders, however, will fall not within the ambit of one of the substantive rights guaranteed by the ECHR but only within that of the right to freedom of movement guaranteed by Article 2 of Protocol No. 4 to the ECHR, which has not been ratified by Switzerland.

In contrast, the equality and non-discrimination guarantees of the ICCPR do provide protection. The ICCPR contains, in Article 12, a guarantee of the right to freedom of movement. Therefore, any measures falling within the scope of protection of this right, including exclusion orders under the Federal Act on Foreign Nationals, must conform to the non-discrimination guarantees of Articles 2 and 26, regardless of the reservation entered by Switzerland with regard to the latter provision.

189 See also Heer, 'Die ausländerrechtliche Ein- und Ausgrenzung' (2004), 12.

The UN Human Rights Committee has made it clear that distinctions based on citizenship or residence permit status fall within the prohibition of discrimination based on 'other status' as provided by Articles 2 and 26.[190] However, it does not seem to treat such distinctions as inherently suspect.[191] As a consequence, differences in treatment based on citizenship or residence permit status are permissible 'if the criteria for such differentiation are reasonable and objective and if the aim is to achieve a purpose which is legitimate under the Covenant'.[192]

In summary, under both Swiss law and the ICCPR, the difference in treatment provided for by the Federal Act on Foreign Nationals with regard to exclusion orders is only permissible if there are objective and reasonable grounds for it. One way of justifying the difference in treatment would be to argue that those who, according to the Act, can be excluded from parts of public space are not in a comparable situation to those who cannot be excluded: the latter have an established right to stay in Switzerland, whereas the former do not.[193] However, as explained in Section 6.1.2.4, the existence of a justification must be assessed in relation to *the aim* of the measure under consideration.

It is true that where the aim of an exclusion order is enforcement of the immigration laws, as is the case with orders issued under Article 74(1)(b) and (c) of the Federal Act on Foreign Nationals (which are designed to ensure that expulsion orders can be enforced), a difference in treatment between citizens and (certain) foreign nationals may not only be justified but, indeed, inevitable. In contrast, however, the purpose of exclusion orders under Article 74(1)(a) is not of an immigration law nature. Instead, these orders are meant to serve the protection of public safety and order. As is clear from the legislative history of Article 74(1)(a), this form of exclusion was primarily intended as a tool against illegal drug trafficking;[194] this primary objective is in fact explicitly reflected in the

190 See e.g. *Karakurt* v. *Austria*, Communication No. 965/2000, 29 April 2002, UN Doc. CCPR/C/74/D/965/2000; *Adam* v. *the Czech Republic*, Communication No. 586/1994, 23 July 1996, UN Doc. CCPR/C/57/D/586/1994; *Simunek et al* v. *the Czech Republic*, Communication No. 516/1992, 19 July 1995, UN Doc. CCPR/C/54/D/516/1992; *Gueye* v. *France*, Communication No. 196/1985, 6 April 1989, UN Doc CCPR/C/35/D/196/1985.

191 See ibid.

192 UN Human Rights Committee, General Comment No. 18, UN Doc. HRI/GEN/1/Rev.9 (Vol. I) 195, para. 13.

193 Kälin, 'Zwangsmassnahmen im Ausländerrecht' (1995), 843.

194 Botschaft zum Bundesgesetz über Zwangsmassnahmen im Ausländerrecht vom 22. Dezember 1993, BBl 1994 I, 305, pp. 308–9, 317, 327.

wording of the provision.[195] Accordingly, the Federal Supreme Court has pointed out that exclusion according to Article 74(1)(a) is designed to give the police a tool against foreign nationals who threaten or disturb public safety and order, especially in those areas where the criminal law may not provide sufficient protection.[196] Thus, even though it is contained in the Federal Act on Foreign Nationals, this form of exclusion is in fact not an immigration law measure but a police measure, which arguably to some degree even has a penal character.[197]

In view of this aim of Article 74(1)(a), there is no justification for making a distinction between, on the one hand, a certain category of foreign nationals (in practice predominantly asylum-seekers) and, on the other hand, another category of foreign nationals and Swiss citizens. If exclusion orders are indeed a sensible and appropriate means of protecting public safety and order – in particular of suppressing illegal drug dealing – then there are no objective and reasonable grounds for making them applicable only to the former category of persons but not to the latter.[198] After all, also Swiss citizens and foreign nationals with a short-stay, residence or permanent residence permit can, and in fact sometimes do, engage in drug trafficking or disturb public safety and order in other ways. Citizenship and residence permit status are not reliable indicators of the threat a person poses to public safety and order. If the aim is really the suppression of drug dealing, then everyone should be subject to these measures, as is the case, for instance, with 'drug exclusion zones' in the United States.[199]

As a result, Article 74(1)(a) of the Federal Act on Foreign Nationals violates Article 8(1) of the Swiss Federal Constitution as well as Articles 2 and 26 of the ICCPR. As explained in Section 5.1.4, Article 190 of the Federal Constitution provides that courts (as well as any other

195 AuG, Art. 74(1)(a) ('[D]iese Massnahme dient insbesondere der Bekämpfung des widerrechtlichen Betäubungsmittelhandels.').

196 E.g. Urteil des Bundesgerichts 2A.148/2003 vom 30. Mai 2003, para. 2.2 ('Sie dient einerseits dazu – gerade in Bereichen, die durch das Strafrecht kaum abgedeckt werden können – gegen Ausländer vorgehen zu können, welche die öffentliche Sicherheit und Ordnung stören oder gefährden.') (concerning the older, but identical, Article 13e of the ANAG).

197 See Albrecht, 'Die ausländerrechtlichen Zwangsmassnahmen im Konflikt mit dem Strafrecht' (2009), 234, 240–1, 253.

198 See also Albrecht, 'Die ausländerrechtlichen Zwangsmassnahmen im Konflikt mit dem Strafrecht' (2009), 253–4; Heer, 'Die ausländerrechtliche Ein- und Ausgrenzung' (2004), 13–14; Raselli, 'Die neuen Zwangsmassnahmen im Ausländerrecht im Lichte von Verfassung und Menschenrechten' (1994), 85.

199 See Section 3.3.1.

law-applying authorities) are bound to apply federal acts even if they violate a constitutional norm such as the equality guarantee of Article 8(1). However, as has also been explained, the situation is different with regard to federal acts that violate not only the Constitution but also international law. As a general rule, international law prevails over federal acts.[200] A federal act may, if at all, only then prevail over international law if it was passed after the respective international norm had come into force and if it was parliament's intention to pass an act that violates international law.[201] As far as the present context is concerned, while the relevant provisions of the Federal Act on Foreign Nationals were passed after the ICCPR had come into force, the legislative history suggests that federal parliament intended to design them so that they would *not* violate international law.[202] In any event, even if parliament had intended (or accepted) a violation of international law, the Federal Supreme Court has suggested that international norms guaranteeing human rights prevail even over federal acts that were passed in the knowledge that they violate international law.[203] As a result, Article 74(1)(a) of the Federal Act on Foreign Nationals must not be used: exclusion orders issued under this provision violate the equality and non-discrimination guarantees of Articles 2 and 26 of the ICCPR.

6.2.1.2 Unequal enforcement: distinctions based on race, ethnic origin or religion

Even where exclusion measures directed against criminal behaviour are, as a matter of law, applicable to everyone, they may raise problems with regard to the guarantee of equality and non-discrimination because they are enforced in a selective fashion or because they have a disproportionate impact on particular groups.

For example, in the United States, the Gang Congregation Ordinance of the City of Chicago, which authorised the police to disperse suspected

200 For the most recent decision of the Federal Supreme Court reaffirming this general rule, see BGE 139 I 16, 28–9 (2012). For a summary of the relevant case law, see Bericht des Bundesrates zum Verhältnis von Völkerrecht und Landesrecht vom 5. März 2010, BBl 2010, 2263, pp. 2310–13.

201 BGE 99 Ib 39, 43–5 (1973).

202 Botschaft zum Bundesgesetz über Zwangsmassnahmen im Ausländerrecht vom 22. Dezember 1993, BBl 1994 I, 305, p. 309; Votum Bruno Frick, Amtliches Bulletin Ständerat 1994, p. 110.

203 BGE 125 II 417, 424–6 (1999).

criminal street gang members loitering in any public place,[204] was predominantly used against black people and Latinos.[205] The police officer who arrested Jesus Morales – the man whose legal challenge eventually led to the US Supreme Court decision of *City of Chicago* v. *Morales* – for violating the ordinance admitted that Morales became the subject of suspicion because he was standing on a street corner with other Latino teenagers in a predominantly white neighbourhood.[206] Large parts of the public accordingly perceived the gang dispersal orders as a tool used by the police to order strangers back to their own neighbourhoods, which in Chicago are highly segregated along ethnic lines.[207] The sort of 'drug exclusion zones' described in Section 3.3.1.2 may raise similar problems. An ordinance of the City of Akron prohibiting loitering for drug-related purposes in public places, for example, was shown to have been enforced almost exclusively against African-Americans.[208] The 'drug exclusion zones' of the City of Cincinnati and the 'drug-loitering free zones' of Annapolis were all established in communities with predominantly African-American residents,[209] and accordingly had a greater impact on the latter than other ethnic groups. In the United Kingdom, an equality impact assessment of counter-terrorism powers observed that all forty-eight individuals who by then had been subject to a control order 'would be likely to describe themselves as Muslim'.[210]

If it can be shown in a given case that exclusion measures have been enforced selectively to target, for instance, persons of a certain race or ethnic appearance, this may amount to direct discrimination. As explained in Section 6.1.2.5, a difference in treatment which is based exclusively or to a decisive extent on a person's race or ethnic origin will be extremely difficult ever to justify. However, it will normally be very

[204] Chicago Municipal Code, § 8–4–015. The provision in its original wording of 17 June 1992 was declared unconstitutional by the US Supreme Court in *City of Chicago* v. *Morales*, 527 U.S. 41 (1999) and thereupon amended. The amended version is reproduced in Annex I. See Section 3.3.1.2.

[205] Roberts, 'Foreword: Race, Vagueness, and the Social Meaning of Order-Maintenance Policing' (1999), 775–6.

[206] See Strosnider, 'Anti-Gang Ordinances after City of Chicago v. Morales' (2002), 120–1.

[207] Strosnider, 'Anti-Gang Ordinances after City of Chicago v. Morales' (2002), 121; Roberts, 'Foreword: Race, Vagueness, and the Social Meaning of Order-Maintenance Policing' (1999), 787–9, 824.

[208] *City of Akron* v. *Rowland*, 618 N.E.2d 138, 147–8 (Ohio 1993).

[209] See *Johnson* v. *City of Cincinnati*, 310 F.3d 484, 488 (6th Cir. 2002); *NAACP Anne Arundel County Branch* v. *City of Annapolis*, 133 F.Supp.2d 795, 798 (D. Md. 2001).

[210] Secretary of State for the Home Department, Review of Counter-Terrorism and Security Powers: Equality Impact Assessment, January 2011, Cm 8006, p. 8.

difficult for a complainant to prove this sort of selective enforcement. To use the example referred to above, how can a complainant prove that he was targeted under a Gang Congregation Ordinance because of his Latino appearance if the police officer in question does not admit that this was indeed the reason?

Nevertheless, since *indirect* discrimination is equally prohibited, also exclusion measures that appear to be neutral as they do not involve a difference in treatment must be reviewed for the impact they have on various groups. Where an exclusion measure is shown to have a disproportionate impact on groups defined by reference to suspect criteria such as race, ethnicity or religion, the justification for this difference in outcome must be reviewed with particularly intense scrutiny. Thus, if 'drug exclusion zones' are imposed, they must be reviewed for the impact they have on different ethnic groups and, if it is shown that the likelihood of being subject to a drug exclusion measure is greater for members of one ethnic group as compared to those of others, one must consider whether there are compelling reasons for the respective ratios. Given that the purpose of 'drug exclusion zones' is the prevention of drug-related offences, such compelling reasons may exist if, for instance, it is demonstrated that the drug trade takes place exclusively, or almost exclusively, in particular ethnic neighbourhoods. The same applies to terrorism control orders. As the UN Committee on the Elimination of Racial Discrimination has highlighted, control orders may have a negative impact on certain groups such as Muslims.[211] It has therefore asked the United Kingdom to ensure that any system of terrorism prevention and investigation 'includes safeguards against abuse and the deliberate targeting of certain ethnic and religious groups' and to provide statistical data disaggregated by religious belief and ethnic origin of the individuals subjected to such a system.[212] A disproportionate impact of counter-terrorism measures such as control orders may only then be justified if it is demonstrably the case that the terrorist threat stems exclusively or almost exclusively from the respective religious or ethnic groups.

The situation with regard to these issues is somewhat different in the United States because, as explained in Section 6.1.2.1, the equal

[211] UN CERD, Concluding observations: United Kingdom, 14 September 2011, UN Doc. CERD/C/GBR/CO/18-20, para. 21; UN CERD, List of issues: United Kingdom, 2 August 2011, UN Doc. CERD/C/GBR/Q/18-20, para. 1(f).

[212] UN CERD, Concluding observations: United Kingdom, 14 September 2011, UN Doc. CERD/C/GBR/CO/18-20, para. 21.

protection principle of the Fourteenth and Fifth Amendments requires the showing of a *discriminatory purpose*. As a consequence, claims that exclusion measures are enforced selectively or have a discriminatory impact are typically brought (and considered by courts) as vagueness challenges under the due process clause rather than as equal protection challenges. The core concern behind these challenges and judicial findings, however, is often the danger of racially discriminatory enforcement. Thus, the ordinance of the City of Akron prohibiting loitering for drug-related purposes in public places referred to above was struck down as being too vague, not least because the court opined that 'without definite statutory language, criminal laws are susceptible to arbitrary enforcement, most often to the detriment of racial and ethnic minorities'.[213]

6.2.2 *Anti-social behaviour*

Exclusion measures designed to counter anti-social behaviour may be explicitly directed against those groups that are seen as the main source of such behaviour. Thus, the scope of application of juvenile night curfews is, by law, limited to those below a certain age, raising the question as to the compatibility of such differential treatment established by law with the right to equality and non-discrimination. However, even when exclusion measures directed against anti-social behaviour are equally applicable to everyone, they may raise concerns with regard to the right to equality and non-discrimination because they are primarily enforced against, or have a disproportionate impact on, particular groups such as the homeless, the poor, alcoholics or drug addicts.

6.2.2.1 Unequal laws: distinctions based on age

As explained in Section 3.3.2.3, in all three states under consideration there are (or were) laws in force prohibiting children and juveniles from being in public places after a certain hour. In most large US cities it is today an offence for a person under seventeen (or in some cases eighteen) to be in any public place at night, normally defined as lasting from 10 or 11 pm until 6 am.[214] In Switzerland, several municipalities have adopted curfew laws that make it unlawful for those of compulsory school age (that is, those below sixteen) or, in some cases, those below fifteen to be (or to assemble) in public places after a certain time, normally set at

213 *City of Akron* v. *Rowland*, 618 N.E.2d 138, 146 (Ohio 1993).
214 E.g. Dallas, Texas Code of Ordinances, s. 31–33.

10 pm.[215] In the United Kingdom, the now repealed Section 14 of the Crime and Disorder Act 1998 gave local authorities and the police the authority to ban those under sixteen from being in a public place in a specified area for specified hours between 9 pm and 6 am. All these juvenile curfew laws provide for a difference in treatment based on age: persons below an age set at somewhere between fifteen and eighteen are prohibited from being in public places after a certain hour, whereas everyone over that age is free to go where they want at any time.

To consider whether this difference in treatment is compatible with the right to equality and non-discrimination, one must first determine the degree of intensity with which it should be reviewed. Are distinctions based on age inherently suspect and do they thus require particularly weighty reasons to be justified? International law does not provide a clear-cut answer to this question. The non-discrimination provisions contained in older human rights treaties, including the ICCPR and the ECHR, do not even explicitly list age as one of the prohibited grounds of distinction. The non-discrimination norm of the more recent International Convention on the Protection of the Rights of All Migrant Workers and Members of Their Families (ICRMW), in contrast, does,[216] and adoption by the UN General Assembly of the UN Principles for Older Persons may be an indication that differential treatment of at least that particular age-group could be regarded as inherently suspect.[217] Nevertheless, the most important human rights body for present purposes, the European Court of Human Rights, has so far not identified differential treatment on the basis of age as particularly serious. The same position has been adopted by the British House

[215] Polizeireglement der Stadt Gossau vom 4. November 2008 (18.01), Art. 19 (Nachtrag vom 6. Dezember 2011); Polizeireglement der Gemeinde Visp vom 27. Mai 2009, Art. 12; Polizeireglement der Gemeinden Bad Zurzach, Baldingen, Böbikon, Böttstein, Döttingen, Endingen, Fisibach, Full-Reuenthal, Kaiserstuhl, Klingnau, Koblenz, Leibstadt, Lengnau, Leuggern, Mandach, Mellikon, Rekingen, Rietheim, Rümikon, Schneisingen, Siglistorf, Tegerfelden, Unterendingen und Wislikofen vom 1. April 2008, § 25(2); Gemeindepolizeireglement der Gemeinde Interlaken vom 5. Dezember 2006 (552.11), Art. 9(4); Gemeindepolizeireglement der Gemeinde Urtenen-Schönbühl vom 15. Mai 2006, Art. 6; Polizeiverordnung der Gemeinde Dänikon vom 18. Juni 2008, Art. 27 (aufgehoben durch Urteil des Verwaltungsgerichts des Kantons Zürich VB.2009.00055 vom 30. April 2009).

[216] International Convention on the Protection of the Rights of All Migrant Workers and Members of Their Families (adopted 18 December 1990, entered into force 1 July 2003) 2220 UNTS 3 (ICRMW), Art. 1(1).

[217] UN Principles for Older Persons, UN General Assembly Resolution 46/91, 16 December 1991, UN Doc. A/RES/46/91 (1991).

of Lords. In *R (Carson)* v. *Secretary of State for Work and Pensions* Lord Walker held that age is not a suspect ground of distinction,[218] although Lord Hoffmann thought that '[d]iscrimination on grounds of old age may be a contemporary example of a borderline case'.[219] The US Supreme Court has also concluded that age – at least old age – is not a suspect ground.[220] Laurence Tribe, on the other hand, has argued that childhood should be regarded as a 'semi-suspect classification' entailing some sort of intermediate scrutiny.[221] As far as Switzerland is concerned, age is among the grounds listed in the prohibition of discrimination of Article 8(2) of the Federal Constitution. The prohibition of discrimination based on *young* age is further reinforced by Article 11(1) of the Federal Constitution, which guarantees children and young people the right to special protection of their integrity.[222] Therefore, differences in treatment based on age require a 'qualified justification'. However, as explained in Section 6.1.2.5, this does not mean that courts will treat distinctions based on age as equally suspect as those based on, for example, race.

Apart from the possible suspect nature of the ground of distinction, a further reason supporting intense scrutiny is that the difference in treatment at issue affects fundamental individual interests. As has been explained in Section 5.2, juvenile curfews interfere with a whole range of fundamental rights, including the guarantees of personal liberty and freedom of movement and, depending on the facts of a given case, the freedoms of assembly, expression, religion and association. It is for this reason that numerous courts in the United States have correctly employed a strict scrutiny standard to review juvenile curfews.[223] Other US courts have employed intermediate scrutiny or even only the rational basis test, based on the argument that minors do have fundamental rights but that – due to their immaturity, vulnerability and need for parental guidance – they are subject to greater regulation and control by the state

[218] *R (Carson)* v. *Secretary of State for Work and Pensions*, [2005] UKHL 37, paras 59–60.

[219] Ibid., para. 17.

[220] *Gregory* v. *Ashcroft*, 501 U.S. 452, 470 (1991); *Massachusetts Board of Retirement* v. *Murgia*, 427 U.S. 307, 313 (1976).

[221] Tribe, *American Constitutional Law* (1988), pp. 1588–93; Tribe, 'Childhood, Suspect Classifications, and Conclusive Presumptions' (1975), 32.

[222] See e.g. Auer/Malinverni/Hottelier, *Droit constitutionnel suisse* (2013), Vol. II, p. 508; Peters, 'Diskriminierungsverbote' (2007), 273.

[223] E.g. *Commonwealth* v. *Weston W.*, 913 N.E.2d 832, 842 (Mass. 2009); *Nunez* v. *City of San Diego*, 114 F.3d 935, 945–6 (9th Cir. 1997); *Qutb* v. *Strauss*, 11 F.3d 488, 492 (5th Cir. 1993); *Waters* v. *Barry*, 711 F. Supp. 1125, 1139 (D.D.C. 1989).

than are adults.[224] It is, of course, true that the special needs of children and juveniles may justify the imposition of restrictions that could not be sustained in the case of adults. However, this cannot influence the applicable standard of review: one must first determine the appropriate level of scrutiny by ascertaining whether the individual interest involved is fundamental, and only then should one consider the state's countervailing interest in imposing restrictions.[225] In sum, although the differences in treatment that juvenile curfews involve are not as suspect as, for example, classifications based on race or ethnicity, they must be subject to close judicial scrutiny and require compelling or cogent reasons to be justified.

As pointed out before, the existence of such reasons must be assessed in relation to the aim of the measure under consideration. One objective sometimes adduced in support of juvenile night curfews is the protection of children and youths themselves (from each other and from other persons).[226] Juveniles, it may be argued, are physically and mentally more vulnerable than other persons and thus require a greater degree of protection. This special need for protection is recognised, for example, in Article 11(1) of the Swiss Federal Constitution, which grants children and young people a right to special protection of their integrity and to the facilitation of their development. However, if the aim of night curfews is really the protection of the personal safety of vulnerable people, then age is not an appropriate criterion of distinction. After all, most fifteen-year-olds are considerably less vulnerable than, for example, most old or disabled people, so that curfews would also have to apply to the latter groups of people. The same holds true for the argument that children and juveniles are not able to make critical decisions in an informed, mature manner: this ability is not (solely) a question of age. And even insofar as age does play a role with regard to the issues of vulnerability and immaturity, it is highly questionable whether a general prohibition to be on the streets at certain times is a suitable means of protecting juveniles from harm or from making wrong decisions.[227] In fact, for

224 E.g. *In re A.G.*, 104 Cal. Rptr. 3d 863, 872–3 (Cal. App. 4 2010) (applying intermediate scrutiny); *Ramos* v. *Town of Vernon*, 353 F.3d 171, 181 (2nd Cir. 2003) (applying intermediate scrutiny); *Hutchins* v. *District of Columbia*, 188 F.3d 531, 541 (D.C. Cir. 1999) (applying intermediate scrutiny); *Bykofsky* v. *Borough of Middletown*, 401 F. Supp. 1242, 1254, 1265 (D.C. Pa. 1975) (applying the rational basis test).

225 See also 'Assessing the Scope of Minors' Fundamental Rights' (1984), 1166, footnote 17.

226 See e.g. *Bykofsky* v. *Borough of Middletown*, 401 F. Supp. 1242, 1255 (D.C. Pa. 1975); Gerber Jenni, ' "Abendausgang Kinder" ' (2006), 851.

227 See also 'Assessing the Scope of Minors' Fundamental' (1984), 1175–8.

a large share of juveniles the risk of being harmed is greater at home than on the streets.[228]

In any event, most juvenile curfews have not been enacted to protect children and youths but, as explained in Section 5.3.1.2, primarily as a means of countering anti-social behaviour, which is said to stem to a large extent from juveniles. As is clear from the legislative history of juvenile curfew laws, they are, above all, meant to help reduce noise at night, prevent littering and protect the public from other 'nocturnal mischief by minors',[229] such as causing damage to property.[230] In some cases it has been argued that the respective juvenile curfews also serve to reduce, not only damage to property, but nocturnal crime more generally.[231]

For age to be an appropriate ground of distinction, it would therefore, first of all, have to be shown that there is a nexus between (young) age and these objectives. As far as the reduction of noise and the prevention of littering are concerned, this nexus may well exist: it is quite possible that young people tend to be noisier at night and to litter more than adults. Too often, however, courts only assume that this is the case or they rely on anecdotal evidence instead of well-established facts. A US district court, for example, stated that it was apparent that a juvenile curfew was effective in reducing mischief 'even in the absence of any statistical data'.[232] As far as the reduction of crime is concerned, it is highly questionable whether a nexus does exist. In the United States, for example, of all persons arrested for criminal offences nationwide in 2014, only 9.1 per cent were below the age of eighteen; in contrast, persons between eighteen and twenty-four accounted for 26.8 per cent of arrests, meaning that people from the latter age group seem to be considerably more likely to commit

[228] See e.g. Trollinger, 'The Juvenile Curfew' (1995), 970; *Waters* v. *Barry*, 711 F. Supp. 1125, 1139 (D.D.C. 1989).

[229] *Bykofsky* v. *Borough of Middletown*, 401 F.Supp. 1242, 1255 (D.C. Pa. 1975).

[230] For Switzerland, see e.g. Urteil des Verwaltungsgerichts des Kantons Zürich VB.2009.00055 vom 30. April 2009, E. 4.3, 5.2.2; Gerber Jenni, ' "Abendausgang Kinder" ' (2006), 845. For the United States, see *Bykofsky* v. *Borough of Middletown*, 401 F.Supp. 1242, 1255 (D.C. Pa. 1975). For the United Kingdom, see Crawford, 'Dispersal Powers and the Symbolic Role of Anti-Social Behaviour Legislation' (2008), 767.

[231] E.g. *In re A.G.*, 104 Cal. Rptr. 3d 863, 873 (Cal. App. 4 2010); *Nunez* v. *City of San Diego*, 114 F.3d 935, 946 (9th Cir. 1997); *Qutb* v. *Strauss*, 11 F.3d 488, 492 (5th Cir. 1993); *Johnson* v. *City of Opelousas*, 658 F.2d 1065, 1073 n. 9 (5th Cir. 1981); *Bykofsky* v. *Borough of Middletown*, 401 F.Supp. 1242, 1255 (D.C. Pa. 1975).

[232] *Bykofsky* v. *Borough of Middletown*, 401 F.Supp. 1242, 1256 (D.C. Pa. 1975).

crimes.[233] In view of this, the US Court of Appeals for the Second Circuit concluded that the distinction made by a juvenile curfew between those below an age set at eighteen and those above that age is not a suitable means of preventing crime.[234] In fact, this distinction could even be said to be completely irrational: if anything, curfews would have to be imposed on those between eighteen and twenty-four. In addition, night curfews are likely to primarily deter those juveniles who already tend to behave lawfully, rather than those who engage in anti-social or even violent behaviour.[235]

Furthermore, even insofar as a nexus between young age and one of the aims listed above *can* be established, the difference in treatment between juveniles and non-juveniles could only be justified if the respective curfew is also the least restrictive means (or, in US terminology, narrowly tailored enough) to achieve this aim. As already explained in Section 5.3.2.2, several courts in the United States and Switzerland have convincingly argued that juvenile curfews fail to meet this requirement because their personal scope is overly broad: instead of targeting those responsible for (or at least those most likely to engage in) the harmful activities at issue, they encompass everyone below a certain age. Juvenile curfews can only meet the least restrictive means requirement if, at the very least, they provide for exemptions for legitimate activities (such as school or religious activities, exercising constitutional rights, travelling to or from a social occasion or work and so on) and ensure that they focus on those activities that are most likely to result in anti-social behaviour or crime.[236] Most juvenile curfews fail to do so. As a result, there is no justification for the difference in treatment based on age they involve, meaning that they violate the right to equality and non-discrimination guaranteed by the respective national and international norms.

6.2.2.2 Unequal enforcement: distinctions based on social status and way of life

In the case of exclusion measures directed against anti-social behaviour the risk that they may be enforced selectively or that they may have a disproportionate impact on particular groups of people is even greater

233 Federal Bureau of Investigation, Uniform Crime Report 2014, Table 38, available at www.fbi.gov/about-us/cjis/ucr/crime-in-the-u.s/2014/crime-in-the-u.s.-2014/tables/table-38.
234 *Ramos* v. *Town of Vernon*, 353 F.3d 171, 186 (2nd Cir. 2003).
235 See e.g. *Waters* v. *Barry*, 711 F. Supp. 1125, 1139 (D.D.C. 1989).
236 E.g. *In re A.G.*, 104 Cal. Rptr. 3d 863, 874–7 (Cal. App. 4 2010).

than in the case of exclusion measures primarily directed against criminal behaviour. In fact, some of these measures are quite clearly intended to target particular social groups by prohibiting activities that are typical for them. The most important examples are laws that prohibit sleeping in parts of public space or even simply lying or sitting in particular public places such as on sidewalks or in or near train stations. As pointed out in Section 3.3.2.2, such prohibitions are particularly widespread in the United States and have now also started to be introduced in Switzerland and the United Kingdom. Although such laws are phrased impartially, preventing *anyone* from sleeping or lying or sitting in these places, they affect almost exclusively those who have nowhere else to sleep or lie down or sit, that is, homeless people.[237] The same applies – although perhaps to a lesser extent – to prohibitions of drinking alcohol in public places, which primarily affect those who are addicted to alcohol.

However, also exclusion measures directed against anti-social behaviour that do not prohibit activities that are typical for particular groups of people may raise concerns with regard to their unequal enforcement or impact. In the case concerning the exclusion orders issued under the cantonal Police Act against a group of persons in the City of Berne for assembling to drink alcohol together,[238] the Swiss Federal Supreme Court thought that the prohibition of discrimination was not engaged as it had not been substantiated that the persons concerned constituted a homogenous group sharing a common characteristic such as a particular appearance or life style; they came from different backgrounds, and the fact that they met regularly was not sufficient to make them a protected group.[239] However, the Supreme Court's reasoning disregards the fact – acknowledged by the Cantonal Administrative Court before it – that those primarily affected by exclusion orders issued under the Police Act share the common characteristic of being addicted to alcohol or drugs.[240] In fact, it has been shown that in some Swiss cities the blanket exclusion powers under the cantonal police acts have been used almost exclusively against drug and alcohol addicts meeting in public places.[241] This at least raises the question as to whether these powers are enforced selectively against, or have a disproportionate impact on, people suffering from an addiction. Juvenile night curfews,

[237] See e.g. Beckett/Herbert, *Banished* (2010), pp. 65–7. [238] See Section 4.3.2.1.
[239] BGE 132 I 49, 66–7 (2006).
[240] BVR 2005, 97, pp. 113–14 (Verwaltungsgericht des Kantons Bern).
[241] Litscher/Grossrieder/Mösch-Payot/Schmutz, *Wegweisung aus öffentlichen Stadträumen* (2011), pp. 78–9.

in turn, disproportionally affect young people from poorer backgrounds who tend to spend more time on the streets than more affluent juveniles because they have less private space available to themselves and lack access to private back yards, swimming pools, cars and so on.[242]

Whether these differences regarding the enforcement and impact of the respective exclusion measures are adjudged to be compatible with the right to equality and non-discrimination depends to a significant extent on whether the grounds of distinction involved are regarded as suspect or not. If homelessness, poverty and addiction to drugs or alcohol are qualified as suspect grounds (or, in terms of the Swiss Federal Constitution, as grounds covered by the prohibition of discrimination of Article 8(2)), differences with regard to enforcement or a disproportionate impact will only be permissible if they are supported by very weighty reasons, that is, if there is a qualified justification. In contrast, if these grounds are not characterised as suspect, then courts will be likely to find the respective exclusion measures to be compatible with the right to equality and non-discrimination.

There have so far not been any pronouncements of international human rights bodies, including most importantly the European Court of Human Rights, to the effect that homelessness, poverty or addiction would constitute suspect classifications. In some early cases, the US Supreme Court appeared to use heightened scrutiny to review state measures discriminating against the poor,[243] but it later held that poverty or financial need is not a suspect ground of distinction, although it is in the different contexts of government funding for abortions and financing of public education.[244] Whether this finding implies that also the homeless are not a suspect class is debatable.[245] The British House of Lords has held that homelessness is a personal characteristic and an 'other status' in the sense of Article 14 of the ECHR, but does not seem to treat it as a suspect ground.[246] In Switzerland, the list of prohibited grounds of discrimination of Article 8(2) of the Federal Constitution includes 'social status'

242 Collins/Kearns, 'Under Curfew and Under Siege?' (2001), 400.

243 *Harper* v. *Virginia Board of Elections*, 383 U.S. 663, 668 (1966) ('Lines drawn on the basis of wealth or property, like those of race, are traditionally disfavored.'). See also *Griffin* v. *Illinois*, 351 U.S. 12, 17 (1956).

244 *Kadrmas* v. *Dickinson Public Schools*, 487 U.S. 450, 458 (1988); *Harris* v. *McRae*, 448 U.S. 297, 322–3 (1980); *Maher* v. *Roe*, 432 U.S. 464, 471 (1977); *San Antonio Independent School Dist.* v. *Rodriguez*, 411 U.S. 1, 28–9 (1973).

245 *Pottinger* v. *City of Miami*, 810 F.Supp. 1551, 1578 (S.D. Fla. 1992).

246 *R (RJM)* v. *Secretary of State for Work and Pensions*, [2008] UKHL 63, paras 35–47 (Lord Neuberger).

(*soziale Stellung/situation sociale*) and 'way of life' (*Lebensform/mode de vie*). Although some commentators have maintained that the criterion of 'social status' could include grounds such as poverty and unemployment,[247] case law dealing with this question is sparse and inconclusive.[248] 'Way of life', in turn, is primarily intended to protect homosexuals as well as travellers.[249] In any event, the list of prohibited grounds of Article 8(2) is not exhaustive, so that newly emerging dangers of social exclusion can be taken account of.[250] Rainer Schweizer has argued that also those addicted to alcohol or other substances deserve to fall within its scope of protection.[251]

When deciding whether grounds of distinction such as homelessness, poverty and addiction should be qualified as suspect or not, it is important to keep in mind the reasons for treating some grounds as particularly suspect. These reasons are, first, to provide (heightened) protection from differential treatment based on those characteristics that form important components of a person's identity and cannot (or can hardly) be changed (and are thus closely related to his or her dignity) and, second, to provide such protection for those 'discrete and insular'[252] minorities that have historically been disadvantaged and excluded.[253] From this perspective, it would be difficult to claim that *all* distinctions based on a person's low economic status or addiction to alcohol or drugs should be treated as suspect. It is disputable that these criteria can in all cases be regarded as important components of a person's identity, which he or she cannot be expected to change. Furthermore, not all distinctions based on these criteria involve an attack on the dignity of those persons. Instead, an assessment of these issues must be based on the specific circumstances of a given case. With regard to homelessness, the case for treating it as a general suspect classification is more convincing. The homeless have been subjected to a history of unequal treatment, which arguably involves an attack on

[247] Auer/Malinverni/Hottelier, *Droit constitutionnel suisse* (2013), Vol. II, pp. 511–12; Kiener/Kälin, *Grundrechte* (2013), p. 432; Hangartner, 'Besprechung des Bundesgerichtsentscheides BGE 135 I 49' (2009), 507–8; Biaggini, *Kommentar BV* (2007), p. 106; Peters, 'Diskriminierungsverbote' (2007), 276.

[248] In BGE 135 I 49, 58 (2008) and BGE 136 I 309, 313 (2010) the Federal Supreme Court explicitly left open the question as to whether dependency on social welfare falls under Article 8(2), although in the latter case it seemed to suggest that it does not.

[249] Kiener/Kälin, *Grundrechte* (2013), p. 433; Biaggini, *Kommentar BV* (2007), p. 106.

[250] Müller/Schefer, *Grundrechte in der Schweiz* (2008), p. 712.

[251] Schweizer, 'Art. 8' (2014), 227. [252] *Graham* v. *Richardson*, 403 U.S. 365, 372 (1971).

[253] See Section 6.1.2.5.

their dignity, simply for living on the streets.[254] In addition, to live on the streets is for most homeless people a 'way of life' in the sense of Article 8(2) of the Swiss Federal Constitution.[255]

Thus, it is important to consider each individual case on its merits to identify the exact ground of distinction as well as the circumstances of, and especially the reasons for, making that distinction. This is, admittedly, no easy task. Nevertheless, in some cases it may be already evident from the legislative history of an exclusion measure that, although couched in neutral terms, it is designed to specifically target particular groups because this was the very reason for its adoption. In such cases the legislator may be understood to have impliedly requested the police to enforce the respective measure in a selective manner. In the case of *Parr* v. *Municipal Court*, for example, the City Council of Carmel had adopted an ordinance prohibiting sitting on any sidewalks or steps and lying or sitting on any lawns. In a declaration accompanying the ordinance, the Council explained that it was adopted in response to 'an extraordinary influx of undesirable and unsanitary visitors to the City, sometimes known as "hippies"'.[256] Although applicable to anyone, it was thus clear that the prohibition was not meant to be enforced against 'ordinary citizens' but against a particular social group that the declaration described as 'unsanitary' 'transients'.[257] The Supreme Court of California concluded that '[t]he inevitable effect must be discriminatory enforcement consistent with the discriminatory purpose expressed by the council: the police will direct their efforts to the task of ridding Carmel's public property of the menace of the hippies'.[258] In the view of the court, the ordinance encouraged 'discrimination against the members of a cultural minority whose life style is disturbing to the majority'.[259] Accordingly, there was a violation of the equal protection clause of the Fourteenth Amendment. Where an exclusion measure is so clearly designed to be enforced selectively, this is certainly the correct conclusion. A justification for directing exclusion measures designed to prevent anti-social behaviour solely against one particular social group is hardly conceivable.

However, it does not necessarily have to be shown that selective enforcement was on the minds of the framers of the relevant measure.

[254] See also *Pottinger* v. *City of Miami*, 810 F.Supp. 1551, 1578 (S.D. Fla. 1992).

[255] See e.g. the interviews with homeless people in Seattle in Beckett/Herbert, *Banished* (2010), pp. 103–39.

[256] *Parr* v. *Municipal Court*, 3 Cal.3d 861, 863 (Cal. 1971). [257] Ibid. [258] Ibid., 868.

[259] Ibid., 870.

The police of the City of Miami had a policy of arresting homeless people for behaviour such as sleeping, lying down and standing in public places in violation of ordinances prohibiting, among other acts, loitering, obstruction of sidewalks and sleeping in public.[260] The district court seized with the matter reviewed the city's actions with strict scrutiny for their conformity with the equal protection clause: It suggested that there were good reasons for characterising the homeless as a suspect class but left the question open as it thought that, in any event, strict scrutiny must apply due to the fact that the city's actions infringed fundamental rights.[261] As a consequence, the city would have had to be able to demonstrate that the targeting of the homeless for these harmless behaviours served a compelling state interest through the least intrusive means. The court thought that most of the interests advanced by the city – keeping its parks and streets clean, promoting tourism, business and the development of the downtown area – were legitimate but not compelling. This is characteristic of exclusion measures directed against anti-social behaviour, in that these normally pursue public interests that cannot be qualified as particularly strong.[262] Regarding the only interest that *could* be characterised as compelling – preventing crime in public parks – the court found that there was no evidence that homeless people were disproportionately responsible for criminal acts and that there were less intrusive means available to ensure safety in parks, such as increased police patrols.[263] Similarly, with prohibitions of drinking alcohol in public places, it will often be possible to show that these are enforced against alcoholics, punks or other marginal groups, but not against 'ordinary citizens' enjoying a night out or a picnic in a public park.[264] Regardless of whether these distinctions are qualified as suspect or not, it would be difficult to think of *any* public interest that is advanced through such unequal enforcement of exclusion measures.[265]

That there is a similar danger of selective enforcement with regard to blanket exclusion powers was highlighted in the case concerning the exclusion orders issued in the City of Berne. In several cases, the police had justified the exclusion orders with the fact that the persons concerned had been hanging around with other 'marginalised people'

260 *Pottinger* v. *City of Miami*, 810 F.Supp. 1551, 1559–60 (S.D. Fla. 1992).

261 Ibid., 1578–81. 262 See Section 5.3.1.2.

263 *Pottinger* v. *City of Miami*, 810 F.Supp. 1551, 1581–3 (S.D. Fla. 1992). See also Ades, 'The Unconstitutionality of "Antihomeless" Laws' (1989), 625–6.

264 E.g. Beckett/Herbert, *Banished* (2010), pp. 129–30.

265 Finger, *Die offenen Szenen der Städte* (2006), pp. 239–40.

(*Randständige*) (more specifically, alcoholics and punks).[266] Although not finding a violation of the prohibition of discrimination of Article 8(2) of the Federal Constitution, the Cantonal Administrative Court nevertheless observed that the complainants' concern that the exclusion powers could be employed in a discriminatory manner against socially marginalised groups was not unfounded. The court called on the police not to base their decisions on stereotypical assumptions about different social groups, reminding them that merely associating with 'marginalised people' was not a sufficient reason to justify an exclusion order. Instead, it had to be demonstrated that the person concerned had engaged in a specific behaviour resulting in a threat to public safety and order.[267] Given that, as explained above, the exclusion powers under the cantonal police acts are often employed almost solely against drug and alcohol addicts, it is questionable whether police officers are in fact always guided by the behaviour of those concerned, rather than their appearance or affiliation. Is it really true that it is almost exclusively persons addicted to drugs or alcohol who engage in this type of behaviour?

Often, however, it will be difficult to demonstrate that exclusion measures designed to prevent anti-social behaviour are enforced in a selective manner. The City of Seattle passed an ordinance that prohibits sitting or lying on public sidewalks in commercial areas between 7 am and 9 pm.[268] A group of plaintiffs brought legal action, claiming, among other things, that the prohibition violates the equal protection clause of the Fourteenth Amendment by discriminating against homeless people. A district court held that, contrary to what has been argued above, the homeless do not constitute a suspect class and that only individuals who engage in certain conduct, namely sitting or lying on sidewalks in commercial areas during business hours, are targeted under the ordinance.[269] Therefore, the court applied (only) the rational basis test and concluded, rather summarily, that the prohibition was rationally related to the legitimate governmental interest of ensuring pedestrian safety and safeguarding the economic vitality of commercial areas.[270] However, even in cases such as this, where it cannot be shown that an exclusion measure was intentionally designed to target a particular group and there is no evidence of selective enforcement, one must also look at the impact of the respective measure to establish whether there is not

266 BVR 2005, 97, pp. 103–5, 114 (Verwaltungsgericht des Kantons Bern).

267 Ibid., pp. 114–15.

268 Seattle Municipal Code, s. 15.48.040.

269 *Roulette* v. *City of Seattle*, 850 F.Supp. 1442, 1449–50 (W.D. Wash. 1994).

270 Ibid., 1447, 1450.

indirect discrimination. Who exactly is affected by the measure? Is it not the case that a prohibition of sitting or lying on public sidewalks affects almost exclusively homeless people? Jeremy Waldron has argued that the disproportionate impact of such prohibitions is regularly so obvious that it would be disingenuous to claim that they were not intended specifically to target the homeless.[271] If this holds true, then the disproportionate impact of the measure concerned will only be compatible with the right to equality and non-discrimination if there is a justification for it. Is there any evidence that the homeless are a greater threat to 'pedestrian safety' than others and that prohibiting them from sitting or lying on public sidewalks increases 'pedestrian safety'? Given the serious personal consequences of spatial exclusion, does the government interest in 'safeguarding the economic vitality of commercial areas' outweigh the disadvantage imposed on the homeless through such prohibitions? Only if these questions can be answered in the affirmative will there be no violation of the right to equality and non-discrimination.

6.2.2.3 Unequal enforcement: distinctions based on race and ethnic origin

Just as with exclusion measures directed against criminal behaviour, there is a great risk that measures intended to deal with anti-social behaviour may be selectively enforced against, or have a disproportionate impact on, particular racial or ethnic groups.

This applies, for example, to juvenile curfews, especially in the United States and the United Kingdom. As even the proponents of juvenile curfews acknowledge, given limited law enforcement resources, it is virtually impossible to enforce them fully: the police simply cannot stop and check all persons (or even most persons) who potentially are in breach of a juvenile curfew.[272] It is thus inevitable that the police target particular juveniles. There is a great potential that persons will be singled out according to their appearance, which may include their racial or ethnic appearance, or that law enforcement resources will be allocated to focus on particular ethnic neighbourhoods.[273] In Los Angeles, for example, juvenile curfews are deployed selectively and almost exclusively against black and Latino neighbourhoods in South Central (today called

[271] Waldron, 'Homelessness and the Issue of Freedom' (1991), 313.

[272] 'Juvenile Curfew Ordinances and the Constitution' (1977), 111, 148–9.

[273] Trollinger, 'The Juvenile Curfew' (1995), 1002; Federle, 'Children, Curfews, and the Constitution' (1995), 1366. For an example of such a complaint, see *Chase* v. *Twist*, 323 F. Supp. 749 (D.C. Ark. 1970).

South Los Angeles).[274] In New Orleans, in 2011, 93 per cent of juveniles detained at the city's curfew centre were African-American.[275] Given the suspect nature of race and ethnicity as grounds of distinction, it seems inconceivable that a court would not find a violation of the prohibition of discrimination where it can be shown that an individual was singled out because of their racial or ethnic appearance. The concentration of law enforcement efforts on particular ethnic neighbourhoods, in turn, could only be justified if it was demonstrated that juveniles in these neighbourhoods are considerably more likely to breach curfew laws.[276] However, even where curfews are enforced uniformly, they may still be problematic because they entail *indirect* discrimination. As explained in the previous section, juvenile curfews disproportionally affect young people from poorer backgrounds. As there is normally a correlation between economic status and ethnicity, juveniles belonging to ethnic minority groups may be more likely to be subject to curfews than other juveniles.[277] Similarly, research carried out in London has shown that black people were more likely than persons belonging to other ethnic groups to be subject to dispersal orders, which are mainly used against juveniles. However, it is unclear whether this is a consequence of selective enforcement or a case of potential indirect discrimination.[278] In any event, where statistics show that juveniles belonging to a particular ethnic group are more likely to be affected by exclusion measures than other juveniles, the government may be hard pressed to come up with a justification for such disparate effects.

Similar problems are raised by laws that prohibit widely defined behaviours such as 'loitering'. As explained in Section 4.3.2.1, US courts, including the Supreme Court, have repeatedly struck down such prohibitions for being too vague. One of the central concerns for doing so has been the danger that such prohibitions may be enforced in a racially discriminatory manner.[279] As the Supreme Court explained in

[274] Davis, *City of Quartz* (1990), p. 286.

[275] R.A. Vargas, 'New Orleans' curfew enforcement is racially biased, ineffective, critics say', *The Times-Picayune*, 15 March 2013.

[276] In *Qutb* v. *Strauss*, 11 F.3d 488, 496 n. 11 (5th Cir. 1993), the court remarked in a footnote that it could 'envision the constitutionality of a narrowly drawn nocturnal juvenile curfew ordinance that applies only in a municipality's high risk, high crime areas or danger zones'.

[277] Franz, *Ausgehverbot für Jugendliche* (2000), p. 182, footnote 260.

[278] Crawford/Lister, *The Use and Impact of Dispersal Orders* (2007), p. 11.

[279] E.g. *Kolender* v. *Lawson*, 461 U.S. 352, 360 (1983); *Papachristou* v. *City of Jacksonville*, 405 U.S. 156, 170 (1972); *Coates* v. *City of Cincinnati*, 402 U.S. 611, 616 (1971).

Coates v. *City of Cincinnati*, 'such a prohibition, in addition, contains an obvious invitation to discriminatory enforcement against those whose association together is "annoying" because their ideas, their lifestyle, or their physical appearance is resented by the majority of their fellow citizens'.[280] With regard to prohibitions of behaviours such as sleeping or drinking alcohol in public parks, research carried out in Seattle has shown that black people and, even more so, native Americans were considerably more likely to be affected by them than white people. As with the dispersal orders in the United Kingdom, it is not clear whether this reflects a selective enforcement practice or whether the disparate impacts are the consequence of structural inequalities, making this potentially a case of indirect discrimination.[281]

6.2.3 Political protest

Laws designed to prevent political protest from being held in certain parts of public space are not normally explicitly directed against particular groups, but instead apply equally to everyone. However, they may be enforced in a selective manner or they may have a disproportionate impact on certain groups. Of particular concern in this regard are distinctions that are made according to the political views of those banned from protesting in parts of public space.

The guarantees of non-discrimination contained in most human rights treaties, including the ICCPR and the ECHR, explicitly list 'political or other opinion' as one of the prohibited grounds of distinction.[282] Nevertheless, distinctions based on political opinion are not treated as inherently suspect under international human rights law, nor are they in British or US case law. As far as Switzerland is concerned, among the grounds listed in the prohibition of discrimination of Article 8(2) of the Federal Constitution is that of 'ideological or political conviction' (*weltanschauliche oder politische Überzeugung/convictions philosophiques ou politiques*). Any distinctions based on this ground, therefore, require a 'qualified justification'. In addition, distinctions involved by exclusion measures directed against political protest should be reviewed with intense scrutiny because they affect fundamental individual interests, most importantly the rights to freedom of assembly and freedom of expression.[283]

[280] *Coates* v. *City of Cincinnati*, 402 U.S. 611, 616 (1971).
[281] Beckett/Herbert, *Banished* (2010), pp. 67–8.
[282] ICCPR, Arts 2(1) and 26; ECHR, Art. 14. [283] See Sections 5.2.5 and 5.2.6.

Police strategies aimed at denying demonstrators access to potential sites of protest[284] raise concerns of direct discrimination if people are denied access based on their (presumed) political affiliation. For example, in the City of Berne the police stopped thirty-seven individuals on the street and ordered them to keep away from the city centre for the duration of a political event organised by the conservative Swiss People's Party; one of these orders was justified by the police with the fact that they found three political stickers in the rucksack of the person concerned.[285] In the case of *Gsell*, referred to repeatedly before, the order preventing Mario Gsell from travelling to Davos was explained, among other reasons, with the fact that he was travelling with persons who appeared to the police to be 'militant anti-globalisation activists'.[286] The Federal Supreme Court did not seem to object to this explanation. While the issue of discrimination was not raised before the court, in its discussion of the proportionality of the interference with Gsell's right to freedom of expression, it held that the police could not be blamed for having carried out the control of persons 'in a somewhat schematic fashion'.[287] Thus, according to the court, to turn back everyone not clearly identified as not posing a risk was a proportionate means of protecting public safety and order.[288] Similar problems may arise with the police strategy of 'kettling', as the police, when using this strategy, may base their decisions as to whom to allow to leave the contained area on people's apparent political affiliations.

In both of the Swiss cases described above, although in the first one more clearly than in that of *Gsell*, people were denied access to potential sites of protest on the basis of the political views they appeared to subscribe to. Such policing strategies are highly problematic in that they may involve selective enforcement of the law and may thus amount to direct discrimination. Differences in treatment based on political opinion can only be justified if they can be said to pursue a legitimate aim, which in the context of political protest will regularly be the

284 See Section 3.3.3.2.

285 M. Dütschler, 'Polizei hat Politiker unbegründet weggewiesen', *Der Bund*, 9 November 2011.

286 BGE 130 I 369, 386–7 (2004) ('Sie [die Regierung] wies darauf hin, dass er mit Personen unterwegs war, welche der Kantonspolizei den Eindruck erweckten, militanten Globalisierungsgegnern anzugehören.').

287 Ibid., 387 ('Darüber hinaus kann der Polizei an Ort und Stelle nicht vorgeworfen werden, die Personenkontrollen angesichts der allgemein gespannten Lage in etwas schematischer Weise vorgenommen zu haben.').

288 Ibid., 384–7.

protection of public safety and order, in a proportionate manner. For example, the police are allowed – and, indeed, obliged – to prevent a clash between two rival political groups by stopping a march of the first group, if there are clear indications that they are on their way to violently break up an event organised by the second group. In this kind of situation, it may be inevitable for the police to determine membership of the first group based on certain signs of political affiliation (such as banners, clothing or bald heads). In contrast, in the two cases described above, the approach of the police appears too schematic and speculative in that there seemed to be insufficient evidence for assuming the persons concerned had violent intentions. To simply equate certain political views with a tendency to disorderly behaviour and single out everyone who appears to subscribe to these views (or to be affiliated with others who do) is neither a suitable nor the least restrictive means to protect public safety and order. Just because someone carries political stickers or travels with others who look 'militant' does not necessarily mean that they pose a greater threat to public safety and order than anyone else. As already explained in Section 5.3.2.2 in the context of the discussion of the proportionality of interferences with fundamental rights, the sounder approach is the one defined by the House of Lords in the case of *Laporte*. There, their Lordships rejected a schematic approach, instead requiring the police to ascertain on an individual basis the intentions and affiliations of persons intending to gain access to a site of protest.[289]

Laws designed to prevent political protest from taking place in certain parts of public space[290] that are neutral and that are enforced in a perfectly uniform manner may still be problematic from a discrimination perspective if they have a disproportionate impact on those who would like to express particular political opinions. In other words, the issue of indirect discrimination must also be considered. An example of an exclusion measure that, due to the definition of the geographical area where it applies, may disproportionately affect those subscribing to certain political views is that of the 'buffer zones' around abortion clinics as they exist in the United States. Such zones prevent anti-abortionists from holding their protests where they would have the greatest effect, namely in the immediate vicinity of abortion clinics, whereas those in favour of (or not concerned about) abortion will not

[289] See in particular *R (Laporte)* v. *Chief Constable of Gloucestershire Constabulary*, [2006] UKHL 55, para. 154 (Lord Mance).

[290] See Section 3.3.3.1.

be affected by them at all. Thus, a neutral measure that is applied uniformly has a disproportionate impact on those holding a particular political view, meaning that there must be a justification for it. In the case of 'buffer zones', such a justification does exist. The establishment of 'buffer zones' pursues a number of aims that are clearly legitimate, in particular the protection of third persons from being harassed or threatened and of upholding public safety and order.[291] They are undoubtedly a suitable means of achieving these objectives. If they are defined sufficiently narrowly, they may also be the least restrictive measure available to achieve these objectives and can be said to strike a fair balance between the rights of anti-abortion protesters on the one hand and the rights of persons trying to gain access to hospitals and the interests of public safety and order on the other.[292] This finding can be applied to bans on holding protests in particular parts of public space in general: the more narrowly defined the respective area is, the easier it will be for the authorities to demonstrate that a disproportionate impact is justified because the ban advances a legitimate aim in a proportionate manner.

6.3 Conclusion

Dworkin argued that any government that professes to take rights seriously must accept the concepts of human dignity and political equality.[293] Accordingly, everyone has the fundamental right to treatment as an equal, that is, to be treated with the same respect and concern as anyone else.[294] This principle of equal concern not only forms the foundation of individual rights[295] but is the 'sovereign virtue of political community'.[296] For Dworkin, equality implies the political virtue of integrity. Integrity requires the state to act on a single, coherent set of principles,[297] which, among other things, means that the legislature may not pass laws that are based on arbitrary distinctions and the bodies charged with applying the law may not enforce it incoherently.[298] This basic idea is reflected in the various international and national norms guaranteeing equality and non-discrimination discussed in this chapter, which require the state to show that there is a reasonable and objective justification for any differences in treatment or outcome.

291 See Section 5.3.1.3. 292 See Section 5.3.2.2.
293 Dworkin, *Taking Rights Seriously* (1977), pp. 198–9. 294 Ibid., pp. 199, 272–8.
295 Ibid., pp. 272–3. 296 Dworkin, *Sovereign Virtue* (2000), p. 1.
297 Dworkin, *Law's Empire* (1986), p. 166. 298 Ibid., pp. 167, 176–224.

In many instances, exclusion measures fail to meet this requirement. Instead of being applied to individuals who have demonstrably engaged in behaviour that justifies exclusion from public space, they are directed against broadly defined groups of people who are deemed to be more likely than others to engage in offensive conduct if granted access to public space. Thus, it is often sufficient to belong to a certain category of foreign nationals, to be of a certain age, to be homeless or to appear to subscribe to particular political views to be regarded as having the potential for engaging in criminal behaviour, anti-social behaviour or political protest and, as a consequence, to be treated differently with regard to access to public space. Such extensive use of exclusion measures tends to create a 'two-class scheme of access'[299] to public space: unrestricted access for 'ordinary citizens', restricted access for members of those social groups that are categorised as posing a heightened risk. Whereas most people can move freely, marginalised groups are increasingly banned from certain parts of public space, especially inner-city areas. These differentiations not only contravene the fundamental principle that public space should be equally accessible to everyone. Since space is a social product, they also change the very nature of public space: they reinforce the trend, described in Section 2.5.1, towards the 'privatisation of public space' understood as the process whereby cities are fragmented into separate segments and people spend less and less time in commonly shared spaces.

An approach based on the virtue of integrity, in contrast, would establish a coherent set of 'ground rules' for the use of public space that precisely set out, in advance, what is allowed and what is not.[300] These ground rules would apply equally to everyone. Only once it has been shown that someone has violated these rules, could he or she be excluded from public space. Insistence on generally applicable rules – on rules that meet Kant's requirement of universality[301] – would force political actors to take better account of the interests of minority groups and would thus pave the way for a more honest and open democratic debate on what forms of behaviour should or should not be acceptable in public space.

[299] Von Hirsch/Simester, 'Penalising Offensive Behaviour' (2006), 130.
[300] See Crawford, *The Local Governance of Crime* (1997), p. 290.
[301] Kant, *Groundwork of the Metaphysics of Morals* (1998), p. 43.

7

Democracy

Exclusion measures are primarily directed against *immobile* behaviour: juveniles 'hanging around' on street corners, alcoholics sitting in public squares, drug addicts standing around in groups, protesters staging a demonstration or sit-in in front of a government building and so on. Such forms of behaviour, it seems, are no longer compatible with the contemporary conception of the city, which prioritises the traffic and consumption functions of urban public space[1] and reduces the city to a 'mobility machine'.[2] Today, it has become suspicious to stay immobile in urban spaces.[3]

Yet it is exactly immobile behaviour, the mere presence in public space that is crucial for democracy. An illustrative case is the occupation of Tahrir Square in Cairo, which was 'the beating heart and most effective symbol' of the Egyptian revolution of 2011.[4] The protesters achieved democratic progress, not least, by simply being in a public square for an extended period and discussing and propagating ideas there.[5] The publicity effect of being immobile in public space is also the basic idea underlying the 'Occupy movement', which, partly inspired by the 'Arab spring', has occupied countless public places all over the world to protest against a variety of issues.[6] Yet, as will be shown below, not only the occupation of parts of public space to make a political statement but also the mere presence of people who do not pursue any political objective is important for democracy. There must be public space available where people are allowed to be immobile: where they can meet others,

1 Bauman, *Liquid Modernity* (2000), pp. 96–8.

2 Rousseau, 'La ville comme machine à mobilité' (2008).

3 Ibid.

4 'The Different Shades of Tahrir', *Al Jazeera*, 8 February 2011, available at www.aljazeera.com/indepth/spotlight/anger-in-egypt/2011/02/20112811181499676.html.

5 A. El Difraoui, 'Die Rolle der neuen Medien im Arabischen Frühling', *Bundeszentrale für politische Bildung*, 3 November 2011, available at www.bpb.de/internationales/afrika/arabischer-fruehling/52420/die-rolle-der-neuen-medien?p=all.

6 E.g. Welty/Bolton/Nayak/Malone (eds), *Occupying Political Science* (2013).

discuss or simply spend time in public. Permanent mobility inhibits meetings, discussion and exchange.

Thus, by changing the terms of access to (and thus presence in) public space, exclusion measures may affect democracy. On the other hand, it may conform to the will of the democratic majority that certain persons are banned from parts of public space. This chapter aims to explore the various links between exclusion from public space and democracy. Do exclusion measures comply with the precepts of democracy or do they undermine them? Of course, there is no straightforward answer to this question – and certainly not a straightforward *legal* answer. Whereas there are commonly accepted legal standards to assess whether a given measure complies with the requirements of the rule of law or guarantees of liberty and equality, such standards do not exist with regard to democracy. An answer to the question of whether exclusion from public space is desirable or not from the point of view of democracy therefore depends on what one understands democracy to mean and imply. There are different theories and definitions of democracy, emphasising different elements of democracy, so that the answer may differ depending on which elements are given priority. As a further caveat, it must be admitted that an assessment of exclusion measures from the perspective of democracy inevitably involves some degree of speculation about their fundamental long-term consequences. Nevertheless, the chapter tries to at least highlight the most important concerns that exclusion measures raise with regard to democracy.

The chapter starts with an explanation of the notions of democracy that underlie the constitutional systems of the three states at issue, drawing out a number of common key elements (Section 7.1). It then explores the democratic legitimacy of exclusion measures: To what extent can they be said to represent the will of the political community (Section 7.2)? The final, and most substantial, section of the chapter analyses what consequences it may have for democracy if ever larger sections of the population are banned from simply being present in public space (Section 7.3).

7.1 Democracy

Today, the term 'democracy' is widely used as a synonym for good government (or even the 'normal' form of government)[7] and has thus

[7] Sen, 'Democracy as a Universal Value' (1999), 4.

largely lost its contours.[8] This makes it important to be clear about what sort of democracy is referred to in a particular context. Etymologically, democracy signifies rule (*kratos*) by the people (*demos*) and thus refers to that form of government in which sovereignty is vested in the people.[9] That 'all power derives from the people'[10] can, together with the principle of political equality,[11] still be described as the 'core meaning'[12] of democracy today. However, there are numerous ways in which the core idea of popular sovereignty can be implemented and thus a democracy can be organised. What one understands a democracy to be depends on one's political views and the historical context. Accordingly, there are countless models of democracy, and understandings of democracy differ significantly from country to country.[13]

This also holds true for the three states under consideration here: as will become clear from this section, ideas as to what democracy is and implies vary considerably among the United Kingdom, the United States and Switzerland. Nevertheless, there are a number of common elements or principles that typically play a role in the implementation of the idea of popular sovereignty at the institutional level, with one or the other element being given more weight in a given political system. At least two of these elements are of central importance to the systems of democracy of all three states at issue and deserve to be highlighted in the present context. The first is the notion that the main objective of rule by the people is facilitation of individual self-determination (that is, individual freedom) and that, therefore, democracy necessarily implies upholding the rule of law and protection of fundamental rights.[14] As explained in the previous chapters, the rule of law and guarantees of fundamental rights accordingly form key elements of the constitutional

[8] Auer/Malinverni/Hottelier, *Droit constitutionnel suisse* (2013), Vol. I, p. 199; Tschannen, *Staatsrecht der Schweizerischen Eidgenossenschaft* (2011), p. 79; Schmidt, *Demokratietheorien* (2010), pp. 20–1; Dahl, *Democracy and Its Critics* (1989), p. 2; Sartori, *The Theory of Democracy Revisited* (1987), pp. 3–6; Cohen, *Democracy* (1971), pp. 103–4.

[9] See Dahl, *Democracy and Its Critics* (1989), p. 3; Sartori, *The Theory of Democracy Revisited* (1987), pp. 21–38; Cohen, *Democracy* (1971), p. 3.

[10] *City of Eastlake* v. *Forest City*, 426 U.S. 668, 672 (1976).

[11] See e.g. Dahl, *On Political Equality* (2006); Dworkin, *Sovereign Virtue* (2000), pp. 184–210; Dahl, *Democracy and Its Critics* (1989), pp. 30–3, 83–105; Beitz, *Political Equality* (1988).

[12] Diggelmann, *Der liberale Verfassungsstaat und die Internationalisierung der Politik* (2005), pp. 69–70 ('harter Begriffskern').

[13] For good overviews, see Schmidt, *Demokratietheorien* (2010); Held, *Models of Democracy* (2006).

[14] See also Section 4.1.7.

orders of the United Kingdom, the United States and Switzerland. The second common element is the idea of deliberative (or discursive) democracy, that is, the idea that, to be legitimate, political decisions must be the outcome of an exchange of arguments among free and equal citizens committed to the values of rationality and impartiality, in which all those who will be affected by these decisions can participate directly or through their representatives.[15] While deliberative democracy is an old idea (already Athenian democracy could be described as largely deliberative),[16] over the last three decades it has become 'one of the most fashionable ideals in contemporary Western political theory' and is now a central component of all major democratic theories.[17] It is, above all, the work of Jürgen Habermas that has been instrumental in this rise to prominence of deliberative democracy.[18]

7.1.1 United Kingdom

Parliament is the central institution in the British system of democracy. Having evolved from the councils of noblemen and senior clergymen that the medieval kings used to call to seek their counsel and consent,[19] the parliament as it developed in England is one of the oldest legislative bodies in the world. Over the centuries, both representation in parliament and its powers were extended. By the fourteenth century, parliament was believed to represent the entire nation and to express its collective counsel and consent.[20] By the end of the seventeenth century, parliament had won the struggle for power with the crown and its sovereignty was a settled principle.[21] Parliamentary sovereignty implies that there are no legal limitations on its power to legislate.[22] Since 1928, when the right to vote in parliamentary elections was extended to all

15 Elster, 'Introduction' (1998), 8. 16 Ibid., 1–2.

17 Besson/Martí, 'Introduction' (2006), xiii.

18 See especially Habermas, 'Drei normative Modelle der Demokratie' (1992); Habermas, *Faktizität und Geltung* (1992); Habermas, *Theorie des kommunikativen Handelns* (1981).

19 Maddicott, *The Origins of the English Parliament* (2010); Goldsworthy, *The Sovereignty of Parliament* (1999), pp. 22, 28.

20 Maddicott, *The Origins of the English Parliament* (2010), pp. 277–375; Goldsworthy, *The Sovereignty of Parliament* (1999), pp. 28–30, 229.

21 Goldsworthy, *The Sovereignty of Parliament* (1999), pp. 142–65.

22 Barnett, *Constitutional and Administrative Law* (2013), pp. 114–15; Bradley/Ewing, *Constitutional and Administrative Law* (2011), p. 53; Bradley, 'The Sovereignty of Parliament' (2007), 28–9; Dicey, *An Introduction to the Study of the Law of the Constitution* (1959), pp. 39–40.

adults,[23] the House of Commons (as the dominant of the two parliamentary chambers) may be called a truly democratic body.

The United Kingdom is a *representative* (or electoral) democracy: unlike in a direct democracy where citizens participate directly in the political process, they elect politicians to represent them in parliament and act in their interest. It can further be described as a *parliamentary* democracy: unlike in a presidential system, the British government is appointed by parliament rather than being elected by the voters. Accordingly, the government is constitutionally responsible to parliament. When it loses parliament's support, it must resign. It is this accountability of government to a political, democratically elected institution (rather than, as in other constitutional systems, the courts of law) that is celebrated as the central safeguard of British democracy.[24]

That the British concept of democracy is inextricably linked to the liberal ideals of fundamental rights and the rule of law is already apparent from the fact that the struggle for the sovereignty of parliament was a struggle for the rights of the people (or, at least, of the most powerful groups among them): parliament was seen as the most effective protector of these rights against the powers of the monarch, it was the only body that could be trusted never to violate them.[25] That only parliament, elected by the people, can impose restrictions on individual rights was originally thought to be a sufficient safeguard for their protection.[26] However, as the failure of this traditional system to give sufficient protection from misuse of state power became more and more apparent, the Human Rights Act was adopted in 1998. While the Human Rights Act formally adheres to the doctrine of parliamentary sovereignty, it gives courts the 'powerful tool'[27] of interpreting legislation in a way that is compatible with the rights guaranteed by the ECHR as well as the power to issue 'declarations of incompatibility'.[28] This and other developments have led Lord Hope to claim that 'Parliamentary sovereignty is no longer, if it ever was, absolute' and 'that [i]t is no longer right to say that its [parliament's] freedom to legislate admits of no qualification whatever'.[29] Instead, according to his Lordship, it is '[t]he rule of law enforced by the

[23] Representation of the People (Equal Franchise) Act 1928.

[24] Tomkins, *Our Republican Constitution* (2005), pp. 1–6.

[25] Goldsworthy, *The Sovereignty of Parliament* (1999), p. 231.

[26] See Section 5.1.2.

[27] *In Re S (Minors) (Care Order: Implementation of Care Plan)* [2002] UKHL 10, para. 37 (Lord Nicholls).

[28] See Section 5.1.2.

[29] *Jackson* v. *Her Majesty's Attorney General* [2005] UKHL 56, para. 104.

courts [that] is the ultimate controlling factor on which our constitution is based' and it is the rule of law, reinforced by the Human Rights Act, which 'protects the individual from arbitrary government'.[30] Similarly, Baroness Hale argued that there are limits on what a democratically elected parliament may do: 'Democracy is the will of the people, but the people may not will to invade those rights and freedoms which are fundamental to democracy itself.'[31] In any event, also parliament itself, even though its powers are in theory unlimited, feels bound by the rule of law.[32]

The idea that democracy must be deliberative is equally an evident characteristic of the democratic system of the United Kingdom. The important role that parliament is accorded in this system is crucial in this regard. From the very beginning, parliament was understood to be not simply a body representing (parts of) the population but also the central forum for transparent deliberation. The most famous expression of this view is that of Edmund Burke in his speech to the electors of Bristol in 1774, in which he characterised the Parliament of Great Britain as 'a deliberative assembly of one nation'.[33] According to Burke, 'government and legislation are matters of reason and judgment, and not of inclination' and therefore require deliberation and debate.[34] He believed that representatives, who were to be guided by 'the general good, resulting from the general reason of the whole',[35] were better able to reach the 'right' answers than the common people.[36] Decision-makers had to be in direct contact with each other: '[W]hat sort of reason is that [. . .] where those who form the conclusion are perhaps three hundred miles distant from those who hear the arguments?'[37] Furthermore, he opposed binding instructions to representatives: 'Your representative owes you, not his industry only, but his judgment; and he betrays, instead of serving you, if he sacrifices it to your opinion.'[38] Although Burke's views can be criticised, from today's perspective, as elitist, it must be acknowledged that he was concerned with having all the relevant arguments represented in the legislative forum.[39] A century later, John Stuart Mill elaborated on this argument. He conceded that also representatives may fail in their duty to promote the general good. However, according to Mill, deliberation in

[30] Ibid., para. 107.
[31] *R. (Countryside Alliance)* v. *Her Majesty's Attorney General* [2007] UKHL 52, para. 114.
[32] See Section 4.1.2. [33] Burke, *Selected Writings* (1960), p. 115. [34] Ibid. [35] Ibid.
[36] Gargarella, 'Full Representation, Deliberation, and Impartiality' (1998), 263.
[37] Burke, *Selected Writings* (1960), p. 115. [38] Ibid.
[39] Gargarella, 'Full Representation, Deliberation, and Impartiality' (1998), 263–4.

parliament reduced this risk as it fostered self-correction. Thus, representatives were superior to ordinary citizens not because they were more intelligent or higher in virtue but because they could learn from each other: '[T]he representative, if he devotes himself to his duty, has greater opportunities of correcting an original false judgement, than fall to the lot of most of his constituents.'[40] Thus, deliberation is a key value underlying the central institution in the British system of democracy.

7.1.2 *United States*

That the United States was founded to realise the core idea of democracy, namely popular sovereignty, is symbolised by the opening words of the US Constitution ('We the People [. . .] do ordain and establish this Constitution for the United States of America.') as well as by the famous statement of one of its foremost presidents, Abraham Lincoln, who described democracy as 'government of the people, by the people, for the people'.[41]

However, this was never intended to imply that there should be unrestrained majority rule. On the contrary, the founding fathers feared the influence of 'factions' (that is, powerful self-interested groups) and a tyranny of the majority.[42] They were therefore opposed to what James Madison termed 'pure democracy', that is, direct democracy.[43] Instead, they devised an elaborate system of checks and balances to ensure limited government and avoid accumulation of powers. These checks and balances included the separation of powers, judicial review of legislation, representative (rather than direct) democracy and broadening the franchise to prevent powerful factions.[44] Such a system, it was hoped, would be able to produce outcomes that serve the common good, rather than group interests, and, importantly, would effectively protect individual liberties.[45] As a further element to achieve the latter goal, the Bill of

40 Mill, *On Liberty and Other Essays* (1991), p. 380.

41 Abraham Lincoln, 'Nicolay Copy' of the Gettysburg Address, 19 November 1863, available on the website of the Library of Congress, at http://myloc.gov/Exhibitions/gettysburgaddress/exhibitionitems/ExhibitObjects/NicolayCopy.aspx?sc_id=wikip.

42 James Madison, Federalist Paper No. 10. The Federalist Papers are available on the website of the Library of Congress, at http://thomas.loc.gov/home/histdox/fedpapers.html.

43 Ibid.

44 James Madison, Federalist Paper No. 10; Alexander Hamilton or James Madison, Federalist Paper No. 51; Alexander Hamilton, Federalist Paper No. 78. See Section 4.1.3.

45 Ibid.

Rights was added a few years later by way of amendment of the US Constitution.[46] Thus, as in the United Kingdom, the idea of democracy was, from the very beginning, seen as inseparably linked to the rule of law and the protection of fundamental rights.

Most of the institutional devices included in the Constitution were designed not only to ensure limited government but also to institutionalise a system of 'government by discussion',[47] in which decisions would be based on reasons that have been debated in public. Thus, the founding fathers of the United States considered broad public deliberation an essential part of the political system they created at the end of the eighteenth century: they sought, in the words of Cass Sunstein, 'to eliminate the monarchical legacy, based on "nature" and "authority", and to replace it with a republic of reasons'.[48] As Burke, they thought that this was best achieved through a system of representation, which would make it possible 'to refine and enlarge the public views, by passing them through the medium of a chosen body of citizens, whose wisdom may best discern the true interest of their country'.[49] Importantly, they believed that heterogeneity and differences of opinion were beneficial, even essential, as they promoted deliberation.[50] Since existing opinions might reflect insufficient information or partial perspectives, those engaged in democratic discussion should be exposed to an appropriate diversity of views through direct contact with others: they should 'meet others from the different parts of the Union, and consult'[51] and be 'open to the force of argument'.[52] Thus, the whole constitutional system of checks and balances was designed to encourage exchange and debate among citizens as well as different factions and governmental entities. The protection of fundamental rights, in particular the First Amendment guarantee of freedom of speech, can be understood as forming part and parcel of the same effort to realise deliberative democracy.[53] In the view of the framers of the US Constitution, limited government and deliberative government were one and the same.[54]

46 See Sections 4.1.3 and 5.1.3.

47 Sunstein, *Democracy and the Problem of Free Speech* (1995), p. xvi.

48 Sunstein, *The Partial Constitution* (1993), p. 347.

49 James Madison, Federalist Paper No. 10.

50 Sunstein, *The Partial Constitution* (1993), pp. 23–4.

51 Annals of Congress, 1st Cong., 763 (Roger Sherman).

52 Farrand (ed.), *The Records of the Federal Convention of 1787* (1966), Vol. III, p. 479.

53 Sunstein, *Democracy and the Problem of Free Speech* (1995); Sunstein, *The Partial Constitution* (1993), pp. 23, 232–56.

54 Sunstein, *The Partial Constitution* (1993), p. 23.

7.1.3 *Switzerland*

Although the Swiss Federal Constitution refers to the term 'democracy' only incidentally,[55] the democratic element plays a crucial role in the political system of Switzerland and is described as a 'structural principle' (*Strukturprinzip/principe structurel*) of the constitution.[56] The idea of democracy has a long tradition in Switzerland.[57] Mixing various dogmatic strands, it has remained, however, a concept without precise theoretical contours.[58] Democracy, as René Rhinow has put it, is in Switzerland lived rather than taught.[59]

Following the categorisation of Oliver Diggelmann, four different strands or elements making up the Swiss concept of democracy can be distinguished.[60] The first is the idea of citizen participation, which reaches back several centuries.[61] This idea is realised primarily through an elaborate system of direct democratic mechanisms (in particular the referendum and the popular initiative), which allow citizens to participate directly in political processes.[62] That many state organs – most importantly parliaments at the cantonal, municipal and, although to a lesser extent, federal level – are based on the principle of 'militia service' (that is, service on a voluntary, non-professional basis) further contributes to the implementation of the idea of citizen participation.[63] The second element is the central role that consensus plays in the Swiss

[55] Biaggini, 'Ausgestaltung und Entwicklungsperspektiven des demokratischen Prinzips in der Schweiz' (2005), 109.

[56] Auer/Malinverni/Hottelier, *Droit constitutionnel suisse* (2013), Vol. I, p. 199; Tschannen, *Staatsrecht der Schweizerischen Eidgenossenschaft* (2011), pp. 77, 79; Rhinow, 'Grundprobleme der schweizerischen Demokratie' (1984), 143–4, 151–60.

[57] See e.g. Adler, *Die Entstehung der direkten Demokratie* (2006); Kölz, *Neuere schweizerische Verfassungsgeschichte* (1992), pp. 615–30; His, *Geschichte des neuern schweizerischen Staatsrechts: Band 1* (1920), pp. 166–71.

[58] Biaggini, 'Ausgestaltung und Entwicklungsperspektiven des demokratischen Prinzips in der Schweiz' (2005), 110–11.

[59] Rhinow, 'Grundprobleme der schweizerischen Demokratie' (1984), 133 ('Demokratie wird hierzulande gelebt, nicht gelehrt.').

[60] Diggelmann, *Der liberale Verfassungsstaat und die Internationalisierung der Politik* (2005), pp. 76–94. For a different categorisation, see Rhinow, 'Grundprobleme der schweizerischen Demokratie' (1984), 189.

[61] See e.g. Auer (ed.), *Les origines de la démocratie directe en Suisse* (1996).

[62] Grisel, 'Les droits populaires au niveau fédéral' (2001); Grisel, 'Les droits populaires au niveau cantonal' (2001); Hangartner/Kley, *Die demokratischen Rechte in Bund und Kantonen der Schweizerischen Eidgenossenschaft* (2000). For a useful overview in English, see Linder, 'Direct Democracy' (2007).

[63] Neidhart, *Die politische Schweiz* (2002), pp. 289–97; Tschannen, *Stimmrecht und politische Verständigung* (1995), pp. 275–7.

system of democracy. As opposed to, for example, the democratic system of the United Kingdom, which is driven by the competition between the parliamentary majority and the opposition party, one of the defining characteristics of Swiss democracy is the constant effort to ensure that the views of all social groups are represented in decision-making processes and to find solutions that enjoy broad political support.[64] Indeed, Switzerland is often cited as the role model of a 'consensus' or 'bargaining democracy'.[65]

The two further elements of Swiss democracy are those that have been described above as also being characteristic of the British and US systems of democracy: the liberal, rule-of-law-based character of democracy and the notion that democracy must be deliberative.

That the Swiss system of democracy is aimed at facilitating individual freedom is evident from the central role accorded to the key postulates of the *Rechtsstaat* in the Federal Constitution (as well as cantonal constitutions).[66] Most importantly, the division of competencies between the different branches of government (as well as the federal structure of Switzerland) prevent the accumulation of powers, while the constitutional guarantees of fundamental rights protect a sphere free from state interference.[67] Furthermore, the guarantee of a set of direct democratic rights itself provides at least some degree of individual self-determination by ensuring participation in political processes and serves as a further check on state power.[68]

The importance of public deliberation to the Swiss system of democracy has been highlighted by authors such as Jörg Paul Müller,[69] Pierre Tschannen[70] and Martin Scheyli.[71] This importance is reflected, for instance, in the fact that the Federal Constitution describes parliament – the forum for debate *par excellence*[72] – as 'the supreme authority of the Confederation'.[73] Thus, as in the United Kingdom and the United States, the most important political matters are reserved for a body that reaches

64 Linder/Steffen, 'Political Culture' (2007), 26–8; Tschannen, *Stimmrecht und politische Verständigung* (1995), pp. 318–23.
65 Lijphart, *Patterns of Democracy* (1999), p. 33.
66 See Rhinow, 'Grundprobleme der schweizerischen Demokratie' (1984), 187.
67 See Sections 4.1.4 and 5.1.4.
68 Rhinow, 'Grundprobleme der schweizerischen Demokratie' (1984), 162–4.
69 Müller, *Demokratische Gerechtigkeit* (1993).
70 Tschannen, *Stimmrecht und politische Verständigung* (1995).
71 Scheyli, *Politische Öffentlichkeit und deliberative Demokratie nach Habermas* (2000).
72 See Müller, *Demokratische Gerechtigkeit* (1993), p. 161.
73 BV, Art. 148(1) ('Die Bundesversammlung übt [. . .] die oberste Gewalt im Bund aus.').

its decisions through a process of transparent deliberation. Furthermore, the direct democratic machinery can equally be understood as a deliberative tool: it ensures that the political debate is open to as wide a range of arguments and counterarguments as possible by enabling also ordinary citizens to put forward policy proposals and to have a say on specific issues.[74] Direct democratic instruments thus guarantee the flow of communication between, to refer to Habermas' concepts, the informal processes of opinion-making in the public sphere and the institutionalised processes of political decision-making.[75] Since political decision-making depends on the input from informal debates in the public sphere (in particular the identification of social problems through them),[76] everyone must have the same opportunities of effectively participating in these debates: democracy presupposes that the actual conditions of communication are framed in a manner that ensures equality of opportunities.[77] The constitutional guarantees of fundamental rights, in particular the freedoms of expression and assembly, are designed to protect these means of participation, including through informal and spontaneous forms of communication.[78] As in the United States, heterogeneity and differences of opinion are understood to be essential parts of deliberative democracy. Democracy can only function if citizens articulate their particular views, needs and interests. It gives expression to these views, needs and interests so that conflicts become apparent and, in view of the inevitability of heterogeneity, mutually acceptable forms of coexistence can be identified.[79] As Müller has put it, 'in a democracy that takes personal freedom seriously, peculiarity and otherness are not merely tolerated but they function as an *engine* of a constant debate that constitutes the core of this form of government'.[80] This function as an engine, in turn, depends on people's willingness and capacity to put

[74] Scheyli, *Politische Öffentlichkeit und deliberative Demokratie nach Habermas* (2000); Tschannen, *Stimmrecht und politische Verständigung* (1995), especially pp. 446–86; Müller, *Demokratische Gerechtigkeit* (1993), pp. 159–60.

[75] Scheyli, *Politische Öffentlichkeit und deliberative Demokratie nach Habermas* (2000), pp. 179–81.

[76] E.g. Habermas, *Faktizität und Geltung* (1992), pp. 382, 427.

[77] Müller, *Die demokratische Verfassung* (2009), p. 35. See also Müller, *Demokratische Gerechtigkeit* (1993), p. 94.

[78] Tschannen, *Stimmrecht und politische Verständigung* (1995), pp. 430–1.

[79] Müller, *Demokratische Gerechtigkeit* (1993), pp. 35, 154.

[80] Ibid., pp. 35–6 ('In einer Demokratie, die persönliche Freiheit und damit das Partikulare ernst nimmt, sind Besonderheit und Anderssein nicht bloss toleriert, sondern wirken als *Motor* einer ständigen Auseinandersetzung, die den Kern dieser Staatsform ausmacht.') (original emphasis).

themselves in the position of their fellows, in other words, on their empathy.[81]

7.1.4 *International law*

While traditional international law, based on the notion of state sovereignty, did not take a position on the political model adopted by states, 'notions of democracy gradually entered international law through the back door of human rights protection'.[82] The UDHR, proclaimed in 1948, guarantees in Article 21(1) the right to political participation by providing that '[e]veryone has the right to take part in the government of his country, directly or through freely chosen representatives'. Explicitly referring to the core meaning of democracy, according to which '[t]he will of the people shall be the basis of the authority of government', it further provides in Article 21(3) that 'this will shall be expressed in periodic and genuine elections which shall be by universal and equal suffrage and shall be held by secret vote or by equivalent free voting procedures'. The ICCPR of 1966, which binds the majority of states, including those under consideration here, contains almost identical provisions in its Article 25, as does the ADHR in Article 20. The link between the right to political participation and the protection of fundamental rights has been emphasised by the UN General Assembly, which has pointed out that 'the right of everyone to take part in the government of his or her country is a crucial factor in the effective enjoyment by all of a wide range of other human rights and fundamental freedoms'.[83] Similarly, the Vienna Declaration and Programme of Action, adopted by the World Conference on Human Rights in 1993, states that '[d]emocracy, development and respect for human rights and fundamental freedoms are interdependent and mutually reinforcing'.[84] Nevertheless, claims that there exists under general international law a right to democratic governance[85] are probably premature, as state practice in this respect remains inconsistent.[86]

[81] Ibid., p. 67.

[82] Wouters/de Meester/Ryngaert, 'Democracy and International Law' (2004), 7.

[83] UN General Assembly Resolution 43/157, 8 December 1988, UN Doc. A/RES/43/157, para. 2.

[84] Vienna Declaration and Programme of Action, adopted at the World Conference on Human Rights, 25 June 1993, UN Doc. A/CONF.157/23, para. 15.

[85] See most famously Franck, 'The Emerging Right to Democratic Governance' (1992).

[86] E.g. Wheatley, 'Democracy in International Law' (2002).

In Europe, in contrast, such a right does exist, as is confirmed by all the major regional organisations.[87] For example, as far as the Council of Europe is concerned, notwithstanding that the right to free elections is only guaranteed by an additional protocol rather than the ECHR itself,[88] the democratic ideal can be said to permeate the Convention in every respect.[89] The framers intended the ECHR as a means 'to ensure that the States of the Members of the Council of Europe are democratic, and remain democratic'.[90] Accordingly, the European Court of Human Rights has repeatedly observed that '[d]emocracy constitutes a fundamental element of the "European public order"' and that 'the Convention was in fact designed to maintain and promote the ideals and values of a democratic society'.[91] From this it has drawn the fundamental conclusion that 'democracy is the only political model contemplated by the Convention and, accordingly, the only one compatible with it'.[92] Democracy, according to the European Court, means that '[o]nly institutions created by and for the people may be vested with the powers and authority of the State' and requires that the people are given the last word on the content and implementation of the laws to which they are subject.[93] Just as the constitutional orders of the three states under consideration, the ECHR establishes a clear connection between democracy and fundamental freedoms by stating in its Preamble that the latter are best maintained 'by an effective political democracy'.[94] Conversely, the Code of Good Practice in Electoral Matters, adopted under the auspices of the Council of Europe, makes it clear that the very existence of democracy is impossible without

[87] For a brief overview, see ibid., pp. 234–5.

[88] Protocol to the Convention for the Protection of Human Rights and Fundamental Freedoms (adopted 20 March 1952, entered into force 18 May 1954) 213 UNTS 262, Art. 3.

[89] Jean-Paul Costa, President of the European Court of Human Rights, 'The Links between Democracy and Human Rights under the Case-Law of the European Court of Human Rights', speech held in Helsinki on 5 June 2008, p. 1. See also Marks, 'The European Convention on Human Rights and Its "Democratic Society"' (1995).

[90] Council of Europe, *Collected Edition of the 'travaux préparatoires' of the European Convention on Human Rights* (1975–1985), Vol. 2, p. 60 (Ungoed-Thomas). For a detailed discussion, see Bates, *The Evolution of the European Convention on Human Rights* (2010), pp. 44–76.

[91] *Ždanoka* v. *Latvia* [GC], no. 58278/00, 16 March 2006, ECHR 2006-IV, 29, para. 98 (citing further case law).

[92] Ibid.

[93] *Refah Partisi (the Welfare Party) and others* v. *Turkey*, nos 41340/98; 41342/98; 41343/98; 41344/98, 31 July 2001, para. 43.

[94] ECHR, preambular para. 4.

respect for human rights.[95] Finally, again similarly as in the United Kingdom, the United States and Switzerland, the understanding of democracy underlying the ECHR is seen as necessarily implying a certain openness to the views and opinions of others. Without 'pluralism, tolerance and broadmindedness', the European Court stated as early as 1976, there cannot be a democratic society.[96]

7.2 The democratic legitimacy of exclusion measures

From the perspective of democracy, measures excluding people from public space may be claimed to be a good thing if and insofar as they are based on norms that were passed by a democratically elected body and/or in a direct democratic process. That certain persons are denied access to public space can then be said to conform to the will of the people. This is perhaps the most obvious, and traditional, way of establishing the democratic legitimacy of a given measure: to trace its roots back to a law created by the democratic legislator. However, as should be clear from what has been said in the previous section, whether a measure is good or bad from the democratic point of view depends not only on what body created the respective legal norm but on a variety of factors. That state action is based on a norm passed in the ordinary legislative process (that is, in Swiss legal terminology, a 'law in the formal sense')[97] does not automatically mean that it has great democratic legitimacy. As will be explained in more detail below, for a variety of reasons, a public authority applying such a norm may have wide scope of discretion, making it difficult to claim that its action represents the will of the democratic lawmaker. On the other hand, it is not always desirable from the perspective of democracy that the legislator regulates all details in advance. Especially where the factual situation to be regulated is subject to change, it may be preferable to have open norms that can gradually be substantiated by the authorities applying the law, taking account of the different interests affected at the relevant stages.[98] In short, the democratic legitimacy of

[95] European Commission for Democracy through Law (Venice Commission), Code of Good Practice in Electoral Matters: Guidelines and Draft Explanatory Report, Opinion No. 190/2002, CDL-AD (2002) 23 rev, para. 60.

[96] *Handyside* v. *The United Kingdom*, no. 5493/72, 7 December 1976, Series A no. 24, para. 49.

[97] See Section 4.2.1.

[98] See Tschannen, *Stimmrecht und politische Verständigung* (1995), pp. 523–4.

state action cannot be reduced to the question as to the existence of an authorising norm in a law passed by the legislator.[99]

Nevertheless, that there is some basis in a law passed by the legislator is the minimum requirement that must be met so that an exclusion measure may be said to enjoy democratic legitimacy. For example, as Lord Bingham pointed out in the case of *Laporte*, described in detail in Section 4.2.3.2, if it is thought to be necessary to give the police the power to keep away people from potential sites of demonstrations, then such a change should not be effected through broad interpretation of the existing powers of the police by the courts. Rather, such an extension 'calls in the first instance for the wide consultation and inquiry and democratic consideration which should characterise the legislative process, not the more narrowly focused process of judicial decision'.[100]

Some exclusion measures fail to meet even this minimum requirement for democratic legitimacy. As explained in Section 4.2.3.2, in many instances the police have banned people from accessing parts of public space without there being an explicit legal authority for doing so. In Switzerland, the police have relied, in the absence of an explicit legal authority, on the *polizeiliche Generalklausel* to exclude people from certain parts of public space. The *polizeiliche Generalklausel* is enshrined in the Federal Constitution[101] as well as in many cantonal constitutions[102] and cantonal police acts,[103] so that it cannot be argued that police action based on it lacks any basis whatsoever in a law passed by a democratic body. Nevertheless, since that legal basis is very vague and does not expressly provide for the power of the police to ban people from public space, exclusion measures based on it certainly cannot be said to enjoy a high degree of democratic legitimacy. The same applies to exclusion measures in the United States, such as the closing off of downtown Seattle during the WTO conference, which are based on vaguely circumscribed emergency powers that allow the executive branch 'to protect the public peace and safety' or some similar formulation.[104]

99 Schindler, *Verwaltungsermessen* (2010), pp. 248–50.

100 *R (Laporte)* v. *Chief Constable of Gloucestershire Constabulary* [2006] UKHL 55, para. 52.

101 BV, Art. 36(1), sentence 3 and Art. 185(3).

102 See e.g. for the Canton of Berne: Verfassung des Kantons Bern vom 6. Juni 1993 (SR 131.212), Art. 28(1); for the Canton of Appenzell Ausserrhoden: Verfassung des Kantons Appenzell Ausserrhoden vom 30. April 1995 (SR 131.224.1), Art. 23(3).

103 See e.g. for the Canton of Zurich: Polizeigesetz vom 23. April 2007 (LS 550.1), § 9; for the Canton of Berne: Polizeigesetz vom 8. Juni 1997 (BSG 551.1), Art. 22.

104 See Section 4.2.3.2.

Finally, in the United Kingdom, the police have invoked their common-law power to prevent breaches of the peace to ban people from parts of public space. Not only is this power as vague as the respective powers in Switzerland and the United States, but it is, in addition, merely part of common law rather than an act passed by the democratic legislator. The respective British exclusion measures therefore lack any democratic legitimacy. In sum, since in all of these cases the question of whether – and, if yes, when and to what extent – the police should have the power to exclude people from public space has never been (explicitly) answered by the democratic lawmaker the respective measures fail to meet the minimum requirement for democratic legitimacy.

Other exclusion measures, in contrast, are based on laws that have been enacted through the democratic legislative process. As can be seen from Annex I, the most important norms explicitly authorising exclusion from public space are contained in laws passed by, in the case of the United Kingdom, the Westminster parliament, in the case of the United States, state parliaments or city councils and, in the case of Switzerland, parliaments at the federal, cantonal or city level or municipal assemblies. In Switzerland, laws passed by parliaments are, in addition, regularly subject to either a mandatory referendum, meaning that they must be put to a popular vote, or an optional referendum, meaning that a certain number of persons eligible to vote may ask for them to be put to a popular vote.[105] Thus, it could be argued that exclusion measures that are authorised by a law, against which no referendum has been brought or which has been approved by a majority in a popular vote, enjoy especially strong democratic legitimacy. Some of the new cantonal police acts providing for blanket exclusion powers were approved by relatively strong majorities of voters. In the Canton of Berne, for example, 64.6 per cent of voters approved the Police Act,[106] in the Canton of Zurich 74.7 per cent.[107] Similarly, ratification of the revised version of the Hooligan Concordat was supported by a strong majority of 85.5 per cent of voters in the

[105] For the federal level, see Hangartner/Kley, *Die demokratischen Rechte in Bund und Kantonen der Schweizerischen Eidgenossenschaft* (2000), pp. 375–431. For the cantonal level, see ibid., pp. 661–93.

[106] See Litscher/Grossrieder/Mösch-Payot/Schmutz, *Wegweisung aus öffentlichen Stadträumen* (2011), p. 67.

[107] Kanton Zürich, Statistisches Amt, Abstimmungsresultate, Abstimmung vom 24. Februar 2008: Referendum gegen den Beschluss des Kantonsrates vom 23. April 2007 für das Polizeigesetz, available at www.statistik.zh.ch/internet/justiz_inneres/statistik/de/wahlen_abstimmungen/abstimmungsarchiv.html.

Canton of Zurich.[108] However, since these pieces of legislation provided for numerous new measures apart from exclusion from public space and touched on a range of contentious issues, a vote for or against the respective law cannot be interpreted simply as a vote for or against granting the police a power of exclusion from public space. This is not to argue that exclusion measures would not find the approval of voters, but simply to point out that inferences about the (direct) democratic legitimacy of such measures should be approached with caution.

Even where exclusion measures are based on laws enacted in the democratic legislative process, this does not automatically mean that they enjoy strong democratic legitimacy. Where an authorising norm is drafted vaguely and broadly and thus grants those applying it a significant degree of discretion, the crucial decisions and determinations may, in practice, be entrusted more to the law-applying body than the democratic lawmaker. As explained in Section 4.3.2, such vague and open norms are characteristic of laws regulating police action, including in the context of police measures aiming at the exclusion of people from public space. The police have been given broadly defined powers to remove and keep away from public places anyone 'posing a danger to public safety and order', understood in a broad sense as including behaviours that undermine the appearance of orderliness and safety of these places; those 'causing harassment or distress to others' can equally be banned from accessing parts of public space; and very vaguely defined forms of behaviour in public places, such as 'loitering', have been prohibited and thus entail exclusion.[109] By using such vague and open clauses, the legislator refers to the moral ideas and value judgments about acceptable forms of behaviour of an anonymous (presumed) majority that are not the result of public deliberation and have not been approved in a proper democratic process. It is then left to those applying the respective norms, that is, the executive branch or, in the case of the British IPNAs and CBOs, a (not democratically elected) judiciary, to speculate about the feelings of that 'majority', to define what amounts to 'posing a danger to public order', to determine what may be seen as 'causing harassment or distress to others'. This is not to say that it is

[108] Kanton Zürich, Statistisches Amt, Abstimmungsresultate, Abstimmung vom 9. Juni 2013: Gesetz über den Beitritt zum Konkordat über Massnahmen gegen Gewalt anlässlich von Sportveranstaltungen (Änderung vom 5. November 2012), available at www.statistik.zh.ch/internet/justiz_inneres/statistik/de/wahlen_abstimmungen/abstimmungsarchiv.html.

[109] Section 4.3.2.1.

necessarily wrong for the legislator to employ open and vague norms: as was explained in Section 4.3.2, when it comes to the regulation of police action, the use of such clauses is – at least to some extent – unavoidable. However, it should then also be acknowledged that the democratic legitimacy of exclusion measures that are based on such norms is rather limited.

This democratic deficit is perhaps most striking with the 'two-step' or 'hybrid prohibitions' such as the British ASBOs, IPNAs and CBOs. As has been pointed out in Section 4.4.1, these orders allow courts to prohibit a person from engaging in forms of behaviour that are normally perfectly legal on the mere basis that this person has acted 'in an anti-social manner'. They thus effectively involve a delegation of powers of criminalisation from parliament to the judiciary, leaving citizens with reduced opportunities to voice objections through democratic channels.[110] In fact, courts can criminalise, and indeed already have criminalised, behaviours that parliament explicitly did not want to make illegal.[111] As Peter Ramsay has sharply stated, such 'a power of unelected judges, responding to the initiative of local authority officials, to limit the basic civil rights of individual citizens on the basis of a discretionary evaluation of those citizens' disposition towards each other's feelings of security [...] is on its face inconsistent with the rule of general laws that has characterised the civilization known as representative democracy'.[112]

In sum, the democratic legitimacy of exclusion measures depends on a number of factors and is in many instances not particularly strong. In addition, as will be pointed out in the following section, by altering the conditions of access to public space, such measures may negatively affect the very conditions of democracy in that they undermine its liberal and its deliberative character. This is a further reason to conclude that the democratic legitimacy of exclusion measures, understood in a comprehensive way as referring to all different elements of democracy taken together, is rather weak.

7.3 The consequences of exclusion measures for democracy

Even when exclusion measures can be said to truly reflect the will of the majority, this does not necessarily mean that they are desirable

110 Simester/von Hirsch, 'Regulating Offensive Conduct through Two-Step Prohibitions' (2006), 180.

111 Ibid., 191.

112 Ramsay, 'Substantively Uncivilized ASBOs' (2010), 763. See also Ramsay, *The Insecurity State* (2012), pp. 223–5.

from the democratic point of view. Even a measure that represents the majority will of the people may, in the long term, be detrimental to democracy because it undermines the conditions that are necessary for it to operate successfully.[113] As will be explained in more detail below, these conditions of democracy are linked to its liberal and deliberative aspects described above. The liberal element of democracy implies that there must be effective protection of individual liberties from majority rule, as the main objective of democracy is, after all, facilitation of individual self-determination. The deliberative element of democracy implies that all members of a political community must have equal opportunities to participate, and therefore also to be present, in public life.

Both of these conditions of democracy, in turn, are heavily dependent on the availability and free accessibility of public space. Certain liberties, such as the freedoms of expression and assembly, can only be meaningfully exercised in public space, while most others are, at the very least, considerably facilitated by the availability of public space as a forum of communication and exchange. Likewise, public space as the material part of the public sphere represents a central arena of discursive interaction: it offers all citizens equal opportunities of physically 'coming together as a public' to deliberate about their common affairs.[114]

Democracy is thus closely interlinked with public space.[115] It is no coincidence that one of the earliest forms of publicly accessible space, the agora in ancient Athens, where up to 6,000 people gathered to discuss public affairs and conduct legal disputes,[116] today stands as a symbol of the origins of the democratic tradition.[117] Similarly, the *Landsgemeinde* (that is, the assembly of eligible citizens in a public place for purposes of voting and electing) as it emerged in Switzerland in the late Middle Ages and still exists today in two cantons is often characterised as the very embodiment of Swiss (direct) democracy.[118] As John R. Parkinson has astutely observed, contemporary theorists of the public sphere often fail to appreciate the degree to which democratic activities (still) depend on

[113] For a comprehensive treatment of the conditions of democracy, see Cohen, *Democracy* (1971), pp. 101–202.

[114] Habermas, *Strukturwandel der Öffentlichkeit* (1990), p. 86. See Section 2.1.5.

[115] Parkinson, *Democracy and Public Space* (2012), especially pp. 71–89.

[116] See Sennett, *Flesh and Stone* (1994), pp. 52–8.

[117] Kohler/Thürer, 'Der Liberale und der öffentliche Raum' (2005), 133.

[118] See Helg, *Die schweizerischen Landsgemeinden* (2007); Adler, *Die Entstehung der direkten Demokratie* (2006); Möckli, *Die schweizerischen Landsgemeinde-Demokratien* (1986); Carlen, *Die Landsgemeinde in der Schweiz* (1976).

being 'grounded' in actual physical space.[119] So that democracy can be realised and flourish, it must be possible for people to exercise their political and civil rights in public space (Section 7.3.1) and, perhaps less obviously but equally fundamentally, simply to be present in public space (Section 7.3.2). By changing the terms of access to public space, exclusion measures may therefore also undermine the conditions of democracy.

7.3.1 *Exercise of political and civil rights in public space and democracy*

The more obvious way in which exclusion from public space may harm democracy is by preventing political rights, such as the right to vote or the right to collect signatures, or civil rights, such as the right to freedom of expression or the right to freedom of assembly, from being exercised.

That exclusion measures interfere with political rights understood in the narrow sense as rights of direct participation in the political process is rather rare, but there may be (and there have been) such instances. Thus, people who are subject to a complete ban of accessing certain areas may thereby be prevented from collecting signatures in these areas or even from casting their vote because the ballot box is situated there. Similarly, juvenile night curfews may prevent those youths who are already eligible to vote from attending and thus voting in, for example, city council meetings or caucuses.[120]

What is in practice of more importance is that exclusion measures often interfere with civil rights by preventing political activities in public space such as protest, leafleting or demonstrations. As explained in Section 3.3.3, in the case of numerous exclusion measures, such prevention of political activities is the very reason for their adoption.

It is widely recognised in the literature on democratic theory that respect for and effective protection of civil rights, foremost among them the rights to freedom of expression and freedom of assembly, are necessary conditions of democracy.[121] Empirical research seems to confirm that the realisation of democracy depends on the effective protection

119 Parkinson, *Democracy and Public Space* (2012), p. 24.

120 See *Maquoketa* v. *Russell*, 484 N.W.2d 179, 185 (Iowa 1992).

121 E.g. Sunstein, *Democracy and the Problem of Free Speech* (1995); Müller, *Demokratische Gerechtigkeit* (1993), pp. 175–7; Habermas, *Strukturwandel der Öffentlichkeit* (1990), pp. 326–33; Auer, 'Problèmes fondamentaux de la démocratie suisse' (1984), 40–2; Cohen, *Democracy* (1971), p. 122; Bäumlin, *Die rechtsstaatliche Demokratie* (1954), pp. 104–12.

of these freedoms.[122] Not only from a liberal perspective but also from a perspective that emphasises the deliberative aspects of democracy, the eminent importance of rights that protect the free expression and exchange of ideas and information, including in public places, for the functioning of democracy is obvious. Through expressive acts in public, such as marches, demonstrations, vigils or leafleting, the attention of a great number and wide variety of fellow citizens can be drawn to a particular issue, idea or argument.[123]

This link between the protection of fundamental rights, in particular the freedoms of expression and assembly, and democracy has been confirmed by international human rights bodies as well as the highest courts of the three states under consideration. The European Court of Human Rights characterises freedom of expression as 'one of the essential foundations of [a democratic] society' and 'one of the basic conditions for its progress' and thus attaches central importance to it.[124] Freedom of assembly has been equally described as a foundational element of a democratic society by the Strasbourg institutions.[125] The link between these freedoms and democracy has, accordingly, also been emphasised by English courts. Lord Steyn, for example, has described freedom of expression as 'the lifeblood of democracy',[126] while freedom of assembly is according to Lord Hope 'essential to the proper functioning of a modern democracy'.[127] In Switzerland, the Federal Supreme Court has pointed out that freedom of expression is the foundation of any democratic state. According to the court, this freedom is indispensable to the full exercise of democracy and therefore deserves to be given 'a privileged treatment' by the authorities.[128] Just as the Strasbourg institutions, the Federal Supreme Court has also emphasised the crucial importance of the freedom of assembly for a democratic society.[129] According to the court, it is part of Swiss democracy that political events, including sometimes larger ones, are held on public ground.[130] As courts in the other jurisdictions, US courts have

122 Schmidt, *Demokratietheorien* (2010), pp. 381–6, 419.

123 Müller, *Demokratische Gerechtigkeit* (1993), p. 176.

124 *Handyside* v. *The United Kingdom*, no. 5493/72, 7 December 1976, Series A no. 24, para. 49.

125 *Güneri et autres c. Turquie*, nos 42853/98; 43609/98; 44291/98, 12 July 2005, para. 76 (only available in French); *Rassemblement jurassien & Unité jurasienne* v. *Switzerland*, no. 8191/78, admissibility decision of 10 October 1979, 17 DR 93, p. 119.

126 *R* v. *Secretary of State for the Home Department, ex parte Simms* [2000] 2 AC 115, 126.

127 *R. (Countryside Alliance)* v. *Her Majesty's Attorney General* [2007] UKHL 52, para. 56.

128 BGE 96 I 586, 592 (1970). See Jaag, '"Preferred Freedoms"' (1996), 367–8.

129 BGE 96 I 219, 223–4 (1970).

130 BGE 107 Ia 64, 69 (1981).

highlighted the crucial role that freedom of expression plays in a democratic society. The Supreme Court, for example, has proclaimed 'that freedom to think as you will and to speak as you think are means indispensable to the discovery and spread of political truth', 'that, without free speech and assembly, discussion would be futile' and 'that public discussion is a political duty'.[131] Therefore, according to the court, this freedom enjoys 'a preferred position'.[132]

Exclusion from public space has been used in two main ways to restrict political speech and protest. First, special zones have been created where protest is severely restricted or even completely prohibited. These zones include, for example, in Switzerland and the United Kingdom, the squares in front of the respective national parliament buildings and, in the United States, specified areas around abortion clinics.[133] Second, in all three states at issue policing strategies have been introduced in recent years that aim at keeping demonstrators away from potential sites of protest by either denying them access to these sites and the surrounding areas, which may extend to the whole downtown area of a city or the entire territory of a municipality, or containing them in a small cordoned-off area ('kettling').[134]

As explained above, many of these measures are incompatible with guarantees of fundamental rights.[135] In this sense, they can be said to undermine the *liberal* aspect of democracy. Beyond this, these exclusion measures are also problematic with regard to their effects on the *deliberative* element of democracy. For centuries, vital parts of political discourse have always taken place on public ground. As the US Supreme Court observed in its famous statement in *Hague* v. *CIO*, streets and parks, 'time out of mind, have been used for purposes of assembly, communicating thoughts between citizens, and discussing public questions'.[136] As no other forum, public streets and squares support crucial characteristics of the non-coercive, symmetrical 'ideal speech situation' (*ideale Sprechsituation*) in the sense of Habermas[137] and Robert Alexy:[138] immediacy of participation, reality of the experience for a maximum number of

[131] *Whitney* v. *California*, 274 U.S. 357, 375 (1927) (Brandeis, J., concurring).
[132] *Murdock* v. *Pennsylvania*, 319 U.S. 105, 115 (1943). [133] See Section 3.3.3.1.
[134] See Section 3.3.3.2. [135] See Sections 5.3.1.3, 5.3.2.2 and 6.2.3.
[136] *Hague* v. *CIO*, 307 U.S. 496, 515 (1939).
[137] See especially Habermas, *Philosophische Texte* (2009), pp. 259–69. For a useful summary of Habermas' concept of the 'ideal speech situation', see Alexy, *Theorie der juristischen Argumentation* (1996), pp. 155–61.
[138] Alexy, *Theorie der juristischen Argumentation* (1996), pp. 238–42.

people, autonomy due to limited external (state or social) control.[139] For smaller political groups who have only limited access (or no access at all) to other public fora such as the mass media, the holding of protest activities in public places such as streets and squares may be the only effective way of expressing their views, participating in the public exchange of arguments and influencing the democratic decision-making process.[140] The Swiss Federal Supreme Court was therefore correct to emphasise that minorities who cannot make themselves sufficiently heard through the existing democratic channels and who lack the means to reach the broad public are especially reliant on the possibility to hold demonstrations in public places in order to draw public attention to an issue.[141]

This central function played in a democracy by political protest in public space may be inhibited or even disabled by exclusion measures. Since location is crucial to political protest, protest can be silenced not only by prohibiting it but also by denying (potential) protesters access to certain areas.[142] From the perspective of the deliberative aspect of democracy, protest activities against a high-level international meeting, for example, are meaningless unless they can take place in the vicinity of the meeting site and are thus visible to those attending the meeting and the media present there. Similarly, public accessibility of parliament buildings, as well as their surroundings, is a hallmark of a democracy: in a democratic state, parliamentarians should not be insulated from the public.[143] Yet, for security reasons, in the last decade or so access to parliament buildings has been restricted all over the world, including in the United States.[144] In the United Kingdom and Switzerland, protest in the areas surrounding the respective parliament buildings has been subject to severe limitations.[145] Thus, '[w]here once assembly buildings symbolized openness and accessibility, most are now protected by heavy perimeter security'.[146] Where, as with the partial ban on protest on the Bundesplatz in Berne, such prohibitions are explained on the basis that parliamentarians, once elected, must be allowed 'to deliberate in freedom and without pressure',[147] this reflects an overly narrow

139 See Tschannen, *Stimmrecht und politische Verständigung* (1995), pp. 433–4.
140 Müller/Schefer, *Grundrechte in der Schweiz* (2008), p. 571; Saxer, *Die Grundrechte und die Benutzung öffentlicher Strassen* (1988), pp. 85, 154–5.
141 BGE 100 Ia 392, 400 (1974). 142 See Section 5.2.6.2.
143 Parkinson, *Democracy and Public Space* (2012), pp. 122–72. 144 Ibid., pp. 133–40.
145 See Section 3.3.3.1. 146 Parkinson, *Democracy and Public Space* (2012), p. 140.
147 Votum Laubacher Otto, Amtliches Bulletin Nationalrat 2007, p. 635 ('Ziel dieses Verbotes ist es, den eidgenössischen Räten, den gewählten Vertretern des Souveräns, die Möglichkeit zu geben, in aller Freiheit und ohne Druck zu tagen.').

understanding of democracy. Election of parliament every four years is not the only channel through which the will of the people may be expressed. Instead (deliberative) democracy presupposes a constant exchange of arguments among as many members of the community as possible.

Thus, citizens should not be prevented from expressing and exchanging their views, including to/with parliamentarians, but, on the contrary, should be encouraged to do so. In contrast, where, as with the 'buffer zones' around abortion clinics in the United States, exclusion measures are narrowly defined and limited to what is strictly required to achieve their objectives and still allow protesters to make their point in an effective manner, they are much less problematic from the perspective of democracy.

7.3.2 *Mere presence in public space and democracy*

In addition to their rather obvious impact on democracy through restricting the exercise of civil and political rights in public space, exclusion measures may undermine the conditions of democracy also in a less obvious, but perhaps even more fundamental way. As has been pointed out in Chapter 3, with the rise and extension of exclusion measures, ever larger sections of the population are banned from simply being in ever larger parts of public space for ever longer periods of time. Not only criminal behaviour but also numerous forms of conduct that, over the last few years, have come to be described as 'anti-social' may entail exclusion from public space. This development may undermine several conditions of democracy that, taking up Carl Cohen's terminology, may be called 'psychological conditions' of democracy: tolerance, empathy and the sense of 'we' within a heterogeneous community that are necessary for a democracy to operate.[148]

7.3.2.1 The 'psychological conditions' of democracy

Cohen has argued that there are a number of 'psychological conditions' of democracy: 'traits of character and habits of mind that members of a community must possess if they are to make democracy work'.[149] According to Cohen, one – and perhaps the most important – of these conditions is tolerance.[150] The notion of tolerance reaches back to ancient times. However, it was only in the Age of Enlightenment that

[148] Cohen, *Democracy* (1971), p. 170. [149] Ibid. [150] Ibid., pp. 184–7.

the idea that tolerance constitutes a civic virtue (rather than merely a duty or measure imposed by some authority) developed.[151] Tolerance now came to be seen as a necessary condition of liberal democracy and thus, together with the rise of liberalism, equally rose in prominence.[152] Today, it is widely acknowledged in academic writing,[153] as well as in the case law of the European Court of Human Rights,[154] that a democratic society cannot exist without tolerance. In particular, since heterogeneity and otherness are beneficial, indeed essential, for democracy,[155] citizens of a democracy must be tolerant of non-conforming behaviour. Already John Stuart Mill argued that 'the mere example of non-conformity, the mere refusal to bend the knee to custom, is itself a service'[156] and Cohen has observed that '[w]here the citizens are not disposed to tolerate non-conformity, participation in government may be wide, but it is likely to be superficial'.[157] The availability and general accessibility of public streets, squares, parks and so on is crucial for the development of tolerance. It is in public space that we become accustomed to meeting strangers and learn to find ways to accommodate living with them.[158] A social order in which 'enforced exposure to alternative perspectives'[159] in public is part of daily life nurtures tolerance.

Furthermore, democracy presupposes empathy. The deliberative element of democracy requires that all participants in a discourse put themselves in the position of those who will be affected by the action or norm under discussion.[160] Thus, although members of a democratic society must not agree with each other, they must be willing and able, in spite of potential social or cultural differences, to adopt the perspective of their fellow citizens, to comprehend their situation, to feel for them, to empathise with them.[161] However, one can only empathise with others if

151 Frenzel, 'Das Dilemma einer Idee' (1974).

152 Ibid., 15–17; Biedenkopf, 'Toleranz in der Demokratie' (1974), 163–4.

153 E.g. Haller/Kölz/Gächter, *Allgemeines Staatsrecht* (2013), pp. 71–2; Dreier, 'Der freiheitliche Verfassungsstaat als riskante Ordnung' (2010), 37–8; Walzer, *On Toleration* (1997); Biedenkopf, 'Toleranz in der Demokratie' (1974); von Oertzen, 'Die Grundlagen der Demokratie' (1974).

154 *Handyside* v. *The United Kingdom*, no. 5493/72, 7 December 1976, Series A no. 24, para. 49.

155 See Sections 7.1.2 and 7.1.3.

156 Mill, *On Liberty and Other Essays* (1991), p. 74.

157 Cohen, *Democracy* (1971), p. 184.

158 Jacobs, *The Death and Life of Great American Cities* (1974), pp. 66–84.

159 Phillips, 'Pluralism, Solidarity, and Change' (1994), 249.

160 Habermas, *Faktizität und Geltung* (1992), p. 564; Habermas, *Erläuterungen zur Diskursethik* (1991), pp. 153–4, 157. See also Müller, *Demokratische Gerechtigkeit* (1993), p. 58.

161 Müller, *Demokratische Gerechtigkeit* (1993), p. 67.

one knows they exist and one has, at the very least, a rough idea of the situation they are in. It is impossible to feel empathy with people one never encounters in one way or the other (although not necessarily in a physical sense). It is in the public sphere – and above all in physical public space – that it is possible for all sorts of people, including members of marginal groups, to become visible, to be represented. This, in turn, allows the other members of the community to develop empathy with them. As Parkinson has put it, 'spaces in which one can encounter the *demos* in all its variety have an important democratic function – they help us see and recognize others and make us more willing to take their right to make claims on us seriously when we encounter them in political debate'.[162]

Beyond tolerance and empathy, democracy also requires what Ernst-Wolfgang Böckenförde has called the social-psychological condition of a '*gemeinsames Wir-Bewusstsein*', that is, a shared consciousness of 'we'.[163] 'Strong democracy', Benjamin Barber has argued, 'mandates a permanent confrontation between the *me* as citizen and the "Other" as citizen, forcing *us* to think in common and act in common'.[164] People can only develop such a 'sense of being mutually affected'[165] if there is a minimum of social integration. Again, it is in public space that it is possible to make the everyday encounters that allow for the development of at least a minimal degree of social solidarity, a basic sense of 'we'.[166]

In addition to fostering tolerance, empathy and a sense of 'we', encounters in public space make visible the consequences of political developments, including those that are democratically legitimised.[167] When we meet, for example, beggars, homeless people or drug addicts in a public street, we cannot fail to acknowledge the existence of economic and social problems such as poverty, homelessness or addiction. It is only in public space that we are forced to confront these problems in such immediacy. Thus, encounters in public space also have a deeply political dimension: they force citizens to face the impacts of developments to which they, as members of a democratic society, contribute themselves.[168]

162 Parkinson, *Democracy and Public Space* (2012), p. 67.
163 Böckenförde, 'Demokratie als Verfassungsprinzip' (2004), 473.
164 Barber, *Strong Democracy* (1984), p. 153 (original emphases).
165 Parkinson, *Democracy and Public Space* (2012), p. 47.
166 Siehr, *Das Recht am öffentlichen Raum* (2016), pp. 215–25.
167 Kohn, *Brave New Neighborhoods* (2004), p. 8; Gusy, 'Polizei und private Sicherheitsdienste im öffentlichen Raum' (2001), 351.
168 Ibid.

Democracy thus depends on spaces where it is possible to encounter – sometimes also unexpectedly – a diversity of persons and situations, that is, spaces that are frequented by the general public. As explained above, already early political thinkers such as Burke, Mill and the founding fathers of the United States understood that democracy inevitably had to be deliberative and thus depended on a heterogeneous citizenry who were in contact with each other. In the words of Mill: 'It is hardly possible to overstate the value, in the present low state of human improvement, of placing human beings in contact with other persons dissimilar to themselves, and with modes of thought and action unlike those with which they are familiar.'[169]

Sociologists and urbanists have observed that random contact with strangers on public streets and squares is important for people's personal growth as well as for social integration. Richard Sennett has argued that city life should be organised in a way that ensures that people encounter, face-to-face, dissimilar people.[170] It is only through such processes of encountering the unknown and having to deal with the dissimilarities that, according to Sennett, people grow.[171] Civility, which for him involves treating others as if they were strangers and forging a social bond upon that distance, is best developed in urban public spaces. In fact, he points out, the terms 'civility' and 'city' have a common root etymologically. For, '[t]he city is that human settlement in which strangers are most likely to meet.'[172] In her famous book *The Death and Life of Great American Cities*, Jane Jacobs has similarly described the social benefits of random contacts in public space,[173] pointing out that their sum 'is a feeling for the public identity of people, a web of public respect and trust'[174] and 'the small change from which a city's wealth of public life may grow'.[175] The German sociologists Hartmut Häussermann and Wilhelm Heitmeyer have, accordingly, both described the city as an '*Integrationsmaschine*' ('machine for integration').[176]

Habermas equally understands communication among strangers in the public sphere to be a central mechanism to achieve social

[169] Mill, 'Principles of Political Economy' (1963–1991), 594.
[170] Sennett, *The Uses of Disorder* (1992), especially pp. 137–9.
[171] Sennett, *The Fall of Public Man* (1992), p. 295; Sennett, *The Uses of Disorder* (1992).
[172] Sennett, *The Fall of Public Man* (1992), p. 264.
[173] Jacobs, *The Death and Life of Great American Cities* (1974), pp. 66–84.
[174] Ibid., p. 67. [175] Ibid., p. 83.
[176] Heitmeyer, 'Versagt die "Integrationsmaschine" Stadt?' (1998); Häussermann, 'Die Stadt und die Stadtsoziologie' (1995), 96.

integration.[177] However, as already pointed out in Section 2.1.5, his concept of the public sphere remains distinctly aspatial and abstract. Yet it is in actual, physical public space that encounters with others develop their fullest force and the idea of deliberative democracy can most efficiently be turned into practice. It was Hannah Arendt who most clearly elaborated this function of public space as the physical context in which democratic politics can arise. For Arendt, democracy is only possible where individuals share an actual common world in which public concerns can emerge and be debated.[178] People must be able to see each other and to talk to each other in the public realm, so that differences and commonalities can become apparent.[179] Since plurality is a human condition and *the* condition of all political life,[180] it is also 'the condition *sine qua non* for that space of appearance which is the public realm': public space must necessarily be a heterogeneous space.[181] Like the founding fathers of the United States such as Thomas Jefferson, whom she approvingly quotes, Arendt believed that it is this shared, public space that makes it possible that distinct individuals can become a political community.[182] The social cohesion of a political community is not the result of some set of common values but of the world that the members of this community establish in common: the spaces they inhabit together, the practices they share.[183] An important consequence of Arendt's understanding of politics as inherently linked to public space is that one cannot be part of politics without 'appearing in public', that is, without in some sense being present in public space.[184] Accordingly, she finds it typical that a common element of tyrannies is the banishment of the citizens from the public realm.[185]

The crucial function that public space fulfils by providing a forum for encounter and exchange among a heterogeneous public has also been highlighted in contemporary democratic theory. If contact with others remains limited to that within the boundaries of homogenous groups, Christoph Möllers has argued, this leads to cognitive and moral narrow-

[177] See Calhoun, 'Information Technology and the International Public Sphere' (2004), 246.
[178] See d'Entrèves, 'Hannah Arendt and the Idea of Citizenship' (1992), 152.
[179] Arendt, *Between Past and Future* (1961), pp. 220–1.
[180] Arendt, *The Human Condition* (1998), p. 7. [181] Ibid., p. 220.
[182] Arendt, *On Revolution* (1963), pp. 256–9.
[183] Arendt, *The Human Condition* (1998), pp. 52–3, 197–9. See also d'Entrèves, 'Hannah Arendt and the Idea of Citizenship' (1992), 153.
[184] Arendt, *The Human Condition* (1998), pp. 50, 198. See also d'Entrèves, 'Hannah Arendt and the Idea of Citizenship' (1992), 153.
[185] Arendt, *The Human Condition* (1998), pp. 221, 224.

mindedness. Democracy needs 'spaces of social generality' (*Räume gesellschaftlicher Allgemeinheit*), '[p]laces where people of different age, sex and social origin meet'.[186] To establish and to frequent such places is, according to Möllers, a democratic form of self-education to democracy.[187] Similarly, Iris Marion Young has maintained that democratic politics depends on 'a heterogeneous public, in which persons stand forth with their differences acknowledged and respected, though perhaps not completely understood, by others'.[188] This, in turn, necessitates the existence of spaces and forums to which everyone has access, places 'where people stand and sit together, interact and mingle, or simply witness one another'[189] and where one will thus 'encounter and hear from those who are different, whose social perspectives, experience and affiliations are different'.[190] '[N]o persons, actions, or aspects of a person's life', Young concludes, 'should be forced into privacy.'[191]

But it is probably the work of Cass Sunstein that demonstrates most thoroughly the central role that a heterogeneous public and exposure to a wide variety of people and views play in a democracy.[192] Importantly, Sunstein makes it clear that not only exposures to other people's views and arguments are valuable to democracy but also exposures to *experiences*, such as, simply, encountering people from different social classes: 'Public forums make it more likely that people will not be able to wall themselves off from their fellow citizens. People will get a glimpse, at least, of the lives of others.'[193] Similarly, not only exposures that are chosen or foreseeable are beneficial but also those that are *unplanned* and even those that are *unwanted*: those that one would avoid if one could, such as encounters with homeless people asking for money.[194] Such exposures are important for democracy because, first, they promote mutual understanding among citizens and safeguard against fragmentation of society into separate groups whose members only interact with members of the same group.[195] Second, they ensure that citizens share a range of common experiences, which provide a form of social glue and a sense of a common enterprise. This, in turn, will facilitate efforts to solve shared problems.[196] As explained in Section 7.1.2, already the

[186] Möllers, *Demokratie* (2008), p. 37 ('Orte, an denen sich Personen verschiedenen Alters, Geschlechts, sozialer Herkunft begegnen, sind wichtig und selten.').
[187] Ibid. [188] Young, *Justice and the Politics of Difference* (1990), p. 119.
[189] Ibid., p. 240. [190] Ibid., p. 119. [191] Ibid., p. 120.
[192] Sunstein, *republic.com* (2001); Sunstein, *The Partial Constitution* (1993), pp. 23–4.
[193] Sunstein, *republic.com* (2001), pp. 33–4. [194] Ibid., pp. 32–4.
[195] Ibid., pp. 8–9, 23–88. [196] Ibid., pp. 9, 23–50, 89–103.

US founding fathers, which Sunstein quotes at length,[197] understood that a heterogeneous society needs a system of deliberative democracy which ensures that citizens meet, and interact with, each other.

7.3.2.2 Exclusion measures and the 'psychological conditions' of democracy

The function of public space as a forum for encounter and exchange among a heterogeneous public contrasts starkly with that of private spaces (such as gated communities) and semi-public spaces (such as shopping centres). Private and semi-public spaces are designed to produce a sensation of similarity, a '"we" feeling' within a *homogeneous* community.[198] As a consequence, they reduce the kinds of otherness that are found to be bearable: in these forms of space, the presence of different types of people becomes a subject of concern.[199] The less one is confronted with others, however, the less one understands what their behaviour signifies and the more difficult it becomes to tolerate them and empathise with them: spatial separation leads to alienation.[200] The trend towards the privatisation of public space may thus undermine the development of people's capacity to accommodate living with others, the development of the 'public sense of self' on which democracy relies.[201] Ultimately, the privatisation of public space may result in people withdrawing from actual, active participation in community life.[202]

As explained above, exclusion measures may be understood as one aspect of the broader process of privatisation of public space: it is one element of the attempt to adapt public space to the new ideal of semi-public space with its controlled, safe and clean environment.[203] Through exclusion from public space, the number of unplanned or unwanted encounters with others can be reduced, the risk of potentially uncomfortable experiences minimised. By eliminating 'all that might convey a feeling of difference',[204] public space can be made to produce a sensation of similarity within a homogeneous community similar to

[197] Ibid., pp. 37–43, 105, 155, 200–1.
[198] Sennett, *The Uses of Disorder* (1992), pp. 39, 68–73.
[199] Frug, 'The Emergence of Private Cities in America' (1999), 585; Heitmeyer, 'Versagt die "Integrationsmaschine" Stadt?' (1998), 452; Sennett, *The Uses of Disorder* (1992), pp. 27–49.
[200] Wehrheim, *Die überwachte Stadt* (2012), p. 236; Heitmeyer, 'Versagt die "Integrationsmaschine" Stadt?' (1998).
[201] Frug, 'The Emergence of Private Cities in America' (1999), 586.
[202] Sennett, *The Uses of Disorder* (1992), pp. 41–2, 82.
[203] See Sections 2.5.1 and 3.2.
[204] Sennett, *The Uses of Disorder* (1992), p. 36.

that experienced in private and semi-public spaces. This trend towards the elimination of the risk of encounters and experiences that are seen as not desirable may be reflective of a parallel trend in the media where new technologies have made it possible for consumers to read, see and hear exactly what they want, to 'filter out' to an unprecedented degree all information and views that are seen as uninteresting or undesirable.[205]

This tendency to protect users of public space from encounters they may find undesirable poses similar problems for democracy as the filtering possibilities offered by new media technologies. As explained above, Sunstein has demonstrated that it is crucial for democracy that citizens are exposed to unplanned, random encounters and to information they would not have chosen in advance, as well as that they all share a range of common experiences. The consequence of exclusion measures, however, is that ever larger sections of the population (in particular all those alleged to be a source of anti-social behaviour) disappear from the most frequented parts of public space, namely inner city areas. Similar to prisoners, they become invisible to society, even though they have not committed a crime and, indeed, are not even suspected of having committed one.

By becoming invisible in public space, these groups cease to be represented in our images of the polity. Without appearing in public, without being seen and heard by others, Arendt argued, one cannot be part of politics.[206] Social groups that are not visible are not included in our 'mental map' of 'the public' and are thus not recognised as proper members of the *demos*. For example, one of the reasons why disabled people are socially and politically marginalised is that most of us rarely encounter a disabled person in public and, as a consequence, their needs are not sufficiently taken into account in public decision-making.[207] Thus, to be represented, people must make themselves visible and recognised, be it in public space, be it in the non-physical part of the public sphere.

Yet those who are most often subject to exclusion measures belong to exactly those groups of people that either do not have any access to the virtual dimension of the public sphere at all or, at the very least, lack the means to make efficient use of it: marginalised groups such as the homeless, drug addicts, alcoholics, youths from disadvantaged backgrounds

[205] Sunstein, *republic.com* (2001).
[206] Arendt, *The Human Condition* (1998), pp. 50, 198.
[207] Parkinson, *Democracy and Public Space* (2012), p. 184.

and so on.[208] The only possibility for the homeless to represent themselves as members of the polity is by being present in public places.[209] Similarly, the desire to be seen, to be somehow represented in public may in many cases be exactly the reason why groups of youths linger in public places.

By having a particularly inhibitory effect on marginalised groups, exclusion measures may undermine the deliberative element of democracy. As explained before, this element of democracy requires, among other things, that everyone should have the same opportunities of effectively participating in societal discourse.[210] This implies that a democratic politics must take account of, and provide voice for, different social groups.[211] Public space, and the public sphere more generally, must be structured so as to be equally accessible for different groups and accommodating of difference: everyone must have equal opportunities of being present and visible in the public sphere. By targeting those groups that are already among the most marginalised in terms of access to the public sphere, exclusion measures run counter to this requirement.

According to Don Mitchell, exclusion from public space may, ultimately, lead to a situation in which the very legitimacy as members of the polity of those who are excluded is put in doubt. With regard to homeless people who are excluded from public space he argues that, since they cease to be represented in public, 'they are banished to a realm outside of politics because they are banished from the gathering places of the city'.[212] That exclusion from certain parts of public space amounts to complete exclusion from the democratic community is, in this generality, too strong a claim. What can be said, however, is that exclusion measures deeply affect a person's participation in, and thus also membership of, a democratic society. For it is through interaction with other members that a person's membership of their society is affirmed, both in the eyes of the person herself and those of the rest of society. The ability to interact, in turn, depends on freedom of movement and access to public space.[213]

This explains why those subject to exclusion measures often *experience* their exclusion from parts of public space as exclusion from the democratic community. In an interview, a person subject to such a measure in Seattle described its effects on him as follows: 'Just being kicked out of

[208] See Section 2.3.5. [209] Mitchell, 'The End of Public Space?' (1995), 115.
[210] See Section 7.1.3. [211] Young, *Justice and the Politics of Difference* (1990), p. 227.
[212] Mitchell, *The Right to the City* (2003), p. 141.
[213] Simester/von Hirsch, 'Regulating Offensive Conduct through Two-Step Prohibitions' (2006), 183.

a public place, it's kinda embarrassing. Not only embarrassing, but I dunno, but yeah, being kicked out of society it's like you're just no longer socially acceptable. Like you're not really a member of society.'[214] Another one characterised his reaction to the exclusion measure imposed on him as follows: 'How does it make me feel? At that particular time, two years ago, I felt like I was a noncitizen.'[215] These reactions provoked by exclusion measures in those subject to them already go a long way to demonstrating the serious implications that such measures may have for democracy.

In addition to their direct impacts on those subject to them, however, exclusion measures also entail far-reaching wider consequences. By banning large sections of the population from the most frequented parts of public space, they prevent (or least considerably reduce) the possibility of random encounters with a wide variety of fellow citizens that, as explained above, are so crucial for a democracy. When we no longer meet diverse social groups such as juveniles or beggars on street corners, we will find it harder to develop the capacity for tolerance. When we no longer encounter homeless people on the streets, we will find it harder to empathise with them. When we no longer see alcoholics in public parks, we will find it harder to acknowledge the existence of the problem of alcoholism and will be less likely to think about its reasons and ways of addressing it. In other words, exclusion from public space may undermine the tolerance, empathy and sense of a common enterprise in a heterogeneous society without which a democracy cannot exist.

7.4 Conclusion

It is important for a democracy that its public streets, squares, parks and so on are attractive. Public space can only fulfil its central functions for a democratic society described in this chapter if its members use it regularly as a forum for encounter and exchange. Citizens must be able to feel safe and at ease in public space, they should not avoid certain streets, or even whole neighbourhoods, out of a feeling of insecurity or uncertainty. However, it is highly doubtful that exclusion from public space is an appropriate means to maintain the attractiveness of public space and that it could thus be described as beneficial for democracy.

[214] Beckett/Herbert, *Banished* (2010), p. 124. [215] Ibid., p. 129.

First, the democratic legitimacy of exclusion measures is not as strong as it may appear at first sight. For some exclusion measures there is no explicit legal authority whatsoever in an act passed by the democratic lawmaker. And where explicit norms authorising exclusion from public space do exist, they are typically drafted in a way that grants those applying them a significant degree of discretion, so that the key determinations are, in reality, entrusted more to the law-applying body than the democratic law-maker.

Second, exclusion from public space may actually be detrimental to democracy because it undermines the conditions that are necessary for it to operate successfully. Whereas exclusion measures directed against criminal behaviour are largely unproblematic in this regard, those directed against political protest regularly restrict the exercise of civil and political rights on which the functioning of any democracy relies. Exclusion measures directed against anti-social behaviour, in turn, lead to the banning of large sections of the population from the most frequented parts of public space, which may have a detrimental effect on the 'psychological conditions' of democracy: the tolerance, empathy and basic sense of a common enterprise on which any democracy depends.

This is not to say, of course, that states that ban people from parts of public space are undemocratic, but merely to highlight that, in the long term, exclusion measures may have serious implications for democracy. A democratic state should not adopt measures that help citizens to wall themselves off from the opinions and concerns of their fellow citizens. Public space is one of the best practice grounds for democracy: it is here, in public space, that people learn how to confront others, how to deal and negotiate with them. Democracy benefits from the presence of members of the whole spectrum of society, including marginalised groups, in public space. Thus, the state should not try to minimise random encounters in public space but should, on the contrary, encourage them. In a democracy, access to public space must be as free and equal for everyone as possible.

At a more general level, it is questionable whether the objective of ensuring that people feel safe and at ease in public space, and thus use it widely, may be achieved primarily through state intervention, more specifically through laws enforced by the police. Given that 'public space', in its function as the central part of the public sphere, also stands symbolically for a certain form of interaction between the different members of a democratic society, it seems more likely that, to use Uwe Volkmann's words, 'the recapture of the commons' cannot be delegated to the police or other state authorities.[216] In a democracy, care for public space is, first of all, a civic responsibility.[217] Therefore, the task of maintaining public space in its function as such must by definition be approached as a common project of citizens rather than to be delegated to the state.

[216] Volkmann, 'Die Rückeroberung der Allmende' (2000).

[217] Kohler/Thürer, 'Der Liberale und der öffentliche Raum' (2005), 133. See also Section 9.2.

8

A right (of access) to public space?

That people must 'reclaim public space' is one of the most influential political slogans of the last few years. Several worldwide political movements that have emerged of late, including the 'Occupy' and the 'Reclaim the Streets' movements, have put the need to reclaim public space at the heart of their agendas. These calls for its reappropriation are a reaction to the process of fundamental transformation that public space – not least due to the proliferation of exclusion measures – has been (and still is) undergoing.

Underlying the idea that there is a need to reclaim public space is the notion that people have (or should have) a right to be in public space – and thus to occupy it, to appropriate it. Is this notion more than a political slogan? Does the law guarantee a 'right to public space' and, if yes, what exactly does this right encompass? If not, is there a need to legally guarantee such a right? These are the questions that constitute the focus of this chapter. It should be noted, however, that the chapter does not intend to provide a comprehensive treatment of these questions. Instead, it concentrates on the role of exclusion from public space in this context, exploring, in particular, whether an explicit legal guarantee of a right to public space would make a difference with regard to exclusion measures.

Drawing together some of the main arguments developed in previous parts of the book, the chapter first briefly shows how exclusion measures contribute to the decline of public space as the space of liberty, equality, tolerance and democracy and then how, as a reaction to this decline, calls for a right to public space have emerged (Section 8.1). The main part of the chapter considers whether, *de lege lata*, there is such a right to public space, be it understood in the sense of a right of access to public space, be it understood in the sense of a right to the existence of public space (Section 8.2). Finally, the chapter explores whether, *de lege ferenda*, there is a need for an explicit guarantee of the right to public space. What would be the consequences for exclusion measures if such an explicit guarantee of this right, understood in the sense of a right of access to public space, existed (Section 8.3)?

8.1 'Reclaiming public space'?

8.1.1 Exclusion measures and the decline of public space

Chapters 5 to 7 have confirmed and illustrated the proposition made at the beginning of this book[1] that liberty, equality, tolerance and democracy crucially depend on the availability of space that is accessible to everyone. Free and equal access to public space is a foundational element of any liberal democracy.

Yet public space as it was once understood is disappearing. As explained in Section 2.5, public space has recently undergone and is still undergoing a process of fundamental transformation. As a consequence of developments such as suburbanisation, the growth of private (and often gated) communities and the proliferation of semi-public space, cities are increasingly fragmented into separate enclaves and people spend less and less time in commonly shared spaces. The remaining public spaces, mostly inner-city areas, are 'upgraded' by assimilating them to the ideal of semi-public space and by subjecting them to regulations that are similar to those applicable in privately owned space ('privatisation of public space'). Furthermore, due to the new emphasis on prevention and order maintenance in the 'security society', public space is surveilled and controlled to an unprecedented degree. As a result, public space is losing its character as the space of liberty, equality, tolerance and democracy.

The adoption of exclusion measures plays a central role in this transformation of public space. By extending the power to deny people access to a given place – originally thought of as the very essence of *private* spaces – to public space, exclusion measures form an important element of the 'privatisation of public space'. In addition, by focusing on the appearance of particular spaces, allowing for the management of risks by dislocating them and conveying a strong symbolic message, they constitute a central tool in the control arsenal of the 'security society'. The preceding analysis of exclusion measures has shown that, as a key element of the process of transformation of public space, they contribute

[1] See Section 2.3.

in several ways to the decline of public space as the space of liberty, equality, tolerance and democracy.

Liberties cannot be exercised in a vacuum: 'to be free to do something, one needs a place at which to do it.'[2] Without access to public space, none of the freedoms described in Chapter 5 can be exercised in a meaningful manner. Yet ever larger sections of the population are banned from ever larger parts of public space for ever longer periods of time, often simply because they are alleged to have engaged in anti-social behaviour or because they want to protest. Exclusion measures thus undermine the character of public space as the *space of liberty*.

Public space is defined by the very fact that it is equally accessible to everyone. Equality is thus immanent to the concept of public space. Yet by specifically targeting, or disproportionately impacting on, particular groups of people (including foreign nationals, juveniles, homeless people, alcohol and drug addicts, racial or ethnic minorities and those subscribing to particular political views), exclusion measures reinforce the trend towards the fragmentation and segregation of cities. Marginalised groups are increasingly banned from inner-city areas. Exclusion measures thus undermine the character of public space as the *space of equality*.

Exclusion measures typically target forms of conduct that used to be regarded as legitimate, and therefore tolerated, but that are now said to contribute to the decline of public order or to be likely to cause harassment, distress or offence to others. Yet in public space people have to tolerate that others exercise their liberties, even if it is in a controversial, confrontational or asocial manner. By banning people from public space simply because others may regard their behaviour as offensive, exclusion measures undermine the character of public space as the *space of tolerance*.

Public space as the physical part of the public sphere is the most important arena for the exercise of those fundamental rights that are at the heart of any democratic system and a central forum for encounter and exchange among a heterogeneous public. In a democracy, all members of society must have the possibility to exercise their civil and political rights in public space as well as to simply be visible in public space, so as to be represented in our images of the polity. Exclusion measures prevent considerable sections of the population from doing so by banning them from the most frequented parts of public space. Thereby they undermine the character of public space as the *space of democracy*.

[2] Von Hirsch/Shearing, 'Exclusion from Public Space' (2000), 84.

In sum, the adoption of exclusion measures is deeply implicated in the decline of public space as the space of liberty, equality, tolerance and democracy. Exclusion measures undermine the fundamental notion that public space is freely accessible to everyone and, since space is a social product,[3] thus alter the very nature of public space. If there is no space left that is accessible to everyone, then there is no public space left – at least not in the sense this concept has traditionally been understood.

8.1.2 Reaction: claims for a right to public space

As a reaction to this transformation of public space, of which the proliferation of exclusion measures forms an important part, there have been repeated calls for 'reclaiming public space' in recent years. The 'Right to the City' (*Recht auf Stadt/droit à la ville*) movement, which originates from the United States and Latin America but has also grown in strength in Europe, has played a central role in formulating and promoting these calls.[4]

'The right to the city' is an idea coined by the French philosopher Henri Lefebvre in his book of the same name (*Le droit à la ville*), published in 1968.[5] For Lefebvre, cities were necessarily public: places of social interaction and exchange among a heterogeneous public.[6] He defined the right to the city as the right 'to urban life, to renewed centrality, to places of encounter and exchange, to life rhythms and time uses, enabling the full and complete usage of these moments and places'.[7] Thus, the right to the city 'would affirm, on the one hand, the right of users to make known their ideas on the space and time of their activities in the urban area; it would also cover the right to the use of the center, a privileged place, instead of being dispersed and stuck into ghettos'.[8]

3 See Section 2.1.1.

4 For the US 'Right to the City' movement, see the website of the Right to the City Alliance, at www.righttothecity.org. On the 'Right to the City' movement in Brazil, see Pindell, 'Finding a Right to the City' (2006). For the 'Recht auf Stadt' movement in Switzerland, see the website www.rechtaufstadt.ch.

5 Lefebvre, *Le droit à la ville* (1968/1972). An English translation can be found in Lefebvre, *Writings on Cities* (1996).

6 See Mitchell, *The Right to the City* (2003), p. 18.

7 Lefebvre, *Writings on Cities* (1996), p. 179. For the French original, see Lefebvre, *Le droit à la ville* (1968/1972), p. 146: 'Parmi ces droits en formation figure le droit à la ville (non pas à la ville ancienne mais à la ville urbaine, à la centralité rénovée, aux lieux de rencontres et d'échanges, aux rythmes de vie et emplois du temps permettant l'usage plein et entier de ces moments et lieux, etc.).'

8 Lefebvre, *Writings on Cities* (1996), p. 34.

A number of authors, most prominently among them the social theorist David Harvey, who has been a prominent figure at various World Social Forums, later took up Lefebvre's idea of a right to the city.[9] Harvey claims that the right to the city, which includes but goes beyond a right of access to urban resources,[10] is a human right, indeed, 'one of the most precious yet most neglected of our human rights'.[11] While definitions of the meaning and content of the right to the city vary widely, for many authors its very essence is the right to public space.[12] Numerous, often interlinked, social movements that have formed over the last decade or so have put the right to public space at the centre of their agendas. Apart from the 'Right to the City' movement, the 'Reclaim the Streets' and, most recently, the 'Occupy Wall Street' (or simply 'Occupy') movements have all called for a 'right to public space'[13] or a 'right to occupy public space'.[14]

While the 'right to the city' and the 'right to public space' were originally conceived primarily as slogans and political ideals,[15] there have now been some first attempts to convert them into legal standards.

In 2000, a network of municipalities called European Conference Cities for Human Rights adopted the European Charter for the Safeguarding of Human Rights in the City.[16] More than 400 European cities have since signed this European Charter and thus committed themselves to making human rights a guideline of their municipal policies.[17] Article I of the European Charter proclaims a 'right to the city', with 'the city' being defined as 'a collective space belonging to all who live in it'. Especially relevant for the present context is Article IX(3), which provides that '[t]he city offers public spaces for the organisation of open meetings and informal gatherings. It ensures free access to these spaces for everyone, provided regulations are adhered to.' At the global

9 Harvey, 'The Right to the City' (2008); Harvey, 'The Right to the City' (2003).

10 Harvey, 'The Right to the City' (2008), 23; Harvey, 'The Right to the City' (2003), 939.

11 Harvey, 'The Right to the City' (2008), 23.

12 Pizzolatto Konzen, 'The City and Its Public Spaces' (2011), 277–8.

13 See the website http://times-up.org/index.php?page=reclaim-the-streets.

14 See the website http://occupywallst.org/article/everyone-has-right-occupy-space-safely/.

15 Harvey, 'The Right to the City' (2008), 40.

16 European Charter for the Safeguarding of Human Rights in the City, approved in St. Denis on 18 May 2000, available at www.uclg-cisdp.org/sites/default/files/CISDP%20Carta%20Europea%20Sencera_baixa_3.pdf.

17 See the information on the European Charter on the website of the Institut de Drets Humans De Catalunya, at www.uclg-cisdp.org/en/right-to-the-city/european-charter.

level, various NGOs and civil society networks have elaborated, in the context of the World Social Forums, the World Charter on the Right to the City.[18] Intended 'as an aid in the process of recognition of the right to the city in the international human rights system',[19] the World Charter was adopted in 2004. Similar to the European Charter for the Safeguarding of Human Rights in the City, it proclaims in its Article I that '[e]veryone has a right to the city' and that '[t]he city is a culturally rich and diversified cultural space that belongs to all the inhabitants', while Article IX obliges cities 'to make public areas available for open meetings and informal gatherings'. In 2010, the World Federation of the umbrella organisation United Cities and Local Governments adopted the Global Charter-Agenda for Human Rights in the City.[20] This Charter-Agenda also guarantees a 'right to the city' in its first article, which, among other rights, includes the right of all city inhabitants 'to available spaces and resources to practice an active citizenship'. According to Article VII(2), every city 'ensures that all inhabitants have free access to public meeting places and facilitates the creation of such places'.

The notion of a right to the city and a related right to public space has also become increasingly popular and influential within the UN. UNESCO and UN-HABITAT both supported the drafting of the World Charter on the Right to the City.[21] In its 2010/2011 report on the state of the world's cities, UN-HABITAT recommends giving every resident the 'right to the city' in which they live and states that '[c]ities must create enabling environments that provide equal access or entitlement to, and enjoyment of, basic and public services, public spaces and all kinds of benefits and opportunities for everyone'.[22]

Proclamations of a right to the city and a right to public space remain, at the international level, primarily symbolic so far. None of the charters and other documents referred to above is legally binding. In large parts, the charters read like wish lists of often quite vaguely defined, widely diverse policies that are said to be desirable at the city level. In fact, at least in some cases, these proclamations do not even appear to be *intended* to be more than symbolic. For instance, the UN-HABITAT report expressly states that '[t]he "right to the city" must not be viewed as a new legal instrument, but instead subsumes a wide range of universally recognized

[18] World Charter on the Right to the City, adopted in Quito and Barcelona in 2004.
[19] Ibid., preambular para. 6.
[20] Global Charter-Agenda for Human Rights in the City, adopted in Florence in 2010, available at www.uclg-cisdp.org/en/right-to-the-city/world-charter-agenda.
[21] UN-HABITAT, *State of the World's Cities 2010/2011* (2008), p. 123. [22] Ibid., p. 133.

human rights into a single claim for enforcement in urban areas.'[23] In contrast, the World Charter on the Right to the City understands the 'right to the city' it proclaims as a collective right of all city inhabitants that imposes a wide range of obligations on local authorities and national governments, and it explicitly calls for 'recognition of the right to the city in the international human rights system'.[24]

At the national level, there have been efforts in a few (mainly Latin American) states to give formal recognition to the right to the city in domestic law.[25] With regard to Germany, Angelika Siehr, after a thorough review of the current transformation of public space referred to in the previous section, makes a detailed case for a constitutionally guaranteed right (of access) to public space.[26]

These calls for a 'right to the city' and a related 'right to public space' raise the question as to whether these rights should be treated as more than mere political slogans: Should they be guaranteed in law? Given the scope of this book, the remainder of the chapter will concentrate on the second, more specific of these rights, that is, the right to public space. This right may be understood in two ways: first, as a right of *access* to public space and/or, second, as a right to the *existence* of public space. Does such a right exist in the law of the United Kingdom, the United States and/or Switzerland (Section 8.2)? If not, would it be helpful to legally guarantee such a right (Section 8.3)?

8.2 *De lege lata*: is there a right to public space?

Neither international law nor the domestic law of the United Kingdom, the United States or Switzerland explicitly guarantee a right to *access* public space. This section explores whether, despite this lack of an explicit guarantee, there is nevertheless such a right in these three states. Given the decline of public space and the proliferation of semi-public space, a further question is of pressing interest: Is there a right to public space in the sense of a right to the *existence* of public space? Such a right could be understood as, first, imposing a duty on the state to provide a 'minimum amount' of space that is publicly accessible and/or, second, implying a right of access to semi-public (or even private) space. Since this book deals with measures relating to *already existing* and *'proper'*

[23] Ibid., p. 122. [24] World Charter on the Right to the City, preambular para. 6.
[25] For an overview, see UN-HABITAT, *State of the World's Cities 2010/2011* (2008), p. 124.
[26] Siehr, *Das Recht am öffentlichen Raum* (2016).

(rather than semi-) public space, a thorough examination of the right to the existence (and thus provision) of public space is beyond its scope. This issue will therefore only be dealt with very summarily.

8.2.1 United Kingdom

Once a piece of land has been dedicated to public use or dedication to public use can be presumed because of long uninterrupted use by the public,[27] then every member of the public has a corresponding right of access to this piece of land. The most important part of public space, the highways, for example, are defined in English common law as ways 'over which there exists a public right of passage, that is to say a right for all Her Majesty's subjects at all seasons of the year freely and at their will to pass and repass without let or hindrance'.[28] This right encompasses use of the highway 'for such reasonable and usual activities as are consistent with the general public's primary right to use the highway for purposes of passage and repassage'.[29] 'Reasonable use' of the highway is not limited to a narrow traffic function but understood broadly; it includes activities that would be qualified as 'extended common use' (*gesteigerter Gemeingebrauch/usage accru*) in Swiss law, such as marches, processions or groups of people standing in the street and singing.[30] Even the holding of public assemblies may be covered. Dicey famously claimed that, since each individual has a right 'to go where he pleases' and 'to walk down the High Street or to go on to a common', 10,000 individuals in common have the right to hold a public meeting.[31] While this conclusion may be too absolute, the House of Lords has ruled that, at least as long as they are peaceful and non-obstructive, demonstrations fall within the scope of the right to reasonable use of the highways.[32]

Unlike in Switzerland, the state does not have comprehensive sovereignty over all public ground. Instead, public entities have the same private-law rights with regard to the land they own as private landowners do. They only have sovereign powers to the limited extent that such powers have been created through legislation.[33] Thus, whereas in Switzerland the

[27] See Section 2.1.1.3. [28] *Halsbury's Laws of England* (1988–2008), Vol. 21, para. 1.
[29] *DPP* v. *Jones (Margaret)*, [1999] 2 AC 240, 255 (Lord Irvine).
[30] Ibid., 280–1 (Lord Clyde).
[31] Dicey, *An Introduction to the Study of the Law of the Constitution* (1959), p. 271.
[32] *DPP* v. *Jones (Margaret)*, [1999] 2 AC 240.
[33] See e.g. Greater London Authority Act 1999, ss 383–5 (with regard to Trafalgar Square and Parliament Square).

focus is still very much on the fact that streets are a domain for the exercise of sovereign state power,[34] in the United Kingdom the public nature of streets derives exclusively from the fact that the rights of the respective landowner – be it a private party, be it a public entity – are subject to the general public's right to access and use them.[35] This right to access public space belongs to 'any member of the public'.[36] The corresponding obligation on the state is understood as a negative obligation not to interfere with the right rather than a positive duty to make available the relevant part of public space. In keeping with the common law system of 'residual liberty', according to which people are free to do whatever they please unless it is expressly prohibited by law,[37] the right to access public space may be exercised to the extent there is no conflict with any explicit prohibitions, such as those criminalising certain forms of trespass.[38] In addition, since a wide range of activities in public space fall within the scope of the rights of the ECHR,[39] the right of access to public space is today also protected by the positive guarantees of the Convention, although to a more limited extent than under common law.

This right of access to public space only relates to places that have already been made accessible to the public and does not imply a right to the *existence* of public space: there are no legal authorities suggesting that it implies a duty of the state to make available to the public certain places not yet open to the public or to provide some 'minimum amount' of public space. Nor is there a right of access to semi-public space. As explained in Section 2.5.1, the Court of Appeal has held that a private shopping centre owner is to be treated like any private property owner and thus has an unchallengeable discretion to deny permission to enter the centre as part of his trespass powers. Members of the public do not have a right to enter and use shopping centres.[40] Similarly, in *Appleby* v. *United Kingdom*, a case concerning a privately owned town centre, the European Court of Human Rights concluded that there was no need for 'the automatic creation of rights of entry to private property'.[41]

[34] See Section 8.2.3.

[35] On this difference, see Thurnheer, *Demonstrationsfreiheit in England und der Schweiz* (2010), pp. 116, 132–3, 160, 172–3.

[36] *Ex parte Lewis*, (1888) 21 QBD 191, 196.

[37] *Beatty* v. *Gillbanks*, (1882) 9 QBD 308; *Entick* v. *Carrington*, (1765) 19 St Tr 1030. See also Section 5.1.2.

[38] E.g. Criminal Justice and Public Order Act 1994, ss 68, 70; SOCPA 2005, s. 128.

[39] See Section 5.2.

[40] *CIN Properties Ltd* v. *Rawlins*, [1995] 39 EG 148 (CA).

[41] *Appleby and others* v. *The United Kingdom*, no. 44306/98, 6 May 2003, ECHR 2003-VI, 185, para. 47.

8.2.2 *United States*

As in the United Kingdom, once a piece of land has been dedicated for use by the public at large, then all members of the public have a right to access it and use it in a reasonable manner.[42] As explained in Section 2.4.3, the US Supreme Court made it clear very early that reasonable use of streets, sidewalks and squares is not limited to their traffic function but that they also serve as fora for communication and debate – indeed, that they are the 'traditional' or 'quintessential public fora'.[43] In *Schneider* v. *State of New Jersey*, decided in 1939, it proclaimed that 'the streets are natural and proper places for the dissemination of information and opinion; and one is not to have the exercise of his liberty of expression in appropriate places abridged on the plea that it may be exercised in some other place.'[44]

The courts have consistently stressed that municipal (and other public) authorities hold the streets of their communities in trust for the public and must keep them open and available for the use of the public.[45] This has led the Supreme Court of California to proclaim that '[t]he streets of a city belong to the people of the state',[46] although, in a strict legal sense, this is not quite correct, since ownership lies with public authorities or private landowners.[47] Accordingly, and as opposed to the situation in Switzerland where the use of public goods has traditionally been dealt with as an administrative law issue,[48] in the United States the question of access to public streets and other parts of public space has always been regarded as a fundamental rights – and thus a constitutional law – issue. Courts have emphasised that the use of public streets is 'not a mere privilege',[49] but a 'common and fundamental',[50] 'inherent'[51] and 'absolute and paramount'[52] right, although they have rarely explained what the exact source of this right is. The Supreme Court of Colorado, in a case concerning a juvenile curfew, held that the rights to freedom of movement and to use the public streets are 'basic values inherent in a free

[42] See e.g. *Harper* v. *City of Wichita Falls*, 105 S.W.2d 743, 750 (Tex. Civ. App. 1937).
[43] *Perry Education Assn.* v. *Perry Local Educators' Assn.*, 460 U.S. 37, 45 (1983).
[44] *Schneider* v. *State of New Jersey*, 308 U.S. 147, 163 (1939).
[45] E.g. ibid., 160; *City of Dalton* v. *Staten*, 201 Ga. 754, 755; 41 S.E.2d 145, 146 (Ga. 1947); *City of Elmhurst* v. *Buettgen*, 394 Ill. 248, 251; 68 N.E.2d 278, 281 (Ill. 1946).
[46] *Ex parte Daniels*, 183 Cal. 636, 639 (Cal. 1920).
[47] See Section 2.4.3.
[48] See Section 8.2.3.
[49] *Escobedo* v. *State Dept. of Motor Vehicles*, 35 Cal.2d 870, 875 (Cal. 1950).
[50] Ibid.
[51] *Ocean Beach Hotel Co.* v. *Town of Atlantic Beach*, 2 So.2d 879, 884 (Fla. 1941).
[52] *Swinson* v. *Cutter Realty Co.*, 156 S.E. 545, 546 (N.C. 1931).

society' and are thus protected by the Colorado Constitution and the due process clause of the Fourteenth Amendment to the US Constitution.[53] Similarly, in the case of Patricia Johnson concerning the 'drug exclusion zones' in Cincinnati,[54] the US Court of Appeals for the Sixth Circuit ruled that the due process clause protects 'a right of access' to 'public spaces'.[55] This right of access to public space belongs to the general public and thus to all persons, whether residents of the respective municipality or not.[56] All members of the public have an equal right to use the streets in a reasonable manner.[57]

As in the United Kingdom, there are no legal authorities that would suggest that this right of access to public space implies a right that certain pieces of land are made available for use of the public. There is, in other words, no right to the *existence* of public space. As far as access to semi-public space is concerned, it has already been pointed out in Section 2.5.1 that the jurisprudence of US courts on this issue is inconsistent and often conflicting. As a general rule, there is more recognition than in the United Kingdom or Switzerland that owners of shopping centres or other semi-public spaces should not have complete discretion to deny access to their property but that they must accommodate, at least to some extent, the rights of members of the public. Nevertheless, there is no firmly established, general right of access to semi-public space.

8.2.3 Switzerland

As explained above, Swiss law characterises streets, squares, parks and so on as *öffentliche Sachen im Gemeingebrauch/domaine public* ('public goods in common use').[58] The Swiss doctrine and jurisprudence concerning the use of such public goods has been heavily influenced by concepts developed in Germany during a time when an authoritarian model of government prevailed.[59] The streets and other public ground have traditionally been seen as a paradigmatic domain for the

[53] *People in Interest of J.M.*, 768 P.2d 219, 221 (Colo. 1989). [54] See Chapter 1.

[55] *Johnson* v. *City of Cincinnati*, 310 F.3d 484, 503 (6th Cir. 2002).

[56] E.g. *City of Elmhurst* v. *Buettgen*, 68 N.E.2d 278, 281 (Ill. 1946); *City of Milwaukee* v. *Milwaukee Electric Ry. & Light Co.*, 180 N.W. 339, 342 (Wis. 1920).

[57] *Escobedo* v. *State Dept. of Motor Vehicles*, 35 Cal.2d 870, 876 (Cal. 1950); *People* v. *Galena*, 70 P.2d 724, 727 (Cal. Super. 1937).

[58] See Sections 2.1.1.3 and 2.4.1.

[59] Saxer, *Die Grundrechte und die Benutzung öffentlicher Strassen* (1988), p. 48; Imboden, 'Das Gesetz als Garantie rechtsstaatlicher Verwaltung' (1971), 6–12.

discretionary exercise of unrestricted state power,[60] and regulation of their use has been informed by an almost exclusively administrative law-focussed understanding of the respective legal positions.[61] Permission to use public ground was, and often still is, understood to be a positive action by the state.[62] Since fundamental rights were thought to impose only a negative obligation on the state not to interfere, this meant that public ground was largely beyond the protection of the constitution.[63] Furthermore, the purpose of streets and squares was essentially reduced to their traffic and transport function.[64] Any forms of use of the streets that did not serve this purpose could therefore be qualified as *gesteigerter Gemeingebrauch/usage accru* ('extended common use')[65] and could thus be subject to a permission requirement.

As a consequence of this traditional understanding, the predominant view of courts and commentators was that there is no subjective right of access to public ground, even if it is only for purposes of *Gemeingebrauch/usage commun* ('common use'),[66] that is, use that conforms to the purpose of the good in question and does not significantly impede the simultaneous use by others.[67] In fact, the Federal Supreme

[60] Saladin, *Grundrechte im Wandel* (1982), pp. 250–1, 323–4; Saladin, 'Unerfüllte Bundesverfassung?' (1974), 322–3; Imboden, 'Das Gesetz als Garantie rechtsstaatlicher Verwaltung' (1971), 7.

[61] Saxer, *Die Grundrechte und die Benutzung öffentlicher Strassen* (1988), p. 121.

[62] See e.g. BGE 127 I 164, 169 (2001) ('In der Zwischenzeit hat die rein defensiv verstandene Natur in diesem Zusammenhang an Gewicht verloren, und es wird ein gewisses Leistungselement anerkannt. Die Meinungs- und Versammlungsfreiheit gebietet in gewissen Grenzen, dass öffentlicher Grund zur Verfügung gestellt wird.'); BGE 77 I 279, 287 (1951) ('In der Bewilligung des gesteigerten Gemeingebrauchs einer öffentlichen Sache, d.h. in einer über den gewöhnlichen, jedem Bürger offenstehenden Gemeingebrauch hinausgehenden Nutzung zu persönlichen Zwecken, läge aber eine positive Leistung des Staates.').

[63] See BGE 100 Ia 392, 399 (1974); Malinverni, 'L'exercice des libertés idéales sur le domaine public' (2004), 30–1, 34–5; Saxer, *Die Grundrechte und die Benutzung öffentlicher Strassen* (1988), p. 121; Malinverni, 'L'exercice des libertés sur le domaine public' (1983), 145–7; Saladin, *Grundrechte im Wandel* (1982), pp. 250–1.

[64] E.g. BGE 100 Ia 392, 396 (1974) ('Die Benützung der Strasse zum Verkehr unter Einschluss des kurzfristigen Abstellens von Fahrzeugen und Waren bildet die Hauptform des Gemeingebrauchs öffentlicher Verkehrswege.'). See Saxer, *Die Grundrechte und die Benutzung öffentlicher Strassen* (1988), pp. 121–3.

[65] On the distinction between 'common use' and 'extended common use', see Section 2.4.1.

[66] See BGE 93 I 638, 645 (1967); BGE 79 I 199, 205 (1953); BGE 73 I 209, 215 (1947); Moser, *Der öffentliche Grund und seine Benützung* (2011), p. 233 and the numerous references cited there; Saxer, *Die Grundrechte und die Benutzung öffentlicher Strassen* (1988), pp. 58, 203.

[67] See Section 2.4.1.

Court entertained the idea that even activities that may be qualified as 'common use' could be subject to a permission requirement[68] – an idea that is contrary to the very notion of 'common use'.[69] However, from about the early 1970s there started to be increased recognition that the regulation of the use of public ground is not beyond the reach of the constitution. Not least due to the influence of the US 'public forum' doctrine,[70] it was now accepted that the streets and squares are not only devoted to traffic but also serve as fora for communication and exchange.[71] Certain forms of 'common use' of public ground were now held to be protected by specific fundamental rights, such as the rights to freedom of expression, economic freedom and personal liberty.[72] In recent years, academic commentators as well as the Federal Supreme Court have explicitly maintained that, as far as it concerns the exercise of fundamental rights, there is a *unbedingter Anspruch* (unconditional right) to 'common use' of public ground.[73]

However, as explained in Section 2.4.1, any use of public ground that is more intense than that for which the good in question was originally intended for or that significantly impedes the simultaneous use by others is characterised as *gesteigerter Gemeingebrauch* ('extended common use') and can be subject to a permission requirement. As a general rule, there is no right to 'extended common use' and thus to be granted a respective permission.[74] The public authorities enjoy wide discretion in deciding on requests for permission and, once granted, permissions can be revoked without compensation.[75] From about the mid-1970s, the Federal Supreme Court started to recognise that, as far as 'extended common use' of public ground is essential for the exercise of one's fundamental rights, there is a *bedingter Anspruch/droit conditionnel* ('conditional right') to be granted permission.[76] The right is described as being only

[68] BGE 109 Ia 208, 210–11 (1983).

[69] Moser, *Der öffentliche Grund und seine Benützung* (2011), p. 216; Tschannen, *Stimmrecht und politische Verständigung* (1995), p. 434.

[70] Saxer, *Die Grundrechte und die Benutzung öffentlicher Strassen* (1988), p. 124.

[71] Thurnheer, *Demonstrationsfreiheit in England und der Schweiz* (2010), pp. 184–6; Saxer, *Die Grundrechte und die Benutzung öffentlicher Strassen* (1988), pp. 121–45. The turning point in the case law of the Federal Supreme Court was probably BGE 96 I 586 (1970).

[72] See Moser, *Der öffentliche Grund und seine Benützung* (2011), pp. 235–6.

[73] BGE 138 I 274, 282 (2012); Kiener/Kälin, *Grundrechte* (2013), p. 209; Moser, *Der öffentliche Grund und seine Benützung* (2011), p. 530.

[74] Tschannen/Zimmerli/Müller, *Allgemeines Verwaltungsrecht* (2014), p. 486; Moser, *Der öffentliche Grund und seine Benützung* (2011), p. 254.

[75] Moser, *Der öffentliche Grund und seine Benützung* (2011), pp. 254, 405.

[76] See Section 2.4.1.

'conditional' because a wide range of other interests, including various public interests and the interests of third persons, need to be taken into account and may prevail over the applicant's interests.[77] The authorities enjoy wide discretion in weighing these interests.[78]

Overall, due to the state's comprehensive, ownership-like authority over public goods, the regulation of the use of public ground is still in many ways treated as a special domain in Swiss law. Permission to use public ground is predominantly conceptualised as a positive state action, a benefit, at least insofar as the use amounts to 'extended common use'.[79] Restrictions imposed by public authorities on the use of public ground must meet less stringent requirements with regard to their legal basis than is normally the case, not only as far as 'extended common use'[80] but also as far as 'common use' is concerned.[81] Furthermore, the case law concerning the use of public ground is quite incoherent as it largely fails to comprehensively address the constitutional law dimensions raised by the use of public ground.[82] Courts still tend to emphasise the traffic function of public streets and squares, often ignoring their important role as fora for communication and exchange.[83] According to an often-used standard formula, activities on public ground that amount to 'extended common use', such as demonstrations, can be subject to 'more far-reaching restrictions' than would otherwise be the case (that is, than would be the case on private ground).[84]

As in the United Kingdom and the United States, there is no right to the *existence* of public space. The Federal Supreme Court has stated explicitly that the (conditional) right to use public ground only relates to already existing public goods or facilities.[85] The state is thus not obliged to create new such goods or facilities.[86] Nor is there an obligation on the state to

[77] Moser, *Der öffentliche Grund und seine Benützung* (2011), pp. 529–30, 532–8.

[78] Ibid., pp. 535–6.

[79] BGE 127 I 164, 168–9 (2001). See Malinverni, 'L'exercice des libertés idéales sur le domaine public' (2004), 30–1, 34; Wyss, 'Appell und Abschreckung' (2002), 396.

[80] See Section 4.2.1; Moser, *Der öffentliche Grund und seine Benützung* (2011), pp. 255–61.

[81] Moser, *Der öffentliche Grund und seine Benützung* (2011), pp. 237–9.

[82] Hangartner, 'Besprechung des Bundesgerichtsentscheides BGE 135 I 302' (2010), 100–1. For examples of the different approaches used by the Federal Supreme Court, see Louis/Schindler, 'Verwaltungsrecht und Grundrechte als "Türen" zum öffentlichen Raum' (2013).

[83] Tschannen, *Stimmrecht und politische Verständigung* (1995), pp. 433–8.

[84] E.g. BGE 127 I 164, 169 (2001) ('weiter gehenden Beschränkungen unterworfen werden'); Häfelin/Haller/Keller, *Schweizerisches Bundesstaatsrecht* (2012), p. 152. See Thurnheer, 'Duldung freier Meinungsäusserung als positive staatliche Leistung?' (2006).

[85] BGE 138 I 274, 282–3 (2012). [86] Ibid., 282; BGE 122 I 279, 284 (1996).

make certain pieces of land available for use of the public or to maintain the extent to which ground is open for use of the public.[87] The question of access to semi-public space has not yet been addressed in any systematic way by the courts or in academic writing. While the Federal Supreme Court has held that there is a 'conditional right' to use publicly accessible parts of train stations for purposes of political advertising,[88] this finding relates to parts of train stations that are owned by the state-owned Swiss Federal Railway company (a public entity) and thus constitute 'proper' public space rather than semi-public space.[89] As explained before, the European Court of Human Rights has ruled that there is no right to access privately owned shopping centres,[90] and it seems unlikely that Swiss courts would go beyond the European Court's jurisprudence and conclude that such a right does exist.

8.2.4 Result

Although not guaranteed explicitly, a right of *access* to public space does exist in all three states at issue. In the United Kingdom and the United States, this right is accepted as more or less *self-evident*: it is understood to be part of people's 'residual liberty' to do anything that is not prohibited and, respectively, a 'basic value inherent in a free society'. In the United Kingdom, the right to access public space may be derived not only from the common law system of 'residual liberty' but also from the very definition of what a highway is and, today, from the positive guarantees of human rights contained in the ECHR. In the United States, if courts see a need at all to refer to the sources of the right of access to public space, they may point to the due process clause of the Fourteenth Amendment to the US Constitution or liberties guaranteed by the respective state constitutions. In Switzerland, in stark contrast, access to public space was originally not thought to be a right held by members of the public.

[87] Urteil des Bundesgerichts 2P.191/2004 vom 10. August 2005, E. 1.2, in (2006) 107 *Schweizerisches Zentralblatt für Staats- und Verwaltungsrecht* 254; BGE 122 I 279, 284 (2006). See Moser, *Der öffentliche Grund und seine Benützung* (2011), pp. 233–4.

[88] BGE 138 I 274 (2006).

[89] See Section 2.1.1.3. However, at least according to the Federal Office of Transport, also (certain parts of) privately owned train stations must be accessible to the public. Verfügung 042/2011-10-27/332 des Bundesamtes für Verkehr vom 23. November 2011, E. 4 and 7 (on file with author).

[90] *Appleby and others* v. *The United Kingdom*, no. 44306/98, 6 May 2003, ECHR 2003-VI, 185, para. 47. See Section 2.5.1.

The recognition of an unconditional right to 'common use' of public ground for the exercise of fundamental rights, which may be guaranteed by the Federal Constitution or the ECHR, was a relatively recent development. And even today the right to use public ground is characterised as being merely 'conditional' if the form of use at issue is classified as 'extended common use'.

In contrast, there is no right to public space in the sense of a right to the *existence* of public space. In none of the three legal systems under consideration is the state obliged to provide a 'minimum amount' of space that is publicly accessible. Furthermore, there is only fleeting recognition of a right of access to semi-public space. Some US courts have ruled that owners of shopping centres or other semi-public spaces must accommodate the rights of members of the public, but the relevant case law is inconsistent. Neither the European Court of Human Rights nor UK or Swiss courts have recognised the existence of a right of access to semi-public space.

8.3 *De lege ferenda*: is there a need for a right to public space?

In view of the fact that in all three states at issue the right to access public space is understood to be (only) a right that *implicitly* follows from people's 'residual liberty' and/or from other legally guaranteed fundamental rights, is there a need for an *explicit* constitutional guarantee of the right of access to public space? Could such an explicit, separate right of access to public space serve as a counterweight to the current trend towards the creation of ever more exclusion measures? These questions constitute the focus of Section 8.3.1. Given the trend towards the privatisation of public space, understood in the sense that we spend less and less time in commonly shared spaces, the question as to whether there is a need for a right to public space in the sense of a right to the *existence* of public space is equally pressing. However, since the sort of exclusion measures that are the subject of the present study apply to already existing and proper (as opposed to semi-) public space, this question is beyond the scope of this study and will thus only be touched upon very briefly (Section 8.3.2).

8.3.1 A right of access to public space?

Claims for new human or fundamental rights typically arise as a reaction to specific experiences of violation: long-felt grievances are framed as normative claims.[91] Only once an interest or good is thought to be under threat does a need for its (special) legal protection emerge. This also holds true for the calls for a right (of access) to public space, which, as explained in Section 8.1, have arisen as a reaction to the decline of public space as the space of liberty, equality, tolerance and democracy.

These calls for a right (of access) to public space have an interesting parallel in recent claims for a right (of access) to the Internet. As free access to, and use of, the Internet has come under increasing threat, there have been assertions in recent years that there is a need for an explicit human or fundamental right to the Internet, including access to it.[92] Michael L. Best, for example, has claimed that the Internet, and thus access to it, 'should be a human right in and of itself'.[93] The UN Human Rights Council has called upon states 'to promote and facilitate access to the Internet',[94] the UN Human Rights Committee has asked states to ensure that individuals have access to Internet-based information dissemination systems,[95] the UN Special Rapporteur on the promotion and protection of the right to freedom of opinion and expression has stated that 'ensuring universal access to the Internet should be a priority for all States'[96] and a joint declaration of several special rapporteurs maintains that 'States are under a positive obligation to facilitate universal access to the Internet.'[97] These statements have been interpreted by some commentators – prematurely, in my view – as UN endorsement of a human right to Internet access.[98] At the level of national law, a number of states,

[91] Bob, *The International Struggle for New Human Rights* (2008).

[92] See von Lewinski, 'Recht auf Internet' (2011).

[93] Best, 'Can the Internet be a Human Right?' (2004), 24.

[94] UN Human Rights Council Resolution No. 20/8, 5 July 2012, UN Doc. A/HRC/20/2, para. 3.

[95] UN Human Rights Committee, General Comment No. 34, UN Doc. CCPR/C/GC/34 (12 September 2011), para. 15.

[96] Report of the UN Special Rapporteur on the promotion and protection of the right to freedom of opinion and expression, 16 May 2011, UN Doc. A/HRC/17/27, para. 85. See also Report of the UN Special Rapporteur on the promotion and protection of the right to freedom of opinion and expression, 10 August 2011, UN Doc. A/66/290, paras 61–3.

[97] UN Special Rapporteur on Freedom of Opinion and Expression, OSCE Representative on Freedom of the Media, OAS Special Rapporteur on Freedom of Expression and ACHPR Special Rapporteur on Freedom of Expression and Access to Information, Joint Declaration on Freedom of Expression and the Internet, 1 June 2011, available at www.oas.org/en/iachr/expression/showarticle.asp?artID=848&lID=1.

[98] E.g. 'United Nations report: Internet access is a human right', *LA Times*, 3 June 2011; D. Kravets, 'U.N. Report Declares Internet Access a Human Right', *Wired*, 3 June 2011, available at www.wired.com/2011/06/internet-a-human-right/; 'UN deems Internet access a basic human right', *Global Post*, 6 July 2012, available at www.globalpost.com

including Finland[99] and Spain,[100] have made access to a broadband connection a legally guaranteed right.[101]

That there is a temptation to create a corresponding new human or fundamental right of access to public space – be it at the international or national level – is understandable. However, this temptation should be resisted. Such a move, it is argued here, would only contribute to the 'proliferation'[102] and 'overproduction of human rights'[103] and would have no added value.

As explained in the previous section, a right of access to public space already exists in all three states at issue. Although not guaranteed explicitly and separately, this right follows from the common law concept of 'residual liberty' and/or, respectively, from various explicitly guaranteed fundamental rights. While talk of a 'right (of access) to public space' may be useful for political and symbolic reasons, from the legal point of view there is therefore no need for an explicit and separate guarantee of such a right in the United Kingdom, the United States or Switzerland.

An analysis of the subject area that constitutes the focus of this study – exclusion measures – confirms that an explicit guarantee of a right of access to public space is not needed. As shown in Section 5.2, there already exist a wide range of fundamental rights that provide protection against exclusion from public space: any exclusion measure will fall within the scope of at least one of these rights.

Also in this respect the parallel to the alleged human or fundamental right to Internet access is revealing. From a legal point of view, there is no

/dispatch/news/politics/diplomacy/120706/un-deems-internet-access-basic-human-right-0.

99 Decree of the Ministry of Transport and Communications on the minimum rate of a functional Internet access as a universal service (732/2009) (original: Liikenne- ja viestintäministeriön asetus tarkoituksenmukaisen internet-yhtyeden vähimmäisnopeudesta yleispalvelussa), FINLEX, 22 October 2009, available at www.finlex.fi/en/laki/kaannokset/2009/en20090732. See D. Reisinger, 'Finland makes 1Mb broadband access a legal right', *BBC News*, 1 July 2010, available at www.bbc.com/news/10461048.

100 See 'Spain govt to guarantee legal right to broadband', *Reuters*, 17 November 2009, available at www.reuters.com/article/2009/11/17/spain-telecoms-idUSLH61554320091117.

101 For the situation in other states, see Report of the UN Special Rapporteur on the promotion and protection of the right to freedom of opinion and expression, 16 May 2011, UN Doc. A/HRC/17/27, para. 65.

102 Kapur, 'Human Rights in the 21st Century' (2006), 665; Donnelly, *Universal Human Rights in Theory and Practice* (2003), 221; Alston, 'Conjuring Up New Human Rights' (1984), 607.

103 Baxi, 'Voices of Suffering and the Future of Human Rights' (1998), 139–41.

need for an explicit, separate right to access the Internet. Internet access is already protected by a number of existing fundamental rights. Having carried out a survey of the legislation of twenty Council of Europe member states, including Switzerland and the United Kingdom, the European Court of Human Rights observed that '[t]he right to Internet access is considered to be inherent in the right to access information and communication protected by national Constitutions'[104] and concluded that a measure interfering with a person's access to the Internet accordingly also falls within the scope of Article 10 of the ECHR, the freedom of expression.[105] Beyond the freedom of expression, measures interfering with people's access to the Internet may also be covered by a range of other fundamental rights, such as, for example, the right to education, the right to work, the right to family life or the right to freedom of assembly.[106] Calls for a human or fundamental right to Internet access are a reaction to the repeated violations of these existing rights. If respect for these already legally guaranteed rights can be ensured, these calls will fade away.

The same holds true for public space. As long as the guarantees of fundamental rights set out in Section 5.2 are complied with and the character of public space as the space of liberty, equality, tolerance and democracy is preserved, no one will see a need for the creation of a separate right (of access) to public space. Thus, those who are concerned about the resurgence of exclusion from public space in recent years should simply insist that any exclusion measures comply with existing guarantees of fundamental rights as well as the rule of law. To oppose the proliferation of exclusion measures with the creation of a right of access to public space would be a purely symbolic reaction to measures that, as explained before, have themselves a strong symbolic component.[107] Instead, public space, just as the Internet, should be regarded not as a right in its own respect, but as a means: it enables individuals to exercise their fundamental rights and serves as a 'catalyst'

[104] *Yildirim* v. *Turkey*, no. 3111/10, 18 December 2012, ECHR 2012, para. 31.

[105] Ibid., paras 46–55.

[106] E.g. Report of the UN Special Rapporteur on the promotion and protection of the right to freedom of opinion and expression, 16 May 2011, UN Doc. A/HRC/17/27, para. 62; UN Special Rapporteur on Freedom of Opinion and Expression, OSCE Representative on Freedom of the Media, OAS Special Rapporteur on Freedom of Expression and ACHPR Special Rapporteur on Freedom of Expression and Access to Information, Joint Declaration on Freedom of Expression and the Internet, 1 June 2011, available at www.oas.org/en/iachr/expression/showarticle.asp?artID=848&lID=1.

[107] See Section 3.2.

that enhances their ability to do so, thus contributing to the *realisation* of fundamental rights.[108]

It is true that, as explained in Section 8.2.3, in Switzerland the implicit right to use public ground is characterised as only being 'conditional' if the use concerned is classified as 'extended common use'. However, there is no need to create an explicit, separate guarantee of the right of access to public space to address this problem.

Instead, one should try to overcome the traditional approach still permeating Swiss jurisprudence and parts of legal scholarship that treats the regulation of the use of public ground as a special legal domain. According to this traditional approach, the state has a comprehensive, ownership-like authority over public goods; already the mere permission to use public ground is, regardless of the specific obligations it may entail for the state, conceptualised as a positive state action.[109] It is this kind of thinking that forms the basis of the view that individuals may only be granted a 'conditional right' to use public ground for certain purposes. This approach is best overcome, not by creating a new right, but by insisting on an interpretation of the existing legal framework that takes account of the fact that public goods 'belong' (although not in the sense of legal ownership) to the people, rather than some government authority. Thus, use of public ground is not a benefit graciously granted by the state. In other words, the starting point of any interpretation of the legal framework regulating the use of public ground should be that it is in the very nature of public space to be open for everyone. As in the United Kingdom and the United States where this is understood to be self-evident, it should be accepted that the general rule is that people are free to be on, and to use, public ground as long as there are no prohibitions in law preventing them from doing so.

Viewed from a perspective that emphasises that public ground 'belongs' to the people rather than the state, it becomes clear that individuals who want to use public streets or squares to, for instance, hold a protest, in fact do not ask for a positive action by the state but simply demand that it abstains from interfering.[110] After all, if it is true that, as

108 See Report of the UN Special Rapporteur on the promotion and protection of the right to freedom of opinion and expression, 16 May 2011, UN Doc. A/HRC/17/27, para. 22.

109 See Section 8.2.3.

110 See Thurnheer, 'Duldung freier Meinungsäusserung als positive staatliche Leistung?' (2006), 946; Burgi, 'Art. 8 GG und die Gewährleistung des Versammlungsorts' (1993), 636.

Walter Jellinek once put it, 'the streets belong to the people',[111] then the people may use them freely: what already belongs to the people does not need to be asked for as a state benefit.[112] The European Court of Human Rights seems to support the position that use of public ground concerns a negative rather than a positive state obligation. In *Women on Waves c. Portugal*, the Portuguese authorities denied a ship carrying political activists permission to enter Portugal's territorial waters. The court characterised the territorial waters as a space that – unlike, for example, government buildings – was 'public and open by its very nature' and held that the denial of access to these waters concerned a *negative* duty on the state not to interfere with the applicants' freedom of expression, rather than a positive obligation.[113] The same reasoning would seem to have to apply to public streets and squares, which are equally public and open by their very nature. In a more recent decision, the court, although not expressing a final view on this point, even entertained the idea that the (non-)authorisation of the use of public billboards for a poster campaign might be characterised as involving a negative, rather than a positive obligation.[114]

It is true, of course, that use of public ground presupposes and entails positive action by the state: streets must be maintained and cleaned, demonstrations may make it necessary for traffic to be diverted and police forces to be deployed and so on. Yet this does not mean, as often seems to be assumed,[115] that every time an individual or a group of individuals want to use public ground, this must be qualified as a request for positive action by the state. Otherwise, there would be no negative liberties at all, as there is no fundamental right that does not require the state, at some stage and to some extent, to take positive action. Viewed from this perspective, one may question whether a generalised distinction between negative liberties and rights to positive state action makes sense at all. In any event, even if one was to insist on the distinction, the past and future provision and maintenance of public infrastructure must be distinguished from the question of what exactly an

111 Jellinek, *Verwaltungsrecht* (1966), p. 490 ('Die Strasse gehört nun einmal dem "Volke".').

112 Siehr, *Das Recht am öffentlichen Raum* (2016), p. 405.

113 *Women on Waves et autres c. Portugal*, no. 31276/05, 3 February 2009, para. 40 (only available in French, Portuguese and Russian) ('un espace public et ouvert de par sa nature même').

114 *Mouvement raëlien suisse* v. *Switzerland* [GC], no. 16354/06, 13 July 2012, ECHR 2012, paras 49–51.

115 E.g. Moser, *Der öffentliche Grund und seine Benützung* (2011), pp. 404–5.

individual demands from the state at the moment he or she wants to use public ground. If all that an individual asks for is that he or she is left alone to, for example, hold a protest on publicly accessible ground, the corresponding obligation on the state is a negative, not a positive one.[116]

Linked to this misleading approach of characterising *any sort of* permission to use public ground as a positive state action is the equally misconceived idea that, as far as 'extended common use' is concerned, the right of individuals to use public ground is only 'conditional'. This qualification suggests a distinction between 'conditional' and 'unconditional' rights that is untenable. Apart from very few absolute rights, such as the prohibition of torture, no right is 'unconditional' in the sense that it cannot be limited.[117] Or, to put it the other way round: apart from these very few absolute rights, all fundamental rights, whether they are exercised on public ground or elsewhere, can be limited as long as the usual limitation requirements, set out in Section 5.3, are met.[118] Thus, if one was consistent, on this basis all rights would have to be qualified as 'conditional'. For example, regardless of whether an assembly is held on public ground or on private property, the state can in both cases impose certain restrictions (for reasons of public safety, prevention of noise emissions etc.). It is thus wrong to qualify, as has been done, the right to freedom of assembly as 'conditional' as far as it is to be exercised on public ground and to contrast it with an allegedly 'unconditional' right to assemble on private premises.[119] Both the right to hold an assembly on private property and the right to access and use public places to assemble there exist unconditionally, but can be limited. Of course, there may be more reasons to impose restrictions on an assembly if it is held on public ground, as a wider range of interests need to be taken account of and coordinated. However, this alone does not mean that the corresponding right is turned into a 'conditional right'.

In summary, the concept of a 'conditional right' to use public ground prevalent in Swiss law is unfounded and should be abandoned. As in the United Kingdom and the United States, there is an implicit right to access

[116] Siehr, *Das Recht am öffentlichen Raum* (2016), p. 404.

[117] See also Reich, *Grundsatz der Wirtschaftsfreiheit* (2011), pp. 98–9.

[118] See also Wolf, 'Wirtschaftsfreiheit und Nutzung öffentlicher Sachen' (2001), 435.

[119] Moser, *Der öffentliche Grund und seine Benützung* (2011), p. 529 ('Während sich aus der Versammlungsfreiheit ein (ungeschmälerter) Anspruch darauf ergibt, auf privatem Grund eine Versammlung ungestört von staatlicher Einmischung abhalten zu können, ergibt sich aus diesem Grundrecht bloss ein "bedingter Anspruch" darauf, die Versammlung auf öffentlichem Grund durchführen zu können.').

and use public ground for the exercise of fundamental rights, which may be restricted but is not in any way 'conditional'. This right already exists and there is no need for a new, explicit guarantee of the right of access to public space.

Instead, what is needed – in all three states at issue – is greater awareness that access to public space is, not least, also a constitutional law issue.[120] Liberty, equality, tolerance and democracy are central values underlying the constitutions of all three states. As a consequence, laws regulating the use of public space must be drafted, interpreted and applied in a manner that takes account of the fact that these central constitutional values vitally depend on individuals having free access to public space. Legislators as well as courts and other law-applying authorities must better acknowledge that, just as the Internet, public space is a key 'enabler' of fundamental rights.[121] As is better recognised in the United Kingdom and the United States than in Switzerland, the 'default position' in a liberal democracy based on the rule of law is that individuals are free to do what they want: to use the Internet, to be on public streets and squares and so on. They do not need to be able to point to a norm explicitly guaranteeing them the respective right. That individuals have a right to access public space is inherent in the very notion of public space and the corresponding subcategories such as 'highway', 'public goods in common use' and so on. If a right of individuals to access the relevant pieces of land did not exist, these pieces of land would not constitute public space. The state may limit the right of certain individuals to access certain parts of public space. However, it is up to the state to create the legal basis for doing so and to justify why, in a given case, an exclusion measure needs to be imposed. It is not up to individuals to demonstrate that there is a legal basis authorising them to be in public space.

8.3.2 A right to the existence of public space?

The (implicit) right of access to public space is only meaningful if there is any public space left. Yet while the law in force in the United Kingdom, the United States and Switzerland (implicitly) guarantees the right of

[120] See also Tschannen, *Stimmrecht und politische Verständigung* (1995), p. 434.

[121] Report of the UN Special Rapporteur on the promotion and protection of the right to freedom of opinion and expression, 16 May 2011, UN Doc. A/HRC/17/27, paras 22 and 67.

access to public space, it does not guarantee, as shown in Section 8.2, the *existence* of (sufficient) public space.

There used to be no need for a right to the existence of public space as long as public space was not in danger of disintegration. Today, however, factors such as the growth of private communities, suburbanisation and, perhaps most importantly, the proliferation of semi-public space lead to an increasing privatisation of public space: cities are more and more fragmented into separate private segments and people spend less and less time in commonly shared spaces.[122] It is not least as a reaction to these developments that the calls for a 'right to the city' and a 'right to public space' have arisen, which accordingly must also be understood as calls for a right to the *existence* of public space. The question of whether such a right should be guaranteed by law is now also starting to be taken up by legal scholars, although a comprehensive study addressing the situation in one of the jurisdictions at issue is still outstanding.[123]

There are two basic ways in which the existence of public space could be legally secured. First, public authorities could be obliged to ensure that there is a certain overall 'minimum amount' of space that is publicly accessible or, at least, that those spaces that are currently open to the public remain publicly accessible. Second, the state could 'open up' semi-public space (or even certain parts of private space) to the public by granting individuals a legally guaranteed right to access and use semi-public (or private) spaces for certain purposes and ensuring that this right can be enforced against the respective private landowners.

As explained in Section 8.2, neither has been done in one of the three states at issue: there is no right to the existence of public space in these states. Therefore, there may indeed be good reasons to claim that there is now a need to either create an explicit right to the existence of public space or, at the very least, to reinterpret the existing legal framework in a manner that ensures the continued existence of publicly accessible space. However, since the present study focuses on exclusion measures that prevent access to existing, 'proper' public space, the question as to the need to guarantee a right to the existence of public space falls outside its scope and cannot be further pursued here.

[122] See Section 2.5.1.
[123] For Germany, see Siehr, *Das Recht am öffentlichen Raum* (2016).

8.4 Conclusion

The concern that space that is freely and equally accessible to everyone may be slowly disappearing has prompted repeated calls for a 'right to public space' in recent years – calls that have gained a lot of attention. These calls are legitimate and understandable. They are legitimate insofar as public space – not least as a consequence of the adoption of ever more exclusion measures – is indeed increasingly losing its character as the space of liberty, equality, tolerance and democracy. They are understandable insofar as they have proved to be powerful slogans that have succeeded in mobilising a great deal of support for the respective political and social movements and causes.

However, from a legal point of view, there is no need for such a right in the United Kingdom, the United States or Switzerland, at least if this right is understood as a right of access to public space. For, although not guaranteed explicitly, a right of access to public space is already implicitly recognised in the legal systems of these three states. To create an explicit guarantee of the right to access public space would therefore amount to a largely symbolic move, which would make no real difference with regard to the issue of exclusion from public space.

Not every new social phenomenon necessitates the creation of a new right. This also holds true for the phenomenon of the resurgence of exclusion from public space. The fundamental rights that already exist would provide sufficient protection, if only law-makers and those applying the law better recognised the vital role that free and equal access to public space plays in a liberal democracy. Laws regulating access to public space must be drafted, interpreted and applied in a manner that takes account of the fact that public space is a key 'enabler' and 'catalyst' of liberty, equality, tolerance and democracy. As a consequence, it must also be acknowledged that exclusion from public space is a measure that affects the foundational elements of liberal democracy and, as such, constitutes a constitutional law issue.

9

Synthesis

This final chapter first summarises the book's main findings (Section 9.1). It then offers a short outlook to the future, exploring whether the maintenance of public space is a task that can and should be delegated to the police or, more generally, the state or whether, instead, it should be viewed primarily as a civic responsibility (Section 9.2).

9.1 Conclusion: exclusion measures in conflict with liberal democracy

Hardly ever used (or even known) twenty years ago, exclusion from public space has today become an instrument that is employed on a routine basis. The power to ban people from parts of public space is now included as a standard measure in, for example, cantonal police acts in Switzerland, anti-social behaviour legislation in the United Kingdom and laws designed to prevent various types of offences in the United States. Whereas throughout most of the twentieth century the general rule was that state authorities such as the police could only send away individuals from a specific location for a short time to deal with urgent situations, the new powers authorise them to prevent people from accessing large parts of public space (whole neighbourhoods, municipalities, city centres, cities or even regions) for extended periods of time (several weeks, months, years or even permanently), regardless of the urgency of the situation. These new exclusion measures are employed widely against all sorts of people – every year, tens of thousands are subject to exclusion from public space in the three states examined in this study. And, these numbers are set to rise further, as there is a clear trend towards increased use of exclusion measures.

This rise of exclusion from public space to a standard tool of state intervention must be understood as forming part of the current transformation of public space. Due to the privatisation of public space, in particular the proliferation of semi-public space and the assimilation of urban public places to the new ideal of semi-public space, the separation between privately owned space and public space has started to blur to an extent that it has become difficult to tell whether one is in private or public space. As a consequence, rules of behaviour that previously only applied in private and semi-public space (such as prohibitions of sitting or lying on the floor or of spitting) have been extended to public space. From this perspective, it is only logical that the key power to enforce these behavioural standards, namely the power to deny others access to the respective place (in other words, the power of exclusion), has also been transposed from privately owned space to public space. This transposition has been facilitated by the shift towards the 'security society': not only has the new preventive logic reinforced the pressure to suppress a wide range of behaviours that are believed to undermine the appearance of public space as a safe and clean environment, but also has the increased control of public space in the 'security society' – and the new technical possibilities it offers – made it much easier to enforce these stricter behavioural standards.

As a consequence, a wide range of behaviours in public space that used to be in the grey area between criminalisation and no state intervention at all have come to be seen as warranting some kind of reaction by the state. The prevailing view now is that 'something needs to be done' even against these borderline cases – that certain forms of behaviour, and thus certain categories of people, simply cannot be tolerated in (certain parts of) public space: potential sex offenders, gang members and football hooligans, drug addicts, alcoholics, homeless people, juveniles at night, protesters and so on. Exclusion from public space is thought to be a convenient, uncomplicated, effective tool to deal with a range of social problems by protecting the average user of public space from undesirable confrontations. As its underlying idea is exclusion rather than inclusion, it does not entail rehabilitation or reintegration efforts and so the cost for the public – so it seems – is low.

However, this new standard tool of state intervention raises serious concerns with regard to fundamental principles that have been engrained in the constitutional systems of the three states reviewed in this study over centuries – and may be characterised as essential values of liberal democracy – that have not yet received the attention they are due.

Exclusion measures have often been adopted based on breach-of-the-peace powers and the *polizeiliche Generalklausel*, respectively, instead of an explicit legal authority. This runs counter to the principle of legality, the central element of the *rule of law*. Especially in Switzerland, courts, including the Federal Supreme Court, have been too willing to accept resort to exclusion measures by the police despite the absence of an explicit legal basis, making it necessary for the European Court of Human Rights to step in. The rule must be that the requirement of an explicit legal authority can only be waived where this is necessary to deal with a serious, imminent threat that simply could not have been anticipated. With regard to the vast majority of exclusion measures, this is not the case as they are designed to deal with standard situations such as anti-social behaviour or common forms of political protest that are perfectly predictable. Where exclusion norms do exist, according to the requirement of sufficient precision, they must be drafted so that people know what kinds of behaviour will entail exclusion from public space and so as to grant those enforcing them as little discretion as possible. Norms that authorise exclusion of everyone posing a danger to 'public safety and order', as they are common in Switzerland, or of everyone 'causing harassment or distress to others', as they are widespread in Switzerland and the United Kingdom, are particularly problematic in this regard, as they make it virtually impossible for people to foresee what types of conduct will trigger their application. Invalidating various prohibitions of vaguely defined behaviour, the US Supreme Court has rightly emphasised that norms authorising exclusion from public space must not only be clearly drafted but, in order to prevent arbitrary enforcement, must also impose substantial limits on the discretion of those applying them. In addition, they must set out in as much detail as possible the terms of exclusion measures, establishing specific limitations on their geographical and temporal scope. Finally, as far as the procedural aspects of the rule of law are concerned, there is a danger that exclusion measures may be used to circumvent the procedural safeguards applicable in criminal proceedings, and they often undermine people's ability to gain access to an effective remedy.

There is more to *liberty* than the right to be left alone. Virtually all our freedoms have a social dimension. As such, they can only be meaningfully exercised if we have access to public space: to places where we can meet and reach others. Measures banning people from accessing (parts of) public space therefore regularly amount to an interference with at least one – and often several – of the fundamental rights guaranteed in the United Kingdom, the United States and Switzerland as well as by international law. Of course, there are legitimate aims that may justify restrictions on access to public space. For example, the state may have to impose such restrictions to prevent certain groups of people from 'taking over' parts of public space in a manner that makes it impossible for others to use them or to ensure safe access to abortion clinics. In contrast, protection from mere feelings such as annoyance, distress or fear does not constitute a legitimate aim for excluding people from public space. Given the extended temporal and geographical scope of many contemporary exclusion measures, they regularly have to be qualified as serious interferences. Accordingly, it is often questionable whether exclusion from public space can be said to be a proportionate means of achieving the legitimate aims referred to above. This especially applies to exclusion measures directed against anti-social behaviour: allowing for the preventive exclusion from public space of everyone who may engage in certain, often very vaguely defined, forms of behaviour, they affect large groups of people who have not been convicted of any criminal offence. But also exclusion measures directed against political protest that render it impossible for protesters to reach their intended audience will frequently amount to disproportionate interferences with fundamental rights. Such measures include, for example, prohibitions of political protest that are not limited to narrowly defined zones around particular critical locations but extend to entire squares or areas as well as the temporary blocking of access to city centres or municipalities.

The adoption of exclusion measures involves the creation of a two-class scheme of access to public space, which may conflict with the 'constitutional essential' of *equality*. Depending on whether a given person appears to be an 'ordinary citizen' or looks like, say, a homeless person, exactly the same action – for instance, drinking a beer in a public park – may have radically different consequences: no consequence at all in the first instance, exclusion from certain parts of public space for several weeks or months in the second instance. Similarly, in Switzerland, dealing in a small amount of drugs will typically entail no consequence beyond criminal prosecution for a citizen, whereas certain foreign nationals may, in addition, be banned permanently from a whole town, region or canton. Differences in treatment (or outcome) with regard to access to public space are only compatible with the right to equality and non-discrimination if the state can show that there is a reasonable and objective justification for them. Many exclusion measures fail to meet this requirement. Instead of being applied to individuals who have demonstrably engaged in behaviour that justifies exclusion from public space, they are directed against anyone deemed to be particularly likely to engage in criminal behaviour, anti-social behaviour or political protest because he or she belongs to a certain category of foreign nationals, is of a certain age, homeless or addicted or appears to subscribe to particular political views.

Finally, by changing the terms of access to – and thus presence in – public space, exclusion measures may have serious implications for *democracy*. The democratic legitimacy of many exclusion measures is not as strong as it might appear at first sight: where norms authorising exclusion from public space exist at all, they typically grant those applying them a significant degree of discretion, so that in reality the key determinations are made by law-applying authorities rather than democratic legislators. In fact, by undermining its liberal and deliberative elements, exclusion from public space may even be detrimental to democracy. Exclusion measures directed against political protest regularly restrict the exercise of civil and political rights on which the functioning of any democracy depends. Measures directed against anti-social behaviour, in turn, result in the banning of large sections of the population from the most frequented parts of public space, which may undermine the tolerance, empathy and sense of a common enterprise without which a democracy cannot exist.

Although it is difficult to draw generalised comparisons between different types of exclusion from public space, applying the typology elaborated in this study, those measures that are directed against *criminal behaviour* may be said to be the least problematic. They generally do not raise concerns with regard to democracy. If they are imposed by a court as an additional restriction to prevent reoffending following a conviction in the normal criminal process, they will normally meet the requirements for restricting guarantees of liberty. However, given their typically very wide personal scope, the lack of an individualised assessment and the seriousness of the restrictions they involve, especially exclusion measures imposed on *potential* offenders may amount to disproportionate interferences with fundamental rights. Exclusion measures directed against criminal behaviour may also conflict with the constitutional value of equality. This holds especially true when they only apply to particular categories of people, such as (certain) foreign nationals, or if they are intended to stigmatise the persons subject to them, as is often the case with, for instance, measures directed against sex offenders.

Exclusion measures directed against *political protest* have repeatedly been adopted without there being any explicit legal basis for doing so, running counter to the requirements that follow from the rule of law.

Where such measures cover entire squares, city centres, towns or municipalities, they will regularly fail to meet the proportionality requirement and thus amount to impermissible restrictions of fundamental rights such as the freedom of expression and the freedom of assembly. Since a democratic society vitally depends on the exercise of these freedoms, exclusion measures directed against political protest may, by undermining its liberal and deliberative elements, also harm democracy.

The most problematic type of exclusion from public space is that directed against *anti-social behaviour*. Intended to contribute to the restoration of the integrity of public space and to provide an instrument to deal with a wide range of social problems, the legal norms authorising this type of exclusion regularly fail to meet the requirement of sufficient precision inherent in the rule of law. In addition, exclusion measures directed against anti-social behaviour frequently conflict with guarantees of liberty. Many of them serve to protect from mere feelings rather than to pursue an aim that is recognised as legitimate. Despite the fact that the public interest in the prevention of rather minor disorder and incivilities is not particularly weighty, such measures tend to have a very broad personal, temporal and geographical scope, raising concerns with regard to their proportionality. Exclusion measures designed to prevent anti-social behaviour may also be incompatible with the right to equality and non-discrimination: some of them are explicitly directed against particular categories of persons, such as juveniles, while others are primarily enforced against, or have a disproportionate impact on, groups such as the homeless, the poor, alcoholics or drug addicts. Finally, preventing large sections of the population from accessing the most frequented parts of public space, such measures may have a detrimental effect on the 'psychological conditions' of democracy.

The rise of exclusion from public space to a standard tool of state intervention is a development that can be observed in all three states considered in this study, posing similar problems regarding its compatibility with the fundamental values and principles of liberal democracy in all of them. Nevertheless, there are some important differences with regard to the approaches prevalent in Switzerland, the United Kingdom and the United States – and thus also with regard to the concerns these approaches raise. Having said this, it is, of course, impossible to characterise one or the other state as being more or less in compliance with liberal democratic values.

In *Switzerland*, exclusion measures were originally often adopted based on the *polizeiliche Generalklausel* rather than any explicit legal basis. Even though, from the late 1990s, powers authorising the police to exclude people from public space started to be included in most cantonal police acts, concerns with regard to compliance with the rule of law persist: these powers are typically very broadly defined, giving the police wide scope of discretion and making it difficult for people to foresee what forms of conduct may entail exclusion. These blanket exclusion powers are employed extensively to deal with all sorts of undesirable behaviours and thus result in the exclusion of whole categories of people (in particular drug addicts, alcoholics and 'difficult' juveniles) from inner-city areas, which is problematic from the perspectives of liberty and democracy – even more so, considering that these powers are also used to keep away demonstrators from potential sites of protest. The existence of an even more far-reaching exclusion power under federal law that is only applicable to certain categories of foreign nationals, in turn, is not reconcilable with the principle of equality.

As in Switzerland, in the *United Kingdom* exclusion from public space is regularly based on police powers, be it explicit ones such as the dispersal powers under the Anti-social Behaviour, Crime and Policing Act 2014, be it the general power to prevent a breach of the peace under common law. In addition, various pieces of legislation authorise courts to ban people from accessing public space as part of, for example, IPNAs, football banning orders, sexual risk orders or serious crime prevention orders, regardless of whether the persons concerned have been convicted of any offence. Almost as broadly drafted as the cantonal police powers in Switzerland and equally widely deployed (including against political protesters), especially the IPNA and dispersal powers raise similar concerns as the former with regard to their compatibility with the requirement of sufficient precision, their conformity with guarantees of liberty and their implications for democracy. In addition, unequal enforcement of these powers and, respectively, their disproportionate impacts may conflict with the right to equality and non-discrimination.

In the *United States*, in contrast, the main form of excluding people from public space is by way of prohibitions: either certain groups of people are prohibited from being present in (parts of) public space (as with juvenile curfews) or certain, often broadly defined, forms of behaviour in public space (such as sitting or lying) are prohibited. As far as compliance with requirements following from the rule of law is concerned, the US Supreme Court, invalidating various prohibitions entailing exclusion from public space for being too vague, has established rather strict standards, requiring a substantial degree of precision as well as safeguards to prevent arbitrary enforcement. Similarly, the US approach regarding exclusion measures directed against political protest is, in general, more protective of the freedoms of expression and assembly than that prevalent in Switzerland and the United Kingdom. The Supreme Court's jurisprudence on 'buffer zones' to regulate anti-abortion demonstrations may even be described as exemplary, as it displays a remarkable awareness of the importance of location for protest. On the other hand, certain categories of people are in the United States subject to exclusion measures that involve very significant restrictions of liberty, also raising the question as to the justification of such uneven treatment: young persons are banned from being in any public place at night in the vast majority of US cities, sex offenders are regularly prevented from accessing large parts of public space for their lifetime, persons previously arrested for a drug offence are banned from whole neighbourhoods and so on.

Space is a social product. Just as the existence and implementation of legal guarantees of liberty and equality turn a given space into a *public* space, the adoption of exclusion measures may deprive a given space of its truly public nature: rights produce public space, whereas limitations of rights reduce it. That spaces change their character happens regularly and is, by itself, not a problem. However, at the very least, such changes to the character of spaces should be intentional and deliberate. Exclusion measures, in contrast, are typically introduced on an *ad hoc* basis as seemingly convenient tools to address pressing social problems. The fundamental implications these measures have for the character of the spaces concerned and for the essential values of liberal democracy set out in this book are rarely, if ever, discussed or even considered. By changing the nature of public space – where and how we go through it, what and whom we see there – exclusion measures also change the character of a liberal democratic society. If, for instance, being immobile in urban public places is treated as suspicious and may entail exclusion, people – or certain groups of people – will be deterred from engaging in immobile behaviour there. As a consequence, although this may never have been the intention and without us even realising it, some parts of space may slowly lose their character as truly public space: as the space of liberty, equality, tolerance and democracy.

There is no need to create a new, explicit right of access to public space as a reaction to this fundamental transformation of public space. Although not guaranteed explicitly, this right is already implicitly recognised in the legal systems of the United Kingdom, the United States and Switzerland. To create a separate guarantee of the right to access public space would amount to a largely symbolic move and have no real added value. Instead, what is necessary, but also sufficient, is that the legal framework regulating the use of public space is drafted, interpreted and applied in a manner that takes account of the fact that public space is a key 'catalyst' of liberty, equality, tolerance and democracy. The fundamental rights that already exist would provide sufficient protection from the proliferation of exclusion measures, if lawmakers and those applying the law better recognised the vital role that free and equal access to public space plays in a liberal democracy.

9.2 Outlook: the importance of civic responsibility

I have repeatedly described public space as the space of liberty, equality, tolerance and democracy. Public space is not merely a location or a physical object but a social product and a symbolic figure – a figure that stands for a particular vision of social interaction. As such, public space depends on people behaving in a certain way when they are present there. Public space can only maintain its character as the sphere that 'belongs' to everyone and is equally accessible to everyone if those using it impose restraint on themselves in order to enable all others to make the same use of it.[1] Parts of public space where this restraint is missing, where particular groups of people become so dominant that others stop using them, lose their character as truly communal space. Thus, it is important to ensure that public space is not 'appropriated' by particular groups such as criminal street gangs, drug or alcohol addicts, homeless people, juveniles or political protesters. 'Ordinary citizens' must feel safe and at ease in public space so that they do not withdraw from it.

It must be stressed, therefore, that the argument developed in this study, namely that many exclusion measures are incompatible with the fundamental values and principles of liberal democracy, should not be misunderstood as a plea for complete permissiveness, for simply accepting all sorts of behaviour in public space. There are clear limits to what is acceptable in public space.

However, to some extent, these limits are already set by the criminal law. To the extent that they are not (that is, as far as forms of behaviour

[1] Volkmann, 'Die Rückeroberung der Allmende' (2000), 362.

are concerned that are not sufficiently grave to deserve criminalisation), state intervention to enforce proper behaviour in public space is, in most cases, not the appropriate approach.

As a general rule, it must be for citizens themselves to look after public space and intervene against anti-social behaviour: maintenance of public space is, first and foremost, a civic responsibility. It cannot be delegated to the police or other public authorities. Where public space has lost its character as a space that is equally accessible to everyone, the task of restoring it must be taken on by the people themselves. Jane Jacobs has highlighted the central role that civility and civic responsibility play for city life as follows:

> The first thing to understand is that the public peace – the sidewalk and street peace – of cities is not kept primarily by the police, necessary as police are. It is kept primarily by an intricate, almost unconscious, network of voluntary controls and standards among the people themselves, and enforced by the people themselves. [. . .] No number of police can enforce civilization where the normal, casual enforcement of it has broken down.[2]

Civility and civic responsibility cannot be imposed by the state, it must be learned. People have to learn how to confront, and interact with, others in the public realm, how to find ways to accommodate living with them, how to negotiate and resolve conflicts over the use of public space. These are skills that cannot be taught by state authorities but must be acquired by the people themselves. People can only learn civility, however, if they are accustomed to meeting strangers in the public realm, if they are used to being confronted with otherness. From this perspective, the adoption of exclusion measures is in fact counterproductive: as one element of the broader process of privatisation of public space, it leads to a reduction in the number of encounters between strangers and thus undermines the conditions necessary for people to acquire the skills of civility and civic responsibility. The more people expect that the state will enforce proper behaviour in public space, the more wary of any form of behaviour that deviates from the norm, and the less willing to intervene themselves, they become.

This is not to say that the state has no role whatsoever in maintaining and, where necessary, restoring the character of public space. However, at least in a liberal democracy, the contribution that the state can make to these objectives is limited. As mentioned above, the

[2] Jacobs, *The Death and Life of Great American Cities* (1974), p. 41.

state can, first of all, make the most serious types of behaviour in public space criminal offences and, retrospectively, sanction any violations of these prohibitions. Beyond this, it may also adopt a range of preventive measures to promote respectful behaviour in public space and encourage people to use public space by ensuring that they experience all parts of it as safe, clean and inviting as possible. For example, the state may make sure that public streets, squares, pathways, subways and so on are designed so that they are accessible for everyone and appear inviting rather than intimidating; it may see to it that there are sufficient means for maintaining and keeping clean and tidy public streets, squares, parks and other parts of public space; it may improve street lightning; it may carry out educational campaigns informing citizens about existing and non-existing dangers; or it may deploy social workers on the streets to support marginalised groups and avoid conflicts in public places.

In contrast, a state that understands itself to be a liberal democracy may take preventive action that interferes with guarantees of fundamental rights only in exceptional circumstances. Only within the narrow constraints described in this book may the state ban individuals from accessing (parts of) public space on the ground that they might behave there in an unacceptable manner: any such bans must, for example, have a legal basis that is sufficiently precise, pursue a legitimate aim, meet the requirement of proportionality and be compatible with the right to equality and non-discrimination. It is the existence of these constraints on state action that characterise a liberal democracy. A state whose arsenal of tools is limited to those of a liberal democracy cannot impose 'the good life'. Or, to use a famous dictum of Ernst-Wolfgang Böckenförde, '[t]he liberal secular state lives on premises that it cannot itself guarantee.'[3] The freedoms granted to people must be regulated from within society. The state cannot guarantee these inner regulating forces by way of legal compulsion and authoritative command, without abandoning its liberal nature.[4]

Thus, one should not expect that the creation of ever new laws and police measures can solve all the problems affecting public space. On the other hand, there is no point in creating a new legal guarantee of the right of access to public space as a reaction to the decline of public space.

[3] Böckenförde, *Staat, Gesellschaft, Freiheit* (1976), p. 60 ('Der freiheitliche, säkularisierte Staat lebt von Voraussetzungen, die er selbst nicht garantieren kann.').

[4] Ibid.

Instead, one must accept that there are clear limits to what the law can achieve. Maintaining or restoring the character of public space as the space of liberty, equality, tolerance and democracy is not a goal that can be reached through the state, the police or the law. In the end, only the people themselves can 'reclaim public space'.

BIBLIOGRAPHY

Works without a named author are listed at the end.

AAS KATJA FRANKO/GUNDHUS HELENE OPPEN/LOMELL HEIDI MONK (eds), *Technologies of Insecurity: The Surveillance of Everyday Life* (London: Routledge) (2008).

ABRAHAM HENRY J./PERRY BARBARA A., *Freedom and the Court: Civil Rights and Liberties in the United States* (Lawrence: University Press of Kansas) (2003) (8th ed.).

ADES PAUL, 'The Unconstitutionality of "Antihomeless" Laws: Ordinances Prohibiting Sleeping in Outdoor Public Areas as a Violation of the Right to Travel' (1989) 77 *California Law Review* 595–628.

ADLER BENJAMIN, *Die Entstehung der direkten Demokratie: Das Beispiel der Landsgemeinde Schwyz 1789–1866* (Zürich: Verlag Neue Zürcher Zeitung) (2006).

ADLER JEFFREY S., 'A Historical Analysis of the Law of Vagrancy' (1989) 27 *Criminology* 209–229.

ALBRECHT HANS-JÖRG, 'Kriminalitätsumfang, Opferrisiken und Kriminalitätsfurcht' in Kunz Karl-Ludwig/Moser Rupert (eds), *Innere Sicherheit und Lebensängste* (Bern: Haupt) (1997) 37–84.

ALBRECHT PETER, 'Die ausländerrechtlichen Zwangsmassnahmen im Konflikt mit dem Strafrecht' (2009) *Basler juristische Mitteilungen* 229–255.

ALBRECHT PETER-ALEXIS, *Der Weg in die Sicherheitsgesellschaft: Auf der Suche nach staatskritischen Absolutheitsregeln* (Berlin: Berliner Wissenschafts-Verlag) (2010).

ALDER JOHN, *Constitutional and Administrative Law* (Basingstoke: Palgrave Macmillan) (2013) (9th ed.).

ALEINIKOFF ALEXANDER T., 'Constitutional Law in the Age of Balancing' (1987) 96 *Yale Law Journal* 943–1005.

ALEXANDER MARK C., 'Attention, Shoppers: The First Amendment in the Modern Shopping Mall' (1999) 41 *Arizona Law Review* 1–47.

ALEXY ROBERT, *Theorie der juristischen Argumentation: die Theorie des rationalen Diskurses als Theorie der juristischen Begründung* (Frankfurt am Main: Suhrkamp) (1996) (3rd ed.).

Alexy Robert, *A Theory of Constitutional Rights* (Oxford: Oxford University Press) (2002).

Allan T. R. S., *Law, Liberty, and Justice: The Legal Foundations of British Constitutionalism* (Oxford: Clarendon Press) (1993).

Allan T. R. S., 'The Rule of Law as the Rule of Reason: Consent and Constitutionalism' (1999) 115 *Law Quarterly Review* 221–244.

Alston Philip, 'Conjuring Up New Human Rights: A Proposal for Quality Control' (1984) 78 *American Journal of International Law* 607–621.

Altwicker Tilmann, *Menschenrechtlicher Gleichheitsschutz* (Heidelberg: Springer) (2011).

Amos Merris, *Human Rights Law* (Oxford: Hart) (2006).

Arendt Hannah, *Between Past and Future: Six Exercises in Political Thought* (London: Faber and Faber) (1961).

Arendt Hannah, *On Revolution* (New York: Viking Press) (1963).

Arendt Hannah, *The Human Condition* (Chicago: University of Chicago Press) (1998) (2nd ed.).

Aristotle, *The Nicomachean Ethics of Aristotle* (London: JM Dent) (1911).

Aristotle, *Politics* (Oxford: Clarendon Press) (1962).

Arthurs H. W., 'Rethinking Administrative Law: A Slightly Dicey Business' (1979) 17 *Osgoode Hall Law Journal* 1–45.

Ashworth Andrew/Gardner John/Morgan Rod/Smith A.T.H/von Hirsch Andrew/Wasik Martin, 'Neighbouring on the Oppressive: The Government's "Anti-Social Behaviour Order" Proposals' (1998) 16 *Criminal Justice* 7.

Ashworth Andrew/Zedner Lucia, 'Defending the Criminal Law: Reflections on the Changing Character of Crime, Procedure and Sanctions' (2008) 2 *Criminal Law and Philosophy* 21–51.

Auer Andreas, 'Problèmes fondamentaux de la démocratie suisse' (1984) 103 *Zeitschrift für Schweizerisches Recht* 1–110.

Auer Andreas, 'Direkte Demokratie und Rechtsstaat' in Biaggini Giovanni/Müller Georg/Müller Jörg Paul/Uhlmann Felix (eds), *Demokratie, Regierungsreform, Verfassungsfortbildung: Symposium für René Rhinow zum 65. Geburtstag* (Basel: Helbing Lichtenhahn) (2009) 31–42.

Auer Andreas (ed.), *Les origines de la démocratie directe en Suisse: Die Ursprünge der schweizerischen direkten Demokratie* (Bâle: Helbing & Lichtenhahn) (1996).

Auer Andreas/Malinverni Giorgio/Hottelier Michel, *Droit constitutionnel suisse* (Berne: Stämpfli) (2013) (3rd ed.).

Augé Marc, *Non-lieux: Introduction à une anthropologie de la surmodernité* (Paris: Seuil) (1992).

Axer Peter, *Die Widmung als Schlüsselbegriff des Rechts der öffentlichen Sachen: Zur Identität des Rechts der öffentlichen Sachen als Rechtsgebiet* (Berlin: Duncker & Humblot) (1994).

BAER SUSANNE, 'Dignity, Liberty, Equality: A Fundamental Rights Triangle of Constitutionalism' (2009) 59 *University of Toronto Law Journal* 417–468.

BAGDIKIAN BEN H., *The New Media Monopoly* (Boston: Beacon Press) (2004).

BAINS CHIRAAG, 'Next-Generation Sex Offender Statutes: Constitutional Challenges to Residency, Work, and Loitering Restrictions' (2007) 42 *Harvard Civil Rights – Civil Liberties Law Review* 483–499.

BALL TERENCE/DAGGER RICHARD, *Political Ideologies and the Democratic Ideal* (Boston: Longman) (2011) (8th ed.).

BARAK AHARON, *Proportionality: Constitutional Rights and Their Limitations* (Cambridge: Cambridge University Press) (2012).

BARBER BENJAMIN R., *Strong Democracy: Participatory Politics for a New Age* (Berkeley: University of California Press) (1984).

BARENDT ERIC, *Freedom of Speech* (Oxford: Oxford University Press) (2005) (2nd ed.).

BARNETT HILAIRE, *Constitutional and Administrative Law* (London: Routledge) (2013) (10th ed.).

BARR HEATHER, 'More Like Disneyland: State Action, 42 U.S.C. § 1983, and Business Improvement Districts in New York' (1997) 28 *Columbia Human Rights Law Review* 393–429.

BARR ROBERT/PEASE KEN, 'Crime Placement, Displacement, and Deflection' (1990) 12 *Crime and Justice* 277–318.

BATES ED, 'History' in Moeckli Daniel/Shah Sangeeta/Sivakumaran Sandesh (eds), *International Human Rights Law* (Oxford: Oxford University Press) (2014) (2nd ed.) 15–33.

BATES ED, *The Evolution of the European Convention on Human Rights: From Its Inception to the Creation of a Permanent Court of Human Rights* (Oxford: Oxford University Press) (2010).

BAUMAN ZYGMUNT, *Liquid Modernity* (Cambridge: Polity Press) (2000).

BAUMANN FELIX, 'Inhalt und Tragweite der Bewegungsfreiheit' (2004) *Schweizerisches Zentralblatt für Staats- und Verwaltungsrecht* 505–535.

BAUMANN FELIX, *Das Grundrecht der persönlichen Freiheit in der Bundesverfassung: unter besonderer Berücksichtigung der geistigen Unversehrtheit* (Zürich: Schulthess) (2011).

BÄUMLIN RICHARD, *Die rechtsstaatliche Demokratie* (Zürich: Polygraphischer Verlag) (1954).

BÄUMLIN RICHARD, 'Der schweizerische Rechtsstaatsgedanke' (1965) 101 *Zeitschrift des Bernischen Juristenvereins* 81–102.

BAXI UPENDRA, 'Voices of Suffering and the Future of Human Rights' (1998) 8 *Transnational Law & Contemporary Problems* 125–169.

BAYEFSKY ANNE F., 'The Principle of Equality or Non-Discrimination in International Law' (1990) 11 *Human Rights Law Journal* 1–34.

Beatty David M., *The Ultimate Rule of Law* (Oxford: Oxford University Press) (2004).

Beaulac Stéphane, 'The Rule of Law in International Law Today' in Palombella Gianluigi/Walker Neil (eds), *Relocating the Rule of Law* (Oxford: Hart) (2009) 197–223.

Beck Ulrich, *Risikogesellschaft: Auf dem Weg in eine andere Moderne* (Frankfurt a. M.: Suhrkamp) (1986).

Beck Ulrich, *Risk Society: Towards a New Modernity* (London: Sage) (1996).

Beckett Katherine/Herbert Steve, *Banished: The New Social Control in Urban America* (Oxford: Oxford University Press) (2010).

Beetham David, 'Liberal Democracy and the Limits of Democratization' in Held David (ed.), *Prospects for Democracy: North, South, East, West* (Cambridge: Polity Press) (1993) 55–73.

Beitz Charles R., *Political Equality: An Essay in Democratic Theory* (Princeton: Princeton University Press) (1988).

Belina Bernd, *Raum, Überwachung, Kontrolle: Vom staatlichen Zugriff auf städtische Bevölkerung* (Münster: Verlag Westfälisches Dampfboot) (2006).

Bell John S., 'Comparative Administrative Law' in Reimann Mathias/ Zimmermann Reinhard (eds), *The Oxford Handbook of Comparative Law* (Oxford: Oxford University Press) (2006) 1259–1286.

Benhabib Seyla, *Situating the Self: Gender, Community and Postmodernism in Contemporary Ethics* (New York: Routledge) (1992).

Bernhardt Rudolf, 'Eigenheiten und Ziele der Rechtsvergleichung im öffentlichen Recht' (1964) 24 *Zeitschrift für ausländisches öffentliches Recht und Völkerrecht* 431–452.

Besson Samantha, 'The Reception Process in Ireland and the United Kingdom' in Keller Helen/ Stone Sweet Alec (eds), *A Europe of Rights: The Impact of the ECHR on National Legal Systems* (Oxford: Oxford University Press) (2008) 31–106.

Besson Samantha/Martí José Luis, 'Introduction' in Besson Samantha/ Martí José Luis (eds), *Deliberative Democracy and Its Discontents* (Aldershot: Ashgate) (2006) xiii–xxxi.

Best Michael L., 'Can the Internet be a Human Right?' (2004) 4 *Human Rights & Human Welfare* 23–31.

Biaggini Giovanni, 'Ausgestaltung und Entwicklungsperspektiven des demokratischen Prinzips in der Schweiz' in Bauer Hartmut/Huber Peter M./ Sommermann Karl-Peter (eds), *Demokratie in Europa* (Tübingen: Mohr Siebeck) (2005) 107–137.

Biaggini Giovanni, 'Grundlagen und Grundzüge staatlichen Verfassungsrechts: Schweiz' in Bogdandy Armin von/Cruz Villalón Pedro/Huber Peter M. (eds), *Handbuch Ius Publicum Europaeum, Bd. 1: Grundlagen und*

Grundzüge staatlichen Verfassungsrechts (Heidelberg: C.F. Müller) (2007) 565–623.

Biaggini Giovanni, *Kommentar BV: Bundesverfassung der Schweizerischen Eidgenossenschaft* (Zürich: Orell Füssli) (2007).

Bichovsky Aude, *Prévention de la violence commise par les spectateurs lors de manifestations sportives: Étude des mesures préventives et de la responsabilité de l'organisateur à la lumière du droit comparé, du droit suisse et du droit associatif* (Bâle, Bruxelles: Helbing Lichtenhahn; Bruylant) (2009).

Biedenkopf Kurt, 'Toleranz in der Demokratie' in Schultz Uwe (ed.), *Toleranz: Die Krise der demokratischen Tugend und sechzehn Vorschläge zu ihrer Überwindung* (Reinbek bei Hamburg: Rowohlt) (1974) 162–174.

Billias George Athan (ed.), *American Constitutionalism Abroad: Selected Essays in Comparative Constitutional History* (New York: Greenwood Press) (1990).

Birtles William, 'The Common Law Power of the Police to Control Public Meetings' (1973) 36 *Modern Law Review* 587–599.

Black Henry Campbell, *Black's Law Dictionary* (St. Paul: West) (1951) (4th ed.).

Blackburn Robert/Polakiewicz Jörg (eds), *Fundamental Rights in Europe: The European Convention on Human Rights and Its Member States, 1950–2000* (Oxford: Oxford University Press) (2001).

Blackstone William, *Commentaries on the Laws of England* (New York: Oceana) (1967).

Blakely Edward J./Snyder Mary Gail, *Fortress America: Gated Communities in the United States* (Washington DC: Brookings Institution Press) (1999).

Bob Clifford A., *The International Struggle for New Human Rights* (Philadelphia, PA: University of Pennsylvania Press) (2008).

Böckenförde Ernst-Wolfgang, 'Entstehung und Wandel des Rechtsstaatsbegriffs' in Ehmke Horst/Schmid Carlo/Scharoun Hans (eds), *Festschrift für Adolf Arndt* (Frankfurt a. M.: Europäische Verlagsanstalt) (1969) 53–76.

Böckenförde Ernst-Wolfgang, *Staat, Gesellschaft, Freiheit: Studien zur Staatstheorie und zum Verfassungsrecht* (Frankfurt a. M.: Suhrkamp) (1976).

Böckenförde Ernst-Wolfgang, 'Demokratie als Verfassungsprinzip' in Isensee Josef/Kirchhof Paul (eds), *Handbuch des Staatsrechts der Bundesrepublik Deutschland: Band II: Verfassungsstaat* (Heidelberg: C.F. Müller) (2004) (3rd ed.) 429–496.

Boers Klaus, *Kriminalitätsfurcht: über den Entstehungszusammenhang und die Folgen eines sozialen Problems* (Pfaffenweiler: Centaurus-Verlagsgesellschaft) (1991).

Bogdandy Armin von, 'The Past and Promise of Doctrinal Constructivism – A Strategy for Responding to the Challenges Facing Constitutional

Scholarship in Europe' (2009) 7 *International Journal of Constitutional Law* 364–400.

Bogdandy Armin von/Cassese Sabino/Huber Peter M. (eds), *Handbuch Ius Publicum Europaeum, Bd. 3: Verwaltungsrecht in Europa: Grundlagen* (Heidelberg: C.F. Müller) (2010).

Bogdandy Armin von/Cassese Sabino/Huber Peter M. (eds), *Handbuch Ius Publicum Europaeum, Bd. 4: Verwaltungsrecht in Europa: Wissenschaft* (Heidelberg: Müller) (2011).

Bogdandy Armin von/Cruz Villalón Pedro/Huber Peter M. (eds), *Handbuch Ius Publicum Europaeum, Bd. 1: Grundlagen und Grundzüge staatlichen Verfassungsrechts* (Heidelberg: C.F. Müller) (2007).

Bogdandy Armin von/Cruz Villalón Pedro/Huber Peter M. (eds), *Handbuch Ius Publicum Europaeum, Bd. 2: Offene Staatlichkeit – Wissenschaft vom Verfassungsrecht* (Heidelberg: C.F. Müller) (2008).

Bourdieu Pierre, 'Physischer, sozialer und angeeigneter physischer Raum' in Wentz Martin (ed.), *Stadt-Räume* (Frankfurt a. M.: Campus) (1991) 25–34.

Bowling Benjamin, 'The Rise and Fall of New York Murder: Zero Tolerance or Crack's Decline?' (1999) 39 *British Journal of Criminology* 531–554.

Boyd-Barrett Oliver, 'U.S. Global Cyberspace' in Schuler Douglas/Day Peter (eds), *Shaping the Network Society: The New Role of Civil Society in Cyberspace* (Cambridge, Mass.: MIT Press) (2004) 19–42.

Bradley A. W./Ewing K. D., *Constitutional and Administrative Law* (Harlow: Pearson) (2011) (15th ed.).

Bradley Anthony, 'The Sovereignty of Parliament – Form or Substance?' in Jowell Jeffrey/Oliver Dawn (eds), *The Changing Constitution* (Oxford: Oxford University Press) (2007) (6th ed.) 25–58.

Breitbach Michael, 'Für die Abschaffung der Bannmeile' (1998) 31 *Kritische Justiz* 238–245.

Breitenmoser Stephan, *Der Schutz der Privatsphäre gemäss Art. 8 EMRK* (Basel: Helbing & Lichtenhahn) (1986).

Briffault Richard, 'A Government for Our Time? Business Improvement Districts and Urban Governance' (1999) 99 *Columbia Law Review* 365–477.

Brunner Otto, *Land und Herrschaft: Grundfragen der territorialen Verfassungsgeschichte Österreichs im Mittelalter* (Darmstadt: Wissenschaftliche Buchgesellschaft) (1970).

Bullinger Martin, *Öffentliches Recht und Privatrecht: Studien über Sinn und Funktionen der Unterscheidung* (Stuttgart: W. Kohlhammer Verlag) (1968).

Bundesamt Für Berufsbildung und Technologie, *Digitale Spaltung in der Schweiz: Bericht zuhanden des Bundesrates* (June 2004).

Burgi Martin, 'Art. 8 GG und die Gewährleistung des Versammlungsorts' (1993) 46 *Die Öffentliche Verwaltung* 633–642.

Burke Edmund, *Selected Writings* (New York: Modern Library) (1960).

Calhoun Craig, 'Tiananmen, Television and the Public Sphere: Internationalization of Culture and the Beijing Spring of 1989' (1989) 2 *Public Culture* 54–71.

Calhoun Craig, 'Information Technology and the International Public Sphere' in Schuler Douglas/Day Peter (eds), *Shaping the Network Society: The New Role of Civil Society in Cyberspace* (Cambridge, Mass.: MIT Press) (2004) 229–251.

Calhoun Craig (ed.), *Habermas and the Public Sphere* (Cambridge, Mass.: MIT Press) (1993).

Carlen Louis, *Die Landsgemeinde in der Schweiz: Schule der Demokratie* (Sigmaringen: Thorbecke) (1976).

Carlen Louis, *Recht, Geschichte und Symbol: Aufsätze und Besprechungen* (Hildesheim: Weidmann) (2002).

Carmona Matthew/Magalhães Claudio de/Hammond Leo, *Public Space: The Management Dimension* (Abingdon: Routledge) (2008).

Carpano Eric, *État de droit et droits européens: l'évolution du modèle de l'état de droit dans le cadre de l'européanisation des systèmes juridiques* (Paris: Harmattan) (2005).

Carpignano Paolo/Andersen Robin/Aronowitz Stanley/Difazio William, 'Chatter in the Age of Electronic Reproduction: Talk Television and the "Public Mind"' (1990) 25/26 *Social Text* 33–55.

Cavigelli Nina, 'Kooperationen zwischen öffentlicher Hand und Privaten in der Stadtentwicklung – Eine Übersicht und allgemeine Erkenntnisse' (19 August 2007), available at www.vlp-aspan.ch/fr/node/49601.

Chambliss William J., 'A Sociological Analysis of the Law of Vagrancy' (1964) 12 *Social Problems* 67–77.

Chemerinsky Erwin, *Constitutional Law* (New York: Aspen Publishers) (2009) (3rd ed.).

Choudhury Tufyal, 'Interpreting the Right to Equality under Article 26 of the International Covenant on Civil and Political Rights' (2003) *European Human Rights Law Review* 24–52.

Clarke Ronald, 'Situational Crime Prevention: Its Theoretical Basis and Practical Scope' in Tonry Michael/Morris Norval (eds), *Crime and Justice* (Chicago: University of Chicago Press) (1983) 225–256.

Clarke Ronald, 'Situational Crime Prevention' in Tonry Michael/Farrington David P. (eds), *Building a Safer Society: Strategic Approaches to Crime Prevention* (Chicago: University of Chicago Press) (1995) 91–150.

Clarke Ronald, 'Situational Prevention, Criminology, and Social Values' in von Hirsch Andrew/Garland David/Wakefield Alison (eds), *Ethical and Social Perspectives on Situational Crime Prevention* (Oxford: Hart) (2000) 97–112.

Coffin Jennifer Niles, 'The United Mall of America: Free Speech, State Constitutions, and the Growing Fortress of Private Property' (2000) 33 *University of Michigan Journal of Law Reform* 615–649.

Cohen Carl, *Democracy* (Athens: University of Georgia Press) (1971).

Cohen Felix S., 'Dialogue on Private Property' (1954) 9 *Rutgers Law Review* 357–387.

Cohen Lizabeth, 'From Town Center to Shopping Center: The Reconfiguration of Community Marketplaces in Postwar America' (1996) 101 *The American Historical Review* 1050–1081.

Cohen Stanley, *Visions of Social Control: Crime, Punishment and Classification* (Cambridge: Polity Press) (1985).

Cohen William/Danelski David J./Yalof David A., *Constitutional Law: Civil Liberty and Individual Rights* (Westbury: Foundation Press) (2007) (6th ed.).

Cohen-Eliya Moshe/Porat Iddo, 'American Balancing and German Proportionality: The Historical Origins' (2010) 8 *International Journal of Constitutional Law* 263–286.

Cohn Margit/Grimm Dieter, '"Human Dignity" as a Constitutional Doctrine' in Tushnet Mark/Fleiner Thomas/Saunders Cheryl (eds), *Routledge Handbook of Constitutional Law* (Abingdon: Routledge) (2013) 193–203.

Cole Danny, 'The Effect of a Curfew Law on Juvenile Crime in Washington, D.C.' (2003) 27 *American Journal of Criminal Justice* 217–232.

Collins Damian C. A./Kearns Robin A., 'Under Curfew and Under Siege? Legal Geographies of Young People' (2001) 32 *Geoforum* 389–403.

Commager Henry Steele, 'America and the Enlightenment' in Barlow J. Jackson/Levy Leonard W./Masugi Ken (eds), *The American Founding: Essays on the Formation of the Constitution* (New York: Greenwood Press) (1988) 247–273.

Compaine Benjamin M. (ed.), *The Digital Divide: Facing a Crisis or Creating a Myth?* (Cambridge, Mass.: MIT Press) (2001).

Constantinesco Léontin-Jean, *Rechtsvergleichung: Band II: Die rechtsvergleichende Methode* (Köln: Heymann) (1972).

Cook Ian R., 'Policing, Partnerships, and Profits: The Operations of Business Improvement Districts and Town Center Management Schemes in England' (2010) 31 *Urban Geography* 453–478.

Cornu Gérard (ed.), *Vocabulaire juridique* (Paris: Quadrige/PUF) (2007) (8th ed.).

Corwin Edward S., 'The Doctrine of Due Process of Law Before the Civil War' (1911) 24 *Harvard Law Review* 366–385.

COSTA PIETRO, 'The Rule of Law: A Historical Introduction' in Costa Pietro/ Zolo Danilo (eds), *The Rule of Law: History, Theory and Criticism* (Dordrecht: Springer) (2007) 73–149.

COTTIER THOMAS, *Die Verfassung und das Erfordernis der gesetzlichen Grundlage* (Diessenhofen: Rüegger) (1983).

COUNCIL OF EUROPE, *Collected Edition of the "travaux préparatoires" of the European Convention on Human Rights* (The Hague: Martinus Nijhoff) (1975–1985).

CRAIG PAUL P., 'Appendix 5: The Rule of Law', in House of Lords Select Committee on the Constitution, Relations between the executive, the judiciary and Parliament, HL Paper 151 (2006–2007) 97–106.

CRAIG PAUL P., 'Formal and Substantive Conceptions of the Rule of Law: An Analytical Framework' (1997) *Public Law* 467–487.

CRAIG PAUL P., *Administrative Law* (London: Sweet & Maxwell) (2012) (7th ed.).

CRAWFORD ADAM, *The Local Governance of Crime: Appeals to Community and Partnerships* (Oxford: Clarendon Press) (1997).

CRAWFORD ADAM, 'Dispersal Powers and the Symbolic Role of Anti-Social Behaviour Legislation' (2008) 71 *Modern Law Review* 753–784.

CRAWFORD ADAM, 'From the Shopping Mall to the Street Corner: Dynamics of Exclusion in the Governance of Public Space' in Crawford Adam (ed.), *International and Comparative Criminal Justice and Urban Governance: Convergence and Divergence in Global, National and Local Settings* (Cambridge: Cambridge University Press) (2011) 483–518.

CRAWFORD ADAM/LISTER STUART, *The Use and Impact of Dispersal Orders: Sticking Plasters and Wake-up Calls* (Bristol: Policy Press) (2007).

CRAWFORD JAMES, *Brownlie's Principles of Public International Law* (Oxford: Oxford University Press) (2012) (8th ed.).

CRAWFORD MARGARET, 'The World in a Shopping Mall' in Sorkin Michael (ed.), *Variations on a Theme Park: The New American City and the End of Public Space* (New York: Hill and Wang) (1992) 3–30.

CRONIN THOMAS E., *Direct Democracy: The Politics of Initiative, Referendum, and Recall* (Cambridge, Mass.: Harvard University Press) (1989).

DAHL ROBERT A., *Democracy and Its Critics* (New Haven: Yale University Press) (1989).

DAHL ROBERT A., *On Political Equality* (New Haven: Yale University Press) (2006).

DAVID RENÉ/BRIERLEY JOHN E. C., *Major Legal Systems in the World Today: An Introduction to the Comparative Study of Law* (London: Stevens) (1985) (3rd ed.).

DAVID RENÉ/JAUFFRET-SPINOSI CAMILLE, *Les grands systèmes de droit contemporains* (Paris: Dalloz) (2003) (11th ed.).

DAVIS KENNETH CULP, 'A New Approach to Delegation' (1968) 36 *University of Chicago Law Review* 713–733.

DAVIS MIKE, *City of Quartz: Excavating the Future in Los Angeles* (London: Verso) (1990).

DEARBORN CHARLES H., III, 'The Domestic Legal Effect of Declarations That Treaty Provisions Are Not Self-Executing' (1979) 57 *Texas Law Review* 233–251.

DELEUZE GILLES, 'Postscript on the Societies of Control' (1992) 59 *October* 3–7.

D'ENTRÈVES MAURIZIO PASSERIN, 'Hannah Arendt and the Idea of Citizenship' in Mouffe Chantal (ed.), *Dimensions of Radical Democracy: Pluralism, Citizenship, Community* (London: Verso) (1992) 145–168.

DICEY ALBERT VENN, *An Introduction to the Study of the Law of the Constitution* (Basingstoke: Macmillan) (1959) (10th ed.).

DIGGELMANN OLIVER, *Der liberale Verfassungsstaat und die Internationalisierung der Politik: Veränderungen von Staat und Demokratie in der Schweiz* (Bern: Stämpfli) (2005).

DONNELLY JACK, *Universal Human Rights in Theory and Practice* (Ithaca: Cornell University Press) (2003) (2nd ed.).

DORSEN NORMAN/ROSENFELD MICHEL/SAJÓ ANDRÁS/BAER SUSANNE, *Comparative Constitutionalism: Cases and Materials* (St. Paul, MN: Thomson/West) (2010) (2nd ed.).

DRAPKIN ISRAEL, *Crime and Punishment in the Ancient World* (Lexington: Lexington Books) (1989).

DREIER HORST, 'Der freiheitliche Verfassungsstaat als riskante Ordnung' (2010) *Rechtswissenschaft* 11–38.

DUBBER MARKUS D., *The Police Power: Patriarchy and the Foundations of American Government* (New York: Columbia University Press) (2005).

DUBBER MARKUS D., 'Comparative Criminal Law' in Reimann Mathias/ Zimmermann Reinhard (eds), *The Oxford Handbook of Comparative Law* (Oxford: Oxford University Press) (2006) 1287–1325.

DUBBER MARKUS D., 'The Legality Principle in American and German Criminal Law: An Essay in Comparative Legal History' (2010), available at http://papers.ssrn.com/sol3/papers.cfm?abstract_id=1735966.

DUBBER MARKUS D./VALVERDE MARIANA (eds), *Police and the Liberal State* (Stanford: Stanford University Press) (2008).

DUBS HANS, 'Die Forderung der optimalen Bestimmtheit belastender Rechtsnormen' (1974) 93 *Zeitschrift für Schweizerisches Recht* 223–247.

DÜRR ROLF ROBERT, *Die Polizeiliche Generalklausel* (Zürich: Juris Druck + Verlag) (1967).

DWORKIN RONALD, 'Political Judges and the Rule of Law' (64) 1978 *Proceedings of the British Academy* 259–287.

DWORKIN RONALD, *Taking Rights Seriously* (London: Duckworth) (1977).

DWORKIN RONALD, *Law's Empire* (London: Fontana Press) (1986).

DWORKIN RONALD, *Sovereign Virtue: The Theory and Practice of Equality* (Cambridge, Mass.: Harvard University Press) (2000).

Egli Patricia, 'Grundrechte: Aktuelle Entwicklungen im Sicherheits- und Polizeirecht' (2012) *Sicherheit & Recht* 193–214.

Eissen Marc-André, 'The Principle of Proportionality in the Case-Law of the European Court of Human Rights' in Macdonald Ronald John/et al (eds), *The European System for the Protection of Human Rights* (Dordrecht: Nijhoff) (1993) 125–146.

Ellickson Robert C., 'Controlling Chronic Misconduct in City Spaces: Of Panhandlers, Skid Rows, and Public-Space Zoning' (1996) 105 *Yale Law Journal* 1165–1248.

Elster Jon, 'Introduction' in Elster Jon (ed.), *Deliberative Democracy* (Cambridge: Cambridge University Press) (1998) 1–18.

Ely John Hart, *Democracy and Distrust: A Theory of Judicial Review* (Cambridge, Mass.: Harvard University Press) (1980).

Emsley Clive, *The English Police: A Political and Social History* (Hemel Hempstead: Harvester Wheatsheaf) (1991).

Ericson Richard V./Haggerty Kevin D., *Policing the Risk Society* (Oxford: Clarendon Press) (1997).

Errass Christoph, 'Art. 22' in Ehrenzeller Bernhard/Schindler Benjamin/ Schweizer Rainer J./Vallender Klaus A. (eds), *Die schweizerische Bundesverfassung: St. Galler Kommentar* (Zürich/St. Gallen: Dike) (2014) (3rd ed.) 500–523.

Ewing K. D./Gearty C. A., *The Struggle for Civil Liberties: Political Freedom and the Rule of Law in Britain 1914–1945* (Oxford: Oxford University Press) (2000).

Fallon Richard H., '"The Rule of Law" as a Concept in Constitutional Discourse' (1997) 97 *Columbia Law Review* 1–56.

Fallon Richard H., *The Dynamic Constitution: An Introduction to American Constitutional Law* (Cambridge: Cambridge University Press) (2004).

Farrand Max (ed.), *The Records of the Federal Convention of 1787* (New Haven: Yale University Press) (1966).

Farrell Robert C., 'Successful Rational Basis Claims in the Supreme Court from the 1971 Term through Romer v. Evans' (1999) 32 *Indiana Law Review* 357–419.

Federle Katherine Hunt, 'Children, Curfews, and the Constitution' (1995) 73 *Washington University Law Quarterly* 1315–1368.

Feeley Malcolm/Simon Jonathan, 'Actuarial Justice: The Emerging New Criminal Law' in Nelken David (ed.), *The Futures of Criminology* (London: Sage) (1994) 173–201.

Feldman David, 'The King's Peace, the Royal Prerogative and Public Order: The Roots and Early Development of Binding Over Powers' (1988) 47 *Cambridge Law Journal* 101–128.

Feldman David, 'The Developing Scope of Article 8 of the European Convention on Human Rights' (1997) *European Human Rights Law Review* 265–274.

Feldman David, 'Human Dignity as a Legal Value: Part 1' (1999) *Public Law* 682–702.

Feldman David, 'Proportionality and the Human Rights Act 1998' in Ellis Evelyn (ed.), *The Principle of Proportionality in the Laws of Europe* (Oxford: Hart) (1999) 117–144.

Feldman David, 'Human Dignity as a Legal Value: Part 2' (2000) *Public Law* 61–76.

Feldman David, 'Property and Public Protest' in Meisel Frank/Cook Peter (eds), *Property and Protection: Essays in Honour of Brian Harvey* (Oxford: Hart) (2000) 31–59.

Feldman David, *Civil Liberties and Human Rights in England and Wales* (Oxford: Oxford University Press) (2002) (2nd ed.).

Feldman David, 'Political Rights' in Feldman David (ed.), *English Public Law* (Oxford: Oxford University Press) (2009) (2nd ed.) 419–451.

Fernandez Esteban Maria Luisa, *The Rule of Law in the European Constitution* (The Hague: Kluwer Law International) (1999).

Finger Thorsten, *Die offenen Szenen der Städte: Gefahrenabwehr-, kommunal- und straßenrechtliche Massnahmen zur Wahrung eines integren öffentlichen Raums* (Berlin: Duncker & Humblot) (2006).

Flammer August/Alsaker Françoise, *Entwicklungspsychologie der Adoleszenz: Die Erschliessung innerer und äusserer Welten im Jugendalter* (Bern: Huber) (2002).

Fleiner Fritz, *Entstehung und Wandlung moderner Staatstheorien in der Schweiz: akademische Antrittsrede* (Zürich: Orell Füssli) (1916).

Fleiner Thomas, *Die Delegation als Problem des Verfassungs- und Verwaltungsrechts: Ein rechtsvergleichender Beitrag zur Rechtsprechung auf dem Gebiet der Gewaltentrennung* (Freiburg: Universitätsverlag Freiburg) (1972).

Fleiner Thomas/Ivanov Daniela, *Die Umsetzung der Rechtsweggarantie gemäss Art. 29a BV im interkantonalen Recht: Rechtsgutachten* (Freiburg) (2007).

Foote Caleb, 'Vagrancy-Type Law and Its Administration' (1956) 104 *University of Pennsylvania Law Review* 603–650.

Force Robert, 'Decriminalization of Breach of the Peace Statutes: A Nonpenal Approach to Order Maintenance' (1972) 46 *Tulane Law Review* 367–494.

Fox Susannah, 'Americans Living with Disability and Their Technology Profile' (2011), available at http://pewinternet.org/Reports/2011/Disability.aspx.

Franck Thomas M., 'The Emerging Right to Democratic Governance' (1992) 86 *American Journal of International Law* 46–91.

Frankenberg Günter, 'Critical Comparisons: Re-thinking Comparative Law' (1985) 26 *Harvard International Law Journal* 411–455.

Franz Oliver, *Ausgehverbot für Jugendliche ("Juvenile Curfew") in den USA: Reformdiskussion und Gesetzgebung seit dem 19. Jahrhundert* (Baden-Baden: Nomos) (2000).

Fraser Nancy, 'Rethinking the Public Sphere: A Contribution to the Critique of Actually Existing Democracy' (1990) 25/26 *Social Text* 56–80.

Fredman Sandra, 'From Deference to Democracy: The Role of Equality under the Human Rights Act 1998' (2006) 122 *Law Quarterly Review* 53–81.

Fredman Sandra, *Discrimination Law* (Oxford: Oxford University Press) (2011) (2nd ed.).

Frenzel Ivo, 'Das Dilemma einer Idee: Ein historischer Rückblick' in Schultz Uwe (ed.), *Toleranz: Die Krise der demokratischen Tugend und sechzehn Vorschläge zu ihrer Überwindung* (Reinbek bei Hamburg: Rowohlt) (1974) 7–21.

Freund Ernst, *The Police Power: Public Policy and Constitutional Rights* (Chicago: Callaghan) (1904).

Frowein Jochen Abr/Peukert Wolfgang, *Europäische Menschenrechtskonvention: EMRK-Kommentar* (Kehl: N.P. Engel Verlag) (2009) (3rd ed.).

Frug Gerald, 'The Geography of Community' (1996) 48 *Stanford Law Review* 1047.

Frug Gerald, 'The Emergence of Private Cities in America' (1999) 32 *Kritische Justiz* 578–586.

Fuller Lon L., *The Morality of Law* (New Haven: Yale University Press) (1969).

Gächter Thomas, 'Allgemeine Grundrechtslehren' in Biaggini Giovanni/Gächter Thomas/Kiener Regina (eds), *Staatsrecht* (Zürich/St. Gallen: Dike) (2011) 410–439.

Gallant Kenneth S., *The Principle of Legality in International and Comparative Criminal Law* (Cambridge: Cambridge University Press) (2009).

Gallie W. B., 'Essentially Contested Concepts' (1956) 56 *Proceedings of the Aristotelian Society* 167–198.

Galligan Denis James, *Discretionary Powers: A Legal Study of Official Discretion* (Oxford: Clarendon Press; Oxford University Press) (1986).

Gamma Marco, *Möglichkeiten und Grenzen der Privatisierung polizeilicher Gefahrenabwehr* (Bern: Verlag Paul Haupt) (2000).

Gander Christine, 'Sicherheit und Demonstrationen – Grenzen eines Grundrechts' (2008) *Sicherheit & Recht* 67–76.

Gardbaum Stephen, 'The Structure and Scope of Constitutional Rights' in Ginsburg Tom/Dixon Rosalind (eds), *Comparative Constitutional Law* (Cheltenham: Edward Elgar) (2011) 387–405.

Gargarella Roberto, 'Full Representation, Deliberation, and Impartiality' in Elster Jon (ed.), *Deliberative Democracy* (Cambridge: Cambridge University Press) (1998) 260–280.

Garland David, *The Culture of Control: Crime and Social Order in Contemporary Society* (Oxford: Oxford University Press) (2001).

Garner Bryan A. (ed.), *Black's Law Dictionary* (St. Paul: West) (2009) (9th ed.)

Garofalo James, 'Victimization and the Fear of Crime' (1979) 16 *Journal of Research in Crime and Delinquency* 80–97.

Garzoni Fernando, 'Die Rechtsstaatsidee im schweizerischen Staatsdenken des 19. Jahrhunderts' (Dissertation, Zürich 1952).

Gasser Karin, *Kriminalpolitik oder City-Pflege? Bedeutungsstrukturen polizeilicher Strategien im öffentlichen Raum der Stadt Bern* (Bern: Stämpfli) (2004).

Gearty Conor, *Civil Liberties* (Oxford: Oxford University Press) (2007).

Gerber Jenni Regula, '"Abendausgang Kinder" – rechtliche Überlegungen zu einer polizeilichen Vorschrift' (2006) *Praxis des Familienrechts* 845–860.

Geuss Raymond, *Public Goods, Private Goods* (Princeton: Princeton University Press) (2001).

Giddens Anthony, *The Consequences of Modernity* (Cambridge: Polity Press) (1990).

Giddens Anthony, *Modernity and Self-Identity* (Stanford: Stanford University Press) (1991).

Glasze Georg, 'Privatisierung öffentlicher Räume? – Einkaufszentren, Business Improvement Districts und geschlossene Wohnkomplexe' (2001) 75 *Berichte zur deutschen Landeskunde* 160–177.

Glenn H. Patrick, *Legal Traditions of the World: Sustainable Diversity in Law* (Oxford: Oxford University Press) (2014) (5th ed.).

Global Justice Clinic (NYU School of Law) and Walter Leitner International Human Rights Clinic at the Leitner Center for International Law and Justice (Fordham Law School), 'Suppressing Protest: Human Rights Violations in the U.S. Response to Occupy Wall Street' (2012), available at http://chrgj.org/wp-content/uploads/2012/10/suppressingprotest.pdf.

Goldstein Paul, *Real Property* (Mineola: Foundation Press) (1984).

Goldsworthy Jeffrey, *The Sovereignty of Parliament: History and Philosophy* (Oxford: Oxford University Press) (1999).

Goodman Maxine D., 'Human Dignity in Supreme Court Constitutional Jurisprudence' (2006) 84 Nebraska Law Review 740–794.

Goold Benjamin, *CCTV and Policing: Public Area Surveillance and Police Practices in Britain* (Oxford: Oxford University Press) (2004).

Gozzi Gustavo, 'Rechtsstaat and Individual Rights in German Constitutional History' in Costa Pietro/Zolo Danilo (eds), *The Rule of Law: History, Theory and Criticism* (Dordrecht: Springer) (2007) 237–259.

Grabenwarter Christoph/Pabel Katharina, *Europäische Menschenrechtskonvention* (München: C.H. Beck) (2012) (5th ed.).

Gray Kevin, 'Property in Thin Air' (1991) 50 *Cambridge Law Journal* 252–307.

Gray Kevin/Gray Susan Francis, *Land Law* (Oxford: Oxford University Press) (2011) (7th ed.).

Gray Susan Francis/Gray Kevin, 'Civil Rights, Civil Wrongs and Quasi-Public Space' (1999) *European Human Rights Law Review* 46–102.

Greer Steven, *The Exceptions to Articles 8 to 11 of the European Convention on Human Rights* (Strasbourg: Council of Europe) (1997).

Grisel André, *Traité de droit administratif* (Neuchâtel: Ides et Calendes) (1984).

GRISEL ETIENNE, 'Les droits populaires au niveau cantonal' in Thürer Daniel/Aubert Jean-François/Müller Jörg Paul (eds), *Verfassungsrecht der Schweiz* (Zürich: Schulthess) (2001) 397–411.

GRISEL ETIENNE, 'Les droits populaires au niveau fédéral' in Thürer Daniel/Aubert Jean-François/Müller Jörg Paul (eds), *Verfassungsrecht der Schweiz* (Zürich: Schulthess) (2001) 383–396.

GRISEL ETIENNE, *Egalité: Les garanties de la Constitution fédérale du 18 avril 1999* (Berne: Stämpfli) (2009) (2nd ed.).

GROTE RAINER, 'Rule of Law, Rechtsstaat and "Etat de droit"' in Starck Christian (ed.), *Constitutionalism, Universalism and Democracy – A Comparative Analysis: The German Contributions to the Fifth World Congress of the International Association of Constitutional Law* (Baden-Baden: Nomos) (1999) 269–306.

GUNTHER GERALD, 'The Supreme Court 1971 Term – Foreword: In Search of Evolving Doctrine on a Changing Court' (1972) 86 *Harvard Law Review* 1–48.

GUSY CHRISTOPH, 'Polizei und private Sicherheitsdienste im öffentlichen Raum: Trennlinien und Berührungspunkte' (2001) 92 *Verwaltungsarchiv* 344–367.

GUSY CHRISTOPH, 'Der öffentliche Raum – Ein Raum der Freiheit, der (Un-) Sicherheit und des Rechts' (2009) 64 *Juristenzeitung* 217–224.

HÄBERLE PETER, 'Gemeineuropäisches Verfassungsrecht' (1991) *Europäische Grundrechte Zeitschrift* 261–274.

HABERMAS JÜRGEN, *Theorie des kommunikativen Handelns* (Frankfurt a. M.: Suhrkamp) (1981).

HABERMAS JÜRGEN, *Strukturwandel der Öffentlichkeit: Untersuchungen zu einer Kategorie der bürgerlichen Gesellschaft: mit einem Vorwort zur Neuauflage 1990* (Frankfurt a. M.: Suhrkamp) (1990) (2nd ed.).

HABERMAS JÜRGEN, *Erläuterungen zur Diskursethik* (Frankfurt am Main: Suhrkamp) (1991).

HABERMAS JÜRGEN, 'Drei normative Modelle der Demokratie: Zum Begriff deliberativer Demokratie' in Münkler Herfried (ed.), *Die Chancen der Freiheit: Grundprobleme der Demokratie* (München: Piper) (1992) 11–24.

HABERMAS JÜRGEN, *Faktizität und Geltung: Beiträge zur Diskurstheorie des Rechts und des demokratischen Rechtsstaats* (Frankfurt a. M.: Suhrkamp) (1992) (2nd ed.).

HABERMAS JÜRGEN, *The Structural Transformation of the Public Sphere: An Inquiry Into a Category of Bourgeois Society* (Cambridge: Polity Press) (1992).

HABERMAS JÜRGEN, *Between Facts and Norms: Contributions to a Discourse Theory of Law and Democracy* (Cambridge: Polity Press) (1996).

HABERMAS JÜRGEN, *Philosophische Texte: Band 2: Rationalitäts- und Sprachtheorie* (Frankfurt am Main: Suhrkamp) (2009).

HACKWORTH JASON, *The Neoliberal City: Governance, Ideology, and Development in American Urbanism* (Ithaca: Cornell University Press) (2006).

HAEFLIGER ARTHUR, *Alle Schweizer sind vor dem Gesetze gleich: Zur Tragweite des Artikels 4 der Bundesverfassung* (Bern: Stämpfli) (1985).

HÄFELIN ULRICH/HALLER WALTER/KELLER HELEN, *Schweizerisches Bundesstaatsrecht* (Zürich: Schulthess) (2012) (8th ed.).

HÄFELIN ULRICH/MÜLLER GEORG/UHLMANN FELIX, *Allgemeines Verwaltungsrecht* (Zürich: Schulthess; Dike) (2010) (6th ed.).

HAGEMANN HANS-RUDOLF, *Basler Rechtsleben im Mittelalter* (Basel: Helbing Lichtenhahn) (1981).

HALE CHRIS, 'The Structural Determinants of Fear of Crime: An Analysis Using Census and Crime Survey Data from England and Wales' (1994) 3 *International Review of Victimology* 211–233.

HALL TIM/HUBBARD PHIL (eds), *The Entrepreneurial City: Geographies of Politics, Regime and Representation* (Chichester: John Wiley and Sons) (1998).

HALLER WALTER, 'Menschenwürde, Recht auf Leben und persönliche Freiheit' in Merten Detlef/Papier Hans-Jürgen (eds), *Handbuch der Grundrechte in Deutschland und Europa: Band VII/2: Grundrechte in der Schweiz und in Liechtenstein* (Heidelberg: C.F. Müller) (2007) 199–228.

HALLER WALTER, *The Swiss Constitution in a Comparative Context* (Zürich/St. Gallen: Dike) (2009).

HALLER WALTER/KÖLZ ALFRED/GÄCHTER THOMAS, *Allgemeines Staatsrecht* (Basel: Helbing Lichtenhahn Verlag) (2013) (5th ed.).

HANGARTNER YVO, 'Recht auf Rechtsschutz' (2002) *Aktuelle Juristische Praxis* 131–155.

HANGARTNER YVO, 'Besprechung des Bundesgerichtsentscheides BGE 132 I 7' (2006) *Aktuelle Juristische Praxis* 740–742.

HANGARTNER YVO, 'Unmittelbare Anwendbarkeit völker- und verfassungsrechtlicher Normen' (2007) 126 *Zeitschrift für Schweizerisches Recht* 137–158.

HANGARTNER YVO, 'Besprechung des Bundesgerichtsentscheides BGE 135 I 49' (2009) *Aktuelle Juristische Praxis* 505–509.

HANGARTNER YVO, 'Besprechung des Bundesgerichtsentscheides BGE 135 I 302' (2010) *Aktuelle Juristische Praxis* 100–102.

HANGARTNER YVO/KLEY ANDREAS, *Die demokratischen Rechte in Bund und Kantonen der Schweizerischen Eidgenossenschaft* (Zürich: Schulthess) (2000).

HANSON DONALD W., *From Kingdom to Commonwealth: The Development of Civic Consciousness in English Political Thought* (Cambridge, Mass.: Harvard University Press) (1970).

HARCOURT BERNARD E, *Illusion of Order: The False Promise of Broken Windows Policing* (Cambridge, Mass.: Harvard University Press) (2001).

HARRIS DAVID/O'BOYLE MICHAEL/BATES ED/BUCKLEY CARLA, *Harris, O'Boyle & Warbrick: Law of the European Convention on Human Rights* (Oxford: Oxford University Press) (2014) (3rd ed.).

HARVEY DAVID, 'The Right to the City' (2003) 27 *International Journal of Urban and Regional Research* 939–941.

HARVEY DAVID, 'The Right to the City' (2008) 53 *New Left Review* 23–40.

HÄUSSERMANN HARTMUT, 'Die Stadt und die Stadtsoziologie: Urbane Lebensweise und die Integration des Fremden' (1995) 5 *Berliner Journal für Soziologie* 89–98.

HAYEK FRIEDRICH AUGUST VON, *The Constitution of Liberty* (Chicago: Chicago University Press) (1960).

HEALEY PATSY, 'On Creating the "City" as a Collective Resource' (2002) 39 *Urban Studies* 1777–1792.

HEER MARKUS, 'Die ausländerrechtliche Ein- und Ausgrenzung – ein problematischer Versuch, Sicherheit zu gewinnen' in Camprubi Madeleine (ed.), *Angst und Streben nach Sicherheit in Gesetzgebung und Praxix* (Zürich: Schulthess) (2004) 1–27.

HEITMEYER WILHELM, 'Versagt die "Integrationsmaschine" Stadt? – Zum Problem der ethnisch-kulturellen Segregation und ihrer Konfliktfolgen' in Heitmeyer Wilhelm/Dollase Rainer/Backes Otto (eds), *Die Krise der Städte: Analysen zu den Folgen desintegrativer Stadtentwicklung für das ethnisch-kulturelle Zusammenleben* (Frankfurt a. M.: Suhrkamp) (1998) 443–467.

HELD DAVID, *Models of Democracy* (Cambridge: Polity Press) (2006).

HELG FELIX, *Die schweizerischen Landsgemeinden: Ihre staatsrechtliche Ausgestaltung in den Kantonen Appenzell Ausserrhoden, Appenzell Innerrhoden, Glarus, Nidwalden und Obwalden* (Zürich, Basel, Genf: Schulthess) (2007).

HENKIN LOUIS, 'Plenary Session: The U.S. Constitution in Its Third Century: Foreign Affairs' (1991) 85 *American Society of International Law Proceedings* 191–192.

HENKIN LOUIS, 'U.S. Ratification of Human Rights Conventions: The Ghost of Senator Bricker' (1995) 89 *American Journal of International Law* 341–350.

HENSLER BEAT, 'Strafe ohne Strafrecht: Die poenale Wirkung von verwaltungsrechtlichen Massnahmen, insbesondere am Beispiel der Präventivmassnahmen des Hooligangesetzes (BWIS) bzw. Hooligankonkordats' (2011) *Sicherheit & Recht* 37–44.

HERSHKOVITZ LINDA, 'Tiananmen Square and the Politics of Place' (1993) 12 *Political Geography* 395–420.

HERTIG RANDALL MAYA, 'Commercial Speech under the European Convention on Human Rights: Subordinate or Equal?' (2006) 6 *Human Rights Law Review* 53–86.

HEUSCHLING LUC, *État de droit, Rechtsstaat, Rule of Law* (Paris: Dalloz) (2002).

His Eduard, *Geschichte des neuern schweizerischen Staatsrechts: Band 1: Die Zeit der Helvetik und der Vermittlungsakte, 1798–1813* (Basel: Helbing & Lichtenhahn) (1920).

His Eduard, *Geschichte des neuern schweizerischen Staatsrechts: Band 3: Der Bundesstaat von 1848–1914* (Basel: Helbing & Lichtenhahn) (1938).

Hobbes Thomas, *Leviathan* (Oxford: Oxford University Press) (1998).

Holt James Clarke, *Magna Carta* (Cambridge: Cambridge University Press) (2015) (3rd ed.).

Holzhauer Heinz, 'Landesverweisung (Verbannung)' in Erler Adalbert/ Kaufmann Ekkehard (eds), *Handwörterbuch zur deutschen Rechtsgeschichte* (Berlin: Schmidt) (1971–1998) cols 1436–1448.

Horder Jeremy (ed.), *Homicide Law in Comparative Perspective* (Oxford: Hart) (2007).

Horowitz Susan M., 'A Search for Constitutional Standards: Judicial Review of Juvenile Curfew Ordinances' (1991) 24 *Columbia Journal of Law & Social Problems* 381–417.

Horwitz Morton J., 'The History of the Public/Private Distinction' (1982) 130 *University of Pennsylvania Law Review* 1423–1428.

Hottelier Michel, 'La réglementation du domaine public à Genève' (2002) *La Semaine Judiciaire* 123–175.

Hottelier Michel, 'Grundrechtskonkurrenzen und Grundrechtskollisionen' in Merten Detlef/Papier Hans-Jürgen (eds), *Handbuch der Grundrechte in Deutschland und Europa: Band VII/2: Grundrechte in der Schweiz und in Liechtenstein* (Heidelberg: C.F. Müller) (2007) 121–140.

Howell Philip, 'Public Space and the Public Sphere: Political Theory and the Historical Geography of Modernity' (1993) 11 *Environment and Planning D: Society and Space* 303–322.

Huber Hans, 'Grundrechte und Polizeigewalt' (1952) 53 *Schweizerisches Zentralblatt für Staats- und Verwaltungsrecht* 233–241.

Huber Hans, 'Über den Grundsatz der Verhältnismässigkeit im Verwaltungsrecht' (1977) 96 *Zeitschrift für Schweizerisches Recht* 1–29.

Hugi Yar Thomas, 'Zwangsmassnahmen im Ausländerrecht' in Uebersax Peter/ Rudin Beat/Hugi Yar Thomas/Geiser Thomas (eds), *Ausländerrecht: Eine umfassende Darstellung der Rechtsstellung von Ausländerinnen und Ausländern in der Schweiz – von A(syl) bis Z(ivilrecht)* (Basel: Helbing Lichtenhahn) (2009) 417–519.

Huisman Wim/Koemans Monique, 'Administrative Measures in Crime Control' (2008) 1 *Erasmus Law Review* 121–143.

Humphrey John, 'The International Bill of Rights: Scope and Implementation' (1976) 17 *William and Mary Law Review* 527–541.

Hutchinson Allan C./Monahan Patrick J., 'Democracy and the Rule of Law' in Hutchinson Allan C./Monahan Patrick J. (eds), *The Rule of Law: Ideal or Ideology* (Toronto: Carswell) (1987) 97–123.

Hutson James H., *The Sister Republics: Die Schweiz und die Vereinigten Staaten von 1776 bis heute* (Bern: Stämpfli) (1992).

Imboden Max, *Schweizerische Verwaltungsrechtsprechung: die Rechtsgrundsätze der Verwaltungspraxis, erläutert an Entscheiden der Verwaltungsbehörden und Gerichte; Bd. I* (Basel: Helbing & Lichtenhahn) (1960).

Imboden Max, 'Das Gesetz als Garantie rechtsstaatlicher Verwaltung (1954)' in Imboden Max (ed.), *Staat und Recht: Ausgewählte Schriften und Vorträge* (Basel: Helbing & Lichtenhahn) (1971) 3–33.

Imperatori Martino, 'Art. 94' in Niggli Marcel Alexander/Wiprächtiger Hans (eds), *Basler Kommentar Strafrecht I: Art. 1–110 StGB und Jugendstrafgesetz* (Basel: Helbing Lichtenhahn) (2013) (3rd ed.) 1879–1885.

Innes Martin/Jones Vanessa, *Neighbourhood Security and Urban Change* (York) (2006).

Institut für Landes- und Stadtentwicklungsforschung des Landes Nordrhein-Westfalen (ed.), *Im Mittelpunkt der Städte: Sicherheit und Aufenthaltsqualität – Strategien für den Erfolg urbaner Zentren* (Dortmund) (2001).

Ishay Micheline R., *The History of Human Rights: From Ancient Times to the Globalization Era* (Berkeley, Calif.: University of California Press) (2008) (2nd ed.).

Jaag Tobias, 'Gemeingebrauch und Sondernutzung öffentlicher Sachen' (1992) 93 *Schweizerisches Zentralblatt für Staats- und Verwaltungsrecht* 145–168.

Jaag Tobias, '"Preferred Freedoms" im schweizerischen Verfassungsrecht' in Zen-Ruffinen Piermarco/Auer Andreas (eds), *De la constitution: études en l'honneur de Jean-François Aubert* (Bâle: Helbing & Lichtenhahn) (1996) 355–370.

Jackson John H., 'United States' in Jacobs Francis Geoffrey/Roberts Shelley (eds), *The Effect of Treaties in Domestic Law* (London: Sweet & Maxwell) (1987) 141–169.

Jackson John H., 'Status of Treaties in Domestic Legal Systems: A Policy Analysis' (1992) 86 *American Journal of International Law* 310–340.

Jackson Vicki C., 'Being Proportional About Proportionality' (2004) 21 *Constitutional Commentary* 803–859.

Jackson Vicki C., *Constitutional Engagement in a Transnational Era* (Oxford: Oxford University Press) (2010).

Jackson Vicki C., 'Comparative Constitutional Law: Methodologies' in Rosenfeld Michel/Sajó András (eds), *The Oxford Handbook of Comparative Constitutional Law* (Oxford: Oxford University Press) (2012) 54–74.

JACOBS JANE, *The Death and Life of Great American Cities* (Harmondsworth: Penguin Books) (1974).

JACOBSOHN GARY JEFFREY, 'Constitutional Values and Principles' in Rosenfeld Michel/Sajó András (eds), *The Oxford Handbook of Comparative Constitutional Law* (Oxford: Oxford University Press) (2012) 777–791.

JEFFRIES JOHN CALVIN, 'Legality, Vagueness, and the Construction of Penal Statutes' (1985) 71 *Virginia Law Review* 189–245.

JELLINEK WALTER, *Verwaltungsrecht* (Bad Homburg v.d. Höhe: Gehlen) (1966) (3rd ed.).

JENNINGS IVOR, *The Law and the Constitution* (London: University of London Press) (1933).

JOHNS CLAUDE HERMANN WALTER, *The Oldest Code of Laws in the World: The Code of Laws Promulgated by Hammurabi, King of Babylon, B.C. 2285–2242* (Union, N.J.: Lawbook Exchange) (2000).

JOWELL JEFFREY, 'Is Equality a Constitutional Principle?' (1994) *Current Legal Problems* 1–18.

JOWELL JEFFREY, 'Beyond the Rule of Law: Towards Constitutional Judicial Review' (2000) *Public Law* 671–683.

JOWELL JEFFREY, 'The Rule of Law and Its Underlying Values' in Jowell Jeffrey/ Oliver Dawn (eds), *The Changing Constitution* (Oxford: Oxford University Press) (2007) (6th ed.) 5–24.

JOWELL JEFFREY, 'The Rule of Law' in Jowell Jeffrey/Oliver Dawn/ Colm O'Cinneide (eds), *The Changing Constitution* (Oxford: Oxford University Press) (2015) (8th ed.) 13–37.

KADISH SANFORD H., 'Methodology and Criteria in Due Process Adjudication – A Survey and Criticism' (1957) 66 *Yale Law Journal* 319–363.

KÄGI WERNER, 'Zur Entwicklung des Schweizerischen Rechtsstaates seit 1848' (1952) 71 *Zeitschrift für Schweizerisches Recht* 173–236.

KÄGI WERNER, 'Rechtsstaat und Demokratie (Antinomie und Synthese)' in *Demokratie und Rechtsstaat: Festgabe zum 60. Geburtstag von Zaccaria Giacometti* (Zürich: Polygraphischer Verlag) (1953) 107–142.

KÄLIN WALTER, 'Zwangsmassnahmen im Ausländerrecht: Materielles Recht' (1995) *Aktuelle Juristische Praxis* 835–853.

KÄLIN WALTER, 'Ausländerdiskriminierung' in Ehrenzeller Bernhard/ Mastronardi Philippe/Schaffhauser René/Schweizer Rainer J./ Vallender, Klaus A. (eds), *Der Verfassungsstaat vor neuen Herausforderungen: Festschrift für Yvo Hangartner* (St. Gallen: Dike) (1998) 561–583.

KÄLIN WALTER/KIENER REGINA/MÜLLER MARKUS/TSCHANNEN PIERRE/ TSCHENTSCHER AXEL, 'Die staatsrechtliche Rechtsprechung des Bundesgerichts in den Jahren 2004 und 2005' (2005) 141 *Zeitschrift des Bernischen Juristenvereins* 633–703.

Kälin Walter/Lienhard Andreas/Wyttenbach Judith, *Auslagerung von sicherheitspolizeilichen Aufgaben auf private Sicherheitsunternehmen*, Zeitschrift für Schweizerisches Recht, Beiheft 46 (Basel: Helbing Lichtenhahn) (2007).

Kalven Harry, 'The Concept of the Public Forum: Cox v. Louisiana' (1965) *Supreme Court Review* 1–32.

Kant Immanuel, *Gesammelte Schriften: Akademie Ausgabe*, Hrsg.: Bd. 1–22 Preussische Akademie der Wissenschaften, Bd. 23 Deutsche Akademie der Wissenschaften zu Berlin, ab Bd. 24 Akademie der Wissenschaften zu Göttingen (Berlin) (1900).

Kant Immanuel, *The Metaphysical Elements of Justice: Part 1 of the Metaphysics of Morals* (Indianapolis: Bobbs-Merrill) (1965).

Kant Immanuel, *Groundwork of the Metaphysics of Morals* (Cambridge: Cambridge University Press) (1998).

Kapur Ratna, 'Human Rights in the 21st Century: Take a Walk on the Dark Side' (2006) 28 *Sydney Law Review* 665–687.

Kaufmann Mathias/Walti Stephanie, 'Die polizeiliche Generalklausel - eine schillernde Rechtsfigur' in Youssef Omar Abo /Töndury Andrea (eds), *Der Schutz polizeilicher Güter: Entwicklungen und Spannungsfelder* (Zürich: Dike) (2011) 59–85.

Keller Helen, *Rezeption des Völkerrechts: Eine rechtsvergleichende Studie zur Praxis des U.S. Supreme Court, des Gerichtshofes der Europäischen Gemeinschaften und des schweizerischen Bundesgerichts in ausgewählten Bereichen* (Berlin: Springer) (2003).

Keller Helen/Stone Sweet Alec (eds), *A Europe of Rights: The Impact of the ECHR on National Legal Systems* (Oxford: Oxford University Press) (2008).

Keller Helen/Stone Sweet Alec, 'Assessing the Impact of the ECHR on National Legal Systems' in Keller Helen/Stone Sweet Alec (eds), *A Europe of Rights: The Impact of the ECHR on National Legal Systems* (Oxford: Oxford University Press) (2008) 677–710.

Keller Helen, 'Rechtsgleichheit und Diskriminierungsverbot' in Biaggini Giovanni/Gächter Thomas/Kiener Regina (eds), *Staatsrecht* (Zürich/St. Gallen: Dike) (2011) 503–519.

Keller Helen/Bürli Nicole, 'Überdenken der polizeilichen Generalklausel bei Vorliegen staatlicher Schutzpflichten' (2011) *Aktuelle Juristische Praxis* 1143–1152.

Kelling George L./Coles Catherine M., *Fixing Broken Windows: Restoring Order and Reducing Crime in Our Communities* (New York: Touchstone) (1996).

Kersten Jens/Meinel Florian, 'Grundrechte in privatisierten öffentlichen Räumen' (2007) 62 *Juristenzeitung* 1127–1134.

Kiener Regina/Kälin Walter, *Grundrechte* (Bern: Stämpfli) (2013) (2nd ed.).

Kiener Regina/Lanz Raphael, 'Amerikanisierung des schweizerischen Rechts – und ihre Grenzen: "Adversarial Legalism" und schweizerische Rechtsordnung' (2000) 119 *Zeitschrift für Schweizerisches Recht* 155–174.

Kiener Regina/Rütsche Bernhard/Kuhn Mathias, *Öffentliches Verfahrensrecht* (Zürich/St. Gallen: Dike) (2012).

Killias Martin/Kuhn André/Aebi Marcelo F., *Grundriss der Kriminologie: Eine europäische Perspektive* (Bern: Stämpfli) (2011) (2nd ed.).

Kirby Michael, 'Transnational Judicial Dialogue, Internationalisation of Law and Australian Judges' (2008) 9 *Melbourne Journal of International Law* 171–189.

Klatt Matthias/Meister Moritz, *The Constitutional Structure of Proportionality* (Oxford: Oxford University Press) (2012).

Kleinstüber Hans J., 'Habermas and the Public Sphere: From a German to a European Perspective' (2001) 8 *The Public* 95–108.

Kley Andreas, 'Art. 29a' in Ehrenzeller Bernhard/Schindler Benjamin/ Schweizer Rainer J./Vallender Klaus A. (eds), *Die schweizerische Bundesverfassung: St. Galler Kommentar* (Zürich/St. Gallen: Dike) (2014) (3rd ed.) 677–692.

Klug Francesca, *Values for a Godless Age: The Story of the UK's New Bill of Rights* (London: Penguin Books) (2000).

Köbler Gerhard, *Juristisches Wörterbuch: für Studium und Ausbildung* (München: Vahlen) (2007) (14th ed.).

Kohler Georg, 'Was ist Öffentlichkeit? Zur Bestimmung eines unübersichtlichen Wortfeldes' (1999) 58 *Studia philosophica* 197–217.

Kohler Georg/Thürer Daniel, 'Der Liberale und der öffentliche Raum: Gespräch zwischen Georg Kohler und Daniel Thürer' in Thürer Daniel (ed.), *Kosmopolitisches Staatsrecht: Grundidee Gerechtigkeit* (Zürich: Schulthess) (2005) 133–148.

Kohn Margaret, *Brave New Neighborhoods: The Privatization of Public Space* (New York: Routledge) (2004).

Kölz Alfred, 'Die Bedeutung der Französischen Revolution für das schweizerische öffentliche Recht und politische System – eine Skizze' (1989) 108 *Zeitschrift für Schweizerisches Recht* 497–516.

Kölz Alfred, *Neuere schweizerische Verfassungsgeschichte: Ihre Grundlinien vom Ende der Alten Eidgenossenschaft bis 1848* (Bern: Stämpfli) (1992).

Kölz Alfred (ed.), *Quellenbuch zur neueren schweizerischen Verfassungsgeschichte: Band I: Ihre Grundlinien vom Ende der Alten Eidgenossenschaft bis 1848* (Bern: Stämpfli) (1992).

Kölz Alfred (ed.), *Quellenbuch zur neueren schweizerischen Verfassungsgeschichte: Band II: Von 1848 bis in die Gegenwart* (Bern: Stämpfli) (1996).

Kölz Alfred, *Der Weg der Schweiz zum modernen Bundesstaat: Historische Abhandlungen, 1789, 1798, 1848, 1998* (Chur: Rüegger) (1998).

Kölz Alfred, *Neuere schweizerische Verfassungsgeschichte: Ihre Grundlinien in Bund und Kantonen seit 1848* (Bern: Stämpfli) (2004).

Komlosy Andrea, 'Der Staat schiebt ab – Zur nationalstaatlichen Konsolidierung von Heimat und Fremde im 18. und 19. Jahrhundert' in Hahn Sylvia/ Komlosy Andrea/Reiter Ilse (eds), *Ausweisung, Abschiebung, Vertreibung in Europa: 16.–20. Jahrhundert* (Innsbruck: Studien-Verlag) (2006) 87–114.

Kommers Donald P./Niehaus Stephanie E., 'An Introduction to American Equal Protection Law' in Wolfrum Rüdiger (ed.), *Gleichheit und Nichtdiskriminierung im nationalen und internationalen Menschenrechtsschutz* (Berlin: Springer) (2003) 25–57.

Kriele Martin, *Einführung in die Staatslehre: die geschichtlichen Legitimitätsgrundlagen des demokratischen Verfassungsstaates* (Reinbek: Rowohlt) (1975).

Kumm Mattias, 'The Idea of Socratic Contestation and the Right to Justification: The Point of Rights-Based Proportionality Review' (2010) 4 *Law and Ethics of Human Rights* 141–175.

Langworthy Robert H./Travis III Lawrence F., *Policing in America: A Balance of Forces* (New York: Macmillan) (1994).

Läpple Dieter, 'Gesellschaftszentriertes Raumkonzept' in Wentz Martin (ed.), *Stadt-Räume* (Frankfurt a. M.: Campus) (1991) 35–46.

Lauterpacht Hersch, *An International Bill of the Rights of Man* (New York: Columbia University Press) (1945).

Law David S., 'Generic Constitutional Law' (2005) 89 *Minnesota Law Review* 652–751.

Law David S./Chang Wen-Chen, 'The Limits of Global Judicial Dialogue' (2011) 86 *Washington Law Review* 523–577.

Law David S./Versteeg Mila, 'The Evolution and Ideology of Global Constitutionalism' (2011) 99 *California Law Review* 1163–1253.

Law David S./Versteeg Mila, 'The Declining Influence of the United States Constitution' (2012) 87 *New York University Law Review* 762–858.

Law Jonathan/Martin Elizabeth A. (eds), *Oxford Dictionary of Law* (Oxford: Oxford University Press) (2009) (7th ed.).

Lazarus Liora, 'Mapping the Right to Security' in Goold Benjamin/Lazarus Liora (eds), *Security and Human Rights* (Oxford: Hart) (2007) 325–346.

Lefebvre Henri, *Le droit à la ville – suivi de Espace et politique* (Paris: Anthropos; Seuil) (1968/1972).

Lefebvre Henri, *Writings on Cities* (Malden Mass: Blackwell) (1996).

Lefebvre Henri, *The Production of Space* (Malden: Blackwell) (2008).

Legnaro Aldo, 'Konturen der Sicherheitsgesellschaft: Eine polemisch-futurologische Skizze' (1997) 25 *Leviathan* 271–284.

Legnaro Aldo, 'Die Stadt, der Müll und das Fremde – Plurale Sicherheit, die Politik des Urbanen und die Steuerung der Subjekte' (1998) 30 *Kriminologisches Journal* 262–283.

Lepsius Oliver, *Verwaltungsrecht unter dem Common Law: Amerikanische Entwicklungen bis zum New Deal* (Tübingen: Mohr Siebeck) (1997).

Lester Anthony, 'The Overseas Trade in the American Bill of Rights' (1988) 88 *Columbia Law Review* 537–561.

Levi Ron, 'Making Counter-Law: On Having No Apparent Purpose in Chicago' (2009) 49 *British Journal of Criminology* 131–149.

Levy Leonard W., 'The Bill of Rights' in Barlow J. Jackson/Levy Leonard W./ Masugi Ken (eds), *The American Founding: Essays on the Formation of the Constitution* (New York: Greenwood Press) (1988) 295–327.

Lewinski Kai v., 'Recht auf Internet' (2011) *Rechtswissenschaft* 70–94.

Lienhard Andreas/Häsler Philipp, 'Verfassungsrechtliche Grundlagen des Sicherheitsrechts' in Schweizer Rainer J. (ed.), *Sicherheits- und Ordnungsrecht des Bundes* (Basel: Helbing Lichtenhahn) (2008) 95–154.

Lienhard Andreas/Zielniewicz Agata, 'Zum Anwendungsbereich des bundesrätlichen Notrechts' (2012) 113 *Schweizerisches Zentralblatt für Staats- und Verwaltungsrecht* 111–142.

Lijphart Arend, *Patterns of Democracy: Government Forms and Performance in Thirty-Six Countries* (New Haven: Yale University Press) (1999).

Lillich Richard B., 'Civil Rights' in Meron Theodor (ed.), *Human Rights in International Law* (New York: Oxford University Press) (1984) 115–170.

Lindenberg Michael/Schmidt-Semisch Henning, 'Sanktionsverzicht statt Herrschaftsverlust: Vom Übergang in die Kontrollgesellschaft' (1995) 27 *Kriminologisches Journal* 2–17.

Lindenberg Michael/Schmidt-Semisch Henning, 'Komplementäre Konkurrenz in der Sicherheitsgesellschaft: Überlegungen zum Zusammenwirken staatlicher und kommerzieller sozialer Kontrolle' (2000) 83 *Monatsschrift für Kriminologie und Strafrechtsreform* 306–319.

Linder Wolf, 'Direct Democracy' in Klöti Ulrich/Knoepfel Peter/ Kriesi Hanspeter/Linder Wolf/Papadopoulos Yannis/Sciarini Pascal (eds), *Handbook of Swiss Politics* (Zürich: Neue Zürcher Zeitung Publishing) (2007) (2nd ed.) 101–120.

Linder Wolf/Steffen Isabelle, 'Political Culture' in Klöti Ulrich/ Knoepfel Peter/Kriesi, Hanspeter/Linder Wolf/Papadopoulos Yannis/ Sciarini Pascal (eds), *Handbook of Swiss Politics* (Zürich: Neue Zürcher Zeitung Publishing) (2007) (2nd ed.) 15–34.

Linsi Christian, 'Verfassungsrechtliche Zuständigkeit des Bundes für den Erlass von Polizeirecht' (2008) *LeGes* 465–493.

Litscher Monika/Grossrieder Beat/Mösch-Payot Peter/Schmutz Marco, *Wegweisung aus öffentlichen Stadträumen* (Luzern: Hochschule Luzern – Soziale Arbeit) (2011).

Livingston Debra, 'Police Discretion and the Quality of Life in Public Places – Courts, Communities, and the New Policing' (1997) 97 *Columbia Law Review* 551–672.

Livingstone Stephen, 'Article 14 and the Prevention of Discrimination in the European Convention on Human Rights' (1997) *European Human Rights Law Review* 25–34.

Locke John, *Two Treatises of Government* (Cambridge: Cambridge University Press) (1998).

Lorenz Priska, 'Der Wegweisungsartikel im Sicherheitsdiskurs der Stadt Bern' in Caviezel Urezza/Fredrich Bettina/Wastl-Walter Doris (eds), *Geographien der (Un-)Sicherheit: Forschungsbericht 15* (Bern: Geographisches Institut, Universität Bern) (2011) 11–29.

Louis Patrik/Schindler Benjamin, 'Verwaltungsrecht und Grundrechte als "Türen" zum öffentlichen Raum' (2013) *Aktuelle Juristische Praxis* 796–806.

Loveland Ian, 'The Constitutionalisation of Political Libels in English Common Law' (1998) *Public Law* 633–646.

Low Setha, *Behind the Gates: Life, Security, and the Pursuit of Happiness in Fortress America* (New York: Routledge) (2003).

Lyon David, *Surveillance Studies: An Overview* (Cambridge: Polity Press) (2007).

MacCormick D. Neil, 'Der Rechtsstaat und die rule of law' (1984) *Juristenzeitung* 65–70.

Macdonald Stuart, 'A Suicidal Woman, Roaming Pigs and a Noisy Trampolinist: Refining the ASBO's Definition of "Anti-Social Behaviour"' (2006) 69 *Modern Law Review* 183–213.

MacKinnon Catharine A., 'Disputing Male Sovereignty: On United States v. Morrison' (2000) 114 *Harvard Law Review* 135–177.

Maddicott John Robert, *The Origins of the English Parliament, 924–1327* (Oxford: Oxford University Press) (2010).

Mahlmann Matthias, 'Human Dignity and Autonomy in Modern Constitutional Orders' in Rosenfeld Michel/Sajó András (eds), *The Oxford Handbook of Comparative Constitutional Law* (Oxford: Oxford University Press) (2012) 370–396.

Mahon Pascal, 'Art. 5' in Aubert Jean-François/Mahon Pascal (eds), *Petit commentaire de la Constitution fédérale de la Confédération suisse du 18 avril 1999* (Zurich: Schulthess) (2003) 39–51.

Mahon Pascal, 'Art. 7' in Aubert Jean-François/Mahon Pascal (eds), *Petit commentaire de la Constitution fédérale de la Confédération suisse du 18 avril 1999* (Zurich: Schulthess) (2003) 67–71.

Malinverni Giorgio, *La liberté de réunion: Etude de droit constitutionnel suisse* (Genève: Librairie de l'Université Georg et Cie) (1981).

Malinverni Giorgio, 'L'exercice des libertés sur le domaine public' in Aubert Jean-François/Bois Philippe (eds), *Mélanges André Grisel:*

Recueil de travaux offert à M. André Grisel (Neuchâtel: Ides et Calendes) (1983) 145–159.

Malinverni Giorgio, 'L'exercice des libertés idéales sur le domaine public' in Bellanger François/Tanquerel Thierry (eds), *Le domaine public* (Genève: Schulthess) (2004) 25–41.

Malinverni Giorgio, 'Meinungs-, Medien- und Informationsfreiheit' in Merten Detlef/Papier Hans-Jürgen (eds), *Handbuch der Grundrechte in Deutschland und Europa: Band VII/2: Grundrechte in der Schweiz und in Liechtenstein* (Heidelberg: C.F. Müller) (2007) 379–403.

Mallett William J., 'Managing the Post-Industrial City: Business Improvement Districts in the United States' (1994) 26 *Area* 276–287.

Maravall José María/ Przeworski Adam (eds), *Democracy and the Rule of Law* (Cambridge: Cambridge University Press) (2003).

Marks Susan, 'The European Convention on Human Rights and Its "Democratic Society"' (1995) 66 *British Year Book of International Law* 209–238.

Martenet Vincent, *Géométrie de l'égalité* (Bruxelles: Bruylant) (2003).

Mastronardi Philippe, *Strukturprinzipien der Bundesverfassung?* (Basel) (1988).

Mastronardi Philippe, *Verfassungslehre: Allgemeines Staatsrecht als Lehre vom guten und gerechten Staat* (Bern: Haupt) (2007).

Mathews Jud/Stone Sweet Alec, 'All Things in Proportion? American Rights Review and the Problem of Balancing' (2011) 60 *Emory Law Journal* 797–875.

Mathis Lukas, 'Die Ausübung politischer Rechte auf Bahnhofsarealen' *Jusletter*, 12. Dezember 2011, available at http://jusletter.weblaw.ch/juslissues/2011/644/_9820.html.

Mathys Hans, *Zum Begriff des Störers im Polizeirecht* (Zürich: Juris-Verlag) (1974).

Matthews Roger, 'Developing More Effective Strategies for Curbing Prostitution' (1990) *Security Journal* 182–187.

Mattmüller Markus, 'Allmend – Version vom 17. Mai 2001' *Historisches Lexikon der Schweiz*, available at www.hls-dhs-dss.ch/textes/d/D13704.php.

McBride Jeremy, 'Proportionality and the European Convention on Human Rights' in Ellis Evelyn (ed.), *The Principle of Proportionality in the Laws of Europe* (Oxford: Hart) (1999) 23–35.

McCrudden Christopher, 'A Common Law of Human Rights?: Transnational Judicial Conversations on Constitutional Rights' (2000) 20 *Oxford Journal of Legal Studies* 499–532.

McCrudden Christopher, 'Human Dignity and Judicial Interpretation of Human Rights' (2008) 19 *European Journal of International Law* 655–724.

McKechnie William Sharp, *Magna Carta: A Commentary on the Great Charter of King John* (Union, N.J.: Lawbook Exchange) (2000) (2nd ed.).

McLynn Frank, *Crime and Punishment in Eighteenth-Century England* (London: Routledge) (1989).

Mead David, 'Of Kettles, Cordons and Crowd Control: Austin v Commissioner of Police for the Metropolis and the Meaning of "Deprivation of Liberty"' (2009) *European Human Rights Law Review* 376–394.

Mead David, *The New Law of Peaceful Protest: Rights and Regulation in the Human Rights Act Era* (Oxford: Hart) (2010).

Meier-Hayoz Arthur, *Berner Kommentar zum schweizerischen Privatrecht, Band IV: Das Sachenrecht, 1. Abteilung: Das Eigentum, 2. Teilband: Grundeigentum I, Artikel 655–679 ZGB* (Bern: Stämpfli) (1965) (3rd ed.).

Merrills J. G., *The Development of International Law by the European Court of Human Rights* (Manchester: Manchester University Press) (1993) (2nd ed.).

Metzger Peter, *Schweizerisches juristisches Wörterbuch* (Basel: Helbing Lichtenhahn) (2005).

Meyer-Ladewig Jens, *Europäische Menschenrechtskonvention: EMRK: Handkommentar* (Baden-Baden, Basel: Nomos; Helbing Lichtenhahn) (2011) (3rd ed.).

Miaskowski August von, *Die schweizerische Allmend in ihrer geschichtlichen Entwickelung vom 13. Jahrhundert bis zur Gegenwart* (Leipzig: Duncker & Humblot) (1879).

Michaels Ralf, 'The Functional Method of Comparative Law' in Reimann Mathias/Zimmermann Reinhard (eds), *The Oxford Handbook of Comparative Law* (Oxford: Oxford University Press) (2006) 339–382.

Michelman Frank I., 'Rawls on Constitutionalism and Constitutional Law' in Freeman Samuel (ed.), *The Cambridge Companion to Rawls* (New York: Cambridge University Press) (2002) 394–425.

Mill John Stuart, 'Principles of Political Economy: With Some of Their Applications to Social Philosophy: Part II' in Robson John M. (ed.), *The Collected Works of John Stuart Mill* (Toronto: University of Toronto Press) (1963–1991).

Mill John Stuart, *On Liberty and Other Essays* (Oxford: Oxford University Press) (1991).

Miller Fred D., 'The Rule of Law in Ancient Greek Thought' in Sellers Mortimer (ed.), *The Rule of Law in Comparative Perspective* (Dordrecht: Springer) (2010) 11–18.

Milz Katharina, *Die Bedeutung Sozialer Netzwerke in der arabischen Welt: Länderbericht der Konrad-Adenauer-Stiftung e.V.* (July 2011), available at www.kas.de/rpg/de/publications/23306/.

Mitchell Don, 'The End of Public Space? People's Park, Definitions of the Public, and Democracy' (1995) 85 *Annals of the Association of American Geography* 108–133.

Mitchell Don, 'The Liberalization of Free Speech: Or, How Protest in Public Space is Silenced' (2003) 4 *Stanford Agora*, available at http://agora.stanford.edu/agora/volume4/mitchell.shtml.

Mitchell Don, *The Right to the City: Social Justice and the Fight for Public Space* (New York: The Guilford Press) (2003).

Möckli Silvano, *Die schweizerischen Landsgemeinde-Demokratien* (St. Gallen: Institut für Politikwissenschaft) (1986).

Moeckli Daniel, *Human Rights and Non-discrimination in the 'War on Terror'* (Oxford: Oxford University Press) (2008).

Moeckli Daniel, 'Bettelverbote: Einige rechtsvergleichende Überlegungen zur Grundrechtskonformität' (2010) 111 *Schweizerisches Zentralblatt für Staats- und Verwaltungsrecht* 537–574.

Moeckli Daniel, 'Equality and Non-Discrimination' in Moeckli Daniel/ Shah Sangeeta/Sivakumaran Sandesh (eds), *International Human Rights Law* (Oxford: Oxford University Press) (2014) (2nd ed.) 157–173.

Moeckli Daniel/Keller Raphael, 'Wegweisungen und Rayonverbote – ein Überblick' (2012) *Sicherheit & Recht* 231–245.

Mohler Markus, 'Zur Anfechtbarkeit polizeilicher intervenierender Realakte unter dem Gesichtspunkt der Rechtsweggarantie gemäss Art. 29a BV' (2007) *Aktuelle Juristische Praxis* 461–472.

Mohler Markus, 'Vernetzung von Sicherheit' in Schweizer Rainer J. (ed.), *Sicherheits- und Ordnungsrecht des Bundes* (Basel: Helbing Lichtenhahn) (2008) 521–624.

Mohler Markus H.F, *Grundzüge des Polizeirechts in der Schweiz* (Basel: Helbing Lichtenhahn) (2012).

Möller Kai, *The Global Model of Constitutional Rights* (Oxford: Oxford University Press) (2012).

Möllers Christoph, *Demokratie – Zumutungen und Versprechen* (Berlin: Wagenbach) (2008).

Montesquieu Charles Secondat de, *De l'esprit des lois* (Paris: Les Belles Lettres) (1950–1961).

Moor Pierre, *Droit administratif III: L'organisation des activités administratives. Les biens de l'Etat* (Berne: Staempfli) (1992).

Moor Pierre, 'Principes de l'activité étatique et responsabilité de l'Etat' in Thürer Daniel/Aubert Jean-François/Müller Jörg Paul (eds), *Verfassungsrecht der Schweiz* (Zürich: Schulthess) (2001) 265–283.

Moor Pierre/Flückiger Alexandre/Martenet Vincent, *Droit administratif I: Les fondements* (Berne: Stämpfli) (2012) (3rd ed.).

Moor Pierre/Poltier Etienne, *Droit administratif II: Les actes administratifs et leur contrôle* (Berne: Stämpfli) (2011) (3rd ed.).

Moser André Werner, *Der öffentliche Grund und seine Benützung: im Lichte der bundesgerichtlichen Rechtsprechung und unter besonderer Berücksichtigung der Rechtslage im Kanton Bern* (Bern: Stämpfli) (2011).

Moser Hans Peter, 'Besprechung von BGE 100 Ia 392' (1975) 76 *Schweizerisches Zentralblatt für Staats- und Verwaltungsrecht* 262–271.

Muir William K., *Police: Streetcorner Politicians* (Chicago: University of Chicago Press) (1979).

Müller Georg, *Inhalt und Formen der Rechtssetzung als Problem der demokratischen Kompetenzordnung* (Basel: Helbing & Lichtenhahn) (1979).

Müller Georg, 'Der Gleichheitssatz' (1989) 47 *Veröffentlichungen der Vereinigung der Deutschen Staatsrechtslehrer* 37–62.

Müller Joël O., 'Das revidierte Konkordat über Massnahmen zur Bekämpfung der Gewalt an Sportveranstaltungen vom 2. Februar 2012 ("Hooligan-Konkordat")' (2013) *recht* 109–121.

Müller Jörg Paul, *Demokratische Gerechtigkeit: Eine Studie zur Legitimität politischer und rechtlicher Ordnung* (München: Deutscher Taschenbuch Verlag) (1993).

Müller Jörg Paul, 'Rule of Law – Rechtsstaat' in Häberle Peter/Müller Jörg Paul (eds), *Menschenrechte und Bürgerrechte in einer vielgestaltigen Welt: Wissenschaftliche Begegnung einiger Freunde von Thomas Fleiner zu Ehren seines 60. Geburtstages* (Basel: Helbing & Lichtenhahn) (2000) 37–47.

Müller Jörg Paul, 'Allgemeine Bemerkungen zu den Grundrechten' in Thürer Daniel/Aubert Jean-François/Müller Jörg Paul (eds), *Verfassungsrecht der Schweiz* (Zürich: Schulthess) (2001).

Müller Jörg Paul, 'Geschichtliche Grundlagen, Zielsetzung und Funktionen der Grundrechte' in Merten Detlef/Papier Hans-Jürgen (eds), *Handbuch der Grundrechte in Deutschland und Europa: Band VII/2: Grundrechte in der Schweiz und in Liechtenstein* (Heidelberg: C.F. Müller) (2007) 3–30.

Müller Jörg Paul, *Die demokratische Verfassung: Von der Selbstbestimmung der Menschen in den notwendigen Ordnungen des Zusammenlebens* (Zürich: Verlag Neue Zürcher Zeitung) (2009) (2nd ed.).

Müller Jörg Paul/Schefer Markus, *Grundrechte in der Schweiz: Im Rahmen der Bundesverfassung, der EMRK und der UNO-Pakte* (Bern: Stämpfli) (2008) (4th ed.).

Müller Markus, 'Die Rechtsweggarantie: Chancen und Risiken' (2004) *Zeitschrift des Bernischen Juristenvereins* 161–197.

Müller Markus/Jenni Christoph, 'Die polizeiliche Generalklausel – Ein Institut mit Reformbedarf' (2008) *Sicherheit & Recht* 4–18.

Muller Pierre, 'Le principe de la proportionnalité' (1978) 97 *Revue de droit suisse* 197–274.

Mumford Lewis, *The City in History: Its Origins, Its Transformations, and Its Prospects* (New York: Harcourt, Brace & World) (1961).

Nash Jennifer C., 'From Lavender to Purple: Privacy, Black Women, and Feminist Legal Theory' (2005) 11 *Cardozo Women's Law Journal* 303–330.

national Law Center on Homelessness & Poverty and National Coalition for the Homeless, 'Homes Not Handcuffs: The Criminalization of Homelessness in U.S. Cities' (July 2009), available at www.nationalhomeless .org/publications/crimreport/index.html.

Neeson J. M., *Commoners: Common Right, Enclosure and Social Change in England, 1700–1820* (Cambridge: Cambridge University Press) (1993).

Neidhart Leonhard, *Die politische Schweiz: Fundamente und Institutionen* (Zürich: Verlag Neue Zürcher Zeitung) (2002).

Nellis Mike, '24/7/365: Mobility, Locatability, and the Satellite Tracking of Offenders' in Aas Katja Franko/Oppen Gundhus Helene/Monk Lomell Heidi (eds), *Technologies of Insecurity: The Surveillance of Everyday Life* (London: Routledge) (2008) 105–124.

Neuman Gerald L., 'Human Dignity in United States Constitutional Law' in Simon Dieter/Weiss Manfred (eds), *Zur Autonomie des Individuums: Liber Amicorum Spiros Simitis* (Baden-Baden: Nomos Verlagsgesellschaft) (2000) 249–271.

Neumann Franz, *Behemoth: The Structure and Practice of National Socialism* (London: Victor Gollancz) (1942).

Neuner Claudia, *Zulässigkeit und Grenzen polizeilicher Verweisungsmassnahmen* (Berlin: Duncker & Humblot) (2003).

Nolte Georg, 'Gleichheit und Nichtdiskriminierung' in Wolfrum Rüdiger (ed.), *Gleichheit und Nichtdiskriminierung im nationalen und internationalen Menschenrechtsschutz* (Berlin: Springer) (2003) 235–252.

Nowak John E./Rotunda Ronald D., *Constitutional Law* (St. Paul: West) (2004) (7th ed.).

Nowlin Christopher, 'The Protection of Morals Under the European Convention for the Protection of Human Rights and Fundamental Freedoms' (2002) 24 *Human Rights Quarterly* 264–286.

Oertzen Peter von, 'Die Grundlagen der Demokratie' in Schultz Uwe (ed.), *Toleranz: Die Krise der demokratischen Tugend und sechzehn Vorschläge zu ihrer Überwindung* (Reinbek bei Hamburg: Rowohlt) (1974) 195–208.

Oesch Matthias, *Differenzierung und Typisierung: Zur Dogmatik der Rechtsgleichheit in der Rechtsetzung* (Bern: Stämpfli) (2008).

Rainey Bernadette/Wicks Elizabeth/Ovey Clare, *Jacobs, White & Ovey: The European Convention on Human Rights* (Oxford: Oxford University Press) (2014) (6th ed.).

Parkinson John R., *Democracy and Public Space: The Physical Sites of Democratic Performance* (Oxford: Oxford University Press) (2012).

Paton-Simpson Elizabeth, 'Privacy and the Resonable Paranoid: The Protection of Privacy in Public Places' (2000) 50 *University of Toronto Law Journal* 305–346.

Paust Jordan J., 'Human Dignity as a Constitutional Right: A Jurisprudentially Based Inquiry into Criteria and Content' (1984) 27 *Howard Law Journal* 145–225.

Pearson Geoff, 'Hybrid Law and Human Rights – Banning and Behaviour Orders in the Appeal Courts' (2006) 27 *Liverpool Law Review* 125–145.

Pech Laurent, 'The Rule of Law as a Constitutional Principle of the European Union' (2009), available at http://papers.ssrn.com/sol3/papers.cfm?abstract_id=1463242.

Peerenboom Randall, *China's Long March Toward Rule of Law* (Cambridge: Cambridge University Press) (2002).

Peters Anne, 'Diskriminierungsverbote' in Merten Detlef/Papier Hans-Jürgen (eds), *Handbuch der Grundrechte in Deutschland und Europa: Band VII/2: Grundrechte in der Schweiz und in Liechtenstein* (Heidelberg: C.F. Müller) (2007) 255–299.

Peters Anne/Altwicker Tilmann, *Europäische Menschenrechtskonvention: Mit rechtsvergleichenden Bezügen zum deutschen Grundgesetz* (München: C.H. Beck) (2012).

Phillips Anne, 'Pluralism, Solidarity, and Change' in Weeks Jeffrey (ed.), *The Lesser Evil and the Greater Good: The Theory and Politics of Social Diversity* (London: Rivers Oram Press) (1994) 235–252.

Pindell Ngai, 'Finding a Right to the City: Exploring Property and Community in Brazil and in the United States' (2006) 39 *Vanderbilt Journal of Transnational Law* 435–479.

Pizzolatto Konzen Lucas, 'The City and Its Public Spaces: The Legal Dimension Explored Sociologically' (2011) 34 *Diálogos de Saberes* 273–288.

Polyviou Polyvios G., *The Equal Protection of the Laws* (London: Duckworth) (1980).

Rachor Frederik, 'Polizeihandeln' in Lisken Hans/Denninger Erhard (eds), *Handbuch des Polizeirechts: Gefahrenabwehr, Strafverfolgung, Rechtsschutz* (München: Beck) (2012) (5th ed.) 284–600.

Radbruch Gustav, 'Gesetzliches Unrecht und übergesetzliches Recht' (1946) 1 *Süddeutsche Juristen-Zeitung* 105–108.

Ramsay Peter, 'The Theory of Vulnerable Autonomy and the Legitimacy of the Civil Preventative Order' (2008) *LSE Working Papers*, available at www.lse.ac.uk/collections/law/wps/WPS2008-01_Ramsay.pdf.

Ramsay Peter, 'Substantively Uncivilized ASBOs' (2010) *Criminal Law Review* 761–763.

Ramsay Peter, *The Insecurity State: Vulnerable Autonomy and the Right to Security in the Criminal Law* (Oxford: Oxford University Press) (2012).

Rao Neomi, 'Three Concepts of Dignity in Constitutional Law' (2011) 86 *Notre Dame Law Review* 183–271.

Raselli Niccolò, 'Die neuen Zwangsmassnahmen im Ausländerrecht im Lichte von Verfassung und Menschenrechten' (1994) *Asyl* 79–88.

RAWLS JOHN, *Political Liberalism* (New York: Columbia University Press) (1993).

RAWLS JOHN, *A Theory of Justice* (Oxford: Oxford University Press) (1999).

RAWLS JOHN, 'Reply to Alexander and Musgrave' in Clayton Matthew/Williams Andrew (eds), *The Ideal of Equality* (Basingstoke: Macmillan) (2000) 21–40.

RAZ JOSEPH, 'The Rule of Law and Its Virtue' (1977) 93 *Law Quarterly Review* 195–211.

REICH JOHANNES, *Grundsatz der Wirtschaftsfreiheit: Evolution und Dogmatik von Art. 94 Abs. 1 und 4 der Bundesverfassung der Schweizerischen Eidgenossenschaft vom 18. April 1999* (Zürich/St. Gallen: Dike) (2011).

REINHARD HANS, *Allgemeines Polizeirecht: Aufgaben, Grundsätze und Handlungen* (Bern: Paul Haupt) (1993).

REYNOLDS K. MICHAEL/SEYDLITZ RUTH/JENKINS PAMELA, 'Do Juvenile Curfew Laws Work? A Time-Series Analysis of the New Orleans Law' (2000) 17 *Justice Quarterly* 205–230.

RHINOW RENÉ, *Rechtsetzung und Methodik: rechtstheoretische Untersuchungen zum gegenseitigen Verhältnis von Rechtsetzung und Rechtsanwendung* (Basel: Helbing & Lichtenhahn) (1979).

RHINOW RENÉ, 'Grundprobleme der schweizerischen Demokratie' (1984) 103 *Zeitschrift für Schweizerisches Recht* 113–273.

RICHLI PAUL, 'Zum Rechtsschutz gegen verfügungsfreies Staatshandeln in der Totalrevision der Bundesrechtspflege' (1998) *Aktuelle Juristische Praxis* 1426–1442.

RICHTER DAGMAR, '"Befriedete Bezirke" und andere demonstrationsfreie Zonen – Kategorienbildung und Problemtypologie anhand in- und ausländischen Versammlungsrechts' in Cremer Hans-Joachim/Giegerich Thomas/Richter Dagmar/Zimmermann Andreas (eds), *Tradition und Weltoffenheit des Rechts: Festschrift für Helmut Steinberger* (Berlin: Springer) (2002) 899–982.

RIEDER ANDREAS, *Form oder Effekt? Art. 8 Abs. 2 BV und die ungleichen Auswirkungen staatlichen Handelns* (Bern: Stämpfli) (2003).

RITTER WERNER, *Das Erfordernis der genügenden Bestimmtheit – dargestellt am Beispiel des Polizeirechts* (Chur: Verlag Rüegger AG) (1994).

RIVERS JULIAN, 'Proportionality and Variable Intensity of Review' (2006) 65 *Cambridge Law Journal* 174–207.

ROBERTS DOROTHY E., 'Foreword: Race, Vagueness, and the Social Meaning of Order-Maintenance Policing' (1999) 89 *Journal of Criminal Law and Criminology* 775–836.

ROBERTS PAUL, 'Penal Offence in Question: Some Reference Points for Interdisciplinary Conversation' in von Hirsch Andrew/Simester A. P. (eds), *Incivilities: Regulating Offensive Behaviour* (Oxford: Hart) (2006) 1–56.

ROSE CAROL, 'The Comedy of the Commons: Custom, Commerce, and Inherently Public Property' (1986) 53 *University of Chicago Law Review* 711–781.

ROSENFELD MICHEL, 'Rule of Law versus Rechtsstaat' in Häberle Peter/Müller Jörg Paul (eds), *Menschenrechte und Bürgerrechte in einer vielgestaltigen Welt: Wissenschaftliche Begegnung einiger Freunde von Thomas Fleiner zu Ehren seines 60. Geburtstages* (Basel: Helbing & Lichtenhahn) (2000) 49–71.

ROSENFELD MICHEL, 'The Rule of Law and the Legitimacy of Constitutional Democracy' (2000) 74 *Southern California Law Review* 1307–1351.

ROTHMAN DAVID J., Perfecting the Prison - United States, 1789–1865' in Morris Norval/Rothman David J. (eds), *The Oxford History of the Prison: The Practice of Punishment in Western Society* (New York: Oxford University Press) (1995) 111–127.

ROUSSEAU JEAN-JACQUES, *Du contrat social* (Paris: Gallimard) (2007).

ROUSSEAU MAX, 'La ville comme machine à mobilité' (2008) *Métropoles*, available at http://metropoles.revues.org/2562.

RUEFLE WILLIAM/REYNOLDS KENNETH MIKE, 'Keep Them at Home: Juvenile Curfew Ordinances in 200 American Cities' (1996) XV *American Journal of Police* 63–84.

RUTLAND ROBERT ALLEN, *The Birth of the Bill of Rights: 1776–1791* (Chapel Hill: University of North Carolina Press) (1955).

SALADIN PETER, 'Unerfüllte Bundesverfassung?' (1974) 93 *Zeitschrift für Schweizerisches Recht* 307–338.

SALADIN PETER, *Grundrechte im Wandel: Die Rechtsprechung des Schweizerischen Bundesgerichts zu den Grundrechten in einer sich ändernden Umwelt* (Bern: Stämpfli) (1982) (3rd ed.).

SANTORO EMILIO, 'The Rule of Law and the "Liberties of the English": The Interpretation of Albert Venn Dicey' in Costa Pietro/Zolo Danilo (eds), *The Rule of Law: History, Theory and Criticism* (Dordrecht: Springer) (2007) 153–199.

SARINE L. ELIZABETH, 'Regulating the Social Pollution of Systemic Discrimination Caused by Implicit Bias' (2012) 100 *California Law Review* 1359–1399.

SARTORI GIOVANNI, *The Theory of Democracy Revisited* (Chatham: Chatham House Publishers) (1987).

SAUER BARBARA, *Das Recht der Vollzugspolizeien von Bund und Kantonen in der Schweiz: Eine vergleichende Untersuchung aus der Perspektive der bundesdeutschen Polizeirechtsordnung* (Würzburg: Ergon Verlag) (2007).

SAXER URS, *Die Grundrechte und die Benutzung öffentlicher Strassen: Eine Untersuchung der Bundesgerichtspraxis, unter Berücksichtigung deutscher Entscheidungen* (Zürich: Schulthess) (1988).

SCHEFER MARKUS, *Die Kerngehalte von Grundrechten: Geltung, Dogmatik, inhaltliche Ausgestaltung* (Bern: Stämpfli) (2001).

Schefer Markus, *Die Beeinträchtigung von Grundrechten: Zur Dogmatik von Art. 36 BV* (Bern: Stämpfli) (2006).

Schewe Christoph S., *Das Sicherheitsgefühl und die Polizei: Darf die Polizei das Sicherheitsgefühl schützen?* (Berlin: Duncker & Humblot) (2008).

Scheyli Martin, *Politische Öffentlichkeit und deliberative Demokratie nach Habermas: Institutionelle Gestaltung durch direktdemokratische Beteiligungsformen?* (Baden-Baden, Bern: Nomos) (2000).

Schindler Benjamin, *Verwaltungsermessen: Gestaltungskompetenzen der öffentlichen Verwaltung in der Schweiz* (Zürich/St. Gallen: Dike) (2010).

Schindler Benjamin, '100 Jahre Verwaltungsrecht in der Schweiz' (2011) 130 *Zeitschrift für Schweizerisches Recht* 331–437.

Schindler Benjamin, 'Rechtsschutz im Polizeirecht: Eine Standortbestimmung' (2012) *Sicherheit & Recht* 215–221.

Schindler Dietrich, 'Die Staatslehre in der Schweiz' (1976) 25 *Jahrbuch des öffentlichen Rechts der Gegenwart* 255–279.

Schlink Bernhard, 'Proportionality (1)' in Rosenfeld Michel/Sajó András (eds), *The Oxford Handbook of Comparative Constitutional Law* (Oxford: Oxford University Press) (2012) 718–737.

Schmid Gerhard/Uhlmann Felix, 'Idee und Ausgestaltung des Rechtsstaates' in Thürer Daniel/Aubert Jean-François/Müller Jörg Paul (eds), *Verfassungsrecht der Schweiz* (Zürich: Schulthess) (2001) 223–232.

Schmidt Manfred G., *Demokratietheorien: Eine Einführung* (Wiesbaden: VS Verlag für Sozialwissenschaften) (2010).

Schmitz Thomas, *Strassen- und polizeirechtliches Vorgehen gegen Randgruppen (Bettler, Land- und Stadtstreicher)* (München: Herbert Utz Verlag) (2003).

Schubert Ernst, *Räuber, Henker, arme Sünder: Verbrechen und Strafe im Mittelalter* (Darmstadt: Wissenschaftliche Buchgesellschaft) (2007).

Schucht Carsten, *Generalklausel und Standardmassnahme: Ein Beitrag zur Bestimmung der Reichweite des Befugnistyps Generalklausel bei nicht typisierten (Standard-)Massnahmen am Beispiel von Platzverweisung, Aufenthaltsverbot, Wohnungsverweisung, körperlicher Untersuchung, Verbringungsgewahrsam und Meldeauflage* (Stuttgart: Boorberg) (2010).

Schuler Douglas/ Day Peter (eds), *Shaping the Network Society: The New Role of Civil Society in Cyberspace* (Cambridge, Mass.: MIT Press) (2004).

Schwander Marianne, *Häusliche Gewalt: Situation kantonaler Massnahmen aus rechtlicher Sicht: Bericht im Auftrag des eidgenössischen Büros für die Gleichstellung von Frau und Mann* (Bern) (2006).

Schwarze Jürgen, *Europäisches Verwaltungsrecht* (Baden-Baden: Nomos) (2005) (2nd ed.).

Schweizer Rainer J., 'Entwicklungen im Polizeirecht von Bund und Kantonen' (1997) *Aktuelle Juristische Praxis* 379–385.

Schweizer Rainer J., 'Recht auf Ehe und Familie' in Merten Detlef/Papier Hans-Jürgen (eds), *Handbuch der Grundrechte in Deutschland und Europa: Band VII/2: Grundrechte in der Schweiz und in Liechtenstein* (Heidelberg: C.F. Müller) (2007) 327–349.

Schweizer Rainer J., 'Art. 8' in Ehrenzeller Bernhard/Schindler Benjamin/ Schweizer Rainer J./Vallender Klaus A. (eds), *Die schweizerische Bundesverfassung: St. Galler Kommentar* (Zürich/St. Gallen: Dike) (2014) (3rd ed.) 201–236.

Schweizer Rainer J., 'Art. 36' in Ehrenzeller Bernhard/Schindler Benjamin/ Schweizer Rainer J./Vallender Klaus A. (eds), *Die schweizerische Bundesverfassung: St. Galler Kommentar* (Zürich/St. Gallen: Dike) (2014) (3rd ed.) 822–842.

Schweizer Rainer J./Müller Lucien, 'Zwecke, Möglichkeiten und Grenzen der Gesetzgebung im Polizeibereich' (2008) *LeGes* 379–399.

Schweizer Rainer J./Sutter Patrick/Widmer Nina, 'Grundbegriffe' in Schweizer Rainer J. (ed.), *Sicherheits- und Ordnungsrecht des Bundes* (Basel: Helbing Lichtenhahn) (2008) 53–94.

Schwerhoff Gerd, 'Vertreibung als Strafe – Der Stadt- und Landesverweis im Ancien Régime' in Hahn Sylvia/Komlosy Andrea/Reiter Ilse (eds), *Ausweisung, Abschiebung, Vertreibung in Europa: 16.–20. Jahrhundert* (Innsbruck: Studien-Verlag) (2006) 48–72.

Sedler Robert A., 'The Role of "Intent" in Discrimination Analysis' in Loenen Titia/Rodrigues Peter R. (eds), *Non-Discrimination Law: Comparative Perspectives* (The Hague: Kluwer Law International) (1999) 91–103.

Selmi Michael, 'Indirect Discrimination: a Perspective From the United States' in Loenen Titia/Rodrigues Peter R. (eds), *Non-Discrimination Law: Comparative Perspectives* (The Hague: Kluwer Law International) (1999) 213–222.

Sen Amartya, 'Democracy as a Universal Value' (1999) 10 *Journal of Democracy* 3–17.

Sennett Richard, *The Fall of Public Man* (New York: Norton) (1992).

Sennett Richard, *The Uses of Disorder: Personal Identity and City Life* (New York: Norton) (1992).

Sennett Richard, *Flesh and Stone: The Body and the City in Western Civilization* (New York: W.W. Norton) (1994).

Servon Lisa J., *Bridging the Digital Divide: Technology, Community, and Public Policy* (Oxford: Wiley-Blackwell) (2002).

Sessar Klaus/Herrmann Heike/Keller Wolfgang/Weinrich Martin/ Breckner Ingrid, *Insecurities in European Cities: Crime-Related Fear Within the Context of New Anxieties and Community-Based Crime Prevention* (December 2004), available at www2.jura.uni-hamburg.de/instkrim/kriminologie/Projekte/INSEC/InSec%20Final%20Report.pdf.

Shaw Malcolm N., *International Law* (Cambridge: Cambridge University Press) (2014) (7th ed.).

Shute Stephen, 'New Civil Preventative Orders: Sexual Offences Prevention Orders, Foreign Travel Orders, Risk of Sexual Harm Orders' (2004) *Criminal Law Review* 417–440.

Siegel Stephen A., 'The Origin of the Compelling State Interest Test and Strict Scrutiny' (2006) 48 *American Journal of Legal History* 355–407.

Siehr Angelika, *Das Recht am öffentlichen Raum: Theorie des öffentlichen Raumes und rechtsdogmatische Probleme seiner Nutzung im Spiegel kommunikativer Freiheitsrechte* (Tübingen: Mohr Siebeck) (forthcoming 2016) (manuscript on file with author; page references refer to the unpublished manuscript).

Simester A. P./von Hirsch Andrew, 'Rethinking the Offense Principle' (2002) 8 *Legal Theory* 269–295.

Simester A. P./von Hirsch Andrew, 'Regulating Offensive Conduct through Two-Step Prohibitions' in von Hirsch Andrew/Simester A. P. (eds), *Incivilities: Regulating Offensive Behaviour* (Oxford: Hart) (2006) 173–194.

Singelnstein Tobias, 'Jeder ist verdächtig: Das neue gesellschaftliche Verständnis von Sicherheit und Bedrohung als Grundlage sozialer Kontrolle' (2007) 46 *Vorgänge: Zeitschrift für Bürgerrechte und Gesellschaftspolitik* 118–126.

Singelnstein Tobias/Stolle Peer, *Die Sicherheitsgesellschaft: Soziale Kontrolle im 21. Jahrhundert* (Wiesbaden: VS Verlag für Sozialwissenschaften) (2012) (3rd ed.).

Skogan Wesley Gordon, *Disorder and Decline: Crime and the Spiral of Decay in American Neighborhoods* (Berkeley, Calif.: University of California Press) (1992).

Slaughter Anne-Marie, 'A Global Community of Courts' (2003) 44 *Harvard International Law Journal* 191–219.

Slaughter Anne-Marie, *A New World Order* (Princeton: Princeton University Press) (2004).

Sloss David, 'The Domestication of International Human Rights: Non-Self-Executing Declarations and Human Rights Treaties' (1999) 24 *Yale Journal of International Law* 129–221.

Smith Neil, 'Degeneracy in Theory and Practice: Spatial Interactionism and Radical Eclecticism' (1981) 5 *Progress in Human Geography* 111–118.

Smith Neil, 'Global Social Cleansing: Postliberal Revanchism and the Export of Zero Tolerance' (2001) 28 *Social Justice* 68–74.

Smith Neil, 'New Globalism, New Urbanism: Gentrification as Global Urban Strategy' (2002) 34 *Antipode* 427–450.

Sohn Louis, 'The Human Rights Law of the Charter' (1977) 12 *Texas International Law Journal* 129–140.

Soòs Robert/Vögeli Christoph, 'BWIS-Massnahmen gegen Gewalt an Sportveranstaltungen: Top oder Flop – Das Rayonverbot und die Meldeauflage in der Praxis' (2008) *Sicherheit & Recht* 156–161.

Spielmann Dean, 'Jurisprudence of the European Court of Human Rights and the Constitutional Systems of Europe' in Rosenfeld Michel/Sajó András (eds), *The Oxford Handbook of Comparative Constitutional Law* (Oxford: Oxford University Press) (2012) 1231–1252.

Spierenburg Pieter, 'The Body and the State – Early Modern Europe' in Morris Norval/Rothman David J. (eds), *The Oxford History of the Prison: The Practice of Punishment in Western Society* (New York: Oxford University Press) (1995) 49–77.

Spoendlin Kaspar, *Die verfassungsmässige Garantie der persönlichen Freiheit* (Zürich: Schulthess) (1945).

Starck Christian, 'Rechtsvergleichung im öffentlichen Recht' (1997) 52 *Juristenzeitung* 1021–1030.

Steiker Carol S., 'Punishment and Procedure: Punishment Theory and the Criminal-Civil Procedural Divide' (1997) 85 *Georgetown Law Journal* 775–819.

Steinhardt Ralph G., 'The Role of International Law as a Canon of Domestic Statutory Construction' (1990) 43 *Vanderbilt Law Review* 1103–1197.

Stern Klaus, 'Die öffentliche Sache' (1964) 21 *Veröffentlichungen der Vereinigung der Deutschen Staatsrechtslehrer* 183–228.

Stolleis Michael, 'Rechtsstaat' in Erler Adalbert/Kaufmann Ekkehard (eds), *Handwörterbuch zur deutschen Rechtsgeschichte* (Berlin: Schmidt) (1971–1998) 367–375.

Stone Richard, 'Breach of the Peace: The Case for Abolition' (2001) *Web Journal of Current Legal Issues*, available at www.bailii.org/uk/other/journals/WebJCLI/2001/issue2/stone2.html.

Stone Sweet Alec/Mathews Jud, 'Proportionality Balancing and Global Constitutionalism' (2008) 47 *Columbia Journal of Transnational Law* 72–164.

Stott Clifford/Pearson Geoff, 'Football Banning Orders, Proportionality, and Public Order Policing' (2006) 45 *Howard Journal* 241–254.

Strasser Othmar, *Polizeiliche Zwangsmassnahmen* (Zürich: Schulthess) (1981).

Strebel Helmut, 'Vergleichung und vergleichende Methode im öffentlichen Recht' (1964) 24 *Zeitschrift für ausländisches öffentliches Recht und Völkerrecht* 405–430.

Strosnider Kim, 'Anti-Gang Ordinances after City of Chicago v. Morales: The Intersection of Race, Vagueness Doctrine, and Equal Protection in the Criminal Law' (2002) 39 *American Criminal Law Review* 101–146.

Stuntz William J., 'Crime Talk and Law Talk' (1995) 23 *Reviews in American History* 153–158.

Sullivan E. Thomas/Frase Richard S., *Proportionality Principles in American Law: Controlling Excessive Government Actions* (Oxford: Oxford University Press) (2009).

Sullivan Kathleen M./Feldman Noah, *Constitutional Law* (Westbury: Foundation Press) (2013) (18th ed.).

Sunstein Cass R., *The Partial Constitution* (Cambridge, Mass.: Harvard University Press) (1993).

Sunstein Cass R., *Democracy and the Problem of Free Speech* (New York: The Free Press) (1995).

Sunstein Cass R., *republic.com* (Princeton, N.J.: Princeton University Press) (2001).

Tamanaha Brian Z., *On the Rule of Law: History, Politics, Theory* (Cambridge: Cambridge University Press) (2004).

Tanquerel Thierry, *Manuel de droit administratif* (Genève: Schulthess) (2011).

Teitel Ruti, 'Comparative Constitutional Law in a Global Age' (2003) 117 *Harvard Law Review* 2570–2596.

Teitel Ruti, 'Humanity Law: A New Interpretive Lens on the International Sphere' (2008) 77 *Fordham Law Review* 667–702.

Teitel Ruti, *Humanity's Law* (Oxford: Oxford University Press) (2011).

tenBroek Jacobus, *Equal Under Law: The Antislavery Origins of the Fourteenth Amendment* (New York: Collier Books) (1965).

Thaler Daniel, 'Hooliganismus und Sport' in Arter Oliver/Baeriswyl Bruno/Baddeley Margareta (eds), *Sport und Recht: 3. Tagungsband* (Bern: Stämpfli) (2006) 245–330.

Thieme Hans, *Die Funktion der Regalien im Mittelalter* (Darmstadt: Wissenschaftliche Buchgesellschaft) (1968).

Thompson E. P., *Whigs and Hunters: The Origin of the Black Act* (London: Penguin Books) (1990).

Thürer Daniel, 'Das Störerprinzip im Polizeirecht' (1983) 102 *Zeitschrift für Schweizerisches Recht* 463–486.

Thürer Daniel, 'Verfassungsrecht und Völkerrecht' in Thürer Daniel/Aubert Jean-François/Müller Jörg Paul (eds), *Verfassungsrecht der Schweiz* (Zürich: Schulthess) (2001) 179–206.

Thürer Daniel, 'Kosmopolitische Verfassungsentwicklungen' in Thürer Daniel (ed.), *Kosmopolitisches Staatsrecht: Grundidee Gerechtigkeit* (Zürich: Schulthess) (2005) 3–39.

Thurnheer Simon, 'Duldung freier Meinungsäusserung als positive staatliche Leistung? – Zur Natur und Tragweite der "weitergehenden Einschränkungen" von Kundgebungen auf öffentlichem Grund' (2006) *Aktuelle Juristische Praxis* 943–948.

Thurnheer Simon, *Demonstrationsfreiheit in England und der Schweiz: Eine vergleichende Untersuchung und ein Beitrag zur Grundrechtsdogmatik* (Zürich: Schulthess) (2010).

THURNHERR DANIELA, 'The Reception Process in Austria and Switzerland' in Keller Helen/Stone Sweet Alec (eds), *A Europe of Rights: The Impact of the ECHR on National Legal Systems* (Oxford: Oxford University Press) (2008) 311–391.

TOMKINS ADAM, *Our Republican Constitution* (Oxford: Hart) (2005).

TRIBE LAURENCE H., 'Childhood, Suspect Classifications, and Conclusive Presumptions: Three Linked Riddles' (1975) 39 *Law and Contemporary Problems* 8–37.

TRIBE LAURENCE H., *American Constitutional Law* (Mineola: Foundation Press) (1988) (2nd ed.).

TROCHSLER-HUGENTOBLER CARMEN/LOBSIGER ADRIAN, 'Polizeiliche Befugnisse und Handlungsformen' in Schweizer Rainer J. (ed.), *Sicherheits- und Ordnungsrecht des Bundes* (Basel: Helbing Lichtenhahn) (2008) 279–336.

TROLLINGER TONA, 'The Juvenile Curfew: Unconstitutional Imprisonment' (1995) 4 *William and Mary Bill of Rights Journal* 949–1003.

TSCHANNEN PIERRE, *Stimmrecht und politische Verständigung: Beiträge zu einem erneuerten Verständnis von direkter Demokratie* (Basel: Helbing & Lichtenhahn) (1995).

TSCHANNEN PIERRE, '"Öffentliche Sittlichkeit": Sozialnormen als polizeiliches Schutzgut?' in Bovay Benoît/Son Nguyen Minh (eds), *Mélanges en l'honneur de Pierre Moor* (Berne: Staempfli) (2005) 553–568.

TSCHANNEN PIERRE, *Staatsrecht der Schweizerischen Eidgenossenschaft* (Bern: Stämpfli) (2011) (3rd ed.).

TSCHANNEN PIERRE/ZIMMERLI ULRICH/Müller Markus, *Allgemeines Verwaltungsrecht* (Bern: Stämpfli) (2014) (4th ed.).

TUSHNET MARK, 'The Possibilities of Comparative Constitutional Law' (1999) 108 *Yale Law Journal* 1225–1309.

TUSHNET MARK, 'Comparative Constitutional Law' in Reimann Mathias/Zimmermann Reinhard (eds), *The Oxford Handbook of Comparative Law* (Oxford: Oxford University Press) (2006) 1225–1257.

TUSSMAN JOSEPH/TENBROEK JACOBUS, 'The Equal Protection of the Laws' (1949) 37 *California Law Review* 341–381.

U.S. DEPARTMENT OF JUSTICE, *Curfew: An Answer to Juvenile Delinquency and Victimization?* (April 1996).

UHLMANN FELIX, 'Verfahrensgrundrechte' in Biaggini Giovanni/Gächter Thomas/Kiener Regina (eds), *Staatsrecht* (Zürich/St. Gallen: Dike) (2011) 527–537.

UN-HABITAT, *State of the World's Cities 2010/2011: Bridging the Urban Divide* (2008), available at www.unhabitat.org/pmss/listItemDetails.aspx?publicationID=2917.

VILLIGER MARK E., *Handbuch der Europäischen Menschenrechtskonvention (EMRK): unter besonderer Berücksichtigung der schweizerischen Rechtslage* (Zürich: Schulthess) (1999) (2nd ed.).

Volkmann Uwe, 'Broken Windows, Zero Tolerance und das deutsche Ordnungsrecht' (1999) *Neue Zeitschrift für Verwaltungsrecht* 225–232.

Volkmann Uwe, 'Die Rückeroberung der Allmende' (2000) *Neue Zeitschrift für Verwaltungsrecht* 361–368.

von Hirsch Andrew/ Simester A. P. (eds), *Incivilities: Regulating Offensive Behaviour* (Oxford: Hart) (2006).

von Hirsch Andrew/Simester A. P., 'Penalising Offensive Behaviour: Constitutive and Mediating Principles' in von Hirsch Andrew/Simester A. P. (eds), *Incivilities: Regulating Offensive Behaviour* (Oxford: Hart) (2006) 115–131.

von Hirsch Andrew/Shearing Clifford, 'Exclusion from Public Space' in von Hirsch Andrew/Garland David/Wakefield Alison (eds), *Ethical and Social Perspectives on Situational Crime Prevention* (Oxford: Hart) (2000) 77–96.

Wacquant Loïc, *Prisons of Poverty* (Minneapolis: University of Minnesota Press) (2009).

Wade William/Forsyth Christopher, *Administrative Law* (Oxford: Oxford University Press) (2014) (11th ed.).

Waechter Kay, 'Rechtsgütergewichtung und wahre sowie eingebildete Bedrohungen' (1999) 114 *Deutsches Verwaltungsblatt* 809–815.

Wakefield Alison, 'Situational Crime Prevention in Mass Private Property' in von Hirsch Andrew/Garland David/Wakefield Alison (eds), *Ethical and Social Perspectives on Situational Crime Prevention* (Oxford: Hart) (2000) 125–145.

Waldmann Bernhard, *Das Diskriminierungsverbot von Art. 8 Abs. 2 BV als besonderer Gleichheitssatz* (Bern: Stämpfli) (2003).

Waldron Jeremy, 'Homelessness and the Issue of Freedom' (1991) 39 *UCLA Law Review* 295–324.

Waldron Jeremy, 'Is the Rule of Law an Essentially Contested Concept (in Florida)?' (2002) 21 *Law and Philosophy* 137–164.

Waldron Jeremy, 'The Rule of International Law' (2006) 30 *Harvard Journal of Law & Public Policy* 15–30.

Waldron Jeremy, *Dignity, Rank, and Rights* (New York: Oxford University Press) (2012).

Walker Samuel, *The Police in America* (New York: McGraw-Hill) (1992) (2nd ed.).

Wallin Luke, 'The Stranger on the Green' in Light Andrew/Smith Jonathan M. (eds), *Philosophy and Geography II: The Production of Public Space* (Lanham: Rowman & Littlefield) (1998) 99–113.

Walzer Michael, *On Toleration* (New Haven: Yale University Press) (1997).

Watts Arthur, 'The Legal Position in International Law of Heads of States, Heads of Governments and Foreign Ministers' (1994-III) 247 *Recueil des Cours: Collected Courses of the Hague Academy of International Law* 9–130.

Weber Albrecht, 'Rechtsstaatsprinzip als gemeineuropäisches Verfassungsprinzip' (2008) 63 *Zeitschrift für öffentliches Recht* 267–292.

Weber Claus (ed.), *Creifelds Rechtswörterbuch* (München: Beck) (2007) (19th ed.).

Weber Jack K., 'The King's Peace: A Comparative Study' (1989) 10 *Journal of Legal History* 135–160.

Weber-Dürler Beatrice, 'Grundrechtseingriffe' in Zimmerli Ulrich (ed.), *Die neue Bundesverfassung: Konsequenzen für Praxis und Wissenschaft: Berner Tage für die juristische Praxis – BTJP 1999* (Bern: Stämpfli) (2000) 131–155.

Weber-Dürler Beatrice, 'Rechtsgleichheit' in Thürer Daniel/Aubert Jean-François/Müller Jörg Paul (eds), *Verfassungsrecht der Schweiz* (Zürich: Schulthess) (2001) 657–675.

Weber-Dürler Beatrice, 'Gleichheit' in Merten Detlef/Papier Hans-Jürgen (eds), *Handbuch der Grundrechte in Deutschland und Europa: Band VII/2: Grundrechte in der Schweiz und in Liechtenstein* (Heidelberg: C.F. Müller) (2007) 229–253.

Wehrheim Jan, *Die überwachte Stadt: Sicherheit, Segregation und Ausgrenzung* (Opladen: Barbara Budrich) (2012) (3rd ed.).

Welty Emily/Bolton Matthew/Nayak Meghana/Malone Christopher (eds), *Occupying Political Science: The Occupy Wall Street Movement from New York to the World* (Basingstoke: Palgrave Macmillan) (2013).

Westen Peter, 'The Empty Idea of Equality' (1982) 95 *Harvard Law Review* 537–596.

Wheatley Steven, 'Democracy in International Law: A European Perspective' (2002) 51 *International and Comparative Law Quarterly* 225–248.

Wickersham George W., 'The Police Power, a Product of the Rule of Reason' (1914) 27 *Harvard Law Review* 297–316.

Widmer Paul, 'Der Einfluss der Schweiz auf die amerikanische Verfassung von 1787' (1988) 38 *Schweizerische Zeitschrift für Geschichte* 359–389.

Widmer Raphael, 'Vereinbarkeit besonderer Zentren für renitente Asylbewerber mit der Bewegungsfreiheit und den Garantien beim Freiheitsentzug' (2013) *Sicherheit & Recht* 17–28.

Wiegand Wolfgang, 'Die Rezeption amerikanischen Rechts' in Jenny Guido/Kälin Walter (eds), *Die schweizerische Rechtsordnung in ihren internationalen Bezügen: Festgabe zum Schweizerischen Juristentag 1988* (Bern: Stämpfli) (1988) 229–262.

Wiegand Wolfgang, 'The Reception of American Law in Europe' (1991) 39 *American Journal of Comparative Law* 229–248.

Wilms Heinrich, 'Der Menschenwürdebegriff in der neuen schweizerischen Bundesverfassung im Vergleich zu Deutschland und den Vereinigten Staaten' in Cremer Hans-Joachim/Giegerich Thomas/Richter Dagmar/

Zimmermann, Andreas (eds), *Tradition und Weltoffenheit des Rechts: Festschrift für Helmut Steinberger* (Berlin: Springer) (2002) 1015–1041.

Wilson James Q./Kelling George L., 'Broken Windows: The Police and Neigborhood Safety' (1982) *The Atlantic Monthly* 29–38.

Winkler Adam, 'Fatal in Theory and Strict in Fact: An Empirical Analysis of Strict Scrutiny in the Federal Courts' (2006) 59 *Vanderbilt Law Review* 793–871.

Wohlers Wolfgang/Trunz Mirjam, 'Hooliganismus-Bekämpfung: Kann die Schweiz von England lernen?' (2011) *Causa Sport* 176–202.

Wolf Burkard J., 'Wirtschaftsfreiheit und Nutzung öffentlicher Sachen – Widersprüchliches aus dem Bundesgericht' (2001) *Aktuelle Juristische Praxis* 430–437.

Wormuth Francis D./Mirkin Harris G., 'The Doctrine of the Reasonable Alternative', (1964) 9 *Utah Law Review* 254–307.

Wouters Jan/Meester Bart de/Ryngaert Cedric, 'Democracy and International Law', in Leuven Interdisciplinary Research Group on International Agreements and Development, Working Paper No. 5 (2004).

Wyss Martin Philipp, *Öffentliche Interessen – Interessen der Öffentlichkeit?: Das öffentliche Interesse im schweizerischen Staats- und Verwaltungsrecht* (Bern: Stämpfli) (2001).

Wyss Martin Philipp, 'Appell und Abschreckung: Verfassungsrechtliche Beobachtungen zur Versammlungsfreiheit' (2002) *Schweizerisches Zentralblatt für Staats- und Verwaltungsrecht* 393–410.

Wyssmann Ursula, *Nutzungskonflikte im öffentlichen Raum: Dargestellt am Beispiel des Bahnhofs Bern* (Zürich/St. Gallen: Dike) (2009).

Young Iris Marion, *Justice and the Politics of Difference* (Princeton: Princeton University Press) (1990).

Young Jock, *The Exclusive Society: Social Exclusion, Crime and Difference in Late Modernity* (London: Sage) (1999).

Zangl Bernhard, 'Is there an Emerging International Rule of Law?' (2005) 13 *European Review* 73–91.

Zedner Lucia, 'Seeking Security by Eroding Rights: The Side-stepping of Due Process' in Goold Benjamin/Lazarus Liora (eds), *Security and Human Rights* (Oxford: Hart) (2007) 257–275.

Zedner Lucia, *Security* (Abingdon: Routledge) (2009).

Ziegler Andreas R., *Einführung in das Völkerrecht* (Bern: Stämpfli) (2011) (2nd ed.).

Zimmerli Ulrich, 'Der Grundsatz der Verhältnismässigkeit im öffentlichen Recht' (1978) 97 *Zeitschrift für Schweizerisches Recht* 1–131.

Zimmerli Ulrich, 'Zum Gesetzmässigkeitsprinzip im Verwaltungsrecht' (1984) *recht* 73–83.

Zimmerli Ulrich, 'Versammlungsfreiheit' in Merten Detlef/Papier Hans-Jürgen (eds), *Handbuch der Grundrechte in Deutschland und Europa: Band VII/2:*

Grundrechte in der Schweiz und in Liechtenstein (Heidelberg: C.F. Müller) (2007) 473–489.

Zolo Danilo, 'The Rule of Law: A Critical Reappraisal' in Costa Pietro/ Zolo Danilo (eds), *The Rule of Law: History, Theory and Criticism* (Dordrecht: Springer) (2007) 3–71.

Zückert Hartmut, *Allmende und Allmendaufhebung: Vergleichende Studien zum Spätmittelalter bis zu den Agrarreformen des 18./19. Jahrhunderts* (Stuttgart: Lucius & Lucius) (2003).

Zünd Andreas/Errass Christoph, 'Die polizeiliche Generalklausel' (2011) 147 *Zeitschrift des Bernischen Juristenvereins* 261–293.

Zweigert Konrad/Kötz Hein, *Einführung in die Rechtsvergleichung: auf dem Gebiete des Privatrechts* (Tübingen: Mohr) (1996) (3rd ed.).

'Curfew Ordinances and the Control of Nocturnal Juvenile Crime' (1958) 107 *University of Pennsylvania Law Review* 66–102.

'The Void-for-Vagueness Doctrine in the Supreme Court' (1960) 109 *University of Pennsylvania Law Review* 67–116.

'Juvenile Curfew Ordinances and the Constitution' (1977) 76 *Michigan Law Review* 109–153.

'Assessing the Scope of Minors' Fundamental Rights – Juvenile Curfews and the Constitution' (1984) 97 *Harvard Law Review* 1163–1181.

Halsbury's Laws of England (London: Lexis Nexis Butterworths) (1988–2008) (4th ed.).

'Symposium: The Ratification of the International Covenant on Civil and Political Rights' (1993) 42 *DePaul Law Review* 1167–1412.

'Juvenile Curfews and Gang Violence – Exiled on Main Street' (1994) 107 *Harvard Law Review* 1693–1710.

'The Shopping Centre Industry: Its Importance to the UK Economy' (1999) 17 (5/6) *Facilities*.

'Making Outcasts out of Outlaws: The Unconstitutionality of Sex Offender Registration and Criminal Alien Detention' (2004) 117 *Harvard Law Review* 2731–2752.

ANNEX I

Overview of the most important exclusion norms

This annex reproduces the text of the most important legal norms authorising exclusion from public space in the United Kingdom, the United States and Switzerland in their original language (in the case of Swiss federal legislation in German). The sources indicated refer to the respective federal, cantonal, state or municipal collections of laws. With regard to the United Kingdom, all legislation is available from the respective government website (www.legislation.gov.uk). With regard to the United States and Switzerland, virtually all cantonal, state and municipal collections referred to in this annex are equally available online. The collection of Swiss federal legislation is available at www.admin.ch/bundes recht. Where a norm cited in this annex was amended after adoption of the law in which it is contained, the date of amendment is indicated.

United Kingdom

Football Spectators Act 1989 (as amended by the Football Disorder Act 2000): Football banning orders

s. 14A Banning orders made on conviction of an offence

(1) This section applies where a person (the 'offender') is convicted of a relevant offence.
(2) If the court is satisfied that there are reasonable grounds to believe that making a banning order would help to prevent violence or disorder at or in connection with any regulated football matches, it must make such an order in respect of the offender.
(3) If the court is not so satisfied, it must in open court state that fact and give its reasons.
(4) A banning order may only be made under this section—
    (a) in addition to a sentence imposed in respect of the relevant offence, or
    (b) in addition to an order discharging him conditionally.
(5) A banning order may be made as mentioned in subsection (4)(b) above in spite of anything in sections 12 and 14 of the Powers of the Criminal Courts (Sentencing) Act 2000 (which relate to orders discharging a person absolutely or conditionally and their effect).

(6) In this section, 'the court' in relation to an offender means—
   (a) the court by or before which he is convicted of the relevant offence, or
   (b) if he is committed to the Crown Court to be dealt with for that offence, the Crown Court.

s. 14B Banning orders made on a complaint

(1) An application for a banning order in respect of any person may be made by the chief officer of police for the area in which the person resides or appears to reside, if it appears to the officer that the condition in subsection (2) below is met.
(2) That condition is that the respondent has at any time caused or contributed to any violence or disorder in the United Kingdom or elsewhere.
(3) The application is to be made by complaint to a magistrates' court.
(4) If—
   (a) it is proved on the application that the condition in subsection (2) above is met, and
   (b) the court is satisfied that there are reasonable grounds to believe that making a banning order would help to prevent violence or disorder at or in connection with any regulated football matches, the court must make a banning order in respect of the respondent.

s. 14F Period of banning orders

(1) Subject to the following provisions of this Part, a banning order has effect for a period beginning with the day on which the order is made.
(2) The period must not be longer than the maximum or shorter than the minimum.
(3) Where the order is made under section 14A above in addition to a sentence of imprisonment taking immediate effect, the maximum is ten years and the minimum is six years; and in this subsection 'imprisonment' includes any form of detention.
(4) In any other case where the order is made under section 14A above, the maximum is five years and the minimum is three years.
(5) Where the order is made under section 14B above, the maximum is three years and the minimum is two years.

s. 14G Additional requirements of orders

(1) A banning order may, if the court making the order thinks fit, impose additional requirements on the person subject to the order in relation to any regulated football matches.
(2) The court by which a banning order was made may, on an application made by—
   (a) the person subject to the order, or

(b) the person who applied for the order or who was the prosecutor in relation to the order, vary the order so as to impose, replace or omit any such requirements.

(3) In the case of a banning order made by a magistrates' court, the reference in subsection (2) above to the court by which it was made includes a reference to any magistrates' court acting for the same petty sessions area as that court.

s. 14J Offences

(1) A person subject to a banning order who fails to comply with—
(a) any requirement imposed by the order, or
(b) any requirement imposed under section 19(2B) or (2C) below, is guilty of an offence.

(2) A person guilty of an offence under this section is liable on summary conviction to imprisonment for a term not exceeding six months, or a fine not exceeding level 5 on the standard scale, or both.

Powers of Criminal Courts (Sentencing) Act 2000: Curfew orders and exclusion orders

s. 37 Curfew orders

(1) Where a person is convicted of an offence, the court by or before which he is convicted may (subject to sections 34 to 36 above) make an order requiring him to remain, for periods specified in the order, at a place so specified.

[. . .]

(3) A curfew order may specify different places or different periods for different days, but shall not specify—
(a) periods which fall outside the period of six months beginning with the day on which it is made; or
(b) periods which amount to less than two hours or more than twelve hours in any one day.

[. . .]

s. 40A Exclusion orders

(1) Where a person is convicted of an offence, the court by or before which he is convicted may (subject to sections 34 to 36 above) make an order prohibiting him from entering a place specified in the order for a period so specified of not more than two years.

[. . .]

Sexual Offences Act 2003 (as amended by the Anti-social Behaviour, Crime and Policing Act 2014): SHPOs and sexual risk orders

s. 103A Sexual harm prevention orders: applications and grounds

(1) A court may make an order under this section (a 'sexual harm prevention order') in respect of a person ('the defendant') where subsection (2) or (3) applies to the defendant.
(2) This subsection applies to the defendant where—
 (a) the court deals with the defendant in respect of—
  (i) an offence listed in Schedule 3 or 5, or
  (ii) a finding that the defendant is not guilty of an offence listed in Schedule 3 or 5 by reason of insanity, or
  (iii) a finding that the defendant is under a disability and has done the act charged against the defendant in respect of an offence listed in Schedule 3 or 5,

 and

 (b) the court is satisfied that it is necessary to make a sexual harm prevention order, for the purpose of—
  (i) protecting the public or any particular members of the public from sexual harm from the defendant, or
  (ii) protecting children or vulnerable adults generally, or any particular children or vulnerable adults, from sexual harm from the defendant outside the United Kingdom.
(3) This subsection applies to the defendant where—
 (a) an application under subsection (4) has been made in respect of the defendant and it is proved on the application that the defendant is a qualifying offender, and
 (b) the court is satisfied that the defendant's behaviour since the appropriate date makes it necessary to make a sexual harm prevention order, for the purpose of—
  (i) protecting the public or any particular members of the public from sexual harm from the defendant, or
  (ii) protecting children or vulnerable adults generally, or any particular children or vulnerable adults, from sexual harm from the defendant outside the United Kingdom.

[...]

s. 103C SHPOs: effect

(1) A sexual harm prevention order prohibits the defendant from doing anything described in the order.

(2) Subject to section 103D(1), a prohibition contained in a sexual harm prevention order has effect—
   (a) for a fixed period, specified in the order, of at least 5 years, or
   (b) until further order.

[. . .]

s. 122A Sexual risk orders: applications, grounds and effect

(1) A chief officer of police or the Director General of the National Crime Agency ('the Director General') may by complaint to a magistrates' court apply for an order under this section (a 'sexual risk order') in respect of a person ('the defendant') if it appears to the chief officer or the Director General that the following condition is met.
(2) The condition is that the defendant has, whether before or after the commencement of this Part, done an act of a sexual nature as a result of which there is reasonable cause to believe that it is necessary for a sexual risk order to be made.

[. . .]

(6) On an application under subsection (1), the court may make a sexual risk order if it is satisfied that the defendant has, whether before or after the commencement of this Part, done an act of a sexual nature as a result of which it is necessary to make such an order for the purpose of—
   (a) protecting the public or any particular members of the public from harm from the defendant, or
   (b) protecting children or vulnerable adults generally, or any particular children or vulnerable adults, from harm from the defendant outside the United Kingdom.
(7) Such an order—
   (a) prohibits the defendant from doing anything described in the order;
   (b) has effect for a fixed period (not less than 2 years) specified in the order or until further order.

[. . .]

Serious Organised Crime and Police Act 2005: Demonstrations in vicinity of Parliament

s. 132 Demonstrating without authorisation in designated area (repealed by Police Reform and Social Responsibility Act 2011)

(1) Any person who—
   (a) organises a demonstration in a public place in the designated area, or

(b) takes part in a demonstration in a public place in the designated area, or
(c) carries on a demonstration by himself in a public place in the designated area,

is guilty of an offence if, when the demonstration starts, authorisation for the demonstration has not been given under section 134(2).

[. . .]

(7) In this section and in sections 133 to 136—
(a) 'the designated area' means the area specified in an order under section 138,
(b) 'public place' means any highway or any place to which at the material time the public or any section of the public has access, on payment or otherwise, as of right or by virtue of express or implied permission,

[. . .]

s. 138 The designated area (repealed by Police Reform and Social Responsibility Act 2011)

(1) The Secretary of State may by order specify an area as the designated area for the purposes of sections 132 to 137.
(2) The area may be specified by description, by reference to a map or in any other way.
(3) No point in the area so specified may be more than one kilometre in a straight line from the point nearest to it in Parliament Square.

Serious Crime Act 2007: Serious Crime Prevention Orders

s. 1 Serious crime prevention orders

(1) The High Court in England and Wales may make an order if—
(a) it is satisfied that a person has been involved in serious crime (whether in England and Wales or elsewhere); and
(b) it has reasonable grounds to believe that the order would protect the public by preventing, restricting or disrupting involvement by the person in serious crime in England and Wales.

[. . .]

(3) An order under this section may contain—
(a) such prohibitions, restrictions or requirements; and
(b) such other terms;

as the court considers appropriate for the purpose of protecting the public by preventing, restricting or disrupting involvement by the person concerned in serious crime in England and Wales or (as the case may be) Northern Ireland.

[...]

s. 5 Type of provision that may be made by orders

(1) This section contains examples of the type of provision that may be made by a serious crime prevention order but it does not limit the type of provision that may be made by such an order.

[...]

(3) Examples of prohibitions, restrictions or requirements that may be imposed on individuals (including partners in a partnership) by serious crime prevention orders include prohibitions or restrictions on, or requirements in relation to—

[...]

(d) the premises to which an individual has access;

(e) the use of any premises or item by an individual;

(f) an individual's travel (whether within the United Kingdom, between the United Kingdom and other places or otherwise).

[...]

(7) In this Part—

[...]

'premises' includes any land, vehicle, vessel, aircraft or hovercraft.

[...]

s. 16 Duration of orders

[...]

(2) An order is not to be in force for more than 5 years beginning with the coming into force of the order.

[...]

Policing and Crime Act 2009: Gang injunctions

s. 34 Injunctions to prevent gang-related violence

(1) A court may grant an injunction under this section if 2 conditions are met.

(2) The first condition is that the court is satisfied on the balance of probabilities that the respondent has engaged in, or has encouraged or assisted, gang-related violence.

(3) The second condition is that the court thinks it is necessary to grant the injunction for either or both of the following purposes—

(a) to prevent the respondent from engaging in, or encouraging or assisting, gang-related violence;
(b) to protect the respondent from gang-related violence.

(4) An injunction under this section may (for either or both of those purposes)—
(a) prohibit the respondent from doing anything described in the injunction;
(b) require the respondent to do anything described in the injunction.
[...]

s. 35 Contents of injunctions

(1) This section applies in relation to an injunction under section 34.
(2) The prohibitions included in the injunction may, in particular, have the effect of prohibiting the respondent from—
(a) being in a particular place;
(b) being with particular persons in a particular place;
(c) being in charge of a particular species of animal in a particular place;
(d) wearing particular descriptions of articles of clothing in a particular place;
(e) using the internet to facilitate or encourage violence.

[...]

s. 36 Contents of injunctions: supplemental

[...]
(2) The injunction may not include a prohibition or requirement that has effect after the end of the period of 2 years beginning with the day on which the injunction is granted ('the injunction date').

[...]

Terrorism Prevention and Investigation Measures Act 2011

s. 2 Imposition of terrorism prevention and investigation measures

(1) The Secretary of State may by notice (a 'TPIM notice') impose specified terrorism prevention and investigation measures on an individual if conditions A to E in section 3 are met.

[...]

s. 3 Conditions A to E

(1) Condition A is that the Secretary of State is satisfied, on the balance of probabilities, that the individual is, or has been, involved in terrorism-related activity (the 'relevant activity').

(2) Condition B is that some or all of the relevant activity is new terrorism-related activity.
(3) Condition C is that the Secretary of State reasonably considers that it is necessary, for purposes connected with protecting members of the public from a risk of terrorism, for terrorism prevention and investigation measures to be imposed on the individual.
(4) Condition D is that the Secretary of State reasonably considers that it is necessary, for purposes connected with preventing or restricting the individual's involvement in terrorism-related activity, for the specified terrorism prevention and investigation measures to be imposed on the individual.
(5) Condition E is that—
    (a) the court gives the Secretary of State permission under section 6, or
    (b) the Secretary of State reasonably considers that the urgency of the case requires terrorism prevention and investigation measures to be imposed without obtaining such permission.
(6) In this section 'new terrorism-related activity' means—
    (a) if no TPIM notice relating to the individual has ever been in force, terrorism-related activity occurring at any time (whether before or after the coming into force of this Act);
    (b) if only one TPIM notice relating to the individual has ever been in force, terrorism-related activity occurring after that notice came into force; or
    (c) if two or more TPIM notices relating to the individual have been in force, terrorism-related activity occurring after such a notice came into force most recently.

[. . .]

Schedule 1, para. 3 Exclusion measure

(1) The Secretary of State may impose restrictions on the individual entering—
    (a) a specified area or place, or
    (b) a place or area of a specified description.
(2) The Secretary of State may, in particular, impose any of the following requirements in respect of a specified area or place or a specified description of an area or place—
    (a) a requirement not to enter without the permission of the Secretary of State;
    (b) a requirement to give notice to the Secretary of State before entering;
    (c) a requirement not to enter unless other specified conditions are met.

Anti-social Behaviour, Crime and Policing Act 2014: IPNAs

s. 1 Power to grant injunctions

(1) A court may grant an injunction under this section against a person aged 10 or over ('the respondent') if two conditions are met.
(2) The first condition is that the court is satisfied, on the balance of probabilities, that the respondent has engaged or threatens to engage in anti-social behaviour.
(3) The second condition is that the court considers it just and convenient to grant the injunction for the purpose of preventing the respondent from engaging in anti-social behaviour.
(4) An injunction under this section may for the purpose of preventing the respondent from engaging in anti-social behaviour—
 (a) prohibit the respondent from doing anything described in the injunction;
 (b) require the respondent to do anything described in the injunction.
(5) Prohibitions and requirements in an injunction under this section must, so far as practicable, be such as to avoid—
 (a) any interference with the times, if any, at which the respondent normally works or attends school or any other educational establishment;
 (b) any conflict with the requirements of any other court order or injunction to which the respondent may be subject.
(6) An injunction under this section must—
 (a) specify the period for which it has effect, or
 (b) state that it has effect until further order.

 In the case of an injunction granted before the respondent has reached the age of 18, a period must be specified and it must be no more than 12 months.
(7) An injunction under this section may specify periods for which particular prohibitions or requirements have effect.
(8) An application for an injunction under this section must be made to—
 (a) a youth court, in the case of a respondent aged under 18;
 (b) the High Court or the county court, in any other case.

[. . .]

s. 2 Meaning of 'anti-social behaviour'

(1) In this Part 'anti-social behaviour' means—
 (a) conduct that has caused, or is likely to cause, harassment, alarm or distress to any person,

(b) conduct capable of causing nuisance or annoyance to a person in relation to that person's occupation of residential premises, or
(c) conduct capable of causing housing-related nuisance or annoyance to any person.

[...]

Anti-social Behaviour, Crime and Policing Act 2014: CBOs

s. 22 Power to make orders

(1) This section applies where a person ('the offender') is convicted of an offence.
(2) The court may make a criminal behaviour order against the offender if two conditions are met.
(3) The first condition is that the court is satisfied, beyond reasonable doubt, that the offender has engaged in behaviour that caused or was likely to cause harassment, alarm or distress to any person.
(4) The second condition is that the court considers that making the order will help in preventing the offender from engaging in such behaviour.
(5) A criminal behaviour order is an order which, for the purpose of preventing the offender from engaging in such behaviour—
   (a) prohibits the offender from doing anything described in the order;
   (b) requires the offender to do anything described in the order.
(6) The court may make a criminal behaviour order against the offender only if it is made in addition to—
   (a) a sentence imposed in respect of the offence, or
   (b) an order discharging the offender conditionally.

s. 25 Duration of order etc.

[...]
(4) In the case of a criminal behaviour order made before the offender has reached the age of 18, the order period must be a fixed period of—
   (a) not less than 1 year, and
   (b) not more than 3 years.
(5) In the case of a criminal behaviour order made after the offender has reached the age of 18, the order period must be—
   (a) a fixed period of not less than 2 years, or
   (b) an indefinite period (so that the order has effect until further order).

[...]

Anti-social Behaviour, Crime and Policing Act 2014: Dispersal powers

s. 35 Directions excluding a person from an area

(1) If the conditions in subsections (2) and (3) are met and an authorisation is in force under section 34, a constable in uniform may direct a person who is in a public place in the locality specified in the authorisation—
  (a) to leave the locality (or part of the locality), and
  (b) not to return to the locality (or part of the locality) for the period specified in the direction ('the exclusion period').

(2) The first condition is that the constable has reasonable grounds to suspect that the behaviour of the person in the locality has contributed or is likely to contribute to—
  (a) members of the public in the locality being harassed, alarmed or distressed, or
  (b) the occurrence in the locality of crime or disorder.

(3) The second condition is that the constable considers that giving a direction to the person is necessary for the purpose of removing or reducing the likelihood of the events mentioned in subsection (2)(a) or (b).

(4) The exclusion period may not exceed 48 hours.
The period may expire after (as long as it begins during) the period specified in the authorisation under section 34.

(5) A direction under this section—
  (a) must be given in writing, unless that is not reasonably practicable;
  (b) must specify the area to which it relates;
  (c) may impose requirements as to the time by which the person must leave the area and the manner in which the person must do so (including the route).

(6) The constable must (unless it is not reasonably practicable) tell the person to whom the direction is given that failing without reasonable excuse to comply with the direction is an offence.

[. . .]

s. 39 Offences

(1) A person given a direction under section 35 who fails without reasonable excuse to comply with it commits an offence.

(2) A person guilty of an offence under subsection (1) is liable on summary conviction—
  (a) to imprisonment for a period not exceeding 3 months, or
  (b) to a fine not exceeding level 4 on the standard scale,

[. . .]

Anti-social Behaviour, Crime and Policing Act 2014: Public spaces protection orders

s. 59 Power to make orders

(1) A local authority may make a public spaces protection order if satisfied on reasonable grounds that two conditions are met.
(2) The first condition is that—
  (a) activities carried on in a public place within the authority's area have had a detrimental effect on the quality of life of those in the locality, or
  (b) it is likely that activities will be carried on in a public place within that area and that they will have such an effect.
(3) The second condition is that the effect, or likely effect, of the activities—
  (a) is, or is likely to be, of a persistent or continuing nature,
  (b) is, or is likely to be, such as to make the activities unreasonable, and
  (c) justifies the restrictions imposed by the notice.
(4) A public spaces protection order is an order that identifies the public place referred to in subsection (2) ('the restricted area') and—
  (a) prohibits specified things being done in the restricted area,
  (b) requires specified things to be done by persons carrying on specified activities in that area, or
  (c) does both of those things.
(5) The only prohibitions or requirements that may be imposed are ones that are reasonable to impose in order—
  (a) to prevent the detrimental effect referred to in subsection (2) from continuing, occurring or recurring, or
  (b) to reduce that detrimental effect or to reduce the risk of its continuance, occurrence or recurrence.
(6) A prohibition or requirement may be framed—
  (a) so as to apply to all persons, or only to persons in specified categories, or to all persons except those in specified categories;
  (b) so as to apply at all times, or only at specified times, or at all times except those specified;
  (c) so as to apply in all circumstances, or only in specified circumstances, or in all circumstances except those specified.

[. . .]

s. 60 Duration of orders

(1) A public spaces protection order may not have effect for a period of more than 3 years, unless extended under this section.

[. . .]

United States

Sex offender laws

Code of Georgia

§ 42-1-15. Restriction on registered offenders residing, working, or loitering within certain distance of child care facilities, churches, schools, or areas where minors congregate; penalty for violations; civil causes of action

(a) As used in this Code section, the term:

(1) 'Individual' means a person who is required to register pursuant to Code Section 42-1-12.

[...]

[...]

(d) Notwithstanding any ordinance or resolution adopted pursuant to Code Section 16-6-24 or subsection (d) of Code Section 16-11-36, it shall be unlawful for any individual to loiter, as prohibited by Code Section 16-11-36, at any child care facility, school, or area where minors congregate.

[...]

(g) Any individual who knowingly violates this Code section shall be guilty of a felony and shall be punished by imprisonment for not less than ten nor more than 30 years.

[...]

§ 42-8-35. Terms and conditions of probation; supervision

(a) The court shall determine the terms and conditions of probation and may provide that the probationer shall:

[...]

(14) Wear a device capable of tracking the location of the probationer by means including electronic surveillance or global positioning satellite systems. DCS shall assess and collect fees from the probationer for such monitoring at levels set by regulation of the Board of Community Supervision;

[...]

(b) In determining the terms and conditions of probation for a probationer who has been convicted of a criminal offense against a victim who is a minor or dangerous sexual offense as those terms are defined in Code Section 42-1-12, the court may provide that the probationer shall be:

(1) Prohibited from entering or remaining present at a victim's school, place of employment, place of residence, or other specified place at times when a victim is present or from loitering in areas where minors congregate, child care facilities, churches, or schools as those terms are defined in Code Section 42-1-12;

[. . .]

[. . .]

Plainfield, Indiana, Ordinance No. 16–2002 (An Ordinance to Establish Rules and Regulations for Parks and Other Recreational Areas in the Town of Plainfield, Indiana)

Section 18 Prohibited Persons

Individuals listed on *State of Indiana Sex Offender Registry* published and disseminated by the Indiana Criminal Justice Institute are prohibited from all parks and other recreational areas of the Town of Plainfield.

Gang loitering laws

Chicago Municipal Code

§ 8-4-015 Gang loitering (new version as amended in 2000)

(a) Whenever a police officer observes a member of a criminal street gang engaged in gang loitering with one or more other persons in any public place designated for the enforcement of this section under subsection (b), the police officer shall, subject to all applicable procedures promulgated by the superintendent of police:
  (i) inform all such persons that they are engaged in gang loitering within an area in which loitering by groups containing criminal street gang members is prohibited;
  (ii) order all such persons to disperse and remove themselves from within sight and hearing of the place at which the order was issued; and
  (iii) inform those persons that they will be subject to arrest if they fail to obey the order promptly or engage in further gang loitering within sight or hearing of the place at which the order was issued during the next eight hours.

(b) The superintendent of police shall by written directive designate areas of the city in which the superintendent has determined that enforcement of this section is necessary because gang loitering has enabled criminal street gangs to establish control over identifiable areas, to intimidate others from entering those areas, or to conceal illegal activities. [. . .]

(c) The superintendent shall by written directive promulgate procedures to prevent the enforcement of this section against persons who are engaged in collective advocacy activities that are protected by the Constitution of the United States or the State of Illinois.

(d) As used in this section:

(1) *Gang loitering* means remaining in any one place under circumstances that would warrant a reasonable person to believe that the purpose or effect of that behavior is to enable a criminal street gang to establish control over identifiable areas, to intimidate others from entering those areas, or to conceal illegal activities.

[...]

(5) *Public place* means the public way and any other location open to the public, whether publicly or privately owned.

(e) Any person who fails to obey promptly an order issued under subsection (a), or who engages in further gang loitering within sight or hearing of the place at which such an order was issued during the eight-hour period following the time the order was issued, is subject to a fine of not less than $100.00 and not more than $500.00 for each offense, or imprisonment for not more than six months for each offense, or both. A second or subsequent offense shall be punishable by a mandatory minimum sentence of not less than five days imprisonment.

In addition to or instead of the above penalties, any person who violates this section may be required to perform up to 120 hours of community service pursuant to section 1-4-120 of this Code.

[...]

'Drug-exclusion zones'

Cincinnati Municipal Code

§ 755–5. Civil Exclusion. (repealed)

A person is subject to exclusion for a period of ninety (90) days from the public streets, sidewalks, and other public ways in all drug-exclusion zones designated in Chapter 755 if that person has been arrested or otherwise taken into custody within any drug-exclusion zone for drug abuse or any drug abuse-related activities including the following crimes:

1. Corrupting another with drugs in violation of Ohio Revised Code Section 2925.02.
2. Trafficking in drugs in violation of Ohio Revised Code Section 2925.03.
3. Drug abuse in violation of Ohio Revised Code Section 2925.11 (except for a minor misdemeanor violation).
4. Possessing drug abuse instruments in violation of Ohio Revised Code Section 2925.12.
5. Drug paraphernalia offenses in violation of Ohio Revised Code Section 2925.14.
6. Illegal processing of drug documents in violation of Ohio Revised Code Section 2925.23.

7. Abusing harmful intoxicants in violation of Ohio Revised Code Section 2925.31.
8. Trafficking in harmful intoxicants in violation of Ohio Revised Code Section 2925.32.
9. Offenses involving counterfeit controlled substances in violation of Ohio Revised Code Section 2925.37.

The aforesaid 90-day exclusion will cease immediately if the person arrested or otherwise taken into custody for the crimes listed above is subsequently acquitted of the charge(s), said charge(s) is/are dismissed, or the charge(s) is/are no longer being pursued by law enforcement.

Additionally, any person arrested or otherwise taken into custody for any crimes listed above who is subsequently convicted thereof in a court of law for that offense is subject to exclusion for a one (1) year period from the date of such conviction from the public streets, sidewalk, and other public ways in all drug-exclusion zones designated in Chapter 755.

If a person excluded from a drug-exclusion zone is found therein during the exclusion period, that person is subject to immediate arrest for criminal trespass pursuant to Ohio Revised Code Section 2911.21, a misdemeanor of the fourth degree.

Charter and Code of the City of Portland, Oregon

14B.20.010 Drug-Free Zones.

[...]

B. Drug-free zones are those areas of the City as designated by the City Council under Chapter 14B.20 of this Code, which are areas where the number of arrests where there was probable cause to believe a person has committed any of the offenses enumerated in Section 14B.20.030 for a twelve (12) month period within the 18 months preceding its designation is significantly higher than that for other similarly sized geographic areas of the City that are not located within a drug-free zone.

14B.20.030 Civil Exclusion. (Amended by Ordinance No. 180213, effective June 14, 2006.)

A. A person is subject to exclusion under the process described in this chapter for a period of ninety (90) days from any public right of way and park within a drug-free zone designated in Code Chapter 14B.20 if that person has been arrested and either cited to appear in court for charging or lodged in jail for presentation to a magistrate for charging based upon probable cause to believe that the person has committed any of the following offenses within that drug-free zone, unless the offense was committed entirely within a private residence:

[. . .]

B. A one (1) year exclusion from any public right of way and park within a drug-free zone shall take effect upon the day after conviction for any of the offenses enumerated in Subsection A of this Section if that offense was committed within that drug-free zone and the person was both given actual notice prior to the exclusion that the City would impose a one-year exclusion upon conviction and notified of the right of appeal and the process for initiating an appeal.

[. . .]

14B.20.040 Issuance of Exclusion Notices.

The Chief of Police and/or designees are the persons in charge of the public rights of way and parks in the drug-free zones for purposes of issuing notices of exclusion in accordance with this Chapter.

General loitering laws

Charleston, South Carolina, Code of Ordinances

Sec. 21–108.— Loitering

(a) *Loitering.* No person shall loiter or prowl in a place, at a time or in a manner not usual for law abiding individuals under circumstances that warrant alarm for the safety of persons or property in the vicinity. Among the circumstances which may be considered in determining whether such alarm is warranted is the fact that the actor takes flight upon appearance of a police officer, refuses to identify himself or manifestly endeavors to conceal himself or any object. [. . .]

[. . .]

(j) *Penalty; continuing violations.* Any person who is convicted of any violation of this section, the court before whom an offender shall be tried may sentence him to pay a fine not exceeding the maximum fine permitted by law or serve a term not exceeding thirty (30) days in jail, or both. Each day any violation of this ordinance shall continue shall constitute a separate offense.

(k) *Court order on jurisdictional limits.* In addition to the penalty that may be imposed pursuant to subsection (j) above, any person who is arrested for and/or convicted of violating any provision of this section may be subject to an order of the court which shall impose a jurisdictional limit on said person prohibiting his presence in a specific geographic area of the City of

Charleston. Failure to comply with the court order shall constitute a violation of the court order and shall result in the following:

(1) in the case of a bond where jurisdictional limits have been imposed, the bond may be revoked and the person shall be incarcerated until trial; and/or

(2) in the case of a sentence where jurisdictional limits have been imposed, the suspended sentence may be revoked and the person shall be incarcerated until he has served the original sentence imposed by the court without any portion thereof suspended.

Prohibitions of sleeping, lying, sitting or drinking alcohol

Reno, Nevada, Municipal Code

Sec. 8.12.015.— Sitting or lying down on public sidewalks in the downtown redevelopment district prohibited.

[. . .]

(b) Except as otherwise provided in this section, no person shall sit or lie down upon a public sidewalk, or upon a blanket, chair, stool, or any other object placed upon a public sidewalk in the Downtown Reno Regional Center, which shall be defined as the area within the exterior boundary bounded by the following named streets: [. . .]

(c) The prohibition in subsection (b) shall not apply to any person:

(1) Sitting or lying down on a public sidewalk due to a medical emergency;

(2) Who, as the result of a disability, utilizes a wheelchair, walker or similar device to move about the public sidewalk;

(3) Operating or patronizing a commercial establishment conducted on the public sidewalk pursuant to a street use permit; or a person participating in or attending a parade, festival, performance, rally, demonstration, meeting, or similar event conducted on the public sidewalk pursuant to a street use or other applicable permit.

(4) Sitting on a chair or bench located on the public sidewalk which is supplied by a public agency or by the abutting private property owner; or

(5) Sitting on a public sidewalk with a bus stop zone while waiting for public or private transportation.

[. . .]

Juvenile curfews

Dallas, Texas Code of Ordinances

Sec. 31–33 CURFEW HOURS FOR MINORS

(a) Definitions. In this section:
  (1) CURFEW HOURS means:
    (A) 11:00 p.m. on any Sunday, Monday, Tuesday, Wednesday, or Thursday until 6:00 a.m. of the following day;
    (B) 12:01 a.m. until 6:00 a.m. on any Saturday or Sunday; and
    (C) 9:00 a.m. until 2:30 p.m. on any Monday, Tuesday, Wednesday, Thursday, or Friday.
  [...]
  (3) ESTABLISHMENT means any privately-owned place of business operated for a profit to which the public is invited, including but not limited to any place of amusement or entertainment.
  [...]
  (6) MINOR means any person under 17 years of age.
  [...]
  (9) PUBLIC PLACE means any place to which the public or a substantial group of the public has access and includes, but is not limited to, streets, highways, and the common areas of schools, hospitals, apartment houses, office buildings, transport facilities, and shops.
  [...]
(b) Offenses.
  (1) A minor commits an offense if he remains in any public place or on the premises of any establishment within the city during curfew hours.
  (2) A parent or guardian of a minor commits an offense if he knowingly permits, or by insufficient control allows, the minor to remain in any public place or on the premises of any establishment within the city during curfew hours.
  (3) The owner, operator, or any employee of an establishment commits an offense if he knowingly allows a minor to remain upon the premises of the establishment during curfew hours.
(c) Defenses.
  (1) It is a defense to prosecution under Subsection (b) that the minor was:
    (A) accompanied by the minor's parent or guardian;
    (B) on an errand at the direction of the minor's parent or guardian, without any detour or stop;
    (C) in a motor vehicle involved in interstate travel;
    (D) engaged in an employment activity, or going to or returning home from an employment activity, without any detour or stop;

(E) involved in an emergency;
(F) on the sidewalk abutting the minor's residence or abutting the residence of a next-door neighbor if the neighbor did not complain to the police department about the minor's presence, except that this defense does not apply to a violation of the curfew hours described in Subsection (a)(1)(C) of this section;
(G) attending an official school, religious, or other recreational activity supervised by adults and sponsored by the city of Dallas, a civic organization, or another similar entity that takes responsibility for the minor, or going to or returning home from, without any detour or stop, an official school, religious, or other recreational activity supervised by adults and sponsored by the city of Dallas, a civic organization, or another similar entity that takes responsibility for the minor;
(H) exercising First Amendment rights protected by the United States Constitution, such as the free exercise of religion, freedom of speech, and the right of assembly; or
(I) married or had been married or had disabilities of minority removed in accordance with Chapter 31 of the Texas Family Code.

[. . .]

(e) Penalties.
(1) A person who violates a provision of this chapter is guilty of a separate offense for each day or part of a day during which the violation is committed, continued, or permitted. Each offense, upon conviction, is punishable by a fine not to exceed $500.

[. . .]

[. . .]

'Buffer zones'

Massachusetts General Laws

Chapter 266, s. 120E1/2 (2007; repealed)

(a) For the purposes of this section, 'reproductive health care facility' means a place, other than within or upon the grounds of a hospital, where abortions are offered or performed.
(b) No person shall knowingly enter or remain on a public way or sidewalk adjacent to a reproductive health care facility within a radius of 35 feet of any portion of an entrance to, exit from, or driveway of a reproductive health care facility, or within the area within a rectangle created by extending the outside boundaries of any entrance to, exit from, or

driveway of, a reproductive health care facility in straight lines to the point where such lines intersect the sideline of the street in front of such entrance, exit or driveway. This subsection shall not apply to the following:

(1) persons entering or leaving such facility;
(2) employees or agents of such facility acting within the scope of their employment;
(3) law enforcement, ambulance, firefighting, construction, utilities, public works and other municipal agents acting within the scope of their employment;
(4) persons using the public sidewalk or street right-of-way adjacent to such facility solely for the purpose of reaching a destination other than such facility.

[. . .]

'Bubble laws'

Colorado Revised Statutes

§ 18-9-122. Preventing passage to and from a health care facility— engaging in prohibited activities near facility

[. . .]

(3) No person shall knowingly approach another person within eight feet of such person, unless such other person consents, for the purpose of passing a leaflet or handbill to, displaying a sign to, or engaging in oral protest, education, or counseling with such other person in the public way or sidewalk area within a radius of one hundred feet from any entrance door to a health care facility. Any person who violates this subsection (3) commits a class 3 misdemeanor.

[. . .]

Emergency powers

Seattle, Local Proclamation of Civil Emergency Order Number 3, 1 December 1999: Limited curfew imposed in a portion of the City: all persons, subject to limited exceptions, prohibited from entering the portion of downtown Seattle described in the order

A limited curfew is imposed in the portion of the City within the following boundaries: Starting on the corner of 4th Avenue and Lenora Street, then proceeding south on 4th Avenue to Seneca Street, then east on Seneca Street to the I-5 freeway, then north along the I-5 freeway to Boren Avenue, then north on Boren Avenue to Pine Street, then west on Pine Street to 6th Avenue, then north on 6th Avenue to Lenora Street, then west on Lenora Street to, and concluding at 4th Avenue and Lenora, as shown on the attached map.

Switzerland

Ausgrenzung gemäss Ausländergesetz

Bundesgesetz über die Ausländerinnen und Ausländer (Ausländergesetz, AuG) vom 16. Dezember 2005, SR 142.20

Art. 74 Ein- und Ausgrenzung

1 Die zuständige kantonale Behörde kann einer Person die Auflage machen, ein ihr zugewiesenes Gebiet nicht zu verlassen oder ein bestimmtes Gebiet nicht zu betreten,
wenn:

a. sie keine Kurzaufenthalts-, Aufenthalts- oder Niederlassungsbewilligung besitzt und sie die öffentliche Sicherheit und Ordnung stört oder gefährdet; diese Massnahme dient insbesondere der Bekämpfung des widerrechtlichen Betäubungsmittelhandels; oder
b. ein rechtskräftiger Weg- oder Ausweisungsentscheid vorliegt und konkrete Anzeichen befürchten lassen, dass die betroffene Person nicht innerhalb der Ausreisefrist ausreisen wird, oder sie die ihr angesetzte Ausreisefrist nicht eingehalten hat;
c. die Ausschaffung aufgeschoben wurde (Art. 69 Abs. 3).

2 Diese Massnahmen werden von der Behörde des Kantons angeordnet, der für den Vollzug der Weg- oder Ausweisung zuständig ist. Für Personen, welche sich in den Empfangsstellen oder in besonderen Zentren nach Artikel 26 Absatz 1bis AsylG aufhalten, ist der Standortkanton zuständig. Das Verbot, ein bestimmtes Gebiet zu betreten, kann auch von der Behörde des Kantons erlassen werden, in dem dieses Gebiet liegt.

3 Gegen die Anordnung dieser Massnahmen kann bei einer kantonalen richterlichen Behörde Beschwerde geführt werden. Die Beschwerde hat keine aufschiebende Wirkung.

Rayonverbote gemäss Konkordat über Massnahmen gegen Gewalt anlässlich von Sportveranstaltungen

Konkordat über Massnahmen gegen Gewalt anlässlich von Sportveranstaltungen vom 15. November 2007; Änderung vom 2. Februar 2012 ('Hooligankonkordat')

Art. 1 Zweck

Die Kantone treffen in Zusammenarbeit mit dem Bund zur Verhinderung gewalttätigen Verhaltens vorbeugende polizeiliche Massnahmen nach diesem Konkordat, um frühzeitig Gewalt anlässlich von Sportveranstaltungen zu erkennen und zu bekämpfen.

Art. 2 Definition gewalttätigen Verhaltens

1 Gewalttätiges Verhalten und Gewalttätigkeiten liegen namentlich vor, wenn eine Person im Vorfeld einer Sportveranstaltung, während der Veranstaltung oder im Nachgang dazu folgende Straftaten begangen oder dazu angestiftet hat:

a. Strafbare Handlungen gegen Leib und Leben nach den Artikeln 111–113, 117, 122, 123, 125 Absatz 2, 126 Abs. 1, 129, 133, 134 des Strafgesetzbuches (StGB);
b. Sachbeschädigungen nach Artikel 144 StGB;
c. Nötigung nach Artikel 181 StGB;
d. Brandstiftung nach Artikel 221 StGB;
e. Verursachung einer Explosion nach Artikel 223 StGB;
f. Gefährdung durch Sprengstoffe und giftige Gase in verbrecherischer Absicht nach Artikel 224 StGB
g. Öffentliche Aufforderung zu Verbrechen oder zur Gewalttätigkeit nach Art. 259 StGB;
h. Landfriedensbruch nach Artikel 260 StGB;
i. Gewalt und Drohung gegen Behörden und Beamte nach Artikel 285 StGB;
j. Hinderung einer Amtshandlung nach Artikel 286 StGB.

2 Als gewalttätiges Verhalten gilt ferner die Gefährdung der öffentlichen Sicherheit durch das Mitführen oder Verwenden von Waffen, Sprengmitteln, Schiesspulver oder pyrotechnischen Gegenständen an Sportstätten, in deren Umgebung sowie auf dem An- und Rückreiseweg.

Art. 3 Nachweis gewalttätigen Verhaltens

1 Als Nachweis für gewalttätiges Verhalten nach Artikel 2 gelten:

a. entsprechende Gerichtsurteile oder polizeiliche Anzeigen;

b. glaubwürdige Aussagen oder Bildaufnahmen der Polizei, der Zollverwaltung, des Sicherheitspersonals oder der Sportverbände und— vereine;
c. Stadionverbote der Sportverbände oder— vereine;
d. Meldungen einer zuständigen ausländischen Behörde.

2 Aussagen nach Absatz 1 Buchstabe b sind schriftlich festzuhalten und zu unterzeichnen.

[. . .]

Art. 4 Rayonverbot

1 Einer Person, die sich anlässlich von Sportveranstaltungen nachweislich an Gewalttätigkeiten gegen Personen oder Sachen beteiligt hat, kann der Aufenthalt in einem genau umschriebenen Gebiet im Umfeld von Sportveranstaltungen (Rayon) zu bestimmten Zeiten verboten werden. Die zuständige Behörde bestimmt, für welche Rayons das Verbot gilt.

2 Das Rayonverbot wird für eine Dauer von einem bis zu drei Jahren verfügt. Es kann Rayons in der ganzen Schweiz umfassen.

3 Das Verbot kann von den folgenden Behörden verfügt werden:

a. von der zuständigen Behörde im Kanton, in dem die Gewalttätigkeit erfolgte;
b. von der zuständigen Behörde im Kanton, in dem die betroffene Person wohnt;
c. von der zuständigen Behörde im Kanton, in dem der Klub seinen Sitz hat, zu dem die betroffene Person in Beziehung steht.

Der Vorrang bei sich konkurrenzierenden Zuständigkeiten folgt der Reihenfolge der Aufzählung in diesem Absatz.

4 Die Schweizerische Zentralstelle Hooliganismus (Zentralstelle) und das Bundesamt für Polizei fedpol können den Erlass von Rayonverboten beantragen.

Art. 5 Verfügung über ein Rayonverbot

1 In der Verfügung über ein Rayonverbot sind die Geltungsdauer und der räumliche Geltungsbereich festzulegen. Der Verfügung sind Angaben beizufügen, die es der betroffenen Person erlauben, genaue Kenntnis über die vom Verbot erfassten Rayons zu erhalten.

2 Die verfügende Behörde informiert umgehend die übrigen in Art. 4 Abs. 3 und 4 erwähnten Behörden.

3 Für den Nachweis der Beteiligung an Gewalttätigkeiten gilt Artikel 3.

Massnahmen gemäss StGB

Schweizerisches Strafgesetzbuch vom 21. Dezember 1937, SR 311.0

Art. 67b Kontakt- und Rayonverbot

1 Hat jemand ein Verbrechen oder Vergehen gegen eine oder mehrere bestimmte Personen oder gegen Personen einer bestimmten Gruppe begangen und besteht die Gefahr, dass er bei einem Kontakt zu diesen Personen weitere Verbrechen oder Vergehen begehen wird, so kann das Gericht für eine Dauer bis zu fünf Jahren ein Kontakt- und Rayonverbot verhängen.

2 Mit dem Kontakt- und Rayonverbot kann das Gericht dem Täter verbieten:

[...]

b. sich einer bestimmten Person zu nähern oder sich in einem bestimmten Umkreis ihrer Wohnung aufzuhalten;

c. sich an bestimmten Orten, namentlich bestimmten Strassen, Plätzen oder Quartieren, aufzuhalten.

3 Für den Vollzug des Verbots kann die zuständige Behörde technische Geräte einsetzen, die mit dem Täter fest verbunden sind. Diese können insbesondere der Feststellung des Standortes des Täters dienen.

4 Das Gericht kann für die Dauer des Verbots Bewährungshilfe anordnen.

5 Es kann das Verbot auf Antrag der Vollzugsbehörden jeweils um höchstens fünf Jahre verlängern, wenn dies notwendig ist, um den Täter von weiteren Verbrechen und Vergehen gegen Minderjährige oder andere besonders schutzbedürftige Personen abzuhalten.

Ersatzmassnahmen gemäss StPO

Schweizerische Strafprozessordnung (Strafprozessordnung, StPO) vom 5. Oktober 2007, SR 312.0

Art. 237 Allgemeine Bestimmungen

1 Das zuständige Gericht ordnet an Stelle der Untersuchungs- oder der Sicherheitshaft eine oder mehrere mildere Massnahmen an, wenn sie den gleichen Zweck wie die Haft erfüllen.

2 Ersatzmassnahmen sind namentlich:

[...]

c. die Auflage, sich nur oder sich nicht an einem bestimmten Ort oder in einem bestimmten Haus aufzuhalten;

[...]

3 Das Gericht kann zur Überwachung solcher Ersatzmassnahmen den Einsatz technischer Geräte und deren feste Verbindung mit der zu überwachenden Person anordnen.

[...]

Schutz der Persönlichkeit gemäss ZGB

Schweizerisches Zivilgesetzbuch vom 10. Dezember 1907, SR 210

Art. 28*b* Gewalt, Drohungen oder Nachstellungen

1 Zum Schutz gegen Gewalt, Drohungen oder Nachstellungen kann die klagende Person dem Gericht beantragen, der verletzenden Person insbesondere zu verbieten:

1. sich ihr anzunähern oder sich in einem bestimmten Umkreis ihrer Wohnung aufzuhalten;
2. sich an bestimmten Orten, namentlich bestimmten Strassen, Plätzen oder Quartieren, aufzuhalten;
3. mit ihr Kontakt aufzunehmen, namentlich auf telefonischem, schriftlichem oder elektronischem Weg, oder sie in anderer Weise zu belästigen.

[...]

Wegweisungsartikel in kantonalen Polizeigesetzen

Bern, Polizeigesetz vom 8. Juni 1997, BSG 551.1

Art. 29 Wegweisung, Fernhaltung

1 Die Kantonspolizei kann Personen von einem Ort vorübergehend wegweisen oder fern halten, wenn

a sie ernsthaft und unmittelbar gefährdet sind;
b der begründete Verdacht besteht, dass sie oder andere, die der gleichen Ansammlung zuzurechnen sind, die öffentliche Sicherheit und Ordnung gefährden oder stören;
c sie Einsätze zur Wiederherstellung oder Aufrechterhaltung der öffentlichen Sicherheit und Ordnung, insbesondere durch Polizeikräfte, Feuerwehr oder Rettungsdienste behindern;
d sie die Kantonspolizei an der Durchsetzung vollstreckbarer Anordnungen hindern oder stören oder sich einmischen oder
e sie die Erfüllung polizeilicher Aufgaben vereiteln oder zu vereiteln versuchen,

f sie eine oder mehrere andere Personen in der psychischen, physischen oder sexuellen Integrität gefährden oder ernsthaft drohen, jene an Leib und Leben zu verletzen, insbesondere in Fällen häuslicher Gewalt.

2 Sie verfügt mit der Wegweisung und der Fernhaltung die zum Vollzug notwendigen Massnahmen. Die Verfügung nach Buchstabe f wird auch dem Opfer eröffnet.

3 Beschwerden gegen Wegweisungs- und Fernhalteverfügungen haben keine aufschiebende Wirkung. Artikel 68 Absätze 4 und 5 des Gesetzes vom 23. Mai 1989 über die Verwaltungsrechtspflege (VRPG) bleiben vorbehalten.

Graubünden, Polizeigesetz des Kantons Graubünden vom 20. Oktober 2004, BR 613.000

Art. 12 Wegweisung und Fernhaltung

1 Die Kantonspolizei kann zur Wahrung der Sicherheit und Ordnung sowie zur Gefahrenabwehr ereignisbezogen die notwendigen Massnahmen anordnen.

2 Insbesondere kann sie

a) Personen anweisen, einen bestimmten Ort oder ein bestimmtes Gebiet zu verlassen;
b) das Betreten von Objekten, Grundstücken oder Gebieten untersagen;
c) den Aufenthalt in Objekten, Grundstücken oder Gebieten untersagen.

3 Sie kann bei Nichtbefolgung der Anweisung diese mit den erforderlichen und angemessenen Mitteln durchsetzen.

Zürich, Polizeigesetz (PolG) vom 23. April 2007, LS 550.1

§ 33. Wegweisung und Fernhaltung

Die Polizei darf eine Person von einem Ort wegweisen oder für längstens 24 Stunden fernhalten,

a. wenn die Person oder eine Ansammlung von Personen, der sie angehört, die öffentliche Sicherheit und Ordnung gefährdet,
b. wenn die Person oder eine Ansammlung von Personen, der sie angehört, Dritte erheblich belästigt, gefährdet oder unberechtigterweise an der bestimmungsgemässen Nutzung des öffentlich zugänglichen Raumes hindert,
c. wenn Einsatzkräfte wie Polizei, Feuerwehr oder Rettungskräfte behindert oder gefährdet sind,
d. wenn die Person selber ernsthaft und unmittelbar gefährdet ist,
e. zur Wahrung der Rechte von Personen, insbesondere zur Wahrung der Pietät.

§ 34. Wegweisung und Fernhaltung mittels Verfügung

1 Widersetzt sich eine Person der angeordneten Wegweisung oder Fernhaltung, darf die Polizei sie zu einer Polizeidienststelle bringen und ihr dort mittels Verfügung verbieten, den betreffenden Ort zu betreten.
2 In besonderen Fällen, namentlich wenn eine Person wiederholt von einem Ort weggewiesen oder ferngehalten werden musste, darf die Polizei das Verbot unter Androhung der Straffolgen von Art. 292 StGB für höchstens 14 Tage verfügen.
3 Die Verfügung legt die Dauer und den räumlichen Geltungsbereich der Massnahme fest.
4 In Fällen von Abs. 2 kann die Verfügung innert fünf Tagen nach ihrer Mitteilung beim Haftrichter angefochten werden. Dem Lauf der Rechtsmittelfrist und der Einreichung des Rechtsmittels kommen keine aufschiebende Wirkung zu. Im Übrigen gelten für das Verfahren sinngemäss die Bestimmungen des Gewaltschutzgesetzes vom 19. Juni 2006.

Basel-Stadt, Gesetz betreffend die Kantonspolizei des Kantons Basel-Stadt (Polizeigesetz, PolG) vom 13. November 1996, SG 510.100

§ 42 Wegweisung und Fernhaltung

1 Die Kantonspolizei kann vorübergehend Personen von einem Ort wegweisen oder fernhalten, wenn sie
1. ernsthaft und unmittelbar gefährdet sind;
2. Einsätze zur Wiederherstellung oder Aufrechterhaltung der öffentlichen Sicherheit und Ordnung, insbesondere durch Polizeikräfte, Feuerwehr oder Rettungsdienste, behindern;
3. die Kantonspolizei an der Durchsetzung vollstreckbarer Anordnungen hindern.

§ 42a Befristeter Platzverweis (eingefügt am 15. Oktober 2008)

1 Die Kantonspolizei kann eine Person von einem bestimmten öffentlichen Ort für höchstens 72 Stunden wegweisen, wenn diese Person
1. Dritte gefährdet oder Dritten mit einer ernsthaften Gefährdung droht;
2. durch ihr Verhalten die unmittelbare Gefahr einer gewalttätigen Auseinandersetzung schafft.
2 Die betroffene Person kann formlos innert 10 Tagen den Erlass einer Verfügung verlangen.
3 In schwerwiegenden Fällen, namentlich wenn eine Person
1. Dritte in ihrer körperlichen Integrität verletzt;
2. gefährliche Gegenstände oder Waffen mit sich führt;

3. an einer gewalttätigen Auseinandersetzung aktiv teilnimmt

sowie bei wiederholter Wegweisung oder im Falle der Missachtung einer Wegweisung kann die Kantonspolizei das Verbot unter Androhung der Straffolgen gemäss Art. 292 des Schweizerischen Strafgesetzbuches für höchstens einen Monat verfügen. In der Verfügung sind insbesondere der Ort, von welchem eine Person weggewiesen wird, die Dauer und die Gründe der Wegweisung anzugeben.

4 Die Polizei informiert die weggewiesene Person über adäquate Beratungsstellen.

République et canton de Genève, Loi sur la police (LPol) du 26 octobre 1957, RSG F 1 05

Section 2 Mesures d'éloignement (eingefügt am 27. August 2009)

Art. 22A Motifs (eingefügt am 19. Februar 2009, Bustabe b geändert am 16. Dezember 2009)

La police peut éloigner une personne d'un lieu ou d'un périmètre déterminé, si:

a) elle-même ou un rassemblement de personnes auquel elle participe menace l'ordre ou la sécurité publics;
b) elle-même ou un rassemblement de personnes auquel elle participe importune sérieusement des tiers;
c) elle se livre à la mendicité;
d) elle participe à des transactions portant sur des biens dont le commerce est prohibé, notamment des stupéfiants.

Art. 22B Décision (eingefügt am 19. Februar 2009)

1 La police peut signifier verbalement une mesure d'éloignement valable 24 heures et conduire la personne hors du lieu ou du périmètre concerné.

2 Lorsque les circonstances le justifient, notamment parce que la personne a violé une mesure d'éloignement signifiée verbalement, la police peut la conduire dans un poste ou un bureau de police pour lui notifier une décision écrite.

3 La décision écrite, prononcée par un officier de police, doit mentionner:
a) la durée de la mesure d'éloignement, qui ne peut excéder 3 mois;
b) la désignation exacte du lieu ou du périmètre interdit;
c) une description sommaire du comportement justifiant la décision;
d) le fait que la décision est signifiée sous la menace des peines de l'article 292 du code pénal;

e) l'indication selon laquelle la décision peut, dans les 30 jours, faire l'objet d'un recours à la chambre administrative de la Cour de justice;
f) l'indication selon laquelle la décision est toutefois exécutoire nonobstant recours.

Art. 22 C Effet suspensif (eingefügt am 19. Februar 2009)

La décision écrite est immédiatement exécutoire nonobstant recours. L'article 66, alinéa 2, de la loi sur la procédure administrative, du 12 septembre 1985, est réservé.

Ausgeh- bzw. Ansammlungsverbote in Polizeiverordnungen der Gemeinden

Gemeindepolizeireglement der Gemeinde Interlaken vom 5. Dezember 2006 (552.11)

Art. 9 Benützung von öffentlichem Grund

[...]
4 Schulpflichtige Kinder dürfen sich nach 22 Uhr nicht ohne Begleitung der Inhabenden der elterlichen Gewalt oder der zuständigen Erziehenden auf öffentlichen Strassen und Plätzen aufhalten.
[...]

Polizeiverordnung der Gemeinde Dänikon vom 18. Juni 2008

Art. 27 (aufgehoben durch Urteil des Verwaltungsgerichts des Kantons Zürich VB.2009.00055 vom 30. April 2009)

Schulpflichtigen Jugendlichen ist es untersagt sich nach 22.00 Uhr ohne Begleitung der Inhaber der elterlichen Sorge in Ansammlungen auf öffentlichen Strassen oder Plätzen aufzuhalten.

Verbot des Sitzens und Liegens

Reglement betreffend die Benützung des städtischen Teils des Bahnhofs Bern vom 1. Juni 2008 (Bahnhofreglement; BHR) (SSSB 732.21)

Art. 2 Vorrangige Nutzung und allgemeine Einschränkungen

[...]
2 Zum Schutz des städtischen Teils des Bahnhofs als Verkehrsweg sind in der Christoffel- und der Neuengass-Unterführung sowie in den

entsprechenden Zugängen und Eintrittsbereichen die folgenden Nutzungen untersagt:

[...]

b. Sitzen und Liegen auf Boden und Treppen;

[...]

g. Ungebührliches Verhalten gegenüber anderen Benutzerinnen und Benutzern des städtischen Teils des Bahnhofs;

h. Lautes Abspielen von Tonträgern;

Politische Kundgebungen

Stadt Bern, Reglement über Kundgebungen auf öffentlichem Grund vom 20. Oktober 2005 (Kundgebungsreglement; KgR) (SSSB 143.1)

Art. 6 Kundgebungen auf dem Bundesplatz

1 Kundgebungen auf dem Bundesplatz werden für folgende Zeiten nicht bewilligt:

a. Sessionswochen des eidgenössischen Parlaments für die Zeit von Montag bis Freitag;

b. dortige Marktzeiten, namentlich von Wochenmarkt, Zibelemärit und Graniummärit.

2 Über Ausnahmen in Einzelfällen entscheidet der Gemeinderat.

ANNEX II

Typology of exclusion norms

Legal basis	Targeted behaviour	Mode of exclusion	Excluded behaviour	Geographical scope	Temporal scope
United Kingdom					
Football Spectators Act 1989 (as amended by the Football Disorder Act 2000), s. 14A in connection with s. 14 F	Violence or disorder in connection with football matches	Power of the court (convicting court)	Any behaviour specified by the court, including mere presence	Any specified place	Between 3 and 10 years
Football Spectators Act 1989 (as amended by the Football Disorder Act 2000), s. 14B in connection with s. 14 F	Violence or disorder in connection with football matches	Power of the court (magistrates' court)	Any behaviour specified by the court, including mere presence	Any specified place	Between 2 and 3 years
Powers of Criminal Courts (Sentencing) Act 2000, s. 40A	Presence of convicted offenders in public places	Power of the court	Mere presence	Any specified place	Up to 2 years
Sexual Offences Act 2003, ss 103A–103 K (SHPOs)	Posing sexual harm by convicted offenders	Power of the court (convicting court)	Any behaviour specified by the court	Any specified place or area	No limit; minimum 5 years
Sexual Offences Act 2003, ss 122A–122 K (sexual risk orders)	Posing sexual harm by any person	Power of the court (magistrates' court)	Any behaviour specified by the court	Any specified place or area	No limit; minimum 2 years

(cont.)

Legal basis	Targeted behaviour	Mode of exclusion	Excluded behaviour	Geographical scope	Temporal scope
SOCPA 2005, ss 132–138 (repealed)	Demonstrations in vicinity of Parliament	Authorisation requirement	Demonstrating without prior authorisation	Designated area (up to one kilometre from Parliament Square)	Permanent
Serious Crime Act 2007, s. 1	Serious crime	Power of the court	Any behaviour specified by the court, including mere presence	Any 'premises' specified by the court	Up to 5 years
Policing and Crime Act 2009, ss 34–50	Gang-related violence	Power of the court	Mere presence	Any particular place	Up to 2 years
Terrorism Prevention and Investigation Measures Act 2011, ss 2–5	Terrorism-related activity	Police power (Home Secretary) / Power of the court	Behaviour specified by the Home Secretary, including mere presence	Any specified area or place	One year (renewable by one year)
Anti-social Behaviour, Crime and Policing Act 2014, s. 1 (IPNAs)	Anti-social behaviour	Power of the court	Any behaviour specified by the court, including mere presence	Unlimited	No limit
Anti-social Behaviour, Crime and Policing Act 2014, s. 22 (CBOs)	Anti-social behaviour	Power of the court (convicting court)	Any behaviour specified by the court, including mere presence	Unlimited	No upper limit, minimum two years

Anti-social Behaviour, Crime and Policing Act 2014, s. 35 (dispersal powers)	Anti-social behaviour	Police power	Mere presence	Any locality specified by a senior police officer	Up to 48 hours
United States					
Code of Georgia, s. 42-1-15	Loitering by registered sex offenders near areas with children	Prohibition	Loitering near areas with children	In proximity of any childcare facility, school or area where minors congregate	Permanent
Code of Georgia, s. 42-8-35	Presence/ loitering of convicted sex offenders near areas with children	Power of the court	Mere presence; loitering	Any specified place at times when a victim is present; areas where minors congregate, child care facilities, churches, and schools	No limit
Chicago Municipal Code, § 8-4-015	Loitering by criminal street gang members	Police power	Mere presence	‘within sight and hearing of the place at which the order was issued’	8 hours

(cont.)

Legal basis	Targeted behaviour	Mode of exclusion	Excluded behaviour	Geographical scope	Temporal scope
Cincinnati Municipal Code, § 755–5 (repealed)	Drug abuse and drug abuse-related activities	Prohibition	Mere presence	Public streets, sidewalks, and other public ways in all drug-exclusion zones (designated areas with a higher incidence of drug-related activity)	90 days in case of arrest for drug abuse-related activities; one year in case of subsequent conviction
Charter and Code of the City of Portland, ss 14B.20.010 – 14B.20.070	Drug abuse and drug abuse-related activities	Prohibition	Mere presence	Public streets and parks in all designated drug-free zones	90 days in case of arrest for drug abuse-related activities; one year in case of conviction
Charleston Code of Ordinances, s. 21–108	Loitering 'at a time or in a manner not usual for law abiding individuals'	Prohibition	Loitering 'at a time or in a manner not usual for law abiding individuals'	Any place	Permanent
Reno Municipal Code, s. 8.12.015	Sitting or lying down on public sidewalks	Prohibition	Sitting or lying down on public sidewalks	Public sidewalks in the downtown redevelopment district	Permanent

Dallas Code of Ordinances, s. 31–33	Presence of persons under 17 in public places	Prohibition	Mere presence	Any public place or the premises of any establishment within the city	Between 11 pm and 6 am on Sundays to Thursdays; and 12:01 am and 6 am on Saturdays and Sundays; and 9 am and 2:30 pm on Mondays to Fridays
Massachusetts General Laws, Chapter 266, s. 120E1/2 (2007; repealed)	Demonstrations near reproductive health care facilities	Prohibition	Mere presence	Public ways or sidewalks adjacent to a reproductive health care facility within a radius of 35 feet of any portion of an entrance, exit or driveway of a reproductive health care facility	Permanent

(cont.)

Legal basis	Targeted behaviour	Mode of exclusion	Excluded behaviour	Geographical scope	Temporal scope
Colorado Revised Statutes, § 18-9-122 (1998)	Demonstrations near health care facilities	Prohibition	Approaching another person for the purpose of passing a leaflet or handbill to, displaying a sign to, or engaging in oral protest, education, or counseling with such other person	Zone of 8 feet around the other person when within a radius of 100 feet from any entrance door to a health care facility	Permanent
Seattle, Local Proclamation of Civil Emergency Order Number 3, 1999	Demonstration against WTO in downtown Seattle	Prohibition	Mere presence	A portion of the City of Seattle as specified on the attached map	No limit
Switzerland					
AuG, Art. 74	Disturbance of, or threat to, public safety and order by foreign nationals without leave to stay	Police power	Mere presence	Any specified area	No limit

Konkordat über Massnahmen gegen Gewalt anlässlich von Sportveranstaltungen, Art. 4	Violence against persons or property at sports events	Police power	Mere presence	Specified area near location of sports events	Up to 1 year (up to 3 years under the revised version of the Concordat)
StGB, Art. 67b	Presence of convicted offenders in the vicinity of potential victims	Power of the court	Mere presence	Any specified place	Up to 5 years (renewable)
Bern, Polizeigesetz, Art. 29	Disturbance of, or threat to, public safety and order	Police power	Any behaviour specified by the police, including mere presence	Any place	'Temporarily'
Graubünden, Polizeigesetz, Art. 12	Disturbance of, or threat to, public safety and order	Police power	Any behaviour specified by the police, including mere presence	Any specified place or area	No limit
Zürich, Polizeigesetz, § 33	– Endangering public safety and order – Endangering or serious harassing third persons	Police power	Any behaviour specified by the police, including mere presence	Any place	Up to 24 hours; up to 14 days in 'special cases'

(cont.)

Legal basis	Targeted behaviour	Mode of exclusion	Excluded behaviour	Geographical scope	Temporal scope
Gemeinde Interlaken, Gemeindepolizei-reglement, Art. 9(4)	Presence of youths of compulsory school age in public places	Prohibition	Mere presence	Any public streets and squares	After 10 pm
Stadt Bern, Reglement betreffend die Benützung des städtischen Teils des Bahnhofs Bern, Art. 2	Various forms of anti-social behaviour, including sitting and lying on the ground, improper behaviour	Prohibition	Various forms of anti-social behaviour, including sitting and lying on the ground, improper behaviour	Parts of train station that are property of the city; entrances to train station	Permanent
Stadt Bern, Reglement über Kundgebungen auf öffentlichem Grund, Art. 6	Demonstrations on Bundes-platz (square in front of the parliament building)	Prohibition (with possibility of exceptions)	Demonstrating	Bundesplatz	Monday to Friday during those weeks parliament is sitting; during times when the market is held

INDEX

CAMBRIDGE STUDIES IN INTERNATIONAL AND COMPARATIVE LAW

Books in the series

129 *Exclusion from Public Space*
Daniel Moeckli

128 *Provisional Measures before International Courts and Tribunals*
Cameron Miles

127 *Humanity at Sea: Maritime Migration and the Foundations of International Law*
Itamar Mann

126 *Beyond Human Rights: The Legal Status of the Individual in International Law*
Anne Peters

125 *The Doctrine of Odious Debt in International Law: A Restatement*
Jeff King

124 *Static and Evolutive Treaty Interpretation: A Functional Reconstruction*
Christian Djeffal

123 *Civil Liability in Europe for Terrorism-Related Risk*
Lucas Bergkamp, Michael Faure, Monika Hinteregger and Niels Philipsen

122 *Proportionality and Deference in Investor-State Arbitration: Balancing Investment Protection and Regulatory Autonomy*
Caroline Henckels

121 *International Law and Governance of Natural Resources in Conflict and Post-Conflict Situations*
Daniëlla Dam-de Jong

120 *Proof of Causation in Tort Law*
Sandy Steel

119 *The Formation and Identification of Rules of Customary International Law in International Investment Law*
Patrick Dumberry

118 *Religious Hatred and International Law: The Prohibition of Incitement to Violence or Discrimination*
Jeroen Temperman

117 *Taking Economic, Social and Cultural Rights Seriously in International Criminal Law*
Evelyne Schmid

116 *Climate Change Litigation: Regulatory Pathways to Cleaner Energy?*
Jacqueline Peel and Hari Osofsky

115 *Mestizo International Law: A global intellectual history 1842–1933*
Arnulf Becker Lorca

114 *Sugar and the Making of International Trade Law*
Michael Fakhri

113 *Strategically-created Treaty Conflicts and the Politics of International Law*
Surabhi Ranganathan

112 *Investment Treaty Arbitration as Public International Law: Procedural Aspects and Implications*
Eric De Brabandere

111 *The New Entrants Problem in International Fisheries Law*
Andrew Serdy

110 *Substantive Protection under Investment Treaties: A Legal and Economic Analysis*
Jonathan Bonnitcha

109 *Popular Governance of Post-Conflict Reconstruction: The Role of International Law*
Matthew Saul

108 *Evolution of International Environmental Regimes: The Case of Climate Change*
Simone Schiele

107 *Judges, Law and War: The Judicial Development of International Humanitarian Law*
Shane Darcy

106 *Religious Offence and Human Rights: The Implications of Defamation of Religions*
Lorenz Langer

105 *Forum Shopping in International Adjudication: The Role of Preliminary Objections*
Luiz Eduardo Ribeiro Salles

104 *Domestic Politics and International Human Rights Tribunals: The Problem of Compliance*
Courtney Hillebrecht

103 *International Law and the Arctic*
Michael Byers

102 *Cooperation in the Law of Transboundary Water Resources*
Christina Leb

101 *Underwater Cultural Heritage and International Law*
Sarah Dromgoole

100 *State Responsibility: The General Part*
James Crawford

99 *The Origins of International Investment Law*
Kate Miles

98 *The Crime of Aggression under the Rome Statute of the International Criminal Court*
Carrie McDougall

97 *Crimes against Peace and International Law*
Kirsten Sellars

96 *The Non-Legal in International Law*
Fleur Johns

95 *Armed Conflict and Displacement: The Protection of Refugees and Displaced Persons under International Humanitarian Law*
Mélanie Jacques

94 *Foreign Investment and the Environment in International Law*
Jorge Viñuales

93 *The Human Rights Treaty Obligations of Peacekeepers*
Kjetil Larsen

92 *Cyberwarfare and the Laws of War*
Heather Harrison Dinniss

91 *The Right to Reparation in International Law for Victims of Armed Conflict*
Christine Evans

90 *Global Public Interest in International Investment Law*
Andreas Kulick

89 *State Immunity in International Law*
Xiaodong Yang

88 *Reparations and Victim Support in the International Criminal Court*
Conor McCarthy

87 *Reducing Genocide to Law: Definition, Meaning, and the Ultimate Crime*
Payam Akhavan

86 *Decolonizing International Law: Development, Economic Growth and the Politics of Universality*
Sundhya Pahuja

85 *Complicity and the Law of State Responsibility*
Helmut Philipp Aust

84 *State Control over Private Military and Security Companies in Armed Conflict*
Hannah Tonkin

83 *'Fair and Equitable Treatment' in International Investment Law*
Roland Kläger

82 *The UN and Human Rights: Who Guards the Guardians?*
Guglielmo Verdirame

81 *Sovereign Defaults before International Courts and Tribunals*
Michael Waibel

80 *Making the Law of the Sea: A Study in the Development of International Law*
James Harrison

79 *Science and the Precautionary Principle in International Courts and Tribunals: Expert Evidence, Burden of Proof and Finality*
Caroline E. Foster

78 *Transition from Illegal Regimes in International Law*
Yaël Ronen

77 *Access to Asylum: International Refugee Law and the Globalisation of Migration Control*
Thomas Gammeltoft-Hansen

76 *Trading Fish, Saving Fish: The Interaction between Regimes in International Law*
Margaret Young

75 *The Individual in the International Legal System: Continuity and Change in International Law*
Kate Parlett

74 *'Armed Attack' and Article 51 of the UN Charter: Evolutions in Customary Law and Practice*
Tom Ruys

73 *Theatre of the Rule of Law: Transnational Legal Intervention in Theory and Practice*
Stephen Humphreys

72 *Science and Risk Regulation in International Law*
Jacqueline Peel

71 *The Participation of States in International Organisations: The Role of Human Rights and Democracy*
Alison Duxbury

70 *Legal Personality in International Law*
Roland Portmann

69 *Vicarious Liability in Tort: A Comparative Perspective*
Paula Giliker

68 *The Public International Law Theory of Hans Kelsen: Believing in Universal Law*
Jochen von Bernstorff

67 *Legitimacy and Legality in International Law: An Interactional Account*
Jutta Brunnée and Stephen J. Toope

66 *The Concept of Non-International Armed Conflict in International Humanitarian Law*
Anthony Cullen

65 *The Principle of Legality in International and Comparative Criminal Law*
Kenneth S. Gallant

64 *The Challenge of Child Labour in International Law*
Franziska Humbert

63 *Shipping Interdiction and the Law of the Sea*
Douglas Guilfoyle

62 *International Courts and Environmental Protection*
Tim Stephens

61 *Legal Principles in WTO Disputes*
Andrew D. Mitchell

60 *War Crimes in Internal Armed Conflicts*
Eve La Haye

59 *Humanitarian Occupation*
Gregory H. Fox

58 *The International Law of Environmental Impact Assessment: Process, Substance and Integration*
Neil Craik

57 *The Law and Practice of International Territorial Administration: Versailles to Iraq and Beyond*
Carsten Stahn

56 *United Nations Sanctions and the Rule of Law*
Jeremy Farrall

55 *National Law in WTO Law: Effectiveness and Good Governance in the World Trading System*
Sharif Bhuiyan

54 *Cultural Products and the World Trade Organization*
Tania Voon

53 *The Threat of Force in International Law*
Nikolas Stürchler

52 *Indigenous Rights and United Nations Standards*
Alexandra Xanthaki

51 *International Refugee Law and Socio-Economic Rights*
Michelle Foster

50 *The Protection of Cultural Property in Armed Conflict*
Roger O'Keefe

49 *Interpretation and Revision of International Boundary Decisions*
Kaiyan Homi Kaikobad

48 *Multinationals and Corporate Social Responsibility: Limitations and Opportunities in International Law*
Jennifer A. Zerk

47 *Judiciaries within Europe: A Comparative Review*
John Bell

46 *Law in Times of Crisis: Emergency Powers in Theory and Practice*
Oren Gross and Fionnuala Ní Aoláin

45 *Vessel-Source Marine Pollution: The Law and Politics of International Regulation*
Alan Tan

44 *Enforcing Obligations Erga Omnes* in International Law
Christian J. Tams

43 *Non-Governmental Organisations in International Law*
Anna-Karin Lindblom

42 *Democracy, Minorities and International Law*
Steven Wheatley

41 *Prosecuting International Crimes: Selectivity and the International Law Regime*
Robert Cryer

40 *Compensation for Personal Injury in English, German and Italian Law: A Comparative Outline*
Basil Markesinis, Michael Coester, Guido Alpa, Augustus Ullstein

39 *Dispute Settlement in the UN Convention on the Law of the Sea*
Natalie Klein

38 *The International Protection of Internally Displaced Persons*
Catherine Phuong

37 *Imperialism, Sovereignty and the Making of International Law*
Antony Anghie

35 *Necessity, Proportionality and the Use of Force by States*
Judith Gardam

34 *International Legal Argument in the Permanent Court of International Justice: The Rise of the International Judiciary*
Ole Spiermann

32 *Great Powers and Outlaw States: Unequal Sovereigns in the International Legal Order*
Gerry Simpson

31 *Local Remedies in International Law, Second Edition*
C. F. Amerasinghe

30 *Reading Humanitarian Intervention: Human Rights and the Use of Force in International Law*
Anne Orford

29 *Conflict of Norms in Public International Law: How WTO Law Relates to Other Rules of International Law*
Joost Pauwelyn

27 *Transboundary Damage in International Law*
Hanqin Xue

25 *European Criminal Procedures*
Edited by Mireille Delmas-Marty and John Spencer

24 *The Accountability of Armed Opposition Groups in International Law*
Liesbeth Zegveld

23 *Sharing Transboundary Resources: International Law and Optimal Resource Use*
Eyal Benvenisti

22 *International Human Rights and Humanitarian Law*
René Provost

21 *Remedies Against International Organisations*
Karel Wellens

20 *Diversity and Self-Determination in International Law*
Karen Knop

19 *The Law of Internal Armed Conflict*
Lindsay Moir

18 *International Commercial Arbitration and African States: Practice, Participation and Institutional Development*
Amazu A. Asouzu

17 *The Enforceability of Promises in European Contract Law*
James Gordley

16 *International Law in Antiquity*
David J. Bederman

15 *Money Laundering: A New International Law Enforcement Model*
Guy Stessens

14 *Good Faith in European Contract Law*
Reinhard Zimmermann and Simon Whittaker

13 *On Civil Procedure*
J. A. Jolowicz

12 *Trusts: A Comparative Study*
Maurizio Lupoi

11 *The Right to Property in Commonwealth Constitutions*
Tom Allen

10 *International Organizations Before National Courts*
August Reinisch

9 *The Changing International Law of High Seas Fisheries*
Francisco Orrego Vicuña

8 *Trade and the Environment: A Comparative Study of EC and US Law*
Damien Geradin

7 *Unjust Enrichment: A Study of Private Law and Public Values*
Hanoch Dagan

6 *Religious Liberty and International Law in Europe*
Malcolm D. Evans

5 *Ethics and Authority in International Law*
Alfred P. Rubin

4 *Sovereignty Over Natural Resources: Balancing Rights and Duties*
Nico Schrijver

3 *The Polar Regions and the Development of International Law*
Donald R. Rothwell

2 *Fragmentation and the International Relations of Micro-States: Self-determination and Statehood*
Jorri Duursma

1 *Principles of the Institutional Law of International Organizations*
C. F. Amerasinghe

Lightning Source UK Ltd.
Milton Keynes UK
UKOW06n2218180617
303574UK00009B/136/P

9 781107 154650